Internetworking Troubleshooting Handbook, Second Edition

Cisco Systems et al.

Cisco Press
201 West 103rd Street
Indianapolis, IN 46290 USA

Internetworking Troubleshooting Handbook, Second Edition

Cisco Systems et al.

Copyright© 2001 Cisco Systems, Inc.

Cisco Press logo is a trademark of Cisco Systems, Inc.

Published by:
Cisco Press
201 West 103rd Street
Indianapolis, IN 46290 USA

Printed in the United States of America 1 2 3 4 5 6 7 8 9 0   04 03 02 01

First Printing February 2001

Library of Congress Cataloging-in-Publication Number: 00-105172

ISBN: 1-58705-005-6

Warning and Disclaimer

This book is designed to provide information about internetworking troubleshooting. Every effort has been made to make this book as complete and as accurate as possible, but no warranty or fitness is implied.

The information is provided on an "as is" basis. The authors, Cisco Press, and Cisco Systems, Inc., shall have neither liability nor responsibility to any person or entity with respect to any loss or damages arising from the information contained in this book or from the use of the discs or programs that may accompany it.

The opinions expressed in this book belong to the authors and are not necessarily those of Cisco Systems, Inc.

Trademark Acknowledgments

All terms mentioned in this book that are known to be trademarks or service marks have been appropriately capitalized. Cisco Press or Cisco Systems, Inc., cannot attest to the accuracy of this information. Use of a term in this book should not be regarded as affecting the validity of any trademark or service mark.

Feedback Information

At Cisco Press, our goal is to create in-depth technical books of the highest quality and value. Each book is crafted with care and precision, undergoing rigorous development that involves the unique expertise of members from the professional technical community.

Readers' feedback is a natural continuation of this process. If you have any comments regarding how we could improve the quality of this book, or otherwise alter it to better suit your needs, you can contact us through e-mail at ciscopress@mcp.com. Please make sure to include the book title and ISBN in your message.

We greatly appreciate your assistance.

Publisher	John Wait
Executive Editor	John Kane
Cisco Systems Project Managers	Edie Quiroz
	Janet Ramey
Cisco Systems Program Manager	Bob Anstey
Managing Editor	Patrick Kanouse
Acquisitions Editors	Tracy Hughes
	Kathy Trace
Technical Editors	Anthony Bruno
	James Enin-okut
	Brian Garland
Senior Editor	Jennifer Chisholm
Copy Editor	Krista Hansing
Compositor	Steve Gifford
Cover Designer	Louisa Klucznick
Indexer	Cheryl Landis

CISCO SYSTEMS

Corporate Headquarters
Cisco Systems, Inc.
170 West Tasman Drive
San Jose, CA 95134-1706
USA
http://www.cisco.com
Tel: 408 526-4000
       800 553-NETS (6387)
Fax: 408 526-4100

European Headquarters
Cisco Systems Europe
11 Rue Camille Desmoulins
92782 Issy-les-Moulineaux
Cedex 9
France
http://www-
europe.cisco.com
Tel: 33 1 58 04 60 00
Fax: 33 1 58 04 61 00

Americas Headquarters
Cisco Systems, Inc.
170 West Tasman Drive
San Jose, CA 95134-1706
USA
http://www.cisco.com
Tel: 408 526-7660
Fax: 408 527-0883

Asia Pacific Headquarters
Cisco Systems Australia,
Pty., Ltd
Level 17, 99 Walker Street
North Sydney
NSW 2059 Australia
http://www.cisco.com
Tel: +61 2 8448 7100
Fax: +61 2 9957 4350

Cisco Systems has more than 200 offices in the following countries. Addresses, phone numbers, and fax numbers are listed on the Cisco web site at www.cisco.com/go/offices

Argentina • Australia • Austria • Belgium • Brazil • Bulgaria • Canada • Chile • China • Colombia • Costa Rica • Croatia • Czech Republic • Denmark • Dubai, UAE • Finland • France • Germany • Greece • Hong Kong • Hungary • India • Indonesia • Ireland • Israel • Italy • Japan • Korea • Luxembourg • Malaysia • Mexico • The Netherlands • New Zealand • Norway • Peru • Philippines • Poland • Portugal • Puerto Rico • Romania • Russia • Saudi Arabia • Scotland • Singapore • Slovakia • Slovenia • South Africa • Spain • Sweden • Switzerland • Taiwan • Thailand • Turkey • Ukraine • United Kingdom • United States • Venezuela • Vietnam • Zimbabwe

Contents at a Glance

Contents

Preface

Because of the rapid and ongoing developments in the field of networking, accurate troubleshooting information is an ever sought-after commodity. Because of this, the Cisco Press *Internetworking Troubleshooting Handbook* is a valuable resource for networking professionals throughout the industry.

For the second edition of this book, we gathered together a team of troubleshooting experts who thoroughly revised the material in each of the technology areas to include the most current and relevant troubleshooting information and solutions available today. Their goal and ours was to provide networking professionals with a guide containing solutions to the problems encountered in the field in a format that is easy to apply. We hope that this publication meets that goal.

Audience

The *Internetworking Troubleshooting Handbook* was written as a resource for anyone working in the field of networking who needs troubleshooting reference information. We anticipate that the information in this publication will assist users in solving specific technology issues and problems that they encounter in their existing environments.

Acknowledgments

The second edition of this unique guide is the outcome of a collaborative effort by a team of talented network troubleshooting experts headed by Cisco Systems Technical Assistance Center (TAC) manager, Janet Ramey. Contributors to this edition include the following current and former TAC Customer Support Engineers (in alphabetical order):

Karim Benhabeje (CCIE #5010)

Gerald Burgess (CCIE# 4540)

Russ Emerson (CCIE #4206)

Tim Gage (CCIE #3492)

Brian Hutchins-Knowles(CCIE #4794)

William M. Lee II

Geraldine Nadela

Nilesh Panicker

Yongxia (Annie) Shi

Francois Tallet (CCIE #3539)

Tom Tobias (CCIE #6257)

Robert Vigil (CCIE #1905)

Russ White (CCIE #2635)

Robert Wright (CCIE #1050)

Gilbert Yip (CCIE #5070)

Other contributors include the following:

Kevin Burgess

Mike Crane

Steve Dussault

Marion Jackson

Johnson Liu

William R. Wagner

Document Conventions

In this publication, the following conventions are used:

- Commands and keywords appear in **boldface**.
- New, important terms are *italicized* when accompanied by a definition or discussion of the term.
- **Note** is used to denote additional, helpful suggestions or references that otherwise do not appear in this book.

Our intent in updating this material and presenting it via Cisco Press is to deliver practical information to our customer community and the networking community at large. It is our hope that you find this material useful in your daily operations.

The authors acknowledge that many current and former Cisco employees contributed to building the content of this publication. Key participants included Jim Young, Amir Khan, John Wright, Keith Redfield, Won Lee, Pasvorn Boonmark, Steve Cunningham, Nga Vu, Imran Qureshi, Atif Khan, Arun Sastry, John Bashinski, Dave Katz, Dino Farinacci, Larry Bowden, Praveen Akkiraju, Steve Russell, Srinivas Vegesna, Phil Remaker, Priscilla Oppenheimer, Bruce Pinsky, Joanna Gardner, Dennis Peng, Charlie Justus, Morris Ng, Sue Phelan, Mark Allen, Ivan Chan, Dennis Wind, Rasa Elena Lorenzana, Cerafin Castillo, John Chong, Jeff Schults, Jack Nichols, and Dianne Dunlap.

The nature of this publication's development required substantial management support to coordinate the subject matter and expert time spent in creating the material. The authors acknowledge Joe Pinto, Brad Wright, Doug Allred, and Charles Baugh as instrumental management sponsors who recognized the importance of this kind of material to customers and nurtured its creation during its early development stages.

Principal authors of the first edition of this book were H. Kim Lew, Spank McCoy, Kathleen Wallace, Tim Stevenson, and Kevin Downes.

Introduction to Troubleshooting

## CHAPTER 1

Troubleshooting Overview

Dependency on network resources has grown tremendously over the past ten years. In today's world, a company's success is highly dependent on its network availability. As a result, companies are increasingly less tolerant of network failures. Therefore, network troubleshooting has become a crucial element to many organizations.

Not only has the dependency for network grown, but the industry also is moving toward increasingly complex environments, involving multiple media types, multiple protocols, and often interconnection to unknown networks. These unknown networks may be defined as a transit network belonging to a Internet service provider (ISP), or a telco that interconnects private networks. The convergence of voice and video into data networks has also added to the complexity and the importance of network reliability.

More complex network environments mean that the potential for connectivity and performance problems in internetworks is high, and the source of problems is often elusive.

Symptoms, Problems, and Solutions

Failures in internetworks are characterized by certain symptoms. These symptoms might be general (such as clients being incapable of accessing specific servers) or more specific (routes not existing in a routing table). Each symptom can be traced to one or more problems or causes by using specific troubleshooting tools and techniques. After being identified, each problem can be remedied by implementing a solution consisting of a series of actions.

This book describes how to define symptoms, identify problems, and implement solutions in generic environments. You should always apply the specific context in which you are troubleshooting to determine how to detect symptoms and diagnose problems for your specific environment.

General Problem-Solving Model

When you're troubleshooting a network environment, a systematic approach works best. An unsystematic approach to troubleshooting can result in wasting valuable time and resources, and can sometimes make symptoms even worse. Define the specific symptoms, identify all potential problems that could be causing the symptoms, and then systematically eliminate each potential problem (from most likely to least likely) until the symptoms disappear.

Figure 1-1 illustrates the process flow for the general problem-solving model. This process flow is not a rigid outline for troubleshooting an internetwork; it is a foundation from which you can build a problem-solving process to suit your particular environment.

Figure 1-1   *General Problem-Solving Model*

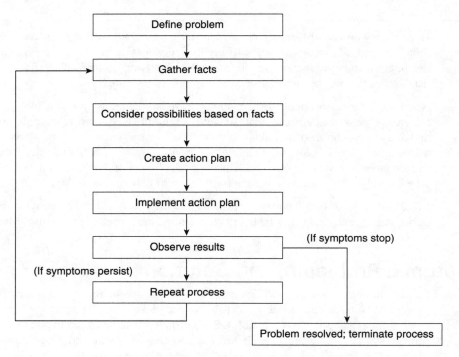

The following steps detail the problem-solving process outlined in Figure 1-1:

Step 1   When analyzing a network problem, make a clear problem statement. You should define the problem in terms of a set of symptoms and potential causes.

To properly analyze the problem, identify the general symptoms and then ascertain what kinds of problems (causes) could result in these symptoms. For example, hosts might not be responding to service requests from clients (a symptom). Possible causes might include a misconfigured host, bad interface cards, or missing router configuration commands.

Step 2 Gather the facts that you need to help isolate possible causes.

Ask questions of affected users, network administrators, managers, and other key people. Collect information from sources such as network management systems, protocol analyzer traces, output from router diagnostic commands, or software release notes.

Step 3 Consider possible problems based on the facts that you gathered. Using the facts, you can eliminate some of the potential problems from your list.

Depending on the data, for example, you might be able to eliminate hardware as a problem so that you can focus on software problems. At every opportunity, try to narrow the number of potential problems so that you can create an efficient plan of action.

Step 4 Create an action plan based on the remaining potential problems. Begin with the most likely problem, and devise a plan in which only one variable is manipulated.

Changing only one variable at a time enables you to reproduce a given solution to a specific problem. If you alter more than one variable simultaneously, you might solve the problem, but identifying the specific change that eliminated the symptom becomes far more difficult and will not help you solve the same problem if it occurs in the future.

Step 5 Implement the action plan, performing each step carefully while testing to see whether the symptom disappears.

Step 6 Whenever you change a variable, be sure to gather results. Generally, you should use the same method of gathering facts that you used in Step 2 (that is, working with the key people affected, in conjunction with utilizing your diagnostic tools).

Step 7 Analyze the results to determine whether the problem has been resolved. If it has, then the process is complete.

Step 8 If the problem has not been resolved, you must create an action plan based on the next most likely problem in your list. Return to Step 4, change one variable at a time, and repeat the process until the problem is solved.

NOTE   If you exhaust all the common causes and actions—either those outlined in this book or ones that you have identified for your environment—you should contact your Cisco technical support representative.

Preparing for Network Failure

It is always easier to recover from a network failure if you are prepared ahead of time. Possibly the most important requirement in any network environment is to have current and accurate information about that network available to the network support personnel at all times. Only with complete information can intelligent decisions be made about network change, and only with complete information can troubleshooting be done as quickly and as easily as possible.

During the process of network troubleshooting, the network is expected to exhibit abnormal behavior. Therefore, it is always a good practice to set up a maintenance time window for troubleshooting to minimize any business impact. Always document any changes being made so that it is easier to back out if troubleshooting has failed to identify the problem within the maintenance window.

To determine whether you are prepared for a network failure, answer the following questions:

- Do you have an accurate physical and logical map of your internetwork?

  Does your organization or department have an up-to-date internetwork map that outlines the physical location of all the devices on the network and how they are connected, as well as a logical map of network addresses, network numbers, subnetworks, and so forth?

- Do you have a list of all network protocols implemented in your network?

  For each of the protocols implemented, do you have a list of the network numbers, subnetworks, zones, areas, and so on that are associated with them?

- Do you know which protocols are being routed?

  For each routed protocol, do you have correct, up-to-date router configuration?

- Do you know which protocols are being bridged?

  Are any filters configured in any bridges, and do you have a copy of these configurations?

- Do you know all the points of contact to external networks, including any connections to the Internet?

  For each external network connection, do you know what routing protocol is being used?

- Do you have an established baseline for your network?

  Has your organization documented normal network behavior and performance at different times of the day so that you can compare the current problems with a baseline?

If you can answer yes to all questions, you will be able to recover from a failure more quickly and more easily than if you are not prepared. Lastly, for every problem solved, be sure to document the problems with solutions provided. This way, you will create a problem/answer database that others in your organization can refer to in case similar problems occur later. This will invariably reduce the time to troubleshoot your networks and, consequently, minimize your business impact.

## CHAPTER 2

Troubleshooting Tools

This chapter presents information about the wide variety of tools available to assist you in troubleshooting your internetwork. This includes information on using router diagnostic commands, Cisco network management tools, and third-party troubleshooting tools.

Using Router Diagnostic Commands

Cisco routers provide numerous integrated commands to assist you in monitoring and troubleshooting your internetwork. The following sections describe the basic use of these commands:

- The **show** commands help monitor installation behavior and normal network behavior, as well as isolate problem areas.
- The **debug** commands assist in the isolation of protocol and configuration problems.
- The **ping** commands help determine connectivity between devices on your network.
- The **trace** commands provide a method of determining the route by which packets reach their destination from one device to another.

Using show Commands

The **show** commands are powerful monitoring and troubleshooting tools. You can use the **show** commands to perform a variety of functions:

- Monitor router behavior during initial installation
- Monitor normal network operation
- Isolate problem interfaces, nodes, media, or applications
- Determine when a network is congested
- Determine the status of servers, clients, or other neighbors

The following are some of the most commonly used **show** commands:

- **show version**—Displays the configuration of the system hardware, the software version, the names and sources of configuration files, and the boot images.

- **show running-config**—Displays the router configuration currently running.

- **show startup-config**—Displays the router configuration stored in nonvolatile RAM (NVRAM).

- **show interfaces**—Displays statistics for all interfaces configured on the router or access server. The resulting output varies, depending on the network for which an interface has been configured.

- **show controllers**—Displays statistics for interface card controllers.

- **show flash**—Displays the layout and contents of Flash memory.

- **show buffers**—Displays statistics for the buffer pools on the router.

- **show memory summary**—Displays memory pool statistics and summary information about the activities of the system memory allocator, and gives a block-by-block listing of memory use.

- **show process cpu**—Displays information about the active processes on the router.

- **show stacks**—Displays information about the stack utilization of processes and interrupt routines, as well as the reason for the last system reboot.

- **show cdp neighbors**—Provides a degree of reachability information of directly connected Cisco devices. This is an extremely useful tool to determine the operational status of the physical and data link layer. Cisco Discovery Protocol (CDP) is a proprietary data link layer protocol.

- **show debugging**—Displays information about the type of debugging that is enabled for your router.

You can always use the **?** at command line for a list of subcommands.

Like the **debug** commands, some of the **show** commands listed previously are accessible only at the router's privileged exec mode (enable mode). This will be explained further in the "Using **debug** commands" section.

Hundreds of other **show** commands are available. For details on using and interpreting the output of specific **show** commands, refer to the Cisco Internetwork Operating System (IOS) command references.

Using debug Commands

The **debug** privileged exec commands can provide a wealth of information about the traffic being seen (or *not* seen) on an interface, error messages generated by nodes on the network, protocol-specific diagnostic packets, and other useful troubleshooting data. To access and list the privileged exec commands, enter this code:

```
Router> enable
Password: XXXXXX
Router# ?
```

Note the change in the router prompts here. The # prompt (instead of the normal > prompt) indicates that you are in the privileged exec mode (enable mode).

CAUTION Exercise care when using **debug** commands. Many **debug** commands are processor-intensive and can cause serious network problems (such as degraded performance or loss of connectivity) if they are enabled on an already heavily loaded router. When you finish using a **debug** command, remember to disable it with its specific **no debug** command (or use the **no debug all** command to turn off all debugging).

Use **debug** commands to isolate problems, not to monitor normal network operation. Because the high processor overhead of **debug** commands can disrupt router operation, you should use them only when you are looking for specific types of traffic or problems, and have narrowed your problems to a likely subset of causes.

Output formats vary with each **debug** command. Some generate a single line of output per packet, and others generate multiple lines of output per packet. Some generate large amounts of output, and others generate only occasional output. Some generate lines of text, and others generate information in field format.

To minimize the negative impact of using **debug** commands, follow this procedure:

Step 1 Use the **no logging console** global configuration command on your router. This command disables all logging to the console terminal.

Step 2 Telnet to a router port and enter the **enable** exec command. The **enable** exec command places the router in the privileged exec mode. After entering the **enable** password, you receive a prompt that consists of the router name with a # symbol.

Step 3 Use the **terminal monitor** command to copy **debug** command output and system error messages to your current terminal display.

By redirecting output to your current terminal display, you can view **debug** command output remotely, without being connected through the console port.

If you use **debug** commands at the console port, character-by-character processor interrupts are generated, maximizing the processor load already caused by using **debug**.

If you intend to keep the output of the **debug** command, spool the output to a file. The procedure for setting up such a **debug** output file is described in the *Debug Command Reference*.

This book refers to specific **debug** commands that are useful when troubleshooting specific problems. Complete details regarding the function and output of **debug** commands are provided in the *Debug Command Reference*.

In many situations, using third-party diagnostic tools can be more useful and less intrusive than using **debug** commands. For more information, see the section "Third-Party Troubleshooting Tools," later in this chapter.

Using the ping Commands

To check host reachability and network connectivity, use the **ping** command, which can be invoked from both user exec mode and privileged exec mode. After you log in to the router or access server, you are automatically in user exec command mode. The exec commands available at the user level are a subset of those available at the privileged level. In general, the user exec commands enable you to connect to remote devices, change terminal settings on a temporary basis, perform basic tests, and list system information. The **ping** command can be used to confirm basic network connectivity on AppleTalk, ISO Connectionless Network Service (CLNS), IP, Novell, Apollo, VINES, DECnet, or XNS networks.

For IP, the **ping** command sends Internet Control Message Protocol (ICMP) Echo messages. ICMP is the Internet protocol that reports errors and provides information relevant to IP packet addressing. If a station receives an ICMP Echo message, it sends an ICMP Echo Reply message back to the source.

The extended command mode of the **ping** command permits you to specify the supported IP header options. This allows the router to perform a more extensive range of test options. To enter **ping** extended command mode, enter **yes** at the extended commands prompt of the **ping** command.

It is a good idea to use the **ping** command when the network is functioning properly to see how the command works under normal conditions and so that you have something to compare against when troubleshooting.

For detailed information on using the **ping** and extended **ping** commands, refer to the *Cisco IOS Configuration Fundamentals Command Reference*.

Using the trace Commands

The **trace** user exec command discovers the routes that a router's packets follow when travelling to their destinations. The **trace** privileged exec command permits the supported IP header options to be specified, allowing the router to perform a more extensive range of test options.

The **trace** command works by using the error message generated by routers when a datagram exceeds its time-to-live (TTL) value. First, probe datagrams are sent with a TTL value of 1. This causes the first router to discard the probe datagrams and send back "time exceeded" error messages. The **trace** command then sends several probes and displays the round-trip time for each. After every third probe, the TTL is increased by 1.

Each outgoing packet can result in one of two error messages. A "time exceeded" error message indicates that an intermediate router has seen and discarded the probe. A "port unreachable" error message indicates that the destination node has received the probe and discarded it because it could not deliver the packet to an application. If the timer goes off before a response comes in, **trace** prints an asterisk (*).

The **trace** command terminates when the destination responds, when the maximum TTL is exceeded, or when the user interrupts the trace with the escape sequence.

As with **ping**, it is a good idea to use the **trace** command when the network is functioning properly to see how the command works under normal conditions and so that you have something to compare against when troubleshooting.

For detailed information on using the **trace** and extended **trace** commands, refer to the *Cisco IOS Configuration Fundamentals Command Reference*.

Using Cisco Network Management Tools

Cisco offers the CiscoWorks 2000 family of management products that provide design, monitoring, and troubleshooting tools to help you manage your internetwork.

The following internetwork management tools are useful for troubleshooting internetwork problems:

- CiscoView provides dynamic monitoring and troubleshooting functions, including a graphical display of Cisco devices, statistics, and comprehensive configuration information.
- Internetwork Performance Monitor (IPM) empowers network engineers to proactively troubleshoot network response times utilizing real-time and historical reports.
- The TrafficDirector RMON application, a remote monitoring tool, enables you to gather data, monitor activity on your network, and find potential problems.

- The VlanDirector switch management application is a management tool that provides an accurate picture of your VLANs.

CiscoView

CiscoView graphical management features provide dynamic status, statistics, and comprehensive configuration information for Cisco internetworking products (switches, routers, hubs, concentrators, and access servers). CiscoView aids network management by displaying a physical view of Cisco devices and color-coding device ports for at-a-glance port status, allowing users to quickly grasp essential information. Features include the following:

- Graphical displays of Cisco products from a central location, giving network managers a complete view of Cisco products without physically checking each device at remote sites
- A continuously updated physical view of routers, hubs, switches, or access servers in a network, regardless of physical location
- Updated real-time monitoring and tracking of key information and data relating to device performance, traffic, and usage, with metrics such as utilization percentage, frames transmitted and received, errors, and a variety of other device-specific indicators
- The capability to modify configurations such as trap, IP route, virtual LAN (VLAN), and bridge configurations

Internetwork Performance Monitor

IPM is a network management application that enables you to monitor the performance of multiprotocol networks. IPM measures the response time and availability of IP networks on a hop-by-hop (router-to-router) basis. It also measures response time between routers and the mainframe in Systems Network Architecture (SNA) networks.

Use IPM to perform the following tasks:

- Troubleshoot problems by checking the network latency between devices
- Send Simple Network Management Protocol (SNMP) traps and SNA alerts when a user-configured threshold is exceeded, when a connection is lost and re-established, or when a timeout occurs
- Analyze potential problems before they occur by accumulating statistics, which are used to model and predict future network topologies
- Monitor response time between two network end points

The IPM product is composed of three parts: the IPM server, the IPM client application, and the response time reporter (RTR) feature of the Cisco IOS software.

The TrafficDirector RMON Application

The *TrafficDirector* advanced packet filters let users monitor all seven layers of network traffic. Using Cisco IOS embedded RMON agents and SwitchProbe standalone probes, managers can view enterprise-wide network traffic from the link, network, transport, or application layers. The TrafficDirector multilayer traffic summary provides a quick, high-level assessment of network loading and protocol distributions. Network managers then "zoom in" on a specific segment, ring, switch port, or trunk link and apply real-time analysis and diagnostic tools to view hosts, conversations, and packet captures.

TrafficDirector threshold monitoring enables users to implement a proactive management environment. First, thresholds for critical Management Information Base (MIB) variables are set within the RMON agent. When these thresholds are exceeded, traps are sent to the appropriate management station to notify the network administrator of an impending problem.

The VlanDirector Switch Management Application

The *VlanDirector* switch management application simplifies VLAN port assignment and offers other management capabilities for VLANs. VlanDirector offers the following features for network administrators:

- Accurate representation of the physical network for VLAN design and configuration verification

- Capability to obtain VLAN configuration information on a specific device or link interface

- Discrepancy reports on conflicting configurations

- Capability to troubleshoot and identify individual device configurations that are in error with system-level VLANs

- Quick detection of changes in VLAN status of switch ports

- User authentication and write protection security

Third-Party Troubleshooting Tools

In many situations, third-party diagnostic tools can be more useful than commands that are integrated into the router. For example, enabling a processor-intensive **debug** command can be disastrous in an environment experiencing excessively high traffic levels. However, attaching a network analyzer to the suspect network is less intrusive and is more likely to yield useful information without interrupting the operation of the router. The following are some typical third-party troubleshooting tools used for troubleshooting internetworks:

- Volt-ohm meters, digital multimeters, and cable testers are useful in testing the physical connectivity of your cable plant.

- Time domain reflectors (TDRs) and optical time domain reflectors (OTDRs) are devices that assist in the location of cable breaks, impedance mismatches, and other physical cable plant problems.

- Breakout boxes, fox boxes, and BERTs/BLERTs are useful for troubleshooting problems in peripheral interfaces.

- Network monitors provide an accurate picture of network activity over a period of time by continuously tracking packets crossing a network.

- Network analyzers such as sniffers decode problems at all seven OSI layers and can be identified automatically in real time, providing a clear view of network activity and categorizing problems by criticality.

Volt-Ohm Meters, Digital Multimeters, and Cable Testers

Volt-ohm meters and *digital multimeters* are at the lower end of the spectrum of cable-testing tools. These devices measure parameters such as AC and DC voltage, current, resistance, capacitance, and cable continuity. They are used to check physical connectivity.

Cable testers (scanners) also enable you to check physical connectivity. Cable testers are available for shielded twisted-pair (STP), unshielded twisted-pair (UTP), 10BaseT, and coaxial and twinax cables. A given cable tester might be capable of performing any of the following functions:

- Test and report on cable conditions, including near-end crosstalk (NEXT), attenuation, and noise

- Perform TDR, traffic monitoring, and wire map functions

- Display Media Access Control (MAC)–layer information about LAN traffic, provide statistics such as network utilization and packet error rates, and perform limited protocol testing (for example, TCP/IP tests such as **ping**)

Similar testing equipment is available for fiber-optic cable. Because of the relatively high cost of this cable and its installation, fiber-optic cable should be tested both before installation (on-the-reel testing) and after installation. Continuity testing of the fiber requires either a visible light source or a reflectometer. Light sources capable of providing light at the three predominant wavelengths—850 nanometers (nm), 1300 nm, and 1550 nm—are used with power meters that can measure the same wavelengths and test attenuation and return loss in the fiber.

TDRs and OTDRs

At the top end of the cable testing spectrum are *TDRs*. These devices can quickly locate open and short circuits, crimps, kinks, sharp bends, impedance mismatches, and other defects in metallic cables.

A TDR works by bouncing a signal off the end of the cable. Opens, shorts, and other problems reflect the signal back at different amplitudes, depending on the problem. A TDR measures how much time it takes for the signal to reflect and calculates the distance to a fault in the cable. TDRs can also be used to measure the length of a cable. Some TDRs can also calculate the propagation rate based on a configured cable length.

Fiber-optic measurement is performed by an OTDR. OTDRs can accurately measure the length of the fiber, locate cable breaks, measure the fiber attenuation, and measure splice or connector losses. An OTDR can be used to take the signature of a particular installation, noting attenuation and splice losses. This baseline measurement can then be compared with future signatures when a problem in the system is suspected.

Breakout Boxes, Fox Boxes, and BERTs/BLERTs

Breakout boxes, fox boxes, and *bit/block error rate testers* (*BERTs/BLERTs*) are digital interface testing tools used to measure the digital signals present at PCs, printers, modems, the channel service unit/digital service unit (CSU/DSU), and other peripheral interfaces. These devices can monitor data line conditions, analyze and trap data, and diagnose problems common to data communication systems. Traffic from data terminal equipment (DTE) through data communications equipment (DCE) can be examined to help isolate problems, identify bit patterns, and ensure that the proper cabling has been installed. These devices cannot test media signals such as Ethernet, Token Ring, or FDDI.

Network Monitors

Network monitors continuously track packets crossing a network, providing an accurate picture of network activity at any moment, or a historical record of network activity over a period of time. They do not decode the contents of frames. Monitors are useful for baselining, in which the activity on a network is sampled over a period of time to establish a normal performance profile, or baseline.

Monitors collect information such as packet sizes, the number of packets, error packets, overall usage of a connection, the number of hosts and their MAC addresses, and details about communications between hosts and other devices. This data can be used to create profiles of LAN traffic as well as to assist in locating traffic overloads, planning for network expansion, detecting intruders, establishing baseline performance, and distributing traffic more efficiently.

Network Analyzers

A *network analyzer* (also called a *protocol analyzer*) decodes the various protocol layers in a recorded frame and presents them as readable abbreviations or summaries, detailing which layer is involved (physical, data link, and so forth) and what function each byte or byte content serves.

Most network analyzers can perform many of the following functions:

- Filter traffic that meets certain criteria so that, for example, all traffic to and from a particular device can be captured
- Time stamp-captured data
- Present protocol layers in an easily readable form
- Generate frames and transmit them onto the network
- Incorporate an "expert" system in which the analyzer uses a set of rules, combined with information about the network configuration and operation, to diagnose and solve, or offer potential solutions to, network problems

Hardware, Booting, and Media Problems

## CHAPTER 3

Troubleshooting Hardware and Booting Problems

This chapter provides procedures for troubleshooting hardware and booting problems. Although it provides specific procedures for some Cisco products, always refer to your hardware installation and maintenance publication for more detailed information about your specific platform, including descriptions of specific LEDs, configuration information, and additional troubleshooting information.

This chapter begins with the following sections on hardware problems:

- **Cisco 7500 Series Startup**—Describes hardware and boot process troubleshooting for Cisco 7500 series routers

- **Cisco 7000 Series Startup**—Describes hardware and boot process troubleshooting for Cisco 7000 series routers

- **Cisco 4000 Series Startup**—Describes hardware and boot process troubleshooting for Cisco 4000 series routers

- **Cisco 2500 Series Startup**—Describes hardware and boot process troubleshooting for Cisco 2500 series routers

- **Catalyst 5000 Series Startup**—Describes hardware and boot process troubleshooting for Catalyst 5000 series LAN switches

- **Catalyst 2900 Series Startup**—Describes hardware and boot process troubleshooting for Catalyst 2900 series LAN switches

- **Testing and Verifying Replacement Parts**—Provides suggested actions when swapping router hardware

- **Catalyst 6000 Series Startup**—Describes hardware and boot process troubleshooting for Catalyst 6000 series LAN switches

- **Cisco 2600 Series Startup**—Describes hardware and boot process troubleshooting for Cisco 2600 series routers

- **Cisco 3600 Series Startup**—Describes hardware and boot process troubleshooting for Cisco 3600 series routers

- **Catalyst 4000 Series Startup**—Describes hardware and boot process troubleshooting for Catalyst 4000 series LAN switches

The remaining sections describe symptoms, problems, and solutions for Flash boot, network boot using TFTP, ROM boot, and other bootup problems:

- Booting: Router Fails to Boot from Flash Memory
- Booting: Vector Error Occurs When Booting from Flash Memory
- Booting: Router Partially Boots from Flash and Displays Boot Prompt
- Booting: Router Cannot Network boot from TFTP Server
- Booting: Router Cannot Network boot from Another Router
- Booting: Timeouts and Out-of-Order Packets Prevent Network booting
- Booting: Invalid Routes Prevent Network booting
- Booting: Client ARP Requests Timeout During Network boot
- Booting: Undefined Load Module Error When Network booting
- Booting: Router Hangs After ROM Monitor Initializes
- Booting: Router Is Stuck in ROM Monitor Mode
- Booting: Scrambled Output When Booting from ROM
- Booting: Local Timeouts Occur When Booting from ROM
- Booting: Unresponsive Terminal Connection to Unconfigured Access Server

Booting the Router

Cisco routers can initialize the system (boot) in four ways:

- **Network boot**—Routers can boot from a server using the Trivial File Transfer Protocol (TFTP), the DEC Maintenance Operation Protocol (MOP), or the Remote Copy Protocol (RCP) across any of the supported media types (such as Ethernet, Token Ring, Fiber Distributed Data Interface [FDDI], High-Speed Serial Interface [HSSI], and serial lines).
- **Flash memory**—Routers can boot from Flash memory, a nonvolatile storage medium that can be electrically erased and reprogrammed.
- **ROM**—Routers can boot a system from built-in read-only memory (ROM).
- **PC Flash memory card**—Routers can boot from a removable Flash memory card.

This section provides general information about router booting.

Network Booting Tips

During network booting sessions, routers behave like hosts. They route via proxy Address Resolution Protocol (ARP), Serial Line Address Resolution Protocol (SLARP) information, Internet Control Message Protocol (ICMP) redirects, or a default gateway. When network booting, routers ignore dynamic routing information, static IP routes, and bridging information. As a result, intermediate routers are responsible for handling ARP and User Datagram Protocol (UDP) requests correctly. For serial and HSSI media, ARP is not used.

Before network booting from a server, you should **ping** the server from the ROM software. If you cannot **ping** the server, follow the procedures described in the section "Booting: Router Cannot Network boot from TFTP Server," later in this chapter. If you still cannot **ping** the server, there is probably a server configuration or hardware problem. Refer to your TFTP server documentation, or contact your technical support representative for assistance.

Fault-Tolerant Boot Strategies

Although network booting is useful, network or server failures can make network booting impossible. After you have installed and configured the router's Flash memory, configure the boot sequence for the router to reduce the impact of a server or network failure. The following order is recommended:

1   Boot an image from Flash memory.

2   Boot an image using a network boot.

3   Boot from a ROM image.

The following is an example of how to configure a router with a fault-tolerant boot sequence.

```
goriot# configure terminal
Enter configuration commands, one per line.  End with CNTL/Z.
goriot(config)# boot system flash gsxx
goriot(config)# boot system gsxx 131.108.1.101
goriot(config)# boot system rom
goriot(config)# ^Z
goriot#
%SYS-5-CONFIG_I: Configured from console by console
goriot# copy running-config startup-config
[ok]
goriot#
```

Using this strategy, a router has three sources from which to boot: Flash memory, network boot, and ROM. Providing alternative sources can help to mitigate any failure of the TFTP server or the network.

NOTE	The configuration register must be set to allow ROM image booting after failed network booting attempts. For more information, refer to the hardware configuration manual for your platform.

Timeouts and Out-of-Order Packets

When network booting, a client might need to retransmit requests before receiving a response to an ARP request. These retransmissions can result in timeouts and out-of-order packets.

Timeouts (shown as periods in a network booting display) and out-of-order packets (shown as uppercase O's) do not necessarily prevent a successful network boot. It is acceptable to have either or both timeouts or out-of-order packets occur during the network boot process.

The following examples show console output from network booting sessions that were successful even though timeouts and out-of-order packets occurred (exclamation points represent successfully received packets):

```
Booting gs3-bfx from 131.108.1.123: !.!!!!!!!!!!!!!!!!!!!!!!!
Booting gs3-bfx from 131.108.1.123: !O.O!!!!!!!!!!!!!!!!!!!!!!!
```

If a network boot generates excessive out-of-order packets and timeouts, problems might result. These problems are discussed later in this chapter, in the section "Booting: Timeouts and Out-of-Order Packets Prevent Network booting."

Information for Technical Support

If you cannot resolve your booting problem using the procedures outlined in this chapter, collect the following information for your technical support representative:

- ROM images. (Use the **show version** exec command.)
- Programmable ROM labels. (This information is printed on the physical chip, and an example is shown in Figure 3-1.)

Figure 3-1 *An Example of a Boot ROM Label—Boot ROM Version 11.1(2)*

```
U30 v11 1(2)
RS P2-ROMMON
O17-2111-04
Cisco Systems
```

- NVRAM configurations for client and adjacent routers.
- Debugging output from adjacent routers using the following privileged exec commands:

  — **debug ip packet**

  — **debug arp**

  — **debug ip udp**

  — **debug tftp**

For more information about these **debug** commands, refer to the *Debug Command Reference*.

Troubleshooting Hardware

This section discusses procedures for connectivity problems related to booting. It describes specific booting symptoms, the problems that are likely to cause each symptom, and the solutions to those problems.

Cisco 7500 Series Startup

When you start up a Cisco 7500 series router, the following should occur:

- The AC (or DC) OK LED should go on immediately and should remain on as long as the system is receiving power.
- The blower should be operating.
- The Route Switch Processor (RSP) and front-panel Normal LEDs should go on (to indicate normal system operation) and should remain on during system operation; the CPU Halt LED should remain off.
- The Enabled LED on each interface processor should go on (to indicate that the RSP has completed initialization of the interface processor).

When the 7500 series system has initialized successfully, the system banner should be displayed on the console screen. If it is not displayed, make sure that the console terminal is properly connected to the RSP console port and that the terminal is set correctly. The system banner should look similar to the following:

```
System Bootstrap, Version 4.6(5), SOFTWARE
Copyright (c) 1986-1995 by cisco Systems
RSP2 processor with 16384 Kbytes of memory
### [...] ###
F3: 2012356+47852+194864 at 0x1000
```

```
                 Restricted Rights Legend
Use, duplication, or disclosure by the Government is
subject to restrictions as set forth in subparagraph
(c) of the Commercial Computer Software - Restricted
Rights clause at FAR sec. 52.227-19 and subparagraph
(c) (1) (ii) of the Rights in Technical Data and Computer
Software clause at DFARS sec. 252.227-7013.
                 cisco Systems, Inc.
                 170 Tasman Drive
                 San Jose, CA 95134
GS Software (RSP-K), Version 10.3(571) [fc3], RELEASE SOFTWARE
Copyright (c) 1986-1995 by cisco Systems, Inc.
[...]
Press RETURN to get started!
```

If a problem occurs, try to isolate the problem to a specific subsystem. The Cisco 7500 series routers have the following subsystems:

- **Power subsystem**—Includes power supplies, external power cable, and backplane

- **Cooling subsystem**—Depending on your system, includes the following:

  — **Cisco 7505**—Fan tray, fan tray spare with six individual fans, and fan control board

  — **Cisco 7507**—Chassis blower

  — **Cisco 7513**—Blower module, including blower, blower-speed control board, front-panel LEDs, and the module itself

- **Processor subsystem**—Depending on your system, includes all interface processors and either the RSP1 or the RSP2

Table 3-1 outlines the areas where Cisco 7500 series startup problems may occur and describes solutions to those problems.

Table 3-1   *Hardware: Cisco 7500 Series Startup Problems and Solutions*

Possible Problem Area	Solution	
Power subsystem	Step 1	Check to see whether the blower is operating and that LEDs on the processor modules are on. If the blower and LEDs are on but the Power Supply LED is off, there is probably a faulty Power Supply LED.
	Step 2	Make sure that the power switch is set correctly to the on position.
	Step 3	Make sure that the power source, power cable, and power supply are functioning correctly. Swap parts to see whether one of the components is faulty.
	Step 4	Ensure that the blower module is seated properly. Make sure that the blower control board edge connector is inserted fully in the backplane socket.

Table 3-1 *Hardware: Cisco 7500 Series Startup Problems and Solutions (Continued)*

Possible Problem Area	Solution
Cooling subsystem	**Step 1** Check to see whether the blower is operating when you start up the system. If the blower is not operating, there might be a problem with the blower or the +24 V DC power:
	• If the Output Fail LED is on, there might be a problem with the +24V DC supply to the blower or fan tray at either the power supply or the blower control board.
	• If the blower is not operating and the Output Fail LED is off, ensure that the blower module is seated properly. Ensure that the blower control board edge connector is inserted fully in the backplane socket.
	Step 2 If the system and blower start up but shut down after about 2 minutes, one or more fans might have failed or might be operating out of tolerance. You will probably see an error message similar to the following:
| | ```
%ENVM-2-FAN: Fan has failed, shutdown in 2
minutes
``` |
| | If the blower or the blower control board fails, you must replace the blower module. |
| | **Step 3** If you see the following message at startup, the system has detected an overtemperature condition or out-of-tolerance power inside the chassis: |
| | ```
Queued messages:
%ENVM-1-SHUTDOWN: Environmental Monitor
initiated shutdown
``` |
	If an environmental shutdown results from an out-of-tolerance power condition, the Output Fail LED goes on before the system shuts down.
	This shutdown message might also indicate a faulty component or temperature sensor. Before the system shuts down, use the **show environment** or **show environment table** commands to display the internal chassis environment.
	Step 4 Ensure that heated exhaust air from other equipment is not entering the inlet vents and that there is sufficient clearance around the chassis to allow cooling air to flow.

continues

Table 3-1 *Hardware: Cisco 7500 Series Startup Problems and Solutions (Continued)*

Possible Problem Area	Solution	
Processor subsystem	**Step 1**	Check the RSP[1] LEDs. If no LEDs come on, ensure that the power supplies and blower are functioning properly.
	Step 2	Check the seating of the RSP. If the RSP is not seated properly, it will hang the system.
	Step 3	If the RSP CPU Halt LED is on, the system has detected a processor hardware failure. Contact a technical support representative for instructions.
	Step 4	Check to see whether the RSP Normal LED is on, indicating that the system software has initialized successfully and that the system is operational.
	Step 5	Check the Enabled LED on each interface processor. This LED should go on when the RSP has initialized the interface processor.
	Step 6	If the Enabled LED on an individual interface processor is off, the interface processor might have pulled away from the backplane. If the interface processors are not seated properly, they will hang the system.

[1]RSP = Route Switch Processor

Cisco 7000 Series Startup

When you start up a Cisco 7000 series router, the following should occur:

- The DC OK LED should go on and should remain on as long as the system is receiving source power.
- The fans should be operating.
- The Route Processor (RP) Normal LED should go on and stay on to indicate normal system operation; the Halt CPU LED should remain off.
- The Enabled LED on the Switch Processor (SP) or Silicon Switch Processor (SSP) and each interface processor should go on when the RP has completed initialization of the interface processor or SP (or SSP) for operation.

When the system has initialized successfully, the system banner should be displayed on the console screen. If it is not displayed, make sure that the console terminal is properly connected to the RP console port and that the terminal is set correctly. The system banner should look similar to the following:

```
System Bootstrap, Version 4.6(5), SOFTWARE
Copyright (c) 1986-1995 by cisco Systems
RP1 processor with 16384 Kbytes of memory
### [...] ###
F3: 2012356+47852+194864 at 0x1000


                    Restricted Rights Legend

Use, duplication, or disclosure by the Government is
subject to restrictions as set forth in subparagraph
(c) of the Commercial Computer Software - Restricted
Rights clause at FAR sec. 52.227-19 and subparagraph
(c) (1) (ii) of the Rights in Technical Data and Computer
Software clause at DFARS sec. 252.227-7013.

                 cisco Systems, Inc.
                 170 West Tasman Drive
                 San Jose, California 95134-1706

GS Software (GS7), Version 10.3(1) [fc3], RELEASE SOFTWARE
Copyright (c) 1986-1995 by cisco Systems, Inc.

RP1 (68040) processor with 16384K bytes of memory.
[...]

Press RETURN to get started!
```

If problems occur, try to isolate the problem to a specific subsystem. The Cisco 7000 series routers have the following subsystems:

- **Power subsystem**—Includes power supplies, fans, external power cable, and internal power harness that connects to the backplane

- **Cooling subsystem**—Depending on your system, includes the following:

  — **Cisco 7000**—Chassis blower

  — **Cisco 7010**—Fan tray assembly, including six individual fans, the fan control board, and the tray itself

- **Processor subsystem**—Includes the RP, SP (or SSP), and all interface processors

Table 3-2 outlines the areas where Cisco 7000 series startup problems may occur and describes solutions to those problems.

Table 3-2   *Hardware: Cisco 7000 Series Startup Problems and Solutions*

Possible Problem Area	Solution	
Power subsystem	**Step 1**	Check to see whether the DC OK LED is on.
	Step 2	If the LED is not on but the fans are operating and LEDs on the processor modules are on, the Power Supply LED might be faulty.
	Step 3	If the LED is not on and there is no other activity, make sure that the power switch is fully in the on position.
	Step 4	Make sure that the power source, power cable, and power supply are functioning correctly. Swap parts to see whether one of the components is faulty.
	Step 5	Ensure that the fan tray is seated properly. Make sure that the fan control board edge connector is inserted fully in the backplane socket.
Cooling subsystem	**Step 1**	Check to see whether the fans are operating.
	Step 2	If the fans are not operating and the DC OK LED is off, there might be a problem with the +24V DC power.
	Step 3	Ensure that the fan tray is seated properly. Make sure that the fan control board edge connector is inserted fully in the backplane socket.
	Step 4	If the system and the fans start up but shut down after about 2 minutes, one or more fans has failed or is operating out of tolerance. You will see an error message similar to the following: `%ENVM-2-FAN: Fan array has failed, shutdown in 2 minutes` If one or more fans or the fan control board fails, you must replace the fan tray.

	Step 5	If you see the following error message, the system has detected an overtemperature condition or out-of-tolerance power inside the chassis:
		
		`Queued messages:`
		`%ENVM-1-SHUTDOWN: Environmental Monitor`
		`initiated shutdown`
		
		If an environmental shutdown results from an out-of-tolerance power condition, the DC OK LED will go off before the system shuts down.

Table 3-2   *Hardware: Cisco 7000 Series Startup Problems and Solutions (Continued)*

Possible Problem Area		Solution
Cooling subsystem *(continued)*		This shutdown message could also indicate a faulty component or temperature sensor. Use the **show environment** or **show environment table** command to display the internal chassis environment.
	Step 6	Make sure that heated exhaust air from other equipment is not entering the inlet vents, and that there is sufficient clearance around the chassis to allow cooling air to flow.
Processor subsystem	Step 1	Check to see whether the RP[1] LEDs come on when system power is turned on.
	Step 2	If none of the RP LEDs come on, make sure that both the fan and the power supply are functioning properly.
	Step 3	If the power supply and fans appear operational but none of the RP LEDs are on, an improperly connected RP, SP[2] (or SSP[3]), or interface processor might have hung the bus.
	Step 4	If the SP (or SSP) Enabled LED is off but any of the RP LEDs are on, make sure that the SP (or SSP) is seated in its slot properly.
	Step 5	Check to see whether the Boot Error LED is on. If the LED is on, the system software is incapable of starting up. If you have a spare RP with the system software ROMs installed, replace the installed RP with the spare to see whether the system will boot.
	Step 6	Check to see whether the RP CPU Halt LED is on. If it is, the system has detected a processor hardware failure. Contact a technical support representative for more information.
	Step 7	Check to see whether all interface processor Enabled LEDs are on.
	Step 8	If the Enabled LED on an individual interface processor is off, make sure that the interface processor has not pulled away from the backplane.

[1]RP = Route Processor

[2]SP = Switch Processor

[3]SSP = Silicon Switch Processor

Cisco 4000 Series Startup

When you start up a Cisco 4000 series router, the following should occur:

- The System OK LED should come on and stay on as long as power is supplied.

- The fans should be operating.

When the system has initialized successfully, the system banner should be displayed on the console screen. The system banner should look similar to the following:

```
System Bootstrap, Version 4.14(9), SOFTWARE
Copyright (c) 1986-1994 by cisco Systems
4000 processor with 16384 Kbytes of main memory

Loading xx-j-mz.112-0.15 at 0x4A790, size = 3496424 bytes [OK]
F3: 8988+3487404+165008 at 0x12000
Self decompressing the image : ###[...]#### [OK]

                  Restricted Rights Legend

Use, duplication, or disclosure by the Government is
subject to restrictions as set forth in subparagraph
(c) of the Commercial Computer Software - Restricted
Rights clause at FAR sec. 52.227-19 and subparagraph
(c) (1) (ii) of the Rights in Technical Data and Computer
Software clause at DFARS sec. 252.227-7013.

            cisco Systems, Inc.
            170 West Tasman Drive
            San Jose, California 95134-1706



Cisco Internetwork Operating System Software
IOS (tm) 4000 Software (XX-J-M), Version 11.2(0.15), BETA TEST SOFTWARE
Copyright (c) 1986-1996 by cisco Systems, Inc.
Compiled Wed 03-Jul-96 01:21 by susingh
Image text-base: 0x00012000, data-base: 0x006F6494


cisco 4000 (68030) processor (revision 0xA0) with 16384K/4096K bytes of memory.
Processor board ID 5007155
G.703/E1 software, Version 1.0.
Bridging software.
SuperLAT software copyright 1990 by Meridian Technology Corp).
X.25 software, Version 2.0, NET2, BFE and GOSIP compliant.
TN3270 Emulation software (copyright 1994 by TGV Inc).
Basic Rate ISDN software, Version 1.0.
2 Ethernet/IEEE 802.3 interfaces.
4 Serial network interfaces.
8 ISDN Basic Rate interfaces.
128K bytes of non-volatile configuration memory.
4096K bytes of processor board System flash (Read/Write)

Press RETURN to get started!
```

If problems occur, try to isolate the problem to a specific subsystem. The Cisco 4000 series routers have the following subsystems:

- **Power subsystem**—This subsystem includes the power supply and the wiring.
- **Cooling subsystem**—This subsystem includes the blower assembly, which should come on when power is applied.
- **Network processor modules (NPMs)**—This subsystem includes all NPMs installed in the router chassis.
- **System cables**—This subsystem includes all the external cables that connect the router to the network.

Table 3-3 outlines the areas where Cisco 4000 series startup problems may occur and describes solutions to those problems.

Table 3-3   *Hardware: Cisco 4000 Series Startup Problems and Solutions*

Possible Problem Area	Solution	
Power and cooling subsystems	Step 1	Check to see whether the blower is operating. If it is not, check the AC power input, AC power source, router circuit breaker, and power supply cable.

	Step 2	If the system shuts down after being on a short time, check the power supply. If the power supply appears operational, the router might have shut down due to overheating. Check the console for error messages similar to the following:
		
		`%SYS-1-OVERTEMP: System detected`
		`OVERTEMPERATURE condition. Please resolve`
		`cooling problem immediately!`
		
		Make sure that the fans are working and that there is no air blockage to cooling vents.

	Step 3	If the system partially boots but LEDs do not light, contact your technical support representative.
NPMs[1] and cables	Step 1	Make sure that NPMs are properly connected to the motherboard connector.
	Step 2	Check the external cables.
	Step 3	Check the processor or software for proper configuration.
	Step 4	Check the external console connection and verify that the console baud rate is correct.

[1]NPMs = network processor modules

Cisco 2500 Series Startup

When you start up a Cisco 2500 series router, the following should occur:

- The System OK LED should come on and stay on as long as power is supplied.

- The fans should be operating.

When the system has initialized successfully, the system banner should be displayed on the console screen. The system banner should look similar to the following:

```
System Bootstrap, Version (3.3), SOFTWARE
Copyright (c) 1986-1993 by cisco Systems
2500 processor with 16384 Kbytes of main memory

Unknown or ambiguous service arg - udp-small-servers
Unknown or ambiguous service arg - tcp-small-servers
Booting igs-in-l.110-9 from Flash address space
F3: 3844616+90320+228904 at 0x3000060


                  Restricted Rights Legend

Use, duplication, or disclosure by the Government is
subject to restrictions as set forth in subparagraph
(c) of the Commercial Computer Software - Restricted
Rights clause at FAR sec. 52.227-19 and subparagraph
(c) (1) (ii) of the Rights in Technical Data and Computer
Software clause at DFARS sec. 252.227-7013.


          cisco Systems, Inc.
          170 West Tasman Drive
          San Jose, California 95134-1706



Cisco Internetwork Operating System Software
IOS (tm) 3000 Software (IGS-IN-L), Version 11.0(9), RELEASE SOFTWARE (fc1)
Copyright (c) 1986-1996 by cisco Systems, Inc.
Compiled Tue 11-Jun-96 01:15 by loreilly
Image text-base: 0x03020F8C, data-base: 0x00001000

cisco 2500 (68030) processor (revision A) with 16384K/2048K bytes of memory.
Processor board ID 01062462, with hardware revision 00000000
Bridging software.
X.25 software, Version 2.0, NET2, BFE and GOSIP compliant.
Basic Rate ISDN software, Version 1.0.
1 Ethernet/IEEE 802.3 interface.
2 Serial network interfaces.
1 ISDN Basic Rate interface.
32K bytes of non-volatile configuration memory.
4096K bytes of processor board System flash (Read ONLY)


Press RETURN to get started!
```

If problems occur, try to isolate the problem to a specific subsystem. The Cisco 2500 series routers have the following subsystems:

- **Power subsystem**—This subsystem includes the power supply and the wiring.

- **Cooling subsystem**—This subsystem includes the fan, which should go on when power is applied.

- **Network interfaces**—This subsystem includes all network interfaces, such as Ethernet, Token Ring, serial, or ISDN Basic Rate Interface (BRI).
- **System cables**—This subsystem includes all the external cables that connect the router to the network.

Table 3-4 outlines the areas where Cisco 2500 series startup problems may occur and describes solutions to those problems.

Table 3-4   *Hardware: Cisco 2500 Series Startup Problems and Solutions*

Possible Problem Area	Solution	
Power and cooling subsystems	Step 1	If the Power LED is off, make sure that the power supply is plugged in to the wall receptacle and that the cable from the power supply to the router is connected.
	Step 2	If the system shuts down after being on a short time, there might have been a thermal-induced shutdown caused by a faulty fan, or the power to the system might have been lost. Ensure that the system is receiving power and that the chassis intake and exhaust vents are clear.
	Step 3	If the system does not boot up but LEDs are on, check the 12V power supply.
	Step 4	If the system partially boots but LEDs are not on, check the 5V power supply.
Network interfaces and cables	Step 1	If a network interface is not recognized by the system, check the interface cable connection and the LED on the network interface.
	Step 2	If a network interface is recognized but will not initialize, check the interface cable connection.
	Step 3	If the system will not boot properly or constantly, or if it intermittently reboots, there might be a processor or software problem. Make sure that DRAM SIMM modules are seated properly.
	Step 4	If the system boots but the console screen is frozen, check the external console connection and verify that the console baud rate is correct.
	Step 5	If the system powers on and boots with a particular interface disconnected, check the network interface connection.

Catalyst 5000 Series Startup

When you start up a Catalyst 5000 series LAN switch, the following should occur:

- The PS1 and PS2 LEDs on the supervisor engine module faceplate should be green.

- The system fan assembly should be operating, and the Fan LED on the supervisor engine module should come on.

- The Status LED on the supervisor engine module and all interfaces should be orange until the boot is complete.

When the system boot is complete, the supervisor engine module should initialize the switching modules. The status LED on each switching module goes on when initialization has been completed, and the console screen displays a script and system banner similar to the following:

```
        ATE0
ATS0=1
Catalyst 5000 Power Up Diagnostics
Init NVRAM Log
LED Test
ROM CHKSUM
DUAL PORT RAM r/w
RAM r/w
RAM address test
Byte/Word Enable test
RAM r/w 55aa
RAM r/w aa55
EARL test
BOOTROM Version 1.4, Dated Dec  5 1995 16:49:40
BOOT date: 00/00/00 BOOT time: 03:18:57
SIMM RAM address test
SIMM Ram r/w 55aa
SIMM Ram r/w aa55
Start to Uncompress Image ...
IP address for Catalyst not configured
BOOTP will commence after the ports are online
Ports are coming online ...
Cisco Systems Console
```

If problems occur, try to isolate the problem to a specific subsystem. The Catalyst 5000 series LAN switches have the following subsystems:

- **Power subsystem**—This subsystem includes the power supplies and power supply fans.

- **Cooling subsystem**—This subsystem includes the chassis fan assembly, which should be operating when the system power is on.

- **Processor and interface subsystem**—This subsystem includes the supervisor engine module (which contains the system operating software), the network interfaces, and all associated cabling.

Table 3-5 outlines the areas where Catalyst 5000 series startup problems may occur and describes solutions to those problems.

Table 3-5   *Hardware: Catalyst 5000 Series Startup Problems and Solutions*

Possible Problem Area	Solution	
Power subsystem	Step 1	Check to see whether the PS1 LED is on. If it is not, ensure that the power supply is connected properly and is flush with the back of the chassis. Make sure that captive installation screws are tight.
	Step 2	Check the AC source and the power cable. Connect the power cord to another power source, if one is available, and turn the power back on. If the LED fails to go on after you connect the power supply to a new power source, replace the power cord.
	Step 3	If the LED fails to go on when the switch is connected to a different power source with a new power cord, the power supply is probably faulty. If a second power supply is available, install it in the second power supply bay, and contact a customer service representative for further instructions.
	Step 4	Repeat these steps for the second power supply, if present.
Cooling subsystem	Step 1	Check to see whether the Fan LED on the supervisor engine module is green. If it is not, check the power subsystem to see whether it is operational.
	Step 2	If the Fan LED is red, the fan assembly might not be seated properly in the backplane. To ensure that the fan assembly is seated properly, loosen the captive installation screws, remove the fan assembly, and reinstall it. Tighten all captive installation screws, and restart the system.
	Step 3	If the Fan LED is still red, the system has probably detected a fan assembly failure. Contact a technical support representative for assistance.

continues

Table 3-5   *Hardware: Catalyst 5000 Series Startup Problems and Solutions (Continued)*

Possible Problem Area	Solution	
Processor and interface subsystem	**Step 1**	Check the supervisor engine module Status and Link LEDs. These should both be green if all diagnostic and self-tests were successful and ports are operational. For more information about interpreting the supervisor engine module LEDs, refer to the user guide for your switch.
	Step 2	Check the LEDs on individual interface modules. In most cases, these should be green (or should flicker green, in the case of Transmit and Receive LEDs) if the interface is functioning correctly. For detailed information on interpreting interface module LEDs, refer to the user guide for your switch.
	Step 3	Check all cabling and connections. Replace any faulty cabling.

Catalyst 2900 Series Startup

When you start up a Catalyst 2900 series LAN switch, the following should occur:

- The PS LED on the supervisor engine module faceplate should come on and stay green while power is applied to the system.

- The system fan assembly and Fan LED should come on and stay on while power is applied to the system.

- The Status LED on the supervisor engine module and on each interface should be orange until the boot is complete.

When the system boot is complete, the supervisor engine module initializes the switching modules. The status LED on each switching module goes on when initialization has been completed, and the console screen displays a script and system banner similar to the following:

```
BOOTROM Version 2.1, Dated May 22 1996 15:17:09

Boot date: 05/22/96 BOOT time: 15:17:09

Executing from RAM


Cisco Systems Console

Sending RARP request with address 00:40:0b:a0:05:b8

Sending bootp request with address 00:40:0b:a0:05:b8

Sending RARP request with address 00:40:0b:a0:05:b8

Sending bootp request with address 00:40:0b:a0:05:b8
```

```
No bootp or rarp response received
```

```
Enter password:
```

If problems occur, try to isolate the problem to a specific subsystem. The Catalyst 2900 series LAN switches have the following subsystems:

- **Power subsystem**—This subsystem includes the power supplies and power supply fans.

- **Cooling subsystem**—This subsystem includes the chassis fan assembly, which should be operating when the system power is on.

- **Processor and interface subsystem**—This subsystem includes the supervisor engine module (which contains the system operating software), the network interfaces, and all associated cabling.

Table 3-6 outlines the areas where Catalyst 2900 series startup problems may occur and describes solutions to those problems.

Table 3-6   *Hardware: Catalyst 2900 Series Startup Problems and Solutions*

Possible Problem Area	Solution	
Power subsystem	**Step 1**	Check the Power LED. If it is off, ensure that the power supply cord is not damaged and that it is properly attached to the power supply and to an AC receptacle.
	Step 2	If the LED is red, the power supply has detected an anomaly or voltage outage and needs to be serviced. Contact your technical support representative for instructions.
Cooling subsystem	**Step 1**	Check to see whether the Fan LED on the supervisor engine module is green. If it is not, check the power subsystem to see whether it is operational.
	Step 2	If the Fan LED is red, contact a technical support representative for assistance.
Series processor and interface subsystem	**Step 1**	Check the supervisor engine module Status and Link LEDs. These should both be green if all diagnostic and self-tests were successful and ports are operational. For more information about interpreting the supervisor engine module LEDs, refer to the user guide for your switch.
	Step 2	Check the LEDs on individual interface modules. In most cases, these should be green (or should flicker green, in the case of transmit and receive LEDs) if the interface is functioning correctly. For detailed information on interpreting interface module LEDs, refer to the user guide for your switch.
	Step 3	Check all cabling and connections. Replace any faulty cabling.

Testing and Verifying Replacement Parts

If you are replacing a part or card to remedy a suspected problem, make only one change at a time.

To test a system, start with a simple hardware configuration and add one card at a time until a failed interface appears or is isolated. Use a simple software configuration, and test connectivity using a **ping** test.

If you determine that a part or card replacement is required, contact your sales or technical support representative. Specific instructions concerning part or card installation are outlined in the configuration note provided with the replacement.

For modular routers, make sure that you seat all cards correctly. Check the seating of cards if the system is not booting properly. Use the ejector levers to reseat all processor modules, and then reboot.

CAUTION   Before accessing the chassis interior and removing any cards, turn off power to the chassis. Use extreme caution around the chassis. Potentially harmful voltages are present.

CAUTION   To prevent damage to components that are sensitive to electrostatic discharge (ESD), attach ESD protection before opening a chassis. Make certain that the power cord is connected but that power is off. ESD damage prevention guidelines are provided in the hardware installation and maintenance publication for your router.

If a part replacement appears to solve a problem, reinstall the suspect part to verify the failure. *Always* double-check a repair.

Troubleshooting Booting Problems

This section discusses troubleshooting procedures for connectivity problems related to booting. It describes specific booting symptoms, the problems that are likely to cause each symptom, and the solutions to those problems.

Booting: Router Fails to Boot from Flash Memory

Symptom: When a user is booting a router from Flash memory, the boot process appears to complete, but the router does not route traffic or communicate with neighbors. In addition, exec commands might or might not appear to function.

Table 3-7 outlines the problems that might cause this symptom and describes solutions to those problems.

Table 3-7   *Booting: Router Fails to Boot from Flash Memory*

Possible Problem	Solution	
Incorrect or corrupted image (exec does not function)	**Step 1**	Check the configuration register using the **show version** exec command. Set the register to boot from Flash memory. For information about configuration register settings, refer to your hardware installation and maintenance documentation.
	Step 2	Power-cycle the router.
	Step 3	Within the first 60 seconds of booting, press the Break key to access the ROM monitor.
	Step 4	At the ROM monitor prompt (>), enter **o/r 0x1** to set the configuration register to boot from ROM.
	Step 5	Enter **i** to reinitialize the router, which causes the router to enter setup mode.
	Step 6	Obtain the correct system image. If necessary, contact your technical support representative to determine which image is correct.
	Step 7	After the correct image is identified, use the **copy tftp flash** privileged exec command at the router to retrieve the image.
	Step 8	Check the configuration register using the **show version** exec command. Set the register to boot from Flash memory.
	Step 9	Use the **show running-config** privileged exec command to see whether the router configuration contains the **boot system flash** global configuration command.
		Note: Issuing the **copy running-config startup-config** command at this point on a Cisco 2500, Cisco 3000, Cisco 4000, or Cisco 7000 series will overwrite the configuration. Make sure that you have a backup of your configuration file.
	Step 10	Include the **boot system flash** command, if it is not in the configuration. Be sure to use the **copy running-config startup-config** command after this change.
	Step 11	Enter the **reload** privileged exec command to restart the router.
		Syntax:
		The following is the syntax for the **reload** command:
		`reload [text] I [in [hh:]mm [text]] I [at hh:mm` `[month day I day month] [text]] I [cancel]`

continues

Table 3-7   *Booting: Router Fails to Boot from Flash Memory (Continued)*

Possible Problem	Solution

Incorrect or corrupted image (exec does not function) *(continued)*	**Examples:**
	
	The following example illustrates how to use the **reload** command to immediately reload the software on the router:
	
	`Router# reload`
	
	The following example illustrates how to use the **reload** command to reload the software on the router in 10 minutes:
	
	`Router# reload in 10`
	`Router# Reload scheduled for 11:57:08 PDT Fri Apr`
	`21 1996 (in 10 minutes)`
	`Proceed with reload? [confirm]`
	`Router#`

Incorrect or corrupted image (exec functions)	**Step 1** Obtain the correct system image. If necessary, contact your technical support representative to determine which image is appropriate. **Step 2** Use the **copy tftp flash** privileged exec command to retrieve the image. **Step 3** Check the configuration register using the **show version** exec command. Set the register to boot from Flash memory. For information about configuration register settings, refer to your hardware installation and maintenance documentation. **Step 4** Use the **show running-config** privileged exec command to determine whether the active configuration contains the **boot system flash** global configuration command. Use the **show startup-config** privileged exec command to determine whether **the boot system flash** command is included in the configuration stored in NVRAM[1]. **Step 5** Include the **boot system flash** command, if it is not in the configuration. Be sure to use the **copy running-config startup-config** privileged exec command to save your modification after this change. **Step 6** Enter the **reload** privileged exec command to restart the router. **Syntax:** The following is the syntax for the **reload** command: `reload [text]	[in [hh:]mm [text]]	[at hh:mm` `[month day	day month] [text]]	[cancel]`  **Examples:**  The following example illustrates how to use the **reload** command to immediately reload the software on the router:  `Router# reload`

Table 3-7   *Booting: Router Fails to Boot from Flash Memory (Continued)*

Possible Problem	Solution
Incorrect or corrupted image (exec functions) *(continued)*	The following example illustrates how to use the **reload** command to reload the software on the router in 10 minutes: ``` Router# reload in 10 Router# Reload scheduled for 11:57:08 PDT Fri Apr 21 1996 (in 10 minutes) Proceed with reload? [confirm] Router# ```

[1]NVRAM = nonvolatile random-access memory

Booting: Vector Error Occurs When Booting from Flash Memory

Symptom: Vector errors occur when a user is booting a router from Flash memory.

Table 3-8 outlines the problems that might cause this symptom and describes solutions to those problems.

Table 3-8   *Booting: Vector Error Occurs When Booting from Flash Memory*

Possible Problem	Solution	
Compressed system image	Step 1	Power-cycle the router.
	Step 2	Within the first 60 seconds of booting, press the Break key to access the ROM monitor.
	Step 3	At the ROM monitor prompt (>), enter **o/r** to set the configuration register to boot from ROM.
	Step 4	Enter **b** to boot the router. The router enters setup mode.
	Step 5	Press **Ctrl-C** to bypass the setup.
	Step 6	Enter the **configure memory** privileged exec command.
	Step 7	Obtain an uncompressed system image. From the router prompt, use the privileged exec command **copy flash tftp** to send the compressed image back to the TFTP[1] server. Decompress the image at the TFTP server. This cannot be done at the router.
	Step 8	Use the **copy tftp flash** privileged exec command at the router to retrieve the uncompressed image. The following is an example of the use of the **copy tftp flash** command: ``` router# copy flash tftp filename ```

continues

Table 3-8   *Booting: Vector Error Occurs When Booting from Flash Memory (Continued)*

Possible Problem	Solution
Compressed system image *(continued)*	The router asks you for the IP address of the TFTP server and the name of the image file that you are copying to the server. A sample of the output for this command using IP address 131.108.10.6 and filename ic92130n follows:

```
IP address of remote host [255.255.255.255]? 131.108.10.6
Name of file to copy []? ic92130n
writing ic92130n !!!!!!!!!!!!!!!!!!!!!!!!!!!!!!!!!!!!!!!!!!!!!!!!
router#
```

Step 9   Check the configuration register using the **show version** exec command. Set the router to boot from Flash memory.

Step 10   Use the **show running-config** privileged exec command to determine whether the router configuration includes the **boot system flash** global configuration command in the correct order with respect to the other **boot system** commands.

Note: The **boot system** global configuration commands are saved in the order in which they were entered. The most recent entry goes to the bottom of the list. For the recommended ordering, refer to the section "Fault-Tolerant Boot Strategies," earlier in this chapter.

Step 11   Configure the **boot system flash** command, if it is missing. Confirm that the order **of boot system** commands is correct. Use the **copy running-config startup-config** command to save this change. The required syntax is as follows:

```
copy running-config {rcp | startup-config | tftp |
file-id} (Cisco 7000, Cisco 7200, and Cisco 7500
series only)
```

Syntax description:

rcp—Specifies a copy operation to a network server using RCP.

startup-config—Specifies the configuration used for initialization as the destination of the copy operation. The Cisco 4500 series cannot use this keyword.

tftp—Specifies a TFTP server as the destination of the copy operation.

file-id—Specifies *device:filename* as the destination of the copy operation. The device argument is optional, but when it is used, the colon (:) is required.

Step 12   Enter the **reload** privileged exec command to restart the router.

Router hardware problem	Troubleshoot router hardware as discussed earlier in this chapter.

[1]TFTP = Trivial File Transfer Protocol

Booting: Router Partially Boots from Flash and Displays Boot Prompt

Symptom: When a user is booting a Cisco 2000, Cisco 2500, Cisco 3000, or Cisco 4000 series router from Flash memory, the boot process halts and the console displays the boot prompt [**router(boot)>**]. In addition, the router does not route, although exec commands might appear to be operational.

Table 3-9 outlines the problems that might cause this symptom and describes solutions to those problems.

Table 3-9   *Booting: Router Partially Boots from Flash and Displays Boot Prompt*

Possible Problem	Solution	
No system image in Flash memory	**Step 1**	Use the **show flash** exec command to determine whether an image exists in Flash memory.
	Step 2	If no image exists, use the **copy tftp flash** privileged exec command to copy the system image from your TFTP[1] server to the router's Flash memory. The following is an example of the use of the **copy tftp flash** command:
		`router# `**`copy flash tftp`**` filename`
		The router asks you for the IP address of the TFTP server and the name of the image file that you are copying to the server. A sample of the output for this command using IP address 131.108.10.6 and filename ic92130n follows:
		``` IP address of remote host [255.255.255.255]? 131.108.10.6 Name of file to copy []? ic92130n writing ic92130n !! router# ```
	Step 3	Enter the **reload** privileged exec command to reboot the router.
		Syntax:
		The following is the syntax for the **reload** command:
		`reload [text]	[in [hh:]mm [text]]	[at hh:mm [month day	day month] [text]]	[cancel]`
		Examples:
		The following example illustrates how to use the **reload** command to immediately reload the software on the router:
		`Router# `**`reload`**
		The following example illustrates how to use the **reload** command to reload the software on the router in 10 minutes:
		``` Router# reload in 10 Router# Reload scheduled for 11:57:08 PDT Fri Apr 21 1996 (in 10 minutes) Proceed with reload? [confirm] Router# ```

continues

Table 3-9 *Booting: Router Partially Boots from Flash and Displays Boot Prompt (Continued)*

Possible Problem	Solution
Missing **boot system flash** global configuration command	**Step 1** Use the **show running-config** privileged exec command to determine whether the configuration includes a **boot system flash** global configuration command entry. Use the **show startup-config** privileged exec command to determine whether the **boot system flash** command is included in the configuration stored in NVRAM.[2]
	Step 2 Check the order of the **boot system** commands. For the recommended ordering, refer to the section "Fault-Tolerant Boot Strategies," earlier in this chapter.
	Step 3 Add the **boot system flash** command or reorder the **boot system** commands, if necessary.
	Step 4 Save the configuration change to NVRAM using the **copy running-config startup-config** privileged exec command. The required syntax is as follows: ```copy running-config {rcp	startup-config	tftp	file-id} (Cisco 7000, Cisco 7200, and Cisco 7500 series only)```
Missing **boot system flash** global configuration command *(continued)*	**Syntax description:** • **rcp**—Specifies a copy operation to a network server using RCP. • **startup-config**—Specifies the configuration used for initialization as the destination of the copy operation. The Cisco 4500 series cannot use this keyword. • **tftp**—Specifies a TFTP server as the destination of the copy operation. • *file-id*—Specifies a *device:filename* as the destination of the copy operation. The device argument is optional, but when it is used, the colon (:) is required.
Misconfigured configuration register	Use the **show version** exec command to check the configuration register setting. Make sure that it is set to boot from Flash memory. Refer to your hardware installation and maintenance publication for details regarding configuration register settings.

[1]TFTP = Trivial File Transfer Protocol

[2]NVRAM = nonvolatile random-access memory

Booting: Router Cannot Network Boot from TFTP Server

Symptom: Router cannot boot from a TFTP server. The router tries to obtain its system image over the network but fails.

The following output is an example of a failed network boot session:

```
Booting gs3-bfx..........[failed]
```

Table 3-10 outlines the problems that might cause this symptom and describes solutions to those problems.

Table 3-10   *Booting: Router Cannot Network Boot from TFTP Server*

Possible Problem	Solution
Network is disconnected or isolated	**Step 1** Boot the router from ROM or Flash memory, if possible.
	Step 2 Use the **ping** exec command to send a message to the broadcast address (255.255.255.255).
	Step 3 If there is no response from the server, use the **show arp** exec command to look for an entry in the ARP table that is associated with the server.
	Step 4 Use the **show ip route** exec command to view the IP routing table. Look for an entry in the table for the network or subnet of the server.

Sample display:

The following is sample output from the **show ip route** command when entered without an address:

```
Router# show ip route
Codes: I - IGRP derived, R - RIP derived, O - OSPF derived
C - connected, S - static, E - EGP derived, B - BGP derived
candidate default route, IA - OSPF inter area route
Gateway of last resort is 131.119.254.240 to network 129.140.0.0
O E2 150.150.0.0 [160/5] via 131.119.254.6, 0:01:00, Ethernet2
E    192.67.131.0 [200/128] via 131.119.254.244, 0:02:22,
    Ethernet2
O E2 192.68.132.0 [160/5] via 131.119.254.6, 0:00:59, Ethernet2
O E2 130.130.0.0 [160/5] via 131.119.254.6, 0:00:59, Ethernet2
E    128.128.0.0 [200/128] via 131.119.254.244, 0:02:22,
    Ethernet2
E    129.129.0.0 [200/129] via 131.119.254.240, 0:02:22,
    Ethernet2
E    192.65.129.0 [200/128] via 131.119.254.244, 0:02:22,
    Ethernet2
```

If a path to a boot server exists, a disconnected network is not the problem. If no path exists, make sure that a path is available before again attempting to network boot.

continues

Table 3-10   *Booting: Router Cannot Network Boot from TFTP Server (Continued)*

Possible Problem	Solution	
TFTP server is down	Step 1	Check the TFTP server to determine whether it is up and running. You can do this by attempting to make a TFTP connection from the boot server to itself. The connection will be successful if the TFTP server is running.
	Step 2	If the TFTP server is not running, initialize it. The initialization process will vary depending on the type of boot server.
		For a BSD UNIX server, check the /etc/inetd.conf file. If the TFTP server is not included in this file, add the appropriate line and cause inetd to reload its configuration.
Router image is in the wrong directory	Step 1	Look at the server configuration file to see whether it points to the directory in which the router image is located.
	Step 2	Move the router image to the correct directory, if necessary.
	Step 3	Make sure that the /tftpboot directory is reachable over the network.
Router system image file permissions are incorrect	Step 1	Check the permissions of the system image file.
	Step 2	If necessary, change the permissions for the file. On a UNIX boot server, set the permissions for the file to owner read/write, group read, and global read (the UNIX command for setting these permissions is **chmod 644** *filename*).
Protocol address is bad	Step 1	Check the server configuration file to make sure that the IP address of the host is correct.
	Step 2	Change the configuration, if it is incorrect.
Default gateway specification is missing or has been misconfigured	Step 1	Use the **show running-config** privileged exec command to view the router configuration. Check for the **ip default-gateway** global configuration command, which defines a default gateway.
		Syntax:
		ip default-gateway *ip-address*
		Syntax description:
		ip-address—IP address of the router.
	Step 2	If the command is missing, add it to the configuration. If the command is present, make sure that it specifies the correct IP address.

Table 3-10   *Booting: Router Cannot Network Boot from TFTP Server (Continued)*

Possible Problem	Solution	
Boot system command has been misconfigured	**Step 1**	Use the **show running-config** privileged exec command to view the router configuration. Check the boot server address (IP address of a TFTP server or MAC[1] address of a MOP[2] server) that is configured on the router.
	Step 2	If the address is specified incorrectly, specify the correct boot server address using the **boot system** global configuration command.
Wrong filename is specified	**Step 1**	Use the **show running-config** privileged exec command to view the router configuration. Check the boot filename that is configured on the router.
	Step 2	Make sure that the filename is specified correctly. Change the filename, if necessary. Check the host documentation for details about setting the name of the system image on the TFTP server.
	Step 3	Some versions of the ROM are case-sensitive. Try changing the case of the filename. Contact your technical support representative for more information.
Configuration register setting is incorrect	To network boot from a server, you must set the configuration register properly. The specific configuration for network booting depends on the platform that is being booted.	
	Step 1	Check the configuration register setting for your system.
	Step 2	Determine whether you want to manually or automatically network boot from a TFTP server.
		To manually network boot, the configuration register must be set to 0x0; otherwise, you will be network booting using the default system image name or the image specified by the **boot system** global configuration command.
	Refer to the Cisco IOS configuration guides and command references, and your hardware installation and maintenance publications, for more details about setting the configuration register.	

[1]MAC = Media Access Control

[2]MOP = Maintenance Operation Protocol

Booting: Router Cannot Network Boot from Another Router

Symptom: A router cannot boot properly when a user is booting from another router that is acting as a TFTP server.

NOTE   This symptom can be caused by any of the problems outlined in the sections on network booting in this chapter. This section focuses on problems with a router that is acting as a TFTP server.

Table 3-11 outlines the problems that might cause this symptom and describes solutions to those problems.

Table 3-11   *Booting: Router Cannot Network Boot from Another Router*

Possible Problem	Solution	
Missing or incorrect **tftp-server** global configuration command	**Step 1**	Use the **show running-config** privileged exec command to determine whether the **tftp-server system** global configuration command is missing or incorrectly specified.
	Step 2	Add or modify the **tftp-server system** global configuration command as necessary on the router acting as the TFTP server. Specify the name of a file in Flash memory.
Incomplete image in Flash memory	Use the **show flash** exec command to determine whether the image is incomplete. This display might show that the image is deleted and might indicate the reason.	
	The following is an example of **show flash** output indicating that the image is deleted:	
| | ```
babar# show flash
2048K bytes of flash memory sized on embedded
flash.
File  name/status
xx-k.914-0.16
  1  xx3-confg
  2  xx-k.91-4.2 [deleted] [invalid cksum]
[0/2097152 bytes free/total]
``` | |
```

Table 3-11   *Booting: Router Cannot Network Boot from Another Router (Continued)*

Possible Problem	Solution
Incorrect image in Flash memory	**Step 1** A "wrong system software" message is displayed when a router attempts to boot an incorrect image. In this case, the router is being booted from the ROM monitor.
	The following is an example of the ROM monitor output after an attempt to boot an incorrect image:

```
b gs3-klingon 131.108.9.40
Booting gs3-klingon from
131.108.9.40:!!!!!!!!!!!!!!!!!!!!!!!!!!!!!!!!!!!!!!!!!!!!!!!!!
!!!!!!!!!!!!!!!!!!!!!!!!!!!!!!!O!!!!!!!!!!!!!!!!!!!!!!!!!!!!!!!
!!!!!!!!!!!!!!!!!!!!!!!!!!!!!!!!!!!!!!!!!!!!!!!!!!!!!!!!!!!!!!!
!!!!!!!!!!!!!!!!!!!!!!!!!!!!!!!!!!!!!!!!!!!!!!!!!!!!!!!!!!!!!!!
!!!!!!!!!!!!!!!!!!!!!!!!!!!!!!!!!!!!!!!!!!.!!!!!!!!!!!!!!!!!!!!
!!!!!!!!!!!!!!!!!!!!!!!!!!!!!!!!!!!!!!!!!!!!!!!!!!!!!!!!!!!!!!!
!!!!!!!!!!!!!!!!!!!!!!!!!!!!!!!!!!!!!!!!!!!!!!!!!!!!!!!!!!!!!!!
!!!!!!!!!!!!!!!!!!!!!!!!!!!!!!!!!!!!!!!!!!!!
[OK - 2056792/3394950 bytes]
F3: 2011628+45132+192972 at 0x1000
Wrong system software for this hardware
```

Step 2 Obtain the correct image. If necessary, contact your technical support representative to determine which image is correct.

Step 3 When you identify the correct image, use the **copy tftp flash** privileged exec command to retrieve the image.

Booting: Timeouts and Out-of-Order Packets Prevent Network Booting

Symptom: Timeouts or out-of-order packets prevent successful network booting. The number of timeouts and out-of-order packets indicated on the router's console display might vary.

The following example shows a network booting session that contains excessive timeouts and out-of-order packets:

```
Booting gs3-bfx from 131.108.1.123: !0.0!.0..0!!!000.0!!.0.0.....
```

The client router might boot in this situation. However, when excessive timeouts and out-of-order packets occur, there is probably a network problem, and network booting (as well as network service availability) might be inconsistent.

Table 3-12 outlines the problems that might cause this symptom and describes solutions to those problems.

Table 3-12 *Booting: Timeouts and Out-of-Order Packets Prevent Network Booting*

Possible Problem	Solution	
Link is saturated	Step 1	Boot the router from ROM and **ping** the TFTP server. Determine whether timeouts and out-of-order packets appear.
	Step 2	Check local network concentrators for excessive collisions on the same network. If there are excessive collisions, reorganizing your network topology might help reduce collisions.
	Step 3	Use the **show interfaces** exec command on routers in the path, or place a network analyzer between the router and server. Look for dropped packets and output errors.
	Step 4	If approximately 15 percent or more of the traffic is being dropped, or if any output errors occur, congestion might be the problem.
	Step 5	Wait until the traffic subsides before attempting to network boot the router. If the problem is chronic, increase bandwidth or move the server closer to the router being booted.
Link is down	Step 1	Check the continuity of the path from the booting router to the boot server using **ping** or **trace** exec commands.
	Step 2	If a break is found, restore the link and attempt to network boot again.

Booting: Invalid Routes Prevent Network Booting

Symptom: Invalid routes prevent successful network booting. If the router is sending packets over an invalid path, a message similar to one of the following is displayed on the console:

```
Booting gs3-bfx!0000..........[timed out]

Booting gs3-bfx!.0.0.0.0..........[timed out]

Booting gs3-bfx!!!!!!!!!!!0000000000..........[timed out]
```

In some cases, there might be an initial response from a server, but the network boot sequence still fails. The boot message would be similar to the following:

```
Booting gs3-bfx!..........[failed]
```

Table 3-13 outlines the problems that might cause this symptom and describes solutions to those problems.

Table 3-13   *Booting: Invalid Routes Prevent Network Booting*

Possible Problem	Solution	
Bad routing paths on neighbor routers	Step 1	Verify that neighbor routers can **ping** the server.
	Step 2	Use the **trace** exec command to determine the path to the server.
	Step 3	Use the **show arp**[1] privileged exec command to examine the ARP tables, or the **show ip route** privileged exec command to view the IP routing table. Verify that the server is listed and that the routing table entries are appropriate.
	Step 4	Use the **clear arp-cache** and **clear ip-route** privileged exec commands to force the router to repopulate its ARP and routing tables.
	Step 5	Try to network boot the router again.
Problems caused by multiple paths	Step 1	Shut down all extra interfaces except the one over which you intend to network boot the router.
	Step 2	Use the **no ip proxy-arp** interface configuration command on all neighboring routers to disable their capability to provide proxy ARP responses. Make this change with care because it can cause problems for other network traffic. If you do not want to disable proxy ARP, boot the router from ROM and configure the **ip default-gateway** global configuration command.
	Step 3	Try to network boot the router again.

[1] ARP = Address Resolution Protocol

Booting: Client ARP Requests Timeout During Network Boot

Symptom: Client ARP requests a timeout during a network boot. If the router does not receive an ARP response, a message similar to the following is displayed on the console:

```
Booting gs3-bfx.........[timed out]
```

Table 3-14 outlines the problems that might cause this symptom and describes solutions to those problems.

Table 3-14   *Booting: Client ARP Requests Timeout During Network Boot*

Possible Problem	Solution	
Intermediate routers have ARP filtering enabled	**Step 1**	Boot the router from ROM.
	Step 2	Make sure that you can **ping** the server from the router.
	Step 3	Use the copy **running-config tftp** privileged exec command to test TFTP connectivity to the server.
	Step 4	If the preceding steps are successful, check the configuration at the intermediate router using the **show arp** exec command.
	Step 5	Enable the **debug arp** privileged exec command to determine whether neighbor proxy ARP responses are being generated.
		Caution: Because debugging output is assigned high priority in the CPU process, it can render the system unusable. For this reason, use **debug** commands only to troubleshoot specific problems or during troubleshooting sessions with Cisco technical support staff. Moreover, it is best to use **debug** commands during periods of lower network traffic and fewer users. Debugging during these periods decreases the likelihood that increased **debug** command processing overhead will affect system use.
	Step 6	If the neighbor is not sending proxy ARP responses and its configuration contains the **no ip proxy-arp** interface configuration command, disable ARP filtering by removing the entry.
		Note that proxy ARP is enabled by default.
	Step 7	If you need to have a **no ip proxy-arp** entry in the neighbor router configurations, use the **ip default-gateway** global configuration command on the router to specify a default gateway.
IP helper address on intermediate router is missing or has been misconfigured	**Step 1**	Check the configurations of all routers in the path. Make sure that all intermediate routers have an IP helper address specified that points to the TFTP server.
		Syntax:
		`ip helper-address address`
		Syntax description:
		address—Destination broadcast or host address to be used when forwarding UDP[1] broadcasts. You can have more than one helper address per interface.
	Step 2	Include helper addresses as required using the **ip helper-address** interface configuration command.
		If you are unicasting to your server, you do not need to use the IP helper address, but if you are broadcasting to 255.255.255.255 (by omitting the IP address of the server), add the **ip helper-address** command on the neighboring router interface used in the network booting broadcast.

[1]UDP = User Datagram Protocol

Booting: Undefined Load Module Error When Network Booting

Symptom: An undefined load module error occurs during a network boot. The console display indicates an "undefined load module" error, and the router is incapable of booting.

Table 3-15 outlines the problem that might cause this symptom and describes solutions to that problem.

Table 3-15   *Booting: Undefined Load Module Error When Network Booting*

Possible Problem	Solution	
Filename mismatch	**Step 1**	If you are booting manually, refer to the user guide for your router to see the proper command-line format.
	Step 2	Check the router configuration file. Compare the filename specified in the **boot system** *filename* [*address*] global configuration command entry with the actual router image filename. Make sure that they match.
	Step 3	If the filenames differ, change the name in the configuration file.
		Remember to use the router image filename in the **boot system** global configuration command specification and the configuration filename with the **boot host** and **boot network** global configuration commands.

Booting: Router Hangs After ROM Monitor Initializes

Symptom: When a user is booting a Cisco 7000 series, AGS+, AGS, ASM-CS, MGS, IGS, or CGS router from ROM, the system hangs after the ROM monitor initializes.

Table 3-16 outlines the problems that might cause this symptom and describes solutions to those problems.

Table 3-16   *Booting: Router Hangs After ROM Monitor Initializes*

Possible Problem	Solution	
EPROM[1] size setting is incorrect	**Step 1**	Power down the system.
	Step 2	Inspect EPROM size jumpers. Refer to the hardware installation and maintenance publication for your router to determine the proper setting.
	Step 3	Move jumpers as required.

continues

Table 3-16 *Booting: Router Hangs After ROM Monitor Initializes (Continued)*

Configuration register is not set correctly	**Step 1**	Check your configuration settings (boot ROM jumpers and software configuration). If no jumper is set at bit 0, and no other boot field is defined, you must reconfigure your system so that it can boot properly.
	Step 2	To enable your router to boot properly, do one of the following:

- Configure the software configuration register of the router using the **config-register value** global configuration command. (This applies to the IGS, Cisco 2500, Cisco 3000, and Cisco 7000 platforms running Cisco IOS Release 10.0 or later in the EPROM.)
- Set the boot ROM jumper to permit booting.
- Include the correct boot system global configuration commands to boot the system.
- Set bit 0 to a value of 1 to force booting from ROM.

Refer to the Cisco IOS configuration guides and command references, as well as your hardware installation and maintenance publications, for more information about configuring your router for the various booting options.

[1]EPROM = erasable programmable read-only memory

Booting: Router Is Stuck in ROM Monitor Mode

Symptom: Router is stuck in ROM monitor mode. When a user is booting a router from ROM, the system boots into ROM monitor mode but does not boot the complete system image.

Table 3-17 outlines the problems that might cause this symptom and describes solutions to those problems.

Table 3-17 *Booting: Router Is Stuck in ROM Monitor Mode*

Possible Problem	Solution	
Configuration register setting is incorrect	**Step 1**	At the ROM monitor prompt (>), enter **b** to boot the system.
	Step 2	If a configuration exists in NVRAM, the system displays the vacant message. Press the Enter key to continue.
		If a configuration does not exist in NVRAM, the setup menu appears. Skip the setup process.
	Step 3	Use the **show version** exec command to determine the configuration register setting.

Table 3-17 *Booting: Router Is Stuck in ROM Monitor Mode (Continued)*

Possible Problem	Solution	
Configuration register setting is incorrect *(continued)*	**Step 4**	Look for an invalid configuration register setting. The default is **0x101**, which disables the Break key and forces the router to boot from ROM. A typical "bad" setting has a 0 in the least significant bit (for example, 0x100).
		For details about setting the configuration register, refer to your hardware installation and maintenance publication.
Break key was pressed during boot process	At the ROM monitor prompt, enter **c** to allow the router to continue booting.	
Console cable was inserted or removed during boot process, or console was power-cycled during boot process	**Step 1**	Press the Enter key and wait for the ROM monitor prompt (>).
	Step 2	If the ROM monitor prompt appears, enter **c** at the prompt to continue the booting process.

Booting: Scrambled Output When Booting from ROM

Symptom: When a user is booting from ROM, the router displays indecipherable text output on the console.

Table 3-18 outlines the problems that might cause this symptom and describes solutions to those problems.

Table 3-18 *Booting: Scrambled Output When Booting from ROM*

Possible Problem	Solution	
Wrong terminal speed setting	**Step 1**	Use the monitor setup menu to check the terminal line speed setting for the monitor.
	Step 2	Check the terminal speed configured on the router as specified in the configuration register setting (default is 9600 baud, 8 data bits, 2 stop bits, and no parity).
	Step 3	If the terminal speed of the monitor and the router do not match, modify as necessary.
		Refer to your hardware installation and maintenance documentation for details about setting up the monitor.
Router hardware problem	Check all hardware for damage, including cabling (broken wire), adapters (loose pin), router ports, and so forth. For more information, refer to the information in the "Troubleshooting "Hardware section found earlier in this chapter.	

Booting: Local Timeouts Occur When Booting from ROM

Symptom: "Local timeout" error messages are generated when a user is booting from ROM. The router is incapable of completing its boot process and will not start the ROM monitor.

Table 3-19 outlines the problem that might cause this symptom and describes solutions to that problem.

Table 3-19 *Booting: Local Timeouts Occur When Booting from ROM*

Possible Problem	Solution
EPROM problem	Generally, this problem occurs only if you have just replaced your system EPROMs.
	Step 1 Power down the system.
	Step 2 Inspect each EPROM. Make sure that each EPROM is correctly positioned in the socket (with notches properly aligned) in the correct socket.
	Step 3 If a pin is bent, straighten it carefully. Reinstall the EPROM and power up the system. If a pin breaks off, the EPROM must be replaced.
	Step 4 If an EPROM has been installed backward and power has been applied to it, the EPROM has been damaged and must be replaced.
	Step 5 If local timeouts persist, contact your technical support representative.

Booting: Unresponsive Terminal Connection to Unconfigured Access Server

Symptom: A terminal connected to an unconfigured access server is unresponsive. The terminal, attached to the console port of an unconfigured Cisco access server, displays bootup banners and begins the setup routine, but the user cannot input commands from the terminal keyboard.

Table 3-20 outlines the problems that might cause this symptom and describes solutions to those problems.

Table 3-20   *Booting: Unresponsive Terminal Connection to Unconfigured Access Server*

Possible Problem	Solution	
Flow control configured on the terminal conflicts with the EIA/TIA-232 control signals supported by the access server console port (RJ-45 to DB-25)	Step 1	Check whether flow control is configured on your terminal.
	Step 2	Disable all flow control on the terminal. With flow control enabled, the terminal will wait indefinitely for a CTS signal because the RJ-45 console port on the access server does not assert CTS.
		For information on how to check for and disable flow control on your specific terminal, consult the documentation provided by your terminal manufacturer.
	Step 3	Alternatively, you can "strap," or short, CTS high by providing the proper voltage on the CTS signal lead to make the signal active. Find an unused signal that is known to be active and strap CTS to it. The terminal sees CTS being asserted (indicating that the access server is ready to receive data) and allows input to be entered.
	Step 4	On an already configured access server, another solution is to connect your terminal to the auxiliary port of the access server. The auxiliary port, unlike the console port, asserts CTS, and the terminal will therefore allow input. However, on a new access server with no configuration, this is not an alternative because the bootup banners and setup routine are seen only on the console port.
Hardware problem	Step 1	Check all hardware—including cabling (broken wires), adapters (loose pins), access server ports, and the terminal itself—for damage.
	Step 2	Replace any hardware that is damaged or excessively worn. For more information, refer to the information in the "Troubleshooting Hardware" section found earlier in this chapter.

Catalyst 6000 Series Startup

When you apply power to the Cisco Catalyst 6000, the following boot process should occur:

```
System Bootstrap, Version 5.3(1)
Copyright (c) 1994-1999 by cisco Systems, Inc.
c6k_sup1 processor with 65536 Kbytes of main memory
Autoboot executing command: "boot bootflash:cat6000-sup.5-5-1.bin"
```

```
Uncompressing file:
################################################################################
################################################################################
################################################################################
################################################################################
################################################################################
################################################################################
################################################################################
################################################################################
################################################################################
################################################################################
################################################################################
################################################################################
################################################################################
################################################################################
################################################################################
################################################################################
#########

     System Power On Diagnostics
     DRAM Size ...................64 MB
     Testing DRAM.................Passed
     NVRAM Size ..................512 KB
     Level2 Cache ................Present
     System Power On Diagnostics Complete

     Boot image: bootflash:cat6000-sup.5-5-1.bin

     Running System Diagnostics from this Supervisor (Module 1)
     This may take up to 2 minutes....please wait

     Cisco Systems Console

     2000 Jul 27 16:21:02 %SYS-1-SYS_ENABLEPS: Power supply 1 enabled
     Enter password: 2000 Jul 27 16:21:05 %SYS-5-MOD_PWRON:Module 3 powered up
     2000 Jul 27 16:21:11 %MLS-5-NDEDISABLED:Netflow Data Export disabled
     2000 Jul 27 16:21:12 %MLS-5-MCAST_STATUS:IP Multicast Multilayer Switching is
     enabled
     2000 Jul 27 16:21:12 %SYS-5-MOD_OK:Module 1 is online
     2000 Jul 27 16:21:33 %SYS-5-MOD_OK:Module 3 is online
     2000 Jul 27 16:21:45 %SYS-5-MOD_OK:Module 15 is online
```

How to Recover a Catalyst 6000
from a Corrupted or Missing Boot Image (from CCO)

This Tech Note explains how to recover a Catalyst 6000 family switch from either a
corrupted or missing boot loader image.

Catalyst 6000 switches running Cisco IOS have two boot Flash areas. The boot Flash area
at the supervisor holds the IOS image, and the area at the Multilayer Switch Feature Card
(MSFC) holds the boot loader image. To run IOS on the Catalyst 6000, you need to have
both images installed.

NOTE The boot loader image must reside in the MSFC boot Flash. The IOS image can reside in either the supervisor boot Flash, a Flash card, or a TFTP server.

If the boot loader image either is corrupted or has been deleted from the MSFC boot Flash, the next reload causes the switch to go into ROMMON, and you will be unable to boot the switch to run IOS software on it.

Things to Be Aware of Before You Use the Recovery Procedure

To save time, it's important to understand the terminology, as well as constraints you may encounter when using the procedure.

1 The IOS on the Catalyst 6000 family switch is the single IOS image that runs the Catalyst 6000 family switch, also known as native IOS on the Catalyst 6000. We refer to it as Catalyst 6000 IOS, or Cat IOS. Catalyst 6000 OS software is the image that runs the supervisor and all the L2 switch functions, also known as the hybrid image when used in conjunction with IOS software on the MSFC. We refer to it as Catalyst 6000 OS, or Cat OS.

2 Two CPUs are involved, the supervisor CPU or switch processor (SP), and the MSFC CPU or route processor (RP).

3 When the boot loader image is missing or corrupted, the very next reload or power cycle brings the switch to SP ROMMON mode.

4 Each CPU has its own ROMMON Command Language Interpreter (CLI).

5 From the SP ROMMON, you can load either the Catalyst 6000 IOS or the Catalyst 6000 OS from either slot 0 or boot Flash. Loading the Cat OS version on a system previously running Cat IOS causes the switch configuration to be reset.

6 After you load the Cat IOS image, you get the RP ROMMON prompt. On the other hand, if you load the Cat OS image, you can switch to the RP ROMMON console using the **switch console** command.

7 From the RP ROMMON CLI, you can't access the supervisor boot Flash or slot 0.

8 There are two ways of loading the boot loader image into the MSFC boot Flash: using a Cisco 4500 or 4700 router, or using xmodem. We'll explain both methods in detail in this tech note.

9 When you're running the boot loader image in the MSFC, you get the MSFC **Router(boot)** prompt in boot mode.

10 You must format the MSFC boot Flash from the MSFC **Router(boot)** prompt.

11   After you format the MSFC boot Flash, you must copy the boot loader into it. Be aware of the caveats discussed in the following section when attempting to copy the boot loader image.

Recovery Procedures

You can recover from this situation in two ways:

* **Method 1**—Use a Cisco 4500 or 4700 router to copy the proper boot loader image into the MSFC boot Flash SIMM.

* **Method 2**—Use xmodem with the Modem Out-of-Band (OOB) Protocol to load the boot loader image to the MSFC boot Flash. This procedure requires the Catalyst 6000 Supervisor (CAT OS) image if using boot loader version c6msfc-boot-mz.120-7.XE, or the Catalyst IOS image if using version c6msfc-boot-mz.120-7.XE1, to be running on the Supervisor module. The MSFC boot loader image is approximately 1.8 MB and takes about 45 minutes to load.

You should use this second method only as a disaster recovery procedure, and the following caveats apply:

* The xmodem procedure doesn't save the current switch configuration if you run the Cat OS image on the supervisor, and you were previously running Cat IOS on the switch.

* The xmodem procedure doesn't save the downloaded image into the MSFC boot Flash.

* The xmodem procedure loads and runs the boot loader in the MFSC, and it puts it in boot mode.

    — From boot mode, the MSFC boot Flash must be formatted before you copy the boot loader image into it.

    — You must place the boot loader image that you want to load in supervisor's slot 0.

NOTE   The xmodem procedure has been verified to work with Microsoft Windows Hypertrm program, and minicom under Linux.

If these methods are not successful, contact the Cisco Technical Assistance Center (TAC), and request an RMA for a new boot Flash SIMM with the desired image in it.

NOTE   As it was mentioned earlier, you could use either the Cat OS or Cat IOS image. Which one to use depends on the boot loader version that you are trying to load.

If you are using version c6msfc-boot-mz.120-7.XE, you need to use Cat OS image. If you use boot loader version c6msfc-boot-mz.120-7.XE1 or later, you may use the Cat IOS image. Using release c6msfc-boot-mz.120-7.XE1 or later has major advantages and should be used whenever possible. First, the switch configuration will not be lost by having to load Cat OS in the switch; second, a few extra steps are not necessary, making the process less time-consuming.

The major difference between the releases is the capability to access the supervisor's slot 0 from boot mode. If you load Cat IOS in the supervisor, you will not be able to access slot 0 until you get to release c6msfc-boot-mz.120-7.XE1 or later.

Method 1: Boot Loader Recovery Procedure Using a Cisco 4500/4700 Router

NOTE   The MSFC in ROMMON mode is capable of reading a 4500/4700 router Flash SIMM. However when Cat IOS is running, the MSFC cannot read a 4500/4700 flash SIMM format. Make sure that you format the MSFC boot Flash from boot mode before the boot loader image is put back on it. The following are the typical messages when attempting to read the MSFC's boot Flash when running Cat IOS.

MSFC in ROMMON:

```
rommon 1 > dir bootflash:
    File size Checksum File name
    1597884 bytes (0x1861bc) 0x8334 c6msfc-boot-mz.120-7T.XE1.0.95.bin
```

MSFC in boot mode:

```
Router(boot)# dir bootflash:
Directory of bootflash:/
1 -rw- 1877456 Jan 01 2000 00:08:25 c6msfc-bootdbg-mz
15990784 bytes total (14113200 bytes free)
Router(boot)#
```

MSFC running Cat IOS:

```
IOS4C6K# dir bootflash:
%Error opening bootflash:/ (Bad device info block)
```

The following is the recovery procedure utilizing a 4500/4700 router.

Step 1   Remove the boot Flash from the Catalyst 6000, and put it into the 4500/
4700 router. Ensure that the Flash SIMM from the slot you have selected
does not contain the IOS software running the 4500/4700 router.

Important: After booting up the 4500/4700, you'll need to partition the
Flash, realizing that the boot Flash in the Catalyst 6000 is 16 M.

```
4500Router(config)# partition flash 2 8 16
4500Router(config)# end
4500Router#
00:07:30: %SYS-5-CONFIG_I: Configured from console by console
4500Router# show flash
System flash directory, partition 1:
File Length Name/status
1 4512036 c4500-js-mz.112-17.P
2 3838296 c4500-j-mz.111-20
[8350460 bytes used, 38148 available, 8388608 total]
8192K bytes of processor board System flash (Read/Write)

System flash directory, partition 2:
No files in System flash
[0 bytes used, 16777216 available, 16777216 total]
16384K bytes of processor board System flash (Read/Write)
```

Step 2   Copy the boot loader image into the appropriate system partition.

```
4500Router# copy tftp flash
Partition Size Used Free Bank-Size State Copy Mode
1 8192K 8154K 37K 8192K Read/Write Direct
2 16384K 0K 16384K 8192K Read/Write Direct
[Type ?<NO> for partition directory; ? for full directory; q to
   abort]
Which partition? [default = 1] 2
System flash directory, partition 2:
No files in System flash
[0 bytes used, 16777216 available, 16777216 total]
Address or name of remote host [255.255.255.255]? tftpserver
Source file name? c6msfc-boot-mz.120-7T.XE1.0.95.bin
Destination file name [c6msfc-boot-mz.120-7T.XE1.0.95.bin]?
Accessing file 'c6msfc-boot-mz.120-7T.XE1.0.95.bin' on
   tftpserver...
```

```
    Loading c6msfc-boot-mz.120-7T.XE1.0.95.bin .from 172.17.196.3 (via
       FastEthernet0): ! [OK]
    Erase flash device before writing? [confirm]
    Flash contains files. Are you sure you want to erase? [confirm]
    Copy 'c6msfc-boot-mz.120-7T.XE1.0.95.bin' from server
    as 'c6msfc-boot-mz.120-7T.XE1.0.95.bin' into Flash WITH erase?
       [yes/no] yes
    Erasing device...
eeeeeeeeeeeeeeeeeeeeeeeeeeeeeeeeeeeeeeeeeeeeeeeeeeeeeeeeeeeeeeeee
...erased
    Loading c6msfc-boot-mz.120-7T.XE1.0.95.bin from 172.17.196.3 (via
       FastEthernet0 ):
    !!!!!!!!!!!!!!!!!!!!!!!!!!!!
    [OK - 1599488/16777216 bytes]
    Verifying checksum... OK (0x13AF)
    Flash copy took 00:00:08 [hh:mm:ss]
```

Step 3   When you finish copying the image, take the SIMM back to the same slot in the Catalyst 6000.

Before the system failing, the bootvar in the Catalyst 6000 may have had the following information:

```
C6000-IOS# sh bootvar
BOOT variable = sup-bootflash:c6sup-jsdbg-mz.120-6.5T.XE1.0.90.bin,1;
CONFIG_FILE variable does not exist
BOOTLDR variable = bootflash:c6msfc-boot-mz.120-6.5T.XE1.0.90.bin
Configuration register is 0x2
```

If you did not have the bootldr variable set. you will get the following message and will have to bring up the switch manually:

```
System Bootstrap, Version 5.2(1)CSX
     Copyright (c) 1994-1999 by cisco Systems, Inc.
     c6k_sup1 processor with 65536 Kbytes of main memory
     Autoboot: failed, BOOT string is empty
     rommon 1 >
```

To bring up the switch manually, you should have either the Cat OS or the Cat IOS image in the supervisor's boot Flash or slot 0. To list the content of slot 0 or bootflash, type **dir slot0:** and **dir bootflash:**, respectively. See the following output.

```
    System Bootstrap, Version 5.2(1)CSX
    Copyright (c) 1994-1999 by cisco Systems, Inc.
    c6k_sup1 processor with 65536 Kbytes of main memory
    rommon 1 > dir slot0:
    File size Checksum File name
    1603124 bytes (0x187634) 0x37e92ad5 c6msfc-boot-mz.120-7T.XE1.2.02.bin
    10827684 bytes (0xa537a4) 0xcdcb1ae c6sup-jsdbg-mz.120-7T.XE1.2.02.bin ** Cat
       IOS image **
6174451 bytes (0x5e36f3) 0xb718ee34 cat6000-sup.5-4-0-97.bin ** Cat IOS image **
    1877456 bytes (0x1ca5d0) 0x325c9851 c6msfc-bootdbg-mz ** MSFC boot loader image
       **
    8235 bytes (0x202b) 0x2a825c18 switch.cfg
    rommon 2 > dir bootflash:
    File size Checksum File name
```

```
10827684 bytes (0xa537a4) 0xcdcb1ae c6sup-jsdbg-mz.120-7T.XE1.2.02.bin *** Cat
   IOS image **
1603124 bytes (0x187634) 0x37e92ad5 c6msfc-boot-mz.120-7T.XE1.2.02.bin
```

When you have identified where the image is located, follow the instructions in one of these two sections:

- If you are using boot loader release c6msfc-boot-mz.120-7.XE1 or later, go to the section "Loading the Catalyst IOS Image."

- If you are using boot loader release c6msfc-boot-mz.120-7.XE, go to the section "Loading the Catalyst OS Image."

Come back to this point after you have loaded either the Cat IOS or the Cat OS image.

The RP is at the boot prompt, and you are ready to bring up the switch running Cat IOS. Ensure that you have the config-register set to 0x2 before you reboot. You also may want to check that the right boot variables are set correctly. If they are not, change them to reflect the right image names. See the following example:

```
boot system flash sup-bootflash:c6sup-jsdbg-mz.120-7T.XE1.2.02.bin
boot bootldr bootflash:c6msfc-bootdbg-mz
```

Note: If the boot variables are not set at all, the switch will attempt to boot from the first file in the respective boot Flash.

```
Router(boot)# sh bootvar
BOOT variable =
CONFIG_FILE variable does not exist
BOOTLDR variable =
Configuration register is 0x0
Router(boot)# conf t
Enter configuration commands, one per line. End with CNTL/Z.
Router(boot)(config)# conf
Router(boot)(config)# config-register 0x2
Router(boot)(config)#
Router(boot)#
00:01:14: %SYS-5-CONFIG_I: Configured from console by console
Router(boot)# reload
System configuration has been modified. Save? [yes/no]: n
Proceed with reload? [confirm]
00:01:30: %SYS-5-RELOAD: Reload requested
System Bootstrap, Version 12.0(3)XE, RELEASE SOFTWARE
Copyright (c) 1998 by cisco Systems, Inc.
Cat6k-MSFC platform with 131072 Kbytes of main memory
Self decompressing the image : ################## [OK]
Starting download: 7813530bytes!!!!!!!!!!!!!!!!!!!!!!!!!!!!!!!!!!!!!!!!!!!!!!!!!!!!!
Chksum: Verified!
Self decompressing the image :
############################################################# [OK]
Restricted Rights Legend
Use, duplication, or disclosure by the Government is
subject to restrictions as set forth in subparagraph
(c) of the Commercial Computer Software - Restricted
Rights clause at FAR sec. 52.227-19 and subparagraph
(c) (1) (ii) of the Rights in Technical Data and Computer
Software clause at DFARS sec. 252.227-7013.
cisco Systems, Inc.
170 West Tasman Drive
San Jose, California 95134-1706
```

```
Cisco Internetwork Operating System Software
IOS (tm) c6sup Software (c6sup-JSDBG-M), Version 12.0(7T)XE1(2.02) INTERIM TEST
   SOFTWARE
Copyright (c) 1986-2000 by cisco Systems, Inc.
Compiled Sun 09-Jan-00 21:59 by integ
Image text-base: 0x60020900, data-base: 0x611BE000
cisco Catalyst 6000 (R5000) processor with 122880K/8192K bytes of memory.
Processor board ID SAD03302657
R5000 CPU at 200Mhz, Implementation 35, Rev 2.1, 512KB L2 Cache
Last reset from power-on
Bridging software.
X.25 software, Version 3.0.0.
SuperLAT software (copyright 1990 by Meridian Technology Corp).
TN3270 Emulation software.
96 FastEthernet/IEEE 802.3 interface(s)
2 Gigabit Ethernet/IEEE 802.3 interface(s)
381K bytes of non-volatile configuration memory.
4096K bytes of packet SRAM memory.
16384K bytes of Flash internal SIMM (Sector size 256K).[OK][OK]

Press RETURN to get started!
monvar =
00:00:03: %SYS-3-LOGGER_FLUSHED: System was paused for 00:00:00 to ensure
   console debugging output.
00:00:03: %C6KPWR-4-PSINSERTED: power supply inserted in slot 1.
00:00:03: %C6KPWR-4-PSOK: power supply 1 turned on.
00:00:03: %C6KPWR-4-PSINSERTED: power supply inserted in slot 2.
00:00:03: %C6KPWR-4-PSOK: power supply 2 turned on.
00:00:03: %C6KPWR-4-PSREDUNDANTBOTHSUPPLY: in power-redundancy mode, system is
   operating on both power supplies.
00:01:02: Cannot open bootflash:?
00:04:59:Translating "derby"...domain server (255.255.255.255)
%SYS-SP-5-RESTART: System restarted --
Cisco Internetwork Operating System Software
IOS (tm) c6sup_sp Software (c6sup_sp-SPDBG-M), Version 12.0(7T)XE1(2.02)
   INTERIM TEST SOFTWARE
Copyright (c) 1986-2000 by cisco Systems, Inc.
Compiled Sun 09-Jan-00 22:40 by integ
00:05:02: %SYS-5-CONFIG_I: Configured from memory by console
00:05:02: L3-MGR: l2 flush entry installed
00:05:02: L3-MGR: l3 flush entry installed
00:05:02: %SYS-5-RESTART: System restarted --
Cisco Internetwork Operating System Software
IOS (tm) c6sup Software (c6sup-JSDBG-M), Version 12.0(7T)XE1(2.02) INTERIM TEST
   SOFTWARE
Copyright (c) 1986-2000 by cisco Systems, Inc.
Compiled Sun 09-Jan-00 21:59 by integ
00:05:06: %C6KPWR-SP-4-ENABLED: power to module in slot 3 set on
00:05:07: %C6KPWR-SP-4-ENABLED: power to module in slot 4 set on
00:05:26: %OIR-SP-6-INSCARD: Card inserted in slot 1, interfaces are now online
00:05:31: %OIR-SP-6-INSCARD: Card inserted in slot 3, interfaces are now online
00:05:32: %OIR-SP-6-INSCARD: Card inserted in slot 4, interfaces are now online
derby> en
derby#
```

Method 2: OOB Boot Loader Recovery Procedure Using xmodem

This alternative is recommended only in case of a disaster recovery situation, when no other option is possible.

The first step is to load the Cat IOS or Cat OS image in the supervisor boot Flash. Make sure that you have the Cat OS image either in the supervisor boot Flash, or a Flash card inserted on slot 0, and follow the instructions in the sections "Loading the Catalyst IOS Image" or "Loading the Catalyst OS Image," later in this chapter.

When you have loaded the Cat IOS or Cat OS image loading procedure, make sure that you at the MSFC's ROMMON prompt.

Note: Currently, the MSFC in ROMMON cannot see the supervisor's boot Flash or slot 0.

Also remember to have the boot loader image available in the computer from which you are performing the xmodem download. At this point, you are ready to initiate the xmodem download. It will take between 40 and 45 minutes to complete.

At the MSFC's ROMMON prompt, type the following command:

```
xmodem -s9600 -c
```

The **-s9600** option sets the speed, while the **-c** option performs checksum.

```
System Bootstrap, Version 12.0(3)XE, RELEASE SOFTWARE
Copyright (c) 1998 by cisco Systems, Inc.
Cat6k-MSFC platform with 65536 Kbytes of main memory
rommon 1 >
rommon 1 > xmodem -s9600 -c
Do not start sending the image yet...
Invoke this application for disaster recovery.
Do you wish to continue? y/n [n]: y
Note, if the console port is attached to a modem, both the
console port and the modem must be operating at the same baud
rate. Use console speed 9600 bps for download [confirm]
Download will be performed at 9600. Make sure your terminal
emulator is set to this speed before sending file.
Ready to receive file ...
```

In your terminal emulator, type **send command** or click on the appropriate icon to start the download process. The transfer will take between 40 and 45 minutes to complete.

We have found that the first attempt may fail. If it does, run the **xmodem** command again without resetting the MSFC. At the end of the successful download, you will the following message:

```
Download Complete!
```

When the download has completed, the image will be decompressed and run by the MSFC. The next prompt will be the boot prompt at the MSFC.

```
Self decompressing the image : ###################### [OK]
Restricted Rights Legend
Use, duplication, or disclosure by the Government is
subject to restrictions as set forth in subparagraph
(c) of the Commercial Computer Software - Restricted
Rights clause at FAR sec. 52.227-19 and subparagraph
(c) (1) (ii) of the Rights in Technical Data and Computer
Software clause at DFARS sec. 252.227-7013.
cisco Systems, Inc.
170 West Tasman Drive
San Jose, California 95134-1706
```

```
Cisco Internetwork Operating System Software
IOS (tm) MSFC Software (C6MSFC-BOOT-M), Version 12.0(7T)XE1(1.11) INTERIM TEST
  SOFTWARE
Copyright (c) 1986-1999 by cisco Systems, Inc.
Compiled Tue 28-Dec-99 04:44 by
Image text-base: 0x60008900, data-base: 0x603B2000
cisco Cat6k-MSFC (R5000) processor with 57344K/8192K bytes of memory.
Processor board ID SAD03483410
R5000 CPU at 200Mhz, Implementation 35, Rev 2.1, 512KB L2 Cache
Last reset from power-on
X.25 software, Version 3.0.0.
123K bytes of non-volatile configuration memory.
4096K bytes of packet SRAM memory.
16384K bytes of Flash internal SIMM (Sector size 256K).


Press RETURN to get started!


00:00:04: %SYS-5-RESTART: System restarted --
Cisco Internetwork Operating System Software
IOS (tm) MSFC Software (C6MSFC-BOOT-M), Version 12.0(7T)XE1(1.11) INTERIM TEST
  SOFTWARE
Copyright (c) 1986-1999 by cisco Systems, Inc.
Compiled Tue 28-Dec-99 04:44 by
Router(boot)>
```

The xmodem download did not copy the boot loader image into the MSFC boot Flash. The download simply loaded and uncompressed image to run the MSFC.

The next step is to copy the boot loader image form the supervisor's slot 0 into the MSFC's boot Flash.

From the MSFC boot prompt, you will not be able to see the supervisor's slot 0 or display its contents. You need to remember the boot loader image name so that you can issue the following command:

If you are running the Cat OS image, use:

```
copy sup-slot0:<boot loader image> bootflash:<boot loader image>
```

If you are running the Cat IOS image, use:

```
download slot0:<boot loader image> bootflash:<bootloader image>
```

Note: Remember, the MSFC will not be capable of copying an image from any location other than the supervisor's slot 0.

Now you are ready to bring up the switch running Cat IOS. Ensure you have the config-register set to 0x2 before you reboot and that the right boot variables are correctly set. The following commands set the boot variables:

```
boot system flash sup-bootflash:<CatIOS image>

boot bootldr bootflash:<boot loader image>
```

Loading the Catalyst IOS Image

Load the Cat IOS image by typing the following command:

```
boot <location>:c6sup-jsdbg-mz.120-7T.XE1.2.02.bin
```

In this command, **<location>** is either slot0 or bootflash.

Note: Loading this image will take you directly to the MSFC's ROMMON prompt.

```
rommon 3 > boot bootflash:c6sup-jsdbg-mz.120-7T.XE1.2.02.bin
Self decompressing the image :#######################[OK]
Restricted Rights Legend
Use, duplication, or disclosure by the Government is
subject to restrictions as set forth in subparagraph
(c) of the Commercial Computer Software - Restricted
Rights clause at FAR sec. 52.227-19 and subparagraph
(c) (1) (ii) of the Rights in Technical Data and Computer

Software clause at DFARS sec. 252.227-7013.
cisco Systems, Inc.
170 West Tasman Drive
San Jose, California 95134-1706




Cisco Internetwork Operating System Software
IOS (tm) c6sup_sp Software (c6sup_sp-SPDBG-M), Version 12.0(7T)XE1(2.02)
   INTERIM TEST SOFTWARE
Copyright (c) 1986-2000 by cisco Systems, Inc.
Compiled Sun 09-Jan-00 22:40 by integ
Image text-base: 0x60020900, data-base: 0x60588000
Start as Primary processor
00:00:03: %SYS-3-LOGGER_FLUSHING: System pausing to ensure console debugging
   output.
00:00:03: %OIR-6-CONSOLE: Changing console ownership to route processor




System Bootstrap, Version 12.0(3)XE, RELEASE SOFTWARE

Copyright (c) 1998 by cisco Systems, Inc.

Cat6k-MSFC platform with 131072 Kbytes of main memory

rommon 1 >
```

At this point, the MSFC must run the boot loader image. Display the contents of the MSFC's boot Flash to ensure that the boot loader image is there. Type the following command:

```
rommon 2 > dir bootflash:

File size Checksum File name

1877456 bytes (0x1ca5d0) 0x325c9851 c6msfc-bootdbg-mz
```

Now boot the MSFC using the boot loader image, as follows:

```
rommon 3 > boot bootflash:c6msfc-bootdbg-mz

Self decompressing the image : ################ [OK]
Restricted Rights Legend
Use, duplication, or disclosure by the Government is
subject to restrictions as set forth in subparagraph
(c) of the Commercial Computer Software - Restricted
Rights clause at FAR sec. 52.227-19 and subparagraph
(c) (1) (ii) of the Rights in Technical Data and Computer
Software clause at DFARS sec. 252.227-7013.
cisco Systems, Inc.
170 West Tasman Drive
San Jose, California 95134-1706

Cisco Internetwork Operating System Software

IOS (tm) MSFC Software (C6MSFC-BOOTDBG-M), Experimental Version
   12.1(20000118:211435) [slarson-cosmos_e2 321]
Copyright (c) 1986-2000 by cisco Systems, Inc.
Compiled Wed 19-Jan-00 16:23 by slarson
Image text-base: 0x60008900, data-base: 0x603C4000
cisco Cat6k-MSFC (R5000) processor with 122880K/8192K bytes of memory.
Processor board ID SAD03302657
R5000 CPU at 200Mhz, Implementation 35, Rev 2.1, 512KB L2 Cache
Last reset from power-on
X.25 software, Version 3.0.0.
123K bytes of non-volatile configuration memory.

4096K bytes of packet SRAM memory.
16384K bytes of Flash internal SIMM (Sector size 256K).


Press RETURN to get started!

00:00:04: %SYS-5-RESTART: System restarted --
Cisco Internetwork Operating System Software
IOS (tm) MSFC Software (C6MSFC-BOOTDBG-M), Experimental Version
   12.1(20000118:211435) [slarson-cosmos_e2 321]
Copyright (c) 1986-2000 by cisco Systems, Inc.
Compiled Wed 19-Jan-00 16:23 by slarson
Router(boot)> en
Router(boot)#
```

You now need to format the MSFC's boot Flash and copy the boot loader image from the supervisor's slot 0.

Note: You will not be able to display the contents of slot 0, so you need to remember the boot loader image name to load it from the supervisor's slot 0.

```
Router(boot)# dir slot0:
              ^
% Invalid input detected at '^' marker.
```

First, format MSFC's boot Flash.

```
Router(boot)# format bootflash:
Format operation may take a while. Continue? [confirm]
Format operation will destroy all data in "bootflash:".
Continue? [confirm]
Formatting sector 1
Format of bootflash: complete
```

Copy the boot loader image to the MSFC's boot Flash by typing the following command:

```
download slot0:<boot loader image> bootflash:<boot loader image>
```

See the following output from the last few steps.

```
Router(boot)# download slot0:c6msfc-bootdbg-mz bootflash:c6msfc-bootdbg-mz
Starting download: 1877456
   bytes!!!!!!!!!!!!!!!!!!!!!!!!!!!!!!!!!!!!!!!!!!!!!!!!!!!!!!!!!!!!!!!!!!!!!!!
Chksum: Verified!
Writing image to bootflash:c6msfc-bootdbg-mz
!!!!!!!!!!!!!!!!!!!!!!!!!!!!!!!!!!!!!!!!!!!!!!!!!!!!!!!!!!!!!!!!!!!!!!!!!!!!!!!!

CCCCCCCCCCCCCCCCCCCCCCCCCCCCCCCCCCCCCCCCCCCCCCCCCC

%Download successful

Router(boot)# dir bootflash:

Directory of bootflash:/

1 -rw- 1877456 Jan 01 2000 00:38:56 c6msfc-bootdbg-mz
      15990784 bytes total (14113200 bytes free)
```

At this point, go back to the main recovery procedures to finalize the process.

Loading the Catalyst OS Image

The first step is to load the Cat OS image and then switch consoles from the RP to the SP. The new console will be the MSFC's ROMMON prompt.

Note: Loading this image will not take you directly to the MSFC's ROMMON prompt.

Load Cat OS by typing the following command:

```
boot <location>:<Cat OS image>
```

In this command, **<location>** is either slot 0 or bootflash.

Switch to the MSFC console by typing **switch console** when you are at the Cat OS enable prompt.

```
rommon 1 > boot slot0:cat6000-sup.5-4-0-97.bin

Uncompressing file: ####################################################


System Power On Diagnostics
```

```
DRAM Size ....................64 MB
Testing DRAM.................Passed
Verifying Text Segment .......Passed
NVRAM Size ..................512 KB
Saving NVRAM .................Done
Testing NVRAM ...............Passed
Restoring NVRAM .............Done
Level2 Cache .................Present
Testing Level2 Cache .........Passed
System Power On Diagnostics Complete
Boot image: slot0:cat6000-sup.5-4-0-97.bin
Running System Diagnostics from this Supervisor (Module 1)
This may take up to 2 minutes....please wait
IP address for Catalyst not configured
DHCP/BOOTP will commence after the ports are online
Ports are coming online ...



Cisco Systems Console




2000 Jan 01 01:16:12 %SYS-4-NVLOG:initBootNvram:Bootarea checksum failed:
  0x4525(0x45A5)

Enter password: 2000 Jan 01 01:16:14 %SYS-1-SYS_NORMPWRMGMT:System in normal
  power management operation

2000 Jan 01 01:16:17 %SYS-5-MOD_PWRON:Module 3 powered up

2000 Jan 01 01:16:17 %SYS-5-MOD_PWRON:Module 4 powered up

2000 Jan 01 01:16:27 %MLS-5-NDEDISABLED:Netflow Data Export disabled

2000 Jan 01 01:16:27 %MLS-5-MCAST_STATUS:IP Multicast Multilayer Switching is
  enabled

2000 Jan 01 01:16:28 %SYS-5-MOD_OK:Module 1 is online

2000 Jan 01 01:16:45 %PAGP-5-PORTTOSTP:Port 1/2 joined bridge port 1/2

2000 Jan 01 01:17:01 %SYS-5-MOD_OK:Module 3 is online

2000 Jan 01 01:17:08 %SYS-5-MOD_OK:Module 4 is online



Console> en

Enter password:

Console> (enable) switch console

Trying Router-15...
```

```
Connected to Router-15.

Type 'exit' to switch back...

rommon 1 >
```

At this point, the MSFC must run the boot loader image. Display the contents of the MSFC's boot Flash to ensure that the boot loader image is there. Type the following command:

```
Router(boot)# dir bootflash:

Directory of bootflash:/

1 -rw- 1877456 Jan 01 2000 00:38:56 c6msfc-bootdbg-mz
```

Now boot the MSFC using the boot loader image, as follows:

```
rommon 5 > boot bootflash:c6msfc-bootdbg-mz

Self decompressing the image : ################## [OK]

Restricted Rights Legend

Use, duplication, or disclosure by the Government is

subject to restrictions as set forth in subparagraph

(c) of the Commercial Computer Software - Restricted

Rights clause at FAR sec. 52.227-19 and subparagraph

(c) (1) (ii) of the Rights in Technical Data and Computer

Software clause at DFARS sec. 252.227-7013.

cisco Systems, Inc.

170 West Tasman Drive

San Jose, California 95134-1706




Cisco Internetwork Operating System Software

IOS (tm) MSFC Software (C6MSFC-BOOTDBG-M), Experimental Version
  12.1(20000118:211435) [slarson-cosmos_e2 321]

Copyright (c) 1986-2000 by cisco Systems, Inc.

Compiled Wed 19-Jan-00 16:23 by slarson

Image text-base: 0x60008900, data-base: 0x603C4000

cisco Cat6k-MSFC (R5000) processor with 122880K/8192K bytes of memory.

Processor board ID SAD03302657

R5000 CPU at 200Mhz, Implementation 35, Rev 2.1, 512KB L2 Cache
```

```
Last reset from power-on

X.25 software, Version 3.0.0.

123K bytes of non-volatile configuration memory.

4096K bytes of packet SRAM memory.

16384K bytes of Flash internal SIMM (Sector size 256K).


Press RETURN to get started!


Module online.

00:00:04: %SYS-5-RESTART: System restarted --

Cisco Internetwork Operating System Software

IOS (tm) MSFC Software (C6MSFC-BOOTDBG-M), Experimental Version
    12.1(20000118:211435) [slarson-cosmos_e2 321]

Copyright (c) 1986-2000 by cisco Systems, Inc.

Compiled Wed 19-Jan-00 16:23 by slarson

Router(boot)> en

        download slot0:<boot loader image> bootflash:<boot loader image>
```

You now need to format the MSFC's boot Flash and copy the boot loader image from the supervisor's slot 0.

Note: You will not be able to display the contents of slot 0, so you need to remember the boot loader image name to load it from the supervisor's slot 0.

```
Router(boot)# dir slot0:
                 ^
% Invalid input detected at '^' marker.
```

First, format MSFC's boot Flash.

```
Router(boot)# format bootflash:

Format operation may take a while. Continue? [confirm]

Format operation will destroy all data in "bootflash:". Continue? [confirm]

Formatting sector 1

Format of bootflash: complete
```

Copy the boot loader image to the MSFC's boot Flash by typing the following command:

```
copy sup-slot0:<boot loader image> bootflash:<boot loader image>
```

See the following output from the last few steps.

```
Router(boot)# copy sup-slot0:c6msfc-boot-mz bootflash:c6msfc-boot-mz
```

```
Destination filename [c6msfc-boot-mz]?

Accessing sup-slot0:c6msfc-boot-mz...

Loading slot0:c6msfc-boot-mz from 127.0.0.11 (via EOBC0): !

Loading slot0:c6msfc-boot-mz from 127.0.0.11 (via EOBC0):
!!!!!!!!!!!!!!!!!!!!!!!!!!!!!!!!!!!!!!!!!!!!!!!![OK
- 1603124/3206144 bytes]

Router(boot)# dir bootflash:

Directory of bootflash:/

1 -rw- 1877456 Jan 01 2000 00:38:56 c6msfc-bootdbg-mz

15990784 bytes total (14113200 bytes free)
```

At this point, go back to the main recovery procedures to finalize the process.

Cisco 2600 TFTP Download and Startup

Introduction

This section explains how to recover a Cisco 2600 router from either a corrupted or missing ios image. To gain access to the rommon command line interpreter, hit the break key during the first 15 seconds after the router has been powered on. From the rommon> prompt you may then use the tftpdnld command to tftpboot an ios image to the router.

```
rommon 1 > tftpdnld

Missing or illegal ip address for variable IP_ADDRESS
Illegal IP address.

usage: tftpdnld [-r]
  Use this command for disaster recovery only to recover an image via TFTP.
  Monitor variables are used to set up parameters for the transfer.
  (Syntax: "VARIABLE_NAME=value" and use "set" to show current variables.)
  "ctrl-c" or "break" stops the transfer before flash erase begins.

  The following variables are REQUIRED to be set for tftpdnld:
            IP_ADDRESS: The IP address for this unit
        IP_SUBNET_MASK: The subnet mask for this unit
       DEFAULT_GATEWAY: The default gateway for this unit
           TFTP_SERVER: The IP address of the server to fetch from
             TFTP_FILE: The filename to fetch

  The following variables are OPTIONAL:
          TFTP_VERBOSE: Print setting. 0=quiet, 1=progress(default), 2=verbose
      TFTP_RETRY_COUNT: Retry count for ARP and TFTP (default=7)
          TFTP_TIMEOUT: Overall timeout of operation in seconds (default=7200)
         TFTP_CHECKSUM: Perform checksum test on image, 0=no, 1=yes (default=1)
          FE_SPEED_MODE: 0=10/hdx, 1=10/fdx, 2=100/hdx, 3=100/fdx, 4=Auto(deflt)

  Command line options:
    -r: do not write flash, load to DRAM only and launch image
rommon 2 > IP_ADDERESS=172.18.44.1
```

```
rommon 3 > IP_SUBNET_MASK=255.255.0.0
rommon 4 > DEFAULT_GATEWAY=172.18.44.44
rommon 5 > TFTP_SERVER=172.18.44.44
rommon 6 > TFTP_FILE=c2600-jk2o3s-mz.121-3.T.bin
rommon 7 > tftpdnld

        IP_ADDRESS: 172.18.44.1
    IP_SUBNET_MASK: 255.255.0.0
   DEFAULT_GATEWAY: 172.18.44.44
       TFTP_SERVER: 172.18.44.44
         TFTP_FILE: c2600-jk2o3s-mz.121-3.T.bin

Invoke this command for disaster recovery only.
WARNING: all existing data in all partitions on flash will be lost!
Do you wish to continue? y/n:  [n]:  y
....
Receiving c2600-jk2o3s-mz.121-3.T.bin from 172.18.44.44
!!!!!!!!!!!!!!!!!!!!!!!!!!!!!!!!!!!!!!!!!!!!!!!!!!!!!!!!!!!!!!!!!!!!!!!!!!!!!!!!!
!!!!!!!!!!!!!!!!!!!!!!!!!!!!!!!!!!!!!!!!!!!!!!!!!!!!!!!!!!!!!!!!!!!!!!!!!!!!!!!!!!
!!!!!!!!!!!!!!!!!!!!!!!!!!!!!!!!!!!!!!!!!!!!!!!!!!!!!!!!!!!!!!!!!!!!!!!!!!!!!!!!!!
!!!!!!!!!!!!!!!!!!!!!!!!!!!!!!!!!!!!!!!!!!!!!!!!!!!!!!!!!!!!!!!!!!!!!!!!!!!!!!!!!!
!!!!!!!!!!!!!!!!!!!!!!!!!!!!!!!!!!!!!!!!!!!!!!!!!!!!!!!!!!!!!!!!!!!!!!!!!!!!!!!!!!
!!!!!!!!!!!!!!!!!!!!!!!!!!!!!!!!!!!!!!!!!!!!!!!!!!!!!!!!!!!!!!!!!!!!!!!!!!!!!!!!!!
!!!!!!!!!!!!!!!!!!!!!!!!!!!!!!!!!!!!!!!!!!!!!!!!!!!!!!!!!!!!!!!!!!!!!!!!!!!!!!!!!!
!!!!!!!!!!!!!!!!!!!!!!!!!!!!!!!!!!!!!!!!!!!!!!!!!!!!!!!!!!!!!!!!!!!!!!!!!!!!!!!!!!
!!!!!!!!!!!!!!!!!!!!!!!!!!!!!!!!!!!!!!!!!!!!!!!!!!!!!!!!!!!!!!!!!!!!!!!!!!!!!!!!!!
!!!!!!!!!!!!!!!!!!!!!!!!!!!!!!!!!!!!!!!!!!!!!!!!!!!!!!!!!!!!!!!!!!!!!!!!!!!!!!!!!!
!!!!!!!!!!!!!!!!!!!!!!!!!!!!!!!!!!!!!!!!!!!!!!!!!!!!!!!!!!!!!!!!!!!!!!!!!!!!!!!!!!
!!!!!!!!!!!!!!!!!!!!!!!!!!!!!!!!!!!!!!!!!!!!!!!!!!!!!!!!!!!!!!!!!!!!!!!!!!!!!!!!!!
!!!!!!!!!!!!!!!!!!!!!!!!!!!!!!!!!!!!!!!!!!!!!!!!!!!!!!!!!!!!!!!!!!!!!!!!!!!!!!!!!!
!!!!!!!!!!!!!!!!!!!!!!!!!!!!!!!!!!!!!!!!!!!!!!!!!!!!!!!!!!!!!!!!!!!!!!!!!!!!!!!!!!
!!!!!!!!!!!!!!!!!!!!!!!!!!!!!!!!!!!!!!!!!!!!!!!!!!!!!!!!!!!!!!!!!!!!!!!!!!!!!!!!!!
!!!!!!!!!!!!!!!!!!!!!!!!!!!!!!!!!!!!!!!!!!!!!!!!!!!!!!!!!!!!!!!!!!!!!!!!!!!!!!!!!!
!!!!!!!!!!!!!!!!!!!!!!!!!!!!!!!!!!!!!!!!!!!!!!!!!!!!!!!!!!!!!!!!!!!!!!!!!!!!!!!!!!
!!!!!!!!!!!!!!!!!!!!!!!!!!!!!!!!!!!!!!!!!!!!!!!!!!!!!!!!!!!!!!!!!!!!!!!!!!!!!!!!!!
!!!!!!!!!!!!!!!!!!!!!!!!!!!!!!!!!!!!!!!!!!!!!!!!!!!!!!!!!!!!!!!!!!!!!!!!!!!!!!!!!!
!!!!!!!!!!!!!!!!!!!!!!!!!!!!!!!!!!!!!!!!!!!!!!!!!!!!!!!!!!!!!!!!!!!!!!!!!!!!!!!!!!
!!!!!!!!!!!!!!!!!!!!!!!!!!!!!!!!!!!!!!!!!!!!!!!!!!!!!!!!!!!!!!!!!!!!!!!!!!!!!!!!!!
!!!!!!!!!!!!!!!!!!!!!!!!!!!!!!!!!!!!!!!!!!!!!!!!!!!!!!!!!!!!!!!!!!!!!!!!!!!!!!!!!!
!!!!7
File reception completed.
Copying file c2600-jk2o3s-mz.121-3.T.bin to flash.

Erasing flash at 0x60000000

program flash location 0x60000000
rommon 9 > dir flash:
         File size        Checksum    File name_
  11542120 bytes (0xb01e68)   0xaae4    c2600-jk2o3s-mz.121-3.T.bin_
rommon 10 > reset

System Bootstrap, Version 11.3(2)XA4, RELEASE SOFTWARE (fc1)
Copyright (c) 1999 by cisco Systems, Inc.
TAC:Home:SW:IOS:Specials for info
C2600 platform with 65536 Kbytes of main memory

program load complete, entry point: 0x80008000, size: 0xb01d4c
```

```
Self decompressing the image :
#####################################################################
#####################################################################
#####################################################################
#####################################################################
#####################################################################
#####################################################################
#####################################################################
#####################################################################
#####################################################################
#####################################################################
#####################################################################
#####################################################################
#####################################################################
#####################################################################
####### [OK]


            Restricted Rights Legend

Use, duplication, or disclosure by the Government is
subject to restrictions as set forth in subparagraph
(c) of the Commercial Computer Software - Restricted
Rights clause at FAR sec. 52.227-19 and subparagraph
(c) (1) (ii) of the Rights in Technical Data and Computer
Software clause at DFARS sec. 252.227-7013.

            cisco Systems, Inc.
            170 West Tasman Drive
            San Jose, California 95134-1706



Cisco Internetwork Operating System Software
IOS (tm) C2600 Software (C2600-JK2O3S-M), Version 12.1(3)T,   RELEASE SOFTWARE (fc1)
Copyright (c) 1986-2000 by cisco Systems, Inc.
Compiled Thu 20-Jul-00 01:38 by ccai
Image text-base: 0x80008088, data-base: 0x81381C5C


Compliance with U.S. Export Laws and Regulations - Encryption

This product performs encryption and is regulated for export
by the U.S. Government.

This product is not authorized for use by persons located
outside the United States and Canada that do not have prior
approval from Cisco Systems, Inc. or the U.S. Government.

This product may not be exported outside the U.S. and Canada
either by physical or electronic means without PRIOR approval
of Cisco Systems, Inc. or the U.S. Government.

Persons outside the U.S. and Canada may not re-export, resell,
or transfer this product by either physical or electronic means
without  prior approval of Cisco Systems, Inc. or the U.S.
Government.

cisco 2621 (MPC860) processor (revision 0x102) with 60416K/5120K bytes of memory.
Processor board ID JAD04270DWH (2283097670)
M860 processor: part number 0, mask 49
Bridging software.
X.25 software, Version 3.0.0.
```

```
SuperLAT software (copyright 1990 by Meridian Technology Corp).
TN3270 Emulation software.
Basic Rate ISDN software, Version 1.1.
2 FastEthernet/IEEE 802.3 interface(s)
1 Serial network interface(s)
1 ISDN Basic Rate interface(s)
32K bytes of non-volatile configuration memory.
16384K bytes of processor board System flash (Read/Write)


        --- System Configuration Dialog ---

Would you like to enter the initial configuration dialog? [yes/no]: no


Would you like to terminate autoinstall? [yes]:


Press RETURN to get started!

Passed
00:00:24: %LINK-3-UPDOWN: Interface FastEthernet0/0, changed state to up
00:00:24: %LINK-3-UPDOWN: Interface FastEthernet0/1, changed state to up
00:00:24: %LINK-3-UPDOWN: Interface Serial0/0, changed state to down
00:00:25: %LINEPROTO-5-UPDOWN: Line protocol on Interface FastEthernet0/0, changed
state to up
00:00:25: %LINEPROTO-5-UPDOWN: Line protocol on Interface FastEthernet0/1, changed
state to down
00:00:25: %LINEPROTO-5-UPDOWN: Line protocol on Interface Serial0/0, changed state
to down
00:00:58: %LINK-5-CHANGED: Interface BRI0/0, changed state to administratively down
00:00:59: %LINEPROTO-5-UPDOWN: Line protocol on Interface BRI0/0, changed state to
down
00:00:59: %IP-5-WEBINST_KILL: Terminating DNS process
00:01:00: %LINK-5-CHANGED: Interface Serial0/0, changed state to administratively
down
00:01:00: %LINK-5-CHANGED: Interface FastEthernet0/0, changed state to
administratively down
00:01:00: %LINK-5-CHANGED: Interface FastEthernet0/1, changed state to
administratively down
```

Troubleshooting the Power and Cooling Systems

Check the following items to help isolate the problem:

- When the power switch is in the on position (I) and the power LED is on, make sure that the fan is operating. If not, check the fan.

- If the router shuts down after being on a short time, check the environmental conditions. The router might be overheating, resulting in a thermal-induced shutdown. Verify that the chassis intake and exhaust vents are clear. The operating temperature for the router is 32°F to 104°F (0°C to 40°C). If the router fails to boot but the power LED is on, check the power supply.

- If the router constantly or intermittently reboots, there might be a problem with either
  the processor or the software, or a DRAM single in-line memory module (SIMM)
  might be installed incorrectly.

Cisco 3600 Startup

Introduction

This section explains how to recover a Cisco 3600 router from either a corrupted or missing
ios image. To gain access to the rommon command line interpreter, hit the break key during
the first 15 seconds after the router has been powered on. From the rommon> prompt you
may then use the xmodem command to transfer an ios image to the router via the console
interface of the router.

Xmodem of loading IOS code:

```
rommon 1 > xmodem ?
Do not start the sending program yet...
device does not contain a valid magic number
dir: cannot open device "flash:"

WARNING: All existing data in flash will be lost!
Invoke this application only for disaster recovery.
Do you wish to continue? y/n  [n]:  y
Ready to receive file ? ...

Erasing flash at 0x30000000

program flash location 0x30000000
Download Complete!
program load complete, entry point: 0x80008000, size: 0xa10988
Self decompressing the image :
#####################################################################
#####################################################################
#####################################################################
#####################################################################
#####################################################################
#####################################################################
#####################################################################
#####################################################################
#####################################################################
#####################################################################
######## [OK]


                    Restricted Rights Legend

Use, duplication, or disclosure by the Government is
subject to restrictions as set forth in subparagraph
(c) of the Commercial Computer Software - Restricted
Rights clause at FAR sec. 52.227-19 and subparagraph
(c) (1) (ii) of the Rights in Technical Data and Computer
Software clause at DFARS sec. 252.227-7013.
```

```
            cisco Systems, Inc.
            170 West Tasman Drive
            San Jose, California 95134-1706


Cisco Internetwork Operating System Software
IOS (tm) 3600 Software (C3640-IK2S-M), Version 12.1(3)T,  RELEASE SOFTWARE (fc1)
Copyright (c) 1986-2000 by cisco Systems, Inc.
Compiled Wed 19-Jul-00 20:18 by ccai
Image text-base: 0x60008950, data-base: 0x6116C000


Compliance with U.S. Export Laws and Regulations - Encryption

This product performs encryption and is regulated for export
by the U.S. Government.

This product is not authorized for use by persons located
outside the United States and Canada that do not have prior
approval from Cisco Systems, Inc. or the U.S. Government.

This product may not be exported outside the U.S. and Canada
either by physical or electronic means without PRIOR approval
of Cisco Systems, Inc. or the U.S. Government.

Persons outside the U.S. and Canada may not re-export, resell,
or transfer this product by either physical or electronic means
without  prior approval of Cisco Systems, Inc. or the U.S.
Government.

cisco 3640 (R4700) processor (revision 0x00) with 60416K/5120K bytes of memory.
Processor board ID 19704176
R4700 CPU at 100Mhz, Implementation 33, Rev 1.0
Bridging software.
X.25 software, Version 3.0.0.
SuperLAT software (copyright 1990 by Meridian Technology Corp).
2 FastEthernet/IEEE 802.3 interface(s)
DRAM configuration is 64 bits wide with parity disabled.
125K bytes of non-volatile configuration memory.
16384K bytes of processor board System flash (Read/Write)

SETUP: new interface FastEthernet0/0 placed in "shutdown" state
SETUP: new interface FastEthernet0/1 placed in "shutdown" state


Press RETURN to get started!


00:00:13: %LINK-3-UPDOWN: Interface FastEthernet0/0, changed state to up
00:00:13: %LINK-3-UPDOWN: Interface FastEthernet0/1, changed state to up
00:00:13: %SYS-5-CONFIG_I: Configured from memory by console
00:00:14: %LINEPROTO-5-UPDOWN: Line protocol on Interface FastEthernet0/0, changed
state to down_00:00:14: %LINEPROTO-5-UPDOWN: Line protocol on Interface
FastEthernet0/1, changed state to down
00:00:18: %LINEPROTO-5-UPDOWN: Line protocol on Interface FastEthernet0/0, changed
state to up
00:00:28: %IP-5-WEBINST_KILL: Terminating DNS process
00:00:29: %LINK-5-CHANGED: Interface FastEthernet0/0, changed state to
administratively down
00:00:29: %SYS-5-RESTART: System restarted --
Cisco Internetwork Operating System Software
IOS (tm) 3600 Software (C3640-IK2S-M), Version 12.1(3)T,  RELEASE SOFTWARE (fc1)
Copyright (c) 1986-2000 by cisco Systems, Inc.
```

```
Compiled Wed 19-Jul-00 20:18 by ccai
00:00:30: %LINK-5-CHANGED: Interface FastEthernet0/1, changed state to
administratively down
00:00:30: %LINEPROTO-5-UPDOWN: Line protocol on Interface FastEthernet0/0, changed
state to down
```

Troubleshooting

For more information on troubleshooting the Cisco 3600, you can visit www.cisco.com/ univercd/cc/td/doc/product/access/acs_mod/cis3600/3600ig/3600trou.htm.

Cisco Catalyst 4000 Startup

When applying power to the Cisco Catalyst 4000, the following boot process should occur:

Boot process:

```
WS-X4013 bootrom version 5.4(1), built on 2000.04.04 10:48:54
H/W Revisions:     Crumb: 5    Rancor: 8    Board: 2
Supervisor MAC addresses: 00:02:b9:11:d4:00 through 00:02:b9:11:d7:ff (1024
addresses)
Installed memory: 64 MB
Testing LEDs.... done!
The system will autoboot in 5 seconds.
Type control-C to prevent autobooting.
rommon 1 >
The system will now begin autobooting.
Autobooting image: "bootflash:cat4000.5-5-1.bin"
.....................................................................................
......................############################
Starting Off-line Diagnostics
Mapping in TempFs
Board type is WS-X4013
DiagBootMode value is "post"
Telling ApkPageMan that we have 12288 pages of memory
Loading diagnostics...

Power-on-self-test for Module 1:  WS-X4013
Status: (. = Pass, F = Fail)
uplink port 1: .        uplink port 2: .        eobc port: .
processor: .            cpu sdram: .            rtc: .
eprom: .                nvram: .                flash: .
temperature sensor: .   enet console port: .    switch 0 port 0: .
switch 0 port 1: .      switch 0 port 2: .      switch 0 port 3: .
switch 0 port 4: .      switch 0 port 5: .      switch 0 port 6: .
switch 0 port 7: .      switch 0 port 8: .      switch 0 port 9: .
switch 0 port 10: .     switch 0 port 11: .     switch 0 registers: .
switch 0 sram: .        switch 1 port 0: .      switch 1 port 1: .
switch 1 port 2: .      switch 1 port 3: .      switch 1 port 4: .
switch 1 port 5: .      switch 1 port 6: .      switch 1 port 7: .
switch 1 port 8: .      switch 1 port 9: .      switch 1 port 10: .
switch 1 port 11: .     switch 1 registers: .   switch 1 sram: .
switch 2 port 0: .      switch 2 port 1: .      switch 2 port 2: .
switch 2 port 3: .      switch 2 port 4: .      switch 2 port 5: .
switch 2 port 6: .      switch 2 port 7: .      switch 2 port 8: .
switch 2 port 9: .      switch 2 port 10: .     switch 2 port 11: .
switch 2 registers: .   switch 2 sram: .
```

```
Module 1 Passed

Power-on-self-test for Module 2:  not present
Port status: (. = Pass, F = Fail)

Module 2 Ignored

Power-on-self-test for Module 3:  WS-X4148-RJ
Port status: (. = Pass, F = Fail)
  1: .    2: .    3: .    4: .    5: .    6: .    7: .    8: .
  9: .   10: .   11: .   12: .   13: .   14: .   15: .   16: .
 17: .   18: .   19: .   20: .   21: .   22: .   23: .   24: .
 25: .   26: .   27: .   28: .   29: .   30: .   31: .   32: .
 33: .   34: .   35: .   36: .   37: .   38: .   39: .   40: .
 41: .   42: .   43: .   44: .   45: .   46: .   47: .   48: .
Module 3 Passed

Power-on-self-test for Module 4:  WS-X4148-RJ
Port status: (. = Pass, F = Fail)
  1: .    2: .    3: .    4: .    5: .    6: .    7: .    8: .
  9: .   10: .   11: .   12: .   13: .   14: .   15: .   16: .
 17: .   18: .   19: .   20: .   21: .   22: .   23: .   24: .
 25: .   26: .   27: .   28: .   29: .   30: .   31: .   32: .
 33: .   34: .   35: .   36: .   37: .   38: .   39: .   40: .
 41: .   42: .   43: .   44: .   45: .   46: .   47: .   48: .
Module 4 Passed

Power-on-self-test for Module 5:  not present
Port status: (. = Pass, F = Fail)

Module 5 Ignored

Power-on-self-test for Module 6:  not present
Port status: (. = Pass, F = Fail)

Module 6 Ignored

Exiting Off-line Diagnostics


Cisco Systems, Inc. Console



Enter password:

Console> ena


Enter password:

Console> (enable) sh mod

Mod Slot Ports Module-Type              Model                Sub Status
--- ---- ----- ------------------------ -------------------- --- --------
 1    1    2   1000BaseX Supervisor     WS-X4013             no  ok
 3    3   48   10/100BaseTx Ethernet    WS-X4148-RJ          no  other
 4    4   48   10/100BaseTx Ethernet    WS-X4148-RJ          no  other
```

```
Mod  Module-Name            Serial-Num
---  -------------------    -------------------
1                           JAB0427081F
3                           JAB04110629
4                           JAE041801B5

Mod  MAC-Address(es)                                 Hw     Fw          Sw
---  ------------------------------------------      ------ ----------  -----------------
1    00-02-b9-11-d4-00 to 00-02-b9-11-d7-ff 1.2      5.4(1)     5.5(1)
3    00-01-42-f5-c5-b0 to 00-01-42-f5-c5-df 2.3
4    00-02-16-25-19-40 to 00-02-16-25-19-6f 2.3
Console> (enable) sh mod

Mod  Slot Ports Module-Type            Model             Sub Status
---  ---- ----- ---------------------- ----------------- --- --------
1    1    2     1000BaseX Supervisor   WS-X4013          no  ok
3    3    48    10/100BaseTx Ethernet  WS-X4148-RJ       no  ok
4    4    48    10/100BaseTx Ethernet  WS-X4148-RJ       no  ok

Mod  Module-Name            Serial-Num
---  -------------------    -------------------
1                           JAB0427081F
3                           JAB04110629
4                           JAE041801B5

Mod  MAC-Address(es)                                 Hw     Fw          Sw
---  ------------------------------------------      ------ ----------  -----------------
1    00-02-b9-11-d4-00 to 00-02-b9-11-d7-ff 1.2      5.4(1)     5.5(1)
3    00-01-42-f5-c5-b0 to 00-01-42-f5-c5-df 2.3
4    00-02-16-25-19-40 to 00-02-16-25-19-6f 2.3
Console> (enable)
```

Troubleshooting

For troubleshooting information on the Cisco 4000, visit www.cisco.com/univercd/cc/td/doc/product/lan/cat4000/inst_gd/06trblsh.htm.

Troubleshooting Ethernet

Ethernet was developed by Xerox Corporation's Palo Alto Research Center (PARC) in the 1970s. Ethernet was the technological basis for the IEEE 802.3 specification, which was initially released in 1980. Shortly thereafter, Digital Equipment Corporation, Intel Corporation, and Xerox Corporation jointly developed and released an Ethernet specification (Version 2.0) that is substantially compatible with IEEE 802.3. Together, Ethernet and IEEE 802.3 currently maintain the greatest market share of any local-area network (LAN) protocol. Today, the term *Ethernet* is often used to refer to all carrier sense multiple access collision detect (CSMA/CD) LANs that generally conform to Ethernet specifications, including IEEE 802.3.

When it was developed, Ethernet was designed to fill the middle ground between long-distance, low-speed networks and specialized, computer-room networks carrying data at high speeds for very limited distances. Ethernet is well suited to applications on which a local communication medium must carry sporadic, occasionally heavy traffic at high peak data rates.

Ethernet and IEEE 802.3

Ethernet and IEEE 802.3 specify similar technologies. Both are CSMA/CD LANs. Stations on a CSMA/CD LAN can access the network at any time. Before sending data, CSMA/CD stations "listen" to the network to see if it is already in use. If it is, the station wanting to transmit waits. If the network is not in use, the station transmits. A collision occurs when two stations listen for network traffic, "hear" none, and transmit simultaneously. In this case, both transmissions are damaged, and the stations must retransmit at some later time. Back-off algorithms determine when the colliding stations retransmit. CSMA/CD stations can detect collisions, so they know when they must retransmit. This access method is used by traditional Ethernet and IEEE 802.3 functions in half-duplex mode. (When Ethernet is operated in full-duplex mode, CSMA/CD is not used.) This means that only one station can transmit at a time over the shared Ethernet.

This access method was conceived to offer shared and fair access to multiple network stations/devices. It allows these systems fair access to the Ethernet network through a process of arbitration by dictating how stations attached to this network can access the shared channel. It allows stations to listen before transmitting and can recover if signals collide. This recovery time interval is called a slot time and is based on the round-trip time that it takes to send a 64-byte frame the maximum length of an Ethernet LAN attached by repeaters. Another name for this shared LAN is a *collision domain*. For half-duplex operation, the mode on which traditional Ethernet is based, the size of your collision domain can be limited by the physical limitations of the cabling utilized. Table 4-1 lists the collision domains for 10/100/1000 Mbps.

Table 4-1   *Examples of Traditional Ethernet and IEEE 802.3 Collision Domains*

Traditional Ethernet and 802.3 Collision Domains		
Signaling Speed	**Network Diameter**	
10BaseX	About 280 meters (coax)	Ethernet
10/100BaseX	About 205 meters (twisted pair)	IEEE 802.3b
1000BaseX	About 20 meters (fiber and copper)	IEEE 802.3z

The limitations of the cable itself can create even smaller boundaries.

Because the 64-byte slot time is consistent for 10/100/1000 transmission speeds, this severely limits the scalability for 1000BaseX to operate in a network with a diameter of more than 20 meters. To overcome this obstacle, use carrier extension bits in addition to the Ethernet frame size to extend the time that transmits on the wire. This expands the network diameter to 100 meters per segment, like 100BaseT.

For this system to work, everyone must abide by the same rules. For CSMA/CD the rules are as follows:

1 **Listen**—Stations listen for signals on the wire. If a signal is detected (carrier sense), then stations should not attempt to transmit frame. If a station "hears" another signal on the wire while transmitting the first 64 bytes of a frame, it should recognize that its frame has collided with another.

2 **Collision detect**—If a station detects a collision, it must back off from sending the frame using the truncated back-off algorithm. The back-off algorithm counts the number of collisions, if any, to determine how long a station must wait to retransmit the frame. This algorithm backs off each time that a collision is detected. The goal of this method is to provide the system a way to determine how many stations are trying to transmit simultaneously and then guess when it should be safe to try again. The way that the truncated back-off algorithm tracks and adjusts timers is based on the value of 2^n, where n is the number of collisions encountered during transmission of the

frame. The result is a guess of how many stations may be on the shared channel. This result gets plugged in as a range, counting from zero, for the number of slot times to wait. The algorithm randomly selects a value from this range as shown in Table 4-2.

Table 4-2   *Back-off Algorithm*

2^n value[1]	Actions
2^0–1	Stations either try to retransmit immediately or wait for one slot time.
2^2	Stations randomly wait zero, one, two, or three slot times to retransmit.
2^3	Stations randomly wait from zero to seven slot times.
2^4	. . . you get the point.

[1]2^n where n = the number of collisions

Depending on the number of collisions the algorithm randomly selects to back off, a station could potentially wait a while before retransmitting.

The algorithm collision counter stops incrementing at 10, where the penalty wait time is selected from a range of 0 to 1023 slot times before retransmission. This is pretty bad, but the algorithm will attempt to retransmit the frame up to 16 collisions. Then it just gives up, and a higher-layer network protocol such as TCP/IP will attempt to retransmit the packet. This is an indication that you have some serious errors.

When a station successfully sends a frame, the collision counter (penalty) is cleared (for that frame) and no loner must wait for the back-off time. ("Interface" statistics are not cleared, just the timer is). Any stations with the lowest collisions will be capable of accessing the wire more quickly because they do not have to wait.

Both Ethernet and IEEE 802.3 LANs are broadcast networks. In other words, all stations see all frames, regardless of whether they represent an intended destination. Each station must examine received frames to determine whether the station is a destination. If it is a destination, the frame is passed to a higher protocol layer for appropriate processing.

Differences between Ethernet and IEEE 802.3 standards are subtle. Ethernet provides services corresponding to Layers 1 and 2 of the OSI reference model, whereas IEEE 802.3 specifies the physical layer (Layer 1) and the channel-access portion of the link layer (Layer 2), but does not define a logical link control protocol. Both Ethernet and IEEE 802.3 are implemented in hardware. Typically, the physical manifestation of these protocols is either an interface card in a host computer or circuitry on a primary circuit board within a host computer.

Now, having said all that regarding the regular operation of traditional Ethernet and 802.3, we must discuss where the two separate in features and functionality. The IEEE 802.3 standard was based on traditional Ethernet, but improvements have been made to this current standard. What we have discussed so far will not scale in today's demanding service provider and enterprise networks.

Full-Duplex Operation 10/100/1000

Everything you've read so far dealt with half-duplex operation (CSMA/CD, back-off timers, and so on). Full-duplex mode allows stations to transmit and receive data simultaneously. This makes for more efficient use of the available bandwidth by allowing open access to the medium. Conversely, this mode of operation can function only with Ethernet switching hubs or via Ethernet cross-over cables between interfaces capable of full-duplex Ethernet. Full-duplex mode expects links to be point-to-point links. There are also no collisions in full-duplex mode, so CSMA/CD is not needed.

Autonegotiation

Autonegotiation allows Ethernet devices to automatically configure their interfaces for operation. If the network interfaces supported different speeds or different modes of operation, they will attempt to settle on a lower common denominator. A plain repeater cannot support multiple speeds; it knows only how to regenerate signals. Smart hubs employ multiple repeaters and a switch plane internally to allow stations that support different speeds to communicate. The negotiation is performed only when the system initially connects to the hub. If slower systems are attached to the same smart hub, then faster systems will have to be manually configured for 10 Mbps operation.

To make sure that your connection is operating properly, IEEE 802.3 Ethernet employs normal link pulses (NLPs), which are used for verifying link integrity in a 10BaseT system. This signaling gives you the link indication when you attach to the hub and is performed between two directly connected link interfaces (hub-to-station or station-to-station). NLPs are helpful in determining that a link has been established between devices, but they are not a good indicator that your cabling is free of problems.

An extension of NLPs is fast link pulses. These do not perform link tests, but instead are employed in the autonegotiation process to advertise a device's capabilities. Autonegotiation on 1000BaseX networks works at only 1000 Mbps, so the only feature "negotiated" is for full- or half-duplex operation. There may be new vendor implementations on the market that can autonegotiate speeds 10 to 1000BaseX, but at this time they are not widely deployed.

A backup alternative, called parallel detection, works for 10/100 speeds if autonegotiation is disabled or is unsupported. This is basically a fallback mechanism that springs into action when autonegotiation fails. The interface capable of autonegotiation will configure itself for bare bones 10-Mbps half-duplex operation.

Physical Connections

IEEE 802.3 specifies several different physical layers, whereas Ethernet defines only one. Each IEEE 802.3 physical layer protocol has a name that summarizes its characteristics. The coded components of an IEEE 802.3 physical layer name are shown in Figure 4-1.

Figure 4-1   *IEEE 802.3 Physical Layer Name Components*

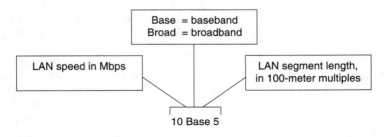

A summary of Ethernet Version 2 and IEEE 802.3 characteristics appears in Tables 4-3 and 4-4.

Table 4-3   *Ethernet Version 2 and IEEE 802.3 Physical Characteristics*

Characteristic	Ethernet Value	IEEE 802.3 Values				
		10Base5	10Base2	1Base5	10BaseT	10Broad36
Data rate (Mbps)	10	10	10	1	10	10
Signaling method	Baseband	Baseband	Baseband	Baseband	Baseband	Broadband
Maximum segment length (m)	500	500	185	250	100	1800
Media	50-ohm coax (thick)	50-ohm coax (thick)	50-ohm coax (thin)	Unshielded twisted-pair wire	Unshielded twisted-pair wire	75-ohm coax
Topology	Bus	Bus	Bus	Star	Star	Star

Table 4-4   *IEEE 802.3 Physical Characteristics*

Characteristic	IEEE 802.3 Values	
	10BaseFX	1000BaseFX
Data rate (Mbps)	100	1000
Signaling method	Baseband	Baseband
Maximum segment length (m)	Repeater 150 m; full-duplex 2000 m Single mode up to 6 to 10 km	Repeater 150 m; full-duplex 2000 m Single mode up to 6 to 10 km
Media	Fiber (single mode or multimode)	Fiber (single mode or multimode)
Topology	Star	Star

There are other 100Base*n* implementations, but they are not widely implemented for various reasons. One particular case in point is 100BaseT4. This system uses four pairs of copper wire and can be used on voice- and data-grade cable. 10/100BaseT systems perform well on Category 5 data-grade cable and use only two pairs of copper wire.

Ethernet is most similar to IEEE 802.3 10Base5. Both of these protocols specify a bus topology network with a connecting cable between the end stations and the actual network medium. In the case of Ethernet, that cable is called a transceiver cable. The *transceiver cable* connects to a transceiver device attached to the physical network medium. The IEEE 802.3 configuration is much the same, except that the connecting cable is referred to as an *attachment unit interface* (AUI), and the transceiver is called a *media attachment unit* (MAU). In both cases, the connecting cable attaches to an interface board (or interface circuitry) within the end station.

Frame Formats

Ethernet and IEEE 802.3 frame formats are shown in Figure 4-2.

Figure 4-2   *Ethernet and IEEE 802.3 Frame Formats*

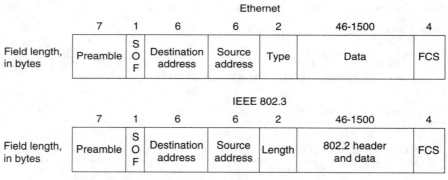

Both Ethernet and IEEE 802.3 frames begin with an alternating pattern of ones and zeros called a *preamble*. The preamble tells receiving stations that a frame is coming.

The byte before the destination address in both an Ethernet and an IEEE 802.3 frame is a start-of-frame (SOF) delimiter. This byte ends with 2 consecutive 1 bits, which serve to synchronize the frame reception portions of all stations on the LAN.

Immediately following the preamble in both Ethernet and IEEE 802.3 LANs are the destination and source address fields. Both Ethernet and IEEE 802.3 addresses are 6 bytes long. Addresses are contained in hardware on the Ethernet and IEEE 802.3 interface cards. The first 3 bytes of the addresses are specified by the IEEE on a vendor-dependent basis, and the last 3 bytes are specified by the Ethernet or IEEE 802.3 vendor. The source address is always a unicast (single node) address, whereas the destination address may be unicast, multicast (group), or broadcast (all nodes).

In Ethernet frames, the 2-byte field following the source address is a type field. This field specifies the upper-layer protocol to receive the data after Ethernet processing is complete.

In IEEE 802.3 frames, the 2-byte field following the source address is a length field, which indicates the number of bytes of data that follow this field and precede the frame check sequence (FCS) field.

Following the type/length field is the actual data contained in the frame. After physical layer and link layer processing is complete, this data will eventually be sent to an upper-layer protocol. In the case of Ethernet, the upper-layer protocol is identified in the type field. In the case of IEEE 802.3, the upper-layer protocol must be defined within the data portion of the frame, if at all. If data in the frame is insufficient to fill the frame to its minimum 64-byte size, padding bytes are inserted to ensure at least a 64-byte frame.

In 802.3 the data field carries a payload header in addition to the payload itself. This header serves the logical link control sublayer of the OSI model and is completely independent of the MAC sublayer and physical layer below it. This header, functionally known as 802.2 encapsulation, contains destination service access point (DSAP) and source service access point (SSAP) information. This will notify higher protocols what type of payload is actually riding in the frame. It functions like the "type" field in traditional Ethernet and is used by upper-layer network protocols such as IPX. Network software developed to support the TCP/IP networking suite uses the type field to determine protocol type in an Ethernet frame. The type field and the LLC header are not replacements for each other, but they serve to offer backward compatibility between network protocol implementations without rewriting the entire Ethernet frame.

After the data field is a 4-byte frame check sequence (FCS) field containing a cyclic redundancy check (CRC) value. The CRC is created by the sending device and is recalculated by the receiving device to check for damage that might have occurred to the frame in transit.

Troubleshooting Ethernet

Table 4-5 provides troubleshooting procedures for common Ethernet media problems.

Table 4-5   *Troubleshooting Procedures for Common Ethernet Media Problems*

Media Problem	Suggested Actions	
Excessive noise	**Step 1**	Use the **show interfaces ethernet** exec command to determine the status of the router's Ethernet interfaces. The presence of many CRC errors but not many collisions is an indication of excessive noise.
	Step 2	Check cables to determine whether any are damaged.
	Step 3	Look for badly spaced taps causing reflections.
	Step 4	If you are using 100BaseTX, make sure you are using Category 5 cabling and not another type, such as Category 3.
Excessive collisions	**Step 1**	Use the **show interfaces ethernet** command to check the rate of collisions. The total number of collisions with respect to the total number of output packets should be around 0.1 percent or less.
	Step 2	Use a TDR to find any unterminated Ethernet cables.
	Step 3	Look for a jabbering transceiver attached to a host. (This might require host-by-host inspection or the use of a protocol analyzer.)
Excessive runt frames	In a shared Ethernet environment, runt frames are almost always caused by collisions. If the collision rate is high, refer to the problem of excessive collisions, earlier in this table.	
	If runt frames occur when collisions are not high or when in a switched Ethernet environment, then they are the result of underruns or bad software on a network interface card.	
	Use a protocol analyzer to try to determine the source address of the runt frames.	
Late collisions[1]	**Step 1**	Use a protocol analyzer to check for late collisions. Late collisions should never occur in a properly designed Ethernet network. They usually occur when Ethernet cables are too long or when there are too many repeaters in the network.
	Step 2	Check the diameter of the network, and make sure that it is within specification.
No link integrity on 10BaseT, 100BaseT4, or 100BaseTX	**Step 1**	Make sure that you are not using 100BaseT4 when only two pairs of wire are available. 100BaseT4 requires four pairs.
	Step 2	Check for a 10BaseT, 100BaseT4, or 100BaseTX mismatch (for example, a card different from the port on a hub).
	Step 3	Determine whether there is cross-connect. (For example, be sure that straight-through cables are not being used between a station and the hub.)
	Step 4	Check for excessive noise (see the problem of excessive noise, earlier in this table).

[1] A late collision is a collision that occurs beyond the first 64 bytes of an Ethernet frame.

When you're troubleshooting Ethernet media in a Cisco router environment, the **show interfaces ethernet** command provides several key fields of information that can assist with isolating problems. The following section provides a detailed description of the **show interfaces ethernet** command and the information that it provides.

show interfaces ethernet

Use the **show interfaces ethernet privileged** exec command to display information about an Ethernet interface on the router:

- show interfaces ethernet unit [accounting]
- **show interfaces ethernet** [*slot | port*] [**accounting**] (for the Cisco 7200 series and Cisco 7500)
- **show interfaces ethernet** [*type slot | port-adapter | port*] (for ports on VIP cards in the Cisco 7500 series routers)

Syntax Description

unit—This must match a port number on the selected interface.

accounting—(Optional) This displays the number of packets of each protocol type that have been sent through the interface.

slot—Refer to the appropriate hardware manual for slot and port information.

port—Refer to the appropriate hardware manual for slot and port information.

port-adapter—Refer to the appropriate hardware manual for information about port adapter compatibility.

Command Mode

Privileged exec

Usage Guidelines

This command first appeared in Cisco IOS Release 10.0. If you do not provide values for the argument *unit* (or *slot* and *port* on the Cisco 7200 series, or *slot* and *port-adapter* on the Cisco 7500 series), the command will display statistics for all network interfaces. The optional keyword **accounting** displays the number of packets of each protocol type that have been sent through the interface.

Sample Display

The following is sample output from the **show interfaces** command for the Ethernet 0 interface:

```
Router# show interfaces ethernet 0
Ethernet 0 is up, line protocol is up
    Hardware is MCI Ethernet, address is aa00.0400.0134 (via 0000.0c00.4369)
            Internet address is 131.108.1.1, subnet mask is 255.255.255.0
            MTU 1500 bytes, BW 10000 Kbit, DLY 1000 usec, rely 255/255, load 1/255
            Encapsulation ARPA, loopback not set, keepalive set (10 sec)
                ARP type: ARPA, PROBE, ARP Timeout 4:00:00
            Last input 0:00:00, output 0:00:00, output hang never
            Output queue 0/40, 0 drops; input queue 0/75, 2 drops
            Five minute input rate 61000 bits/sec, 4 packets/sec
            Five minute output rate 1000 bits/sec, 2 packets/sec
        2295197 packets input, 305539992 bytes, 0 no buffer
        Received 1925500 broadcasts, 0 runts, 0 giants
        3 input errors, 3 CRC, 0 frame, 0 overrun, 0 ignored, 0 abort
            0 input packets with dribble condition detected
        3594664 packets output, 436549843 bytes, 0 underruns
        8 output errors, 1790 collisions, 10 interface resets, 0 restarts
```

Table 4-6 presents **show interfaces ethernet** field descriptions.

Table 4-6   **show interfaces ethernet** *Field Descriptions*

Field	Description
Ethernet . . . is up . . . is administratively down	Indicates whether the interface hardware is currently active and whether it has been taken down by an administrator. "Disabled" indicates that the router has received more than 5,000 errors in a keepalive interval, which is 10 seconds, by default.
line protocol is {*up* | *down* | *administratively down*}	Indicates whether the software processes that handle the line protocol believe that the interface is usable (that is, whether keepalives are successful) or if it has been taken down by an administrator.
Hardware	Specifies the hardware type (for example, MCI Ethernet, SCI, cBus Ethernet) and address.
Internet address	Specifies the Internet address, followed by the subnet mask.
MTU	Gives the maximum transmission unit of the interface.
BW	Gives the bandwidth of the interface in kilobits per second.
DLY	Gives the delay of the interface in microseconds.
rely	Shows reliability of the interface as a fraction of 255 (255/255 is 100 percent reliability), calculated as an exponential average over 5 minutes.
load	Shows load on the interface as a fraction of 255 (255/255 is completely saturated), calculated as an exponential average over 5 minutes.
Encapsulation	Specifies the encapsulation method assigned to interface.

Table 4-6   **show interfaces ethernet** *Field Descriptions (Continued)*

ARP type	Specifies the type of Address Resolution Protocol assigned.
loopback	Indicates whether loopback is set.
keepalive	Indicates whether keepalives are set.
Last input	Gives the number of hours, minutes, and seconds since the last packet was successfully received by an interface. This is useful for knowing when a dead interface failed.
Last output	Gives the number of hours, minutes, and seconds since the last packet was successfully transmitted by an interface.
output	Gives the number of hours, minutes, and seconds since the last packet was successfully transmitted by the interface. This is useful for knowing when a dead interface failed.
output hang	Gives the number of hours, minutes, and seconds (or never) since the interface was last reset because of a transmission that took too long. When the number of hours in any of the "last" fields exceeds 24 hours, the number of days and hours is printed. If that field overflows, asterisks are printed.
Last clearing	Gives the time at which the counters that measure cumulative statistics (such as number of bytes transmitted and received) shown in this report were last reset to zero. Note that variables that might affect routing (for example, load and reliability) are not cleared when the counters are cleared. "***" indicates that the elapsed time is too large to be displayed. "0:00:00" indicates that the counters were cleared more than 231ms (and less than 232ms) ago.
Output queue, input queue, drops	Gives the number of packets in output and input queues. Each number is followed by a slash, the maximum size of the queue, and the number of packets dropped due to a full queue.
Five minute input rate, Five minute output rate	Gives the average number of bits and packets transmitted per second in the past 5 minutes. If the interface is not in promiscuous mode, it senses network traffic it sends and receives (rather than all network traffic). The 5-minute input and output rates should be used only as an approximation of traffic per second during a given 5-minute period. These rates are exponentially weighted averages with a time constant of 5 minutes. A period of four time constants must pass before the average will be within 2 percent of the instantaneous rate of a uniform stream of traffic over that period.
packets input	Gives the total number of error-free packets received by the system.

continues

Table 4-6   **show interfaces ethernet** *Field Descriptions (Continued)*

bytes input	Gives the total number of bytes, including data and MAC encapsulation, in the error-free packets received by the system.
no buffers	Gives the number of received packets discarded because there was no buffer space in the main system. Compare this with the ignored count. Broadcast storms on Ethernet networks and bursts of noise on serial lines are often responsible for no input buffer events.
Received . . . broadcasts	Shows the total number of broadcast or multicast packets received by the interface.
Runts	Gives the number of packets that are discarded because they are smaller than the medium's minimum packet size. For instance, any Ethernet packet that is less than 64 bytes is considered a runt.
giants	Gives the number of packets that are discarded because they exceed the medium's maximum packet size. For example, any Ethernet packet that is greater than 1518 bytes is considered a giant.
input error	Includes runts, giants, no buffer, CRC, frame, overrun, and ignored counts. Other input-related errors can also cause the input error count to be increased, and some datagrams may have more than one error; therefore, this sum may not balance with the sum of enumerated input error counts.
CRC	Indicates that the cyclic redundancy checksum generated by the originating LAN station or far-end device does not match the checksum calculated from the data received. On a LAN, this usually indicates noise or transmission problems on the LAN interface or the LAN bus itself. A high number of CRCs is usually the result of collisions or a station transmitting bad data.
frame	Shows the number of packets received incorrectly having a CRC error and a noninteger number of octets. On a LAN, this is usually the result of collisions or a malfunctioning Ethernet device.
overrun	Shows the number of times that the receiver hardware was incapable of handing received data to a hardware buffer because the input rate exceeded the receiver's capability to handle the data.
ignored	Shows the number of received packets ignored by the interface because the interface hardware ran low on internal buffers. These buffers are different from the system buffers mentioned previously in the buffer description. Broadcast storms and bursts of noise can cause the ignored count to be increased.
input packets with dribble condition detected	Gives the dribble bit error, which indicates that a frame is slightly too long. This frame error counter is incremented just for informational purposes; the router accepts the frame.
packets output	Shows the total number of messages transmitted by the system.

Table 4-6   **show interfaces ethernet** *Field Descriptions (Continued)*

bytes	Shows the total number of bytes, including data and MAC encapsulation, transmitted by the system.
underruns	Gives the number of times that the transmitter has been running faster than the router can handle. This may never be reported on some interfaces.
output errors	Gives the sum of all errors that prevented the final transmission of datagrams out of the interface being examined. Note that this may not balance with the sum of the enumerated output errors because some datagrams may have more than one error, and others may have errors that do not fall into any of the specifically tabulated categories.
collisions	Gives the number of messages retransmitted due to an Ethernet collision. This is usually the result of an overextended LAN (Ethernet or transceiver cable too long, more than two repeaters between stations, or too many cascaded multiport transceivers). A packet that collides is counted only once in output packets.
interface resets	Gives the number of times that an interface has been completely reset. This can happen if packets queued for transmission were not sent within several seconds. On a serial line, this can be caused by a malfunctioning modem that is not supplying the transmit clock signal, or by a cable problem. If the system notices that the carrier detect line of a serial interface is up, but the line protocol is down, it periodically resets the interface in an effort to restart it. Interface resets can also occur when an interface is looped back or shut down.
restarts	Gives the number of times a Type 2 Ethernet controller was restarted because of errors.

Troubleshooting Fiber Distributed Data Interface

The Fiber Distributed Data Interface (FDDI) standard was produced by the ANSI X3T9.5 standards committee in the mid-1980s. During this period, high-speed engineering workstations were beginning to tax the capabilities of existing local-area networks (LANs)—primarily Ethernet and Token Ring. A new LAN was needed that could easily support these workstations and their new distributed applications. At the same time, network reliability was becoming an increasingly important issue as system managers began to migrate mission-critical applications from large computers to networks. FDDI was developed to fill these needs.

After completing the FDDI specification, ANSI submitted FDDI to the International Organization for Standardization (ISO). ISO has created an international version of FDDI that is completely compatible with the ANSI standard version.

Although FDDI implementations are not as common as Ethernet or Token Ring, FDDI has gained a substantial following that continues to increase as the cost of FDDI interfaces diminishes. FDDI is frequently used as a backbone technology as well as a means to connect high-speed computers in a local area.

FDDI Technology Basics

FDDI specifies a 100-Mbps, token-passing, dual-ring LAN using a fiber-optic transmission medium. It defines the physical layer and media-access portion of the link layer, and is roughly analogous to IEEE 802.3 and IEEE 802.5 in its relationship to the Open System Interconnection (OSI) reference model.

Although it operates at faster speeds, FDDI is similar in many ways to Token Ring. The two types of networks share many features, including topology (ring), media-access technique (token passing), and reliability features (redundant rings, for example). For more information on Token Ring and related technologies, refer to Chapter 6, "Troubleshooting Token Ring."

One of the most important characteristics of FDDI is its use of optical fiber as a transmission medium. Optical fiber offers several advantages over traditional copper wiring, including security (fiber does not emit electrical signals that can be tapped), reliability (fiber is immune to electrical interference), and speed (optical fiber has much higher throughput potential than copper cable).

FDDI defines use of two types of fiber: single mode (sometimes called monomode) and multimode. Modes can be thought of as bundles of light rays entering the fiber at a particular angle. *Single-mode fiber* allows only one mode of light to propagate through the fiber, whereas *multimode fiber* allows multiple modes of light to propagate through the fiber. Because multiple modes of light propagating through the fiber may travel different distances (depending on the entry angles), causing them to arrive at the destination at different times (a phenomenon called *modal dispersion*), single-mode fiber is capable of higher bandwidth and greater cable run distances than multimode fiber. Because of these characteristics, single-mode fiber is often used for interbuilding connectivity, and multimode fiber is often used for intrabuilding connectivity. Multimode fiber uses light-emitting diodes (LEDs) as the light-generating devices, whereas single-mode fiber generally uses lasers.

FDDI Specifications

FDDI is defined by four separate specifications (see Figure 5-1):

- **Media Access Control (MAC)**—Defines how the medium is accessed, including frame format, token handling, addressing, an algorithm for calculating a cyclic redundancy check value, and error recovery mechanisms.

- **Physical Layer Protocol (PHY)**—Defines data encoding/decoding procedures, clocking requirements, framing, and other functions.

- **Physical Layer Medium (PMD)**—Defines the characteristics of the transmission medium, including the fiber-optic link, power levels, bit error rates, optical components, and connectors.

- **Station Management (SMT)**—Defines the FDDI station configuration, ring configuration, and ring control features, including station insertion and removal, initialization, fault isolation and recovery, scheduling, and collection of statistics.

Figure 5-1   *FDDI Standards*

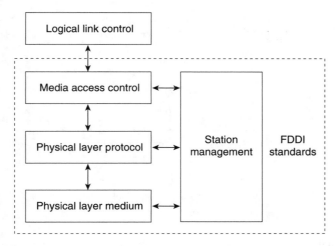

Physical Connections

FDDI specifies the use of dual rings. Traffic on these rings travels in opposite directions. Physically, the rings consist of two or more point-to-point connections between adjacent stations. One of the two FDDI rings is called the *primary ring*; the other is called the *secondary ring*. The primary ring is used for data transmission, and the secondary ring is generally used as a backup.

Class B or single-attachment stations (SASs) attach to one ring; Class A or dual-attachment stations (DASs) attach to both rings. SASs are attached to the primary ring through a concentrator, which provides connections for multiple SASs. The concentrator ensures that failure or power down of any given SAS does not interrupt the ring. This is particularly useful when PCs, or similar devices that frequently power on and off, connect to the ring.

A typical FDDI configuration with both DASs and SASs is shown in Figure 5-2.

Figure 5-2   *FDDI Nodes: DAS, SASs, and Concentrator*

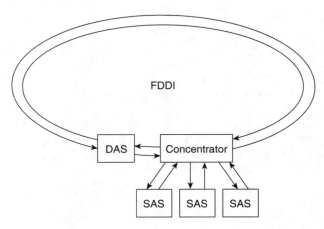

Each FDDI DAS has two ports, designated A and B. These ports connect the station to the dual FDDI ring. Therefore, each port provides a connection for both the primary and the secondary ring, as shown in Figure 5-3.

Figure 5-3   *FDDI DAS Ports*

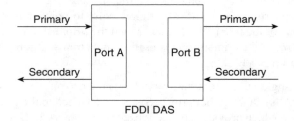

Traffic Types

FDDI supports real-time allocation of network bandwidth, making it ideal for a variety of different application types. FDDI provides this support by defining two types of traffic: synchronous and asynchronous. Synchronous traffic can consume a portion of the 100-Mbps total bandwidth of an FDDI network, and asynchronous traffic can consume the rest. Synchronous bandwidth is allocated to those stations requiring continuous transmission capability. Such capability is useful for transmitting voice and video information, for example. Other stations use the remaining bandwidth asynchronously. The FDDI SMT specification defines a distributed bidding scheme to allocate FDDI bandwidth.

Asynchronous bandwidth is allocated using an eight-level priority scheme. Each station is assigned an asynchronous priority level. FDDI also permits extended dialogues, where stations may temporarily use all asynchronous bandwidth. The FDDI priority mechanism can essentially lock out stations that cannot use synchronous bandwidth and have too low an asynchronous priority.

Fault-Tolerant Features

FDDI provides a number of fault-tolerant features, the most important of which is the *dual ring*. If a station on the dual ring fails or is powered down or if the cable is damaged, the dual ring is automatically wrapped (doubled back onto itself) into a single ring, as shown in Figure 5-4. In this figure, when Station 3 fails, the dual ring is automatically wrapped in Stations 2 and 4, forming a single ring. Although Station 3 is no longer on the ring, network operation continues for the remaining stations.

Figure 5-4   *Station Failure, Ring Recovery Configuration*

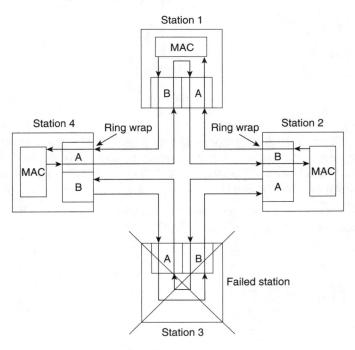

Figure 5-5 shows how FDDI compensates for a wiring failure. Stations 3 and 4 wrap the ring within themselves when wiring between them fails.

Figure 5-5   *Failed Wiring, Ring Recovery Configuration*

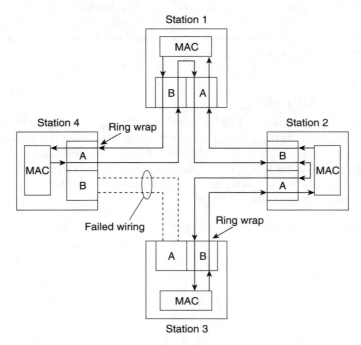

As FDDI networks grow, the possibility of multiple ring failures grows. When two ring failures occur, the ring is wrapped in both cases, effectively segmenting the ring into two separate rings that cannot communicate with each other. Subsequent failures cause additional ring segmentation.

Optical bypass switches can be used to prevent ring segmentation by eliminating failed stations from the ring. This is shown in Figure 5-6.

Figure 5-6   *The Use of an Optical Bypass Switch*

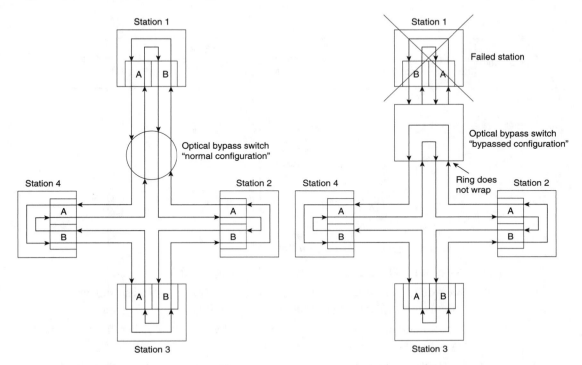

Critical devices such as routers or mainframe hosts can use another fault-tolerant technique called *dual homing* to provide additional redundancy and help guarantee operation. In dual-homing situations, the critical device is attached to two concentrators. One pair of concentrator links is declared the active link; the other pair is declared passive. The passive link stays in backup mode until the primary link (or the concentrator to which it is attached) is determined to have failed. When this occurs, the passive link is automatically activated.

Frame Format

FDDI frame formats (shown in Figure 5-7) are similar to those of Token Ring.

Figure 5-7 *FDDI Frame Format*

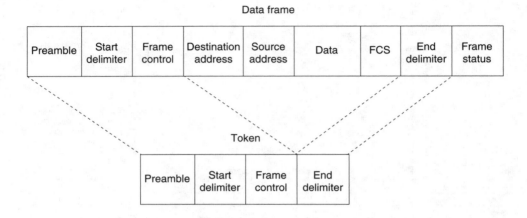

The fields of an FDDI frame are as follows:

- **Preamble**—Prepares each station for the upcoming frame.

- **Start delimiter**—Indicates the beginning of the frame. It consists of signaling patterns that differentiate it from the rest of the frame.

- **Frame control**—Indicates the size of the address fields, whether the frame contains asynchronous or synchronous data, and other control information.

- **Destination address**—Contains a unicast (singular), multicast (group), or broadcast (every station) address. As with Ethernet and Token Ring, FDDI destination addresses are 6 bytes.

- **Source address**—Identifies the single station that sent the frame. As with Ethernet and Token Ring, FDDI source addresses are 6 bytes.

- **Data**—Contains either information destined for an upper-layer protocol or control information.

- **Frame check sequence (FCS)**—Filled by the source station with a calculated cyclic redundancy check (CRC) value dependent on the frame contents (as with Token Ring and Ethernet). The destination station recalculates the value to determine whether the frame may have been damaged in transit. If it has been damaged, the frame is discarded.

- **End delimiter**—Contains nondata symbols that indicate the end of the frame.

- **Frame status**—Allows the source station to determine whether an error occurred and whether the frame was recognized and copied by a receiving station.

CDDI

The high cost of fiber-optic cable has been a major impediment to the widespread deployment of FDDI to desktop computers. At the same time, shielded twisted-pair (STP) and unshielded twisted-pair (UTP) copper wire is relatively inexpensive and has been widely deployed. The implementation of FDDI over copper wire is known as Copper Distributed Data Interface (CDDI).

Before FDDI could be implemented over copper wire, a problem had to be solved. When signals strong enough to be reliably interpreted as data are transmitted over twisted-pair wire, the wire radiates electromagnetic interference (EMI). Any attempt to implement FDDI over twisted-pair wire had to ensure that the resulting energy radiation did not exceed the specifications set in the United States by the Federal Communications Commission (FCC) and in Europe by the European Economic Council (EEC). Three technologies reduce energy radiation:

- **Scrambling**—When no data is being sent, FDDI transmits an idle pattern that consists of a string of binary ones. When this signal is sent over twisted-pair wire, the EMI is concentrated at the fundamental frequency spectrum of the idle pattern, resulting in a peak in the frequency spectrum of the radiated interference. By scrambling FDDI data with a pseudo-random sequence prior to transmission, repetitive patterns are eliminated. The elimination of repetitive patterns results in a spectral peak that is distributed more evenly over the spectrum of the transmitted signal.

- **Encoding**—Signal strength is stronger, and EMI is lower when transmission occurs over twisted-pair wire at lower frequencies. MLT3 is an encoding scheme that reduces the frequency of the transmitted signal. MLT3 switches between three output voltage levels so that peak power is shifted to less than 20 MHz.

- **Equalization**—Equalization boosts the higher frequency signals for transmission over UTP. Equalization can be done on the transmitter (predistortion), at the receiver (postcompensation), or both. One advantage of equalization at the receiver is the ability to adjust compensation as a function of cable length.

Troubleshooting FDDI

This section provides troubleshooting procedures for common FDDI media problems.

Table 5-1 outlines problems commonly encountered on FDDI networks and offers general guidelines for solving those problems.

Table 5-1   *Media Problems: FDDI*

Media Problem	Suggested Actions
Nonfunctional FDDI ring	**Step 1** Use the **show interfaces fddi** exec command to determine the status of the router's FDDI interfaces.
	Step 2 If the **show interfaces fddi** command indicates that the interface and line protocol are up, use the **ping** command between routers to test connectivity.
	Step 3 If the interface and line protocol are up, make sure the MAC addresses of upstream and downstream neighbors are as expected.
	Step 4 If all zeros appear in either of the address fields for these neighbors, there is probably a physical connection problem.
	In this case (or if the status line does *not* indicate that the interface and line protocol are up), check patch-panel connections or use an OTDR[1] or light meter to check connectivity between neighbors. Ensure that signal strength is within specifications.
Upstream neighbor has failed and bypass switch is installed	Bypass switches can cause signal degradation because they do not repeat signals as a normal transceiver does.
	Step 1 Check upstream neighbor to determine whether it is operational.
	Step 2 If the node is down and a bypass switch is in place, resolve any problems found in the upstream neighbor.

[1]OTDR = optical time-domain reflectometer

When you're troubleshooting FDDI media in a Cisco router environment, the **show interfaces fddi** command provides several key fields of information that can assist in isolating problems. The following section provides detailed description of the **show interfaces fddi** command and the information it provides.

show interfaces fddi

To display information about the FDDI interface, use the **show interfaces fddi** exec command:

```
show interfaces fddi number [accounting]
show interfaces fddi [slot | port] [accounting] (Cisco 7000 series and Cisco 7200 series)
show interfaces fddi [slot | port-adapter | port] [accounting] (Cisco 7500 series routers)
```

Syntax Description

- *number*—Port number on the selected interface.

- **accounting**—(Optional) Displays the number of packets of each protocol type that have been sent through the interface.

- *slot*—Refers to the appropriate hardware manual for slot and port information.

- *port*—Refers to the appropriate hardware manual for slot and port information.

- *port-adapter*—Refers to the appropriate hardware manual for information about port adapter compatibility.

Command Mode

exec

Usage Guidelines

This command first appeared in Cisco IOS Release 10.0.

This information was modified in Cisco IOS Release 11.3 to include sample output for FDDI full-duplex, single-mode, and multimode port adapters (PA-F/FD-SM and PA-F/FD-MM).

Sample Displays

The following is a sample partial display of FDDI-specific data from the **show interfaces fddi** command on a Cisco 7500 series router:

```
Router> show interfaces fddi 3/0
Fddi3/0 is up, line protocol is up
  Hardware is cxBus Fddi, address is 0000.0c02.adf1 (bia 0000.0c02.adf1)
  Internet address is 131.108.33.14, subnet mask is 255.255.255.0
  MTU 4470 bytes, BW 100000 Kbit, DLY 100 usec, rely 255/255, load 1/255
  Encapsulation SNAP, loopback not set, keepalive not set
  ARP type: SNAP, ARP Timeout 4:00:00
  Phy-A state is  active, neighbor is   B, cmt signal bits 008/20C, status ILS
  Phy-B state is  active, neighbor is   A, cmt signal bits 20C/008, status ILS
  ECM is in, CFM is thru, — is ring_op
  Token rotation 5000 usec, ring operational 21:32:34
  Upstream neighbor 0000.0c02.ba83, downstream neighbor 0000.0c02.ba83
  Last input 0:00:05, output 0:00:00, output hang never
  Last clearing of "show interface" counters 0:59:10
  Output queue 0/40, 0 drops; input queue 0/75, 0 drops
  Five minute input rate 69000 bits/sec, 44 packets/sec
  Five minute output rate 0 bits/sec, 1 packets/sec
     113157 packets input, 21622582 bytes, 0 no buffer
     Received 276 broadcasts, 0 runts, 0 giants
     0 input errors, 0 CRC, 0 frame, 0 overrun, 0 ignored, 0 abort
     4740 packets output, 487346 bytes, 0 underruns
     0 output errors, 0 collisions, 0 interface resets, 0 restarts
     0 transitions, 2 traces, 3 claims, 2 beacons
```

The following is a sample display of the **show interfaces fddi** command for the full-duplex FDDI port adapter on a Cisco 7500 series router:

```
Router# show interfaces fddi 0/1/0
Fddi0/1/0 is up, line protocol is up
  Hardware is cxBus FDDI, address is 0060.3e33.3608 (bia 0060.3e33.3608)
  Internet address is 2.1.1.1/24
  MTU 4470 bytes, BW 100000 Kbit, DLY 100 usec, rely 255/255, load 1/255
  Encapsulation SNAP, loopback not set, keepalive not set
  ARP type: SNAP, ARP Timeout 04:00:00
  FDX supported, FDX enabled, FDX state is operation
  Phy-A state is maintenance, neighbor is Unknown, status HLS
  Phy-B state is active, neighbor is A, status SILS
  ECM is in, CFM is c_wrap_b, — is ring_op,
  Requested token rotation 5000 usec, negotiated 4997 usec
  Configured tvx is 2500 usec
  LER for PortA = 0A, LER for PortB = 0A ring operational 00:02:45
  Upstream neighbor 0060.3e73.4600, downstream neighbor 0060.3e73.4600
  Last input 00:00:12, output 00:00:13, output hang never
  Last clearing of "show interface" counters never
  Queueing strategy: fifo
  Output queue 0/40, 0 drops; input queue 0/75, 0 drops
  5 minute input rate 0 bits/sec, 0 packets/sec
  5 minute output rate 0 bits/sec, 0 packets/sec
     62 packets input, 6024 bytes, 0 no buffer
     Received 18 broadcasts, 0 runts, 0 giants
     0 input errors, 0 CRC, 0 frame, 0 overrun, 0 ignored, 0 abort
     71 packets output, 4961 bytes, 0 underruns
     0 output errors, 0 collisions, 0 interface resets
     0 output buffer failures, 0 output buffers swapped out
     3 transitions, 0 traces,  100 claims, 0 beacon
```

Table 5-2 describes the **show interfaces fddi** display fields.

Table 5-2   **show interfaces fddi** *Field Descriptions*

Field	Description
Fddi is {*up* | *down* | *administratively down*}	Gives the interface processor unit number and tells whether the interface hardware is currently active and can transmit and receive or whether it has been taken down by an administrator.
line protocol is {*up* | *down*}	Indicates whether the software processes that handle the line protocol consider the interface usable.
Hardware	Provides the hardware type, followed by the hardware address.
Internet address	IP address, followed by subnet mask.
MTU	Maximum transmission unit of the interface.
BW	Bandwidth of the interface in kilobits per second.
DLY	Delay of the interface in microseconds.

Table 5-2   **show interfaces fddi** *Field Descriptions (Continued)*

Field	Description
rely	Reliability of the interface as a fraction of 255 (255/255 is 100 percent reliability), calculated as an exponential average of over five minutes.
load	Load on the interface as a fraction of 255 (255/255 is completely saturated), calculated as an exponential average of over five minutes.
Encapsulation	Encapsulation method assigned to interface.
loopback	Indicates whether loopback is set.
keepalive	Indicates whether keepalives are set.
ARP type	Type of Address Resolution Protocol assigned.
FDX	Displays full-duplex information. Values are **not supported** and **supported**. When the value is **supported**, the display indicates whether full-duplex is enabled or disabled. When enabled, the state of the FDX negotiation process is displayed. The negotiation states only relate to the full-duplex negotiation process. You must also ensure that the interface is up and working by looking at other fields in the **show interfaces fddi** command such as line protocol and —. Negotiation states are • **idle**—Interface is working but not in full-duplex mode yet. If persistent, it could mean that the interface did not meet all negotiation conditions (for example, there are more than two stations in the ring). • **request**—Interface is working but not in full-duplex mode yet. If persistent, it could mean that the remote interface does not support full-duplex or full-duplex is not enabled on the interface. • **confirm**—Transient state. • **operation**—Negotiations completed successfully, and both stations are operating in full-duplex mode.
Phy-{*A* | *B*}	Lists the state the Physical A or Physical B connection is in; one of the following: **off**, **active**, **trace**, **connect**, **next**, **signal**, **join**, **verify**, or **break**.

continues

Table 5-2   **show interfaces fddi** *Field Descriptions (Continued)*

Field	Description
neighbor	State of the neighbor:
	A—Indicates that the CMT[1] process has established a connection with its neighbor. The bits received during the CMT signaling process indicate that the neighbor is a Physical A type DAS[2] or concentrator that attaches to the primary ring IN and the secondary ring OUT when attaching to the dual ring.
	S—Indicates that the CMT process has established a connection with its neighbor and that the bits received during the CMT signaling process indicate that the neighbor is one Physical type in a single-attachment station SAS.[3]
	B—Indicates that the CMT process has established a connection with its neighbor and that the bits received during the CMT signaling process indicate that the neighbor is a Physical B dual attachment station or concentrator that attaches to the secondary ring IN and the primary ring OUT when attaching to the dual ring.
	M—Indicates that the CMT process has established a connection with its neighbor and that the bits received during the CMT signaling process indicate that the router's neighbor is a Physical M-type concentrator serving as a master to a connected station or concentrator.
	unk—Indicates that the network server has not completed the CMT process and, as a result, does not know about its neighbor.
cmt signal bits	Shows the transmitted/received CMT bits. The transmitted bits are **0x008** for a Physical A type and **0x20C** for Physical B type. The number after the slash (**/**) is the received signal bits. If the connection is not active, the received bits are zero (**0**); see the line beginning **Phy-B** in the display. This applies to FDDI processor FIP[4] interfaces only.
status	Status value displayed is the actual status on the fiber. The FDDI standard defines the following values:
	• **LSU**—Line state unknown, the criteria for entering or remaining in any other line state have not been met.
	• **NLS**—Noise line state, entered upon the occurrence of 16 potential noise events without satisfying the criteria for entry into another line state.
	• **MLS**—Master line state, entered upon the receipt of eight or nine consecutive **HQ** or **QH** symbol pairs.

Table 5-2   **show interfaces fddi** *Field Descriptions (Continued)*

Field	Description
status *(continued)*	• **ILS**—Idle line state, entered upon receipt of four or five idle symbols.
	• **HLS**—Halt line state, entered upon the receipt of 16 or 17 consecutive H symbols.
	• **QLS**—Quiet line state, entered upon the receipt of 16 or 17 consecutive Q symbols or when carrier detect goes low.
	• **ALS**—Active line state, entered upon receipt of a **JK** symbol pair when carrier detect is high.
	• **OVUF**—Elasticity buffer overflow/underflow. The normal states for a connected Physical type are **ILS** or **ALS**. If the report displays the **QLS** status, this indicates that the fiber is disconnected from Physical B, or that it is not connected to another Physical type, or that the other station is not running.
ECM is...	ECM is the SMT entity coordination management, which overlooks the operation of CFM and PCM. The ECM state can be one of the following:
	• **out**—Router is isolated from the network.
	• **in**—Router is actively connected to the network. This is the normal state for a connected router.
	• **trace**—Router is trying to localize a stuck beacon condition.
	• **leave**—Router is allowing time for all the connections to break before leaving the network.
	• **path_test**—Router is testing its internal paths.
	• **insert**—Router is allowing time for the optical bypass to insert.
	• **check**—Router is making sure optical bypasses switched correctly.
	• **deinsert**—Router is allowing time for the optical bypass to deinsert.

continues

Table 5-2 **show interfaces fddi** *Field Descriptions (Continued)*

Field	Description
CFM is...	Contains information about the current state of the MAC connection. The configuration management state can be one of the following:
	• **isolated**—MAC is not attached to any Physical type.
	• **wrap_a**—MAC is attached to Physical A. Data is received on Physical A and transmitted on Physical A.
	• **wrap_b**—MAC is attached to Physical B. Data is received on Physical B and transmitted on Physical B.
	• **wrap_s**—MAC is attached to Physical S. Data is received on Physical S and transmitted on Physical S. This is the normal mode for a SAS.
— is...	— (ring management) is the SMT MAC-related state machine. The — state can be one of the following:
	• **isolated**—MAC is not trying to participate in the ring. This is the initial state.
	• **non_op**—MAC is participating in ring recovery, and ring is not operational.
	• **ring_op**—MAC is participating in an operational ring. This is the normal state while the MAC is connected to the ring.
	• **detect**—Ring has been nonoperational for longer than normal. Duplicate address conditions are being checked.
	• **non_op_dup**—Indications have been received that the address of the MAC is a duplicate of another MAC on the ring. Ring is not operational.
	• **ring_op_dup**—Indications have been received that the address of the MAC is a duplicate of another MAC on the ring. Ring is operational in this state.
	• **directed**—MAC is sending beacon frames notifying the ring of the stuck condition.
	• **trace**—Trace has been initiated by this MAC, and the — state machine is waiting for its completion before starting an internal path test.
token rotation	Token rotation value is the default or configured rotation value as determined by the **fddi token-rotation-time** command. This value is used by all stations on the ring. The default is 5,000 microseconds. For FDDI full-duplex, this indicates the value in use prior to entering full-duplex operation.

Table 5-2   **show interfaces fddi** *Field Descriptions (Continued)*

Field	Description
negotiated	Actual (negotiated) target token rotation time.
ring operational	When the ring is operational, the displayed value will be the negotiated token rotation time of all stations on the ring. Operational times are displayed by the number of hours/minutes/ seconds the ring has been up. If the ring is not operational, the message "ring not operational" is displayed.
Configured tvx	Transmission timer.
LER	Link error rate.
Upstream | downstream neighbor	Displays the canonical MAC address of outgoing upstream and downstream neighbors. If the address is unknown, the value will be the FDDI unknown address (**0x00 00 f8 00 00 00**).
Last input	Number of hours, minutes, and seconds since the last packet was successfully received by an interface. Useful for knowing when a dead interface failed.
output	Number of hours, minutes, and seconds since the last packet was successfully transmitted by an interface.
output hang	Number of hours, minutes, and seconds (or never) since the interface was last reset because of a transmission that took too long. When the number of hours in any of the "last" fields exceeds 24 hours, the number of days and hours is printed. If that field overflows, asterisks are printed.
Last clearing	Time at which the counters that measure cumulative statistics (such as number of bytes transmitted and received) shown in this report were last reset to zero. Note that variables that might affect routing (for example, load and reliability) are not cleared when the counters are cleared. *** indicates the elapsed time is too large to be displayed. 0:00:00 indicates the counters were cleared more than 231 ms (and less than 232 ms) ago.
Queueing strategy	First-in, first-out queuing strategy (other queueing strategies you might see are priority-list, custom-list, and weighted fair).
Output queue, input queue, drops	Number of packets in output and input queues. Each number is followed by a slash, the maximum size of the queue, and the number of packets dropped due to a full queue.

continues

Table 5-2   **show interfaces fddi** *Field Descriptions (Continued)*

Field	Description
5 minute input rate, 5 minute output rate	Average number of bits and packets transmitted per second in the past five minutes.
	The five-minute input and output rates should be used only as an approximation of traffic per second during a given five-minute period. These rates are exponentially weighted averages with a time constant of five minutes. A period of four time constants must pass before the average will be within 2 percent of the instantaneous rate of a uniform stream of traffic over that period.
packets input	Total number of error-free packets received by the system.
bytes	Total number of bytes, including data and MAC encapsulation, in the error-free packets received by the system.
no buffer	Number of received packets discarded because there was no buffer space in the main system. Compare with ignored count. Broadcast storms on Ethernet networks and bursts of noise on serial lines are often responsible for no input buffer events.
broadcasts	Total number of broadcast or multicast packets received by the interface.
runts	Number of packets that are discarded because they are smaller than the medium's minimum packet size.
giants	Number of packets that are discarded because they exceed the medium's maximum packet size.
CRC	Cyclic redundancy checksum generated by the originating LAN station or far-end device does not match the checksum calculated from the data received. On a LAN, this usually indicates noise or transmission problems on the LAN interface or the LAN bus itself. A high number of CRCs is usually the result of collisions or a station transmitting bad data.
frame	Number of packets received incorrectly that have a CRC error and a noninteger number of octets. On a LAN, this is usually the result of collisions or a malfunctioning Ethernet device. On an FDDI LAN, this also can be the result of a failing fiber (cracks) or a hardware malfunction.
overrun	Number of times the serial receiver hardware was unable to hand received data to a hardware buffer because the input rate exceeded the receiver's ability to handle the data.

Table 5-2   show interfaces fddi *Field Descriptions (Continued)*

Field	Description
ignored	Number of received packets ignored by the interface because the interface hardware ran low on internal buffers. These buffers are different from the system buffers mentioned previously in the **buffer** description. Broadcast storms and bursts of noise can cause the ignored count to be increased.
packets output	Total number of messages transmitted by the system.
bytes	Total number of bytes, including data and MAC encapsulation, transmitted by the system.
underruns	Number of transmit aborts (when the router cannot feed the transmitter fast enough).
output errors	Sum of all errors that prevented the final transmission of datagrams out of the interface being examined. Note that this might not balance with the sum of the enumerated output errors because some datagrams can have more than one error and others can have errors that do not fall into any of the specifically tabulated categories.
collisions	Because an FDDI ring cannot have collisions, this statistic is always zero.
interface resets	Number of times an interface has been reset. The interface may be reset by the administrator or automatically when an internal error occurs.
restarts	Should always be zero for FDDI interfaces.
output buffer failures	Number of no-resource errors received on the output.
output buffers swapped out	Number of packets swapped to DRAM.
transitions	Number of times the ring made a transition from ring operational to ring nonoperational, or vice versa. A large number of transitions indicates a problem with the ring or the interface.
traces	Indicates the number of times this interface started a trace. Trace count applies to both the FCI, FCIT, and FIP.
claims	Pertains to FCIT and FIP only. Indicates the number of times this interface has been in claim state.
beacons	Pertains to FCIT and FIP only. Indicates the number of times the interface has been in beacon state.

[1]CMT = connection management

[2]DAS = dual-attachment station

[3]SAS = single-attachment station

[4]FIP = FDDI processor

Troubleshooting Token Ring

The Token Ring network was originally developed by IBM in the 1970s. It is still IBM's primary local-area network (LAN) technology, and is second only to Ethernet/IEEE 802.3 in general LAN popularity. The IEEE 802.5 specification is almost identical to, and completely compatible with, IBM's Token Ring network. In fact, the IEEE 802.5 specification was modeled after IBM Token Ring, and continues to shadow IBM's Token Ring development. The term *Token Ring* is generally used to refer to both IBM's Token Ring network and IEEE 802.5 networks.

Token Ring/IEEE 802.5 Comparison

Token Ring and IEEE 802.5 networks are basically quite compatible, but the specifications differ in relatively minor ways. IBM's Token Ring network specifies a star, with all end stations attached to a device called a multistation access unit (MAU), whereas IEEE 802.5 does not specify a topology (although virtually all IEEE 802.5 implementations also are based on a star). Other differences exist, including media type (IEEE 802.5 does not specify a media type, whereas IBM Token Ring networks use twisted-pair wire) and routing information field size. Figure 6-1 summarizes IBM Token Ring network and IEEE 802.5 specifications.

Figure 6-1 *IBM Token Ring Network/IEEE 802.5 Comparison*

	IBM Token Ring Network	IEEE 802.5
Data rates	4 or 16 Mbps	4 or 16 Mbps
Stations/segment	280 (shielded twisted pair) −2 (unshielded twisted pair)	250
Topology	Star	Not specified
Media	Twisted pair	Not specified
Signaling	Baseband	Baseband
Access method	Token passing	Token passing
Encoding	Differential Manchester	Differential Manchester

Token Passing

Token Ring and IEEE 802.5 are the primary examples of token-passing networks. Token-passing networks move a small frame, called a *token*, around the network. Possession of the token grants the right to transmit. If a node receiving the token has no information to send, it simply passes the token to the next end station. Each station can hold the token for a maximum period of time.

If a station possessing the token does have information to transmit, it seizes the token, alters 1 bit of the token (which turns the token into a start-of-frame sequence), appends the information it wishes to transmit, and finally sends this information to the next station on the ring. While the information frame is circling the ring, there is no token on the network (unless the ring supports early token release), so other stations wishing to transmit must wait. Therefore, collisions cannot occur in Token Ring networks. If early token release is supported, a new token can be released when frame transmission is complete.

The information frame circulates the ring until it reaches the intended destination station, which copies the information for further processing. The information frame continues to circle the ring and is finally removed when it reaches the sending station. The sending station can check the returning frame to see whether the frame was seen and subsequently copied by the destination.

Unlike carrier sense multiple access collision detect (CSMA/CD) networks—such as Ethernet—token-passing networks are deterministic. In other words, it is possible to calculate the maximum time that will pass before any end station will be able to transmit. This feature and several reliability features, which are discussed in the section "Fault Management Mechanisms" later in this chapter, make Token Ring networks ideal for applications where delay must be predictable and robust network operation is important. Factory automation environments are examples of such applications.

Physical Connections

IBM Token Ring network stations are directly connected to MAUs, which can be wired together to form one large ring (as shown in Figure 6-2). Patch cables connect MAUs to adjacent MAUs. Lobe cables connect MAUs to stations. MAUs include bypass relays for removing stations from the ring.

Figure 6-2   *IBM Token Ring Network Physical Connections*

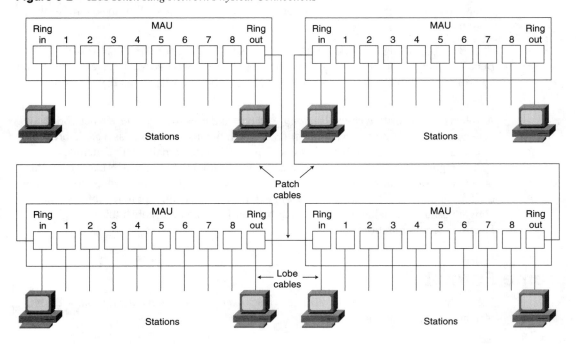

The Priority System

Token Ring networks use a sophisticated priority system that permits certain user-designated, high-priority stations to use the network more frequently. Token Ring frames have two fields that control priority: the *priority field* and the *reservation field*.

Only stations with a priority equal to or higher than the priority value contained in a token can seize that token. Once the token is seized and changed to an information frame, only stations with a priority value higher than that of the transmitting station can reserve the token for the next pass around the network. When the next token is generated, it includes the higher priority of the reserving station. Stations that raise a token's priority level must reinstate the previous priority after their transmission is complete.

Fault Management Mechanisms

Token Ring networks employ several mechanisms for detecting and compensating for network faults. For example, one station in the Token Ring network is selected to be the active monitor. This station, which can potentially be any station on the network, acts as a centralized source of timing information for other ring stations and performs a variety of ring maintenance functions. One of these functions is the removal of continuously circulating frames from the ring. When a sending device fails, its frame may continue to circle the ring. This can prevent other stations from transmitting their own frames and essentially lock up the network. The active monitor can detect such frames, remove them from the ring, and generate a new token.

The IBM Token Ring network's star topology also contributes to overall network reliability. Because all information in a Token Ring network is seen by active MAUs, these devices can be programmed to check for problems and selectively remove stations from the ring if necessary.

A Token Ring algorithm called *beaconing* detects and tries to repair certain network faults. Whenever a station detects a serious problem with the network (such as a cable break), it sends a beacon frame. The beacon frame defines a failure domain, which includes the station reporting the failure, its nearest active upstream neighbor (NAUN), and everything in between. Beaconing initiates a process called *autoreconfiguration*, where nodes within the failure domain automatically perform diagnostics in an attempt to reconfigure the network around the failed areas. Physically, the MAU can accomplish this through electrical reconfiguration.

Frame Formats

Token Ring networks define two frame types: *tokens* and *data/command frames*. Both formats are shown in Figure 6-3.

Figure 6-3   *IEEE 802.5/Token Ring Frame Formats*

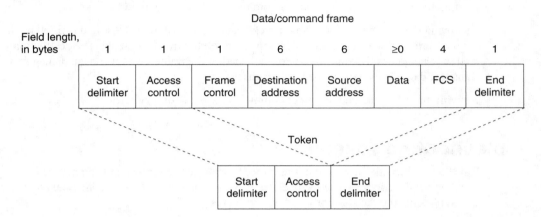

Tokens

Each token is 3 bytes in length and consists of a start delimiter, an access control byte, and an end delimiter.

The start delimiter serves to alert each station to the arrival of a token (or data/command frame). This field includes signals that distinguish the byte from the rest of the frame by violating the encoding scheme used elsewhere in the frame.

The access control byte contains the priority and reservation fields, as well as a token bit (used to differentiate a token from a data/command frame) and a monitor bit (used by the active monitor to determine whether a frame is circling the ring endlessly).

Finally, the end delimiter signals the end of the token or data/command frame. It also contains bits to indicate a damaged frame and a frame that is the last in a logical sequence.

Data/Command Frames

Data/command frames vary in size, depending on the size of the information field. Data frames carry information for upper-layer protocols; command frames contain control information and have no data for upper-layer protocols.

In data/command frames, a frame control byte follows the access control byte. The frame control byte indicates whether the frame contains data or control information. In control frames, this byte specifies the type of control information.

Following the frame control byte are the two address fields, which identify the destination and source stations. As with IEEE 802.3, addresses are 6 bytes in length.

The data field follows the address fields. The length of this field is limited by the ring token holding time, which defines the maximum time a station may hold the token.

Following the data field is the frame check sequence (FCS) field. This field is filled by the source station with a calculated value dependent on the frame contents. The destination station recalculates the value to determine whether the frame may have been damaged in transit. If damage did occur, the frame is discarded.

As with the token, the end delimiter completes the data/command frame.

Troubleshooting Token Ring

This section provides troubleshooting procedures for common Token Ring media problems. It describes a specific Token Ring symptom, the problems that are likely to cause this symptom, and the solutions to those problems.

Media Problems: Token Ring

Table 6-1 outlines problems commonly encountered on Token Ring networks and offers general guidelines for solving those problems.

Table 6-1   *Media Problems: Token Ring*

Media Problem	Suggested Actions	
Nonfunctional Token Ring	**Step 1**	Use the **show interfaces token** command to determine the status of the router's Token Ring interfaces.
	Step 2	If the status line indicates that the interface and line protocol are not up, check the cable from the router to the MAU.[1] Make sure that the cable is in good condition. If it is not, replace it.
	Step 3	If you are performing a new installation, make sure that the MAU has been properly initialized. For information on initializing your MAU, refer to the manufacturer's documentation.
Ring speed mismatch	**Step 1**	Check the ring speed specification on all nodes attached to the Token Ring backbone. The ring speed configured for all stations must be the same (either 4 Mbps or 16 Mbps). Use the **show running-config** privileged exec command to determine which speed is specified on the router.
	Step 2	If necessary, modify ring speed specifications for clients, servers, and routers. On routers, use the **ring-speed** interface configuration command to change the ring speed.
		Change jumpers as needed for modular router platforms that do not support software speed configuration. For more information about ring speed specifications, refer to the hardware installation and maintenance manual for your system.

Table 6-1   *Media Problems: Token Ring (Continued)*

Media Problem	Suggested Actions	
Relay open in MAU	**Step 1**	If an "open lobe fault" message appears on the console at system power up, check the cable connection to the MAU.
	Step 2	Use the **clear interface** privileged exec command to reset the Token Ring interface and reinsert the router into the ring.
		For all Token Ring cards except the CTR and access routers, you must use the **clear interface** command to reinitialize the Token Ring interface if the interface is down.
	Step 3	Use the **show interfaces token** exec command to verify that the interface and line protocol are up.
	Step 4	If the interface is operational, but the "open lobe fault" message persists and the router still cannot connect to the ring, connect the router to a different MAU port.
	Step 5	If the message continues to appear, disconnect all devices from the MAU and reset the MAU's relay with the tool provided by the MAU vendor.
	Step 6	Reattach the router and determine whether it can connect to the ring. If resetting the relay does not solve the problem, try replacing the MAU with one that is known to be operational.
	Step 7	If the router still cannot connect to the ring, check internal cable connections of the router Token Ring cards. Ensure that cables associated with the respective port numbers are correctly wired and that they are not swapped.
	Step 8	If the router still cannot connect to the ring, replace the cables that connect the router to the MAU with working cables.
	Step 9	Use the **clear interface** command to reset the interface and reinsert the router into the ring. Use the **show interfaces token** command to verify that the interface and line protocol are up.
	Step 10	Alternatively, you can connect the router to a spare MAU to which no stations are connected. If the router can attach to the ring, replace the original MAU.
Duplicate MAC[2] address	This problem can arise when routers are using locally administered MAC addresses.	
	Step 1	Use a network analyzer to check the Duplicate Address test frames from a booting station. If the station gets a response, then there is another station already configured with the MAC address of the booting station.
	Step 2	If there are two stations with the same MAC addresses, change the MAC address of one of the stations and reinitialize the node.

continues

Table 6-1   *Media Problems: Token Ring (Continued)*

Media Problem	Suggested Actions	
Congested ring	Step 1	Insert the router during an off-peak period.
	Step 2	If insertion is successful during off-peak periods, but unsuccessful during peak load, segment your internetwork to distribute traffic.
RPS[3] conflict	Step 1	Use the **no lnm rps** interface configuration command to disable the RPS function on the router that you are trying to insert into the ring.
	Step 2	Try to insert the router into the ring.
	Step 3	If you can insert the router with RPS disabled, there is a conflict between RPS implementations. Contact your technical support representative for more information.

[1]MAU = multistation access unit
[2]MAC = Media Access Control
[3]RPS = Ring Parameter Server

show interfaces tokenring

When troubleshooting Token Ring media in a Cisco router environment, you can use the **show interfaces tokenring** command to provide several key fields of information that can assist in isolating problems. This section provides a detailed description of the **show interfaces tokenring** command and the information it provides in Table 6-2.

Use the **show interfaces tokenring** privileged exec command to display information about the Token Ring interface and the state of source route bridging:

```
show interfaces tokenring unit [accounting]
show interfaces tokenring slot | port [accounting] (for the Cisco 7500 series and
    Cisco 7200 series)
show interfaces tokenring [slot | port-adapter | port] (for ports on VIP cards in the
    Cisco 7500 series routers)
```

Syntax Description

- *unit*—Must match the interface port line number.

- **accounting**—(Optional) Displays the number of packets of each protocol type that have been sent through the interface.

- *slot*—Refers to the appropriate hardware manual for slot and port information.

- *port*—Refers to the appropriate hardware manual for slot and port information.

- *port-adapter*—Refers to the appropriate hardware manual for information about port adapter compatibility.

Command Mode

Privileged exec

Usage Guidelines

This command first appeared in Cisco IOS Release 10.0.

The command description was modified in Cisco IOS Release 11.3 to account for support on new full-duplex Token Ring port adapters.

If you do not provide values for the parameters *slot* and *port*, the command will display statistics for all the network interfaces. The optional keyword **accounting** displays the number of packets of each protocol type that have been sent through the interface.

Sample Display

The following is sample output from the **show interfaces tokenring** command:

```
Router# show interfaces tokenring
TokenRing 0 is up, line protocol is up
Hardware is 16/4 Token Ring, address is 5500.2000.dc27 (bia 0000.3000.072b)
            Internet address is 150.136.230.203, subnet mask is 255.255.255.0
            MTU 8136 bytes, BW 16000 Kbit, DLY 630 usec, rely 255/255, load 1/255
            Encapsulation SNAP, loopback not set, keepalive set (10 sec)
    ARP type: SNAP, ARP Timeout 4:00:00
    Ring speed: 16 Mbps
    Single ring node, Source Route Bridge capable
            Group Address: 0x00000000, Functional Address: 0x60840000
            Last input 0:00:01, output 0:00:01, output hang never
            Output queue 0/40, 0 drops; input queue 0/75, 0 drops
            Five minute input rate 0 bits/sec, 0 packets/sec
            Five minute output rate 0 bits/sec, 0 packets/sec
                16339 packets input, 1496515 bytes, 0 no buffer
    Received 9895 broadcasts, 0 runts, 0 giants
    0 input errors, 0 CRC, 0 frame, 0 overrun, 0 ignored, 0 abort
            32648 packets output, 9738303 bytes, 0 underruns
            0 output errors, 0 collisions, 2 interface resets, 0 restarts
            5 transitions
```

Table 6-2 describes the **show interfaces tokenring** display field.

Table 6-2   **show interfaces tokenring** *Field Descriptions*

Field	Description
Token Ring is { *up* | *down* }	Interface is either currently active and inserted into ring (up) or inactive and not inserted (down).
	On the Cisco 7500 series, gives the interface processor type, slot number, and port number.
Token Ring is Reset	Hardware error has occurred.
Token Ring is Initializing	Hardware is up, in the process of inserting the ring.

continues

Table 6-2   **show interfaces tokenring** *Field Descriptions (Continued)*

Field	Description
Token Ring is Administratively Down	Hardware has been taken down by an administrator.
line protocol is {*up* | *down* | *administratively down*}	Indicates whether the software processes that handle the line protocol believe the interface is usable (that is, whether keepalives are successful).
Hardware	Hardware type. **Hardware is Token Ring** indicates that the board is a CSC-R board. **Hardware is 16/4 Token Ring** indicates that the board is a CSC-R16 board. Also shows the address of the interface.
Internet address	Lists the Internet address followed by subnet mask.
MTU	Maximum transmission unit of the interface.
BW	Bandwidth of the interface in kilobits per second.
DLY	Delay of the interface in microseconds.
rely	Reliability of the interface as a fraction of 255 (255/255 is 100 percent reliability), calculated as an exponential average over five minutes.
load	Load on the interface as a fraction of 255 (255/255 is completely saturated), calculated as an exponential average over five minutes.
Encapsulation	Encapsulation method assigned to interface.
loopback	Indicates whether loopback is set.
keepalive	Indicates whether keepalives are set.
ARP type:	Type of Address Resolution Protocol assigned.
Ring speed:	Speed of Token Ring—4 or 16 Mbps.
{*Single ring* | *multiring node*}	Indicates whether a node is enabled to collect and use source routing information (RIF) for routable Token Ring protocols.
Group Address:	Interface's group address, if any. The group address is a multicast address; any number of interfaces on the ring may share the same group address. Each interface may have at most one group address.
Last input	Number of hours, minutes, and seconds since the last packet was successfully received by an interface. Useful for knowing when a dead interface failed.
Last output	Number of hours, minutes, and seconds since the last packet was successfully transmitted by an interface.

Table 6-2   **show interfaces tokenring** *Field Descriptions (Continued)*

Field	Description
output hang	Number of hours, minutes, and seconds (or never) since the interface was last reset because of a transmission that took too long. When the number of hours in any of the "last" fields exceeds 24 hours, the number of days and hours is printed. If that field overflows, asterisks are printed.
Last clearing	Time at which the counters that measure cumulative statistics (such as number of bytes transmitted and received) shown in this report were last reset to zero. Note that variables that might affect routing (for example, load and reliability) are not cleared when the counters are cleared.
	*** indicates the elapsed time is too large to be displayed. 0:00:00 indicates the counters were cleared more than 231 ms (and less than 232 ms) ago.
Output queue, drops **Input queue, drops**	Number of packets in output and input queues. Each number is followed by a slash, the maximum size of the queue, and the number of packets dropped due to a full queue.
Five minute input rate, **Five minute output rate**	Average number of bits and packets transmitted per second in the past five minutes.
	The five-minute input and output rates should be used only as an approximation of traffic per second during a given five-minute period. These rates are exponentially weighted averages with a time constant of five minutes. A period of four time constants must pass before the average will be within 2 percent of the instantaneous rate of a uniform stream of traffic over that period.
packets input	Total number of error-free packets received by the system.
bytes input	Total number of bytes, including data and MAC encapsulation, in the error-free packets received by the system.
no buffer	Number of received packets discarded because there was no buffer space in the main system. Compare with *ignored* count. Broadcast storms on Ethernet networks and bursts of noise on serial lines are often responsible for no input buffer events.
broadcasts	Total number of broadcast or multicast packets received by the interface.
runts	Number of packets that are discarded because they are smaller than the medium's minimum packet size.
giants	Number of packets that are discarded because they exceed the medium's maximum packet size.

continues

Table 6-2   **show interfaces tokenring** *Field Descriptions (Continued)*

Field	Description
CRC	The cyclic redundancy checksum generated by the originating LAN station or far-end device does not match the checksum calculated from the data received. On a LAN, this usually indicates noise or transmission problems on the LAN interface or the LAN bus itself. A high number of CRCs is usually the result of a station transmitting bad data.
frame	Number of packets received incorrectly having a CRC error and a noninteger number of octets.
overrun	Number of times the serial receiver hardware was unable to hand receive data to a hardware buffer because the input rate exceeded the receiver's ability to handle the data.
ignored	Number of received packets ignored by the interface because the interface hardware ran low on internal buffers. These buffers are different than the system buffers mentioned previously in the buffer description. Broadcast storms and bursts of noise can cause the ignored count to be increased.
packets output	Total number of messages transmitted by the system.
bytes output	Total number of bytes, including data and MAC encapsulation, transmitted by the system.
underruns	Number of times that the far-end transmitter has been running faster than the near-end router's receiver can handle. This may never be reported on some interfaces.
output errors	Sum of all errors that prevented the final transmission of datagrams out of the interface being examined. Note that this may not balance with the sum of the enumerated output errors, as some datagrams may have more than one error and others may have errors that do not fall into any of the specifically tabulated categories.
collisions	Because a Token Ring cannot have collisions, this statistic is nonzero only if an unusual event occurred when frames were being queued or taken out of the queue by the system software.
interface resets	The number of times an interface has been reset. The interface may be reset by the administrator or automatically when an internal error occurs.
restarts	Should always be zero for Token Ring interfaces.
transitions	Number of times the ring made a transition from up to down, or vice versa. A large number of transitions indicates a problem with the ring or the interface.

PART III

Troubleshooting Desktop and Enterprise Routing Protocols

Troubleshooting TCP/IP

The sections in this chapter describe common features of TCP/IP and provide solutions to some of the most common TCP/IP problems. The following items will be covered:

- TCP/IP Introduction
- Tools for Troubleshooting IP Problems
- General IP Troubleshooting Theory and Suggestions
- Troubleshooting Basic IP Connectivity
- Troubleshooting Physical Connectivity Problems
- Troubleshooting Layer 3 Problems
- Troubleshooting Hot Standby Router Protocol (HSRP)

TCP/IP Introduction

In the mid-1970s, the Defense Advanced Research Projects Agency (DARPA) became interested in establishing a packet-switched network to provide communications between research institutions in the United States. DARPA and other government organizations understood the potential of packet-switched technology and were just beginning to face the problem that virtually all companies with networks now have—communication between dissimilar computer systems.

With the goal of heterogeneous connectivity in mind, DARPA funded research by Stanford University and Bolt, Beranek, and Newman (BBN) to create a series of communication protocols. The result of this development effort, completed in the late 1970s, was the Internet Protocol suite, of which the Transmission Control Protocol (TCP) and the Internet Protocol (IP) are the two best-known protocols.

The most widespread implementation of TCP/IP is IPv4 (or IP version 4). In 1995, a new standard, RFC 1883—which addressed some of the problems with IPv4, including address space limitations—was proposed. This new version is called IPv6. Although a lot of work has gone into developing IPv6, no wide-scale deployment has occurred; because of this, IPv6 has been excluded from this text.

Internet Protocols

Internet protocols can be used to communicate across any set of interconnected networks. They are equally well suited for local-area network (LAN) and wide-area network (WAN) communications. The Internet suite includes not only lower-layer specifications (such as TCP and IP), but also specifications for such common applications as e-mail, terminal emulation, and file transfer. Figure 7-1 shows some of the most important Internet protocols and their relationships to the OSI reference model.

As an interesting side note, the seven-layer model actually came about *after* TCP/IP. DARPA used a four-layer model instead, which the OSI later expanded to seven layers. This is why TCP/IP doesn't generally fit all that well into the seven-layer OSI model.

Figure 7-1   *The Internet Protocol Suite and the OSI Reference Model*

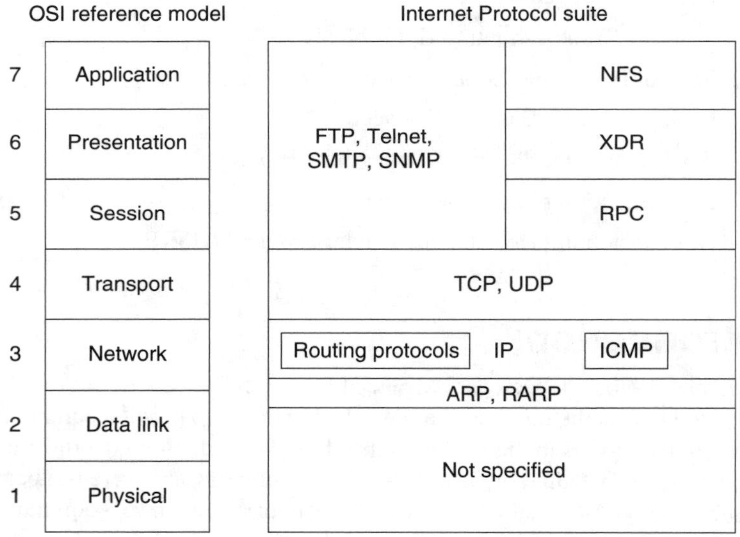

Creation and documentation of the Internet Protocol suite closely resemble an academic research project. The protocols are specified and refined in documents called Requests For Comments (RFCs), which are published, reviewed, and analyzed by the Internet community. Taken together, the RFCs provide a colorful history of the people, companies, and trends that have shaped the development of what is today the world's most popular open-system protocol suite.

The Network Layer

IP is the primary Layer 3 protocol in the TCP/IP suite. IP provides the logical addressing that enables communication across diverse networks. IP also provides fragmentation and reassembly of datagrams and error reporting. Along with TCP, IP represents the heart of the Internet Protocol suite. The IP packet format is shown in Figure 7-2.

Figure 7-2   *The IP Packet Format*

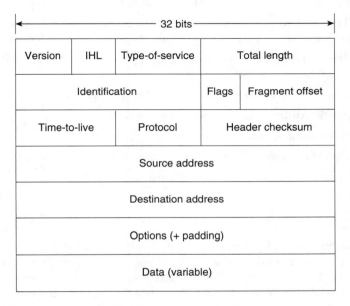

The fields of the IP packet are as follows:

- **Version**—Indicates the version of this IP datagram.
- **IP Header Length (IHL)**—Indicates the datagram header length in 32-bit words.
- **Type-of-Service**—Specifies how a particular upper-layer protocol would like the current datagram to be handled. Datagrams can be assigned various levels of importance using this field.

  Today this field is used primarily to provide quality of service (QoS) capabilities to TCP/IP for applications requiring predictable bandwidth or delay. RFC 2474 describes a method by which the TOS field is replaced by a DS field that is used to provide differentiated services (DiffServ) on networks. This field is split into two parts. The first 6 bits are used for the DSCP codepoint, which is used to differentiate traffic. The last 2 bits, or CU, are ignored by DiffServ-compliant nodes.

- **Total Length**—Specifies the length of the entire IP packet, including data and header, in bytes.

- **Identification**—Consists of an integer identifying this datagram. This field is used to help piece together datagram fragments.

- **Flags**—Consists of 3 bits, of which the low-order 2 bits control fragmentation. One bit specifies whether the packet can be fragmented; the second bit specifies whether the packet is the last fragment in a series of fragmented packets.

- **Time-to-Live**—Maintains a counter that gradually decrements down to zero, at which point the datagram is discarded. This keeps packets from looping endlessly.

- **Protocol**—Indicates which upper-layer protocol receives incoming packets after IP processing is complete.

- **Header Checksum**—Helps ensure IP header integrity.

- **Source Address**—Specifies the sending node.

- **Destination Address**—Specifies the receiving node.

- **Options**—Allows IP to support various options, such as security.

- **Data**—Contains upper-layer information.

Addressing

As with all network layer protocols, the addressing scheme is integral to the process of routing IP datagrams through an internetwork. An IP address is 32 bits in length, divided into either two or three parts. The first part designates the network address, the second part (if present) designates the subnet address, and the final part designates the host address. Subnet addresses are present only if the network administrator has decided that the network should be divided into subnetworks. The lengths of the network, subnet, and host fields are all variable.

Today's Internet does not segment addresses along classful bounds—it is almost entirely classless. The separation between networks and subnets has been effectively eliminated. The requirement to understand network classes and the difference between a network and a subnet remains solely because of configuration and behavioral issues with network devices.

IP addressing supports five different network classes, and the high-order—far-left—bits indicate the network class:

- Class A networks provide 8 bits for the Network Address field. The high-order bit (at far left) is 0.

- Class B networks allocate 16 bits for the Network Address field and 16 bits for the Host Address field. This address class offers a good compromise between network and host address space. The first 2 high-order bits are 10.

- Class C networks allocate 24 bits for the Network Address field. Class C networks provide only 8 bits for the Host field, however, so the number of hosts per network may be a limiting factor. The first 3 high-order bits are 110.

- Class D addresses are reserved for multicast groups, as described formally in RFC 1112. The first 4 high-order bits are 1110.

- Class E addresses are also defined by IP but are reserved for future use. The first 4 high-order bits are 1111.

IP addresses are written in dotted decimal format (for example, 34.10.2.1). Figure 7-3 shows the address formats for Class A, B, and C IP networks.

Figure 7-3   *Class A, B, and C Address Formats*

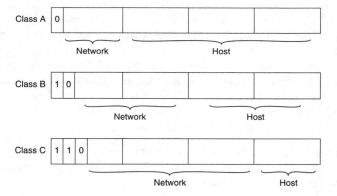

IP networks can also be divided into smaller units called subnets. Subnets provide extra flexibility for network administrators. For example, assume that a network has been assigned a Class B address, and all the nodes on the network currently conform to a Class B address format. Then assume that the dotted decimal representation of this network's address is 172.16.0.0 (all zeros in the Host field of an address specifies the entire network). Rather than change all the addresses to some other basic network number, the administrator can subdivide the network using subnetting. This is done by borrowing bits from the host portion of the address and using them as a subnet field, as shown in Figure 7-4.

Figure 7-4   *Subnet Addresses*

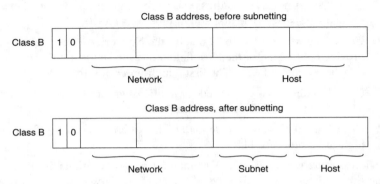

If a network administrator has chosen to use 8 bits of subnetting, the third octet of a Class B IP address provides the subnet number. For example, address 172.16.1.0 refers to network 172.16, subnet 1; address 172.16.2.0 refers to network 172.16, subnet 2; and so on. In today's world, the difference between subnet bits and the natural mask has become blurred, and you will often see only a prefix length that specifies the length of the entire mask (natural mask plus subnet bits). It is still important to understand the difference between the natural network mask, which is determined by the network class, and the subnet mask, because routers sometimes make assumptions based on the natural mask of an address. For example, the natural mask of 10.1.1.1/24 is 8 bits because this is a class A network, even though the subnet mask is 24 bits.

Subnet masks can be expressed in two forms: prefix length (as in /24), or dotted-decimal notation (As in 255.255.255.0). Both forms mean exactly the same thing and can easily be converted to the other, as seen in Example 7-1.

Example 7-1   *Subnet Mask Expressed in Prefix Length and Dotted Decimal*

```
255.255.255.0 = 11111111 11111111 11111111 00000000 = /24 bits (count the ones).
```

On some media (such as IEEE 802 LANs), the correlation between media addresses and IP addresses is dynamically discovered through the use of two other members of the Internet Protocol suite: the Address Resolution Protocol (ARP) and the Reverse Address Resolution Protocol (RARP). ARP uses broadcast messages to determine the hardware Media Access Control (MAC)–layer address corresponding to a particular IP address. ARP is sufficiently generic to allow use of IP with virtually any type of underlying media-access mechanism. RARP uses broadcast messages to determine the Internet address associated with a particular hardware address. RARP is particularly important to diskless nodes, which may not know their IP address when they boot.

Internet Routing

Routing devices in the Internet have traditionally been called gateways—an unfortunate term because elsewhere in the industry, the term *gateway* applies to a device with somewhat different functionality. Gateways (which we will call *routers* from this point on) within the Internet are organized hierarchically.

Dynamic routing protocols, such as RIP and OSPF, provide a means by which routers can communicate and share information about routes that they have learned or are connected to. This contrasts with static routing, in which routes are established by the network administrator and do not change unless they are manually altered. An IP routing table consists of destination address/next-hop pairs. A sample entry, shown in Figure 7-5, is interpreted as meaning, "To get to network 34.1.0.0 (subnet 1 on network 34), the next stop is the node at address 54.34.23.12."

Figure 7-5   *An Example of an IP Routing Table*

Destination address	Next hop
34.1.0.0	54.34.23.12
78.2.0.0	54.34.23.12
147.9.5.0	
17.12.0.0	54.32.12.10
	54.32.12.10

IP routing specifies that IP datagrams travel through internetworks one hop at a time; the entire route is not known at the outset of the journey. Instead, at each stop, the next destination is calculated by matching the destination address within the datagram with an entry in the current node's routing table. Each node's involvement in the routing process consists only of forwarding packets based on internal information, regardless of whether the packets get to their final destination. In other words, IP does not provide for error reporting back to the source when routing anomalies occur. This task is left to other Internet protocols, such as the Internet Control Message Protocol (ICMP) and TCP protocol.

ICMP

ICMP performs a number of tasks within an IP internetwork, the principal of which is reporting routing failures back to the source of a datagram. In addition, ICMP provides helpful messages such as the following:

- Echo and reply messages to test node reachability across an internetwork
- Redirect messages to stimulate more efficient routing

- Time exceeded messages to inform sources that a datagram has exceeded its allocated time to exist within the internetwork

- Router advertisement and router solicitation messages to determine the addresses of routers on directly attached subnetworks

The Transport Layer

The Internet transport layer is implemented by Transport Control Protocol (TCP) and the User Datagram Protocol (UDP). TCP provides connection-oriented data transport, whereas UDP operation is connectionless.

TCP

TCP provides full-duplex, acknowledged, and flow-controlled service to upper-layer protocols. It moves data in a continuous, unstructured byte stream in which bytes are identified by sequence numbers. TCP can support numerous simultaneous upper-layer conversations. The TCP packet format is shown in Figure 7-6.

Figure 7-6   *The TCP Packet Format*

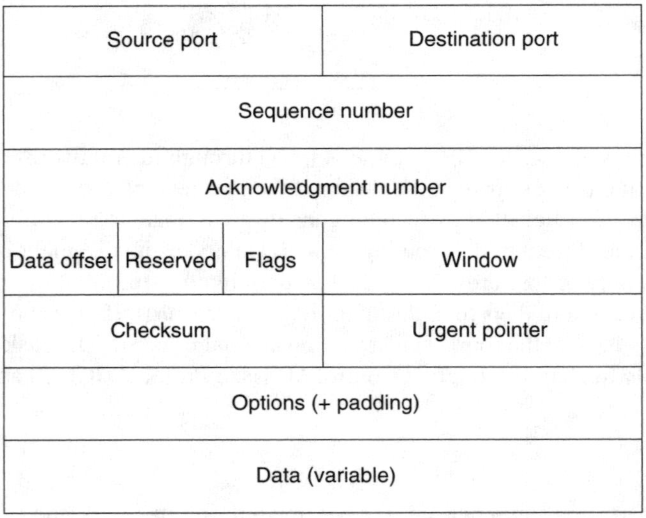

Source port			Destination port	
Sequence number				
Acknowledgment number				
Data offset	Reserved	Flags	Window	
Checksum			Urgent pointer	
Options (+ padding)				
Data (variable)				

The fields of the TCP packet are described here:

- **Source port and destination port**—Identify the points (sockets) at which upper-layer source and destination processes receive TCP services.
- **Sequence number**—Usually specifies the number assigned to the first byte of data in the current message. Under certain circumstances, it can also be used to identify an initial sequence number to be used in the upcoming transmission.
- **Acknowledgment number**—Contains the sequence number of the next byte of data that the sender of the packet expects to receive.
- **Data offset**—Indicates the number of 32-bit words in the TCP header.
- **Reserved**—Is reserved for future use.
- **Flags**—Carries a variety of control information.
- **Window**—Specifies the size of the sender's receive window (buffer space available for incoming data).
- **Checksum**—Provides information used to determine whether the header was damaged in transit.
- **Urgent pointer**—Points to the first urgent data byte in the packet.
- **Options**—Specifies various TCP options.
- **Data**—Contains upper-layer information.

UDP

UDP is a much simpler protocol than TCP and is useful in situations in which the reliability mechanisms of TCP are not necessary. The UDP header has only four fields: Source Port, Destination Port, Length, and UDP Checksum. The Source and Destination Port fields serve the same functions as they do in the TCP header. The Length field specifies the length of the UDP header and data, and the UDP Checksum field allows packet integrity checking. The UDP checksum is optional.

Upper-Layer Protocols

The Internet Protocol suite includes many upper-layer protocols representing a wide variety of applications, including network management, file transfer, distributed file services, terminal emulation, and electronic mail. Table 7-1 maps the best-known Internet upper-layer protocols to the applications that they support.

Table 7-1   *Internet Protocol/Application Mapping (with Common Port Numbers)*

Application	Protocols
WWW browser	HTTP (TCP port 80)
The Hypertext Transfer Protocol (HTTP) is used by Web browsers and servers to transfer the files that make up web pages.	
File transfer	FTP (TCP ports 20 and 21)
The File Transfer Protocol (FTP) provides a way to move files between computer systems. Telnet allows virtual terminal emulation.	
Terminal emulation	Telnet (TCP port 23)
The Telnet protocol provides terminal emulation services over a reliable TCP stream. The Telnet protocol also specifies how a client and server should negotiate the use of certain features and options.	
Electronic mail	SMTP (TCP port 25), POP3 (TCP port 110), IMAP4 (TCP port 143)
The Simple Mail Transfer Protocol (SMTP) is used to transfer electronic mail between mail servers, and is used by mail clients to send mail. Mail clients do not generally use SMTP to receive mail. Instead, they use either the Post Office Protocol version 3 (POP3) or the Internet Message Access Protocol (IMAP); this will be discussed in greater detail later in this chapter.	
Network management	SNMP (UDP port 161)
The Simple Network Management Protocol (SNMP) is a network management protocol used for reporting anomalous network conditions and setting network threshold values.	
Distributed file services	NFS, XDR, RPC (UDP port 111), X Windows (UDP ports 6000-6063)
X Windows is a popular protocol that permits intelligent terminals to communicate with remote computers as if they were directly attached. Network file system (NFS), external data representation (XDR), and remote-procedure call (RPC) combine to allow transparent access to remote network resources.	

These and other network applications use the services of TCP/IP and other lower-layer Internet protocols to provide users with basic network services.

Domain Name System

TCP/IP uses a numeric addressing scheme in which each node is assigned an IP address that is used to route packets to a node on the network. Because it is much easier for people to remember names such as www.somedomain.com instead of 10.1.1.1, a protocol called Domain Name System (DNS) is used to map numbers to names, and vice versa. Most web pages refer to other web pages or links using these names instead of their IP addresses. This provides many advantages; for example, the address can change without breaking any links to a web page if the DNS table is also changed to point to the new address.

Tools for Troubleshooting IP Problems

The tools ping and traceroute, both in the TCP/IP protocol suite, will greatly assist in troubleshooting IP connectivity. Most operating systems and IP implementations come with these tools installed by default. On some UNIX platforms, however, you may need to download and install a traceroute package.

Cisco routers provide a basic method of viewing IP traffic switched through the router called *packet debugging*. Packet debugging enables a user to determine whether traffic is travelling along an expected path in the network or whether there are errors in a particular TCP stream. Although in some cases packet debugging can eliminate the need for a packet analyzer, it should not be considered a replacement for this important tool.

Packet debugging can be very intrusive—in some cases, it can cause a router to become inoperable until physically reset. In other instances, packets that are present on the network and switched through the router may not be reported by packet debugging. Thus, a firm conclusion cannot be drawn that a packet was not sent solely from the output of packet debugging; a network analyzer must be used to accurately make this assessment. *Packet debugging should be used with extreme caution by only advanced operators because it can cause the router to lock up and stop routing traffic, if not used carefully.* The risks of using packet debugging may be compounded by the necessity of disabling fast switching for packet debugging to be effective. As a general rule, packet debugging should not be used on a production router unless you have physical access to the router and are willing to risk it going down.

ping

The ping tool uses the IP ICMP echo request and echo reply messages to test reachability to a remote system. In its simplest form, ping simply confirms that an IP packet is capable of getting to and getting back from a destination IP address (Figure 7-7). This tool generally returns two pieces of information: whether the source can reach the destination (and, by inference, vice versa), and the round-trip time (RTT, typically in milliseconds). The RTT returned by ping should be used only as a comparative reference because it can depend greatly on the software implementation and hardware of the system on which ping is run. If ping fails or returns an unusual RTT, traceroute can be used to help narrow down the problem. It is also possible to vary the size of the ICMP echo payload to test problems related to maximum transmission unit (MTU).

Figure 7-7   *ping Example (pingfig.gif/cdr)*

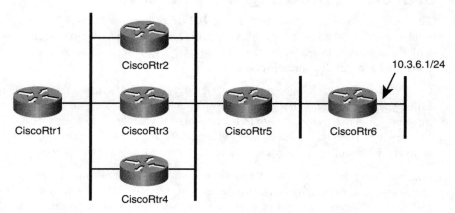

Example 7-2 shows ping returning three values separated with the slash "/," the minimum, average, and maximum RTT. Large differences in these values could indicate network congestion or a network problem. In most cases, the average value accurately portrays the network latency to the destination. By default, ping uses small packets for connectivity testing; the packet size will influence the RTT values. The packet size may be changed in some implementations, including that of Cisco Systems's IOS.

Example 7-2   **ping** *Returning Three Values Separated with the Slash "/," the Minimum, Average, and Maximum RTT*

```
CiscoRtr1>ping 10.3.1.6

Type escape sequence to abort.
Sending 5, 100-byte ICMP Echoes to 10.3.1.6, timeout is 2 seconds:
!!!!!
Success rate is 100 percent (5/5), round-trip min/avg/max = 4/4/4 ms
```

Firewalls and routers can be configured to not allow devices to be pinged but to still permit other types of IP traffic. For this reason, a ping failure between two devices should not be misconstrued as a lack of IP connectivity between those devices. Table 7-2 shows a list of some of the codes returned by the Cisco ping utility, along with their meanings and possible cause.

Table 7-2   *Cisco ping Return Codes*

Code	Meaning	Possible Cause(s)
!	Each exclamation point indicates receipt of an ICMP echo reply.	The ping completed successfully.
.	Each period indicates that the network server timed out while waiting for a reply.	This message can indicate many problems: • ping was blocked by an access list or firewall. • A router along the path did not have a route to the destination and did not send an ICMP destination unreachable message. • A physical connectivity problem occurred somewhere along the path.
U	An ICMP unreachable message was received.	A router along the path did not have a route to the destination address.
C	An ICMP source quench message was received.	A device along the path—possibly the destination—may be receiving to much traffic; check input queues.
&	An ICMP time exceeded message was received.	A routing loop may have occurred.

traceroute

The traceroute utility sends out either ICMP echo request (Windows) or UDP (most implementations) messages with gradually increasing IP TTL values to probe the path by which a packet traverses the network (see Example 7-3). The first packet with the TTL set to 1 will be discarded by the first hop, and the first hop will send back an ICMP TTL exceeded message sourced from its IP address facing the source of the packet. When the machine running the traceroute receives the ICMP TTL exceeded message, it can determine the hop via the source IP address. This continues until the destination is reached. The destination will return either an ICMP echo reply (Windows) or a ICMP port unreachable, indicating that the destination had been reached. Cisco's implementation of traceroute sends out three packets at each TTL value, allowing traceroute to report routers that have multiple equal-cost paths to the destination.

Traceroute can return useful information about TCP/IP connectivity across your network. Table 7-3 shows some of the codes that can be returned by the Cisco traceroute utility, along with their possible cause.

Table 7-3 *Cisco traceroute Return Codes*

Code	Meaning	Possible Cause(s)
nn msec	This gives, for each node, the round-trip time (in milliseconds) for the specified number of probes.	This is normal.
*	The probe timed out.	A device along the path either did not receive the probe or did not reply with an ICMP "packet life exceeded" message.
A	Administratively prohibited.	A device along the path, such as a firewall or router, may be blocking the probe and possibly other or all traffic; check access lists.
Q	Source quench.	A device along the path may be receiving to much traffic; check input queues.
H	An ICMP unreachable message has been received.	A routing loop may have occurred.

Example 7-3 *(Taken from a Cisco Router) traceroute*

```
CiscoRtr1>traceroute 10.3.1.6

Type escape sequence to abort.
Tracing the route to 10.3.1.6

  1 CiscoRtr2 (10.1.1.2) 0 msec
    CiscoRtr3 (10.1.1.3) 0 msec
    CiscoRtr4 (10.1.1.4) 4 msec
  2 CiscoRtr5 (10.2.1.6) 4 msec 4 msec 0 msec
  3 CiscoRtr6 (10.3.1.6) 4 msec 4 msec 4 msec
```

If there had been a problem between CiscoRtr5 and CiscoRtr6, you would have seen the following on a Cisco router:

```
CiscoRtr1>traceroute 10.3.1.6

Type escape sequence to abort.
Tracing the route to 10.3.1.6

  1 CiscoRtr2 (10.1.1.2) 0 msec
    CiscoRtr3 (10.1.1.3) 0 msec
    CiscoRtr4 (10.1.1.4) 4 msec
  2 CiscoRtr5 (10.2.1.6) 4 msec 4 msec 0 msec
  3  *  *  *
  4  *  *  *
```

Although it may also be possible to trace the path between source and destination using ping and the IP record route option, traceroute is preferred because the record route option can alter the way in which packets are forwarded by routers in the network, yielding incorrect path information.

Packet Debugging

The following example is applicable to Cisco 16xx, 25xx, 26xx, 36xx, 40xx, 45xx, 70xx, and 75xx series routers. Consult the Cisco TAC web page www.cisco.com/tac for instructions on using this command on other Cisco router platforms.

CAUTION   The **debug ip packet** command should always be run with an access list to restrict the traffic that it will display. Failure to do so will almost certainly lock up the router. Even with an access list, there is always a possibility that packet debugging will lock up the router. *Do not* run this utility on a router that cannot be brought down or physically reset.

To use the **debug ip packet** command, you must do the following:

1 Enter enable mode.

```
CiscoRtr> enable
CiscoRtr#
```

2 Disable console logging. (This command can be run with console logging, but this increases the likelihood of locking up the router.)

```
CiscoRtr# configure terminal
CiscoRtr(config)# no logging console
CiscoRtr(config)# end
CiscoRtr#
```

3 Enable buffer logging.

```
CiscoRtr# configure terminal
CiscoRtr(config)# logging buffered
CiscoRtr(config)# end
CiscoRtr#
```

4 Turn on logging timestamps with millisecond output.

```
CiscoRtr# configure terminal
CiscoRtr(config)# service timestamps log datetime msec
CiscoRtr(config)# end
CiscoRtr#
```

5 Ensure that the router's CPU is not overloaded. This depends greatly on the amount of traffic to capture and the type of router. As a general rule, a CPU percentage (highlighted here) less than 30 percent should be safe. *Note: This may still cause your router to lock up!*

```
CiscoRtr#show processes cpu
CPU utilization for five seconds: 2%/0%; one minute: 0%; five minutes: 0%
 PID  Runtime(ms)  Invoked  uSecs   5Sec   1Min   5Min TTY Process
   1        2075   308386       6  0.00%  0.00%  0.00%   0 Load Meter
   2         273       55    4963  1.55%  0.18%  0.06%   0 Exec
[snip]
CiscoRtr#
```

6 Disable fast-switching on the inbound and outbound interfaces from which you would like to capture traffic.

```
CiscoRtr#configure terminal
CiscoRtr(config)# interface ethernet 0
CiscoRtr(config-if)# no ip route-cache
CiscoRtr(config-if)# interface ethernet 1
CiscoRtr(config-if)# no ip route-cache
CiscoRtr(config-if)# end
CiscoRtr#
```

7 Create an access list that matches *only* the traffic that you want to capture. In this example, we are using access list 101 to match all DHCP traffic. The number 101 should be replaced with an available IP access list on your router.

```
CiscoRtr#configure terminal
CiscoRtr(config)# access-list 101 permit udp any any eq bootpc
CiscoRtr(config)# access-list 101 permit udp any any eq bootps
CiscoRtr(config)# access-list 101 permit udp any eq bootpc any
CiscoRtr(config)# access-list 101 permit udp any eq bootps any
CiscoRtr(config)# end
CiscoRtr#
```

8 Double-check that the access list exists and is correct. (A nonexistent or incorrect access list can lock up your router.)

```
CiscoRtr#  show ip access-lists
Extended IP access list 101
    permit udp any any eq bootpc
    permit udp any any eq bootps
    permit udp any eq bootpc any
    permit udp any eq bootps any
```

9 Start packet debugging with the access list. (Omitting the access list can lock up your router.)

```
CiscoRtr# debug ip packet 101 detail
```

10 Stop debugging.

```
CiscoRtr# undebug all
```

11 View results in the log.

```
CiscoRtr# show log
Syslog logging: enabled (0 messages dropped, 0 flushes, 0 overruns)
    Console logging: disabled
    Monitor logging: level debugging, 0 messages logged
    Buffer logging: level debugging, 16 messages logged
    Trap logging: level informational, 0 message lines logged


Log Buffer (4096 bytes):

*Mar 16 18:00:10.485: IP: s=0.0.0.0 (Ethernet0), d=255.255.255.255, len
328, rcvd 2
*Mar 16 18:00:10.485:      UDP src=68, dst=67
*Mar 16 18:00:10.485: IP: s=10.1.1.1 (local), d=10.1.2.2 (Ethernet1), len
328, sending
*Mar 16 18:00:10.485:      UDP src=67, dst=67
*Mar 16 18:00:10.492: IP: s=10.1.2.2 (Ethernet1), d=10.1.1.1, len 328,
rcvd 4
*Mar 16 18:00:10.492:      UDP src=67, dst=67
*Mar 16 18:00:10.492: IP: s=10.1.1.1 (local), d=10.1.1.10 (Ethernet0),
len 328, sending
*Mar 16 18:00:10.492:      UDP src=67, dst=68
*Mar 16 18:00:10.510: IP: s=0.0.0.0 (Ethernet0), d=255.255.255.255, len
328, rcvd 2
*Mar 16 18:00:10.510:      UDP src=68, dst=67
*Mar 16 18:00:10.510: IP: s=10.1.1.1 (local), d=10.1.2.2 (Ethernet1), len
328, sending
*Mar 16 18:00:10.510:      UDP src=67, dst=67
*Mar 16 18:00:10.530: IP: s=10.1.2.2 (Ethernet1), d=10.1.1.1, len 328,
rcvd 4
*Mar 16 18:00:10.530:      UDP src=67, dst=67
*Mar 16 18:00:10.530: IP: s=10.1.1.1 (local), d=10.1.1.10 (Ethernet0),
len 328, sending
*Mar 16 18:00:10.530:      UDP src=67, dst=68
```

General IP Troubleshooting Suggestions

This chapter approaches the process of troubleshooting TCP/IP connectivity issues with the assumption that you will have access to the client (or source) and may not have access to the server (or destination). If the problem is determined to be a server issue, you contact the server administrator. If you are the server administrator, you can apply the troubleshooting process in reverse (server to client) to further troubleshoot connectivity issues. This chapter will not address the specifics of troubleshooting server-side IP services; for this, consult the manual or web page for the software or service running on the server.

Because TCP/IP does not store path information in its packets, it is possible for a packet to have a working path from the source to the destination (or vice versa), but not to have a working path in the opposite direction. For this reason, it may be necessary to perform all troubleshooting steps in both directions along an IP path to determine the cause of a connectivity problem.

Narrowing Down the Problem Domain

To efficiently troubleshoot a TCP/IP connectivity problem, it is necessary to identify a single pair of source and destination devices that are exhibiting the connectivity problem. When you've selected the two devices, test to make sure that the problem is actually occurring between these two devices.

Possible problems include these:

- Physical layer issue somewhere along the path
- First-hop Layer 3 connectivity issue, local LAN segment
- Layer 3 IP connectivity issue somewhere along the packet's path
- Name resolution issue

Where to start:

1 Try to ping from the source to destination device by IP address. If the ping fails, verify that you are using the correct address, and try the ping again. If the ping still fails, go to the next section, "Troubleshooting Local Connectivity Problems." Otherwise, proceed to Step 2.

2 Try to ping from the source to the destination device by name. If the ping fails, verify that the name is correctly spelled and that it refers to the destination device, and then try the ping again. If the ping still fails, go to the section "Troubleshooting Domain Name Server Problems," later in this chapter. Otherwise, proceed to Step 3.

3 If you can ping the destination by both name and address, it appears that the problem is an upper-layer problem. Go to the section "Troubleshooting Upper Layer Problems," later in this chapter.

Troubleshooting Local Connectivity Problems

This section describes how to troubleshoot local connectivity problems on LAN segments such as Ethernet or Token Ring. Going through the methodology in this chapter with help determine and resolve problems moving packets on the local LAN segment or to the next-hop router. If the problem is determined to be past the local LAN segment, then you will be referred to the section "Troubleshooting IP Connectivity and Routing Problems," later in this chapter. If the source device is connected via a modem, then you should consult Chapter 16, "Troubleshooting Dialup Connections."

Possible problems include these:

- Configuration problem
- DHCP or BOOTP issue
- Physical layer issue
- Duplicate IP address

Check for Configuration Problems

To begin troubleshooting, display and examine the IP configuration of the source device. The method to determine this information varies greatly from platform to platform. If you are unsure of how to display this information, consult the manual for the device or operating system. Refer to the following examples:

- On a Cisco router, use **show ip interface** and **show running-config**.
- On Windows 95 or 98, use **winipcfg.exe**.
- On Windows 2000 or NT, use **ipconfig.exe**.
- On a UNIX platform, use **ifconfig**.

Examine the configuration, looking specifically for the IP address and subnet mask. On Windows 9x or Windows 2000 platforms, the default gateway address should also be displayed.

If no IP address is configured, verify that this node receives its IP address from BOOTP or DHCP. Otherwise, an IP address should be statically configured for this interface. Configure an address if one is not present. If the source is configured to receive an IP address via DHCP or BOOTP and is not receiving one, make sure that the bootp (IP) helper address is configured on the router interface facing the source device.

If the incorrect IP address, subnet mask, or default gateway is configured, verify that this node receives its IP address from BOOTP or DHCP, and then contact the DHCP or BOOTP administrator. Ask the administrator to troubleshoot the DHCP or BOOTP server's configuration. If the address is statically configured, configure the correct address.

Check for Local Connectivity

If the destination is on the same subnet as the source, try pinging the destination by IP address. If the destination is on a different subnet, then try pinging the default gateway or appropriate next hop obtained from the routing table. If the ping fails, double-check the configuration of the next-hop router to see if the subnet and mask match the source's configuration.

If the configuration is correct, check that the source or next-hop router is capable of pinging any other device on the local LAN segment. If you cannot ping the next-hop address, and if the next-hop address is an HSRP virtual address, try pinging one of the next-hop router's actual IP addresses. If the actual address works but the virtual address does not, you may be experiencing an HSRP issue. Failure to communicate with some or all devices on the LAN segment could indicate a physical connectivity problem, a switch or bridge misconfiguration, or a duplicate IP address.

Ruling Out Duplicate IP Addresses

To rule out a duplicate IP address, you can disconnect the suspect device from the LAN or shut down the suspect interface and then try pinging the device from another device on that same LAN segment. If the ping is successful, then there is another device on that LAN segment using the IP address. You will be able to determine the MAC address of the conflicting device by looking at the ARP table on the device that issued the ping.

If at this point you still do not have local connectivity for either the source or the next-hop router, proceed to the next section.

Troubleshooting Physical Connectivity Problems

This section describes how to troubleshoot Layer 1 and 2 physical connectivity issues on LANs such as Ethernet or Token Ring. For troubleshooting information on dialup links or WAN connections, consult the chapters in Part IV, "Troubleshooting Serial Lines and WAN Connections."

Even though it may seem logical to first troubleshoot at the physical layer, problems can generally be found more quickly by first troubleshooting at Layer 3 and then working backward when a physical problem is found or suspected.

Possible problems include these:

- Configuration is incorrect.
- Cable is faulty or improperly connected.

- Wiring closet cross-connect is faulty or improperly connected.
- Hardware (interface or port) is faulty.
- Interface has too much traffic.

Rule Out a Configuration Problem

Check to make sure that all cables are connected to the appropriate ports. Make sure that all cross-connects are properly patched to the correct location using the appropriate cable and method. Verify that all switch or hub ports are set in the correct VLAN or collision domain and have appropriate options set for spanning tree and other considerations.

Check Cable Connections

Verify that the proper cable is being used. If this is a direct connection between two end systems (for example, a PC and a router) or between two switches, a special crossover cable may be required. Verify that the cable from the source interface is properly connected and is in good condition. If you doubt that the connection is good, reseat the cable and ensure that the connection is secure. Try replacing the cable with a known working cable. If this cable connects to a wall jack, use a cable tester to ensure that the jack is properly wired. Also check any transceiver in use to ensure that it is the correct type, is properly connected, and is properly configured. If replacing the cable does not resolve the problem, try replacing the transceiver if one is being used.

Check the Configuration

Verify that the interface on the device is configured properly and is not shut down. If the device is connected to a hub or switch, verify that the port on the hub or switch is configured properly and is not shut down. Check both speed and duplex.

Check the Network Interface

Most interfaces or NICs will have indicator lights that show whether there is a valid connection; often this light is called the link light. The interface may also have lights to indicate whether traffic is being sent (TX) or received (RX). If the interface has indicator lights that do not show a valid connection, power off the device and reseat the interface card.

Troubleshooting IP Connectivity and Routing Problems

When troubleshooting IP connectivity problems across large networks, it always helps to have a network diagram handy so that you can understand the path that the traffic should take and compare it to the path that it is actually taking.

When IP packets are routed across a network, there is the potential for problems at every hop between the source and the destination, so test connectivity at each hop to determine where it is broken is the logical troubleshooting methodology.

The following could be wrong:

- A router may not have a route to the source or destination.
- The network might have a routing loop or other routing protocol-related problem.
- A physical connectivity problem might have occurred.
- A resource problem on one router might be prohibiting proper router operation. This could possibly be caused by lack of memory, lack of buffers, or lack of CPU.
- A configuration problem might have occurred on a router.
- A software problem might have occurred on a router.
- A packet filter or firewall might be preventing traffic from passing for an IP address or protocol.
- An MTU mismatch problem might have occurred.

Determining Where to Start

The most detailed method to find a problem would obviously be to start at the next hop away from the source and work your way one hop at a time toward the destination, exploring all possible paths along the way. You would then test basic IP connectivity and possibly protocol connectivity from each router forward. Although in some cases this method is the only one available, the process can generally be shortened by first performing a traceroute from the source to the destination to determine the first problematic hop. If the traceroute method does not provide an answer, you will have to fall back to the longer method.

When you have found a starting point, connect to that router via telnet or console, and verify that it is capable of pinging the source and the destination. When doing this, keep in mind that the router will source the ping packet from the interface closest to the ping target. In some cases, you may want to use an extended ping to specify a source interface because the ping target may not know how to get to the default source address; this is common on serial interfaces configured with private addressing.

Check for Resources

If the router appears sluggish or does not respond (echo) to what you are typing quickly, or if you suspect a resource issue, check the router's resources. Check memory using **show memory**; be sure not to have **terminal length 0** configured when doing this, or it make take a long time. Look at how much memory is available in the **largest free** field. If this number is low (less than 5 percent of total router memory), use **show process memory** to identify which process(es) are "holding" the memory.

Sluggish router response can also be caused by CPU overload. This can be checked using **show process cpu**. You will see two percentages listed (such as 75%/24%). The first number is the total CPU utilization for the router, and the second is interrupt-generated processor utilization. If the total CPU utilization is greater than 90 percent for an extended period of time (10 to 15 minutes), then you should investigate what is using all the CPU. **Show process cpu** will show which processes are running and how much CPU they are using. If the CPU is too high, it is possible to lose console and Telnet access to the router.

Although I will not cover all the processes that could possibly be running, a few have special meaning. The IP Input process is tied to process-switched traffic. Some traffic that will frequently cause an increase in process-switched traffic includes broadcast traffic, multicast traffic, routing updates, or traffic destined for an IP address on the router. For example, a broadcast storm will cause IP Input to increase and can cause CPU to jump to 99 percent. You will also see processes for the individual routing protocols such as these:

- IP BGP
- IP EIGRP
- IP OSPF

If a routing protocol is converging, it is possible that one of these processes may increase CPU utilization; in most cases, this is normal.

Check for Connectivity

If you cannot ping from this router to either the source or the destination, check the routing table for a route to the ping target. Keep in mind that it may be desirable for the router to use the default route to this destination, and **ip classless** may need to be configured for this to happen. If there is no route to the ping target, you will need to either troubleshoot your routing protocol, if you are running one, or add a static route to the destination network. The router will need to have both a route to the source and to the destination for communication to succeed.

If ping succeeds only a percentage of the time, look to see if there are multiple paths to the destination. If there are multiple paths, it is possible that one path may be failing while the others are working. This can be symptomatic of a routing loop or physical problem somewhere along the path. The only way to test whether a path is failing is to go to all the next hops and test connectivity from there.

Pings with less than 100 percent success rate can also indicate problematic links or links with high utilization. Look at the interface statistics using **show interface** for outgoing interfaces to see if any have problems. When reviewing statistics, keep in mind that the router may have been collecting information for years; always look at the uptime for the router, reported in **show version**, and the last time that the counters were reset, reported at the top of **show interface**. Generally, the counters can be looked at as an accurate percentage of packets received or sent. If the counters have not been reset in a long time, or if a problem is suspected, the counters should be reset using **clear counters** command, and a new reading should be taken after a reasonable period of time has elapsed. If a problem is detected on a WAN or dialup link, refer to Part IV. If a problem is detected on a LAN connection, see the section "Troubleshooting Physical Connectivity Problems," earlier in this chapter.

Check for ACLs

Check this router for any access lists applied to an interface using **ip access-group**, or any other firewall or packet filters configured. Does the packet filtering permit the desired source/destination to communicate using the requested protocol? If you are unsure, see the section "Troubleshooting Upper-Layer Problems."

Check for Network Address Translation

Check to see if this router is configured for network address translation. If it is, is it supposed to translate packets between the source and destination? Has it been configured correctly?

At this point, you will want to move on to one of the next-hop routers. Record routers that you have already visited on a piece of paper. Also record any problems or questions that arose at the router. This record will help you detect routing loops and will provide useful information if you find it necessary to call for support.

Troubleshooting Upper-Layer Problems

Even though there may be IP connectivity between a source and a destination, problems may still exist for a specific upper-layer protocols such as FTP, HTTP, or Telnet. These protocols ride on top of the basic IP transport but are subject to protocol-specific problems relating to packet filters and firewalls. It is possible that everything except mail will work between a given source and destination. Before troubleshooting at this level, it is important to first establish whether IP connectivity exists between the source and the destination. If IP connectivity exists, then the issue must be at the application layer.

The following could go wrong:

- A packet filter/firewall issue might have arisen for the specific protocol, data connection, or return traffic.
- The specific service could be down on the server.
- An authentication problem might have occurred on the server for the source or source network.
- There could be a version mismatch or incompatibility with the client and server software.

Generic

To troubleshoot an upper-layer protocol connectivity problem, you must understand how it works. You can generally find this information in the latest RFC for the protocol or on the developer's web page. Questions that you should answer to make certain that you understand the protocol include these:

- What IP protocols does the protocol use (TCP, UDP, ICMP, IGMP, or other)?
- What TCP or UDP port numbers are used by the protocol?
- Does the protocol require any inbound TCP connections or inbound UDP packets?
- Does the protocol embed IP addresses in the data portion of the packet?
- Are you running a client or a server for the protocol?

If the protocol embeds IP addresses in the data portion of the packet and you have NAT configured anywhere along the path of the packet, the NAT gateway will need to know how to deal with that particular protocol, or the connection will fail. NAT gateways do not typically change information in the data portion of a packet unless they have been specifically coded to do so. Some examples of protocols that embed IP addresses in the data portion of the packet are FTP, SQLNet, and Microsoft WINs.

If there is a question whether a firewall or router is interfering with the flow of data for a particular application or protocol, you can take several steps to see what exactly is happening. These steps may not all be possible in all situations.

- Move the client outside the firewall or address translation device.
- Verify whether the client can talk to a server on the same subnet as the client.
- Capture a network trace at the client's LAN and on the LAN closest to the server (or, preferably, on the server's LAN, if possible).
- If the service is ASCII-based, you can try Telnetting to the service's port from the router closest to the server; then work backward into the network toward the client.

Hypertext Transport Protocol

HTTP is the protocol used to transfer the files that make up web pages. Although the HTTP specification allows for data to be transferred on port 80 using either TCP or UDP, most implementations use TCP. A secure version of the protocol, SHTTP, uses TCP port 443.

You can test HTTP connectivity using any Telnet application that allows a port number to be specified by Telnetting to the IP address of the destination server on port 80. You should see a hello message, which indicates that you have HTTP connectivity to the server.

FTP

FTP uses two or more TCP connections to accomplish data transfers. To start a session, the FTP client opens a TCP connection to port 21 on the FTP server. This connection is called the *control connection* and is used to pass commands and results between the client and the server. No data, such as file transfers or directory listings, is passed over the control connection; instead, data is transferred over a separate TCP connection created specifically to fulfill that request. This *data connection* can be opened in several different ways:

- **Traditional (or active)**—The FTP server opens a TCP connection back to the client's port 20. This method will not work on a multiuser system because many users may make simultaneous FTP requests, and the system will not be capable of matching incoming FTP data connections to the appropriate user.

- **Multiuser traditional (or active)**—The FTP client instructs the FTP server to open a connection on some random port in the range 1024 through 65535. This method creates a rather large security hole because it requires system administrators to permit inbound TCP connections to all ports greater than 1023. Although firewalls that monitor FTP traffic and dynamically allow inbound connections help close this security hole, many corporate networks do not permit this type of traffic. Most command-line FTP clients default to this method of transfer and offer a **passive** command (or something similar) to switch to passive mode.

- **Passive mode**—The FTP client instructs the FTP server that it wants a passive connection, and the server replies with an IP address and port number to which the FTP client can open a TCP data connection. This method is by far the most secure because it requires no inbound TCP connections to the FTP client. Many corporate networks permit only this type of FTP transfer. Although most of the popular web browsers default to this method of FTP transfer, you shouldn't assume that they do.

You can test the FTP control connection using any Telnet application that allows a port number to be specified. Telnet to the IP address of the destination server using port 21, and you should see a hello message indicating that you have FTP connectivity to the server.

Generally, if a client has connectivity via the control connection but cannot retrieve directory listings or transfer files, there is an issue with opening the data connection. Try specifying passive mode because this is permitted by most firewalls.

Another common problem with FTP is being able to transfer small files but not large files, with the transfer generally failing at the same place or time in every file. Remember that the data connection (and the transfer) will be closed if the control connection closes; because the control connection is typically dormant during large file transfers, it is possible for the connection to close in NAT/PAT environments in which there is a timeout on TCP connections. Increasing the timeout on dormant TCP connections may resolve this problem. If an FTP client is not properly coded, you may also see this problem.

Because FTP file transfers generally create packets of maximum size, an MTU mismatch problem will almost always cause file transfers to fail in a single direction (*gets* may fail, but *puts* may work). This can be caused by a server located on a LAN media that support larger MTUs (such as Token Ring, which can have an MTU of 4096 or larger). Normally this problem is resolved automatically by fragmentation, but misconfigurations or having the IP Don't Fragment option set in the IP datagrams can prevent proper operation.

MAIL (IMAP, POP, and SMTP)

Two types of machines exist in the e-mail universe, and they work in different ways. E-mail servers communicate with each other using the Simple Mail Transport Protocol (SMTP) to send and receive mail. The SMTP protocol transports e-mail messages in ASCII format using TCP; it's possible to connect to an SMTP server by Telnetting to the SMTP port (25). This is a good way to test whether a mail server is reachable.

When a mail server receives a message destined for a local client, it stores that message and waits for the client to collect the mail. There are several ways for mail clients to collect their mail: They can use programs that access the mail server files directly, or they can collect their mail using one of many network protocols. The most popular mail client protocols are POP3 and IMAP4, which both use TCP to transport data. Even though mail clients use these special protocols to collect mail, they almost always use SMTP to send mail. Because two different protocols, and possibly two different servers, are used to send and receive mail, it is possible that mail clients can perform one task and not the other—so you should troubleshoot sending and receiving mail separately.

When verifying the configuration of a mail client, both the mail relay (SMTP) server and mail (POP or IMAP) servers should be verified. The SMTP protocol does not offer much in the way of security and does not require any sort of authentication, so to prevent unauthorized users from bouncing mail messages off their servers, administrators don't often allow hosts that are not part of their network to use their SMTP server to send (or relay) mail.

You can test SMTP, IMAP, and POP connectivity using any Telnet application that allows a port number to be specified. Telnet to the IP address of the destination server using ports 25, 143, and 110 respectively. You should see a hello message, which indicates that you have connectivity to that server.

Telnet

If the Telnet to a particular server fails from one host, try connecting from a router and several other devices. If when Telnetting to a server you do not receive a login prompt, you will want to check the following:

- Are you able to do a reverse DNS lookup on the client's address? Many Telnet servers will not allow connections from IP addresses that have no DNS entry. This is a common problem for DHCP-assigned addresses in which the administrator has not added DNS entries for the DHCP pools.

- It is possible that your Telnet application cannot negotiate the appropriate options and therefore will not connect. On a Cisco router, you can view this negotiation process using **debug telnet**.

- It is possible that Telnet is disabled or has been moved to a port other than 23 on the destination server.

Troubleshooting Domain Name Server Problems

It is possible for IP connectivity to work but for DNS name resolution to fail. To troubleshoot this situation, use one of the following methods to determine whether DNS is resolving the name of the destination:

- Ping the destination by name, and look for an error message indicating that the name could not be resolved.

- If you are working on a UNIX machine, use **nslookup** *<fully-qualified domain name>* to perform a DNS lookup on the destination. If it is successful, the host's address should be displayed:

```
unix% nslookup www.somedomain.com
Server:   localhost
Address:  127.0.0.1

Non-authoritative answer:
Name:     www.somedomain.com
Address:  10.1.1.1
```

If **nslookup** fails, the following output resembles the following sample output:

```
unix% nslookup www.somedomain.com
Server:   localhost
Address:  127.0.0.1

*** localhost can't find www.notvalid.com: Non-existent host/domain
```

If DNS correctly resolves the host's name, go to the section "Narrowing Down the Problem Domain," earlier in this chapter, to start troubleshooting again. Otherwise, continue troubleshooting as follows:

1 Determine which name server you are using; this can be found in different places on each operating system, so if you are unsure of how to find it, consult the device's manual. For examples:

   — On a Cisco router, type **show run** and look for the **name-server**.

   — On Windows 95 or 98, use **winipcfg.exe**.

   — On Windows 2000 or NT, use **ipconfig.exe**.

   — On a UNIX platform, type **cat /etc/resolv.conf** at a command prompt.

2 Verify that you can ping the name server using its IP address. If the ping fails, go to the section "Narrowing Down the Problem Domain," earlier in this chapter, to troubleshoot connectivity between the client and the name server.

3 Verify that you can resolve names within your domain. (For example, if your host is Host1.test.com, you should be able to resolve the names of other hosts in the test.com domain, such as host2.test.com.)

4 Verify that you can resolve one or more domain names outside your domain.

If you cannot resolve names from all domains except that of the destination, there might be a problem with the DNS for the destination host. Contact the administrator of the destination device.

If you cannot resolve names within your domain or a large number of external domains, contact your DNS administrator because there may be a problem with the local DNS (or your host could be using the wrong domain server).

Before Calling Cisco Systems' Technical Assistance Center

Before calling Cisco Systems's Technical Assistance Center (TAC), make sure that you have read through this chapter and completed the actions suggested for your system's problem.

Additionally, do the following and document the results so that the Cisco TAC can better assist you:

• Have a network diagram of your network or affected portion of your network ready. Make sure that all IP addresses and their associated network masks or prefix lengths are listed.

- Have any information that you gathered thus far while troubleshooting available for the TAC engineer.
- If the problem appears to be with only a few—fewer than four—routers, capture the output from **show tech** on these routers.

Dial-in or Telnet access also help considerably in effective problem resolution.

For More Information

For further information, including step-by-step configuration materials and full command examples for most IP-related commands, you can consult the following books and web pages:

- The Technical Assistance Center (TAC) web site on Cisco Connection Online (CCO), at www.cisco.com/tac
- The Cisco IOS online documentation on CCO, at www.cisco.com
- Stevens, W. Richard. *TCP/IP Illustrated, Volume 1*. Addison-Wesley.
- Comer, Douglas E. *Internetworking with TCP/IP, Volume I*. Prentice Hall.

CHAPTER 8

Troubleshooting Novell IPX

NetWare is a network operating system (NOS) and related support services environment created by Novell, Inc., and introduced to the market in the early 1980s. Then, networks were small and predominantly homogeneous, local-area network (LAN) workgroup communication was new, and the idea of a personal computer (PC) was just becoming popular.

Much of NetWare's networking technology was derived from Xerox Network Systems (XNS), a networking system created by Xerox Corporation in the late 1970s.

By the early 1990s, NetWare's NOS market share had risen to between 50 percent and 75 percent. With more than 500,000 NetWare networks installed worldwide and an accelerating movement to connect networks to other networks, NetWare and its supporting protocols often coexisted on the same physical channel with many other popular protocols, including TCP/IP, DECnet, and AppleTalk. Although networks today are predominately IP, there are some legacy Novel IPX traffic.

Novell Technology Basics

As an NOS environment, NetWare specifies the upper five layers of the OSI reference model. The parts of NetWare that occupy the upper five layers of the OSI model are as follows:

- NetWare Core Protocol (NCP)
- Service Advertisement Protocol (SAP)
- Routing Information Protocol (RIP)

NetWare provides file and printer sharing, support for various applications such as electronic mail transfer and database access, and other services. Like other NOSs, such as the network file system (NFS) from Sun Microsystems, Inc., and Windows NT from Microsoft Corporation, NetWare is based on a client/server architecture. In such architectures, clients (sometimes called workstations) request certain services such as file and printer access from servers.

Originally, NetWare clients were small PCs, whereas servers were slightly more powerful PCs. As NetWare became more popular, it was ported to other computing platforms. Currently, NetWare clients and servers can be represented by virtually any kind of computer system, from PCs to mainframes.

A primary characteristic of the client/server system is that remote access is transparent to the user. This is accomplished through remote procedure calls, a process by which a local computer program running on a client sends a procedure call to a remote server. The server executes the remote procedure call and returns the requested information to the local computer client.

Figure 8-1 illustrates a simplified view of NetWare's best-known protocols and their relationship to the OSI reference model. With appropriate drivers, NetWare can run on any media-access protocol. The figure lists those media-access protocols currently supported with NetWare drivers.

Figure 8-1 *NetWare and the OSI Reference Model*

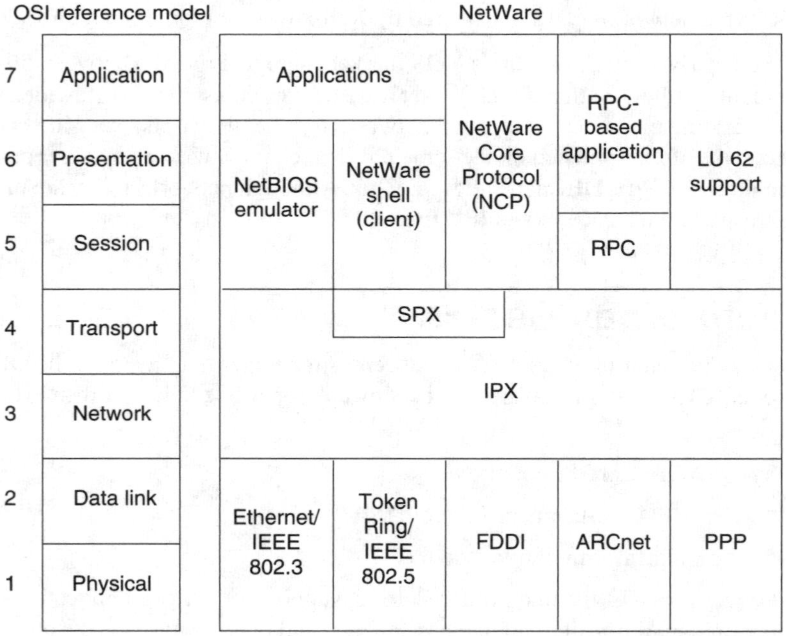

Media Access

NetWare runs on Ethernet/IEEE 802.3, Token Ring/IEEE 802.5, Fiber Distributed Data Interface (FDDI), Copper Distributed Data Interface (CDDI), and ARCnet. NetWare also works over synchronous wide-area network (WAN) links using the Point-to-Point Protocol (PPP).

The Network Layer

Internetwork Packet Exchange (IPX) is Novell's original network layer protocol. When a device to be communicated with is located on a different network, IPX routes the information to the destination through any intermediate networks. Figure 8-2 shows the IPX packet format.

Figure 8-2   *IPX Packet Format*

Checksum
Packet length
Transport control · Packet type
Destination network
Destination node
Destination socket
Source network
Source node
Source socket
Upper-layer data

The fields of the IPX packet are as follows:

- **Checksum**—A 16-bit field that is set to ones.

- **Packet length**—A 16-bit field that specifies the length, in bytes, of the complete IPX datagram. IPX packets can be any length, up to the media maximum transmission unit (MTU) size. There is no packet fragmentation.

- **Transport control**—An 8-bit field that indicates the number of routers that the packet has passed through. When the value of this field reaches 15, the packet is discarded under the assumption that a routing loop might be occurring. With the use of NetWare Links State Protocol (NLSP), an IPX packet can travel up to 127 hops to reach a destination.

- **Packet type**—An 8-bit field that specifies the upper-layer protocol to receive the packet's information. Two common values for this field are 5, which specifies Sequenced Packet Exchange (SPX), and 17, which specifies the NetWare Core Protocol (NCP).

- **Destination network (32-bit field), Destination node (48-bit field), and Destination socket (16-bit field)**—Fields that specify destination information.

- **Source network (32-bit field), Source node (48-bit field), and Source socket (16-bit field)**—Fields that specify source information.

- **Upper-layer data**—Information for upper-layer processes. This section of the packet is also referred to as the Higher Level Protocol Headers headers of the higher level NetWare protocols such as NCP or SPX. These headers occupy the data position of the IPX packet.

Although IPX was derived from XNS, it has several unique features. From the standpoint of routing, the encapsulation mechanisms of these two protocols represent the most important difference. Encapsulation is the process of packaging upper-layer protocol information and data into a frame. For Ethernet, XNS uses standard Ethernet encapsulation, whereas IPX packets are encapsulated in Ethernet Version 2.0 or IEEE 802.3, without the IEEE 802.2 information that typically accompanies these frames. Figure 8-3 illustrates Ethernet, standard IEEE 802.3, and IPX encapsulation.

NOTE   NetWare 4.0 supports encapsulation of IPX packets in standard IEEE 802.3 frames. It also supports Subnetwork Access Protocol (SNAP) encapsulation, which extends the IEEE 802.2 headers by providing a type code similar to that defined in the Ethernet specification.

Figure 8-3   *Ethernet, IEEE 802.3, and IPX Encapsulation Formats*

Ethernet	Standard IEEE 802.3	IPX
Destination address	Destination address	Destination address
Source address	Source address	Source address
Type	Length	Length
Upper-layer data	802.2 header	IPX data
	802.2 data	
CRC	CRC	CRC

To route packets in an internetwork, IPX uses a dynamic routing protocol called the Routing Information Protocol (RIP). Like XNS, RIP was derived from work done at Xerox for the XNS protocol family.

In addition to the difference in encapsulation mechanisms, Novell added a protocol called the Service Advertising Protocol (SAP) to its IPX protocol family. SAP allows nodes that provide services (such as file servers and print servers) to advertise their addresses and the services that they provide.

Novell also supports IBM logical unit (LU) 6.2 network addressable units (NAUs). LU 6.2 allows peer-to-peer connectivity across IBM communication environments. Using NetWare's LU 6.2 capability, NetWare nodes can exchange information across an IBM network. NetWare packets are encapsulated within LU 6.2 packets for transit across the IBM network.

The Transport Layer

Sequenced Packet Exchange (SPX) is the most commonly used NetWare transport protocol. Novell derived this protocol from the XNS Sequenced Packet Protocol (SPP). As with the Transmission Control Protocol (TCP) and many other transport protocols, SPX is a reliable, connection-oriented protocol that supplements the datagram service provided by Layer 3 protocols.

SPX is noted by Novell's documentation as follows: "SPX (Sequenced Packet Exchange) is a protocol within IPXODI. SPX is derived from Novell's IPX using the Xerox Sequenced Packet Protocol. It enhances the IPX protocol by supervising data sent out across the network."

Novell also offers Internet Protocol (IP) support in the form of User Datagram Protocol (UDP)/IP encapsulation of other Novell packets, such as SPX/IPX packets. IPX datagrams are encapsulated inside UDP/IP headers for transport across an IP-based internetwork. NetWare 5.0 runs native IP, but the previous versions can run IP in the form mentioned previously or NetWare/IP.

Upper-Layer Protocols

NetWare supports a wide variety of upper-layer protocols, but several are somewhat more popular than others. The NetWare shell runs in clients (often called workstations in the NetWare community) and intercepts application I/O calls to determine whether they require network access for satisfaction. If they do, the NetWare shell packages the requests and sends them to lower-layer software for processing and network transmission. If they do not require network access, they are simply passed to local I/O resources. Client applications are unaware of any network access required for completion of application calls. NetWare remote procedure call (NetWare RPC) is another more general redirection mechanism supported by Novell.

NCP is a series of server routines designed to satisfy application requests coming from, for example, the NetWare shell. Services provided by NCP include file access, printer access, name management, accounting, security, and file synchronization.

NetWare also supports the Network Basic Input/Output System (NetBIOS) session layer interface specification from IBM and Microsoft. NetWare's NetBIOS emulation software allows programs written to the industry-standard NetBIOS interface to run within the NetWare system.

NetWare application layer services include NetWare Message Handling Service (NetWare MHS), Btrieve, NetWare-loadable modules (NLMs), and various IBM connectivity features. NetWare MHS is a message delivery system that provides electronic mail transport. Btrieve is Novell's implementation of the binary tree (btree) database access mechanism. NLMs are implemented as add-on modules that attach into the NetWare system. NLMs for alternate protocol stacks, communication services, database services, and many other services are currently available from Novell and third parties.

Troubleshooting Novell IPX

This section presents protocol-related troubleshooting information for Novell IPX connectivity and performance problems. It describes specific Novell IPX symptoms, the problems that are likely to cause each symptom, and the solutions to those problems.

The following sections outline the most common issues in Novell IPX networks:

- Novell IPX: Client Cannot Connect to Server on Same LAN
- Novell IPX: Client Cannot Connect to Server on Remote LAN
- Novell IPX: Clients Cannot Connect to Server over Public Switched Network (PSN)
- Novell IPX: Client Cannot Connect to Server over Integrated Services Digital Network (ISDN)
- Novell NetBIOS: Applications Cannot Connect to Server over Router
- IPX RIP: No Connectivity over IPX Routing Information Protocol (RIP) Router
- IPX RIP: Service Advertisement Protocol Updates Not Propagated by Router
- IPX Enhanced IGRP: No Connectivity over IPX Enhanced Interior Gateway Routing Protocol Router
- IPX Enhanced IGRP: Routers Not Establishing Neighbors
- IPX Enhanced IGRP: SAP Updates Not Propagated by Router
- IPX Enhanced IGRP: Router Stuck in Active Mode
- Novell IPX: Intermittent Connectivity
- Novell IPX: Slow Performance

Novell IPX: Client Cannot Connect to Server on Same LAN

Symptom: Clients cannot make connections to servers located on the same LAN. Also, clients cannot connect to servers on remote networks.

Table 8-1 outlines the problems that might cause this symptom and describes solutions to those problems.

Table 8-1   *Novell IPX: Client Cannot Connect to Server on Same LAN*

Possible Problem	Solution
Misconfigured client or server	Verify that the software on both clients and servers is the current version, is configured correctly, and has loaded correctly. On clients, check the network drivers and the configuration specified in the net.cfg file.
	(On servers, make certain that SAPs[1] are being generated properly and that any NLMs[2] are loaded properly. Use the **track on** command to monitor routing and SAP activity.
	Check the encapsulation on clients and servers to make sure that they are not mismatched.
	For specific information on configuring your client or server, refer to the documentation provided with the device.
Not enough user licenses	Make sure that there is a sufficient number of NetWare user licenses available. Use the Monitor utility screen on a NetWare server to see the total number of connections available and the number of connections in use.
Mismatched network numbers	All servers attached to the same cable must bind to the same external network number. If there are mismatched network numbers, packets will not be forwarded properly.
	Watch for error messages on the system console similar to the following:
	• "Router configuration error detected"
	• "Node address claims network x should be y"
	These error messages indicate that a server on the LAN has a conflicting network number. *Node address* is the node address of the network card from which the incorrect address came. *x* is the network number specified in packets received from the node. *y* is the network number configured on the server generating the error.
	All servers on the same LAN must have the same external network number (if they use the same frame type). If the network numbers do not match, reconfigure the conflicting server with the correct external network number.
Client, server, or other hardware problem	Check all NIC[3] cards, transceivers, hub ports, switches, and other hardware. Check all appropriate LEDs to see if there are error indications. Replace any faulty or malfunctioning hardware.
	For information on troubleshooting a client, server, or other hardware problem not related to Cisco routers, refer to the documentation provided with the hardware.

continues

Table 8-1   *Novell IPX: Client Cannot Connect to Server on Same LAN (Continued)*

Possible Problem	Solution	
Media problem	**Step 1**	Check all cabling and connections. Make sure that cables are not damaged and that all connections are correct and make proper contact.
	Step 2	Use the **show interfaces** exec command to check for input or output errors, or other indications of problems on the media.
	Step 3	If the command output shows excessive errors, use the clear **interface counter** privileged exec command to clear the interface counters.
	Step 4	Check the output of the **show interfaces** command again. If the errors are incrementing rapidly, there is probably a problem with the media.
	For more detailed information on troubleshooting media problems, refer to the media troubleshooting chapter that covers the media type used in your network.	

[1]SAP = Service Advertising Protocol
[2]NLM = NetWare-loadable module
[3]NIC = network interface card

Novell IPX: Client Cannot Connect to Server on Remote LAN

Symptom: Clients cannot make connections to servers on another network over one or more routers interconnected by LAN networks. Clients can connect to servers on their local network. Table 8-2 outlines the problems that might cause this symptom and describes solutions to those problems.

NOTE   If clients cannot connect to servers on their local network, refer to the section "Novell IPX: Client Cannot Connect to Server on Same LAN," earlier in this chapter. If there is a WAN network between the local and remote LANs, WAN problems must be considered a source of problems as well. Refer to the IPX-specific WAN problems outlined later in this chapter, or to the general WAN problems outlined in other chapters in this book.

Table 8-2   *Novell IPX: Client Cannot Connect to Server on Remote LAN*

Possible Problem	Solution	
Router interface is down.	**Step 1**	Use the **show interfaces** exec command on the router to check the status of the router interfaces. Verify that the interface and line protocol are up.
	Step 2	If the interface is administratively down, use the **no shutdown interface configuration** command to bring the interface back up. (Q14)
	Step 3	If the interface or line protocol is down, refer to the media troubleshooting chapter that covers the media type used in your network.
Ethernet encapsulation methods are mismatched.	**Step 1**	Use the **show ipx interface** privileged exec command to check the encapsulation type specified in the router configuration. By default, Cisco routers use Novell's Frame Type Ethernet 802.3 encapsulation. (Cisco refers to this as "novell-ether" encapsulation.)
	Step 2	Compare the encapsulation type configured on router interfaces with the encapsulation type that is being used by clients and servers.
	Step 3	If the router uses one encapsulation type but the clients and servers use a different type, then there is a mismatch.
	Change the encapsulation type used on either the clients and servers or the router, as appropriate, so that all devices use the same encapsulation method. On routers, specify the encapsulation type with the **ipx network network encapsulation** *encapsulation-type* interface configuration command. For information on changing the encapsulation type on clients and servers, consult the vendor documentation.	
LIPX[1] problem has occurred.	If you are using NetWare 3.12 or above, and you have LIPX enabled, a client and server could conceivably negotiate a packet size larger than a router could support. This can cause intermediate routers to drop packets. Without LIPX, the server checks the network number for the buffer size request packet from the client, and if the network number is different than the server's (which means that the packet is from another network over a router), it orders clients to use 512 bytes (hard-coded) instead.	
	For information on configuring LIPX, refer to the vendor documentation.	

continues

Table 8-2   *Novell IPX: Client Cannot Connect to Server on Remote LAN (Continued)*

Possible Problem	Solution
Ring speed specification mismatch has occurred.	In a Token Ring environment, all devices must agree on the configured ring speed (4 or 16 Mbps), or connectivity will fail.
	Step 1 Use the **show interfaces token** exec command on the router. Look for the ring speed value in the output. Compare this value with the ring speed specification on Novell servers.
	Step 2 If the ring speeds do not match, change the server or router configuration, as appropriate, so that all stations agree on the ring speed. On routers, use the **ring-speed** interface configuration command to change the **ring speed**. For information about configuring the ring speed on Novell servers, consult the vendor documentation.
Duplicate node numbers on routers are present.	**Step 1** Use the **show running-config** privileged exec command to examine the current configuration of each router in the path.
	Step 2 Check the node number specified in the **ipx routing** *node* global configuration command. The node number is either a user-specified node number or the MAC address of the first Ethernet, Token Ring, or FDDI^2 interface card in the router.
	Step 3 The node number configured on each router must be unique. If the number is the same on multiple routers, enter the **no ipx routing** global configuration command to disable IPX routing on the router.
	Step 4 Reinitialize **IPX routing** by entering the **ipx routing** command (do not specify a node number). Use the **show running-config** command to verify that the rest of the IPX configuration is still correct.
Duplicate network numbers are present.	Every network number must be unique throughout the entire Novell IPX internetwork. A duplicate network number will prevent packets from being forwarded properly.
	Step 1 Use the **show ipx servers** and the **show ipx route** privileged exec commands. Check the output of these commands for server addresses that have been learned from the wrong interface.
	For example, if you know that you have a server on the local network with network number 3c.0000.0c01.2345, and the **show** command output shows that this server is located on a remote network, there is probably a server on the remote network that's using the same network number.
	Step 2 If you suspect a duplicate network number, use a process of elimination to identify the misconfigured server. This can be difficult, particularly if you do not have access to every network device in the Novell IPX internetwork. When you have identified the misconfigured server, modify the server configuration to eliminate the duplicate network number.

Table 8-2   *Novell IPX: Client Cannot Connect to Server on Remote LAN (Continued)*

Possible Problem	Solution
Router hardware problem has occurred.	Check all router ports, interface processors, and other router hardware. Make sure that cards are seated properly and that no hardware is damaged. Replace faulty or malfunctioning hardware. For detailed information on troubleshooting router hardware problems, refer to Chapter 3, "Troubleshooting Hardware and Booting."
Back-door bridge between segments exists.	**Step 1** Use the **show ipx traffic** exec command on intermediate routers. Determine whether the bad hop count field is incrementing. **Step 2** If the bad hop count counter is incrementing, use a network analyzer to look for packet loops on suspect segments. Look for RIP[3] and SAP updates as well. If a back-door bridge exists, you are likely to see hop counts that increment to 16, at which time the route disappears and reappears unpredictably. **Step 3** Look for packets from known *remote* network numbers that appear on the *local* network. Look for packets whose source address is the MAC[4] address of the remote node instead of the MAC address of the router. **Step 4** Examine packets on each segment. A back door is present on the segment if packets appear whose source address is the MAC address of a remote node instead of that of the router. **Step 5** Remove the back-door bridge to close the loop.
Routing protocol problem has occurred.	Misconfigurations and other routing protocol issues can cause connectivity and performance problems.

[1]LIPX = Large Internet Packet Exchange

[2]FDDI = Fiber Distributed Data Interface

[3]RIP = Routing Information Protocol

[4]MAC = Media Access Control

Novell IPX: Clients Cannot Connect to Server over PSN

Symptom: Clients cannot connect to servers over a packet-switched network (PSN), such as Frame Relay, X.25, or SMDS. Clients can connect to local servers.

Procedures for troubleshooting connectivity problems not specific to PSN environments are described in the section "Novell IPX: Client Cannot Connect to Server on Remote LAN," earlier in this chapter.

Table 8-3 outlines the problems that might cause this symptom and describes solutions to those problems.

Table 8-3   *Novell IPX: Client Cannot Connect to Server over PSN*

Possible Problem	Solution	
Address mapping error	Step 1	Use the **show running-config** privileged exec command to view the configuration of the router.
	Step 2	Depending on your PSN environment, look for any **x25 map ipx**, **frame-relay map ipx**,[1] or **smds static-map ipx**[2] interface configuration command entries in the router configuration.
		• Make sure that the address mapping specified by these commands is correct:
		• For X.25, address mapping maps host protocol addresses to the host's X.121 address.
		• For Frame Relay, address mapping maps a next-hop protocol address and the DLCI[3] used to connect to the address.
		• For SMDS, address mapping defines static entries for SMDS remote peer routers.
		For more information about configuring address maps, refer to the *Cisco IOS Wide Area Networking Configuration Guide and Wide Area Networking Command Reference.*
Encapsulation mismatch	Step 1	Use the **show interfaces** privileged exec command to determine the encapsulation type being used (such as X.25, Frame Relay, or SMDS encapsulation). Look for output similar to the following:
		``` Serial0 is up, line protocol is up Hardware is MCI Serial Internet address is 192.168.54.92 255.255.255.0 MTU 1500 bytes, BW 1544 Kbit, DLY 20000 usec, rely 255/ 255, load 1/255 Encapsulation FRAME-RELAY, loopback not set, keepalive set (10 sec) ```
	Step 2	If an **encapsulation** command is not present, the default is HDLC[4] encapsulation. For PSN interconnection, you must explicitly specify the proper encapsulation type (such as **encapsulation x25** for an X.25 connection).
		Configure the proper encapsulation type, and use the **show interfaces** command to verify that the encapsulation type is correct.
Misconfigured DLCI assignments (Frame Relay only)	Step 1	Use the **show frame-relay map** exec command on the hub router to see the Frame Relay map assignments currently configured.
	Step 2	Check each Frame Relay map statement to ensure that the DLCI assignments are correctly configured. Make sure that you use the DLCIs obtained from your Frame Relay provider. Remember that DLCI values are locally significant.

Table 8-3   *Novell IPX: Client Cannot Connect to Server over PSN (Continued)*

Possible Problem	Solution
Misconfigured LMI[5] type (Frame Relay only)	**Step 1** Use the **debug frame-relay lmi** privileged exec command to see the LMI type being used by the Frame Relay switch.
	Step 2 The LMI type is determined by your Frame Relay provider. Make sure that you use the LMI type specified by the provider.
Full Frame Relay broadcast queue (Frame Relay only)	This problem is most likely to occur on the hub router in a Frame Relay hub-and-spoke topology.
	Step 1 Use the **show interfaces** privileged exec command to check for dropped Frame Relay broadcast frames.
	Step 2 If the number of drops on the broadcast queue is excessively high, increase the size of the queue using the **frame-relay broadcast-queue size byte-rate packet-rate** interface configuration command. **Command syntax:** **frame-relay broadcast-queue** *size byte-rate packet-rate* **Command syntax:** *size*—Number of packets to be held in the broadcast queue. The default is 64 packets. *byte-rate*—Maximum number of bytes to be transmitted per second. The default is 256,000 bytes per second. *packet-rate*—Maximum number of packets to be transmitted per second. The default is 36 packets per second.
Hub router not forwarding SAPs (Frame Relay only)	In a Frame Relay hub-and-spoke topology, SAPs received on one of the hub router's interfaces will not be forwarded back out the same interface because of the split horizon rule, which states that an incoming packet cannot be placed on the same network interface from which it originated, preventing an infinite routing loop if a link fails.
	To allow SAPs to be forwarded appropriately, you must configure subinterfaces on the Frame Relay interface of the hub router. Assign a subinterface to each spoke site. The hub router will treat each subinterface as a physical interface, allowing it to advertise SAPs without violating the split horizon rule. For specific information on configuring subinterfaces, see the *Wide Area Networking Configuration Guide*.
	Note: Other problems can prevent a router from forwarding SAP packets. For more information, see the section "IPX RIP: SAP Updates Not Propagated by Router," later in this chapter.

continues

Table 8-3   *Novell IPX: Client Cannot Connect to Server over PSN (Continued)*

Possible Problem	Solution	
Missing or misconfigured multicast address (SMDS only)	**Step 1**	Use the **show running-config** privileged exec command to view the router configuration. Check for an **smds multicast ipx** interface configuration command entry.
	Step 2	If the command is not present, add it to the configuration. If the command is present, confirm that the multicast address configured is correct. The SMDS multicast address is specified by your SMDS provider.

[1]You can eliminate the need for Frame Relay address maps by using Inverse ARP instead. Use the **frame-relay interface-dlci** *dlci* **broadcast** interface configuration command to configure an interface to use Inverse ARP. For more information about the use of this command, refer to the *Cisco IOS Wide-Area Networking Configuration Guide* and *Wide Area Networking Command Reference*.

[2]DLCI = data-link connection identifier

[3]SMDS = Switched Multimegabit Data Service

[4]HDLC = High-Level Data Link Control

[5]LMI = Local Management Interface

Novell IPX: Client Cannot Connect to Server over ISDN

Symptom: Clients cannot connect to servers over an ISDN link. Clients can connect to local servers.

Procedures for troubleshooting connectivity problems not specific to ISDN environments are described in the section "Novell IPX: Client Cannot Connect to Server on Remote LAN," earlier in this chapter. Procedures for troubleshooting ISDN connectivity problems not specific to IPX environments are described in Chapter 17, "Troubleshooting ISDN Connections."

Table 8-4 outlines the problems that might cause this symptom and describes solutions to those problems.

Novell NetBIOS: Applications Cannot Connect to Server over Router

Symptom: Applications that use Novell NetBIOS (such as Windows 95) cannot connect to servers over a router. Clients cannot connect to servers on the same LAN.

Table 8-4   *Novell IPX: Client Cannot Connect to Server over ISDN*

Possible Problem	Solution	
Static RIP and SAP statements are missing or have been misconfigured.	Step 1	Use the **show running-config** privileged exec command to view the router configuration. Check for **ipx route** and **ipx sap** global configuration command entries.
		Both commands, which specify static routes and static SAP entries, respectively, are required in an ISDN environment so that clients and servers on the local network are aware of clients and servers on the remote network.
	Step 2	If you do not have static routes and static SAP entries configured, configure them using the **ipx route** and **ipx sap** commands. For detailed information on configuring static routes and SAP entries, refer to the *Cisco IOS Network Protocols Configuration Guide, Part 1* and *Network Protocols Command Reference, Part 1.*
Access lists specified in dialer lists have been misconfigured.	Step 1	Use the **show running-config** privileged exec command to view the router configuration. Check the access lists configured for use by dialer lists.
	Step 2	Make sure that the access lists deny only RIP routing updates, SAP advertisements, and Novell serialization packets. If other packets are denied, connectivity problems can occur.
	Step 3	Make sure that access lists end with an **access-list** *access-list-number* **permit –1** statement, which permits all other IPX traffic to trigger the dialer.

Table 8-5 outlines the problems that might cause this symptom and describes solutions to those problems.

Table 8-5   *Novell NetBIOS: Applications Cannot Connect to Server over Router*

Possible Problem	Solution	
Missing **ipx type-20-propagation** commands	Step 1	Use the **debug ipx packet** privileged exec command or a network analyzer to look for Novell packets with a specification of type 20.

continues

Table 8-5 *Novell NetBIOS: Applications Cannot Connect to Server over Router (Continued)*

Possible Problem	Solution
Missing **ipx type-20-propagation** commands *(continued)*	**Caution:** Exercise caution when using the **debug ipx packet** command. Because debugging output is assigned high priority in the CPU process, it can render the system unusable. For this reason, use **debug** commands only to troubleshoot specific problems or during troubleshooting sessions with Cisco technical support staff. Moreover, it is best to use **debug** commands during periods of lower network traffic and fewer users. Debugging during these periods decreases the likelihood that increased **debug** command processing overhead will affect system use.
	Step 2 Use the **show running-config** privileged exec command to check for **ipx type-20-propagation** interface configuration command entries on routers in the path from client to server.
	Step 3 If the **ipx type-20-propagation** command is not present, add it to the interface configuration for every router interface in the path from client to server.
Missing **ipx helper-address** command	**Step 1** Use the **debug ipx packet** privileged exec command or a network analyzer to look for Novell packets with a specification other than type 20 (such as type 0 or type 4). Sometimes applications do not conform to the Novell standard and use packet types other than type 20.
	Caution: Exercise caution when using the **debug ipx packet** command. Because debugging output is assigned high priority in the CPU process, it can render the system unusable. For this reason, use **debug** commands only to troubleshoot specific problems or during troubleshooting sessions with Cisco technical support staff. Moreover, it is best to use **debug** commands during periods of lower network traffic and fewer users. Debugging during these periods decreases the likelihood that increased **debug** command processing overhead will affect system use.
	Step 2 If you see packets other than type 20, use the **show running-config** privileged exec command to view the router configuration. Check to see whether the **ipx helper-address** interface configuration command is configured on the interface to which the client is attached.
	Step 3 If the **ipx helper-address** command is not present, configure it on the router interfaces. Make sure that the helper address is the IPX protocol address of the NetBIOS server that the client needs to reach. The following is the syntax for the **ipx helper-address** command: **ipx helper-address** *network.node*

Table 8-5   *Novell NetBIOS: Applications Cannot Connect to Server over Router (Continued)*

Possible Problem	Solution
Missing **ipx helper-address** command *(continued)*	**Syntax Description:** *network*—Network on which the target IPX server resides. This is an eight-digit hexadecimal number that uniquely identifies a network cable segment. It can be a number in the range 1 to FFFFFFFE. A network number of –1 indicates all-nets flooding. You do not need to specify leading zeros in the network number. For example, for the network number 000000AA, you can enter just **AA**. *node*—Node number of the target Novell server. This is a 48-bit value represented by a dotted triplet of four-digit hexadecimal numbers (xxxx.xxxx.xxxx). A node number of FFFF.FFFF.FFFF matches all servers.
Workstation not running NetBIOS over IPX	Make sure that your workstation is running NetBIOS over IPX, not NetBIOS over another protocol, such as NetBEUI. For information about what protocols your workstation is running, refer to the vendor documentation.

IPX RIP: No Connectivity over IPX RIP Router

Symptom: IPX RIP routers are blocking connections. Clients cannot connect to servers over one or more routers running IPX RIP.

NOTE	Procedures for troubleshooting connectivity problems not specific to IPX RIP routing are described in the section "Novell IPX: Client Cannot Connect to Server on Remote LAN," earlier in this chapter.

Table 8-6 outlines the problems that might cause this symptom and describes solutions to those problems.

Table 8-6   *IPX RIP: No Connectivity over IPX RIP Router*

Possible Problem	Solution	
IPX RIP routing not configured or misconfigured on the router	**Step 1**	Use the **show running-config** privileged exec command to view the router configuration.
	Step 2	Check the configuration to make sure that there is an **ipx routing** global configuration command entry. If there is not, enter the **ipx routing** command to enable IPX routing.
		Issuing the **ipx routing** command on a router automatically enables IPX RIP routing on all interfaces that have a network number assigned to them.

continues

Table 8-6   *IPX RIP: No Connectivity over IPX RIP Router (Continued)*

Possible Problem	Solution	
Missing **ipx network** commands on interface	**Step 1**	Use the **show ipx interface** privileged exec command to view the state of all IPX interfaces.
	Step 2	If the output indicates that there are no interfaces running IPX, or if an interface that should be running IPX is not, you must configure the appropriate interfaces with an IPX address. The Novell server administrator can provide the **IPX network** *number* for the segment to which your router is attached.

To enable IPX protocol processing on an interface, enter the **ipx network** *number* interface configuration command:

ipx network *network* [**encapsulation** *encapsulation-type* [**secondary**]]

Syntax description:

- *network*—Network number. This is an eight-digit hexadecimal number that uniquely identifies a network cable segment. It can be a number in the range 1 to FFFFFFFE. You do not need to specify leading zeros in the network number. For example, for the network number 000000AA, you can enter just **AA**.

- **encapsulation** *encapsulation-type*—(Optional) Type of encapsulation. It can be one of the following values:

  - **arpa**—(For Ethernet interfaces only.) Use Novell's Ethernet II encapsulation. This encapsulation is recommended for networks that handle both TCP/IP and IPX traffic.

  - **hdlc**—(For serial interfaces only.) Use HDLC encapsulation.

  - **novell-ether**—(For Ethernet interfaces only.) Use Novell's Ethernet 802.3 encapsulation. This encapsulation consists of a standard 802.3 MAC header followed directly by the IPX header with a checksum of FFFF. It is the default encapsulation used by NetWare Version 3.11.

  - **sap**—*For Ethernet interfaces:* Use Novell's Ethernet 802.2 encapsulation. This encapsulation consists of a standard 802.3 MAC header followed by an 802.2 LLC header. This is the default encapsulation used by NetWare Version 4.0. *For Token Ring interfaces:* This encapsulation consists of a standard 802.5 MAC header followed by an 802.2 LLC header. *For FDDI interfaces:* This encapsulation consists of a standard FDDI MAC header followed by an 802.2 LLC header.

Table 8-6   *IPX RIP: No Connectivity over IPX RIP Router (Continued)*

Possible Problem	Solution
Missing **ipx network** commands on interface *(continued)*	— **snap**—*For Ethernet interfaces:* Use Novell Ethernet Snap encapsulation. This encapsulation consists of a standard 802.3 MAC header followed by an 802.2 SNAP LLC header. *For Token Ring and FDDI interfaces:* This encapsulation consists of a standard 802.5 or FDDI MAC header followed by an 802.2 SNAP LLC header. — **secondary**—(Optional) Indicates an additional network configured after the first (primary) network.
RIP timer mismatch	You can change RIP timer values changed on servers running NetWare 4.x or later. Mismatches between routers and servers can cause connectivity problems.
	Step 1 Use the **show ipx interfaces** privileged exec command on the router to view the state of IPX interfaces. Look for output similar to the following: ``` C4500#show ipx interface [...] Updates each 60 seconds, aging multiples RIP: 3 SAP: 3 [...] ``` Compare the timer value configured on the router with that configured on Novell servers.
	Step 2 The timer values configured on servers and routers should be the same across the whole IPX network. Reconfigure the router or the servers to bring the timer values into conformance. On the router, use the **ipx update-time** interface configuration command to change the RIP timer interval. For information on changing the timer value configured on Novell servers, consult your server documentation.
Router not propagating RIP updates	**Step 1** Use the **debug ipx routing** activity privileged exec command on the router. Look for routing updates sent by the router out each interface.
	Step 2 If you do not see RIP updates being sent out the interfaces, try disabling RIP routing using the no **ipx routing** global configuration command and then re-enabling it using the **ipx routing** command. Use the **show running-config** command to verify that the rest of the IPX configuration is still correct.
	Step 3 If disabling and re-enabling IPX does not work, try restarting the router.

continues

Table 8-6   *IPX RIP: No Connectivity over IPX RIP Router (Continued)*

Possible Problem	Solution
Misconfigured network filters	**Step 1** Use the **show access-lists** privileged exec command on suspect routers to see whether there are Novell IPX access lists configured.
	Step 2 Use the **show running-config** privileged exec command to view the router configuration. You can see whether access lists are specified in an **ipx input-network-filter** or **ipx output-network-filter** interface configuration command.

Examples:

In the following example, access list 876 controls which networks are added to the routing table when IPX routing updates are received on Ethernet interface 1:

```
access-list 876 permit 1b
interface ethernet 1
ipx input-network-filter 876
```

Routing updates for network 1b will be accepted. Routing updates for all other networks are implicitly denied and are not added to the routing table.

The following example is a variation of the preceding that explicitly denies network 1a and explicitly allows updates for all other networks:

```
access-list 876 deny 1a
access-list 876 permit -1
```

Step 3 If access lists are used by one of these commands, disable the filters using the **no ipx input-network-filter** or **no ipx output-network-filter** commands.

Step 4 Check whether the client can access the server normally. If the connection is successful, one or more access list needs modification.

Step 5 To isolate the problem access list, apply one IPX filter at a time until you can no longer create connections.

Step 6 When the problem access list is isolated, examine each **access-list** statement to see whether it blocks traffic from desired networks. If it does, configure explicit **permit** statements for networks that you want to be advertised normally in updates.

Step 7 After altering the access list, re-enable the filter to make sure that connections between the client and the server still work. Continue testing access lists until all your filters are enabled and the client can still connect to the server.

Table 8-6   *IPX RIP: No Connectivity over IPX RIP Router (Continued)*

Possible Problem	Solution	
Routes not redistributed correctly Routes not redistributed correctly	Step 1	Use the **show ipx route** privileged exec command to see the IPX routing table.
	Step 2	Examine the routing table and make sure that routes have been learned by the expected protocol and from the expected interface.
	Step 3	Use the **show running-config** privileged exec command to view the router configuration. Check each **ipx router** global configuration command entry and the associated **redistribute** commands, if any.
	Step 4	Make certain that redistribution is configured between IPX RIP and the desired protocols. Make sure that all the desired networks are specified for redistribution.
		Note: Route redistribution is enabled automatically between IPX RIP and Enhanced IGRP,[1] and between IPX RIP and NLSP.[2]
		For detailed information on configuring route redistribution, see the *Network Protocols Configuration Guide, Part 1.*
Router not propagating SAPs	For information on troubleshooting this problem, refer to the section "IPX RIP: SAP Updates Not Propagated by Router," later in this chapter.	

[1]Enhanced IGRP = Enhanced Interior Gateway Routing Protocol

[2]NLSP = NetWare Link Services Protocol

IPX RIP: SAP Updates Not Propagated by Router

Symptom: Novell SAP packets are not forwarded through a router running IPX RIP. Clients might be incapable of connecting to servers over one or more routers, or they might intermittently be capable of connecting.

NOTE   Procedures for troubleshooting IPX RIP problems not specific to SAPs are described in the section "IPX RIP: No Connectivity over IPX RIP Router," earlier in this chapter. Additional problems relating to intermittent connectivity problems are described in the section "Novell IPX: Intermittent Connectivity," later in this chapter.

Table 8-7 outlines the problems that might cause this symptom and describes solutions to those problems.

Table 8-7   *IPX RIP: SAP Updates Not Propagated by Router*

Possible Problem	Solution
SAP timer mismatch has occurred.	**Step 1** Use the **show running-config** privileged exec command to view the router configuration. Look for **ipx sap-interval** interface configuration command entries.
	Example:
	In the following example, SAP updates are sent (and expected) on serial interface 0 every 5 minutes:
	``` interface serial 0 ipx sap-interval 5 ```
	Step 2 On LAN interfaces, it is recommended that you use the default SAP interval of 1 minute because the interval on servers cannot be changed. To restore the default value, use the **no ipx sap-interval** command. The following is the syntax for the **ipx sap-interval** command:
	ipx sap-interval *minutes*
	no ipx sap-interval
	Syntax description:
	minutes—Interval, in minutes, between SAP updates sent by the communication server. The default value is 1 minute. If minutes is 0, periodic updates are never sent.
	On serial interfaces, make sure that whatever interval you configure is the same on both sides of the serial link. Use the **ipx sap-interval** interface configuration command to change the SAP interval.
SAP filters have been misconfigured.	**Step 1** Use the **show access-lists** privileged exec command on suspect routers to see whether there are Novell IPX access lists configured. Use the **show running-config** privileged exec command to see whether there are SAP filters that use any of the configured access lists. At the end of this chapter is a list of Novell SAPs that includes the SAP description and hex and decimal values.
	Step 2 If SAP filters are configured, disable them by removing **ipx input-sap-filter** and **ipx output-sap-filter** interface configuration commands as appropriate (using the **no** version of the command).
	Step 3 Use the **debug ipx sap activity** privileged exec command to see whether SAP traffic is forwarded normally. The **debug** command output shows the server name, network number, and MAC address of SAP packets.

Table 8-7   *IPX RIP: SAP Updates Not Propagated by Router (Continued)*

Possible Problem		Solution
SAP filters have been misconfigured. *(continued)*		**Caution**: Because debugging output is assigned high priority in the CPU process, it can render the system unusable. For this reason, use **debug** commands only to troubleshoot specific problems or during troubleshooting sessions with Cisco technical support staff. Moreover, it is best to use **debug** commands during periods of lower network traffic and fewer users. Debugging during these periods decreases the likelihood that increased **debug** command processing overhead will affect system use.
	Step 4	If SAP information is forwarded properly by the router, a SAP filter is causing SAP updates to be dropped by the router.
	Step 5	To isolate the problem SAP filter, re-enable filters one at a time until SAP packets are no longer forwarded by the router.
	Step 6	Change the referenced access list to allow the SAP traffic that you want to be forwarded to pass through the router. Make sure that all necessary ports are configured with an explicit **permit** statement.
	Step 7	Continue enabling filters one at a time, checking to see that SAP traffic is still being forwarded properly until you have verified that all filters are configured properly.
Novell server is not sending SAP updates.	Step 1	Use the **debug ipx sap activity** privileged exec command or a protocol analyzer to look for SAP updates from servers.
		Caution: Because debugging output is assigned high priority in the CPU process, it can render the system unusable. For this reason, use **debug** commands only to troubleshoot specific problems or during troubleshooting sessions with Cisco technical support staff. Moreover, it is best to use **debug** commands during periods of lower network traffic and fewer users. Debugging during these periods decreases the likelihood that increased **debug** command processing overhead will affect system use.
	Step 2	If a server is not sending SAP updates, make sure that the server is attached to the network and is up and running.
	Step 3	Make sure that the server is properly configured to send SAPs. For information on configuring your server software properly, refer to your vendor documentation.

continues

Table 8-7   *IPX RIP: SAP Updates Not Propagated by Router (Continued)*

Possible Problem	Solution
Novell servers are not processing SAP updates as quickly as the router is generating them.	**Step 1** Use the **show interfaces** privileged exec command to check for output drops.
	Step 2 If there are excessive drops, use the **show ipx servers** exec command on the router. Compare the output of this command with the output of the **display servers** system console command on Novell servers.
	Step 3 If the **display servers** output for a Novell server shows only a partial listing of the SAP entries shown by the router, the Novell servers might not be capable of processing SAP updates as quickly as the router is generating them.
	Step 4 Use the **ipx output-sap-delay** interface configuration command to configure the delay between packets in a multipacket SAP update. Novell specifies a delay of 55 ms.
	The following is the syntax for the **ipx output-sap-delay** command:
	ipx output-sap-delay *delay*
	Syntax description:
	• *delay*—Delay, in milliseconds, between packets in a multiple-packet SAP update.

IPX Enhanced IGRP: No Connectivity over IPX Enhanced IGRP Router

Symptom: IPX Enhanced IGRP routers are blocking connections. Clients cannot connect to servers over one or more routers running IPX Enhanced IGRP.

NOTE   Procedures for troubleshooting connectivity problems not specific to IPX Enhanced IGRP routing are described in the section "Novell IPX: Client Cannot Connect to Server on Remote LAN," earlier in this chapter.

Table 8-8 outlines the problems that might cause this symptom and describes solutions to those problems.

Table 8-8   *IPX Enhanced IGRP: No Connectivity over IPX Enhanced IGRP Router*

Possible Problem	Solution
IPX Enhanced IGRP is not configured or is misconfigured on the router.	Unlike IPX RIP, IPX Enhanced IGRP is *not* enabled by default on all interfaces when the **ipx routing** global configuration command is issued.

Step 1   Use the **show running-config** privileged exec command to view the router configuration.

Step 2   Check the configuration to make sure that there is an **ipx routing** global configuration command entry. This command enables IPX routing globally.

Step 3   If the command is not present, use the **ipx routing** global configuration command to enable IPX routing. The following is the syntax for the **ipx routing** command:

ipx routing [*node*]

Syntax description:

- *node*—(Optional) Node number of the router. This is a 48-bit value represented by a dotted triplet of four-digit hexadecimal numbers (xxxx.xxxx.xxxx). It must not be a multicast address.

If you omit *node*, the router uses the hardware MAC address currently assigned to it as its node address. This is the MAC address of the first Ethernet, Token Ring, or FDDI interface card. If no satisfactory interfaces are present in the router (for example, there are only serial interfaces), you must specify *node*.

Step 4   Check the router configuration for an **ipx router eigrp** *autonomous-system-number* global configuration command and associated **ipx network** interface configuration commands.

Step 5   If these commands are not present, configure the Enhanced IGRP process and then assign it to the appropriate interfaces with the **ipx network** commands.

The following example enables RIP on networks 1 and 2, and Enhanced IGRP on network 1:

```
ipx routing
!
interface ethernet 0
 ipx network 1
!
interface ethernet 1
 ipx network 2
!
ipx router eigrp 100
 network 1
```

continues

Table 8-8   *IPX Enhanced IGRP: No Connectivity over IPX Enhanced IGRP Router (Continued)*

Possible Problem	Solution	
The **ipx network** command is missing on the interface.	**Step 1**	Use the **show ipx interface** privileged exec command to view the state of all IPX interfaces.
	Step 2	If the output indicates that there are no interfaces running IPX, or if an interface that should be running IPX is not, you must configure the appropriate interfaces with an IPX address. To enable IPX protocol processing on an interface, enter the **ipx network** *number* interface configuration command.
IPX RIP is not enabled on the network with connected Novell servers.	Novell servers do not understand IPX Enhanced IGRP. You must ensure that IPX RIP is enabled on interfaces connected to LAN segments with attached Novell servers. Use the **show running-config** privileged exec command on suspect routers to view the router configuration. Make sure that any interfaces connected to a LAN segment with attached Novell servers have IPX RIP enabled. It is not necessary to disable the other routing protocol, but running IPX Enhanced IGRP and IPX RIP on the same interface can sometimes create performance problems.	
Filters have been misconfigured.	**Step 1**	Use the **show access-lists** privileged exec command on suspect routers to see whether there are Novell IPX access lists configured.
	Step 2	Use the **show running-config** privileged exec command to view the router configuration. See whether access lists are specified in an **ipx input-network-filter** or **ipx output-network-filter** interface configuration command.
	Step 3	If access lists are used by one of these commands, disable the filters using the **no ipx input-network-filter** or **no ipx output-network-filter** commands.
	Step 4	Check whether the client can access the server normally. If the connection is successful, one or more access lists need modification.
	Step 5	To isolate the problem access list, apply one IPX filter at a time until you can no longer create connections.

Table 8-8   *IPX Enhanced IGRP: No Connectivity over IPX Enhanced IGRP Router (Continued)*

Possible Problem	Solution	
Filters have been misconfigured. *(continued)*	**Step 6**	When the problem access list is isolated, examine each **access-list** statement to see whether it is blocking traffic from desired networks. If it is, configure explicit **permit** statements for networks that you want to be advertised normally in updates.
	Step 7	After altering the access list, re-enable the filter to make sure that connections between the client and the server still work. Continue testing access lists until all your filters are enabled and the client can still connect to the server.
Routes are not redistributed properly.	Route redistribution between IPX Enhanced IGRP autonomous systems and between Enhanced IGRP and other routing protocols is not enabled by default. You must manually configure redistribution between different autonomous systems or routing protocols.	
	Step 1	Use the **show running-config** privileged exec command on any routers that border two Enhanced IGRP autonomous systems. Look for **redistribute** *protocol* IPX-router configuration command entries.
	Step 2	If the command is not present, you must enter the appropriate **redistribute** *protocol* command to allow route redistribution between different autonomous systems or routing protocols.
	For detailed information on configuring route redistribution, see the *Network Protocols Configuration Guide, Part 1*.	
Routers are not establishing neighbors properly.	For information on troubleshooting this problem, see the section "IPX Enhanced IGRP: Routers Not Establishing Neighbors," next.	
Router are not propagating SAPs.	For information on troubleshooting this problem, refer to the section "IPX Enhanced IGRP: SAP Updates Not Propagated by Router," later in this chapter.	

IPX Enhanced IGRP: Routers Not Establishing Neighbors

Symptom: IPX Enhanced IGRP routers do not establish neighbors properly. Routers that are known to be connected do not appear in the neighbor table.

NOTE   Procedures for troubleshooting IPX Enhanced IGRP problems not specific to establishing neighbors are described in the section "IPX Enhanced IGRP: No Connectivity over IPX Enhanced IGRP Router," earlier in this chapter.

Table 8-9 outlines the problems that might cause this symptom and describes solutions to those problems.

Table 8-9   *IPX Enhanced IGRP: Routers Not Establishing Neighbors*

Possible Problem	Solution	
Routers are in different autonomous systems.	**Step 1**	Neighbor relationships will not be established between routers in different autonomous systems. Make sure that the routers that you want to be neighbors are in the same autonomous system.
	Step 2	Use the **show running-config** privileged exec command to view the router configuration. Check the **ipx router eigrp** command entries to see which autonomous systems the router belongs to.
Hello or hold-time timer mismatch has occurred.	**Step 1**	Use the **show running-config** privileged exec command on each router in the network. Look for **ipx hello-interval eigrp** and **ipx hold-time eigrp** interface configuration command entries.
		The values configured by these commands should be the same for all IPX routers in the network.
	Step 2	If any router has a conflicting hello interval or hold-time value, reconfigure it to conform to the rest of the routers on the network.
		You can return these values to their defaults with the **no ipx hello-interval eigrp** and **no ipx hold-time interval eigrp** interface configuration commands.
Link problem has occurred.	**Step 1**	Use the **show interfaces** privileged exec command to check whether the interface is up and functioning correctly.
		The following is sample output from the **show interfaces** command:

```
Router#show interface fastethernet1/0
FastEthernet1/0 is up, line protocol is up
  Hardware is cyBus FastEthernet Interface, address is
0010.5498.d020 (bia 0010.
5498.d020)
    Internet address is 210.84.3.33/24
  MTU 1500 bytes, BW 100000 Kbit, DLY 100 usec, rely 230/
255, load 1/255
    Encapsulation ARPA, loopback not set, keepalive set
(10 sec), hdx, 100BaseTX/FX
```

	Step 2	Use the **show ipx eigrp** neighbors privileged exec command to make sure that all Enhanced IGRP neighbors are shown in the neighbor table.
	Step 3	If not all neighbors are in the neighbor table, there might be a link problem. Refer to other chapters in this book for information on troubleshooting specific link types.

IPX Enhanced IGRP: SAP Updates Not Propagated by Router

Symptom: Novell SAP packets are not forwarded through a router running IPX Enhanced IGRP. Clients might be incapable of connecting to servers over one or more routers, or they might connect only intermittently.

NOTE	Procedures for troubleshooting IPX Enhanced IGRP problems not specific to SAPs are described in the section "IPX Enhanced IGRP: No Connectivity over IPX Enhanced IGRP Router" earlier in this chapter.

Table 8-10 outlines the problems that might cause this symptom and describes solutions to those problems.

Table 8-10   *IPX Enhanced IGRP: SAP Updates Not Propagated by Router*

Possible Problem	Solution	
SAP filters have been misconfigured.	**Step 1**	Use the **show access-lists** privileged exec command on suspect routers to see whether there are Novell IPX access lists configured. Use the **show running-config** privileged exec command to see whether there are SAP filters that use any of the configured access lists. At the end of this chapter is a list of Novell SAPs that includes the SAP description and hex and decimal values.
	Step 2	If SAP filters are configured, disable them by removing **ipx input-sap-filter** and **ipx output-sap-filter** interface configuration commands as appropriate (using the **no** version of the command).
	Step 3	Use the **debug ipx sap** activity privileged exec command to see whether SAP traffic is being forwarded normally. The **debug** command output shows the server name, network number, and MAC address of SAP packets.
		Caution: Because debugging output is assigned high priority in the CPU process, it can render the system unusable. For this reason, use **debug** commands only to troubleshoot specific problems or during troubleshooting sessions with Cisco technical support staff. Moreover, it is best to use **debug** commands during periods of lower network traffic and fewer users. Debugging during these periods decreases the likelihood that increased **debug** command processing overhead will affect system use.
	Step 4	If SAP information is being forwarded properly by the router, a SAP filter is causing SAP updates to be dropped by the router.

continues

Table 8-10 *IPX Enhanced IGRP: SAP Updates Not Propagated by Router (Continued)*

Possible Problem	Solution
SAP filters have been misconfigured. *(continued)*	**Step 5** To isolate the problem SAP filter, re-enable filters one at a time until SAP packets are no longer forwarded by the router.
	Step 6 Change the referenced access list to allow the SAP traffic that you want to be forwarded to pass through the router. Make sure that all necessary ports are configured with an explicit **permit** statement.
	Step 7 Continue enabling filters one at a time, checking to see that SAP traffic is being forwarded properly until you have verified that all filters are configured properly.
SAP updates are being sent incrementally rather than periodically.	Connectivity problems can occur when LAN interfaces are configured to send incremental (not periodic) SAP updates on segments that have attached Novell clients or servers. Incremental SAP updates are sent only when there is a change in the SAP table.
	Step 1 Use the **show running-config** privileged exec command to view the router configuration. Look for **ipx sap-incremental eigrp** interface configuration command entries on interfaces with attached Novell clients or servers.
	Step 2 If the command is present and the interface in question has attached Novell clients or servers, you must disable the **ipx sap-incremental eigrp** command. This command should be configured on an interface only if all the nodes attached to that interface are Enhanced IGRP peers.
Link problem has occurred.	**Step 1** Use the **show interfaces** privileged exec command, and look for drops and interface resets.
	The following is sample output from the **show interfaces** command:

```
Router#show interface fastethernet 1/0
FastEthernet1/0 is up, line protocol is up
Hardware is cyBus FastEthernet Interface, address is
0010.5498.d020 (bia 0010. 5498.d020)
  Internet address is 208.84.3.33/24
  MTU 1500 bytes, BW 100000 Kbit, DLY 100 usec, rely 255/
255, load 1/255
  Encapsulation ARPA, loopback not set, keepalive set
(10 sec), hdx, 100BaseTX/FX
  ARP type: ARPA, ARP Timeout 04:00:00
  Last input 00:00:07, output 00:00:07, output hang never
  Last clearing of "show interface" counters never
  Queueing strategy: fifo
Output queue 0/40, 0 drops; input queue 0/75, 0 drops
```

Table 8-10   *IPX Enhanced IGRP: SAP Updates Not Propagated by Router (Continued)*

Possible Problem		Solution
Link problem has occurred. *(continued)*	**Step 2**	If you see many drops or interface resets, use the **debug ipx sap activity** privileged exec command and then the **clear ipx eigrp neighbor** privileged exec command.
		Caution: Because debugging output is assigned high priority in the CPU process, it can render the system unusable. For this reason, use **debug** commands only to troubleshoot specific problems or during troubleshooting sessions with Cisco technical support staff. Moreover, it is best to use **debug** commands during periods of lower network traffic and fewer users. Debugging during these periods decreases the likelihood that increased **debug** command processing overhead will affect system use.
		If there is a link problem, the **debug ipx sap activity** command will not produce any output.
	Step 3	Refer to the appropriate chapter elsewhere in this book for information on troubleshooting the particular link type. For example, for serial links, refer to Chapter 15, "Troubleshooting Serial Lines."

IPX Enhanced IGRP: Router Stuck in Active Mode

Symptom: An IPX Enhanced IGRP router is stuck in active mode. The router repeatedly sends error messages similar to the following to the console:

```
%DUAL-3-SIA: Route 3c.0800.0c00.4321 Stuck-in-Active
```

NOTE   Occasional messages of this type are not a cause for concern. This is how an Enhanced IGRP router recovers if it does not receive replies to its queries from all its neighbors. However, if these error messages occur frequently, you should investigate the problem.

For a more detailed explanation of Enhanced IGRP active mode, see the section "Enhanced IGRP and Active/Passive Modes," later in this chapter.

Table 8-11 outlines the problems that might cause this symptom and describes solutions to those problems.

Table 8-11 *IPX Enhanced IGRP: Router Stuck in Active Mode*

Possible Problem	Solution	
Active timer value is misconfigured.	**Step 1**	The active timer specifies the maximum period of time that an Enhanced IGRP router will wait for replies to its queries. If the active timer value is set too low, there might not be enough time for all the neighboring routers to send their replies to the active router. A value of 3 (3 minutes, which is the default value) is strongly recommended to allow all Enhanced IGRP neighbors to reply to queries.
	Step 2	Check the configuration of each Enhanced IGRP router using the **show running-config** privileged exec command. Look for a **timers active-time** router configuration command entry.
	Step 3	The value set by the **timers active-time** command should be consistent among routers in the same autonomous system. A value of 3 (3 minutes, which is the default value) is strongly recommended to allow all Enhanced IGRP neighbors to reply to queries.
Interface or other hardware problem has occurred.	**Step 1**	Use the **show ipx eigrp neighbors** exec command, and examine the Uptime and Q Cnt (queue count) fields in the output. The following is sample output from the **show ipx eigrp neighbors** command:

```
Router# show ipx eigrp neighbors
IPX EIGRP Neighbors for process 200
H Address            Interface     Hold Uptime  Q   Seq  SRTT  RTO
                                  (secs) (h:m:s) Cnt Num  (ms)  (ms)
6 90.0000.0c02.096e  Tunnel44444   13   0:30:57 0   21    9    20
5 80.0000.0c02.34f2  Fddi0         12   0:31:17 0   62   14    28
4 83.5500.2000.a83c  TokenRing2    13   0:32:36 0  626   16    32
3 98.0000.3040.a6b0  TokenRing1    12   0:32:37 0   43    9    20
2 80.0000.0c08.cbf9  Fddi0         12   0:32:37 0  624   19    38
1 85.aa00.0400.153c  Ethernet2     12   0:32:37 0  627   15    30
0 82.0000.0c03.4d4b  Hssi0         12   0:32:38 0  629   12    24
```

		If the uptime counter is continually resetting, or if the queue count is consistently high, there might be a hardware problem.
	Step 2	Check the output of the "Stuck-in-Active" error message. The output indicates the general direction of the problem node, but if there are multiple nodes in that direction, the problem could be in any one of them.
	Step 3	Make sure that the suspect router still works. Check the interfaces on the suspect router. Make sure that the interface and line protocol are up, and determine whether the interface is dropping packets. For more information on troubleshooting hardware, see Chapter 3.

Table 8-11   *IPX Enhanced IGRP: Router Stuck in Active Mode (Continued)*

Possible Problem	Solution	
Flapping route has occurred.	**Step 1**	Check for a flapping serial route (caused by heavy traffic load) by using the **show interfaces** privileged exec command. Flapping is a routing problem in which an advertised route between two nodes alternates (flaps) back and forth between two paths due to a network problem that causes intermittent interface failures. You might have a flapping route if there are large numbers of resets and carrier transitions.
	Step 2	If there is a flapping route, queries and replies might not be forwarded reliably. Route flapping caused by heavy traffic on a serial link can cause queries and replies to be lost, resulting in the active timer timing out.
		Take steps to reduce traffic on the link, or increase the bandwidth of the link.
		For more information about troubleshooting serial lines, refer to Chapter 15.

Enhanced IGRP and Active/Passive Modes

An Enhanced IGRP router can be in either passive or active mode. A router is said to be passive for a network when it has an established path to the network in its routing table. The route is in an active state when a router is undergoing a route recomputation. If there are always feasible successors, a route never has to go into active state and avoids a route recomputation.

If the Enhanced IGRP router loses the connection to a network, it becomes active for that network. The router sends out queries to all its neighbors to find a new route. The router remains in active mode until either it has received replies from all its neighbors or the active timer, which determines the maximum period of time a router will stay active, has expired.

If the router receives a reply from each of its neighbors, it computes the new next hop to the network and becomes passive for that network. However, if the active timer expires, the router removes any neighbors that did not reply from its neighbor table, again enters active mode, and issues a "Stuck-in-Active" message to the console.

Novell IPX: Intermittent Connectivity

Symptom: Connectivity between clients and servers is intermittent. Clients might be capable of connecting some of the time, but at other times no connectivity to certain servers or networks is possible.

Table 8-12 outlines the problems that might cause this symptom and describes solutions to those problems.

Table 8-12 *Novell IPX: Intermittent Connectivity*

Possible Problem	Solution
SAP timer mismatch has occurred.	**Step 1** Use the **show running-config** privileged exec command to view the router configuration. Look for **ipx sap-interval** interface configuration command entries.
	Step 2 On LAN interfaces, it is recommended that you use the default SAP interval of 1 minute because the interval on servers cannot be changed. To restore the default value, you can use the **no ipx sap-interval** command.
	On serial interfaces, make sure that whatever interval you configure is the same on both sides of the serial link. Use the **ipx sap-interval** interface configuration command to change the SAP interval.
RIP timer mismatch has occurred.	You can change RIP timer values on servers running NetWare 4.x or later. Mismatches between routers and servers can cause connectivity problems.

	Step 1 Use the **show ipx interfaces** privileged exec command on the router to view the state of IPX interfaces. Look for output similar to the following:
	
	`C4500#show ipx interface`
	`[...]`
	`Updates each 60 seconds, aging multiples RIP:`
	`3 SAP: 3`
	`[...]`
	
	Compare the timer value configured on the router with that configured on Novell servers.

	Step 2 The timer values configured on servers and routers should be the same across the entire IPX network.
	Reconfigure the router or the servers to bring the timer values into conformance. On the router, use the **ipx update-time** interface configuration command to change the RIP timer interval.
	For information on changing the timer value configured on Novell servers, consult your server documentation.

Table 8-12   *Novell IPX: Intermittent Connectivity (Continued)*

Possible Problem	Solution
SAP updates are sent incrementally rather than periodically.	In IPX Enhanced IGRP environments, problems can occur when interfaces are configured to send incremental (not periodic) SAP updates on segments that have attached Novell servers. (Incremental SAP updates are sent only when there is a change in the SAP table.)
	Step 1 Use the **show running-config** privileged exec command to view the router configuration. Check to see whether there are **ipx sap-incremental eigrp** interface configuration command entries enabled on interfaces with attached Novell clients or servers.
	Step 2 If the **incremental** command is present and the interface in question has attached Novell clients or servers, you must disable the **ipx sap-incremental eigrp** command by using the **no** version of the command. This command should be configured on an interface only if all the nodes attached to that interface are Enhanced IGRP peers.
Novell servers not processing SAP updates as quickly as the router is generating them.	**Step 1** Use the **show interfaces** privileged exec command to check for output drops.
	Step 2 If there are excessive drops, use the **show ipx servers** exec command on the router. Compare the output of this command with the output of the **display servers** system console command on Novell servers.
	Step 3 If the **display servers** output for a Novell server shows only a partial listing of the SAP entries shown by the router, the Novell servers might be incapable of processing SAP updates as quickly as the router is generating them.
	Step 4 Use the **ipx output-sap-delay** interface configuration command to configure the delay between packets in a multipacket SAP update. Novell specifies a delay of 55 ms.

continues

Table 8-12 *Novell IPX: Intermittent Connectivity (Continued)*

Possible Problem	Solution
SAP updates are dropped from the hub router's output queue.	Slow serial lines can cause the router to drop SAP packets before they are transmitted.

Step 1 Use the **show interfaces serial** exec command, and examine the output queue drops field. A large number of dropped packets might indicate that SAP updates are being dropped before they can be transmitted across the serial link.

Step 2 Use the **show ipx servers** exec command on the router. Compare the output of this command with the output of the **display servers** system console command on Novell servers.

Step 3 If the **display servers** output for a Novell server shows only a partial listing of the SAP entries shown by the router, the router might be dropping SAP packets from the output queue.

Step 4 Eliminate the forwarding of any SAP updates that are not absolutely necessary. Configure filters using the **ipx input-sap-filter**, **ipx output-sap-filter**, and **ipx router-sap-filter** interface configuration commands, as appropriate.

Step 5 Increasing the output hold queue on the serial interface might also improve performance. Use the **hold-queue** *length* **out** interface configuration command to increase the output **hold queue** *length*. The default output **hold-queue** limit is 100 packets. The general rule when using the **hold-queue** command is to use a small output **hold-queue** limit for slow links. This approach prevents storing packets at a rate that exceeds the transmission capability of the link. For fast links, use a large output **hold-queue** limit. A fast link may be busy for a short time (and thus require the hold queue), but it can empty the output hold queue quickly when capacity returns.

Step 6 If SAP filters and increased queue lengths do not solve the problem, increase the available bandwidth, if possible. Add a second serial line, or obtain a single link with more available bandwidth.[1]

Table 8-12   *Novell IPX: Intermittent Connectivity (Continued)*

Possible Problem	Solution
Router is stuck in active mode (EIGRP only).	If you consistently receive "Stuck-in-Active" messages about a particular network, you probably have a flapping route (typically caused by heavy traffic load).
	Route flapping can cause routes to come and go in the routing table, resulting in intermittent connectivity to some networks.
	Take steps to reduce traffic on the link, or increase the bandwidth of the link.
	For more information about troubleshooting serial lines, refer to Chapter 15.

[1]If increasing the bandwidth is not possible, buffer management might help alleviate the problem. Contact the Cisco Technical Assistance Center for assistance in tuning buffers.

Novell IPX: Slow Performance

Symptom: Slow network performance is experienced in a Novell IPX network.

Table 8-13 outlines the problems that might cause this symptom and describes solutions to those problems.

Table 8-13   *Novell IPX: Slow Performance*

Possible Problem	Solution	
Novell servers are not processing SAP updates as quickly as the router is generating them.	Step 1	Use the **show interfaces** privileged exec command to check for output drops.
	Step 2	If there are excessive drops, use the **show ipx servers** exec command on the router. Compare the output of this command with the output of the **display servers** system console command on Novell servers.
	Step 3	If the **display servers** output for a Novell server shows only a partial listing of the SAP entries shown by the router, the Novell servers might be incapable of processing SAP updates as quickly as the router is generating them.
	Step 4	Use the **ipx output-sap-delay** interface configuration command to configure the delay between packets in a multipacket SAP update. Novell specifies a delay of 55 ms.

continues

Table 8-13 *Novell IPX: Slow Performance (Continued)*

Possible Problem	Solution
Periodic SAP updates are using excessive bandwidth.	In a non-IPX RIP environment (such as on a serial link running Enhanced IGRP), you can reduce SAP traffic by configuring routers to send incremental rather than periodic SAP updates. Incremental SAP updates are sent only when there is a change to the SAP table.
	You should have incremental SAP updates enabled only on interfaces that have no Novell clients or servers attached. Novell clients and servers require periodic SAP updates.
	Use the **ipx sap-incremental eigrp** interface configuration command to enable incremental SAP updates.
IPX RIP and IPX Enhanced IGRP are enabled on the same interface.	Running both IPX Enhanced IGRP and IPX RIP on the same interface is sometimes desired or required in an IPX network. However, doing so can cause performance problems in some cases by creating excess traffic and processor overhead.
	Step 1 Use the **show running-config** privileged exec command to view the router configuration. Check the **network** router configuration commands associated with **ipx router rip** and the **ipx router eigrp** global configuration commands to see whether both routing protocols are enabled on the same interface.
	Step 2 If both protocols are enabled, determine whether one or the other can be disabled without affecting the proper operation of the network. If there is no need for both protocols to be running on the same interface, remove the superfluous configuration commands as appropriate.
Router is stuck in active mode (EIGRP only).	If you consistently receive "Stuck-in-Active" messages about a particular network, you probably have a flapping route (typically caused by heavy traffic load).
	Route flapping can force routers to use a less preferred route, resulting in slower performance.
	Take steps to reduce traffic on the link, or increase the bandwidth of the link.
	For more information about troubleshooting serial lines, refer to Chapter 15.

Novell SAPs

The list of Novell SAPs in Table 8-14 is contributed unverified information from various sources. Novell, in an official capacity, does not and has not provided any of this information.

Table 8-14   *Novell SAPs, Their Descriptions, and Their Decimal and Hex Values*

Decimal	Hex	SAP Description
0	0000	Unknown
1	0001	User
2	0002	User Group
3	0003	Print Queue or Print Group
4	0004	File Server (SLIST source)
5	0005	Job Server
6	0006	Gateway
7	0007	Print Server or Silent Print Server
8	0008	Archive Queue
9	0009	Archive Server
10	000a	Job Queue
11	000b	Administration
15	000F	Novell TI-RPC
23	0017	Diagnostics
32	0020	NetBIOS
33	0021	NAS SNA Gateway
35	0023	NACS Async Gateway or Asynchronous Gateway
36	0024	Remote Bridge or Routing Service
38	0026	Bridge Server or Asynchronous Bridge Server
39	0027	TCP/IP Gateway Server
40	0028	Point to Point (Eicon) X.25 Bridge Server
41	0029	Eicon 3270 Gateway
42	002a	CHI Corp
44	002c	PC Chalkboard
45	002d	Time Synchronization Server or Asynchronous Timer
46	002e	ARCserve 5.0/Palindrome Backup Director 4.x (PDB4)
69	0045	DI3270 Gateway

continues

Table 8-14 *Novell SAPs, Their Descriptions, and Their Decimal and Hex Values (Continued)*

Decimal	Hex	SAP Description
71	0047	Advertising Print Server
74	004a	NetBlazer Modems
75	004b	Btrieve VAP/NLM 5.0
76	004c	Netware SQL VAP/NLM Server
77	004d	Xtree Network Version Netware XTree
80	0050	Btrieve VAP 4.11
82	0052	QuickLink (Cubix)
83	0053	Print Queue User
88	0058	Multipoint X.25 Eicon Router
96	0060	STLB/NLM
100	0064	ARCserve
102	0066	ARCserve 3.0
114	0072	WAN Copy Utility
122	007a	TES-Netware for VMS
146	0092	WATCOM Debugger or Emerald Tape Backup Server
149	0095	DDA OBGYN
152	0098	Netware Access Server (Asynchronous gateway)
154	009a	Netware for VMS II or Named Pipe Server
155	009b	Netware Access Server
158	009e	Portable Netware Server or SunLink NVT
161	00a1	Powerchute APC UPS NLM
170	00aa	LAWserve
172	00ac	Compaq IDA Status Monitor
256	0100	PIPE STAIL
258	0102	LAN Protect Bindery
259	0103	Oracle DataBase Server
263	0107	Netware 386 or RSPX Remote Console
271	010f	Novell SNA Gateway
273	0111	Test Server
274	0112	Print Server (HP)

Table 8-14 *Novell SAPs, Their Descriptions, and Their Decimal and Hex Values (Continued)*

Decimal	Hex	SAP Description
276	0114	CSA MUX (f/Communications Executive)
277	0115	CSA LCA (f/Communications Executive)
278	0116	CSA CM (f/Communications Executive)
279	0117	CSA SMA (f/Communications Executive)
280	0118	CSA DBA (f/Communications Executive)
281	0119	CSA NMA (f/Communications Executive)
282	011a	CSA SSA (f/Communications Executive)
283	011b	CSA STATUS (f/Communications Executive)
286	011e	CSA APPC (f/Communications Executive)
294	0126	SNA TEST SSA Profile
298	012a	CSA TRACE (f/Communications Executive)
299	012b	Netware for SAA
301	012e	IKARUS virus scan utility
304	0130	Communications Executive
307	0133	NNS Domain Server or Netware Naming Services Domain
309	0135	Netware Naming Services Profile
311	0137	Netware 386 Print Queue or NNS Print Queue
321	0141	LAN Spool Server (Vap, Intel)
338	0152	IRMALAN Gateway
340	0154	Named Pipe Server
358	0166	NetWare Management
360	0168	Intel PICKIT Comm Server or Intel CAS Talk Server
369	0171	Unknown
371	0173	Compaq
372	0174	Compaq SNMP Agent
373	0175	Compaq
384	0180	XTree Server or XTree Tools
394	018A	Unknown Running on a Novell Server
432	01b0	GARP Gateway (net research)

continues

Table 8-14   *Novell SAPs, Their Descriptions, and Their Decimal and Hex Values (Continued)*

Decimal	Hex	SAP Description
433	01b1	Binfview (Lan Support Group)
447	01bf	Intel LanDesk Manager
458	01ca	AXTEC
459	01cb	Shiva NetModem/E
460	01cc	Shiva LanRover/E
461	01cd	Shiva LanRover/T
472	01d8	Castelle FAXPress Server
474	01da	Castelle LANPress Print Server
476	01dc	Castille FAX/Xerox 7033 Fax Server/Excel Lan Fax
496	01f0	LEGATO
501	01f5	LEGATO
563	0233	NMS Agent or Netware Management Agent
567	0237	NMS IPX Discovery or LANtern Read/Write Channel
568	0238	NMS IP Discovery or LANtern Trap/Alarm Channel
570	023a	LABtern
572	023c	MAVERICK
574	023e	Unknown Running on a Novell Server
575	023f	Used by 11 various Novell Servers/Novell SMDR
590	024e	NetWare connect
618	026a	Network Management Service (NMS) Console
619	026b	Time Synchronization Server (Netware 4.x)
632	0278	Directory Server (Netware 4.x)
989	03dd	Banyan ENS for Netware Client NLM
772	0304	Novell SAA Gateway
776	0308	COM or VERMED 1
778	030a	Galacticomm's Worldgroup Server
780	030c	Intel Netport 2 or HP JetDirect or HP Quicksilver
800	0320	Attachmate Gateway
807	0327	Microsoft Diagnostics

Table 8-14   *Novell SAPs, Their Descriptions, and Their Decimal and Hex Values (Continued)*

Decimal	Hex	SAP Description
808	0328	WATCOM SQL server
821	0335	MultiTech Systems Multisynch Comm Server
835	2101	Performance Technology Instant Internet
853	0355	Arcada Backup Exec
858	0358	MSLCD1
865	0361	NETINELO
894	037e	Twelve Novell file servers in the PC3M family
895	037f	ViruSafe Notify
902	0386	HP Bridge
903	0387	HP Hub
916	0394	NetWare SAA Gateway
923	039b	Lotus Notes
951	03b7	Certus Anti Virus NLM
964	03c4	ARCserve 4.0 (Cheyenne)
967	03c7	LANspool 3.5 (Intel)
983	03d7	Lexmark printer server (type 4033-011)
984	03d8	Lexmark XLE printer server (type 4033-301)
990	03de	Gupta Sequel Base Server or NetWare SQL
993	03e1	Univel Unixware
996	03e4	Univel Unixware
1020	03fc	Intel Netport
1021	03fd	Print Server Queue
1196	04ac	On-Time Scheduler NLM
1034	040A	ipnServer Running on a Novell Server
1035	040B	Unknown
1037	040D	LVERRMAN Running on a Novell Server
1038	040E	LVLIC Running on a Novell Server

continues

Table 8-14 *Novell SAPs, Their Descriptions, and Their Decimal and Hex Values (Continued)*

Decimal	Hex	SAP Description
1040	0410	Unknown
		Running on a Novell Server
1044	0414	Kyocera
1065	0429	Site Lock Virus (Brightworks)
1074	0432	UFHELP R
1075	0433	Synoptics 281x Advanced SNMP Agent
1092	0444	Microsoft NT SNA Server
1096	0448	Oracle
1100	044c	ARCserve 5.01
1111	0457	Canon GP55
		Running on a Canon GP55 network printer
1114	045a	QMS Printers
1115	045b	Dell SCSI Array (DSA) Monitor
1169	0491	NetBlazer Modems
1200	04b0	CD-Net (Meridian)
1217	04C1	Unknown
1299	0513	Emulux NQA
		Something from Emulex
1312	0520	Site lock checks
1321	0529	Site Lock Checks (Brightworks)
1325	052d	Citrix OS/2 App Server
1343	0535	Tektronix
1344	0536	Milan
1387	056b	IBM 8235 modem server
1388	056c	Shiva LanRover/E PLUS
1389	056d	Shiva LanRover/T PLUS
1408	0580	McAfee's NetShield anti-virus
1466	05BA	Compatible Systems Routers
1569	0621	IBM AntiVirus NLM
1571	0623	Unknown
		Running on a Novell Server

Table 8-14   *Novell SAPs, Their Descriptions, and Their Decimal and Hex Values (Continued)*

Decimal	Hex	SAP Description
1900	076C	Xerox
1947	079b	Shiva LanRover/E 115
1958	079c	Shiva LanRover/T 115
2154	086a	ISSC collector NLMs
2175	087f	ISSC DAS agent for AIX
2857	0b29	Site Lock
3113	0c29	Site Lock Applications
3116	0c2c	Licensing Server
9088	2380	LAI Site Lock
9100	238c	Meeting Maker
18440	4808	Site Lock Server or Site Lock Metering VAP/NLM
21845	5555	Site Lock User
25362	6312	Tapeware
28416	6f00	Rabbit Gateway (3270)
30467	7703	MODEM
32770	8002	NetPort Printers (Intel) or LANport
32776	8008	WordPerfect Network Version
34238	85BE	Cisco Enhanced Interior Routing Protocol (EIGRP)
34952	8888	WordPerfect Network Version or Quick Network Management
36864	9000	McAfee's NetShield antivirus
38404	9604	CSA-NT_MON
46760	b6a8	Ocean Isle Reachout Remote Control
61727	f11f	Site Lock Metering VAP/NLM
61951	f1ff	Site Lock
62723	F503	SCA-NT
64507	fbfb	TopCall III fax server
65535	ffff	Any Service or Wildcard

Troubleshooting AppleTalk

In the early 1980s, as Apple Computer, Inc., was preparing to introduce the Macintosh computer, Apple engineers knew that networks would become a critical need. They wanted to ensure that a Macintosh-based network was a seamless extension of the revolutionary Macintosh user interface. With these two goals in mind, Apple decided to build a network interface into every Macintosh and to integrate that interface into the desktop environment. Apple's new network architecture was called AppleTalk.

Although AppleTalk is a proprietary network, Apple has published AppleTalk specifications in an attempt to encourage third-party development. Today, many companies—including Novell, Inc., and Microsoft Corporation—are successfully marketing AppleTalk-based products.

The original implementation of AppleTalk, which was designed for local workgroups, is now commonly referred to as AppleTalk Phase 1. With the installation of more than 1.5 million Macintosh computers in the first five years of the product's life, however, Apple found that some large corporations were exceeding the built-in limits of AppleTalk Phase 1, so they enhanced the protocol. The enhanced protocol, known as AppleTalk Phase 2, improved the routing capabilities of AppleTalk and allowed AppleTalk to run successfully in larger networks.

AppleTalk Technology Basics

AppleTalk was designed as a client/server distributed network system. In other words, users share network resources (such as files and printers) with other users. Computers supplying these network resources are called *servers*; computers using a server's network resources are called *clients*. Interaction with servers is essentially transparent to the user because the computer itself determines the location of the requested material and accesses it without further information from the user. In addition to their ease of use, distributed systems also enjoy an economic advantage over peer-to-peer systems because important materials can be located in a few, rather than many, locations.

In Figure 9-1, AppleTalk protocols are shown adjacent to the Open System Interconnection (OSI) reference model layers to which they map.

Figure 9-1   *AppleTalk and the OSI Reference Model*

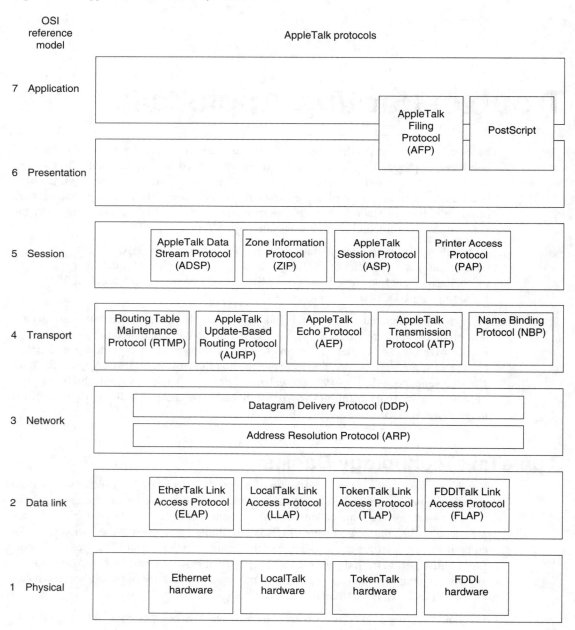

Media Access

Apple designed AppleTalk to be link-layer independent. In other words, it can theoretically run on top of any link-layer implementation. Apple supports a variety of link-layer implementations, including Ethernet, Token Ring, Fiber Distributed Data Interface (FDDI), and LocalTalk. Apple refers to AppleTalk over Ethernet as EtherTalk, to AppleTalk over Token Ring as TokenTalk, and to AppleTalk over FDDI as FDDITalk. The link-layer protocols that support AppleTalk over these media are EtherTalk Link Access Protocol (ELAP), LocalTalk Link Access Protocol (LLAP), TokenTalk Link Access Protocol (TLAP), and FDDITalk Link Access Protocol (FLAP). LocalTalk is Apple's proprietary media-access system. It is based on contention access, bus topology, and baseband signaling, and runs on shielded twisted-pair media at 230.4 kbps. The physical interface is EIA/TIA-422 (formerly RS-422), a balanced electrical interface supported by EIA/TIA-449 (formerly RS-449). LocalTalk segments can span up to 300 meters and support a maximum of 32 nodes.

The Network Layer

This section describes AppleTalk network-layer concepts and protocols. It includes discussion of protocol address assignment, network entities, and AppleTalk protocols that provide OSI reference model Layer 3 functionality.

Protocol Address Assignment

To ensure minimal network administrator overhead, AppleTalk node addresses are assigned dynamically. When a Macintosh running AppleTalk starts up, it chooses a protocol (network-layer) address and checks whether that address is currently in use. If it is not, the new node has successfully assigned itself an address. If the address is currently in use, the node with the conflicting address sends a message indicating a problem, and the new node chooses another address and repeats the process. Figure 9-2 shows the AppleTalk address selection process.

The mechanics of AppleTalk address selection are media dependent. The AppleTalk Address Resolution Protocol (AARP) is used to associate AppleTalk addresses with particular media addresses. AARP also associates other protocol addresses with hardware addresses. When either AppleTalk or any other protocol stack must send a packet to another network node, the protocol address is passed to AARP. AARP first checks an address cache to see whether the relationship between the protocol and the hardware address is already known. If it is, that relationship is passed up to the inquiring protocol stack. If it is not, AARP initiates a broadcast or multicast message inquiring about the hardware address for the protocol address in question. If the broadcast reaches a node with the specified protocol address, that node replies with its hardware address. This information is passed up to the inquiring protocol stack, which uses the hardware address in communications with that node.

Figure 9-2 *The AppleTalk Address Selection Process*

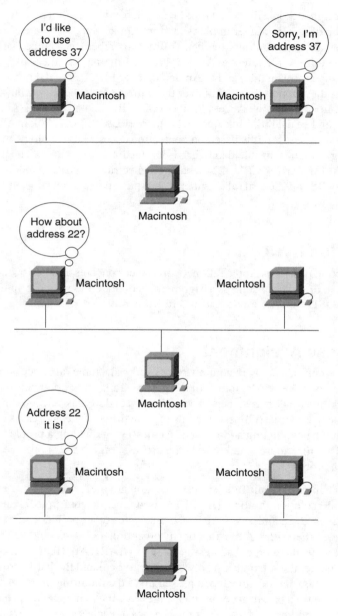

Network Entities

AppleTalk identifies several network entities. The most elemental is a node, which is simply any device connected to an AppleTalk network. The most common nodes are Macintosh computers and laser printers, but many other types of computers are also capable of AppleTalk communication, including IBM PCs, Digital Equipment Corporation VAX computers, and a variety of workstations. The next entity defined by AppleTalk is the network. An AppleTalk network is simply a single logical cable. Although the logical cable is frequently a single physical cable, some sites use bridges to interconnect several physical cables. Finally, an AppleTalk zone is a logical group of (possibly noncontiguous) networks. These AppleTalk entities are shown in Figure 9-3.

Figure 9-3   *AppleTalk Entities*

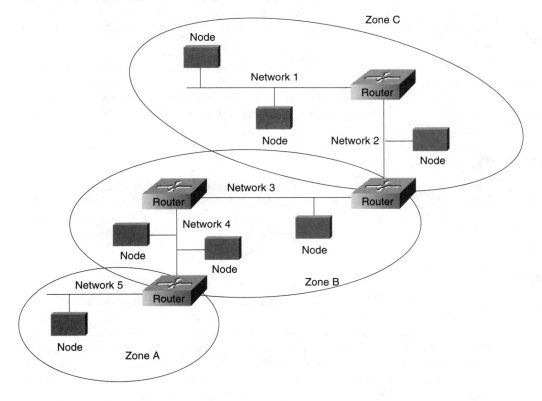

Datagram Delivery Protocol

AppleTalk's primary network-layer protocol is the Datagram Delivery Protocol (DDP). DDP provides connectionless service between network sockets. Sockets can be assigned either statically or dynamically.

AppleTalk addresses, which are administered by the DDP, consist of two components: a 16-bit network number and an 8-bit node number. The two components are usually written as decimal numbers, separated by a period (for example, 10.1 means network 10, node 1). When an 8-bit socket identifying a particular process is added to the network number and node number, a unique process on a network is specified.

AppleTalk Phase 2 distinguishes between nonextended and extended networks. In a nonextended network such as LocalTalk, each AppleTalk node number is unique. Nonextended networks were the sole network type defined in AppleTalk Phase 1. In an extended network such as EtherTalk and TokenTalk, each network number/node number combination is unique.

Zones are defined by the AppleTalk network manager during the router configuration process. Each node in an AppleTalk network belongs to a single specific zone. Extended networks can have multiple zones associated with them. Nodes on extended networks can belong to any single zone associated with the extended network.

The Transport Layer

AppleTalk's transport layer is implemented by several protocols: Routing Table Maintenance Protocol (RTMP), AppleTalk Update Routing Protocol (AURP), AppleTalk Echo Protocol (AEP), AppleTalk Transaction Protocol (ATP), and Name Binding Protocol (NBP).

RTMP

The protocol that establishes and maintains AppleTalk routing tables is RTMP. RTMP routing tables contain an entry for each network that a datagram can reach. Each entry includes the router port that leads to the destination network, the node ID of the next router to receive the packet, the distance in hops to the destination network, and the current state of the entry (good, suspect, or bad). Periodic exchange of routing tables allows the routers in an internetwork to ensure that they supply current and consistent information. Figure 9-4 shows a sample RTMP table and the corresponding network architecture.

Figure 9-4   *A Sample AppleTalk Routing Table*

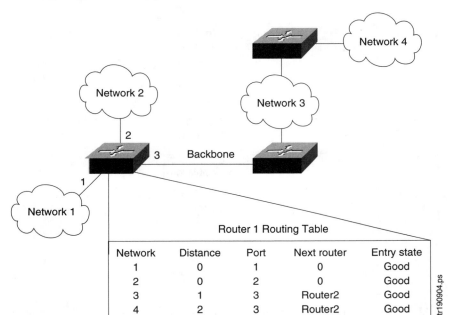

Network	Distance	Port	Next router	Entry state
1	0	1	0	Good
2	0	2	0	Good
3	1	3	Router2	Good
4	2	3	Router2	Good

AppleTalk's NBP associates AppleTalk names (expressed as network-visible entities, or NVEs) with addresses. An NVE is an AppleTalk network-addressable service, such as a socket. NVEs are associated with one or more entity names and attribute lists. Entity names are character strings such as printer@net1, whereas attribute lists specify NVE characteristics.

Named NVEs are associated with network addresses through the process of name binding. Name binding can be done when the user node is first started up, or dynamically, immediately before first use. NBP orchestrates the name binding process, which includes name registration, name confirmation, name deletion, and name lookup.

Zones allow name lookup in a group of logically related nodes. To look up names within a zone, an NBP lookup request is sent to a local router, which sends a broadcast request to all networks that have nodes belonging to the target zone. The Zone Information Protocol (ZIP) coordinates this effort.

ZIP maintains network number-to-zone name mappings in zone information tables (ZITs). ZITs are stored in routers, which are the primary users of ZIP, but end nodes use ZIP during the startup process to choose their zone and to acquire internetwork zone information. ZIP uses RTMP routing tables to keep up with network topology changes. When ZIP finds a routing table entry that is not in the ZIT, it creates a new ZIT entry. Figure 9-5 shows a sample ZIT.

Figure 9-5 *A Sample AppleTalk ZIT*

Network number	Zone
1	My
2	Your
3	Marketing
4	Documentation
5-5	Sales

AURP

AURP allows a network administrator to connect two or more AppleTalk internetworks through a foreign network (such as Transmission Control Protocol/Internet Protocol [TCP/IP]) to form an AppleTalk wide-area network (WAN). The connection is called a tunnel, which functions as a single, virtual data link between the AppleTalk internetworks, as shown in Figure 9-6.

Figure 9-6 *An AppleTalk Tunnel*

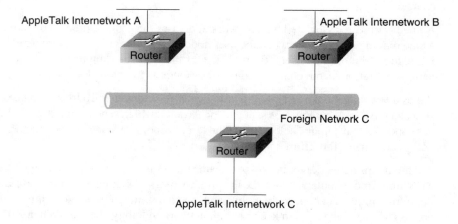

A router that connects an AppleTalk internetwork to a tunnel (that is, a router that runs AURP) is called an *exterior router*. The exterior router sends AppleTalk data packets and routing information through the foreign network by encapsulating the packets with the header information required by the foreign network system. The receiving exterior router removes the foreign header information and sends the packets out the appropriate interface. Packets are encapsulated in User Datagram Protocol (UDP) headers in the initial implementation of AURP.

When only two exterior routers are connected to a tunnel, that tunnel is called a *point-to-point tunnel*. When more than two exterior routers are connected to the tunnel, that tunnel is called a *multipoint tunnel*. If all exterior routers connected to a multipoint tunnel can send packets to each other, the tunnel is said to be *fully connected*. If one or more exterior routers are not aware of other exterior routers, the tunnel is said to be *partially connected*. Each exterior router functions both as an AppleTalk router within its local internetwork and as an end node in the foreign network that connects the AppleTalk internetworks.

The main function of AURP is to maintain accurate routing tables for the entire AppleTalk WAN by the exchange of routing information between exterior routers. In addition, AURP encapsulates AppleTalk data packets with the headers required by the foreign network.

AURP uses the principle of split horizons (which states that it is never useful to send information about a route back in the direction from which the information came) to limit the propagation of routing updates. For that reason, an exterior router sends routing information about only the networks that comprise its local internetwork to other exterior routers connected to the tunnel.

When an exterior router becomes aware of another exterior router on the tunnel, the two exterior routers exchange their lists of network numbers and associated zone information. Thereafter, an exterior router sends routing information only when the following events occur:

- A network is added to the routing table.
- A change in the path to a network causes the exterior router to access that network through its local internetwork rather than through the tunnel or to access that network through the tunnel rather than through the local internetwork.
- A network is removed from the routing table.
- The distance to a network is changed.

When an exterior router receives AppleTalk data packets or routing information that needs to be forwarded over the tunnel, the AURP module converts that information to AURP packets. The AURP packets are encapsulated in the header information required by the foreign network and sent over the tunnel to the destination exterior router, as shown in Figure 9-7.

Figure 9-7 *The AURP Architectural Model*

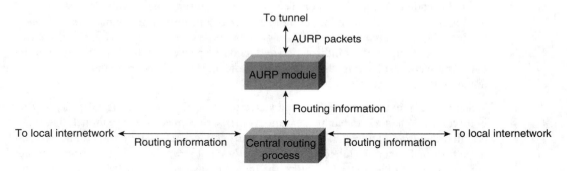

At the destination exterior router, the AURP module removes the headers required by the foreign system from the AURP packets and sends AppleTalk data packets to their final destination. The exterior router uses the AURP packets that contain routing information to update its routing information tables but does not propagate that information to any other exterior router.

NOTE   As defined by Apple Computer, AURP converts RTMP and ZIP packets into AURP packets and vice versa. As implemented by Cisco, AURP converts Enhanced IGRP packets as well as RTMP and ZIP packets.

AEP

AEP is an extremely simple protocol which generates packets that can be used to test the reachability of various network nodes.

ATP

ATP is suitable for transaction-based applications such as those found in banks or retail stores. ATP transactions consist of requests (from clients) and replies (from servers). Each request/reply pair has a particular transaction ID. Transactions occur between two socket clients. ATP uses exactly once (XO) and at-least-once (ALO) transactions. XO transactions are used in situations where performing the transaction more than once would be unacceptable. Banking transactions are examples of transactions that, if performed more than once, result in invalid data.

ATP is capable of most important transport-layer functions, including data acknowledgment and retransmission, packet sequencing, and fragmentation and reassembly. ATP limits message segmentation to eight packets, and ATP packets cannot contain more than 578 data bytes.

Upper-Layer Protocols

AppleTalk supports several upper-layer protocols:

- AppleTalk Data Stream Protocol (ADSP) establishes and maintains full-duplex data streams between two sockets in an AppleTalk internetwork. ADSP is a reliable protocol in that it guarantees that data bytes are delivered in the same order as sent and that they are not duplicated. ADSP numbers each data byte to keep track of the individual elements of the data stream. ADSP also specifies a flow-control mechanism. The destination can essentially slow source transmissions by reducing the size of its advertised receive window. ADSP also provides an out-of-band control message mechanism. Attention packets are used as the vehicle for moving out-of-band control messages between two AppleTalk entities. These packets use a separate sequence number stream to differentiate them from normal ADSP data packets.

- The AppleTalk Session Protocol (ASP) establishes and maintains sessions (logical conversations) between an AppleTalk client and a server.

- AppleTalk's Printer Access Protocol (PAP) is a connection-oriented protocol that establishes and maintains connections between clients and servers. (Use of the term *printer* in this protocol's title is purely historical.)

- The AppleTalk Filing Protocol (AFP) helps clients share server files across a network.

Troubleshooting AppleTalk

This section presents protocol-related troubleshooting information for AppleTalk connectivity and performance problems. In addition to general AppleTalk problems, this chapter also covers AppleTalk Enhanced IGRP, AppleTalk Remote Access (ARA), AURP, and FDDITalk problems.

The section "AppleTalk Configuration and Troubleshooting Tips" discusses preventive measures and tips to help you configure and troubleshoot your AppleTalk internetwork. The remaining sections describe specific AppleTalk symptoms, the problems that are likely to cause each symptom, and the solutions to those problems.

The following sections cover the most common network issues in AppleTalk environments:

- AppleTalk: Users Cannot Access Zones or Services
- AppleTalk: Zones Missing from Chooser
- AppleTalk: No Devices in Chooser
- AppleTalk: Network Services Intermittently Unavailable

- AppleTalk: Old Zone Names Appear in Chooser (Phantom Zones)
- AppleTalk: Connections to Services Drop
- AppleTalk: Interface Fails to Initialize AppleTalk
- AppleTalk: Port Stuck in Restarting or Acquiring Mode
- AppleTalk Enhanced IGRP: Clients Cannot Connect to Servers
- AppleTalk Enhanced IGRP: Routers Not Establishing Neighbors
- AppleTalk Enhanced IGRP: Routes Missing from Routing Table
- AppleTalk Enhanced IGRP: Poor Performance
- AppleTalk Enhanced IGRP: Router Stuck in Active Mode
- AURP: Routes Not Propagated Through AURP Tunnel
- FDDITalk: No Zone Associated with Routes
- ARA: ARA Client Unable to Connect to ARA Server
- ARA: Connection Hangs After "Communicating At..." Message
- ARA: Cannot Send or Receive Data over ARA Dialin Connection
- ARA: Slow Performance from Dialin Connection

AppleTalk Configuration and Troubleshooting Tips

This section offers configuration and troubleshooting tips that can help you prevent or more easily repair problems in AppleTalk internetworks.

It consists of information on preventing AppleTalk problems, preventing internetwork reconfiguration problems, changing zone names, using AppleTalk Discovery Mode, and forcing an interface up to allow a router to start functioning if the network is misconfigured.

Preventing AppleTalk Problems

Table 9-1 lists suggestions to help you avoid problems when configuring a router for AppleTalk.

Table 9-1   *AppleTalk Problem-Prevention Techniques*

Preventive Action	Description
Every router connected to a network must agree on the configuration of that network	Every router on an AppleTalk network (that is, on a single cable segment) must agree on the configuration of the network. Therefore, network numbers, cable ranges, timer values, zone names, and other parameters should be the same for every router on the segment.

Table 9-1   *AppleTalk Problem-Prevention Techniques (Continued)*

Preventive Action	Description
Every network number in an internetwork must be unique	Network numbers must be unique throughout the entire AppleTalk network. Duplicate network numbers can cause connectivity- and performance-related problems.
Upgrade to AppleTalk Phase 2 wherever possible	To minimize interoperability problems, upgrade all router Ethernet interfaces to Phase 2. Phase 1/Phase 2 networks can be problematic, as can nonextended AppleTalk networks.
When you change a router or interface configuration, enable the **debug apple error privileged exec** command to log errors	The **debug apple error privileged exec** command tracks the progress and status of changes in the internetwork and alerts you to any errors. You can also run this command periodically when you suspect network problems. In a stable network, this command returns no output.
	You can establish a syslog server at your site and add the configuration command **appletalk event-logging** to the router. This keeps a running log, with timestamps, of significant events on your network.
	Disable this command with the **no debug apple error** command when you have completed diagnostic activities.
Design your network with attention to the direction in which traffic will flow and minimize the number of different zones in the internetwork	Careful zone mapping can minimize unnecessary NBP[1] traffic. Planning is particularly important in WANs where traffic traversing WAN links (such as X.25) can be quite expensive.
	In System 6, if a user opens the Chooser, the Macintosh continually sends NBP BrReq packets. In System 7, a logarithmic backoff minimizes the amount of traffic generated.
	Give all the backbone/WAN connections the same zone name rather than put them in a zone with a LAN.
	In most internetworks, it is not desirable to have the zone names for all backbone or WAN connections appear in the Chooser list. If you make the zone name of all the WAN links the same (for example, ZZSerial), only that entry appears in the Chooser menu.
Set AppleTalk timers to the default values throughout the internetwork	A stable network almost *never* has nondefault timer values configured. Timers should be consistently set to the *same value* throughout the internetwork, or at a minimum, throughout the backbone of the internetwork. Check with a qualified technical support representative before changing AppleTalk default timer values.

[1]NBP = Name Binding Protocol

Using the test appletalk and ping appletalk Commands

In Cisco IOS Release 11.1 and later, use the **test appletalk privileged exec** command to help identify problem nodes. Use the **nbp** (Name Binding Protocol) options of the command to perform informational lookups of NBP-registered entities. The information returned when using the **nbp** options is useful when AppleTalk zones are listed in the Chooser but services in those zones are unavailable.

When running the **test appletalk** facility, use the confirm option to check that a name of a specified type is registered on a device. For example, **nbp confirm 24279.173 my-mac:AFPServer@engineering** confirms that the name my-mac is registered on the device 24279.173 in the engineering zone. The object type is AFPServer. The syntax for the **nbp confirm** command is as follows:

nbp confirm *appletalk-address* [:skt] *object:type@zone*

The syntax description is as follows:

- *appletalk-address*—AppleTalk network address in the form **network.node**. The argument **network** is the 16-bit network number in the range 1 to 65279. The argument node is the 8-bit node number in the range 0 to 254. Both numbers are decimal.

- :skt—(Optional) Name of socket.

- *object:type*—Name of device and the type of service. The colon (:) between object and type is required.

- *@zone*—Name of the AppleTalk zone where the entity *object:type* resides.

In software releases prior to Cisco IOS Release 11.0, the **ping appletalk** exec command serves a similar function. Use this command to verify that a node is reachable from the router (for example, **ping appletalk 2.24 ping**s AppleTalk node 2.24).

The following display shows input to and output from the user **ping** command:

```
Router> ping appletalk 2.24
Type escape sequence to abort.
Sending 5, 100-byte AppleTalk Echoes to 2.24, timeout is 2 seconds:
!!!!!
Success rate is 100 percent, round-trip min/avg/max = 4/4/8 ms
```

The **ping** privileged exec command also supports several AppleTalk parameters that provide additional troubleshooting capabilities. In particular, use the NBP option when AppleTalk zones are listed in the Chooser but services are not available. If a configuration contains the **appletalk name-lookup-interval** global configuration command, the NBP option of the AppleTalk **ping** function displays nodes by their NBP registration names.

Preventing Internetwork Reconfiguration Problems

Configuration conflicts can occur when zone names or cable range numbers are changed. In particular, problems arise when routing devices about which you are not administratively aware exist on the internetwork.

Many devices can act as routers (for example, Novell servers, Pathworks servers, or UNIX workstations running CAP to do print and file sharing). In general, if you are changing zone names or cable range numbers in your internetwork, shut down all routers so that a Cisco router does not see a conflict and prevent AppleTalk from initializing on the interface.

Before changing the configuration, use the **show appletalk neighbors** exec command to determine on which routers you should disable AppleTalk routing. You should disable AppleTalk on all routers that are on the same network segment and that have sent RTMP updates in the past 10 seconds. Disable AppleTalk routing on all of the appropriate interfaces, wait approximately 10 minutes, and then bring up the seed router.

Changing Zone Names

When changing a zone name on an existing network, perform the following actions:

Step 1 Disable AppleTalk on all router interfaces on the cable for approximately 10 minutes. This allows all routers in the internetwork to age out the network number from their routing tables.

Step 2 Configure the new zone list.

Step 3 Re-enable AppleTalk on all interfaces.

These actions are required because AppleTalk makes no provisions for informing neighbors in the internetwork about a changed zone list. Routers make ZIP queries only when a new (or previously aged-out) network appears on the internetwork.

Adding a new zone to an extended cable configuration prevents the router from bringing up an AppleTalk interface after the interface has been reset. This is because its configuration no longer matches that of its neighbors (that is, it detects a configuration mismatch error).

AppleTalk Discovery Mode

When bringing up an interface on an existing cable where a long zone list is defined, using AppleTalk discovery mode helps you save effort and avoid mistakes.

The following steps outline bringing up an interface in discovery mode:

Step 1 Bring up the interface in discovery mode (using the **appletalk cable-range 0-0** interface configuration command). When a router is in discovery mode, the router changes its configuration to match the advertised cable range if the advertised cable range is different from that configured on the router. The **debug apple events** privileged exec command lets you know when the discovery process is complete by displaying an "operational" message.

Step 2 After discovery is complete, and while in interface configuration mode, enter the **no appletalk discovery** interface configuration command for the specific AppleTalk interface being initialized. This saves the acquired information and forces the configuration to be validated at port startup.

The router should not be in discovery mode for normal operation (it is recommended that discovery mode be used only when initially configuring networks). After the initial configuration, configure all routers for seed, or nondiscovery, mode. If you enable AppleTalk discovery and the interface is restarted, you must have another operational communication server or router on the directly connected network or the interface will not start up. It is not advisable to have all communication servers and routers on a network configured with discovery mode enabled. If all communication servers were to restart simultaneously (for instance, after a power failure), the network would become inaccessible until at least one communication server or router were restarted with discovery mode disabled.

Step 3 Use the **copy running-config startup-config** privileged exec command to save the acquired information to nonvolatile RAM (NVRAM).

Step 4 Verify the configuration with the **show running-config** privileged exec command.

Forcing an Interface Up

In certain situations, you might need to force an interface to come up even though its zone list conflicts with that of another router on the network. You can do this by using the **appletalk ignore-verify-errors** global configuration command. Usually the other router is one over which you have no administrative control but which you know has an incorrect zone list.

The **appletalk ignore-verify-errors** command allows you to bypass the default behavior of an AppleTalk interface. By default, the AppleTalk interface does not come up if its zone list conflicts with that of its neighbors. However, you should use this command with *extreme* caution; bringing up an interface with a zone list that conflicts with that of other routers can cause serious network problems. In addition, the other router *must* be reconfigured at some point so that all the routers in the internetwork agree on the zone list.

After all the AppleTalk routers on the network segment have conforming zone lists, disable the **appletalk ignore-verify-errors** command using the **no** form of the command. For complete information on the **appletalk ignore-verify-errors** global configuration command, see the Cisco IOS *Network Protocols Command Reference, Part 1*.

AppleTalk: Users Cannot Access Zones or Services

Symptom: Users cannot access zones or services that appear in the Chooser. Users might or might not be able to access services on their own network.

Table 9-2 outlines the problems that might cause this symptom and describes solutions to those problems.

Table 9-2   *AppleTalk: Users Cannot Access Zones or Services*

Possible Problems	Solution	
Configuration mismatch	**Step 1**	Use the **show appletalk interface** exec command. Check the output for a "port configuration mismatch" message.
		If the command output contains a "mismatch" message, the router configuration disagrees with that of the listed neighbor.
		If the command output does not include the "mismatch" message, use the **clear apple interface privileged exec** command on the interface in question. If the interface becomes operational after clearing, a configuration mismatch does not exist.
		Enter the **show appletalk interface** exec command again. If its output still contains a "port configuration mismatch" message, check whether all router configurations agree on the network number or cable range and the zone or zone list.
	Step 2	If router configurations disagree on these parameters, alter router configurations to bring all routers into alignment.
	Step 3	If problems persist, put the problem router in discovery mode by specifying the interface configuration command **appletalk address 0.0** on a nonextended network or the **appletalk cable-range 0-0** command on an extended network. This causes the router to get its configuration information from the network.
		For more information about configuration mismatches, see the section "AppleTalk Configuration Mismatches" later in this chapter.

continues

Table 9-2   *AppleTalk: Users Cannot Access Zones or Services (Continued)*

Possible Problems	Solution
Duplicate network numbers or overlapping cable-range	In AppleTalk, network numbers must be unique within an internetwork. If duplicate network numbers exist, packets might not be routed to their intended destinations.
	If AppleTalk services do not appear in the Chooser for particular networks, those networks probably have duplicate network numbers.
	Step 1 Change the network number or cable-range of the suspect network to a unique value using the **appletalk cable-range** interface configuration command.
	Step 2 Use the **show appletalk route privileged** exec command to view the routing table. If the network number or cable-range continues to appear in routing tables, you have found the duplicate (because the other network using that number will continue to send routing updates).
	If the network number or cable-range disappears from the internetwork after 40 seconds, you have not found the duplicate. Change the network number or cable-range specification back to its previous value and try again to isolate the duplicate network number.
	Step 3 If you changed the network number or cable-range on the interface, remember to reenter the zone name and any other interface configurations for AppleTalk on that interface.
Phase 1 and Phase 2 rule violations	**Step 1** Use the **show appletalk globals** exec command to determine whether the internetwork is in compatibility mode.
	Step 2 Enable the **appletalk name-lookup-interval** global configuration command and use the **show appletalk neighbors** exec command to determine which specific neighbor (by NBP[1] name) is in compatibility mode.
	Step 3 To resolve the problem, you can perform one of the following actions:
	• Upgrade AppleTalk Phase 1 routers to AppleTalk Phase 2 and reconfigure the internetwork
	• Ensure that all routers are in compliance with the two Phase 1 and Phase 2 rules
	For more information on Phase 1 and Phase 2 rule violations, see the section "Phase 1 and Phase 2 Rule Violations" later in this chapter.

Table 9-2   *AppleTalk: Users Cannot Access Zones or Services (Continued)*

Possible Problems	Solution	
Misconfigured access lists or other filters	Step 1	Use the **show appletalk access-list** exec command on routers in the path from source to destination.
	Step 2	Disable any access lists (or just those on a particularly suspect router) using the **no appletalk access-group** interface configuration command. If there are distribution lists or other filters configured, disable them.
	Step 3	After disabling access lists, check whether remote zones and services become accessible.
	Step 4	If zones and services are now available, a misconfigured access list is the likely problem. To isolate the problem access list, enable lists one at a time until connectivity fails.
	Step 5	Check the access lists and associated configuration commands for errors. Configure explicit **permit** statements for traffic that you want to pass through the router normally.
	Step 6	If problems persist, there might be more than one misconfigured access list. Continue enabling access lists one at a time and fixing misconfigured access lists until the problem is solved.

[1]NBP = Name Binding Protocol

AppleTalk Configuration Mismatches

A configuration mismatch occurs if all the AppleTalk routers on a given cable do not agree on the configuration of that cable. This means that all routers must have matching network numbers, a matching default zone, and a matching zone list.

To protect against configuration errors that violate this rule, Cisco AppleTalk routers block activation of any port on which a violation of this rule exists. At interface initialization, if other routers on the network do not agree with the way a router is configured, the router does not allow AppleTalk to become operational on that interface. Cisco routers attempt to restart such an interface every two minutes to avoid outages that result from transient conditions.

However, if the router is already operational and another router whose configuration does not match becomes active, the router continues to operate on that interface until the interface is reset. At that point, the interface fails to become active. When the **show appletalk interface** exec command is issued, the router indicates a port configuration mismatch.

The following is sample output from the **show appletalk interface** command when a
configuration mismatch exists:

```
Ethernet 0 is up, line protocol is up
AppleTalk routing disabled, Port configuration mismatch
AppleTalk cable range is 4-5
AppleTalk address is 4.252, Valid
AppleTalk zone is "Maison Vauquer"
AppleTalk port configuration conflicts with 4.156
AppleTalk discarded 8 packets due to input errors
AppleTalk discarded 2 packets due to output errors
AppleTalk route cache is disabled, port initializing
```

Line 2 of the command output shows that routing has been disabled due to a port
configuration mismatch. Line 6 indicates the AppleTalk address of the conflicting router.

You can also display the NBP registered name of the conflicting router, which can simplify
resolution of a port mismatch problem. To see registered NBP names, enable the
appletalk name-lookup-interval global configuration command. This causes the **show
appletalk interface** exec command output to display nodes by NBP registration name.

Phase 1 and Phase 2 Rule Violations

When Phase 1 and Phase 2 routers are connected to the same internetwork, the
internetwork specifications must conform to two rules:

- There can be no wide cable range specifications in the Phase 2 extended portion of the
  internetwork. That is, no cable ranges can span more than a single (unary) network
  number. For example, the cable ranges 2–2, 9–9, and 20–20 are all acceptable. The
  cable ranges 10–12 and 100–104 are not acceptable.

- Multiple zones cannot be assigned to unary cable ranges.

If these rules are not followed, connectivity between the nonextended and extended
portions of an internetwork becomes degraded and might be lost. In particular, services
located on nonextended networks using Phase 1 routers will not be visible on the other side
of the Phase 1 router.

NOTE   On Cisco routers, Phase 1 refers to the router Ethernet interfaces being configured with a
single network address and Ethernet I encapsulation, instead of with a cable-range and
Ethernet SNAP encapsulation. A Cisco router running Software Release 8.2 or later is a
Phase 2–compliant router regardless of how the interfaces are configured.

Another Phase 1 and Phase 2 issue is the handling of NBP packets. Phase 1 AppleTalk has
three types of NBP packets, and Phase 2 AppleTalk has four types of NBP packets. This

difference can lead to communication problems between Phase 1 and Phase 2 routers. Table 9-3 lists the NBP packet types for AppleTalk Phase 1 and Phase 2.

Table 9-3   *Comparison of Phase 1 and Phase 2 NBP Packet Types*

Phase 1 NBP Packet	Phase 2 NBP Packet
BrRq (Broadcast Request)	BrRq (Broadcast Request)
—	FwdReq (Forward Request)
LkUp (Lookup)	LkUp (Lookup)
LkUp-Reply (Lookup Reply)	LkUp-Reply (Lookup Reply)

As shown in Table 9-3, Forward Request packets do not exist in Phase 1. Only Phase 2 routers know what to do with them. Phase 1 routers that receive Forward Request packets simply drop them.

AppleTalk: Zones Missing from Chooser

Symptom: Certain zones do not appear in the Chooser. The zones are not visible from multiple networks. In some cases, when the Chooser is opened, the zone list changes.

Table 9-4 outlines the problems that might cause this symptom and describes solutions to those problems.

Table 9-4   *AppleTalk: Zones Missing from Chooser*

Possible Problems	Solution	
Configuration mismatch	Step 1	Use the **show appletalk interface** exec command. Check the output for a "port configuration mismatch" message.
		If the command output contains a "mismatch" message, the router configuration disagrees with that of the listed neighbor.
		If the command output does not include the "mismatch" message, use the **clear apple interface privileged** exec command on the interface in question. If the interface becomes operational after clearing, a configuration mismatch does not exist.
	Step 2	Enter the **show appletalk interface** exec command again. If its output still contains a "port configuration mismatch" message, check whether all router configurations agree on the network number or cable range and the zone or zone list.
	Step 3	If router configurations disagree on these parameters, alter router configurations to bring all routers into alignment.

continues

Table 9-4   *AppleTalk: Zones Missing from Chooser (Continued)*

Possible Problems	Solution	
Configuration mismatch *(continued)*	Step 4	If problems persist, put the problem router in discovery mode by specifying the interface configuration command **appletalk address 0.0** on a nonextended network or the **appletalk cable-range 0-0** command on an extended network. This causes the router to get its configuration information from the network.
		For more information about configuration mismatches, see the section "AppleTalk Configuration Mismatches" earlier in this chapter.
Misconfigured access lists or other filters	Step 1	Use the **show appletalk access-list** exec command on routers in the path from source to destination.
	Step 2	Disable any access lists (or just those on a particularly suspect router) using the **no appletalk access-group** interface configuration command. If there are distribution lists or other filters configured, disable them.
	Step 3	After disabling access lists, check whether remote zones and services become accessible.
	Step 4	If zones and services are now available, a misconfigured access list is the likely problem. To isolate the problem access list, enable lists one at a time until connectivity fails.
	Step 5	Check the access lists and associated configuration commands for errors. Configure explicit **permit** statements for traffic that you want to pass through the router normally.
	Step 6	If problems persist, there might be more than one misconfigured access list. Continue enabling access lists one at a time and fixing misconfigured access lists until the problem is solved.
Route flapping (unstable route)		Excessive traffic load on internetworks with many routers can prevent some routers from sending RTMP[1] updates every 10 seconds as they should. Because routers begin to age out routes after missing two consecutive RTMP updates, the inconsistent arrival of RTMP updates can result in constant route changes.
	Step 1	Use the **show interfaces** exec command to check the traffic load. Check the load for each interface.
		The following example is output from the **show interfaces** command:

```
Ethernet0 is up, line protocol is up
  Hardware is Lance, address is 0000.0c32.49b1 (bia
    0000.0c32.49b1)
  Internet address is 192.168.52.26/24
  MTU 1500 bytes, BW 10000 Kbit, DLY 1000 usec, rely 255/255,
    load 1/255
  [...]
```

Table 9-4   *AppleTalk: Zones Missing from Chooser (Continued)*

Possible Problems	Solution
Route flapping (unstable route)	The load field displayed in the **show interfaces** command is the load on the interface as a fraction of 255 (255/255 is completely saturated), calculated as an exponential average over five minutes.

Step 2   If the load is less than 50%, reconfiguring timer values might solve the problem by allowing RTMP updates more time to propagate through the network.

If the load is more than 50%, you might need to segment the network to reduce the number of routers (and therefore the amount of traffic) on each network segment.

Step 3   Use the **debug apple events privileged exec** command to determine whether routes are being aged incorrectly. The output should resemble the following:

```
Router#debug apple events
AppleTalk Events debugging is on
Router#
%AT-6-PATHNOTIFY: Ethernet0: AppleTalk RTMP path to
250-250 down; reported bad by 200.41
```

Caution: Because debugging output is assigned high priority in the CPU process, it can render the system unusable. For this reason, use **debug** commands only to troubleshoot specific problems or during troubleshooting sessions with Cisco technical support staff. Moreover, it is best to use **debug** commands during periods of lower network traffic and fewer users. Debugging during these periods decreases the likelihood that increased **debug** command processing overhead will affect system use.

Step 4   If routes are being aged incorrectly, use the **appletalk timers** global configuration command to correct the problem. Suggested timer values are 10, 30, and 90 to start, but do not exceed 10, 40, and 120. The first number must always be 10, and the third value should be three times the second.

You can return the timers to their defaults (10, 20, 60) by using the **no appletalk timers** global configuration command.

Timers should be consistently set to the same value throughout the internetwork, or at a minimum, throughout the backbone of the internetwork.

continues

Table 9-4   *AppleTalk: Zones Missing from Chooser (Continued)*

Possible Problems	Solution
ZIP storm	A ZIP storm occurs when a router propagates a route for which it currently has no corresponding zone name; the route is then propagated by downstream routers.
	Note: Cisco routers provide a firewall against ZIP storms in the internetwork. If a Cisco router receives a routing update from a neighbor, it does not propagate that new route until it receives the accompanying zone name.

Step 1   Use the **show appletalk traffic** command and check the field showing the number of ZIP requests.

The following example is output from the **show appletalk traffic** command:

```
Router#sh apple traffic
[...]
ZIP:    44 received, 35 sent, 6 netinfo
[...]
Router#
```

Compare this output with the output shown by the command 30 seconds later.

Step 2   If the traffic counters for ZIP requests are incrementing very rapidly (by more than 10 every 30 seconds), a ZIP storm is probably occurring.

Use the **debug apple zip privileged exec** command to identify the network for which the zone is being requested by neighboring routers. You can also use the **show apple private exec** command to check the number of pending ZIP requests.

Step 3   Identify the router that injected the network number into the internetwork (and that is causing the excessive ZIP traffic). The **show appletalk traffic** and **show appletalk route** exec commands provide information that can help you find the suspect router.

For example, you can use the **show appletalk route** exec command to view the AppleTalk routing table. Check whether a network shows up in the routing table, even though the display indicates that no zone is set.

If you find a network for which no zone is set, a node on that network is probably not responding to ZIP requests, resulting in the ZIP storm.

Step 4   Determine why the node is not responding to ZIP requests. Access lists or other filters might be the cause. ZIP storms can also result from a defect in the software running on the node. Contact the vendor to determine whether there is a known problem.

Table 9-4   *AppleTalk: Zones Missing from Chooser (Continued)*

Possible Problems	Solution
Too many zones in internetwork	The Chooser in System 6 can display only a limited number of zones, which presents problems in large internetworks that have many zones.
	If the Macintosh is running a version of System 6, upgrade it to System 7 or System 7.5.

[1]RTMP = Routing Table Maintenance Protocol

AppleTalk: No Devices in Chooser

Symptom: Zones appear in the Chooser, but when a service (such as AppleShare) and a zone are selected, no devices appear in the device list.

Table 9-5 outlines the problem that might cause this symptom and describes solutions to that problem.

Table 9-5   *AppleTalk: No Devices in Choose*

Possible Problems	Solution	
Misconfigured access lists	**Step 1**	Use the **show appletalk access-list** exec command on routers in the path from source to destination.
	Step 2	Disable any access lists (or just those on a particularly suspect router) using the **no appletalk access-group** interface configuration command.
	Step 3	After disabling access lists, check whether devices appear in the Chooser.
	Step 4	If devices now appear in the Chooser, a misconfigured access list is probably filtering NBP traffic. To isolate the problem access list, enable lists one at a time until devices no longer appear.
	Step 5	Check the access lists and associated configuration commands for errors. Configure explicit **permit** statements for traffic that you want to pass through the router normally.
	Step 6	If problems persist, there might be more than one misconfigured access list. Continue enabling access lists one at a time and fixing misconfigured access lists until the problem is solved.
		For detailed information about filtering NBP traffic using access lists, refer to the Cisco IOS *Network Protocols Configuration Guide, Part 1.*

continues

AppleTalk: Network Services Intermittently Unavailable

Symptom: Network services are intermittently unavailable. Services come and go without warning.

Table 9-6 outlines the problems that might cause this symptom and describes solutions to those problems.

Table 9-6 *AppleTalk: Network Services Intermittently Unavailable*

Possible Problems	Solution
Duplicate network numbers or overlapping cable-range	In AppleTalk, network numbers must be unique within an internetwork. If duplicate network numbers exist, packets might not be routed to their intended destinations.
	If AppleTalk services do not appear in the Chooser for particular networks, those networks probably have duplicate network numbers.
	Step 1 Change the network number or cable-range of the suspect network to a unique value using the **appletalk cable-range** interface configuration command.
	Step 2 Use the **show appletalk route** privileged exec command to view the routing table. If the network number or cable-range continues to appear in routing tables, you have found the duplicate (because the other network using that number will continue to send routing updates).
	If the network number or cable-range disappears from the internetwork after 40 seconds, you have not found the duplicate. Change the network number or cable-range specification back to its previous value and try again to isolate the duplicate network number.
	Step 3 If you changed the network number or cable-range on the interface, remember to reenter the zone name and any other interface configurations for AppleTalk on that interface.
Route flapping (unstable route)	Excessive traffic load on internetworks with many routers can prevent some routers from sending RTMP updates every 10 seconds as they should. Because routers begin to age out routes after missing two consecutive RTMP updates, the inconsistent arrival of RTMP updates can result in constant route changes.
	Step 1 Use the **show interfaces** exec command to check the traffic load. Check the load for each interface.

Table 9-6 *AppleTalk: Network Services Intermittently Unavailable (Continued)*

Possible Problems	Solution

Route flapping (unstable route) *(continued)*	The following example is output from the **show interfaces** command:
	
	``
	Ethernet0 is up, line protocol is up
	  Hardware is Lance, address is 0000.0c32.49b1 (bia
	0000.0c32.49b1)
	  Internet address is 192.168.52.26/24
	  MTU 1500 bytes, BW 10000 Kbit, DLY 1000 usec, rely
	255/255, load 1/255
	[...]
	``
	
	The load field displayed in the **show interfaces** command is the load on the interface as a fraction of 255 (255/255 is completely saturated), calculated as an exponential average over five minutes.

Step 2	If the load is less than 50%, reconfiguring timer values might solve the problem by allowing RTMP updates more time to propagate through the network. If the load is more than 50%, you might need to segment the network to reduce the number of routers (and therefore the amount of traffic) on each network segment.
Step 3	Use the **debug apple events privileged exec** command to determine whether routes are being aged incorrectly. The output should resemble the following: ``` Router#debug apple events AppleTalk Events debugging is on Router# %AT-6-PATHNOTIFY: Ethernet0: AppleTalk RTMP path to 250-250 down; reported bad by 200.41 ``` The **debug apple events** command is useful for solving AppleTalk network problems because it provides an overall picture of the stability of the network. In a stable network, the **debug apple events** command does not return any information. If, however, the command generates numerous messages, the messages can indicate where the problems might lie. Turning on debug apple events will not cause **apple event-logging** to be maintained in nonvolatile memory. Only turning on **apple event-logging** explicitly will store it in nonvolatile memory. Furthermore, if **apple event-logging** is already enabled, turning on or off debug apple events will not affect **apple event-logging**.

continues

Table 9-6 *AppleTalk: Network Services Intermittently Unavailable (Continued)*

Possible Problems	Solution
Route flapping (unstable route) *(continued)*	**Caution:** Because debugging output is assigned high priority in the CPU process, it can render the system unusable. For this reason, use **debug** commands only to troubleshoot specific problems or during troubleshooting sessions with Cisco technical support staff. Moreover, it is best to use **debug** commands during periods of lower network traffic and fewer users. Debugging during these periods decreases the likelihood that increased **debug** command processing overhead will affect system use.
	Step 4 If routes are being aged incorrectly, use the **appletalk timers** global configuration command to correct the problem. Suggested timer values are 10, 30, and 90 to start, but do not exceed 10, 40, and 120. The first number must always be 10, and the third value should be three times the second.
	You can return the timers to their defaults (10, 20, 60) by using the **no appletalk timers** global configuration command.
	Timers should be consistently set to the same value throughout the internetwork, or at a minimum, throughout the backbone of the internetwork.
ZIP storm	A ZIP storm occurs when a router propagates a route for which it currently has no corresponding zone name; the route is then propagated by downstream routers.
	Note: Cisco routers provide a firewall against ZIP storms in the internetwork. If a Cisco router receives a routing update from a neighbor, it does not propagate that new route until it receives the accompanying zone name.

	Step 1 Use the **show appletalk traffic** command to check the field showing the number of ZIP requests:
	
	 ```Router#sh apple traffic```
	 ```[...]```
	 ```ZIP: 44 received, 35 sent, 6 netinfo```
	 ```[...]```
	 ```Router#```
	
	 Compare this output with the output shown by the command 30 seconds later.

	Step 2 If the traffic counters for ZIP requests are incrementing very rapidly (by more than 10 every 30 seconds) a ZIP storm is probably occurring.

Table 9-6   *AppleTalk: Network Services Intermittently Unavailable (Continued)*

Possible Problems	Solution	
ZIP storm *(continued)*		Use the **debug apple zip** privileged exec command to identify the network for which the zone is being requested by neighboring routers. You can also use the **show apple private exec** command to check the number of pending ZIP requests.
	Step 3	Identify the router that injected the network number into the internetwork (and that is causing the excessive ZIP traffic). The **show appletalk traffic** and **show appletalk route** exec commands provide information that can help you find the suspect router.
		For example, you can use the **show appletalk route** exec command to view the AppleTalk routing table. Check whether a network shows up in the routing table, even though the display indicates that no zone is set.
		If you find a network for which no zone is set, a node on that network is probably not responding to ZIP requests, resulting in the ZIP storm.
	Step 4	Determine why the node is not responding to ZIP requests. Access lists or other filters might be the cause.
		ZIP storms can also result from a defect in the software running on the node. Contact the vendor to determine whether there is a known problem.

AppleTalk: Old Zone Names Appear in Chooser (Phantom Zones)

Symptom: Old AppleTalk zone names continue to appear in the Chooser. Even after zone names are removed from the configuration, "phantom" zones continue to appear in the Chooser.

Table 9-7 outlines the problems that might cause this symptom and describes solutions to those problems.

Table 9-7   *AppleTalk: Old Zone Names Appear in Chooser (Phantom Zones)*

Possible Problems	Solution	
Configuration mismatch	**Step 1**	Use the **show appletalk interface** exec command. Check the output for a "port configuration mismatch" message.If the command output contains a"mismatch" message, the router configuration disagrees with that of the listed neighbor.If the command output does not include the "mismatch" message, use the **clear apple interface privileged** exec command on the interface in question. If the interface becomes operational after clearing, a configuration mismatch does not exist.

continues

Table 9-7   *AppleTalk: Old Zone Names Appear in Chooser (Phantom Zones) (Continued)*

Possible Problems	Solution
Configuration mismatch *(continued)*	**Step 1** Use the **show appletalk interface** exec command. Check the output for a "port configuration mismatch" message.If the command output contains a"mismatch" message, the router configuration disagrees with that of the listed neighbor.If the command output does not include the "mismatch" message, use the **clear apple interface privileged** exec command on the interface in question. If the interface becomes operational after clearing, a configuration mismatch does not exist.
	Step 2 Enter the **show appletalk interface** exec command again. If its output still contains a "port configuration mismatch" message, check whether all router configurations agree on network number or cable range and the zone or zone list.
	Step 3 If router configurations disagree on these parameters, alter router configurations to bring all routers into alignment.
	Step 4 If problems persist, put the problem router in discovery mode by specifying the interface configuration command **appletalk address 0.0** on a nonextended network or the **appletalk cable-range 0-0** command on an extended network. This causes the router to get its configuration information from the network. For more information about configuration mismatches, see the section "AppleTalk Configuration Mismatches" earlier in this chapter.
Invalid zone names in routing table	AppleTalk does not provide a way to update ZIP tables when changing the mapping of zone names to networks or cable ranges. For example, if the zone name for network number 200 is Twilight Zone, but you decide to change the zone to No Parking Zone, the zone name on the interface can be changed, and the new zone name takes effect locally. However, unless you keep network 200 off the internetwork long enough for it to be completely aged out of the routing tables, some routers will continue to use the old zone name (this is called a *phantom zone*). Alternatively, if you cannot keep the network off the internetwork that long, change the underlying network number when you change the zone name of a cable. **Step 1** Use the **show running-config** privileged exec command to view the router configuration. Check the network numbers configured for each AppleTalk interface.

Table 9-7   *AppleTalk: Old Zone Names Appear in Chooser (Phantom Zones) (Continued)*

Possible Problems	Solution	
Invalid zone names in routing table *(continued)*	**Step 2**	Make sure that there are no network numbers configured that were previously assigned to a zone that has been deleted. Change the cable-range using the **appletalk cable-range** interface configuration command or disable the network until it is aged out of routing tables.
	Step 3	Use the **show appletalk zones** command to verify that the zone no longer appears in the zone list.

AppleTalk: Connections to Services Drop

Symptom: Users complain that their AppleTalk sessions suddenly drop for no apparent reason.

Table 9-8 outlines the problem that might cause this symptom and describes solutions to that problem.

Table 9-8   *AppleTalk: Connections to Services Drop*

Possible Problems	Solution	
Route flapping (unstable route)	Excessive traffic load on internetworks with many routers can prevent some routers from sending RTMP updates every 10 seconds as they should. Because routers begin to age out routes after missing two consecutive RTMP updates, the inconsistent arrival of RTMP updates can result in constant route changes.	
	Step 1	Use the **show interfaces** exec command to check the traffic load. Check the load for each interface.
		The following example is output from the **show interfaces** command:
| | | ```
Ethernet0 is up, line protocol is up
Hardware is Lance, address is 0000.0c32.49b1 (bia
  0000.0c32.49b1)
Internet address is 192.168.52.26/24
MTU 1500 bytes, BW 10000 Kbit, DLY 1000 usec, rely 255/
  255, load 1/255
[...]
``` |
| | | The load field displayed in the **show interfaces** command is the load on the interface as a fraction of 255 (255/255 is completely saturated), calculated as an exponential average over five minutes. |

continues
```

Table 9-8 *AppleTalk: Connections to Services Drop (Continued)*

Possible Problems	Solution
Route flapping (unstable route) *(continued)*	**Step 2** If the load is less than 50%, reconfiguring timer values might solve the problem by allowing RTMP updates more time to propagate through the network. If the load is more than 50%, you might need to segment the network to reduce the number of routers (and therefore the amount of traffic) on each network segment. **Step 3** Use the **debug apple events privileged exec** command to determine whether routes are being aged incorrectly. The output should resemble the following: ``` Router#debug apple events AppleTalk Events debugging is on Router# %AT-6-PATHNOTIFY: Ethernet0: AppleTalk RTMP path to 250-250 down; reported bad by 200.41 ``` **Caution:** Because debugging output is assigned high priority in the CPU process, it can render the system unusable. For this reason, use **debug** commands only to troubleshoot specific problems or during troubleshooting sessions with Cisco technical support staff. Moreover, it is best to use **debug** commands during periods of lower network traffic and fewer users. Debugging during these periods decreases the likelihood that increased **debug** command processing overhead will affect system use. **Step 4** If routes are being aged incorrectly, use the **appletalk timers** global configuration command to correct the problem. Suggested timer values are 10, 30, and 90 to start, but do not exceed 10, 40, and 120. The first number must always be 10, and the third value should be three times the second. You can return the timers to their defaults (10, 20, 60) by using the **no appletalk timers** global configuration command. Timers should be consistently set to the same value throughout the internetwork, or at a minimum, throughout the backbone of the internetwork.

AppleTalk: Interface Fails to Initialize AppleTalk

Symptom: Router interface connected to a network will not initialize AppleTalk.

Table 9-9 outlines the problems that might cause this symptom and describes solutions to those problems.

Table 9-9   *AppleTalk: Interface Fails to Initialize AppleTalk*

Possible Problems	Solution	
Configuration mismatch	Step 1	Use the **show appletalk interface** exec command. Check the output for a "port configuration mismatch" message.
		If the command output contains a "mismatch message," the router configuration disagrees with that of the listed neighbor.
		If the command output does not include the "mismatch" message, use the **clear apple interface privileged** exec command on the interface in question. If the interface becomes operational after clearing, a configuration mismatch does not exist.
	Step 2	Enter the **show appletalk interface** exec command again. If its output still contains a "port configuration mismatch" message, check to see whether all router configurations agree on network number or cable range and the zone or zone list.
	Step 3	If router configurations disagree on these parameters, alter router configurations to bring all routers into alignment.
	Step 4	If problems persist, put the problem router in discovery mode by specifying the interface configuration command **appletalk address 0.0** on a nonextended network or the **appletalk cable-range 0-0** command on an extended network. This causes the router to get its configuration information from the network.
		For more information about configuration mismatches, see the section "AppleTalk Configuration Mismatches" earlier in this chapter.

continues

Table 9-9 *AppleTalk: Interface Fails to Initialize AppleTalk (Continued)*

Possible Problems	Solution	
Phase 1 and Phase 2 rule violations	**Step 1**	Use the **show appletalk globals** exec command to determine whether the internetwork is in compatibility mode.
	Step 2	Enable the **appletalk name-lookup-interval** global configuration command and use the **show appletalk neighbors exec** command to determine which specific neighbor (by NBP name) is in compatibility mode.
	Step 3	To resolve the problem, you can perform one of the following actions: • Upgrade AppleTalk Phase 1 routers to AppleTalk Phase 2 and reconfigure the internetwork • Ensure that all routers are in compliance with the two Phase 1 and Phase 2 rules For more information on Phase 1 and Phase 2 rule violations, see the section "Phase 1 and Phase 2 Rule Violations" earlier in this chapter.

AppleTalk: Port Stuck in Restarting or Acquiring Mode

Symptom: A router port is stuck in restarting or acquiring mode (as shown in the output of the **show apple interface** privileged exec command). The router cannot discover routes or poll neighbors on an attached cable.

Table 9-10 outlines the problems that might cause this symptom and describes solutions to those problems.

Table 9-10 *AppleTalk: Port Stuck in Restarting or Acquiring Mode*

Possible Problems	Solution	
Router is in discovery mode, and no seed router exists on the network	**Step 1**	Put the router in nondiscovery mode by assigning a network number or cable range to the problem interface using the **appletalk address** or **appletalk cable-range** interface configuration command.
	Step 2	If the problem persists, consult your technical support representative for more assistance.

Table 9-10   *AppleTalk: Port Stuck in Restarting or Acquiring Mode (Continued)*

Possible Problems	Solution	
Crossed serial circuits with multiple lines between two routers	**Step 1**	Check the physical attachment of serial lines to ensure that they are correctly wired.
	Step 2	If necessary, rewire the lines and check the output of the **show interfaces** and **show appletalk interface** commands to confirm that the interface and line protocol are up.
	Step 3	If the router still cannot find routes, consult your technical support representative for more assistance.
Software problem	If the router issues a message that says "restart port pending," upgrade to the latest system software maintenance release or contact your technical support representative.	

AppleTalk Enhanced IGRP: Clients Cannot Connect to Servers

Symptom: Macintosh clients cannot connect to servers in an AppleTalk Enhanced IGRP network environment.

Table 9-11 outlines the problems that might cause this symptom and describes solutions to those problems.

Table 9-11   *AppleTalk Enhanced IGRP: Clients Cannot Connect to Servers*

Possible Problem	Solution
Routers not establishing neighbors properly	For information on troubleshooting this problem, see the section "AppleTalk Enhanced IGRP: Routers Not Establishing Neighbors" next.
Routes missing from routing table	For information on troubleshooting this problem, see the section "AppleTalk Enhanced IGRP: Routes Missing from Routing Table" later in this chapter.

continues

Table 9-11 *AppleTalk Enhanced IGRP: Clients Cannot Connect to Servers*

Possible Problem	Solution
Appletalk Enhanced IGRP enabled on network with connected Macintosh computers	Macintosh computers do not understand AppleTalk Enhanced IGRP. RTMP must be enabled on interfaces with Macintosh computers on the connected LAN segment. By default, AppleTalk RTMP routes are automatically redistributed into enhanced IGRP, and AppleTalk enhanced IGRP routes are automatically redistributed into RTMP.
	Step 1 Use the **show running-config** privileged exec command on routers to make sure that RTMP is enabled on interfaces connected to LAN segments with connected Macintosh computers.
	Step 2 If RTMP is not enabled, enable it using the **appletalk protocol rtmp** interface configuration command.
	Step 3 If desired, disable AppleTalk Enhanced IGRP on the interface using the **no appletalk protocol eigrp** interface configuration command.

AppleTalk Enhanced IGRP: Routers Not Establishing Neighbors

Symptom: AppleTalk Enhanced IGRP routers do not establish neighbors properly. Routers that are connected do not appear in the neighbor table.

Table 9-12 outlines the problems that might cause this symptom and describes solutions to those problems.

Table 9-12 *AppleTalk Enhanced IGRP: Routers Not Establishing Neighbors*

Possible Problem	Solution
AppleTalk Enhanced IGRP is not globally configured on the appropriate routers	**Step 1** Use the **show running-config** privileged exec command to check the configuration of routers that should be running Enhanced IGRP. Look for **appletalk routing eigrp** global configuration command entries. This command enables AppleTalk Enhanced IGRP routing on the router.
	Step 2 If AppleTalk Enhanced IGRP routing is not enabled on the router, use the **appletalk routing eigrp** *router-id* global configuration command to enable it. Make sure that the router ID is unique throughout the network.
	Step 3 Perform the same actions on other routers that should be running AppleTalk Enhanced IGRP. The router ID must be different for each router.

Table 9-12   *AppleTalk Enhanced IGRP: Routers Not Establishing Neighbors (Continued)*

Possible Problem	Solution
AppleTalk Enhanced IGRP is not enabled on interfaces	Use the **show running-config privileged exec** command on routers that are running Enhanced IGRP. Check the interface configurations for **appletalk protocol eigrp** interface configuration command entries.
	This command must be present in order for an interface to generate AppleTalk Enhanced IGRP hello messages and routing updates.
Timer values are mismatched	**Step 1** Use the **show appletalk eigrp neighbors** exec command. Make sure that all directly connected AppleTalk Enhanced IGRP routers appear in the output.
	Step 2 Examine the uptime field in the **show appletalk eigrp neighbors** output. A continuously resetting uptime counter indicates that hello packets from the neighboring router are arriving sporadically. This might be caused by a timer value mismatch or by hardware problems.
	Step 3 Use the **show interface** exec command to determine whether the interface and line protocol are up. Look for high numbers in the queue fields and excessive drop counts. The queue fields displays the maximum size of the queue and the number of packets dropped due to a full queue.
	If there are many drops, if the queue count is high, or if the interface or line protocol is down, there is probably something wrong with the interface or other hardware. For more information on troubleshooting hardware, see Chapter 3,"Troubleshooting Hardware and Booting Problems," and Chapter 15, "Troubleshooting Serial Line Problems."
	Step 4 Use the **show running-config privileged** exec command on all AppleTalk Enhanced IGRP routers in the network. Look for **appletalk eigrp-timers** interface configuration command entries. The values configured by this command must be the same for all AppleTalk Enhanced IGRP routers on the network.

continues

Table 9-12   *AppleTalk Enhanced IGRP: Routers Not Establishing Neighbors (Continued)*

Possible Problem	Solution	
Timer values are mismatched *(continued)*	**Step 5**	If any routers have conflicting timer values, reconfigure them to conform with the rest of the routers on the network. These values can be returned to their defaults with the **no appletalk eigrp-timers** interface configuration command.
Older version of the Cisco IOS software	If problems persist, upgrade to the latest release of the Cisco IOS software.	

AppleTalk Enhanced IGRP: Routes Missing from Routing Table

Symptom: Routes are missing from the routing table of routers running AppleTalk Enhanced IGRP. Clients (Macintosh computers) on one network cannot access servers on a different network. Clients might or might not be able to connect to servers on the same network. The problem might occur in internetworks running only Enhanced IGRP or in an internetwork running Enhanced IGRP and RTMP.

Table 9-13 outlines the problems that might cause this symptom and describes solutions to those problems.

Table 9-13   *AppleTalk Enhanced IGRP: Routes Missing from Routing Table*

Possible Problem	Solution
Routers not establishing neighbors properly	For information on troubleshooting this problem, see the section "AppleTalk Enhanced IGRP: Routers Not Establishing Neighbors" earlier in this chapter.
AppleTalk Enhanced IGRP is not enabled on interfaces	Use the **show running-config privileged exec** command on routers that are running Enhanced IGRP. Check the interface configurations for **appletalk protocol eigrp** interface configuration command entries. This command must be present in order for an interface to generate AppleTalk Enhanced IGRP hello messages and routing updates.
Older version of the Cisco IOS software	If problems persist, upgrade to the latest release of the Cisco IOS software.

AppleTalk Enhanced IGRP: Poor Performance

Symptom: Network performance in an AppleTalk Enhanced IGRP environment is poor. Connections between clients and servers are slow or unreliable.

Table 9-14 outlines the problems that might cause this symptom and describes solutions to those problems.

Table 9-14   *AppleTalk Enhanced IGRP: Poor Performance*

Possible Problem	Solution
AppleTalk Enhanced IGRP and RTMP are running simultaneously on the same interface	Use the **show running-config privileged exec** command on network routers. Check the interface configurations to determine whether AppleTalk Enhanced IGRP and RTMP are both enabled on the same interface. Running both AppleTalk Enhanced IGRP and RTMP on the same interface increases bandwidth and processor overhead. Determine whether both routing protocols need to be running on the interface and disable one or the other if necessary or desired.
Older version of the Cisco IOS software	If problems persist, upgrade to the latest release of the Cisco IOS software.

AppleTalk Enhanced IGRP: Router Stuck in Active Mode

Symptom: An AppleTalk Enhanced IGRP router is stuck in Active mode. The router repeatedly sends error messages similar to the following to the console:

```
%DUAL-3-SIA: Route 2.24 Stuck-in-Active
```

NOTE	Occasional messages of this type are *not* a cause for concern. This is how an Enhanced IGRP router recovers if it does not receive replies to its queries from all its neighbors. However, if these error messages occur frequently, you should investigate the problem.

For a more detailed explanation of Enhanced IGRP Active mode, see the section "Enhanced IGRP Active/Passive Modes" later in this chapter.

Table 9-15 outlines the problems that might cause this symptom and describes solutions to those problems.

Table 9-15   *AppleTalk Enhanced IGRP: Router Stuck in Active Mode*

Possible Problems	Solution
Active timer value is misconfigured	The active timer determines the maximum period of time that an Enhanced IGRP router will wait for replies to its queries. If the active timer value is set too low, there might not be enough time for all the neighboring routers to send their replies to the Active router.
	Step 1 Check the configuration of each Enhanced IGRP router using the **show running-config privileged** exec command. Look for the **timers active-time** router configuration command entry associated with the **appletalk routing eigrp** global configuration command entry.
	Step 2 The value set by the **timers active-time** command should be consistent among routers in the same autonomous system. A value of 3 (3 minutes, the default value) is strongly recommended to allow all Enhanced IGRP neighbors to reply to queries.
Interface or other hardware problem	**Step 1** If queries and replies are not sent and received properly, the active timer times out and causes the router to issue an error message. Use the **show appletalk eigrp neighbors** exec command and examine the uptime and Q Cnt (queue count) fields in the output.
	The following example is output from the **show appletalk eigrp neighbor** command:
	``` Router#show appletalk eigrp neighbor AT/EIGRP Neighbors for process 1, router id 1 H Address Interface Hold Uptime SRTT RTO Q Seq (sec) (ms) Cnt Num 0 200.41 Et0 10 0:00:37 0 3000 0 2 ```
	If the uptime counter is continually resetting or if the queue count is consistently high, there might be a hardware problem. The uptime counter is the elapsed time, in hours, minutes, and seconds, since the local router first heard from this neighbor.
	Step 2 Determine where the problem is by looking at the output of the "Stuck-in-Active" error message, which indicates the AppleTalk address of the problematic node.
	Step 3 Make sure the suspect router is still functional. Check the interfaces on the suspect router. Make sure the interface and line protocol are up and determine whether the interface is dropping packets.
	For more information on troubleshooting hardware, see Chapter 3, "Troubleshooting Hardware and Booting Problems."

Table 9-15   *AppleTalk Enhanced IGRP: Router Stuck in Active Mode (Continued)*

Possible Problems	Solution
Flapping route	If there is a flapping serial route (caused by heavy traffic load), queries and replies might not be forwarded reliably. Route flapping caused by heavy traffic on a serial link can cause queries and replies to be lost, resulting in the active timer timing out. Take steps to reduce traffic on the link, or increase the bandwidth of the link.
Older version of the Cisco IOS software	If problems persist, upgrade to the latest release of the Cisco IOS software.

Enhanced IGRP Active/Passive Modes

An Enhanced IGRP router can be in either Passive or Active mode. A router is said to be passive for a network when it has an established path to that network in its routing table. The route is in Active state when a router is undergoing a route recomputation. If there are always feasible successors, a route never has to go into Active state and avoids a route recomputation.

If the Enhanced IGRP router loses the connection to a network, it becomes active for that network. The router sends out queries to all its neighbors in order to find a new route to the network. The router remains in Active mode until it has either received replies from *all* its neighbors or until the active timer, which determines the maximum period of time a router will stay active, has expired.

If the router receives a reply from each of its neighbors, it computes the new next hop to the network and becomes passive for that network. However, if the active timer expires, the router removes from its neighbor table any neighbors that did not reply, again enters Active mode, and issues a "Stuck-in-Active" message to the console.

AURP: Routes Not Propagated Through AURP Tunnel

Symptom: AppleTalk routes are not propagated through an AURP tunnel. Routes that are known to exist on one side of the tunnel do not appear in the routing tables of the exterior router on the other side of the tunnel. Changes on the remote network (such as a route going down) are not learned by the exterior router on the other side of the tunnel.

Table 9-16 outlines the problems that might cause this symptom and describes solutions to those problems.

Table 9-16   *AURP: Routes Not Propagated Through AURP Tunnel*

Possible Problems	Solution	
Misconfigured AURP tunnel	Step 1	Use the **show appletalk interfaces** exec command to make sure the tunnel interface is up.
	Step 2	Use the **show running-config privileged** exec command to view the router configuration. Check the **tunnel source** and **tunnel destination** interface configuration command entries.
	Step 3	Exterior routers must have their tunnel interface configured with a **tunnel source** and a **tunnel destination** command. Make sure that the **tunnel destination** command on each router points to the IP address of the remote exterior router's tunnel interface.
Missing **appletalk route-redistribution** command	Step 1	If changes on the remote network are not learned through the tunnel, use the **show running-config privileged** exec command to view the router configuration. Check for an **appletalk route-redistribution** global configuration command entry.
	Step 2	If the command is not present, add it to the configuration.
Problem with underlying IP network		If there are routing problems in the transit network (the IP network through which the AURP tunnel passes), then AppleTalk traffic might have difficulty traversing the tunnel.
		To troubleshoot your TCP/IP network, follow the procedures outlined in Chapter 7, "Troubleshooting TCP/IP."

FDDITalk: No Zone Associated with Routes

Symptom: Routers on an FDDI ring have routes to networks across the ring, but no zones are associated with the routes. The output of the **show appletalk route** command indicates "no zone set" for those routes.

NOTE   On other media, routes with no zone set are the result of other problems, such as ZIP storms. See the sections "AppleTalk: Zones Missing from Chooser" and "AppleTalk: Network Services Intermittently Unavailable" in this chapter for more information.

Table 9-17 outlines the problem that might cause this symptom and describes solutions to that problem.

Table 9-17 *FDDITalk: No Zone Associated with Routes*

Possible Problems	Solution
FDDITalk version mismatch	If any routers in the internetwork are using software releases prior to Cisco IOS Release 10.0, there is a possibility of a FDDITalk version mismatch. Make sure that all routers on the ring are using either pre-FDDITalk or FDDITalk and are not a combination of the two.
	Following are the FDDITalk implementations for each software release:
	• In software releases prior to 9.0(2), routers can use only pre-FDDITalk.
	• In software releases prior to Cisco IOS Release 10.0, routers use the Apple implementation of FDDITalk by default.
	However, if a pre-FDDITalk router exists on the FDDI network, routers fall back to pre-FDDITalk. A router can be forced to use FDDITalk with the **no appletalk pre-fdditalk** interface configuration command.
	• In Cisco IOS Release 10.0 and later, the default is to use the Apple implementation of FDDITalk.
	However, you can force a router to use pre-FDDITalk with the **appletalk pre-fdditalk** interface configuration command.

ARA: ARA Client Unable to Connect to ARA Server

Symptom: An ARA client (such as a Macintosh) attempts to connect to an ARA server (such as a Cisco access server) and cannot initiate a remote session. The user might be able to connect briefly, but the connection is immediately terminated.

Table 9-18 outlines the problems that might cause this symptom and describes solutions to those problems.

Table 9-18 *ARA: ARA Client Unable to Connect to ARA Server*

Possible Problems	Solution	
Missing **arap network** command entry	Step 1	Use the **show running-config** privileged exec command to view the router configuration. If you are running Cisco IOS Release 10.2 or later, look for an **arap network** global configuration command entry.
	Step 2	Configure the **arap network** global configuration command to enable ARA on the router or access server. The syntax for the **arap network** command is as follows:
		arap network [*network-number*] [*zone-name*]

continues

Table 9-18   *ARA: ARA Client Unable to Connect to ARA Server (Continued)*

Possible Problems	Solution	
Missing **arap network** command entry *(continued)*	**Syntax Description:** • *network-number*—(Optional) The AppleTalk network number. The network number must be unique on your AppleTalk network. This network is where all ARAP[1] users appear when they dial in to the network. • *zone-name*—(Optional) The AppleTalk zone name.	
AppleTalk routing is not enabled on the appropriate interfaces	Step 1	Use the **show apple interfaces exec** command to determine whether interfaces are operational and whether AppleTalk routing is enabled on the correct interfaces.
	Step 2	If AppleTalk routing is not enabled on the proper interfaces, enable it where appropriate. Refer to the Cisco IOS *Network Protocols Configuration Guide, Part 1* for detailed information on configuring an interface for AppleTalk routing.
Modem, serial line, or hardware problems	For serial line troubleshooting information, see Chapter 15, "Troubleshooting Serial Lines." For modem troubleshooting information, see Chapter 16, "Troubleshooting Dialup Connections." For hardware troubleshooting information, see Chapter 3, "Troubleshooting Hardware and Booting Problems."	

[1] ARAP = AppleTalk Remote Access Protocol

ARA: Connection Hangs After "Communicating At..." Message

Symptom: An ARA client (for example, a Macintosh) tries to connect to an ARA server (such as a Cisco access server) over client and server modems. The client receives a connect message such as "Communicating at 14.4 Kbps" but then hangs for 10–30 seconds and finally shows a "connection failed" message.

Table 9-19 outlines the problem that might cause this symptom and describes solutions to that problem.

Table 9-19   *ARA: Connection Hangs After "Communicating At..." Message*

Possible Problems	Solution	
MNP4 Link Request packets sent by client ARA stack are responded to by the serving modem instead of the ARA server	Step 1	Check the version numbers of the ARA software on the client and the Cisco IOS software on the access server.
		If you are using ARA version 1.0 or Cisco IOS software prior to Release 10.2, it is advisable to upgrade to ARA 2.0 and Cisco IOS Release 10.2 or later. ARA 2.0 modifies the framing of MNP4 Link Request packets, allowing them to be passed to the access server rather than responded to by the serving modem.

Table 9-19   *ARA: Connection Hangs After "Communicating At..." Message (Continued)*

Possible Problems		Solution
MNP4 Link Request packets sent by client ARA stack are responded to by the serving modem instead of the ARA server *(continued)*	Step 2	If you cannot upgrade your software, try modifying the behavior of the modem to use a LAPM-to-No Error Correction fallback instead of a LAPM-to-MNP4-to-No Error Correction fallback. The modem no longer listens for and respond to MNP4 messages, allowing MNP4 packets to reach the access server.
		Note: Many modems cannot be configured in this manner.
	Step 3	If your modem does not use LAPM error correction, it might be possible to modify *all* ARA client scripts to extend the 500 ms pause before exiting. Configure an additional delay that takes into account the behavior of the *serving* modem.

ARA: Cannot Send or Receive Data over ARA Dialin Connection

Symptom: ARA connections are established, but users cannot send or receive ARA data over the link.

Table 9-20 outlines the problems that might cause this symptom and describes solutions to those problems.

Table 9-20   *ARA: Cannot Send or Receive Data over ARA Dialin Connection*

Possible Causes		Suggested Actions
Missing **arap network** command entry	Step 1	Use the **show running-config** privileged exec command to view the router configuration. If you are running Cisco IOS Release 10.2 or later, look for an **arap network** global configuration command entry.
	Step 2	Configure the **arap network** global configuration command to enable ARA on the router or access server. The syntax for the **arap network** command is as follows:
		arap network [*network-number*] [*zone-name*]
		Syntax Description:
		• *network-number*—(Optional) The AppleTalk network number. The network number must be unique on your AppleTalk network. This network is where all ARAP users appear when they dial in to the network.
		• *zone-name*—(Optional) The AppleTalk zone name.

continues

Table 9-20 *ARA: Cannot Send or Receive Data over ARA Dialin Connection*

Possible Causes	Suggested Actions	
Missing **autoselect** command	Step 1	Use the **show running-config** privileged exec command to view the router configuration. Check to see whether the **autoselect arap** line configuration command is configured on the router.
	Step 2	If the command is not present, add it to the configuration.
MNP5 enabled on answering modem	Step 1	Check to see whether the answering modem has MNP5 error correction enabled.
	Step 2	If MNP5 is enabled on the answering modem, disable it. For information on checking or changing the modem configuration, refer to the modem documentation.
Zone list is empty	Step 1	Use the **show appletalk route** and **show appletalk zones** privileged exec commands to determine whether the router can see its ARA routes and zones.
	Step 2	Use the show **appletalk interface ethernet** exec command and make sure that the output matches your Apple network parameters.
	Step 3	Change the interface configuration as required.
TACACS[1] problem	For information on troubleshooting TACACS problems, refer to Chapter 24, "Troubleshooting CiscoWorks 2000."	

[1]TACACS = Terminal Access Controller Access Control System

ARA: Slow Performance from Dialin Connection

Symptom: Performance on remote dialin ARA sessions is slow.

Table 9-21 outlines the problem that might cause this symptom and describes solutions to that problem.

Table 9-21 *ARA: Slow Performance from Dialin Connection*

Possible Problems	Solution	
Flow control is not enabled, is enabled only on one device (either DTE or DCE), or is misconfigured	Step 1	Configure hardware flow control on the line using the **flowcontrol hardware** line configuration command. Hardware flow control is recommended for access server-to-modem connections.

Table 9-21   *ARA: Slow Performance from Dialin Connection (Continued)*

Possible Problems	Solution
Flow control is not enabled, is enabled only on one device (either DTE or DCE), or is misconfigured *(continued)*	For example, to configure hardware flow control on line 2 of an access server, enter the following commands:

```
C2500(config)#line 2
C2500(config-line)#flowcontrol hardware
```

Note: If you cannot use flow control, limit the line speed to 9600 bps. Faster speeds can result in lost data.

Step 2   After enabling hardware flow control on the access server or router line, initiate a reverse Telnet session to the modem via that line.

For instructions on initiating a reverse Telnet session, see the section "Establishing a Reverse Telnet Session to a Modem" in Chapter 16, "Troubleshooting Dialup Connections."

Step 3   Use a modem command string that includes the RTS/CTS flow command for your modem. This command ensures that the modem is using the same method of flow control (that is, hardware flow control) as the Cisco access server or router. See your modem documentation for exact configuration command syntax.

For more information about troubleshooting access server- to-modem connections, see Chapter 16, "Troubleshooting Dialup Connections." For information on troubleshooting hardware problems, see Chapter 3, "Troubleshooting Hardware and Booting Problems."

## CHAPTER 10

Troubleshooting IBM

This chapter focuses on connectivity and performance problems associated with bridging and routing in IBM-based networks. When troubleshooting IBM-based networks, it is important to have a knowledge of Synchronous Data Link Control (SDLC) and source-route bridging (SRB), as well as data-link switching (DLSw). The following sections provide an overview of DLSw, SDLC, and SRB.

DLSw

Data-link switching was developed to provide support for SNA and NetBIOS in multiprotocol routers. SNA and NetBIOS are basically connection-oriented protocols, so the data link control procedure that they use on the LAN is IEEE 802.2 Logical Link Control (LLC) Type 2. Data-link switching also accommodates SNA protocols over WAN links via the SDLC protocol. For more information about DLSw, refer to RFC 1795, which defines the protocol.

For more information about troubleshooting DLSw problems, refer to the online "DLSw Troubleshooting Guide" at www.cisco.com/warp/customer/697/dlswts1.html.

SDLC

IBM developed the SDLC protocol in the mid-1970s for use in Systems Network Architecture (SNA) environments. SDLC was the first of an important new breed of link-layer protocols based on synchronous, bit-oriented operation. Compared to synchronous character-oriented (for example, Bisync, from IBM) and synchronous byte count–oriented protocols (for example, Digital Data Communications Message Protocol [DDCMP], from Digital Equipment Corporation), bit-oriented synchronous protocols are more efficient, more flexible, and often faster.

After developing SDLC, IBM submitted it to various standards committees. The International Organization for Standardization (ISO) modified SDLC to create the High-Level Data Link Control (HDLC) protocol. The International Telecommunications Union–Telecommunications Standards Section (ITU-T, formerly CCITT) subsequently modified HDLC to create Link Access Procedure (LAP) and then Link Access Procedure, Balanced (LAPB). The Institute of Electrical and Electronic Engineers (IEEE) modified HDLC to create IEEE 802.2. Each of these protocols has become important in its own domain. SDLC remains the SNA primary link-layer protocol for wide-area network (WAN) links.

Technology Basics

SDLC supports a variety of link types and topologies. It can be used with point-to-point and multipoint links, bounded and unbounded media, half-duplex and full-duplex transmission facilities, and circuit-switched and packet-switched networks.

SDLC identifies two types of network nodes:

- **Primary**—Controls the operation of other stations (called secondaries). The primary polls the secondaries in a predetermined order. Secondaries can then transmit if they have outgoing data. The primary also sets up and tears down links and manages the link while it is operational.

- **Secondary**—Is controlled by a primary. Secondaries can send information only to the primary, but they cannot do this unless the primary gives permission.

SDLC primaries and secondaries can be connected in four basic configurations:

- **Point-to-point**—Involves only two nodes, one primary and one secondary.

- **Multipoint**—Involves one primary and multiple secondaries.

- **Loop**—Involves a loop topology, with the primary connected to the first and last secondaries. Intermediate secondaries pass messages through one another as they respond to the requests of the primary.

- **Hub go-ahead**—Involves an inbound and an outbound channel. The primary uses the outbound channel to communicate with the secondaries. The secondaries use the inbound channel to communicate with the primary. The inbound channel is daisy-chained back to the primary through each secondary.

Frame Format

The SDLC frame format is shown in Figure 10-1.

Figure 10-1 *The SDLC Frame Format*

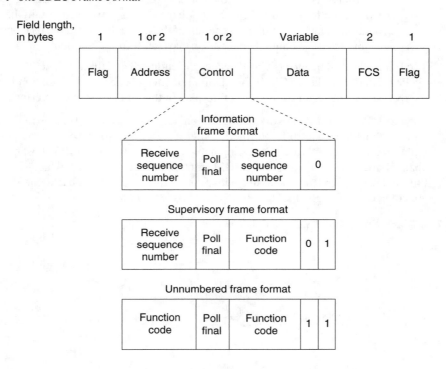

As Figure 10-1 shows, SDLC frames are bounded by a unique flag pattern. The Address field always contains the address of the secondary involved in the current communication. Because the primary is either the communication source or destination, there is no need to include the address of the primary—it is already known by all secondaries.

The Control field uses three different formats, depending on the type of SDLC frame used. The three SDLC frames are described as follows:

- **Information (I) frames**—These frames carry upper-layer information and some control information. Send and receive sequence numbers and the poll final (P/F) bit perform flow and error control. The send sequence number refers to the number of the frame to be sent next. The receive sequence number provides the number of the frame to be received next. Both the sender and the receiver maintain send and receive sequence numbers. The primary uses the P/F bit to tell the secondary whether it requires an immediate response. The secondary uses this bit to tell the primary whether the current frame is the last in its current response.

- **Supervisory (S) frames**—These frames provide control information. They request and suspend transmission, report on status, and acknowledge the receipt of I frames. They do not have an Information field.

- **Unnumbered (U) frames**—As the name suggests, these frames are not sequenced. They are used for control purposes. For example, they are used to initialize secondaries. Depending on the function of the unnumbered frame, its Control field is 1 or 2 bytes. Some unnumbered frames have an Information field.

The frame check sequence (FCS) precedes the ending flag delimiter. The FCS is usually a cyclic redundancy check (CRC) calculation remainder. The CRC calculation is redone in the receiver. If the result differs from the value in the sender's frame, an error is assumed.

A typical SDLC-based network configuration appears in Figure 10-2. As illustrated, an IBM establishment controller (formerly called a cluster controller) in a remote site connects to dumb terminals and to a Token Ring network. In a local site, an IBM host connects (via channel-attached techniques) to an IBM front-end processor (FEP), which can also have links to local Token Ring local-area networks (LANs) and an SNA backbone. The two sites are connected through an SDLC-based 56-kbps leased line.

Figure 10-2 *A Typical SDLC-Based Network Configuration*

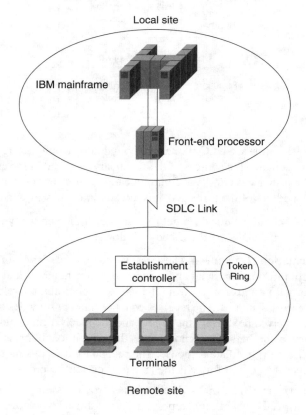

SRB

The SRB algorithm was developed by IBM and proposed to the IEEE 802.5 committee as the means to bridge among all LANs. The IEEE 802.5 committee subsequently adopted SRB into the IEEE 802.5 Token Ring LAN specification.

Since its initial proposal, IBM has offered a new bridging standard to the IEEE 802 committee: the source-route transparent (SRT) bridging solution. SRT bridging eliminates pure SRBs entirely, proposing that the two types of LAN bridges be transparent bridges and SRT bridges. Although SRT bridging has support, SRBs are still widely deployed.

SRB Algorithm

SRBs are so named because they assume that the complete source-to-destination route is placed in all inter-LAN frames sent by the source. SRBs store and forward the frames as indicated by the route appearing in the appropriate frame field. Figure 10-3 illustrates a sample SRB network.

Figure 10-3 *A Sample SRB Network*

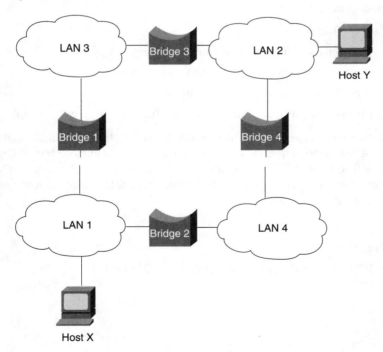

Referring to Figure 10-3, assume that Host X wants to send a frame to Host Y. Initially, Host X does not know whether Host Y resides on the same LAN or a different LAN. To determine this, Host X sends out a test frame. If that frame returns to Host X without a positive indication that Host Y has seen it, Host X must assume that Host Y is on a remote segment.

To determine the exact remote location of Host Y, Host X sends an explorer frame. Each bridge receiving the explorer frame (Bridges 1 and 2, in this example) copies the frame onto all outbound ports. Route information is added to the explorer frames as they travel through the internetwork. When Host X's explorer frames reach Host Y, Host Y replies to each individually using the accumulated route information. Upon receipt of all response frames, Host X chooses a path based on some predetermined criteria.

In the example in Figure 10-3, this process will yield two routes:

- LAN 1 to Bridge 1, to LAN 3, to Bridge 3, to LAN 2
- LAN 1 to Bridge 2, to LAN 4, to Bridge 4, to LAN 2

Host X must select one of these two routes. The IEEE 802.5 specification does not mandate the criteria that Host X should use in choosing a route, but it does make several suggestions, including the following:

- First frame received
- Response with the minimum number of hops
- Response with the largest allowed frame size
- Various combinations of these criteria

In most cases, the path contained in the first frame received will be used.

After a route is selected, it is inserted into frames destined for Host Y in the form of a routing information field (RIF). A RIF is included only in those frames destined for other LANs. The presence of routing information within the frame is indicated by the setting of the most significant bit within the Source Address field, called the routing information indicator (RII) bit.

Frame Format

The IEEE 802.5 RIF is structured as shown in Figure 10-4.

Figure 10-4 *The IEEE 802.5 RIF*

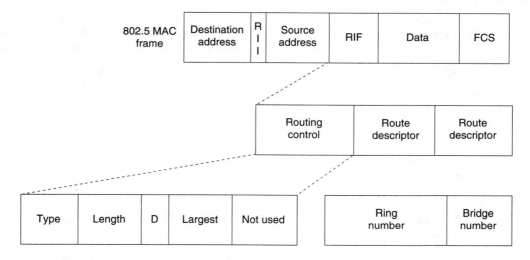

The fields of the RIF are as follows:

- The Routing Control field, which consists of the following subfields:

  — The Type subfield in the RIF indicates whether the frame should be routed to a single node, a group of nodes that make up a spanning tree of the internetwork, or all nodes. The first type is called a specifically routed frame, the second type is called a spanning-tree explorer, and the third type is called an all-paths explorer. The spanning-tree explorer can be used as a transit mechanism for multicast frames. It can also be used as a replacement for the all-paths explorer in outbound route queries. In this case, the destination responds with an all-paths explorer.

  — The Length subfield indicates the total length (in bytes) of the RIF.

  — The D bit indicates the direction of the frame (forward or reverse).

  — The largest field indicates the largest frame that can be handled along this route.

- The Route Descriptor field, of which there can be more than one. Each route descriptor field carries a ring number/bridge number pair that specifies a portion of a route. Routes, then, are simply alternating sequences of LAN and bridge numbers that start and end with LAN numbers.

Troubleshooting IBM

This section focuses on connectivity and performance problems associated with bridging and routing in IBM-based networks. This section covers specific IBM-related symptoms, the problems that are likely to cause each symptom, and the solutions to those problems.

This section covers the most common network issues in IBM networks:

- Local SRB: Host Cannot Connect to Server
- Local RSRB: Routing Does Not Function
- RSRB: Host Cannot Connect to Server (Peers Not Open)
- RSRB: Host Cannot Connect to Server (Peers Open)
- RSRB: Periodic Communication Failures
- RSRB: NetBIOS Client Cannot Connect to Server
- Translational Bridging: Client Cannot Connect to Server
- SRT Bridging: Client Cannot Connect to Server
- SDLC: Router Cannot Communicate with SDLC Device
- SDLC: Intermittent Connectivity
- SDLC: Client Cannot Connect to Host over Router Running SDLLC
- SDLC: Sessions Fail over Router Running STUN
- CIP: CLAW Connection Does Not Come Up
- CIP: No Enabled LED On
- CIP: CIP Will Not Come Online to Host
- CIP: Router Cannot **ping** Host, or Host Cannot **ping** Router
- CIP: Host Cannot Reach Remote Networks
- CIP: Host Running Routed Has No Routes

Local SRB: Host Cannot Connect to Server

Symptom: Connections fail over a router configured as an SRB connecting two or more Token Rings.

Table 10-1 outlines the problems that might cause this symptom and describes solutions to those problems.

Table 10-1   *Local SRB: Host Cannot Connect to Server*

Possible Problem	Solution
Ring number mismatch	A router interface configured for bridging fails to insert into a ring when it detects a ring number mismatch, and it posts an error message to the console.

<table>
<tr><td></td><td>

Step 1   Get the ring number (specified in hexadecimal) from IBM SRBs (either by examining the configuration of other SRBs or from the system administrator).

Step 2   Use the **show running-config** (or simply **show run**) privileged exec command to view the configuration of routers configured as SRBs. Look for **source-bridge** interface configuration command entries that assign ring numbers (displayed in decimal) to the rings that are connected to the router's interfaces.[1]

For example, the following configuration entry shows the entry for local ring 10, bridge number 500, and remote ring 20:

```
source-bridge 10 500 20
```

Note: Parallel bridges situated between the same two rings must have different bridge numbers.

Step 3   Convert IBM SRB ring numbers to decimal, and verify that the ring numbers configured on all internetworking nodes agree.

Step 4   If the ring numbers do not agree, reconfigure the router interface or IBM SRBs so that the ring numbers match. Use the **source-bridge** command to make configuration changes; the syntax is as follows:

source-bridge *source-ring-number bridge-number target-ring-number [conserve-ring]*

Syntax description:

- *source-ring-number*—Ring number for the interface's Token Ring or FDDI[2] ring. It must be a decimal number in the range 1 to 4095 that uniquely identifies a network segment or ring within the bridged Token Ring or FDDI network.

- *bridge-number*—Number that uniquely identifies the bridge connecting the source and target rings. It must be a decimal number in the range 1 to 15.

- *target-ring-number*—Ring number of the destination ring on this router. It must be unique within the bridged Token Ring or FDDI network. The target ring can also be a ring group. This must be a decimal number.

</td></tr>
</table>

continues

Table 10-1   *Local SRB: Host Cannot Connect to Server (Continued)*

Possible Problem	Solution
Ring number mismatch *(continued)*	• *conserve-ring*—(Optional) Keyword to enable SRB over Frame Relay. When this option is configured, the SRB software does not add the ring number associated with the Frame Relay PVC,[3] the partner's virtual ring, to outbound explorer frames. This option is permitted for Frame Relay subinterfaces only.
	Example:
	In the following example, Token Rings 129 and 130 are connected via a router:
	``` interface tokenring 0 source-bridge 129 1 130 ! interface tokenring 1 source-bridge active 130 1 129 ```
End system that does not support RIF[4]	**Step 1** Place a network analyzer on the same ring to which the end system is connected.
	Step 2 Look for RIF frames sent from the end system (RIF frames have the high-order bit of the source MAC[5] address set to 1).
	Step 3 If no RIF frames are found, the end system does not support RIF and cannot participate in source routing.
	If the protocol is routable, you can route the protocol or configure transparent bridging. If you use transparent bridging, be careful not to create loops between the SRB and the transparent bridging domains.
	Step 4 If your environment requires SRB, contact your workstation or server vendor for SRB drivers or for information about setting up your workstation or server to support SRB.
Hop count exceeded	Use the **show** *protocol* **route** command to check the hop count values on routers and bridges in the path. Packets that exceed the hop count are dropped.
	Alternatively, you can enable the **debug source event** privileged exec command to see whether packets are being dropped because the hop count has been exceeded.

Table 10-1   *Local SRB: Host Cannot Connect to Server (Continued)*

Possible Problem	Solution
Hop count exceeded *(continued)*	**Caution:** Because debugging output is assigned high priority in the CPU process, it can render the system unusable. For this reason, use **debug** commands only to troubleshoot specific problems or during troubleshooting sessions with Cisco technical support staff. Moreover, it is best to use **debug** commands during periods of lower network traffic and fewer users. Debugging during these periods decreases the likelihood that increased **debug** command processing overhead will affect system use. Remember to use the **undebug all** command to turn off debugging after troubleshooting. Increase the hop count if it is less than the default value, 7. Otherwise, the network must be redesigned so that no destination is more than seven hops away.
| Router that is not configured to forward spanning explorers | Spanning explorer packets are equivalent to a single-route broadcast. Routers must therefore be configured to route them.<br><br>**Step 1**  Use the **show source-bridge** exec command to determine whether the spanning explorer count is incrementing.<br><br>**Step 2**  If the spanning explorer count is not incrementing, use the **show running-config** privileged exec command on routers to see whether the **source-bridge spanning** interface configuration command is configured. This command configures the router to forward spanning explorers.<br><br>**Step 3**  If the command entry is not present in the configuration, add it to any router that is required to pass spanning explorers. The command syntax is as follows:<br><br>**source-bridge spanning** *bridge-group* [**path-cost** *path-cost*]<br><br>**Syntax description:**<br><br>• *bridge-group*—Number in the range 1 to 9 that you choose to refer to a particular group of bridged interfaces.<br><br>• **path-cost**—(Optional) Path cost for a specified interface.<br><br>• *path-cost*—(Optional) Path cost for the interface. The valid range is 0 to 65535.<br><br>**Example:**<br><br>The following example adds Token Ring 0 to bridge group 1 and assigns a path cost of 12 to Token Ring 0:<br><br>```
interface tokenring 0
 source-bridge spanning 1 path-cost 12
```<br><br>**Step 4**  Use the **show source-bridge** exec command to determine whether explorers are being sent. |

continues
```

Table 10-1   *Local SRB: Host Cannot Connect to Server (Continued)*

Possible Problem	Solution	
Router that is not configured to forward spanning explorers *(continued)*	**Step 5**	If explorers are not being sent, place a network analyzer on the same ring to which the end system is connected.
	Step 6	If you find spanning all-ring frames, use the **show running-config** privileged exec command to make sure that the router is properly configured. If sessions still cannot be established over the SRB, contact your technical support representative for more assistance.

[1]Although you can enter the ring number in hexadecimal or decimal, it always appears in the configuration as a decimal number.

[2]FDDI = Fiber Distributed Data Interface

[3]PVC= permanent virtual circuit

[4]RIF = routing information field

[5]MAC = Media Access Control

Local SRB: Routing Does Not Function

Symptom: Routed protocols are not forwarded properly by routers in a local SRB environment. SRBs bridge traffic normally.

Table 10-2 outlines the problems that might cause this symptom and describes solutions to those problems.

Table 10-2   *Local SRB: Routing Does Not Function*

Possible Problem	Solution	
Routing problem	For detailed information on troubleshooting routing problems, refer to the chapters in this book that cover the routing protocols in question. For example, if you are running Novell IPX, see Chapter 8, "Troubleshooting Novell IPX."	
Missing **multiring** command	**Step 1**	Use the **show running-config** privileged exec command on the router. Look for a **multiring** interface configuration command entry. This command enables the collection and use of RIF information on router interfaces.
	Step 2	If the **multiring** command is not present, add the command to the configuration using the following command:
		`C4000(config-if)#multiring all`

Table 10-2   *Local SRB: Routing Does Not Function (Continued)*

Possible Problem	Solution	
Incomplete ARP[1] table	**Step 1**	Determine whether you can **ping** hosts.
	Step 2	If the host does not respond, use the **show arp** exec command to determine whether an entry for the host exists in the ARP table.
	Step 3	If an entry exists, there is probably a routing problem. Determine whether you have a source-route path to the destination hardware (MAC) address. Use the **show rif** exec command to match the RIF with the hardware address of the host.
	Step 4	If no entry exists, use a network analyzer to see whether ARP requests are getting through to the remote ring and to see whether replies come back.

[1]ARP=Address Resolution Protocol

RSRB: Host Cannot Connect to Server (Peers Not Open)

Symptom: Hosts cannot make connections to servers across a router configured as a remote source-routing bridge (RSRB). The output of the **show source-bridge** privileged exec command shows that SRB peers are not open.

NOTE   If you succeed in getting peers to open, but hosts are still incapable of communicating with servers, refer to the section "RSRB: Host Cannot Connect to Server (Peers Open)," later in this chapter.

Table 10-3 outlines the problems that might cause this symptom and describes solutions to those problems.

Table 10-3   *RSRB: Host Cannot Connect to Server (Peers Not Open)*

Possible Problem	Solution	
Missing or misconfigured **source-bridge remote-peer** command on the router	**Step 1**	Use the **show source-bridge** exec command to check for remote peers.
		If the output shows that peers are open, refer to the section "RSRB: Host Cannot Connect to Server (Peers Open)," later in this chapter.

continues

Table 10-3   *RSRB: Host Cannot Connect to Server (Peers Not Open) (Continued)*

Possible Problem	Solution	
Missing or misconfigured **source-bridge remote-peer** command on the router *(continued)*	**Step 2**	If the output shows that peers are not open, use the **show running-config** privileged exec command to view the router configuration. Verify that two **source-bridge remote-peer** global configuration command entries are present—one should point to the IP address of the local router, and the other should point to the IP address of the remote router.
	Step 3	If either or both of the commands are missing or point to the wrong address, add or modify the commands as required.
		For detailed information about configuring routers for RSRB, see the Cisco *IOS Bridging and IBM Networking Configuration Guide* and *Bridging and IBM Networking Command Reference*.
No route to the remote peer	If you are using TCP[1] or FST[2] encapsulation between the local and remote SRB, follow these steps:	
	Step 1	Test IP connectivity using the extended **ping privileged** exec command. Use the local peer ID as the source address, and the remote peer ID as the destination address.
	Step 2	If the ping fails, use the **show ip route** exec command to view the IP routing table.
	Step 3	If the **show ip route** output does not show a route to the intended remote peer, there is probably an IP routing problem, or a problem with the hardware or cabling in the path from the local to the remote SRB.
		For information on troubleshooting IP routing, refer to Chapter 7, "Troubleshooting TCP/IP." For information about troubleshooting hardware problems, see Chapter 3, "Troubleshooting Hardware and Booting."
Serial link problem	If there is a direct connection between the local and remote SRB (that is, if you are not using FST or TCP encapsulation), follow these steps:	
	Step 1	Check to make sure that the next-hop router is directly adjacent.
	Step 2	If the router is adjacent, perform other tests to ensure that the link is functioning properly. For more information, refer to Chapter 15, "Troubleshooting Serial Lines."
	Step 3	If the next hop is not directly adjacent, redesign your network so that it is.

Table 10-3   *RSRB: Host Cannot Connect to Server (Peers Not Open) (Continued)*

Possible Problem	Solution
End system that is not generating explorer traffic	**Step 1** Use the **show source-bridge** privileged exec command to see whether the explorer count is incrementing.
	Step 2 If the explorer count is not incrementing, use the **show running-config** privileged exec command to view the router configuration. Check for a source-bridge spanning interface configuration command on the local and remote routers.
	Step 3 If the **source-bridge spanning** command is not configured on the routers, configure it on the interfaces connecting the local and remote SRBs. This command is required if the end system is using single-route explorers. The command syntax is as follows:
	source-bridge spanning *bridge-group* [**path-cost** *path-cost*]
	Syntax description:
	• *bridge-group*—Number in the range 1 to 9 that you choose to refer to a particular group of bridged interfaces.
	• **path-cost**—(Optional) Path cost for a specified interface.
	• *path-cost*—(Optional) Path cost for the interface. The valid range is 0 to 65535.
	Example:
	The following example adds Token Ring 0 to bridge group 1 and assigns a path cost of 12 to Token Ring 0:
	``` interface tokenring 0 source-bridge spanning 1 path-cost 12 ```
Encapsulation mismatch	**Step 1** Use the **show interfaces** exec command to verify that the interface and line protocol are up. If the status line indicates any other state, refer to Chapter 15.
	Step 2 Verify that the configured encapsulation type matches the requirements of the network to which the serial interface is attached.
	For example, if the serial interface is attached to a leased line but the configured encapsulation type is Frame Relay, there is an encapsulation mismatch.
	Step 3 To resolve the mismatch, change the encapsulation type on the serial interface to the type appropriate for the attached network— for example, change from frame-relay to hdlc.

continues

Table 10-3   *RSRB: Host Cannot Connect to Server (Peers Not Open) (Continued)*

Possible Problem	Solution	
Hop count exceeded	**Step 1**	Use the **show** *protocol* **route** command to check the hop count values on routers and bridges in the path. Packets that exceed the hop count are dropped.
		Alternatively, you can enable the **debug source event** privileged exec command to see whether packets are being dropped because the hop count has been exceeded.
		Caution: Because debugging output is assigned high priority in the CPU process, it can render the system unusable. For this reason, use **debug** commands only to troubleshoot specific problems or during troubleshooting sessions with Cisco technical support staff. Moreover, it is best to use **debug** commands during periods of lower network traffic and fewer users. Debugging during these periods decreases the likelihood that increased **debug** command processing overhead will affect system use.
	Step 2	Increase the hop count if it is less than the default value, 7. Otherwise, the network must be redesigned so that no destination is greater than seven hops away.

[1]TCP=Transmission Control Protocol
[2]FST=Fast Sequenced Transport

RSRB: Host Cannot Connect to Server (Peers Open)

Symptom: Hosts cannot make connections to servers across a router configured as an RSRB. The output of the **show source-bridge** privileged exec command shows that SRB peers are open.

The following is an example of output from the **show source-bridge** command:

```
ionesco#show source-bridge
[...]
Peers:                    state   lv  pkts_rx   pkts_tx   expl_gn     drops TCP
    TCP 150.136.92.92      -       2       0         0         0       0   0
    TCP 150.136.93.93      open    2*      18        18        3       0   0
[...]
```

Table 10-4 outlines the problems that might cause this symptom and describes solutions to those problems.

Table 10-4   *RSRB: Host Cannot Connect to Server (Peers Open)*

Possible Problem	Solution
End system misconfiguration	**Step 1** If the end system is on the ring local to the router, use the **show lnm station** privileged exec command on the local router. This command lists the stations on the local ring.

The following is an example of the **show lnm station** command:

```
show lnm station [address]
```

Syntax description:

- *address*—(Optional) Address of a specific LNM[1] station

Sample Display:

The following is sample output from the **show lnm station** command when a particular address (in this case, 1000.5abc15) has been specified:

```
Router# show lnm station 1000.5a6f.bc15
isolating error counts
      station       int  ring  loc.   weight   line  inter burst
ac  abort
1000.5a6f.bc15    T1  0001  0000   00 - N   00000 00000 00000
00000 00000
Unique ID:    0000.0000.0000            NAUN: 0000.3000.abc4
Functional: C000.0000.0000             Group: C000.0000.0000
Physical Location:   00000        Enabled Classes:   0000
Allowed Priority:     00000        Address Modifier: 0000
Product ID:       00000000.00000000.00000000.00000000.0000
Ucode Level:      00000000.00000000.0000
Station Status: 00000000.0000
Last transmit status: 00
```

Step 2 Check the command output for the MAC address of the workstation or server. If the MAC address is not present in the output, check the configuration of the end system.

Step 3 If the problem persists, use a network analyzer to check network traffic generated by the end system. If you do not have a network analyzer, use the **debug token-ring** and the **debug source-bridge** commands.

Caution: Using the **debug token-ring** and the **debug source-bridge** commands on a heavily loaded router is not advised. These commands can cause further network degradation or complete network failure if not used judiciously.

Step 4 Check the output of the **debug** commands to see whether the end system is sending traffic to the correct MAC addresses or destination names (in the case of NetBIOS).

continues

Table 10-4   *RSRB: Host Cannot Connect to Server (Peers Open) (Continued)*

Possible Problem	Solution	
End system that does not support RIF	**Step 1**	Place a network analyzer on the same ring to which the end system is connected.
	Step 2	Look for RIF frames sent from the end system (RIF frames have the high-order bit of the source MAC address set to 1).
	Step 3	If no RIF frames are seen, the end system does not support RIF and cannot participate in source routing.
		If the protocol is routable, you can route the protocol or configure transparent bridging. If you use transparent bridging, be careful not to create loops between the SRB and the transparent bridging domains.
	Step 4	If your environment requires SRB, contact your workstation or server vendor for SRB drivers or for information about setting up your workstation or server to support SRB.
Explorer traffic that is not reaching remote ring	**Step 1**	Using a network analyzer or the **debug source-bridge** command, watch network traffic to see whether explorers from the end system reach the remote ring.
	Step 2	If traffic reaches the remote ring successfully, check the configuration of the destination end system (for example, a server) to see why that station does not reply to the explorer traffic from the source.
		If traffic does not reach the remote ring, use the **show source-bridge** command to check ring lists. If information about the ring has not been learned, check router configurations.
	Step 3	If you are using NetBIOS, use the **show netbios name-cache** exec command to see whether traffic is passing through the network properly. If it is not, check router configurations.
		For detailed information about configuring routers for RSRB, refer to the Cisco IOS *Bridging and IBM Networking Configuration Guide* and *Bridging and IBM Networking Command Reference*.

[1]LNM=LAN Network Manager

RSRB: Periodic Communication Failures

Symptom: Communication failures occur periodically over a router configured as an RSRB.

Table 10-5 outlines the problems that might cause this symptom and describes solutions to those problems.

Table 10-5   *RSRB: Periodic Communication Failures*

Possible Problem	Solution	
Misconfigured T1 timers	If you are not using local acknowledgment, misconfigured T1 timers can cause periodic timeouts.	
	Step 1	Use a network analyzer to see how long it takes for packets to travel from one end of the network to the other. (Note: Inserting a network analyzer to a T1 circuit will bring the circuit down.)
	Step 2	Use a **ping** test to the remote router, and note the round-trip delay. Compare this value with the configured T1 timer values on end systems.
	Step 3	If the round-trip delay is close to or exceeds the T1 timer value, acknowledgments are probably being delayed or dropped by the WAN. For delays, increase the T1 configuration on end systems. For drops, check buffers and interface queues.
	Step 4	Enable local acknowledgment to see whether that solves the problem.
WAN link problem	For information on troubleshooting serial line problems, refer to Chapter 15. For information on troubleshooting different WAN environments, refer to the appropriate chapter elsewhere in this book.	

RSRB: NetBIOS Client Cannot Connect to Server

Symptom: NetBIOS clients cannot connect to NetBIOS servers over a router configured as an RSRB.

Table 10-6 outlines the problems that might cause this symptom and describes solutions to those problems.

Table 10-6   *RSRB: NetBIOS Client Cannot Connect to Server*

Possible Problem	Solution	
Incorrect mapping of NetBIOS name cache server-to-client mapping	**Step 1**	For each router on which NetBIOS name caching is enabled, use the **show rif** exec command to determine whether the RIF entry shows the correct path from the router to both the client and the server.

continues

Table 10-6 *RSRB: NetBIOS Client Cannot Connect to Server (Continued)*

Possible Problem	Solution
| Incorrect mapping of NetBIOS name cache server-to-client mapping *(continued)* | The following is an example of the **show rif** exec command:<br><br>```
cantatrice#show rif
Codes: * interface, - static, + remote
Hardware Addr  How   Idle (min)  Routing Information
                                  Field
5C02.0001.4322 rg5        -       0630.0053.00B0
5A00.0000.2333 TR0        3       08B0.0101.2201.0FF0
5B01.0000.4444 -          -       -
0000.1403.4800 TR1        0       -
0000.2805.4C00 TR0        *       -
0000.2807.4C00 TR1        *       -
0000.28A8.4800 TR0        0       -
0077.2201.0001 rg5        10      0830.0052.2201.0FF0
```<br><br>In this display, entries marked with an asterisk (*) are the router's interface addresses. Entries marked with a dash (-) are static entries. Entries with a number denote cached entries. If the RIF timeout is set to something other than the default of 15 minutes, the timeout is displayed at the top of the display. |

Step 2 Use the **show running-config** privileged exec command to view the router configuration. Make sure that the **source-bridge proxy-explorer** interface configuration command is included in the Token Ring configuration. Proxy explorers must be enabled on any interface that uses NetBIOS name caching.

Step 3 Use the **show netbios-cache** exec command to see whether the NetBIOS cache entry shows the correct mappings of server and client names to MAC addresses.

The following is an example of the **show netbios-cache** exec command:

```
cantatrice#show netbios-cache
  HW Addr         Name       How    Idle   NetBIOS Packet
                                            Savings
  1000.5a89.449a  IC6W06_B   TR1    6      0
  1000.5a8b.14e5  IC_9Q07A   TR1    2      0
  1000.5a25.1b12  IC9Q19_A   TR1    7      0
  1000.5a25.1b12  IC9Q19_A   TR1    10     0
  1000.5a8c.7bb1  BKELSA1    TR1    4      0
  1000.5a8b.6c7c  ICELSB1    TR1    -      0
  1000.5a31.df39  ICASC_01   TR1    -      0
  1000.5ada.47af  BKELSA2    TR1    10     0
  1000.5a8f.018a  ICELSC1    TR1    1      0
```
```

Table 10-6   *RSRB: NetBIOS Client Cannot Connect to Server (Continued)*

Possible Problem	Solution
Incorrect mapping of NetBIOS name cache server-to-client mapping *(continued)*	The following are the fields reported by the **show netbios-cache** command: • **show netbios**—Cache field descriptions. • **HW Addr**—MAC address mapped to the NetBIOS name in this entry. • **Name**—NetBIOS name mapped to the MAC address in this entry. • **How**—Interface through which this information was learned. • **Idle**—Period of time (in seconds) since this entry was last accessed. A hyphen in this column indicates that it is a static entry in the NetBIOS name cache. • **NetBIOS Packet Savings**—Number of packets to which local replies were made (thus preventing transmission of these packets over the network).
	Step 4 Use the **show running-config** privileged exec command at each router to examine the mapping of addresses specified in **netbios name-cache** global configuration command entries. The following example shows a configuration in which the NetBIOS server is accessed remotely: ``` source-bridge ring-group 2 rif 0110.2222.3333 0630.021.0030 ring group 2 netbios name-cache 0110.2222.3333 DEF ring-group 2 ```
Misconfigured **source-bridge** command	**Step 1** For each router on which NetBIOS name caching is enabled, use the **show source-bridge** command to obtain the version of the remote connection. The value specified should be 2 or 3. If the value is 1, connections will not get through, and you must modify your configuration.

continues

Table 10-6   *RSRB: NetBIOS Client Cannot Connect to Server (Continued)*

Possible Problem	Solution
Misconfigured **source-bridge** command	**Example:** The following is sample output from the **show source-bridge** command:

```
Router# show source-bridge
Local Interfaces:                     receive           transmit
               srn bn  trn r p s n  max hops    cnt            cnt
drops
TR0             5  1   10 *   *         7        39:1002      23:62923
Ring Group 10:
  This peer: TCP 150.136.92.92
   Maximum output TCP queue length, per peer: 100
  Peers:                      state   lv  pkts_rx  pkts_tx  expl_gn
drops TCP
    TCP 150.136.92.92         -       2     0        0        0   0   0
    TCP 150.136.93.93         open    2*   18       18        3   0   0
Rings:
   bn: 1 rn: 5     local  ma: 4000.3080.844b TokenRing0
fwd: 18
   bn: 1 rn: 2   remote  ma: 4000.3080.8473 TCP 150.136.93.93
fwd: 36
Explorers: ------- input -------            ------- output --
-----
        spanning  all-rings     total     spanning  all-rings
total
   TR0      0          3           3           3         5          8
Router#
```

Step 2   If the router is running a software release prior to Cisco IOS
Release 10.0, specify either version 2 or version 3 in the **source-
bridge remote-peer** interface configuration command. The
syntax is as follows:

source-bridge remote-peer *ring-group tcp ip-address* [*lf size*]
[*local-ack*] [*priority*] [*version number*]

If the router is running Cisco IOS Release 10.0 or later, the
specification of a version is ignored.

For more information, refer to the Cisco IOS *Bridging and IBM
Networking Configuration Guide* and *Bridging and IBM
Networking Command Reference.*

Translational Bridging: Client Cannot Connect to Server

Symptom: Clients cannot communicate over a router configured as a translational bridge.

CAUTION	In certain situations, replacing existing translational bridges with Cisco translational bridges can cause interoperability problems. Some translational bridge implementations map functional addresses between media (such as local-area transport [LAT] functional address 0900.2B00.00FA on Ethernet) to a broadcast address on the Token Ring side (such as C000.FFFF.FFFF). Cisco does not support this functionality. Furthermore, you cannot use translational bridging with any protocol that embeds the MAC address of a station inside the Information field of the MAC frames (examples include IP ARP and Novell IPX).

Table 10-7 outlines the problems that might cause this symptom and describes solutions to those problems.

Table 10-7   *Translational Bridging: Client Cannot Connect to Server*

Possible Problem	Solution	
Media problem	Verify the line using the **show interfaces** exec command. If the interface or line protocol is down, troubleshoot the media. For LAN media, refer to the chapter that covers your media type.	
Ethernet–to–Token Ring address mapping that is misconfigured	**Step 1**	Use the **show bridge** exec command to verify the existence of the Ethernet station. Ethernet and Token Ring addresses use opposite bit ordering schemes. The Token Ring address 0110.2222.3333 is equivalent to the Ethernet address 8008.4444.cccc.
	Step 2	Use the **show spanning** exec command to determine whether the Ethernet port is in forwarding mode.

continues

Table 10-7   *Translational Bridging: Client Cannot Connect to Server (Continued)*

Possible Problem	Solution

Ethernet–to–Token Ring address mapping that is misconfigured *(continued)*	**Example:** The following is sample output from the **show span** command:

```
RouterA> show span
Bridge Group 1 is executing the IBM compatible spanning tree
protocol
   Bridge Identifier has priority 32768, address 0000.0c0c.f68b
   Configured hello time 2, max age 6, forward delay 4
   Current root has priority 32768, address 0000.0c0c.f573
   Root port is 001A (TokenRing0/0), cost of root path is 16
   Topology change flag not set, detected flag not set
   Times:  hold 1, topology change 30, notification 30
           hello 2, max age 6, forward delay 4, aging 300
   Timers: hello 0, topology change 0, notification 0
Port 001A (TokenRing0/0) of bridge group 1 is forwarding. Path
cost 16
   Designated root has priority 32768, address 0000.0c0c.f573
   Designated bridge has priority 32768, address 0000.0c0c.f573
   Designated port is 001B, path cost 0, peer 0
   Timers: message age 1, forward delay 0, hold 0
Port 002A (TokenRing0/1) of bridge group 1 is blocking. Path
cost 16
   Designated root has priority 32768, address 0000.0c0c.f573
   Designated bridge has priority 32768, address 0000.0c0c.f573
   Designated port is 002B, path cost 0, peer 0
   Timers: message age 0, forward delay 0, hold 0
Port 064A (spanRSRB) of bridge group 1 is disabled. Path cost 250
   Designated root has priority 32768, address 0000.0c0c.f573
   Designated bridge has priority 32768, address 0000.0c0c.f68b
   Designated port is 064A, path cost 16, peer 0
   Timers: message age 0, forward delay 0, hold 0
```

A port (spanRSRB) is created with each virtual ring group. The port is disabled until one or more peers go into open state in the ring group.

Step 3   Use the **show rif** exec command to determine whether the target Token Ring station is visible on the internetwork.

When configured for translational bridging, the router extracts the RIF of a packet received from the Token Ring network and saves it in a table. The router then transmits the packet on the Ethernet network. Later, the router reinserts the RIF when it receives a packet destined for the originating node on the Token Ring side.

Table 10-7   *Translational Bridging: Client Cannot Connect to Server (Continued)*

Possible Problem	Solution
Ethernet–to–Token Ring address mapping that is misconfigured *(continued)*	**Example:** The following is sample output from the show rif command: ``` Router# show rif Codes: * interface, - static, + remote Hardware Addr How Idle (min) Routing Information Field 5C02.0001.4322 rg5 - 0630.0053.00B0 5A00.0000.2333 TR0 3 08B0.0101.2201.0FF0 5B01.0000.4444 - - - 0000.1403.4800 TR1 0 - 0000.2805.4C00 TR0 * - 0000.2807.4C00 TR1 * - 0000.28A8.4800 TR0 0 - 0077.2201.0001 rg5 10 0830.0052.2201.0FF0 ``` **Step 4** If Ethernet and Token Ring end systems are visible, statically configure any relevant server MAC addresses in the client configurations so that clients can listen to the server advertisements directly. One case in which static mapping is required is when bridging DEC LAT traffic over a translational bridge. LAT services on Ethernet are advertised on a multicast address that is mapped by some translational bridges to a broadcast address on the Token Ring side. Routers do not support this mapping.
Vendor code mismatch	Older Token Ring implementations require that the vendor code (OUT[1] field) of the SNAP[2] header be 000000. Cisco routers modify this field to be 0000F8 to specify that the frame was translated from Ethernet Version 2 to Token Ring. This can cause problems on older Token Ring networks. Specify the **ethernet-transit-oui** interface configuration command to force the router to make the vendor code field 000000. This change is frequently required when there are IBM 8209s (IBM Token Ring-to-Ethernet translating bridges) in the network. The following is an example of the **ethernet-transit-oui** command: **ethernet-transit-oui** [*90-compatible* | *standard* | *cisco*] **Syntax description:** • *90-compatible*—OUI used 0000F8 by default, when talking to other Cisco routers. It provides the most flexibility. • *standard*—OUI used 000000 when talking to IBM 8209 bridges and other vendor equipment. It does not provide for as much flexibility as the other two choices.

continues

Table 10-7 *Translational Bridging: Client Cannot Connect to Server (Continued)*

Possible Problem	Solution

Vendor code mismatch *(continued)*	• *cisco*—OUI used 00000C, which provided for compatibility with future equipment.
	
	Example:
	
	The following example specifies Cisco's OUI form:
	
	`interface tokenring 0`
	`ethernet-transit-oui cisco`

Cisco and non-Cisco translational bridges in parallel	**Step 1** Check for translational bridges in parallel with the Cisco translational bridge. If there are any parallel non-Cisco translational bridges, loops will probably be created. **Step 2** Because implementing translational bridging defeats the spanning-tree mechanism of both transparent bridging and SRB environments, you must eliminate all loops caused by inserting the translational bridge. A transparent spanning tree and a source-bridge spanning tree cannot communicate with one another.
Trying to bridge protocols that embed MAC addresses in the Information field of the MAC frame (such as IP ARP,[3] Novell IPX, or AARP[4])	If MAC addresses are embedded in the Information field of the MAC frame, bridges will be incapable of reading the address. Bridges will therefore be incapable of forwarding the traffic. **Step 1** If you are attempting to bridge this type of protocol, route the protocol instead. **Step 2** If you still cannot communicate over the router, contact your technical support representative.

[1]OUI=organizationally unique identifier

[2]SNAP=Subnetwork Access Protocol

[3]ARP=Address Resolution Protocol

[4]AARP=AppleTalk Address Resolution Protocol

SRT Bridging: Client Cannot Connect to Server

Symptom: Clients cannot communicate over a router configured to perform SRT bridging. Packets are not forwarded by the SRT bridge.

SRT bridging enables you to implement transparent bridging in Token Ring environments. It is not a means of translating between SRB on a Token Ring and transparent bridging on Ethernet (or other) media.

Table 10-8 outlines the problems that might cause this symptom and describes solutions to those problems.

Table 10-8   *SRT Bridging: Client Cannot Connect to Server*

Possible Problem	Solution
Trying to bridge frames containing RIF from Token Ring network to Ethernet network over an SRT bridge	Use translational bridging instead of SRT bridging to allow SRB-to-transparent bridging translation. Because SRT bridging works only between Ethernet and Token Ring, any packet containing a RIF is dropped when SRT bridging is used.
Attempting to transfer large frame sizes	Problems will occur if Token Ring devices transmit frames exceeding the Ethernet MTU[1] of 1500 bytes. Configure hosts on the Token Ring to generate frame sizes less than or equal to the Ethernet MTU.
Trying to bridge protocols that embed the MAC address in the Information field of the MAC frame (such as IP ARP, Novell IPX, or AARP)	If MAC addresses are embedded in the Information field of the MAC frame, bridges will be incapable of reading the address. Bridges will therefore be incapable of forwarding the traffic. **Step 1** If you are attempting to bridge this type of protocol, route the protocol instead. **Step 2** If you still cannot communicate over the router, contact your technical support representative.
Media problem	Verify the line using the **show interfaces** exec command. If the interface or line protocol is down, troubleshoot the media. For LAN media, refer to the chapter that covers your media type.

[1]MTU=maximum transmission unit

SDLC: Router Cannot Communicate with SDLC Device

Symptom: Router cannot communicate with an IBM SDLC device.

Table 10-9 outlines the problems that might cause this symptom and describes solutions to those problems.

Table 10-9   *SDLC: Router Cannot Communicate with SDLC Device*

Possible Problem	Solution
Physical layer problem	**Step 1** Use the **show interfaces** exec command to determine whether the interface and line protocol are up.
	Step 2 If the interface and line protocol are both up, troubleshoot link-layer problems, as described later in this table.
	Step 3 If the output does not indicate that the interface up and the line protocol up, make sure that the device is powered on. Make sure that all cabling is correct, securely connected, and undamaged. Make sure that the cabling does not exceed the recommended length for the speed of the connection.

continues

Table 10-9   *SDLC: Router Cannot Communicate with SDLC Device (Continued)*

Possible Problem	Solution	
Physical layer problem *(continued)*	**Step 4**	If the interface or line protocol is still down, use a breakout box to check the signals on the line.
		Note: On some Cisco platforms, such as the Cisco 7500 running a recent Cisco IOS release, the output of the **show interfaces** command will indicate the state of line signals.
		If the router is full-duplex DCE,[1] check for DTR[2] and RTS.[3] If these signals are not high, proceed to Step 5. If these signals are high, the interface should be up. If it is not, contact your technical support representative.
		On a Cisco 7500, if the breakout box shows that the DTR and DTS signals are high, but **the show interfaces** command shows that they are not, check the router cabling. In particular, make sure that the 60-pin high-density cable is not plugged in to the router upside-down.
		If the router is half-duplex DCE, check for DTR. If DTR is not high, proceed to Step 5. If DTR is high, the interface should be up. If it is not, contact your technical support representative.
		Note: Half-duplex is not supported on Cisco 7000 series routers.
		If the router is full- or half-duplex DTE, check for CD. If CD is not high, proceed to Step 5. If CD is high, the interface should be up. If it is not, contact your technical support representative.
	Step 5	If the router is full-duplex DCE, make sure that the device is configured for permanent RTS high. If the device does not allow you to configure permanent RTS, set the signal high by strapping DTR from the device side to RTS on the router side (see Figure 10-5).
	Step 6	If the router is DCE, it may be required to provide clock to the device. Make sure that the **clock rate** interface configuration command is present in the router configuration. Use the **show running-config** privileged exec command on the router to view the interface configuration. The following example shows the clock rate information for interface serial 0.
		Example:
		The following example sets the clock rate on the first serial interface to 64000 bits per second:
| | | ```
interface serial 0
  clock rate 64000
``` |
| | | If the router is DTE, it should get clock from an external device. Make sure that a device is providing clock properly. Make sure that the clocking source is the same for all devices. |
```

Table 10-9   *SDLC: Router Cannot Communicate with SDLC Device (Continued)*

Possible Problem	Solution	
Link-layer problem (router is primary)	**Step 1**	Use the **debug sdlc** privileged exec command[4] to see whether the router is sending SNRMs.[5]
		Caution: Because debugging output is assigned high priority in the CPU process, it can render the system unusable. For this reason, use **debug** commands only to troubleshoot specific problems or during troubleshooting sessions with Cisco technical support staff. Moreover, it is best to use **debug** commands during periods of lower network traffic and fewer users. Debugging during these periods decreases the likelihood that increased **debug** command processing overhead will affect system use.
	Step 2	If the router is not sending SNRMs, check the physical layer (see the preceding problem in this table). If the router is sending SNRMs, the device should send UAs[6] in reply.
	Step 3	If the device is not sending UAs, make sure that the addresses of the router and device are correct.
	Step 4	If you are using a V.35 connection, make sure that the SCT/SCTE[7] setting is correct on the interface. The router should use SCTE if the router is DCE, and it should use SCT if the router is DTE.
		The SCT/SCTE setting might be changed with a jumper or with the software configuration **command dce-terminal-timing enable**, depending on the platform. Some platforms do not allow you to change this setting.
		Example:
		The following example prevents phase shifting of the data with respect to the clock:
		``` interface serial 0 dce-terminal-timing enable ```
	Step 5	Make sure that the device and the router are using the same signal coding (NRZ[8] or NRZI[9]). NRZ is enabled by default on the router. To enable NRZI encoding, use the **nrzi-encoding** interface configuration command.
		Example:
		In the following example, serial interface 1 is configured for NRZI encoding:
		``` interface serial 1 nrzi-encoding ```

continues

Table 10-9 *SDLC: Router Cannot Communicate with SDLC Device (Continued)*

Possible Problem	Solution	
Link-layer problem (router is primary) *(continued)*	Step 6	Try reducing the line speed to 9600 bps using the **clock rate** interface configuration command. Use the **clock rate** interface configuration command to configure the clock rate for the hardware connections on serial interfaces such as NIMs[10] and interface processors to an acceptable bit rate.
		Syntax:
		The following is the syntax of the **clock rate** command:
		clock rate *bps*
		Syntax description:
		• *bps*—Desired clock rate in bits per second: 1200, 2400, 4800, 9600, 19200, 38400, 56000, 64000, 72000, 125000, 148000, 250000, 500000, 800000, 1000000, 1300000, 2000000, 4000000, or 8000000
		Example:
		The following example sets the clock rate on the first serial interface to 64,000 bits per second:
| | | ```
interface serial 0
  clock rate 64000
``` |
	Step 7	Make sure that cabling is correct, securely attached, and undamaged.
Link-layer problem (router is secondary)	Step 1	Use the **debug sdlc** privileged exec command to see whether the router is receiving SNRMs.
		Caution: Because debugging output is assigned high priority in the CPU process, it can render the system unusable. For this reason, use **debug** commands only to troubleshoot specific problems or during troubleshooting sessions with Cisco technical support staff. Moreover, it is best to use **debug** commands during periods of lower network traffic and fewer users. Debugging during these periods decreases the likelihood that increased **debug** command processing overhead will affect system use.
	Step 2	If the router is not receiving SNRMs, check the primary device. Make sure that the physical layer is operational (see the problem "Physical layer problem," earlier in this table). If the router is receiving SNRMs, it should send UAs in reply.
	Step 3	If the router is not sending UAs, make sure that the addresses of the router and device are correct.
	Step 4	If you are using a V.35 connection, make sure that the SCT/SCTE setting is correct on the interface. The router should use SCTE if the router is DCE, and should use SCT if the router is DTE.
```

Table 10-9   *SDLC: Router Cannot Communicate with SDLC Device (Continued)*

Possible Problem	Solution
Link-layer problem (router is secondary) *(continued)*	The SCT/SCTE setting might be changed with a jumper or with the software configuration command **dce-terminal-timing enable**, depending on the platform. Some platforms do not allow you to change this setting.

Example:

The following example prevents phase shifting of the data with respect to the clock:

```
interface serial 0
 dce-terminal-timing enable
```

Step 5   Use a breakout box to check for CTS high on the line.

Step 6   Make sure that both the device and the router are using the same signal coding (NRZ or NRZI). NRZ is enabled by default on the router. To enable NRZI encoding, use the **nrzi-encoding** interface configuration command.

Example:

In the following example, serial interface 1 is configured for NRZI encoding:

```
interface serial 1
 nrzi-encoding
```

Step 7   Try reducing the line speed to 9600 bps using the **clock rate** interface configuration command. Use the **clock rate** interface configuration command to configure the clock rate for the hardware connections on serial interfaces such as NIMs and interface processors to an acceptable bit rate.

Syntax:

The following is the syntax of the **clock rate** command:

clock rate *bps*

Syntax description:

- *bps*—Desired clock rate in bits per second: 1200, 2400, 4800, 9600, 19200, 38400, 56000, 64000, 72000, 125000, 148000, 250000, 500000, 800000, 1000000, 1300000, 2000000, 4000000, or 8000000

Example:

The following example sets the clock rate on the first serial interface to 64000 bits per second:

```
interface serial 0
 clock rate 64000
```

continues

Table 10-9   *SDLC: Router Cannot Communicate with SDLC Device (Continued)*

Possible Problem	Solution	
Link-layer problem (router is secondary) *(continued)*	**Step 8**	Make sure that cabling is correct, securely attached, and undamaged.

[1]DCE=data communications equipment

[2]DTR=data terminal ready

[3]RTS=request to send

[4]To reduce the amount of screen output produced by the **debug sdlc** command, configure the **sdlc poll-pause-timer 1000** command to reduce the frequency at which the router sends poll frames. Remember to return this command to its original value (the default is 10 milliseconds).

[5]SNRM=send normal response mode

[6]UA=unnumbered acknowledgment

[7]SCT/SCTE=serial clock transmit/serial clock transmit external

[8]NRZ=nonreturn to zero

[9]NRZI=nonreturn to zero inverted

[10]NIM=network interface module

Figure 10-5   *Strapping DTR to RT*

SDLC: Intermittent Connectivity

Symptom: User connections to hosts time out over a router configured to perform SDLC transport.

Table 10-10 outlines the problem that might cause this symptom and describes solutions to that problem.

Table 10-10 *SDLC: Intermittent Connectivity*

Possible Problem	Solution	
SDLC timing problems	**Step 1**	Place a serial analyzer on the serial line attached to the source station, and monitor packets.
	Step 2	If duplicate packets appear, check the router configuration using **the show running-config** privileged exec command. Check to see whether the **local-ack** keyword is present in the configuration.
	Step 3	If the **local-ack** keyword is missing, add it to the router configuration for SDLC interfaces.
	Step 4	Local acknowledgment parameters can be adjusted in the router, the attached device, or both. Adjust SDLC protocol parameters as appropriate. These parameters are used to customize SDLC transport over various network configurations. In particular, you might need to tune various LLC2 timer values.

The following is a sample configuration using the **local-ack** command:

```
Interface Serial 1
mtu 4400
no ip address
hold-queue 150 in
encapsulation stun
stun group 1
stun sdlc-role primary
sdlc line-speed 19200
sdlc n1 35200
sdlc address 04 echo
stun route address 4 tcp 156.28.11.1 local-ack clockrate
19200
```

For more information about configuring SDLC, refer to the Cisco IOS *Bridging and IBM Networking Configuration Guide* and *Bridging and IBM Networking Command Reference.*

SDLC: Client Cannot Connect to Host over Router Running SDLLC

Symptom: Users cannot open connections to hosts on the other side of a router configured to support SDLC Logical Link Control (SDLLC).

Table 10-11 outlines the problems that might cause this symptom and describes solutions to those problems.

Table 10-11   *SDLC: Client Cannot Connect to Host over Router Running SDLLC*

Possible Problem	Solution	
SDLC physical or data link layer problem	**Step 1**	Use the **show interface** *slot/port* exec command to check the state of the connection with the SDLC device.
	Step 2	Look for USBUSY in the output, which indicates that the router is attempting to establish an LLC connection. If the router is not USBUSY, make sure that the physical and link layers are working properly. For more information, refer to the section "SDLC: Router Cannot Communicate with SDLC Device," earlier in this chapter.
	Step 3	If the router is USBUSY, proceed to the next problem in this table.
Router that is not sending test frames to FEP[1]	**Step 1**	With the **debug sdllc** and **debug llc2 packet** privileged exec commands enabled on the router, check whether the router is sending test frames to the FEP.
		Caution: Because debugging output is assigned high priority in the CPU process, it can render the system unusable. For this reason, use **debug** commands only to troubleshoot specific problems or during troubleshooting sessions with Cisco technical support staff. Moreover, it is best to use **debug** commands during periods of lower network traffic and fewer users. Debugging during these periods decreases the likelihood that increased **debug** command processing overhead will affect system use.
	Step 2	If the router is sending test frames to the FEP, proceed to the next problem in this table.
	Step 3	If the router is not sending test frames to the FEP, use the **show running-config** privileged EXEC command to view the router configuration. Make sure that the **sdllc partner** interface configuration command is present.
	Step 4	If the **sdlc partner** command is not present, add it to the configuration. Make sure that it points to the hardware address of the FEP on the Token Ring. The following is the syntax for the **sdlc partner** command:
		sdlc partner *mac-address sdlc-address*
		Syntax description:
		• *mac-address*—48-bit MAC address of the Token Ring host.
		• *sdlc-address*—SDLC address of the serial device that will communicate with the Token Ring host. The valid range is 1 to FE.

Table 10-11 *SDLC: Client Cannot Connect to Host over Router Running SDLLC (Continued)*

Possible Problem	Solution	
FEP on Token Ring that is not replying to test frames	**Step 1**	With the **debug sdllc** and **debug llc2 packet** privileged exec commands enabled on the router, check whether the FEP is replying to test frames sent by the router.
		Caution: Because debugging output is assigned high priority in the CPU process, it can render the system unusable. For this reason, use **debug** commands only to troubleshoot specific problems or during troubleshooting sessions with Cisco technical support staff. Moreover, it is best to use **debug** commands during periods of lower network traffic and fewer users. Debugging during these periods decreases the likelihood that increased **debug** command processing overhead will affect system use.
	Step 2	If the FEP is responding, proceed to the next problem in this table.
	Step 3	If the FEP is not responding, check the MAC address of the router's partner (the FEP). Make sure that the address is correctly specified in the **sdllc partner** command entry on the router. The following is the syntax of the **sdlc partner** command:
		sdlc partner *mac-address sdlc-address*
		Syntax description:
		• *mac-address*—48-bit MAC address of the Token Ring host.
		• *sdlc-address*—SDLC address of the serial device that will communicate with the Token Ring host. The valid range is 1 to FE.
	Step 4	Check whether RSRB peers are up. If the peers are not open, refer to the section "RSRB: Host Cannot Connect to Server (Peers Not Open)," earlier in this chapter.
	Step 5	If the RSRB peers are up, attach a network analyzer to the Token Ring with the FEP attached, and make sure that the router's test frames are arriving on the ring and that the FEP is replying.

continues

Table 10-11 *SDLC: Client Cannot Connect to Host over Router Running SDLLC (Continued)*

Possible Problem	Solution
XID[2] not sent by router	**Step 1** With the **debug sdllc** and **debug llc2 packet** privileged exec commands enabled on the router, check whether the router is sending XID frames to the FEP.
	Caution: Because debugging output is assigned high priority in the CPU process, it can render the system unusable. For this reason, use **debug** commands only to troubleshoot specific problems or during troubleshooting sessions with Cisco technical support staff. Moreover, it is best to use **debug** commands during periods of lower network traffic and fewer users. Debugging during these periods decreases the likelihood that increased **debug** command processing overhead will affect system use.
	Step 2 If the router is sending XID frames to the FEP, proceed to the next problem in this table.
	Step 3 If the router is not sending XID frames, use the **show running-config** privileged exec command to view the router configuration. Make sure that there is an **sdllc xid** interface configuration command entry present.
	Step 4 If the **sdllc xid** command is not configured on the router, add it to the configuration. The following is the syntax for the **sdlc xid** command:
	sdlc xid *address xid*
	Syntax description:
	• *address*—Address of the SDLC station associated with this interface.
	• *xid*—XID that the Cisco IOS software will use to respond to XID requests that the router receives. This value must be 4 bytes (8 digits) in length and is specified with hexadecimal digits.
	Example:
	The following example specifies an XID value of 01720002 at address C2:
	``` interface serial 0 sdlc xid c2 01720002 ```

Table 10-11 *SDLC: Client Cannot Connect to Host over Router Running SDLLC (Continued)*

Possible Problem	Solution	
FEP not replying to XID	**Step 1**	With the **debug sdllc** and **debug llc2 packet** privileged exec commands enabled on the router, check to see whether the FEP is replying to XID frames from the router.
	Step 2	If the FEP is responding, proceed to the next problem in this table.
	Step 3	If the FEP is not responding, check the XID values configured by the **sdllc xid** command on the router. The values for IDBLK and IDNUM on the router must match the values in VTAM on the FEP. The following is the syntax for the **sdlc xid** command:
		sdlc xid *address xid*
		Syntax description:
		• *address*—Address of the SDLC station associated with this interface.
		• *xid*—XID that the Cisco IOS software will use to respond to XID requests that the router receives. This value must be 4 bytes (8 digits) in length and is specified with hexadecimal digits.
		Example:
		The following example specifies an XID value of 01720002 at address C2:
| | | ```
interface serial 0
  sdlc xid c2 01720002
``` |
| | **Step 4** | Make sure that the XID information on the hosts is properly defined. If a 317X device is a channel-attached gateway, the XID must be 0000000 for IDBLK and IDNUM. |
| Host problem | Check for activation, application problems, VTAM and NCP misconfigurations, configuration mismatches, and other problems on the IBM host. | |

[1]FEP=front-end processor

[2]XID=exchange of identification

Virtual Token Ring Addresses and SDLLC

The **sdllc traddr** command specifies a virtual Token Ring MAC address for an SDLC-attached device (the device that you are spoofing to look like a Token Ring device). The last two hexadecimal digits of the virtual MAC address must be 00. The router then reserves any virtual ring address that falls into the range xxxx.xxxx.xx00 to xxxx.xxxx.xxff for the SDLLC serial interface.
```

As a result, other IBM devices on an internetwork might have an LAA that falls in the same range. This can cause problems if you are using local acknowledgment because routers examine only the first 10 digits of the LAA address of a packet (not the last two, which are considered wildcards).

If the router sees an address that matches an assigned SDLLC LAA address, it automatically forwards that packet to the SDLLC process. This can result in packets being incorrectly forwarded to the SDLLC process and sessions never being established.

NOTE   To avoid assigning conflicting addresses, be certain that you know the LAA naming convention used in the internetwork before assigning a virtual ring address for any SDLLC implementation.

SDLC: Sessions Fail over Router Running STUN

Symptom: SDLC sessions between two nodes fail when they are attempted over a router that is running serial tunnel (STUN).

NOTE   This section discusses troubleshooting procedures for STUN without local acknowledgment (LACK). For STUN with LACK, the procedures are essentially the same, but remember that there are two sessions: one from the primary to the router, and one from the secondary to the router.

Table 10-12 outlines the problems that might cause this symptom and describes solutions to those problems.

Table 10-12   *SDLC: Sessions Fail over Router Running STUN*

Possible Problem	Solution	
Peers that are not open	**Step 1**	Use the **show stun** exec command to see whether the peers are open. If the peers are open, one of the other problems in this table is probably the cause.
		The following is sample output from the **show stun** command:
| | | ```
Router# show stun
This peer: 131.108.10.1
Serial0 -- 3174 Controller for test lab (group 1 [sdlc])
                        state   rx-pkts  tx-pkts drops  poll
   7[ 1] IF Serial1       open    20334    86440      5 8P
  10[ 1] TCP 131.108.8.1   open     6771     7331      0
 all[ 1] TCP 131.108.8.1   open   612301  2338550   1005
``` |
```

Table 10-12 *SDLC: Sessions Fail over Router Running STUN (Continued)*

Possible Problem		Solution
Peers that are not open *(continued)*		In this display, the first entry reports that proxy polling is enabled for address 7, and serial 0 is running with modulus 8 on the primary side of the link. The link has received 20,334 packets, transmitted 86,440 packets, and dropped 5 packets.
	Step 2	If the peers are not open, use the **debug stun** command on the core router to see whether the peers are trying to open. Peers do not open if there is no traffic on the link.
		Caution: Do not enable **debug** commands on a heavily loaded router. Doing so can cause performance and connectivity problems. Use a protocol analyzer or **show** commands instead.
	Step 3	If you do not see the peers trying to open, use the **show interface** exec command to make sure that the interface and line protocol are both up. If they are not both up, there could be a link problem. Proceed to the problem "SDLC physical or link layer problem," later in this table.
	Step 4	If the peers are trying to open, use the **show running-config** privileged exec command to make sure that the **stun route** and other STUN configuration commands are configured correctly. Reconfigure the router, if necessary.
	Step 5	Use the **debug stun packet** privileged exec command on the core router. Look for SNRMs or XIDs being sent.
	Step 6	If you do not see SNRMs or XIDs, there is probably a basic link problem. See the problem "SDLC physical or link layer problem," later in this table.
	Step 7	Check to make sure that no other network problems are occurring, such as interface drops, buffer misses, overloaded Frame Relay switches, and IP routing problems.
SNRMs or XIDs not sent	Step 1	Use the **show stun** command to see whether the peers are open. If the peers are not open, see the preceding problem in this table.
	Step 2	If the peers are open, use the **debug stun packet** privileged exec command on the remote end. Check for SNRMS or XIDs from the primary arriving as NDI packets.
	Step 3	If SNRMs or XIDs are arriving, proceed to the next problem in this table.
	Step 4	If SNRMS or XIDs are not arriving, use the **debug stun packet** command on the core router to see whether SNRMs or XIDs are being sent.

continues

Table 10-12 *SDLC: Sessions Fail over Router Running STUN (Continued)*

Possible Problem		Solution
SNRMs or XIDs not sent *(continued)*	Step 5	If the core router is not sending SNRMs or XIDs, make sure that the physical and link layers are operating properly. See the problem "SDLC physical or link layer problem," later in this table.
	Step 6	If the core router is sending SNRMs or XIDs, use the **show running-config** privileged exec command to make sure that the **stun route** command is properly configured on the router.
	Step 7	Check to make sure that no other network problems are occurring, such as interface drops, buffer misses, overloaded Frame Relay switches, and IP routing problems.
No reply to SNRMs or XIDs	Step 1	Use the **show stun** command to see whether the peers are open. If the peers are not open, see the first problem in this table.
	Step 2	If the peers are open, use the **debug stun packet** privileged exec command on the remote end. Check for SNRMS or XIDs from the primary arriving as NDI packets.
	Step 3	If SNRMs or XIDs are not arriving, refer to the preceding problem in this table.
	Step 4	If SNRMs or XIDs are arriving, make sure that the core router is sending UA or XID responses as SDI packets.
	Step 5	If the router is not sending responses, there might be a link problem. Refer to the problem "SDLC physical or link layer problem," later in this table.
	Step 6	If the router is sending responses, use the **debug stun packet** command to see whether the UA or XID responses are getting back to the primary as SDI packets.
	Step 7	If the responses are not getting back to the primary, use the **show running-config** privileged exec command to make sure that the stun route and other STUN configuration commands are properly configured on the remote router. The following is the syntax for the **stun route** command: **stun route** *address* *address-number* **tcp** *ip-address* [*local-ack*] [*priority*] [*tcp-queue-max*] **Syntax description:** • *address-number*—Is a number that conforms to TCP addressing conventions • *ip-address*—Gives the IP address by which this STUN peer is known to other STUN peers that are using the TCP as the STUN encapsulation

Table 10-12 *SDLC: Sessions Fail over Router Running STUN (Continued)*

Possible Problem	Solution
No reply to SNRMs or XIDs	• *local-ack*—(Optional) Enables local acknowledgment for STUN • *priority*—(Optional) Establishes the four levels used in priority queuing: low, medium, normal, and high • *tcp-queue-max*—(Optional) Sets the maximum size of the outbound TCP queue for the SDLC link **Example:** In the following example, a frame with a source-route address of 10 is propagated using TCP encapsulation to a device with an IP address of 131.108.8.1: `stun route address 10 tcp 131.108.8.1`
	Step 8 Check to make sure that no other network problems are occurring, such as interface drops, buffer misses, overloaded Frame Relay switches, and IP routing problems.
	Step 9 If packets are passed end-to-end in both directions, check end station configurations, duplex settings, configurations, and so forth.
SDLC physical or link layer problem	**Step 1** Use the **show interfaces** exec command on the link connecting to the primary device. Make sure that the interface and the line protocol are both up.
	Step 2 If the interface or line protocol is not up, make sure that the devices are powered up and connected correctly. Check the line to make sure that it is active. Check for clocking, address misconfigurations, correct NRZ or NRZI specifications, and so forth.
	Step 3 Try slowing the clock rate of the connection. Use the **clock rate** interface configuration command to configure the clock rate for the hardware connections on serial interfaces such as NIMs and interface processors to an acceptable bit rate. The following is the syntax of the **clock rate** command: **clock rate** *bps* **Syntax description:** • *bps*—Desired clock rate in bits per second: 1200, 2400, 4800, 9600, 19200, 38400, 56000, 64000, 72000, 125000, 148000, 250000, 500000, 800000, 1000000, 1300000, 2000000, 4000000, or 8000000

continues

Table 10-12 *SDLC: Sessions Fail over Router Running STUN (Continued)*

Possible Problem	Solution
SDLC physical or link layer problem *(continued)*	**Example:** The following example sets the clock rate on the first serial interface to 64000 bits per second: `interface serial 0` `  clock rate 64000` For more information about troubleshooting SDLC physical and link-layer problems, see the section "SDLC: Router Cannot Communicate with SDLC Device," earlier in this chapter.

CIP: CLAW Connection Does Not Come Up

Symptom: Common Link Access for Workstations (CLAW) connections do not come up properly over a Channel Interface Processor (CIP). The output of the **show extended channel slot/port statistics** exec command shows N for CLAW connections, indicating that they are down.

Table 10-13 outlines the problems that might cause this symptom and describes solutions to those problems.

Table 10-13 *CIP: CLAW Connection Does Not Come Up*

Possible Problem	Solution	
TCP/IP not running on host	**Step 1**	Check whether TCP/IP is running on the host.
	Step 2	If TCP/IP is not running, start it.
CIP devices not online to host	**Step 1**	Check the mainframe to see whether the CIP devices are online to the host.
	Step 2	If the CIP devices are not online, vary them online. If devices do not come online, see the section "CIP: CIP Will Not Come Online to Host," later in this chapter.
	Step 3	Check whether the TCP/IP device has been started.
	Step 4	If the device has not been started, start it. **Note:** It might be necessary to stop and start the TCP/IP application to start the device. If you are using obey files, this might not be necessary.
	Step 5	Check the configuration for the CIP in the TCP/IP profile on the host, and check the router configuration for the CIP device.
	Step 6	Use the **moretrace claw** command on the host, either from an obey file or in the TCP/IP profile. This command traces the establishment of CLAW connections and can provide information that is useful for determining causes of connection problems.

CIP: No Enabled LED On

Symptom: The Enabled LED on the CIP card does not come on.

Table 10-14 outlines the problems that might cause this symptom and describes solutions to those problems.

Table 10-14 *CIP: No Enabled LED On*

Possible Problem	Solution	
Hardware problem	Step 1	Check to make sure that the router is plugged in and turned on.
	Step 2	Use the **show version** exec command and see whether the CIP card appears in the output.
	Step 3	If the CIP card appears in the output, the Enabled LED might be faulty.
	Step 4	If the CIP card does not appear in the output, reseat the CIP card, reboot the router, and check the output of the **show version** command again.
Old Cisco IOS release	Step 1	Use the **show version** exec command to find out what version of the Cisco IOS software you are running.
	Step 2	If you are using Cisco IOS software prior to Release 10.2(6), you should upgrade to a more recent version.

CIP: CIP Will Not Come Online to Host

Symptom: The CIP card will not come online to the host.

Table 10-15 outlines the problem that might cause this symptom and describes solutions to that problem.

Table 10-15 *CIP: CIP Will Not Come Online to Host*

Possible Problem	Solution	
CHPID[1] not online to host	Step 1	Make sure that the Enabled LED on the CIP card is on. If it is not on, refer to the section "CIP: No Enabled LED On," earlier in this chapter.
	Step 2	Use the **show extended channel** *slot/port* **subchannel** command, and check for the SIGNAL flag in the output.
	Step 3	If the SIGNAL flag is not present, check whether the CHPID is online to the host. If it is not, configure it to come online.
		Note: On a bus and tag channel, the SIGNAL flag is turned on by OP_OUT being high from the host. On an ESCON channel, the SIGNAL flag is turned on by the presence of light on the channel.
	Step 4	If the CHPID does not come online to the host, check the physical cabling.
	Step 5	If the CIP still does not come online, check the IOCP[2] definitions for the CIP device, and check the router configuration.

[1]CHPID=channel path identifier

[2]IOCP=input/output control program

CIP: Router Cannot ping Host, or Host Cannot ping Router

Symptom: Attempts to **ping** are unsuccessful, either from the CIP card in a router to a host or from a host to the CIP card in a router.

Table 10-16 outlines the problem that might cause this symptom and describes solutions to that problem.

Table 10-16 *CIP: Router Cannot* **ping** *Host, or Host Cannot* **ping** *Router*

Possible Problem	Solution	
Addressing problem between CIP and host	**Step 1**	Verify that the CLAW connection is up by checking the output of the **show extended channel** *slot/port* **statistics** exec command on the router.
	Step 2	If the output shows that CLAW connections are not up (indicated by an N), refer to the section "CIP: CLAW Connection Does Not Come Up," earlier in this chapter.
	Step 3	If the CLAW connections are up (indicated by a Y), issue the **clear counters** privileged exec command. Then attempt a basic **ping** to the host from the router or to the router from the host.
	Step 4	When the ping is completed, use the **show extended channel** *slot/port* **statistics** exec command on the router.
		If you issued the **ping** from the router to the host, the host should have read five 100-byte ICMP echos from the router. The Total Blocks field in the **show** command output should indicate five blocks read. If the host replied, the output should indicate five blocks written.
		If you issued the **ping** from the host to the router, the host should have sent one 276-byte ICMP echo to the router. The Write field should indicate one block written. If the router replied, the output should indicate one block in the Read field.
	Step 5	If this is not the case, there could be an addressing problem between the CIP and the host. Check all IP addresses on the router and in the host TCP/IP profile, and make sure that they are correct.

CIP: Host Cannot Reach Remote Networks

Symptom: Mainframe host cannot access networks across a router.

Table 10-17 outlines the problem that might cause this symptom and describes solutions to that problem.

Table 10-17 *CIP: Host Cannot Reach Remote Networks*

Possible Problem	Solution	
Missing or misconfigured IP routes	**Step 1**	If the mainframe host is incapable of communicating with networks on the other side of the router, try to **ping** the remote network from the router.
		If the **ping** succeeds, proceed to Step 4.
	Step 2	If the **ping** fails, use the **show ip route** privileged exec command to verify that the network is accessible by the router.
	Step 3	If there is no route to the network, check the network and router configuration for problems.
	Step 4	Verify that the host connection is active by pinging the host IP address from the router. If the **ping** is unsuccessful, see the section "CIP: Router Cannot **ping** Host, or Host Cannot **ping** Router," earlier in this chapter.
	Step 5	Issue the **netstat gate** command on the host, and check for a route to the network.
	Step 6	If a route does not exist, make sure that the host is using the address of the CIP in the router as the default route. If it is not, add a GATEWAY statement in the TCP/IP profile that points to the network, or set the CIP in the router as the default route using a DEFAULTNET statement in the TCP/IP profile.

CIP: Host Running Routed Has No Routes

Symptom: A host running routed has no routes to remote networks.

Table 10-18 outlines the problems that might cause this symptom and describes solutions to those problems.

Table 10-18 *CIP: Host Running Routed Has No Routes*

Possible Problem	Solution	
RIP not properly configured on the router	**Step 1**	Use the **show running-config** privileged exec command to view the router configuration. Make sure that RIP is configured on the router. If RIP is not configured, configure it.
	Step 2	Check the configuration to see whether there are **network** statements for each of the networks that should be advertised in RIP updates. If they are missing, add them to the configuration.
	Step 3	Make sure that the **passive-interface** command is not configured on the channel interface.

continues

Table 10-18 *CIP: Host Running Routed Has No Routes (Continued)*

Possible Problem	Solution	
RIP not properly configured on the router *(continued)*	Step 4	If the command is present, remove it using the **no passive-interface** router configuration command.
	Step 5	Make sure there are no **distribute-list** statements filtering RIP routing updates.
| | Step 6 | Check the router configuration to be sure that the **broadcast** keyword has been specified in the **claw** interface configuration command. The following is the **claw** command syntax: <br><br>**claw** *path device-address ip-address host-name device-name host-app device-app* [*broadcast*]<br><br>**Example:**<br><br>The following example shows how to enable IBM channel-attach routing on the CIP port 0, which is supporting a directly connected ESCON channel:<br><br>```
interface channel 3/0
 ip address 198.92.0.1 255.255.255.0
 claw 0100 00 198.92.0.21 CISCOVM EVAL TCPIP TCPIP
``` |
	Step 7	If there is no **broadcast** keyword specified, add it to the configuration.
Host misconfiguration	Step 1	Use the **netstat gate** command on the host. Check whether there are routes learned from RIP updates.
	Step 2	If you do not see RIP routes, verify that the host connection is active by pinging the host IP address from the router.
	Step 3	If the **ping** is unsuccessful, see the section "CIP: Router Cannot **ping** Host, or Host Cannot **ping** Router," earlier in this chapter.
	Step 4	Verify that the *routed* daemon is running on the host.
	Step 5	Use the **show extended channel** *slot/port* **stat** exec command to see whether RIP routing updates are incrementing the counters.
	Step 6	Check the TCP/IP profile on the host to be sure that there are BSDROUTINGPARMS instead of GATEWAY statements.
```

Troubleshooting DECnet

Digital Equipment Corporation (Digital) developed the DECnet protocol family to provide a well-thought-out way for its computers to communicate with one another. The first version of DECnet, released in 1975, allowed two directly attached PDP-11 minicomputers to communicate. In more recent years, Digital has included support for nonproprietary protocols, but DECnet remains the most important of Digital's network product offerings.

DECnet is currently in its fifth major product release (sometimes called *Phase V* and referred to as DECnet/OSI in Digital literature). DECnet Phase V is a superset of the OSI protocol suite and supports all OSI protocols as well as several other proprietary and standard protocols that were supported in previous versions of DECnet. As with past changes to the protocol, DECnet Phase V is compatible with the previous release (Phase IV, in this case).

Digital Network Architecture

Contrary to popular belief, DECnet is not a network architecture at all but is, rather, a series of products conforming to Digital's Digital Network Architecture (DNA). Like most comprehensive network architectures from large systems vendors, DNA supports a large set of both proprietary and standard protocols. The list of DNA-supported technologies grows constantly as Digital implements new protocols. Figure 11-1 illustrates an incomplete snapshot of DNA and the relationship of some of its components to the OSI reference model.

Figure 11-1 *DNA and the OSI Reference Model*

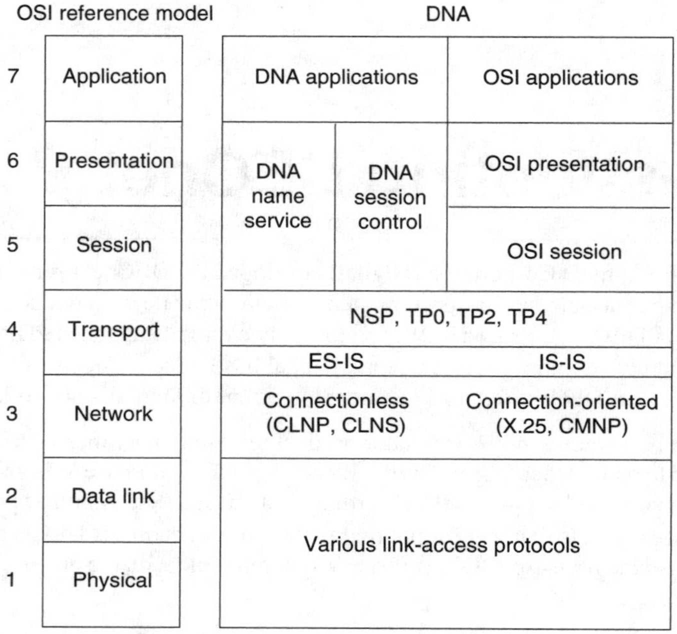

OSI reference model		DNA	
7	Application	DNA applications	OSI applications
6	Presentation	DNA name service	DNA session control	OSI presentation
5	Session			OSI session
4	Transport	NSP, TP0, TP2, TP4	
		ES-IS	IS-IS
3	Network	Connectionless (CLNP, CLNS)	Connection-oriented (X.25, CMNP)
2	Data link	Various link-access protocols	
1	Physical		

As Figure 11-1 shows, DNA supports a variety of media and link implementations. Among these are well-known standards such as Ethernet, Token Ring, Fiber Distributed Data Interface (FDDI), IEEE 802.2, and X.25. DNA also offers a traditional point-to-point link-layer protocol called *Digital Data Communications Message Protocol* (DDCMP) and a 70-Mbps bus used in the VAX cluster called the *computer-room interconnect bus* (CI bus).

The Network Layer

DECnet supports both connectionless and connection-oriented network layers. Both network layers are implemented by OSI protocols. The connectionless implementation uses the Connectionless Network Protocol (CLNP) and the Connectionless Network Service (CLNS). The connection-oriented network layer uses the X.25 Packet-Level Protocol (PLP), which is also known as X.25 Level 3, and the Connection-Mode Network Protocol (CMNP).

Although most of DNA was brought into OSI conformance with DECnet Phase V, DECnet Phase IV routing was already very similar to OSI routing. Phase V DNA routing consists of OSI routing (ES-IS and IS-IS), plus continued support for the DECnet Phase IV routing protocol.

DECnet Phase IV Routing Frame Format

The DECnet Phase IV routing protocol differs from IS-IS in several ways. One difference is in the protocol header. The DNA Phase IV routing layer header is shown in Figure 11-2; IS-IS packet formats are shown in Chapter 12, "Troubleshooting ISO CLNS."

Figure 11-2 *A DNA Phase IV Routing Layer Header*

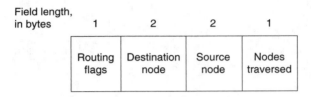

The first field in a DNA Phase IV routing header is the routing flags field, which includes:

- A return-to-sender bit that, if set, indicates that the packet is returning to the source.

- A return-to-sender-request bit that, if set, indicates that request packets should be returned to the source if they cannot be delivered to the destination.

- An intraLAN bit, which is on by default. If the router detects that the two communicating end systems are not on the same subnetwork, it turns the bit off.

- Other bits that indicate header format, whether padding is being used, and other functions.

The destination node and source node fields identify the network addresses of the destination nodes and the source node.

The nodes traversed field shows the number of nodes the packet has traversed on its way to the destination. This field allows implementation of a maximum hop count so that obsolete packets can be removed from the network.

DECnet identifies two types of nodes: end nodes and routing nodes. Both end nodes and routing nodes can send and receive network information, but only routing nodes can provide routing services for other DECnet nodes.

DECnet routing decisions are based on cost, an arbitrary measure assigned by network administrators to be used in comparing various paths through an internetwork environment. Costs are typically based on hop count, media bandwidth, or other measures. The lower the cost, the better the path. When network faults occur, the DECnet Phase IV routing protocol uses cost values to recalculate the best paths to each destination. Figure 11-3 illustrates the calculation of costs in a DECnet Phase IV routing environment.

Figure 11-3 *A DECnet Phase IV Routing Protocol Cost Calculation*

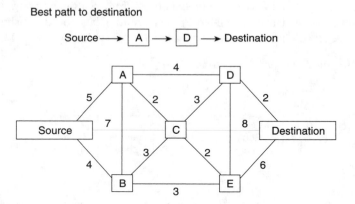

Addressing

DECnet addresses are not associated with the physical networks to which the nodes are connected. Instead, DECnet locates hosts using area/node address pairs. An area's value ranges from 1 to 63, inclusive. A node address can be between 1 and 1023, inclusive. Therefore, each area can have 1023 nodes, and approximately 65,000 nodes can be addressed in a DECnet network. Areas can span many routers, and a single cable can support many areas. Therefore, if a node has several network interfaces, it uses the same area/node address for each interface. Figure 11-4 shows a sample DECnet network with several addressable entities.

Figure 11-4 *Examples of DECnet Addresses*

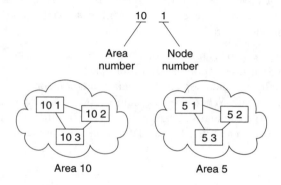

DECnet hosts do not use manufacturer-assigned Media Access Control (MAC)-layer addresses. Instead, network-level addresses are embedded in the MAC-layer address according to an algorithm that multiplies the area number by 1,024 and adds the node number to the product. The resulting 16-bit decimal address is converted to a hexadecimal number and appended to the address AA00.0400 in byte-swapped order, with the least significant byte first. For example, DECnet address 12.75 becomes 12363 (base 10), which equals 304B (base 16). After this byte-swapped address is appended to the standard DECnet MAC address prefix, the resulting address is AA00.0400.4B30.

Routing Levels

DECnet routing nodes are referred to as either Level 1 or Level 2 routers. A Level 1 router communicates with end nodes and with other Level 1 routers in a particular area. Level 2 routers communicate with Level 1 routers in the same area and with Level 2 routers in different areas. Together, Level 1 and Level 2 routers form a hierarchical routing scheme. This relationship is illustrated in Figure 11-5.

Figure 11-5 *DECnet Level 1 and Level 2 Routers*

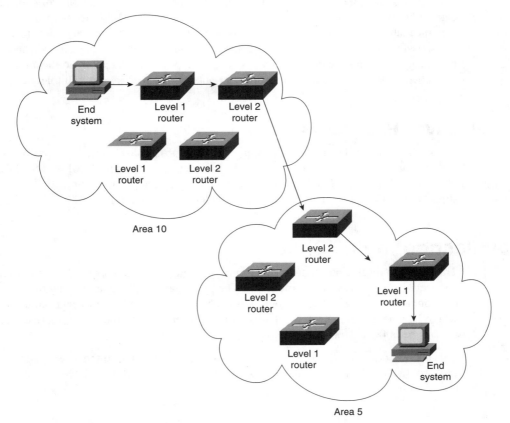

End systems send routing requests to a designated Level 1 router. The Level 1 router with the highest priority is elected to be the designated router. If two routers have the same priority, the one with the larger node number becomes the designated router. A router's priority can be manually configured to force it to become the designated router.

As shown in Figure 11-5, multiple Level 2 routers can exist in any area. When a Level 1 router wishes to send a packet outside its area, it forwards the packet to a Level 2 router in the same area. In some cases, the Level 2 router may not have the optimal path to the destination, but the mesh network configuration offers a degree of fault tolerance not provided by the simple assignment of one Level 2 router per area.

The Transport Layer

The DNA transport layer is implemented by a variety of transports, both proprietary and standard. OSI transports TP0, TP2, and TP4 are supported.

Digital's own Network Services Protocol (NSP) is functionally similar to TP4 in that it offers connection-oriented, flow-controlled service with message fragmentation and reassembly. Two subchannels are supported—one for normal data and one for expedited data and flow control information. Two flow control types are supported—a simple start/stop mechanism where the receiver tells the sender when to terminate and resume data transmission and a more complex flow control technique, where the receiver tells the sender how many messages it can accept. NSP can also respond to congestion notifications from the network layer by reducing the number of outstanding messages it will tolerate.

Upper-Layer Protocols

Above the transport layer, DECnet supports its own proprietary upper-layer protocols as well as standard OSI upper-layer protocols. DECnet application protocols use the DNA session control protocol and the DNA name service. OSI application protocols are supported by OSI presentation- and session-layer implementations.

Troubleshooting DECnet

This section presents protocol-related troubleshooting information for DECnet Phase IV connectivity and performance problems. The procedures outlined apply only to environments in which DECnet routing is enabled on the router, not to environments in which DECnet is being bridged (that is, bridging is enabled on the router interfaces and EtherType 6003 is being passed).

This chapter does not discuss other Digital protocols, such as Maintenance Operation Protocol (MOP), local-area transport (LAT), local-area VAX cluster (LAVC), and local-area systems technology (LAST).

NOTE	For information about troubleshooting ISO CLNS (DECnet Phase V) problems, refer to Chapter 12, "Troubleshooting ISO CLNS."

The section "Using DECnet in a Multiprotocol Environment" discusses possible problems when using DECnet in an internetwork running other protocols as well. The remaining sections describe specific DECnet symptoms, the problems that are likely to cause each symptom, and the solutions to those problems.

The following sections outline the most common network issues in DECnet networks:

- DECnet: Connections to DEC Hosts Fail over Router (End Node Problem)
- DECnet: Connections to DEC Hosts Fail over Router (Router Problem)
- DECnet: End Nodes Cannot Find Designated Router
- DECnet: Router or End Node Sees Incorrect Designated Router
- DECnet: Routers Not Establishing Adjacencies
- DECnet: Routing Node Adjacencies Toggle Up and Down
- DECnet: No Phase IV Connectivity over Phase V Backbone
- DECnet: Poor Performance

NOTE	In some of the symptom discussions that follow, Operator Communication Manager (OPCOM) messages are used to illustrate certain errors. These examples assume that OPCOM is running and event logging is enabled. For more information about event logging, see the section "Configuring a DECnet Node to Log DECnet Events" later in this chapter.

Using DECnet in a Multiprotocol Environment

It is important to remember that DECnet changes the MAC addresses of router interfaces. This behavior can cause problems for other protocols that are already enabled on the router.

If after enabling DECnet on a router interface other protocols (such as Novell IPX or XNS) experience connectivity loss due to address resolution problems, the problem is probably a result of DECnet changing the MAC address of the router interface.

As a rule, enable DECnet on router interfaces first, and then enable other protocols. Otherwise, use the **copy running-config startup-config** command to save the router configuration and then reload the router.

DECnet: Connections to DEC Hosts Fail over Router (End Node Problem)

Symptom: DECnet nodes cannot communicate when attempting to make connections over routers.

NOTE	This section focuses on problems in end nodes. For router-related problems and solutions, see the section "DECnet: Connections to DEC Hosts Fail over Router (Router Problem)" later in this chapter.

Table 11-1 outlines the problems that might cause this symptom and describes solutions to those problems.

Table 11-1   *DECnet: Connections to DEC Hosts Fail over Router (End Node Problem)*

Possible Problem	Solution	
Misconfigured end node	**Step 1**	Check the end node configuration using the **show executor characteristics** NCP[1] command.
	Step 2	Make sure that the end node type (nonrouting Phase IV, routing Phase IV, area), node address, node name, and routing and link parameters are correctly specified.
	Step 3	Check the circuit characteristics using the **show known circuit characteristics** NCP command.
	Step 4	Make sure that the designated router, hello timer, router priority (if the node is a routing node), and other circuit characteristics are properly configured.
		The following **decnet** commands are used to set the designated router, hello timers, and router priority on a Cisco router:
		decnet hello-timer *seconds*
		• *seconds*—Interval at which the Cisco IOS software sends hello messages. It can be a decimal number in the range 1 to 8191 seconds. The default is 15 seconds.
		decnet router-priority *value*
		To elect a designated router to which packets will be sent when no destination is specified, use the **decnet router-priority** interface configuration command.
		• *value*—Priority of the router. This can be a number in the range 0 through 127. The larger the number, the higher the priority. The default priority is 64.

Table 11-1   *DECnet: Connections to DEC Hosts Fail over Router (End Node Problem) (Continued)*

Possible Problem	Solution
Misconfigured end node *(continued)*	**Step 5** Reconfigure the end node if any of the end node or circuit characteristics are misconfigured. For information on configuring end nodes, refer to the vendor documentation.
Host access control rejects connection	With this problem, users see the message "connect failed, access control rejected." This is typically a session-layer problem. **Step 1** Make sure that the following requirements are satisfied: • User-supplied access control information is correct • Proxy access is set up correctly • Proxy database and proxy account are correct **Step 2** Make sure that the user's security access matches the access specifications for the user on the remote systems. **Step 3** If there are problems in any of these areas, make changes as necessary.
Unrecognized object	With this problem, users see the message "connect failed, unrecognized object." **Step 1** Use the **tell** NCP command to determine whether the object is defined on the target node. The syntax of the **tell** command is as follows: **tell** *target-node-name* **show known** *objects* **Step 2** If the object is not defined, log in as superuser and run NCP to define the object with the **set object** NCP command, as follows: **set object** *object-id* **Step 3** After the object is defined, use the **tell** NCP command to determine whether the object has a file specified, as follows: **tell** *target-node-name* **show object** *object-id* **character** **Step 4** Exit NCP and determine whether the file specified for the object exists. **Step 5** If the file for the requested object does not exist, create the file. **Step 6** Make sure the permissions for the specified file are correct.

continues

Table 11-1   *DECnet: Connections to DEC Hosts Fail over Router (End Node Problem) (Continued)*

Possible Problem	Solution
Insufficient resource error	With an insufficient resource error, VMS[2] users see the following message: `% system-E-REMRSC, insufficient system resource at remote node` **Note:** This error message might not indicate a problem. These parameter values can be set intentionally to prevent network connections beyond a certain number. Try tuning the following DEC target system parameters: • SYSGEN parameters: — MAXPROCESSCNT • NCP parameters: — MAXIMUM LINKS — ALIAS MAXIMUM LINKS • AUTHORIZE parameters: — MAXJOBS — MAXACCTJOBS

[1]NCP = Network Control Program
[2]VMS = Virtual Memory System

Configuring a DECnet Node to Log DECnet Events

In addition to the diagnostic tools available on your router, DECnet environments provide a wealth of diagnostic information. DECnet nodes can use the DECnet Event Logging Facility (EVL) to track DECnet events. EVL allows you to monitor significant network events, such as lost packets and circuit failures.

The following steps outline the basic tasks required to enable event logging on a VMS system:

Step 1   Determine whether the OPCOM process is running:

```
$ show system
```

Step 2   If OPCOM does not appear in the list of running processes, enter the following command to start it:

```
$ @sys$system:STARTUP.com OPCOM
```

Step 3   Use the NCP to enable event logging:

```
$ MCR NCP
NCP> SET logging MONITOR KNOWN Events
NCP> DEFINE logging MONITOR KNOWN Events
```

```
NCP> SET logging MONITOR STATE ON
NCP> DEFINE logging MONITOR STATE ON
```

Step 4   Exit NCP:

NCP> **Exit**

Step 5   To monitor network events from a console terminal, enter the following command at the VMS system prompt:

$ REPLY/ENABLE = NETWORK

(This command is equivalent to the **terminal monitor** privileged exec command.)

DECnet: Connections to DEC Hosts Fail over Router (Router Problem)

Symptom: DECnet nodes cannot communicate when attempting to make connections over routers.

NOTE   This section focuses on problems in the router. For end node–related problems and solutions, see the section "DECnet: Connections to DEC Hosts Fail over Router (End Node Problem)" earlier in this chapter.

Table 11-2 outlines the problems that might cause this symptom and describes solutions to those problems.

Table 11-2   *DECnet: Connections to DEC Hosts Fail over Router (Router Problem)*

Possible Problem	Solution	
DECnet is not enabled on router	**Step 1**	Use the **show decnet interface** privileged exec command to see on which interfaces, if any, DECnet is enabled.
	Step 2	If the output shows that DECnet is not enabled, use the **show running-config privileged exec** command to view the router configuration. Determine whether DECnet global and interface command specifications are configured on the router.
	Step 3	Enable DECnet routing on the appropriate routers and interfaces. For detailed information on configuring DECnet, refer to the Cisco IOS *Network Protocols Configuration Guide, Part 2*.

continues

Table 11-2   *DECnet: Connections to DEC Hosts Fail over Router (Router Problem) (Continued)*

Possible Problem	Solution	
Missing **decnet cost** command	Step 1	Make sure that there is a cost configured on DECnet interfaces. Check the configuration for a **decnet cost** *cost-value* interface configuration command entry.
	Step 2	If the command is not present, add the **decnet cost** command for each interface on which DECnet is enabled.
End nodes and router area number mismatch	Step 1	Check the configuration of end nodes and routers on the network segment. Check the area address specified on end nodes and routers.
	Step 2	If an end node is not in the same area as a router on the segment, you must either change the address of the end node to be the same as a router on the segment, or you must reconfigure a router on the segment with the same area number as the end node.
Actual cost to the destination area is more than the configured cost	Step 1	Use the **show decnet interface** exec command to determine the configured maximum cost to the destination area.
	Step 2	Use the **show decnet route exec** command to determine the actual cost to the destination area.
	Step 3	If the actual cost is more than the configured maximum cost, increase the maximum cost configured on the router.
		On Level 1 routers, use the **decnet max-cost** global configuration command to increase the area maximum cost.
		On Level 2 routers, use the **decnet area-max-cost** global configuration command to increase the area maximum cost.
Actual number of hops to the destination is more than the configured maximum number of hops	Step 1	Use the **show decnet interface** command to determine the maximum number of hops allowed for intra-area routing.
	Step 2	Use the **show decnet route** exec command to determine the actual number of hops to the destination as shown in the DECnet routing table.
	Step 3	If the actual number of hops is more than the configured maximum allowed hops, increase the maximum hops configured on the router.
		On Level 1 routers, use the **decnet max-hops** global configuration command to increase the maximum hops.
		On Level 2 routers, use the **decnet area-max-hops** global configuration command to increase the maximum number of hops.

Table 11-2   *DECnet: Connections to DEC Hosts Fail over Router (Router Problem) (Continued)*

Possible Problem	Solution	
Access list is misconfigured	**Step 1**	Use the **show decnet access-list** privileged exec command to determine whether there are DECnet access lists configured on the router.
	Step 2	If there are access lists applied to router interfaces, use the **debug decnet connects** privileged exec command to determine whether important packets are being forwarded properly.
		Caution: Because debugging output is assigned high priority in the CPU process, it can render the system unusable. For this reason, use **debug** commands only to troubleshoot specific problems or during troubleshooting sessions with Cisco technical support staff. Moreover, it is best to use **debug** commands during periods of lower network traffic and fewer users. Debugging during these periods decreases the likelihood that increased **debug** command processing overhead will affect system use.
	Step 3	If packets are being dropped, disable all access lists on the router using the **no decnet access-group** interface configuration command.
	Step 4	Determine whether connections to hosts are now possible. If connections are made successfully, a misconfigured access list is probably the problem.
	Step 5	Enable access lists on the router using the **decnet access-group** interface configuration command. Enable the lists one at a time until connectivity is lost, at which point you have found the problem access list.
	Step 6	Modify the access list as necessary. Make sure to include explicit **permit** statements for traffic that you want to be forwarded normally.
	Step 7	If problems persist, continue the process until you have isolated all problem access lists.

continues

Table 11-2 *DECnet: Connections to DEC Hosts Fail over Router (Router Problem) (Continued)*

Possible Problem	Solution	
Node address out of range	Step 1	Use the **show running-config** privileged exec command to view router configurations. Check to see whether the **decnet max-address** global configuration command has been configured. This command sets the highest DECnet node number allowed in the area.
		Note: The **decnet max-address** command specifies the highest node number allowed in an area, *not* the maximum number of node addresses allowed in an area. For example, if you configure the command **decnet max-address 1000** on a router and you configure a node with a node address of 1001, the address is out of range.
	Step 2	The default maximum address is 1023. However, if another value is configured, the node address might be more than the configured value. If this is the case, increase the maximum address value using the **decnet max-address** command.
Partitioned area		Make sure the network topology has no discontiguous areas. If any discontiguous areas exist, reconfigure the topology by changing area addresses or by creating a path (with a router) to create a contiguous network.
Media problem		For information on troubleshooting serial lines, refer to Chapter 15, "Troubleshooting Serial Lines." For information on troubleshooting LAN media, refer to the media troubleshooting chapter that covers the media type used in your network.

DECnet: End Nodes Cannot Find Designated Router

Symptom: End nodes cannot find a designated router. End nodes cannot access nodes that are on different LANs, but other nodes connected to the same LAN are accessible.

Table 11-3 outlines the problems that might cause this symptom and describes solutions to those problems.

Table 11-3 *DECnet: End Nodes Cannot Find Designated Router*

Possible Problem	Solution	
DECnet not enabled on router	Step 1	Use the **show running-config privileged** exec command to view the router configuration. Determine whether DECnet global configuration and interface command specifications are configured on the router.
	Step 2	Enable DECnet routing on the appropriate routers and interfaces. For detailed information on configuring DECnet, refer to the Cisco IOS Network Protocols Configuration Guide, Part 2.

Table 11-3   *DECnet: End Nodes Cannot Find Designated Router (Continued)*

Possible Problem	Solution	
End nodes and router area number mismatch	Step 1	Check the configuration of end nodes and routers on the network segment. Check the area address specified on end nodes and routers. Use the **show running-config** privileged exec command to view the router configuration.
	Step 2	If an end node is not in the same area as a router on the segment, you must either change the address of the end node to be the same as that of a router on the segment, or you must reconfigure a router on the segment with the same area number as the end node.
Hello packets are not being exchanged	Step 1	Use the **debug decnet adj** privileged exec command to determine whether the router is sending hello packets and whether hellos are being received.
	Step 2	**Caution:** Because debugging output is assigned high priority in the CPU process, it can render the system unusable. For this reason, use **debug** commands only to troubleshoot specific problems or during troubleshooting sessions with Cisco technical support staff. Moreover, it is best to use **debug** commands during periods of lower network traffic and fewer users. Debugging during these periods decreases the likelihood that increased **debug** command processing overhead will affect system use.
	Step 3	If no exchange is occurring, use the **show interfaces** exec command to determine whether the interface input and output queues are full. A full input queue is indicated by a value of 75/75, and a full output queue is indicated by a value of 40/40.
	Step 4	If the queues are full and no hello packets are being exchanged, contact your technical support representative.
	Step 5	If routers are sending hello packets, check end nodes to determine why end nodes are rejecting hello packets.
Media problem	For information on troubleshooting serial lines, refer to Chapter 15, "Troubleshooting Serial Lines." For information on troubleshooting LAN media, refer to the media troubleshooting chapter that covers the media type used in your network.	

DECnet: Router or End Node Sees Incorrect Designated Router

Symptom: Routers and end nodes see an incorrect or an unexpected designated router. If your network requires a specific router to be elected the designated router, allowing another router to become a designated router can cause unpredictable network behavior and can block connectivity in and out of the area.

Table 11-4 outlines the problems that might cause this symptom and describes solutions to those problems.

Table 11-4   *DECnet: Router or End Node Sees Incorrect Designated Router*

Possible Problem	Solution	
Priority of the expected designated router is not configured correctly	**Step 1**	Use the **show decnet interface** exec command to determine which router is the designated router. Note the priority of the router that is shown in the command output.
	Step 2	If the designated router identified in the output is not the correct router, use the **show decnet interface** command on the expected designated router and the actual designated router.
	Step 3	Compare the priority of the actual designated router with that of the expected designated router. The router that you want to be the designated router should have the highest priority.
		Syntax:
	Step 4	If necessary, use the **decnet router-priority** interface configuration command to give a higher priority to a router so that it will be elected the designated router.
		The following is the syntax for the **decnet router-priority** command:
		decnet router-priority *value*
		To elect a designated router to which packets will be sent when no destination is specified, use the **decnet router-priority** interface configuration command.
		Syntax:
		• *value*—Priority of the router. This can be a number in the range 0 through 127. The larger the number, the higher the priority. The default priority is 64.
Multiple routers have the same router priority	**Step 1**	Use the **show decnet interface** command to determine which router is the designated router. Note the priority of the router that is shown in the command output.
	Step 2	Use the **show decnet interface** command on the expected designated router and compare the priorities of the actual and the expected designated routers.
	Step 3	If the routers have the same priority, use the **decnet router-priority** interface configuration command to configure a higher priority on the router that should be elected the designated router.

Table 11-4   *DECnet: Router or End Node Sees Incorrect Designated Router (Continued)*

Possible Problem	Solution
Multiple routers have the same router priority *(continued)*	**Syntax:** The following is the syntax for the **decnet router-priority** command: **decnet router-priority** *value* To elect a designated router to which packets will be sent when no destination is specified, use the **decnet router-priority** interface configuration command. **Syntax:** • *value*—Priority of the router. This can be a number in the range 0 through 127. The larger the number, the higher the priority. The default priority is 64. **Note:** If two routers are configured with the same priority, the router with the higher node number will become the designated router.
Adjacency between nodes is not bidirectional	**Step 1** Use the **show decnet route exec** command to see whether the adjacency with the expected designated router is in a "down" or "initializing" state. **Step 2** Use the **debug decnet adj** privileged exec command to determine whether hello packets are being exchanged. **Caution:** Because debugging output is assigned high priority in the CPU process, it can render the system unusable. For this reason, use **debug** commands only to troubleshoot specific problems or during troubleshooting sessions with Cisco technical support staff. Moreover, it is best to use **debug** commands during periods of lower network traffic and fewer users. Debugging during these periods decreases the likelihood that increased **debug** command processing overhead will affect system use. **Step 3** If a router is not sending hello packets, use the **show interfaces** command to determine whether the interface input and output queues are full. A full input queue is indicated by a value of 75/75, and a full output queue is indicated by a value of 40/40. **Step 4** If the queues are full, and no hello packets are being exchanged, contact your router technical support representative. **Step 5** If routers are sending hello packets, contact end-node administrators to determine why end nodes are rejecting hello packets.

DECnet: Routers Not Establishing Adjacencies

Symptom: Routers do not establish adjacencies with other routers on the same LAN.

Table 11-5 outlines the problems that might cause this symptom and describes solutions to those problems.

Table 11-5 *DECnet: Routers Not Establishing Adjacencies*

Possible Problem	Solution
More than 32 routers on the network	DECnet limits the number of adjacencies that can be established by a router to 32.

Step 1 Enable the **debug decnet events** privileged exec command to determine whether the adjacency is being rejected. Enable this command on one router at a time.

Caution: Because debugging output is assigned high priority in the CPU process, it can render the system unusable. For this reason, use **debug** commands only to troubleshoot specific problems or during troubleshooting sessions with Cisco technical support staff. Moreover, it is best to use **debug** commands during periods of lower network traffic and fewer users. Debugging during these periods decreases the likelihood that increased **debug** command processing overhead will affect system use.

Step 2 If the adjacency is being rejected, reduce the number of adjacent routers or increase the priority of a router that you want to be adjacent so that it has a higher priority than one of the other neighboring routers. An adjacency will be established with the router you want instead of with a router assigned a lower priority.

Syntax:

The following is the syntax to adjust the priority of a router:

decnet router-priority *value*

To elect a designated router to which packets will be sent when no destination is specified, use the **decnet router-priority** interface configuration command.

Syntax Description:

- *value*—Priority of the router. This can be a number in the range 0 through 127. The larger the number, the higher the priority. The default priority is 64.

Table 11-5   *DECnet: Routers Not Establishing Adjacencies (Continued)*

Possible Problem	Solution	
Node address out of range	**Step 1**	Use the **show running-config** privileged exec command to view router configurations. Check to see whether the **decnet max-address** global configuration command has been configured. This command sets the highest DECnet node number allowed in the area.
		Note: The **decnet max-address** command specifies the highest node number allowed in an area, *not* the maximum number of node addresses allowed in an area. For example, if you configure the command **decnet max-address 1000** on a router and you configure a node with a node address of 1001, the address is out of range.
	Step 2	The default maximum address is 1023. However, if another value is configured, the node address might be more than the configured value. If this is the case, increase the maximum address value using the **decnet max-address** command.
Router area number is higher than configured **decnet max-area**	If the area number of a DECnet node (such as a router) is higher than the configured **decnet max-area** value, the adjacency will be reset.	
	Step 1	Use the **show running-config** privileged exec command to view the router configuration. Look for **decnet max-area** global configuration command entries. This command sets the DECnet maximum area number for the router.
		Note: The **decnet max-area** command specifies the highest area value allowed in the network, *not* the maximum number of areas configurable. For example, if you configure the command **decnet max-area 60** and you configure a node with area number 61, the node's area address is out of range.
	Step 2	Use the **show running-config** privileged exec command to find the area number configured on other DECnet routers. Compare the value configured by the **decnet max-area** command to the area numbers of other routers.
	Step 3	If a router's area number is higher than the value configured by the **decnet max-area** global configuration command, reconfigure the **decnet max-area** command so that the DECnet maximum area is higher than the area number of all routers.

Table 11-5 *DECnet: Routers Not Establishing Adjacencies (Continued)*

Possible Problem	Solution	
Adjacency between routers is not bidirectional	**Step 1**	Use the **show decnet route exec** command to see if the adjacency with the expected designated router is in a "down" or "initializing" state.
	Step 2	If you are troubleshooting a nonbroadcast multiaccess network (such as Frame Relay or X.25), make sure that **map** statements are properly configured.
		To establish an address translation for selected nodes, use the **decnet map** global configuration command:
		Syntax:
		decnet *first-network* **map** *virtual-address second-network real-address*
		• *first-network*—DECnet network numbers in the range 0 to 3.
		• *virtual-address*—Numeric DECnet address (10.5, for example).
		• *second-network*—DECnet network number you map to; DECnet numbers range 0 to 3.
		Syntax Description:
		• *real-address*—Numeric DECnet address (10.5, for example).
	Step 3	Use the **debug decnet adj** privileged exec command to determine whether hello packets are being exchanged.
	Step 4	If a router is not sending hello packets, use the **show interfaces** command to determine whether the interface input and output queues are full. A full input queue is indicated by a value of 75/75, and a full output queue is indicated by a value of 40/40.
	Step 5	If the queues are full, and no hello packets are being exchanged, contact your router technical support representative.

DECnet: Routing Node Adjacencies Toggle Up and Down

Symptom: Routing adjacencies toggle up and down. Output such as the following appears repeatedly on the DEC system console:

```
%%%%%%%%%% OPCOM 30-JUN-1993 1:25:07.45 %%%%%%%%%%
Message from user DECNET on The Bay
DECnet event 4.16, adjacency rejected
From NODE 12.1 (The Bay), 30-JUN-1993 1:25:07.45
Circuit UNA-0, Adjacent node = 1.101 (Vax1)
```

```
%%%%%%%%%% OPCOM 30-JUN-1993 1:25:07.46 %%%%%%%%%%
Message from user DECNET on The Bay
DECnet event 4.15, adjacency up
From NODE 12.1 (The Bay), 30-JUN-1993 1:25:07.46
Circuit UNA-0, Adjacent node = 1.12 (Vax2)
```

This output indicates that routers are constantly being added to and removed from the routing table. The OPCOM messages specify DECnet events 4.16 (adjacency rejected) and 4.15 (adjacency up) for specific routing nodes.

Table 11-6 outlines the problems that might cause this symptom and describes solutions to those problems.

Table 11-6   *DECnet: Routing Node Adjacencies Toggle Up and Down*

Possible Problem	Solution	
Total number of routing nodes on network segment is more than 32	DECnet limits the number of adjacencies that can be established by a router to 32.	
	Step 1	Enable the **debug decnet events** privileged exec command to determine whether the adjacency is being rejected. Enable this command on one router at a time.
	Step 2	If the adjacency is being rejected, reduce the number of adjacent routers on the segment.
Hardware problem	Check the error message output to identify the routing node or nodes that are causing the adjacency to toggle.	
	Follow the procedures outlined in Chapter 3, "Troubleshooting Hardware and Booting Problems."	

DECnet: No Phase IV Connectivity over Phase V Backbone

Symptom: Communication between DECnet Phase IV areas separated by an ISO CLNS (Phase V) backbone fails. Phase IV nodes cannot communicate with other Phase IV nodes across a Phase V cloud. However, nodes can communicate with one another within the same Phase IV cloud.

NOTE   For more information about troubleshooting DECnet /OSI internetworks, see Chapter 12, "Troubleshooting ISO CLNS."

Table 11-7 outlines the problems that might cause this symptom and describes solutions to those problems.

Table 11-7   *DECnet: No DECnet Phase IV Connectivity over Phase V Backbone*

Possible Problem	Solution	
Misconfigured addresses	Step 1	Use the **show interfaces** command to confirm that CLNS and DECnet Phase IV are both configured on ISO CLNS backbone routers.
	Step 2	Make sure that the **decnet conversion** global configuration command is configured on backbone routers to allow DECnet Phase IV–to–ISO CLNS conversion.
	Step 3	Use the **show running-config privileged exec** command on backbone routers to verify that DECnet addresses agree with CLNS addresses.
		Two kinds of addresses are easily misconfigured: DECnet addresses, which should be specified in decimal, and CLNS Network Service Access Point addresses, which should be specified in hexadecimal.
		For more information, refer to the section "DECnet Phase IV and ISO CLNS Addresses" later in this chapter.
	Step 4	If the area addresses do not agree, confirm the address specifications and reconfigure the DECnet and CLNS addresses on the router.
		For detailed information on configuring DECnet Phase IV, CLNS, and conversion, refer to the *Cisco IOS Network Protocol Configuration Guide, Part 2.*
ISO CLNS or DECnet not enabled on appropriate interfaces	Step 1	On Phase IV routers bordering the backbone, use the **show clns interface** and **show decnet interface** commands to see which interfaces are running which protocols.
		Verify that DECnet and ISO CLNS are enabled on backbone router interfaces where conversion will occur.
	Step 2	If DECnet is not configured on the correct interfaces, enable it. Make sure you specify the **decnet cost** interface configuration command to assign a cost to the interface. If ISO CLNS routing is not configured on the correct interfaces, use the **clns router** interface configuration command. The full syntax for this command is
		clns *routing*
		Use the **no clns** *routing* command to disable CLNS routing:
		no clns *routing*
		For detailed information on configuring DECnet Phase IV and ISO CLNS, refer to the Cisco IOS *Network Protocol Configuration Guide, Part 2.*

DECnet Phase IV and ISO CLNS Addresses

Address conversion between DECnet Phase IV and ISO CLNS (Phase V) requires that NSAP addresses be Phase IV compatible. If an address can be converted to a valid Phase IV address, it is Phase IV compatible.

To be compatible, the OSI area number must be between 1 and 63 (when converted to decimal) and the OSI station ID must be in the format AA00.0400.*xxxx*. In addition, the OSI area and the DECnet area (calculated from the OSI station ID) must match. This allows the DECnet Phase IV address to be extracted properly from the NSAP.

Table 11-8 shows addresses and their equivalent DECnet Phase IV addresses, and indicates whether the NSAP address is Phase IV compatible and why.

Table 11-8   *OSI NSAP–to–DECnet Phase IV Address Conversion*

OSI NSAP Address (Hex)	OSI Area	DECnet Address (Decimal)	Phase-IV Compatible
49.1111.0012.AA00.0400.0149.20	18	18.257	Yes
49.1111.0009.AA00.0400.BC04.20	9	1.188	No—OSI area does not match the DECnet area
49.1111.0041.AA00.0400.FFFF.20	65	63.1023	No—OSI area is greater than 63
49.1111.000E.AA00.0400.0000.20	14	0.0	No—DECnet address in NSAP station ID is invalid
49.1111.0009.0800.2B05.8297.20	9	—	No—NSAP station ID is not in the proper format (AA00.0400.*xxxx*)

DECnet: Poor Performance

Symptom: Performance in a DECnet network is slow or unreliable. Connections to hosts over one or more routers are periodically inaccessible or drop unexpectedly.

Table 11-9 outlines the problems that might cause this symptom and describes solutions to those problems.

Table 11-9   *DECnet: Poor Performance*

Possible Problem	Solution	
DECnet traffic problem	Step 1	Use the **show decnet traffic** exec command and check the Received and Forwarded fields in the output. In most cases, the values in these fields should match.
	Step 2	If the values do not match, check the Returned, Converted, Access Control Failed, No Route, and Encapsulation Failed fields to see what is causing the performance problem.
	Step 3	If the problem cannot be isolated or solved, contact your technical support representative for assistance.

continues

Table 11-9   *DECnet: Poor Performance (Continued)*

Possible Problem	Solution	
Timer mismatch	**Step 1**	Use the **show decnet interface** exec command on all routers in the network. Verify that the values configured for hello timers and routing update timers are consistent among all routers in the network.
		The following is example output from the **show decnet interface** command:
| | | ```
C4500#show decnet interface
[...]
Ethernet0 is up, line protocol is up,
encapsulation is ARPA
  Interface cost is 50, priority is 64, DECnet
network: 0
  We are the designated router
  Sending HELLOs every 15 seconds, routing
updates 40 seconds
[...]
``` |
	Step 2	If timer values are inconsistent, bring routers into conformance using the **decnet hello-timer** and the **decnet routing-timer** interface configuration commands. The hello timer can be restored to its default, 15 seconds, by using the **no** form of the command.
Media problem	**Step 1**	Use the **show interfaces** exec command and look for CRCs[1] in the output.
	Step 2	If there are CRCs, there is probably a media problem. Refer to the media troubleshooting chapter that covers the media type used in your network.
Input and Output queue drops	**Step 1**	Use the **show interfaces** exec command to check the input and output queues. Look for drops. Each number is followed by a slash, the maximum size of the queue, and the number of packets dropped because the queue is full.
	Step 2	If drops are occurring, contact your technical support representative for assistance.

[1]CRC = cyclic redundancy checks
```

## CHAPTER 12

Troubleshooting ISO CLNS

This chapter presents protocol-related troubleshooting information for International Organization for Standardization (ISO) Connectionless Network Service (CLNS) protocol connectivity and performance problems. ISO CLNS is a network layer standard that is part of the Open System Interconnection (OSI) protocol suite.

The Cisco IOS software supports packet forwarding and routing for ISO CLNS on networks using a variety of data link layers: Ethernet, Token Ring, Fiber Distributed Data Interface (FDDI), and serial. You can use CLNS routing on serial interfaces with High-Level Data Link Control (HDLC), Point-to-Point Protocol (PPP), Link Access Procedure, Balanced (LAPB), X.25, Switched Multimegabit Data Service (SMDS), or Frame Relay encapsulation. To use HDLC encapsulation, you must have a router at both ends of the link. If you use X.25 encapsulation, you must manually enter the network service access point (NSAP)-to-X.121 mapping. The LAPB, X.25, Frame Relay, and SMDS encapsulations interoperate with other vendors.

Cisco's CLNS implementation is also compliant with the Government Open Systems Interconnection Profile (GOSIP) Version 2. As part of its CLNS support, Cisco routers fully support the following ISO and American National Standards Institute (ANSI) standards:

- ISO 9542—Documents the End System-to-Intermediate System (ES-IS) routing exchange protocol.
- ISO 8473—Documents the ISO Connectionless Network Protocol (CLNP).
- ISO 8348/Ad2—Documents NSAP addresses.
- ISO 10589—Documents Intermediate System-to-Intermediate System (IS-IS) Intra-domain Routing Exchange Protocol.

Both the ISO-developed IS-IS routing protocol and Cisco's ISO Interior Gateway Routing Protocol (IGRP) are supported for dynamic routing of ISO CLNS. In addition, static routing for ISO CLNS is supported.

ISO CLNS Technology Basics

The world of OSI networking has a unique terminology:

- *End system* (ES) refers to any nonrouting network device.
- *Intermediate system* (IS) refers to a router.
- *Area* is a group of contiguous networks and attached hosts that are specified by a network administrator or manager to be an area.
- *Domain* is a collection of connected areas. Routing domains provide full connectivity to all end systems within them.

ISO CLNS Addressing

Addresses in the ISO network architecture are referred to as NSAP addresses and network entity titles (NETs). Each node in an OSI network has one or more NETs. In addition, each node has many NSAP addresses. Each NSAP address differs from one of the NETs for that node in only the last byte (see Figure 12-1). This byte is called the *n-selector*. Its function is similar to the port number in other protocol suites.

Cisco's implementation supports all NSAP address formats that are defined by ISO 8348/Ad2; however, Cisco provides dynamic routing (ISO-IGRP or IS-IS routing) only for NSAP addresses that conform to the address constraints defined in the ISO standard for IS-IS (ISO 10589).

An NSAP address consists of two major fields:

- The initial domain part (IDP) is made up of 1-byte AFI and a variable-length initial domain identifier (IDI). The length of the IDI and the encoding format for the domain-specific part (DSP) are based on the value of the authority and format identifier (AFI).
- The DSP is made up of a high-order DSP, an area ID, a system ID, and a 1-byte n-selector.

The key difference between the ISO-IGRP and IS-IS NSAP addressing schemes is in the definition of area addresses. Both use the system ID for Level 1 routing. However, they differ in the way addresses are specified for area routing. An ISO-IGRP NSAP address includes three separate levels for routing: the domain, area, and system ID. An IS-IS address includes two fields: a single continuous area field comprising the domain and area fields defined for ISO-IGRP and the system ID.

Figure 12-1 illustrates the ISO-IGRP NSAP addressing structure.

Figure 12-1 *ISO-IGRP NSAP Addressing Structure*

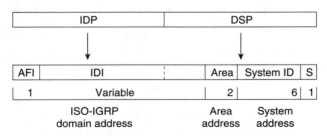

The ISO-IGRP NSAP address is divided into three parts: a domain part, an area address, and a system ID. Domain routing is performed on the domain part of the address. Area routing for a given domain uses the area address. System ID routing for a given area uses the system ID part. The NSAP address is laid out as follows:

- The domain part is of variable length and comes before the area address.
- The area address is the 2 bytes before the system ID.
- The system ID is the 6 bytes before the n-selector.
- The n-selector (S) is the last byte of the NSAP address.

Our ISO-IGRP routing implementation interprets the bytes from the AFI up to (but not including) the area field in the DSP as a domain identifier. The area field specifies the area, and the system ID specifies the system.

Figure 12-2 illustrates the IS-IS NSAP addressing structure.

Figure 12-2 *IS-IS NSAP Addressing Structure*

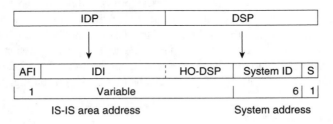

An IS-IS NSAP address is divided into two parts: an area address (AA) and a system ID. Level 2 routing uses the AA. Level 1 routing uses the system ID address. The NSAP address is laid out as follows:

- The n-selector (S) is the last byte of the NSAP address.
- The system ID is found between the area address and the n-selector byte.
- The area address is the NSAP address, not including the system ID and n-selector.

The IS-IS routing protocol interprets the bytes from the AFI up to (but not including) the system ID field in the DSP as an area identifier. The system ID specifies the system.

Addressing Rules

All NSAP addresses must obey the following constraints:

- No two nodes can have addresses with the same NET; that is, addresses can match all but the n-selector (S) field in the DSP.
- ISO-IGRP requires at least 10 bytes of length; 1 for domain, 2 for area, 6 for system ID, and 1 for n-selector.
- Cisco's implementation of IS-IS requires at least 8 bytes; 1 for area, 6 for system ID, and 1 for n-selector.
- No two nodes residing within the same area can have addresses in which the system ID fields are the same.

The following are examples of OSI network and GOSIP NSAP addresses using the ISO-IGRP implementation. The second example is the OSI network NSAP address format:

```
47.0004.004D.0003.0000.0C00.62E6.00
| Domain| Area| System ID| S|
```

Entering Routes

Routes are entered by specifying pairs (NSAP prefix and next-hop NET). NETs are similar in function to NSAP addresses. In the routing table, the best match means the longest NSAP prefix entry that matches the beginning of the destination NSAP address. In Table 12-1, which is an example of a static routing table, the next-hop NETs are listed for completeness but are not necessary to understand the routing algorithm. Table 12-2 offers examples of how the longest matching NSAP prefix can be matched with routing table entries in Table 12-1.

Table 12-1   *Sample Routing Table Entries*

Entry	NSAP Address Prefix	Next-Hop NET
1	47.0005.000c.0001	47.0005.000c.0001.0000.1234.00
2	47.0004	47.0005.000c.0002.0000.0231.00
3	47.0005.0003	47.0005.000c.0001.0000.1234.00
4	47.0005.000c	47.0005.000c.0004.0000.0011.00
5	47.0005	47.0005.000c.0002.0000.0231.00

Table 12-2   *Hierarchical Routing Examples*

Datagram Destination NSAP Address	Table Entry Number Used
47.0005.000c.0001.0000.3456.01	1
47.0005.000c.0001.6789.2345.01	1
47.0004.1234.1234.1234.1234.01	2
47.0005.0003.4321.4321.4321.01	3
47.0005.000c.0004.5678.5678.01	4
47.0005.0001.0005.3456.3456.01	5

Octet boundaries must be used for the internal boundaries of NSAP addresses and NETs.

Troubleshooting ISO CLNS

This section presents protocol-related troubleshooting information for ISO CLNS protocol connectivity and performance problems. It describes specific ISO CLNS symptoms, the problems that are likely to cause each symptom, and the solutions to those problems.

NOTE   Discussions of host configuration problems in this chapter assume that the host is a UNIX system. Equivalent actions might also be applicable to non-UNIX hosts, but the discussions do not specifically address non-UNIX end-station problems.

The following sections cover the most common network issues in ISO CLNS networks:

- ISO CLNS: Host Cannot Access Hosts on Local or Remote Network
- ISO CLNS: Host Cannot Access Hosts in Same Area
- ISO CLNS: Host Cannot Access Hosts in Different Area
- ISO CLNS: Connections Fail Using Certain Protocols
- ISO CLNS: Users Cannot Make Connections over Parallel Path
- ISO CLNS: Redistribution Causes Routing Problems
- ISO CLNS: Poor Performance

ISO CLNS: Host Cannot Access Hosts on Local or Remote Network

Symptom: Hosts cannot communicate with other hosts. Hosts might be located on the local or a remote network. Connections to some hosts on a network might be possible, whereas connections to other hosts on the same network fail.

Table 12-3 outlines the problems that might cause this symptom and describes solutions to those problems.

Table 12-3 *ISO CLNS: Host Cannot Access Hosts on Local or Remote Network*

Possible Problem	Solution	
Missing or misconfigured default gateway specification	**Step 1**	Determine whether a default gateway is specified in the adjacency table of the host attempting to make a connection. Use the following UNIX command: `host% netstat -rn` Check the output of this command for a default gateway specification. **Syntax Description:** • **netstat**—Displays protocol statistics and current TCP/IP[1] network connections • **r**—Displays the contents of the routing table • **n**—Displays addresses and port numbers in numeric form
	Step 2	If the default gateway specification is incorrect, or if it is not present at all, you can change or add a default gateway using the following UNIX command at the local host: `host% route add default address 1` where *address* is the IP address of the default gateway (the router local to the host). The value 1 indicates that the specified gateway is one hop away.
	Step 3	It is recommended that you specify a default gateway as part of the boot process. Specify the ISO CLNS address of the gateway in the following UNIX host file: `/etc/defaultrouter` This filename might be different on your UNIX system.
End system has no Level 1 router	**Step 1**	Use the **show clns neighbors detail** privileged exec command to show all ESs[2] and ISs[3] to which the router is directly connected.
	Step 2	Make sure there is at least one Level 1 router on the same network as the end system.

Table 12-3   *ISO CLNS: Host Cannot Access Hosts on Local or Remote Network (Continued)*

Possible Problem	Solution	
Level 1 router or ES has bad address	Step 1	Verify that the Level 1 router has the same address as the ES.
	Step 2	Verify that all bytes of the NSAP[4] address, up to but not including the system ID, are the same on both the router and the ES. The domain and area addresses must match, and the station IDs must be unique. (The value of the n-selector byte has no impact in this case.)
ES host is not running ES-IS[5] protocol	Step 1	Use the appropriate host commands to verify that an ES-IS process is running. If necessary, initiate the ES-IS process on the host.
	Step 2	Check the adjacency database on the host and verify that it has an entry for its directly connected router.
	Step 3	Use the **debug clns packet** privileged exec command on the Level 1 router to verify that it sees and forwards packets from the ES.
		Caution: Because debugging output is assigned high priority in the CPU process, it can render the system unusable. For this reason, use **debug** commands only to troubleshoot specific problems or during troubleshooting sessions with Cisco technical support staff. Moreover, it is best to use **debug** commands during periods of lower network traffic and fewer users. Debugging during these periods decreases the likelihood that increased **debug** command processing overhead will affect system use.
	Step 4	If necessary, statically configure the router to recognize the ES by using the **clns es-neighbor** interface configuration command. The following is the syntax for the **clns es-neighbor** command:

clns es-neighbor *nsap snpa*

Syntax Description:

- *nsap*—Specific NSAP to map to a specific MAC[6] address.

- *snpa*—Data link (MAC) address.

Example:

The following example defines an ES neighbor on Ethernet interface 0:

```
interface ethernet 0
 clns es-neighbor 47.0004.004D.0055.0000.0C00.A45B.00
0000.0C00.A45B
```

In this case, the end systems with the following NSAP, or NET,[7] are configured with an Ethernet MAC address of 0000.0C00.A45B:

- 47.0004.004D.0055.0000.0C00.A45B.00

continues

Table 12-3 *ISO CLNS: Host Cannot Access Hosts on Local or Remote Network (Continued)*

Possible Problem	Solution

Router between hosts is down	**Step 1** Use the **trace** exec command to check connectivity between routers and the source ES.
	
	Step 2 If the **trace** fails at a router, use the **show clns neighbors** exec command to see which neighboring routers and ESs are recognized.
	
	Sample Display:
	
	The following is sample output from the **show clns neighbors** command. This display is a composite of the **show clns es-neighbor** and **show clns is-neighbor** commands:
	
	```router# show clns neighbors```
	```System Id SNPA Interface State Holdtime Type```
	```Protocol```
	```0000.0000.0007 aa00.0400.6408 Ethernet0 Init 277 IS ES-IS```
	```0000.0C00.0C35 0000.0c00.0c36 Ethernet1 Up 91 L1 IS-IS```
	```0800.2B16.24EA aa00.0400.2d05 Ethernet0 Up 29 L1L2 IS-IS```
	```0800.2B14.060E aa00.0400.9205 Ethernet0 Up 1698 ES ES-IS```
	```0000.0C00.3E51 *HDLC* Serial1 Up 28 L2 IS-IS```
	```0000.0C00.62E6 0000.0c00.62e7 Ethernet1 Up 22 L1 IS-IS```
	```0A00.0400.2D05 aa00.0400.2d05 Ethernet0 Init 24 IS ES-IS```
	
	Step 3 If neighboring routers and end systems are up, perform one of the following procedures:
	
	• For ISO-IGRP,[8] check the routing table and see whether the routes are being learned. Use the **show clns route** exec command to display the routing tables.
	
	• For IS-IS,[9] check the LSP[10] database to see whether the links are being reported in link state advertisements. Check the IS-IS routing table to see whether the routes are being installed in the routing table. Use the **show isis database detail** exec command to display the routing tables.

Route redistribution problem	Misconfigured route redistribution can cause connectivity problems. For specific troubleshooting information, see the section "ISO CLNS: Redistribution Causes Routing Problems" later in this chapter.

[1]TCP/IP = Transmission Control Protocol/Internet Protocol

[2]ES = end system

[3]IS = intermediate system

[4]NSAP = Network service access point

[5]ES-IS = End System-to-Intermediate System

[6]MAC = Media Access Control

[7]NET = network entity title

[8]IGRP = Interior Gateway Routing Protocol

[9]IS-IS = Intermediate System-to-Intermediate System

[10]LSP = Link State Protocol

ISO CLNS: Host Cannot Access Hosts in Same Area

Symptom: Hosts cannot access other hosts in the same area. The hosts might be on the same network or they might be in a different network in the same area.

Table 12-4 outlines the problems that might cause this symptom and describes solutions to those problems.

Table 12-4   *ISO CLNS: Host Cannot Access Hosts in Same Area*

Possible Problem	Solution	
Area address is configured incorrectly on the host	Step 1	Check all Level 1 routing tables and link-state databases.
	Step 2	Verify that the hosts are in the same area.
	Step 3	Check that the NSAP address is entered correctly on the hosts.
Different area addresses are merged into a single area, but the router is configured incorrectly	Step 1	Use the **show running-config** privileged exec command to see router configurations. Check whether multiple area addresses are configured.
	Step 2	If multiple network addresses are configured, verify that the router is configured to support a multihomed area (a single area that has more than one area address; see Figure 12-3).
	Step 3	To communicate, routers must establish a Level 1 adjacency. Therefore, area addresses in a multihomed area must overlap across routers.

For example, in the multihomed area shown in Figure 12-3, to configure Area 1 and Area 2 as a multihomed area, both Router A and Router B must be configured to be in both areas. IS-IS routing supports the assignment of multiple area addresses on the same router. This concept is referred to as *multihoming*. Multihoming provides a mechanism for smoothly migrating network addresses, as follows:

- Splitting up an area—Nodes within a given area can accumulate until they are difficult to manage, cause excessive traffic, or threaten to exceed the usable address space for an area. Multiple area addresses can be assigned so that you can smoothly partition a network into separate areas without disrupting service.

- Merging areas—Use transitional area addresses to merge as many as three separate areas that have a common area address into a single area.

continues

Table 12-4   *ISO CLNS: Host Cannot Access Hosts in Same Area (Continued)*

Possible Problem	Solution
Different area addresses are merged into a single area, but the router is configured incorrectly *(continued)*	• Transition to a different address—You may need to change an area address for a particular group of nodes. Use multiple area addresses to allow incoming traffic intended for an old area address to continue being routed to associated nodes. You must statically assign the multiple area addresses on the router. Cisco currently supports assignment of up to three area addresses on a router. The number of areas allowed in a domain is unlimited. All the addresses must have the same system ID. For example, you can assign one address (area1 plus system ID) and two additional addresses in different areas (area2 plus system ID and area3 plus system ID) where the system ID is the same.
	Step 4 Alternatively, one router can be configured in both areas, while the other router remains configured for a single area. Provided that the area numbers on routers overlap, the routers will establish a Level 1 adjacency, allowing them to communicate.
ES host is not running ES-IS protocol	**Step 1** Use the appropriate host commands to verify that an ES-IS process is running. If necessary, initiate the ES-IS process on the host.
	Step 2 Check the adjacency database on the host and verify that it has an entry for its directly connected router.
	Step 3 Use the **debug clns packet** privileged exec command on the Level 1 router to verify that it sees and forwards packets from the ES. **Caution:** Because debugging output is assigned high priority in the CPU process, it can render the system unusable. For this reason, use **debug** commands only to troubleshoot specific problems or during troubleshooting sessions with Cisco technical support staff. Moreover, it is best to use **debug** commands during periods of lower network traffic and fewer users. Debugging during these periods decreases the likelihood that increased **debug** command processing overhead will affect system use.
	Step 4 If necessary, statically configure the router to recognize the ES by using the **clns es-neighbor** interface configuration command. The following is the syntax for the **clns es-neighbor** command: **clns es-neighbor** *nsap snpa*

Table 12-4   *ISO CLNS: Host Cannot Access Hosts in Same Area (Continued)*

Possible Problem	Solution
ES host is not running ES-IS protocol *(continued)*	**Syntax Description:** • *nsap*—Specific NSAP to map to a specific MAC address. • *snpa*—Data link (MAC) address. **Example:** The following example defines an ES neighbor on Ethernet interface 0: ``` interface ethernet 0 clns es-neighbor 47.0004.004D.0055.0000.0C00.A45B.00 0000.0C00.A45B ```
Route redistribution problem	Misconfigured route redistribution can cause connectivity problems. For specific troubleshooting information, see the section "ISO CLNS: Redistribution Causes Routing Problems" later in this chapter.

Figure 12-3   *Multihomed Area Sample Network*

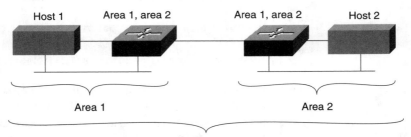

Single area with two area addresses

ISO CLNS: Host Cannot Access Hosts in Different Area

Symptom: Host cannot access hosts in a different area. Hosts in the same area are accessible.

Table 12-5 outlines the problems that might cause this symptom and describes solutions to those problems.

Table 12-5 *ISO CLNS: Host Cannot Access Hosts in Different Area*

Possible Problem	Solution

Level 2 routers are not routing packets to the correct area	**Step 1** Use the **trace** command to verify that Level 1 routers are routing packets to the nearest Level 2 router.
	
	Sample Display:
	
	The following display shows an example of ISO CLNS **trace** output:
	
	``
	router# trace
	Protocol [ip]: clns
	Target CLNS address: thoth
	Timeout in seconds [3]:
	Probe count [3]:
	Minimum Time to Live [1]:
	Maximum Time to Live [30]:
	Type escape sequence to abort.
	Tracing the route to THOTH
	(55.0006.0100.0000.0000.0001.8888.1112.1314.1516)
	   HORUS(55.0006.0100.0000.0000.0001.6666.3132.3334.3536) 32
	msec ! 28 msec
	28 msec !
	   2 ISIS(55.0006.0100.0000.0000.0001.7777.2122.2324.2526)
	56 msec ! 80 msec
	56 msec !
	   3 THOTH(55.0006.0100.0000.0000.0001.8888.1112.1314.1516) 80
	msec ! 80 msec ! 8
	``
	
	Step 2 Use the **trace** exec command to verify that Level 2 routers are routing packets to the correct destination area.
	
	Step 3 If packets are not being routed to the correct area, check the Level 2 routing tables (ISO-IGRP[1]) or the Level 2 link state databases (IS-IS) to see whether the packets are being forwarded to another area.
	
	Step 4 If necessary, reconfigure routers with the correct area addresses and Level 2 (IS-IS) routing information.

ES host is not running ES-IS protocol	**Step 1** Use the appropriate host commands to verify that an ES-IS process is running. If necessary, initiate the ES-IS process on the host. **Step 2** Check the adjacency database on the host and verify that it has an entry for its directly connected router. **Step 3** Use the **debug clns packet** privileged exec command on the Level 1 router to verify that it sees and forwards packets from the ES.

Table 12-5   *ISO CLNS: Host Cannot Access Hosts in Different Area (Continued)*

Possible Problem	Solution
ES host is not running ES-IS protocol *(continued)*	**Caution:** Because debugging output is assigned high priority in the CPU process, it can render the system unusable. For this reason, use **debug** commands only to troubleshoot specific problems or during troubleshooting sessions with Cisco technical support staff. Moreover, it is best to use **debug** commands during periods of lower network traffic and fewer users. Debugging during these periods decreases the likelihood that increased **debug** command processing overhead will affect system use.
	Step 4 If necessary, statically configure the router to recognize the ES by using the **clns es-neighbor** interface configuration command.
Route redistribution problem	Misconfigured route redistribution can cause connectivity problems. For specific troubleshooting information, see the section "ISO CLNS: Redistribution Causes Routing Problems" later in this chapter.

Router between hosts is down	**Step 1** Use the **trace** exec command to check connectivity between routers and the source ES.
	
	Sample Display:
	
	The following display shows an example of ISO CLNS **trace** output.
	
	`router# trace`
	`Protocol [ip]: clns`
	`Target CLNS address: thoth`
	`Timeout in seconds [3]:`
	`Probe count [3]:`
	`Minimum Time to Live [1]:`
	`Maximum Time to Live [30]:`
	`Type escape sequence to abort.`
	`Tracing the route to THOTH`
	`(55.0006.0100.0000.0000.0001.8888.1112.1314.1516)`
	`    HORUS(55.0006.0100.0000.0000.0001.6666.3132.3334.3536) 32`
	`msec ! 28 msec`
	`28 msec !`
	`    2 ISIS(55.0006.0100.0000.0000.0001.7777.2122.2324.2526)`
	`56 msec ! 80 msec`
	`56 msec !`
	`    3 THOTH(55.0006.0100.0000.0000.0001.8888.1112.1314.1516) 80`
	`msec ! 80 msec ! 8`
	
	Step 2 If the **trace** fails at a router, use the **show clns neighbors** exec command to see which neighboring routers and ESs are recognized.

continues

Table 12-5   *ISO CLNS: Host Cannot Access Hosts in Different Area (Continued)*

Possible Problem	Solution	
Router between hosts is down	**Step 3**	If neighboring routers and end systems are up, perform one of the following procedures:
		• For ISO-IGRP, check the routing table and see whether the routes are being learned. Use the **show clns route** exec command to display the routing tables.
		• For IS-IS, check the LSP[2] database to see whether the links are being reported in link state advertisements. Check the IS-IS routing table to see whether the routes are being installed in the routing table. Use the **show isis database detail** exec command to display the routing tables.

[1] IGRP = Interior Gateway Routing Protocol
[2] LSP = Link State Protocol

ISO CLNS: Connections Fail Using Certain Protocols

Symptom: Host connections fail using certain protocols. Hosts might be able to connect to other hosts using some protocols but are unable to connect using others.

Table 12-6 outlines the problems that might cause this symptom and describes solutions to those problems.

Table 12-6   *ISO CLNS: Connections Fail Using Certain Protocols*

Possible Problem	Solution	
Host is not configured to support the service	Verify that the needed protocols are correctly installed and configured on the host system. Consult your vendor's documentation for information on configuring hosts.	
Misconfigured access list	**Step 1**	Use the **trace** exec command to determine the path taken to reach remote hosts.
	Step 2	If you discover a router that is stopping traffic, use the **show access-lists** privileged exec command to see whether any access lists are configured on the router.
	Step 3	Disable all access lists on the router using **no access-group** interface configuration commands on the appropriate interfaces.
	Step 4	Determine whether hosts can now use the protocol in question. If traffic can get through, it is likely that an access list is blocking protocol traffic.
	Step 5	Make sure the access list does not filter traffic from ports that are used by the protocol in question. Configure explicit **permit** statements for traffic that you want the router to forward normally.
	Step 6	Enable the access list and verify that the protocol still functions correctly. If problems persist, continue isolating and analyzing access lists on all routers in the path from source to destination.

ISO CLNS: Users Cannot Make Connections over Parallel Path

Symptom: In environments with multiple paths between networks, when one link goes down, connections across a parallel link are not possible.

NOTE	IS-IS has equal-cost load balancing for both Level 1 and Level 2 routes. If there are parallel paths in an IS-IS network and one goes down, the other should serve as a backup that is ready to be used immediately.

Table 12-7 outlines the problems that might cause this symptom and describes solutions to those problems.

Table 12-7   *ISO CLNS: Users Cannot Make Connections over Parallel Path*

Possible Problem	Solution	
Routing has not converged	Step 1	Use the **show clns route** privileged exec command to view the CLNS routing table. Examine the table for routes listed as "possibly down." This indicates that the routing protocol has not converged.
	Step 2	Wait for the routing protocol to converge. Use the **show clns route** command again to see whether the routes are now up.
		Note: ISO-IGRP does load balancing only for domain prefix routes. If you are doing Level 1 or Level 2 routing in ISO-IGRP, only a single path is maintained. If that path goes down, you must wait for the network to converge before the alternate path is available.
Misconfigured access list	Step 1	Use the **trace** exec command to determine the path taken to reach remote hosts.
	Step 2	If you discover a router that is stopping traffic, use the **show access-lists** privileged exec command to see whether any access lists are configured on the router.
	Step 3	Disable all access lists on the router using **no access-group** interface configuration commands on the appropriate interfaces.
	Step 4	Determine whether hosts can now use the protocol in question. If traffic can get through, it is likely that an access list is blocking protocol traffic.
	Step 5	Make sure the access list does not filter traffic from ports that are used by the protocol in question. Configure explicit **permit** statements for traffic that you want the router to forward normally.
	Step 6	Enable the access list and verify that the protocol still functions correctly. If problems persist, continue isolating and analyzing access lists on all routers in the path from source to destination.

continues

Table 12-7 *ISO CLNS: Users Cannot Make Connections over Parallel Path (Continued)*

Possible Problem	Solution
Hardware or media problem	For information on troubleshooting hardware problems, see Chapter 3. "Troubleshooting Hardware and Booting Problems." For information on troubleshooting media problems, refer to the media troubleshooting chapter that covers the media type used in your network.

ISO CLNS: Redistribution Causes Routing Problems

Symptom: Route redistribution does not work properly and causes routing problems. Traffic does not get through a router that is redistributing routes between two different routing areas or domains—typically IS-IS and ISO-IGRP. Observed symptoms range from poor performance to no communication at all.

Table 12-8 outlines the problems that might cause this symptom and describes solutions to those problems.

Table 12-8 *ISO CLNS: Redistribution Causes Routing Problems*

Possible Problem	Solution
Misordered sequence numbers	The sequence numbers used in **route-map** router configuration commands determine the order in which conditions are tested. Misordered sequence numbers can cause redistribution problems.
	Step 1 Use the **show running-config** privileged exec command to display the router configuration. Look for **route-map** router configuration command entries.
	Step 2 If **route-map** commands are configured, look at the sequence numbers that are assigned. Lower sequence numbers are tested before higher sequence numbers, regardless of the order in which they are listed in the configuration.
	Step 3 If conditions are not being tested in the order you want, you must modify the sequence numbers to change the testing order. The syntax for the **route-map** command to adjust the sequence number is as follows:
	route-map *map-tag* {**permit** | **deny**} *sequence-number*
	Syntax Description:
	• *map-tag*—Meaningful name for the route map. The redistribute command uses this name to reference this route map. Multiple route maps can share the same map tag name. Can either be an expression or a filter set.

Table 12-8   *ISO CLNS: Redistribution Causes Routing Problems (Continued)*

Possible Problem	Solution
Misordered sequence numbers *(continued)*	• **permit**—If the match criteria are met for this route map and **permit** is specified, the route is redistributed as controlled by the set actions. If the match criteria are not met, and permit is specified, the next route map with the same map tag is tested. If a route passes none of the match criteria for the set of route maps sharing the same name, it is not redistributed by that set. • **deny**—If the match criteria are met for the route map and **deny** is specified, the route is not redistributed and no further route maps sharing the same map tag name will be examined. • *sequence-number*—Number that indicates the position a new route map is to have in the list of route maps already configured with the same name. If given with the no form of this command, it specifies the position of the route map that should be deleted.
Missing or misconfigured **default-metric** command	**Step 1** Use the **show running-config** exec command to view the router configuration. Look for a **default-metric** router configuration command entry. **Step 2** If the **default-metric** router configuration command or the **distance** router configuration command is missing, add the appropriate version of the missing command. **Syntax:** The following is the syntax for the **default-metric** command: **default-metric** *number* **Syntax Description:** • *number*—Default metric value appropriate for the specified routing protocol. **Syntax:** The following is the syntax for the **distance** command: **distance** *value* [**clns**] **Syntax Description:** • *value*—Administrative distance, indicating the trustworthiness of a routing information source. This argument has a numeric value between 0 and 255. A higher relative value indicates a lower trustworthiness rating. Preference is given to routes with smaller values. The default, if unspecified, is 110. • **clns**—(Optional) CLNS-derived routes for IS-IS. Refer to the *Cisco IOS Network Protocols Configuration Guide, Part 2 and Network Protocols Command Reference, Part 2*, for information about adjusting ISO CLNS default metrics.

continues

Table 12-8 *ISO CLNS: Redistribution Causes Routing Problems (Continued)*

Possible Problem	Solution

Missing or misconfigured **distance** command	**Step 1** Use the **show running-config** exec command to view the router configuration. Look for a **distance** router configuration command entry.
	
	Step 2 If the **distance** command is missing, configure a distance specification on the router. Use the **distance** router configuration command to configure the administrative distance for CLNS routes learned.
	
	Syntax:
	
	The following is the syntax for the **distance** command:
	
	distance *value* [**clns**]
	
	Syntax Description:
	
	• *value*—Administrative distance, indicating the trustworthiness of a routing information source. This argument has a numeric value between 0 and 255. A higher relative value indicates a lower trustworthiness rating. Preference is given to routes with smaller values. The default, if unspecified, is 110.
	
	• **clns**—(Optional) CLNS-derived routes for IS-IS.
	
	Example:
	
	In the following example, the **distance** value for CLNS routes learned is 90. Preference is given to these CLNS routes rather than routes with the default administrative **distance** value of 110:
	
	`router isis`
	` distance 90 clns`

Redistribution feedback loop exists	Redistribution between an IS-IS cloud and an ISO-IGRP cloud should be performed only at a single point. If it is not, routing information can be advertised back into one of the clouds, causing routing feedback loops.
	
	Examples:
	
	The following example illustrates redistribution of ISO-IGRP routes of Michigan and ISO-IGRP routes of Ohio into the IS-IS area tagged **USA**:
	
	`router isis USA`
	` redistribute iso-igrp Michigan`
	` redistribute iso-igrp Ohio`
	
	The following example illustrates redistribution of IS-IS routes of France and ISO-IGRP routes of Germany into the ISO-IGRP area tagged **Backbone**:
	
	`router iso-igrp Backbone`
	` redistribute isis France`
	` redistribute iso-igrp Germany`

Table 12-8   *ISO CLNS: Redistribution Causes Routing Problems (Continued)*

Possible Problem	Solution
Redistribution feedback loop exists *(continued)*	If you must redistribute at another point, use default metrics to perform the redistribution in one direction only.
	Refer to the Cisco IOS *Network Protocols Configuration Guide, Part 2,* and *Network Protocols Command Reference, Part 2,* for information about adjusting ISO CLNS default metrics.

ISO CLNS: Poor Performance

Symptom: Users experience poor performance or sudden loss of connections. One or more routers might be receiving duplicate routing updates and might see routers and ESs on multiple interfaces.

Table 12-9 outlines the problems that might cause this symptom and describes solutions to those problems.

Table 12-9   *ISO CLNS: Poor Performance*

Possible Problem	Solution	
Multiple ISO-IGRP processes are configured on a single interface	**Step 1**	Use the **show clns interface** exec command to view the interface configuration. Look for multiple ISO-IGRP processes that are configured on a single interface.
	Step 2	If multiple ISO-IGRP processes are configured on a single interface, different Level 2 updates are being sent out through the same interface.
		Multiple Level 2 updates on the same interface can cause congestion problems, especially if the network is large and links are flapping outside the damping intervals. Flapping is a routing problem where an advertised route between two nodes alternates (flaps) back and forth between two paths due to a network problem that causes intermittent interface failures.
	Step 3	Remove one of the ISO-IGRP processes from the interface configuration using the appropriate **no clns router iso-igrp** interface configuration command.

continues

Table 12-9 *ISO CLNS: Poor Performance (Continued)*

Possible Problem	Solution
Bridge or repeater in parallel with router	A bridge or repeater in parallel with a router can cause updates and traffic to be seen from both sides of an interface.

Step 1 Use the **show clns is-neighbors detail** and the **show clns neighbors detail** exec commands to see through which routers and protocols the router's adjacencies were learned.

The following is sample output from the **show clns neighbors detail** command:

```
router# show clns neighbors detail
System Id     SNPA            Interface  State Holdtime Type Protocol
000.0000.0007 aa00.0400.6408  Ethernet0  Init  291      IS   ES-IS
  Area Address(es): 47.0005.80FF.F500.0000.0003.0020
0000.0C00.0C35 0000.0c00.0c36 Ethernet1  Up    94       L1   IS-IS
  Area Address(es): 47.0004.004D.0001 39.0001
0800.2B16.24EA aa00.0400.2d05 Ethernet0  Up    9        L1L2 IS-IS
  Area Address(es): 47.0004.004D.0001
0800.2B14.060E aa00.0400.9205 Ethernet0  Up    1651     ES   ES-IS
  Area Address(es): 49.0040
0000.0C00.3E51 *HDLC*          Serial1    Up    27       L2   IS-IS
  Area Address(es): 39.0004
0000.0C00.62E6 0000.0c00.62e7 Ethernet1  Up    26       L1   IS-IS
  Area Address(es): 47.0004.004D.0001
oA00.0400.2D05 aa00.0400.2d05 Ethernet0  Init  29       IS   ES-IS
  Area Address(es): 47.0004.004D.0001
```

Look for routers that are known to be on a remote network. A router listed in the adjacency table but that is not on a directly connected network indicates a problem.

You can also look for paths to networks (or areas) on multiple interfaces.

Step 2 If you determine that there is a parallel bridge or repeater, remove the device or configure filters that block routing updates from being learned from the device.

Route redistribution problem	Misconfigured route redistribution can cause performance problems. For specific troubleshooting information, see the section "ISO CLNS: Redistribution Causes Routing Problems" earlier in this chapter.

## CHAPTER 13

Troubleshooting Banyan VINES

Banyan Virtual Integrated Network Service (VINES) implements a distributed network operating system based on a proprietary protocol family derived from Xerox Corporation's Xerox Network Systems (XNS) protocols (see Chapter 14, "Troubleshooting XNS"). VINES uses a client/server architecture in which clients request certain services, such as file and printer access, from servers. Along with Novell's NetWare, IBM's LAN Server, and Microsoft's LAN Manager, VINES is one of the best-known distributed system environments for microcomputer-based networks.

VINES Technology Basics

The VINES protocol stack is shown in Figure 13-1.

Figure 13-1 *The VINES Protocol Stack*

OSI reference model	VINES protocol			
7	File services	Print services	StreetTalk	Other applications
6 5	RPC			
4	IPC (datagram)		SPP (stream)	
3	VIP			ARP RTP ICP
2 1	Media-access protocols			

VINES Media Access

The two lower layers of the VINES stack are implemented with a variety of well-known media-access mechanisms, including High-Level Data Link Control (HDLC), Synchronous Data Link Control (SDLC) and derivatives, X.25, Ethernet, and Token Ring.

The Network Layer

VINES uses the VINES Internetwork Protocol (VIP) to perform Layer 3 activities (including internetwork routing). VINES also supports its own Address Resolution Protocol (ARP), its own version of the Routing Information Protocol (RIP) called the Routing Table Protocol (RTP), and the Internet Control Protocol (ICP), which provides exception handling and special routing cost information. ARP, ICP, and RTP packets are encapsulated in a VIP header.

VIP

VINES network-layer addresses are 48-bit entities subdivided into network (32 bits) and subnetwork (16 bits) portions. The network number is better described as a server number because it is derived directly from the server's key (a hardware module that identifies a unique number and the software options for that server). The subnetwork portion of a VINES address is better described as a host number because it is used to identify hosts on VINES networks. Figure 13-2 illustrates the VINES address format.

Figure 13-2 *The VINES Address Format*

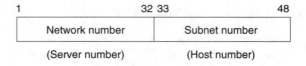

The network number identifies a VINES logical network, which is represented as a two-level tree with the root at a service node. Service nodes, which are usually servers, provide address resolution and routing services to clients, which represent the leaves of the tree. The service node assigns VIP addresses to clients.

When a client is powered on, it broadcasts a request for servers. All servers that hear the request respond. The client chooses the first response and requests a subnetwork (host) address from that server. The server responds with an address consisting of its own network address (derived from its key), concatenated with a subnetwork (host) address of its own choosing. Client subnetwork addresses are typically assigned sequentially, starting with 8001H. Server subnetwork addresses are always 1. The VINES address selection process is shown in Figure 13-3.

Figure 13-3 *The VINES Address Selection Process*

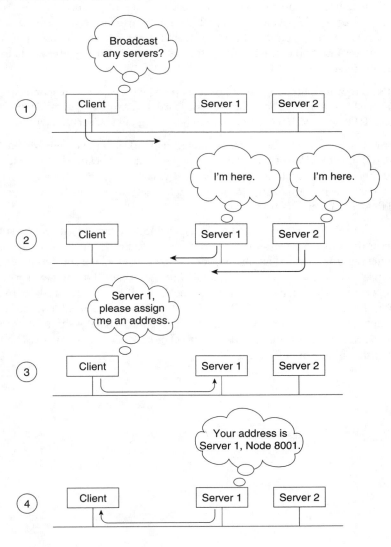

Dynamic address assignment is not unique in the industry (AppleTalk also uses this process), but it is certainly not as common as static address assignment. Because addresses are chosen exclusively by a particular server (whose address is unique as a result of the uniqueness of the hardware key), there is very little chance of a duplicate address (a potentially devastating problem on Internet Protocol [IP] and other networks).

In the VINES network scheme, all servers with multiple interfaces are essentially routers. A client always chooses its own server as a first-hop router, even if another server on the same cable provides a better route to the ultimate destination. A client can learn about other routers by receiving redirect messages from its own server. Because clients rely on their servers for first-hop routing, VINES servers maintain routing tables to help them find remote nodes.

VINES routing tables consist of host/cost pairs, where host corresponds to a network node that can be reached and cost corresponds to a delay, expressed in milliseconds, to get to that node. RTP helps VINES servers find neighboring clients, servers, and routers.

Periodically, all clients advertise both their network-layer and their Media Access Control (MAC)–layer addresses with the equivalent of a hello packet. Hello packets indicate that the client is still operating and network ready. The servers themselves send routing updates to other servers periodically. Routing updates alert other routers to changes in node addresses and network topology.

When a VINES server receives a packet, it checks whether the packet is destined for another server or if it's a broadcast. If the current server is the destination, the server handles the request appropriately. If another server is the destination, the current server either forwards the packet directly (if the server is a neighbor) or routes it to the next server in line. If the packet is a broadcast, the current server checks whether the packet came from the least-cost path. If it did not, the packet is discarded. If it did, the packet is forwarded on all interfaces except the one on which it was received. This approach helps diminish the number of broadcast storms, a common problem in other network environments. The VINES routing algorithm is shown in Figure 13-4.

Figure 13-4 *The VINES Routing Algorithm*

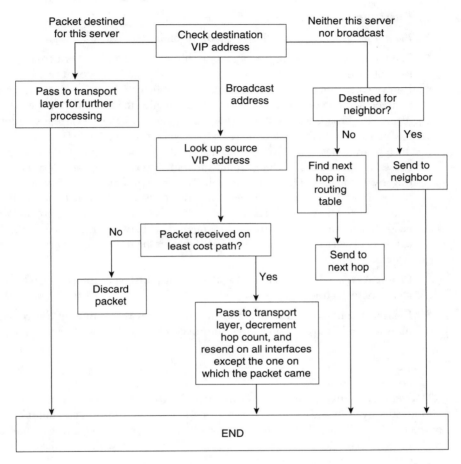

The VIP packet format is shown in Figure 13-5.

Figure 13-5 *The VIP Packet Format*

Field length, in bytes	2	2	1	1	4	2	4	2	Variable
	Check-sum	Packet length	Trans-port control	Protocol type	Destination network number	Destination subnetwork number	Source network number	Source subnetwork number	Data

The fields of a VIP packet are as follows:

- **Checksum**—Used to detect packet corruption.
- **Packet length**—Indicates the length of the entire VIP packet.
- **Transport control**—Consists of several subfields. If the packet is a broadcast packet, two subfields are provided: class (bits 1 through 3) and hop-count (bits 4 through 7). If the packet is not a broadcast packet, four subfields are provided: error, metric, redirect, and hop count. The class subfield specifies the type of node that should receive the broadcast. For this purpose, nodes are broken into various categories having to do with the type of node and the type of link the node is on. By specifying the type of nodes to receive broadcasts, the class subfield reduces the disruption caused by broadcasts. The hop count subfield represents the number of hops (router traversals) the packet has been through. The error subfield specifies whether the ICP protocol should send an exception notification packet to the packet's source if a packet turns out to be unroutable. The metric subfield is set to 1 by a transport entity when it needs to learn the routing cost of moving packets between a service node and a neighbor. The redirect subfield specifies whether the router should generate a redirect (when appropriate).
- **Protocol type**—Indicates the network- or transport-layer protocol for which the metric or exception notification packet is destined.
- **Destination network number**, **Destination subnetwork number**, **Source network number**, and **Source subnetwork number**—Provide VIP address information.

RTP

RTP distributes network topology information. Routing update packets are broadcast periodically by both client and service nodes. These packets inform neighbors of a node's existence and indicate whether the node is a client or a service node. Service nodes also include, in each routing update packet, a list of all known networks and the cost factors associated with reaching those networks.

Two routing tables are maintained: a table of all known networks and a table of neighbors. For service nodes, the table of all known networks contains an entry for each known network except the service node's own network. Each entry contains a network number, a routing metric, and a pointer to the entry for the next hop to the network in the table of neighbors. The table of neighbors contains an entry for each neighbor service node and client node. Entries include a network number, a subnetwork number, the media-access protocol (for example, Ethernet) used to reach that node, a local-area network (LAN) address (if the medium connecting the neighbor is a LAN), and a neighbor metric.

RTP specifies four packet types:

- **Routing update**—Issued periodically to notify neighbors of an entity's existence.
- **Routing request**—Exchanged by entities when they need to learn the network's topology quickly.
- **Routing response**—Contains topological information and is used by service nodes to respond to routing request packets.
- **Routing redirect**—Provides better path information to nodes using inefficient paths.

Each RTP packet has a 4-byte header consisting of the following 1-byte fields:

- **Operation type**—Indicates the packet type.
- **Node type**—Indicates whether the packet came from a service node or a nonservice node.
- **Controller type**—Indicates whether the controller in the node transmitting the RTP packet has a multibuffer controller.
- **Machine type**—Indicates whether the processor in the RTP sender is fast or slow.

Both the controller type and the machine type fields are used for pacing.

ARP

ARP entities are classified as either address resolution clients or address resolution services. Address resolution clients are usually implemented in client nodes, whereas address resolution services are typically provided by service nodes.

An ARP packet has an 8-byte header consisting of a 2-byte packet type, a 4-byte network number, and a 2-byte subnetwork number. There are four packet types: a query request, which is a request for an ARP service; a service response, which is a response to a query request; an assignment request, which is sent to an ARP service to request a VINES internetwork address; and an assignment response, which is sent by the ARP service as a response to the assignment request. The network number and subnet number fields have meaning only in an assignment response packet.

ARP clients and services implement the following algorithm when a client starts up. First, the client broadcasts query request packets. Then, each service that is a neighbor of the client responds with a service response packet. The client then issues an assignment request packet to the first service that responded to its query request packet. The service responds with an assignment response packet containing the assigned internetwork address.

ICP

ICP defines exception notification and metric notification packets. Exception notification packets provide information about network-layer exceptions; metric notification packets contain information about the final transmission used to reach a client node.

Exception notifications are sent when a VIP packet cannot be routed properly, and the error subfield in the VIP header's transport control field is enabled. These packets also contain a field identifying the particular exception by its error code.

ICP entities in service nodes generate metric notification messages when the metric subfield in the VIP header's transport control field is enabled, and the destination address in the service node's packet specifies one of the service node's neighbors.

The Transport Layer

VINES provides three transport-layer services:

- **Unreliable datagram service**—Sends packets that are routed on a best-effort basis but not acknowledged at the destination.

- **Reliable message service**—A virtual-circuit service that provides reliable sequenced and acknowledged delivery of messages between network nodes. A reliable message can be transmitted in a maximum of four VIP packets.

- **Data stream service**—Supports the controlled flow of data between two processes. The data stream service is an acknowledged virtual circuit service that supports the transmission of messages of unlimited size.

Upper-Layer Protocols

As a distributed network, VINES uses the remote-procedure call (RPC) model for communication between clients and servers. RPC is the foundation of distributed service environments. The NetRPC protocol (Layers 5 and 6) provides a high-level programming language that allows access to remote services in a manner transparent to both the user and the application.

At Layer 7, VINES offers file-service and print-service applications, as well as StreetTalk, which provides a globally consistent name service for an entire internetwork.

VINES also provides an integrated applications development environment under several operating systems, including DOS and UNIX. This development environment allows third parties to develop both clients and services that run in the VINES environment.

Troubleshooting Banyan VINES

This section presents protocol-related troubleshooting information for connectivity problems related to Banyan VINES. It describes specific VINES symptoms, the problems that are likely to cause each symptom, and the solutions to those problems.

The following sections describe the most common errors experienced in Banyan VINES networks:

- VINES: Clients Cannot Communicate with Servers over Router
- VINES: Client Cannot Connect to Server over PSN
- VINES: Client on Serverless Network Cannot Connect to Server over PSN

VINES: Clients Cannot Communicate with Servers over Router

Symptom: Clients cannot connect to VINES servers over one or more routers. Clients might or might not be able to connect to servers on their directly connected networks.

Table 13-1 outlines the problems that might cause this symptom and describes solutions to those problems.

Table 13-1   *VINES: Clients Cannot Communicate with Servers over Router*

Possible Problem	Solution	
Router interface is down	**Step 1**	Use the **show interfaces** exec command to check the status of the router interfaces.
	Step 2	If the status line indicates that an interface that should be up is "administratively down," use the **no shutdown** interface configuration command on the interface.
	Refer to the troubleshooting chapter that covers the media type used in your network.	
Hardware or media problem	For information on troubleshooting hardware problems, refer to the troubleshooting chapter that covers the media type used in your network.	
Addressing problem	**Step 1**	On a serverless segment, use the **show vines route** exec command to make sure the router is seeing server network layer addresses.
	Step 2	If the router is not seeing server addresses, make sure that the server and router addresses are correct. To change the address, use the following syntax:
	vines routing [*address* | *recompute*]	

continues

Table 13-1   *VINES: Clients Cannot Communicate with Servers over Router (Continued)*

Possible Problem	Solution
Addressing problem *(continued)*	**Syntax Description:** • *address* (Optional)—Network address of the router. You should specify an address on a router that does not have any Ethernet or FDDI[1] interfaces. You can also specify an address in the unlikely event that two routers map themselves to the same address. • *recompute* (Optional)—Dynamically redetermines the router's network address.
VINES metric value is not specified	**Step 1** Use the **show vines** interface exec command to check the status of VINES interfaces on the router. Make sure all VINES interfaces have the **vines metric** interface configuration command configured. The **metric** command enables VINES processing on the interface. **Step 2** If the **vines-metric** interface configuration command is not configured on the interface, specify the command for the interface. Configure the **vines metric** based on whether the interface is LAN or WAN connected. Suggested metrics for LAN and WAN connections follow: • Ethernet and 16-Mbps Token Ring: **vines-metric 2** • 4-Mbps Token Ring: **vines-metric 4** • T1 line: **vines-metric 35** • Other WAN link: **vines-metric 45**
Missing **vines serverless** or **vines arp-enable** commands	A network that does not have an attached server must be configured with the **vines serverless broadcast** and **vines arp-enable** router configuration commands. **Note:** These commands are enabled by default in Cisco IOS Release 10.3 and later. **Step 1** Use the **show running-config** privileged exec command on routers attached to networks with no VINES servers attached. Look for **vines serverless** and **vines arp-enable** router configuration commands entries. **Step 2** If both the **vines serverless** and the **vines arp-enable** commands are not present, specify the commands for router interfaces in serverless networks.

Table 13-1   *VINES: Clients Cannot Communicate with Servers over Router (Continued)*

Possible Problem	Solution
Missing **vines serverless** or **vines arp-enable** commands *(continued)*	**Syntax:** The following syntax is required to enable **vines serverless**: **vines serverless** [*dynamic* | *broadcast*] **Syntax Description:** • *dynamic* (Optional)—Forward broadcasts toward one server only if there are no servers present on this interface. • *broadcast* (Optional)—Always flood broadcasts out all other router interfaces to reach all servers. **Syntax:** The following syntax is required to enable **vines arp-enable**: **vines arp-enable** [*dynamic*] **Syntax Description:** • *dynamic* (Optional)—Responds to ARP[2] and SARP[3] requests on this interface only if there are no other VINES servers present.
Misconfigured access list	**Step 1** Use the **show vines access-list** privileged exec command on routers in the path from source to destination. This command shows whether there are access lists configured on the router. **Step 2** Disable all access lists configured on the router using **no vines access-group** commands. **Step 3** Test the connection from the client to the server to see whether connections are now possible. If the connection is successful, an access list is blocking traffic. **Step 4** To isolate the problem access list, apply one access list statement at a time until you can no longer create connections.

continues

Table 13-1   *VINES: Clients Cannot Communicate with Servers over Router (Continued)*

Possible Problem	Solution	
Misconfigured access list *(continued)*	Step 5	When the problem list is identified, alter it so that necessary traffic is allowed to pass. On a serverless segment, make sure that well-known ports 0x06 (VINES file service) and 0x0F (StreetTalk) are not filtered. Configure explicit **permit** statements for traffic you want the router to forward.
	Step 6	If problems persist, continue testing for problem access lists on all routers in the path from source to destination.

[1]FDDI = Fiber Distributed Data Interface

[2]ARP = Address Resolution Protocol

[3]SARP = Sequence Address Resolution Protocol

VINES: Client Cannot Connect to Server over PSN

Symptom: Clients cannot connect to VINES servers across a packet-switched network (PSN). Clients can connect to local VINES servers.

Table 13-2 outlines the problems that might cause this symptom and describes solutions to those problems.

Table 13-2   *VINES: Client Cannot Connect to Server over PSN*

Possible Problem	Solution	
Address mapping error	Step 1	Use the **show running-config** privileged exec command to view the configuration of the router.
	Step 2	For X.25 environments, make sure that LAN protocol-to-X.121 address mapping specified in **x25 map vines** interface configuration command entries use the VINES addresses and X.121 addresses of the destination routers. Confirm that the destination addresses used in the command entries are correct.
	Step 3	For Frame Relay environments, make sure that the LAN protocol-to-DLCI[1] address mapping specified in **frame-relay map** command entries use the VINES address of the destination router and the DLCI of the local interface. Confirm that the destination address and the local DLCI used in the command entries are correct.

Table 13-2   *VINES: Client Cannot Connect to Server over PSN*

Possible Problem	Solution	
PVC[2] is not set up	**Step 1**	Use the **show running-config** privileged exec command to view the configuration of the local and remote routers. Make sure there is an **x25 pvc n vines address** interface configuration command specified on the local and remote routers. This command sets up a PVC between the two routers.
	Step 2	If the command is not present, add it to the router configuration.

[1]DLCI = Data Link Connection Identifier
[2]PVC = permanent virtual circuit

VINES: Client on Serverless Network Cannot Connect to Server over PSN

Symptom: Clients on a serverless network (that is, a network segment that has no attached VINES servers) cannot open a connection to a VINES server over a PSN.

Table 13-3 outlines the problems that might cause this symptom and describes solutions to those problems.

Table 13-3   *VINES: Client on Serverless Network Cannot Connect to Server over PSN*

Possible Problem	Solution	
Address mapping error	**Step 1**	Use the **show running-config** privileged exec command to view the configuration of the router.
	Step 2	For X.25 environments, make sure that LAN protocol-to-X.121 address mapping specified in the **x25 map vines** interface configuration command entries use the VINES addresses and X.121 addresses of the destination routers. Confirm that the destination addresses used in the command entries are correct.
		Syntax:
		x25 map *protocol address* [*protocol2 address2*[...[*protocol9 address9*]]] *x121-address* [*option*] **no x25 map** *protocol address x121-address*

continues

Table 13-3 *VINES: Client on Serverless Network Cannot Connect to Server over PSN (Continued)*

Possible Problem	Solution
Address mapping error *(continued)*	**Syntax:** • *protocol*—Protocol type, entered by keyword. As many as nine *protocol* and *address* pairs can be specified in one command line. • *address*—Protocol address. • *x121-address*—X.121 address of the remote host. • *option*—(Optional) Additional functionality that can be specified for originated calls.
	Step 3 For Frame Relay environments, make sure the LAN protocol-to-DLCI[1] address mapping specified in **frame-relay map** command entries use the VINES address of the destination router and the DLCI of the local interface. Confirm that the destination address and the local DLCI used in the command entries are correct. **Syntax:** **frame-relay map** *protocol protocol-address dlci* [*broadcast*] [*ietf* | *cisco*] [*payload-compress* {*packet-by-packet* | *frf9 stac* [*hardware-options*]}] **no frame-relay map** *protocol protocol-address* **Syntax Description:** • *protocol*—Supported protocol, bridging, or logical link control keywords: **appletalk**, **decnet**, **dlsw**, **ip**, **ipx**, **llc2**, **rsrb**, **vines**, and **xns**. • *protocol-address*—Destination protocol address. • *dlci*—DLCI number used to connect to the specified protocol address on the interface. • *broadcast*—(Optional) IETF[2] form of Frame Relay encapsulation. Used when the router or access server is connected to another vendor's equipment across a Frame Relay network. • *cisco*—(Optional) Cisco encapsulation method.

Table 13-3   *VINES: Client on Serverless Network Cannot Connect to Server over PSN (Continued)*

Possible Problem	Solution	
Address mapping error *(continued)*		• *payload-compress packet-by-packet*—(Optional) Enables FRF.9 compression using the **Stacker** method.
		• *compress frf9 stac*—If the CSA is not available, compression is performed in the software installed on the VIP2 (distributed compression). If the router contains a CSA,[3] compression is performed in the CSA hardware (hardware compression). If the VIP2 is not available, compression is performed in the router's main processor (software compression).
		• *hardware-options*—(Optional) One of the following keywords: **distributed**, **software**, or **csa**.
PVC[4] is not set up	Step 1	Use the **show running-config** privileged exec command to view the configuration of the router. Make sure a PVC is set up between the routers on each side of the PSN using the **x25 pvc n vines address** interface configuration command.
	Step 2	If the command is not present, add it to the configuration.
VINES broadcasts are not forwarded across the PSN	Step 1	Use the **show running-config** command to examine the configuration of the router. Make sure the **vines propagate** interface configuration command is configured on the serial interface of the router that provides the serverless packet-switched node service.
	Step 2	If the command is not present, add it to the configuration.
VINES broadcasts not forwarded to all router interfaces	Step 1	Use the **show running-config** privileged exec command to view the router configuration. Check whether the **vines serverless broadcast** interface configuration command is configured on the router.
	Step 2	If the command is not present, configure the router using the **vines serverless broadcast** command. This command configures the router to always flood VINES broadcasts on all interfaces.
		Note: The **vines serverless broadcast** command is enabled by default in Cisco IOS Release 10.3 and later.

[1]DLCI = Data Link Connection Identifier

[2]IETF = Internet Engineering Task Force

[3]CSA = compression service adapter

[4]PVC = permanent virtual circuit

## CHAPTER 14

Troubleshooting XNS

The Xerox Network Systems (XNS) protocols were created by Xerox Corporation in the late 1970s and early 1980s. They were designed to be used across a variety of communication media, processors, and office applications. Several XNS protocols resemble the Internet Protocol (IP) and Transmission Control Protocol (TCP), developed by the Defense Advanced Research Projects Agency (DARPA) for the U.S. Department of Defense (DoD).

Because of its availability and early entry into the market, XNS was adopted by most of the early LAN companies, including Novell, Inc., Ungermann-Bass, Inc. (now a part of Tandem Computers), and 3Com Corporation. Each of these companies has since made various changes to the XNS protocols. Novell added the Service Advertising Protocol (SAP) to permit resource advertisement and modified the OSI Layer 3 protocols (which Novell renamed IPX, for Internetwork Packet Exchange) to run on IEEE 802.3 rather than Ethernet networks. Ungermann-Bass modified Routing Information Protocol (RIP) to support delay as well as hop count and made other small changes. Over time, the XNS implementations for PC networking have become more popular than XNS as it was designed by Xerox.

Although XNS documentation mentions X.25, Ethernet, and High-Level Data Link Control (HDLC), XNS does not expressly define what it refers to as a Level 0 protocol. Like many other protocol suites, XNS leaves media access an open issue, implicitly allowing any such protocol to host the transport of XNS packets over a physical medium.

The Network Layer

The XNS network-layer protocol is called the Internet Datagram Protocol (IDP). IDP performs standard Layer 3 functions, including logical addressing and end-to-end datagram delivery across an internetwork. The format of an IDP packet is shown in Figure 14-1.

Figure 14-1   *The IDP Packet Format*

A - Checksum
B - Length
C - Transport control
D - Packet type
E - Destination network number
F - Destination host number
G - Destination socket number
H - Source network number
I - Source host number
J - Source socket number

The fields of the IDP packet are as follows:

- **Checksum**—A 16-bit field that helps gauge the integrity of the packet after it traverses the internetwork.

- **Length**—A 16-bit field that carries the complete length (including checksum) of the current datagram.

- **Transport control**—An 8-bit field that contains hop count and maximum packet lifetime (MPL) subfields. The hop count subfield is initialized to zero by the source and incremented by one as the datagram passes through a router. When the hop count field reaches 16, the datagram is discarded on the assumption that a routing loop is occurring. The MPL subfield provides the maximum amount of time, in seconds, that a packet can remain on the internetwork.

- **Packet type**—An 8-bit field that specifies the format of the data field.

- **Destination network number**—A 32-bit field that uniquely identifies the destination network in an internetwork.

- **Destination host number**—A 48-bit field that uniquely identifies the destination host.

- **Destination socket number**—A 16-bit field that uniquely identifies a socket (process) within the destination host.

- **Source network number**—A 32-bit field that uniquely identifies the source network in an internetwork.

- **Source host number**—A 48-bit field that uniquely identifies the source host.

- **Source socket number**—A 16-bit field that uniquely identifies a socket (process) within the source host.

IEEE 802 addresses are equivalent to host numbers, so a host that is connected to more than one IEEE 802 network has the same address on each segment. This makes network numbers redundant, but nevertheless useful for routing. Certain socket numbers are well known, meaning that the service performed by the software using them is statically defined. All other socket numbers are reusable.

XNS supports Ethernet Version 2.0 encapsulation for Ethernet and three types of encapsulation for Token Ring: 3Com, Subnet Access Protocol (SNAP), and Ungermann-Bass.

XNS supports unicast (point-to-point), multicast, and broadcast packets. Multicast and broadcast addresses are further divided into directed and global types. Directed multicasts deliver packets to members of the multicast group on the network specified in the destination multicast network address. Directed broadcasts deliver packets to all members of a specified network. Global multicasts deliver packets to all members of the group within the entire internetwork, whereas global broadcasts deliver packets to all internetwork addresses. One bit in the host number indicates a single versus a multicast address. All ones in the host field indicate a broadcast address.

To route packets in an internetwork, XNS uses the dynamic routing scheme RIP. Today, RIP is still in use, but has largely been replaced by more scalable protocols, such as Open Shortest Path First (OSPF) and Border Gateway Protocol (BGP).

The Transport Layer

OSI transport-layer functions are implemented by several protocols. Each of the following protocols is described in the XNS specification as a Layer 2 protocol.

The Sequenced Packet Protocol (SPP) provides reliable, connection-based, flow-controlled packet transmission on behalf of client processes. It is similar in function to the Internet Protocol suite's TCP and the OSI protocol suite's Transport Protocol 4 (TP4).

Each SPP packet includes a sequence number, which is used to order packets and to determine whether any have been duplicated or missed. SPP packets also contain two 16-bit connection identifiers. One connection identifier is specified by each end of the connection. Together, the two connection identifiers uniquely identify a logical connection between client processes.

SPP packets cannot be longer than 576 bytes. Client processes can negotiate use of a different packet size during connection establishment, but SPP does not define the nature of this negotiation.

The Packet Exchange Protocol (PEP) is a request-response protocol designed to have greater reliability than simple datagram service (as provided by IDP, for example), but less reliability than SPP. PEP is functionally similar to the Internet Protocol suite's User Datagram Protocol (UDP). PEP is single-packet based, providing retransmissions but no duplicate packet detection. As such, it is useful in applications where request-response transactions can be repeated without damaging data, or where reliable transfer is executed at another layer.

The Error Protocol (EP) can be used by any client process to notify another client process that a network error has occurred. This protocol is used, for example, in situations where an SPP implementation has identified a duplicate packet.

Upper-Layer Protocols

XNS offers several upper-layer protocols. The Printing Protocol provides print services. The Filing Protocol provides file-access services. The Clearinghouse Protocol provides name services. Each of these three protocols runs on top of the Courier Protocol, which provides conventions for data structuring and process interaction.

XNS also defines Level 4 protocols. These are application protocols but, because they have little to do with actual communication functions, the XNS specification does not include any pertinent definitions for them.

The Level 2 Echo Protocol is used to test the reachability of XNS network nodes and to support functions such as that provided by the **ping** command found in UNIX and other environments.

Troubleshooting XNS

This section presents protocol-related troubleshooting information for XNS connectivity problems. It describes specific XNS symptoms, the problems that are likely to cause each symptom, and the solutions to those problems.

This section covers the most common network issues in XNS environments:

- XNS: Clients Cannot Connect to Servers over Router
- XNS: XNS Broadcast Packets Not Forwarded by Router
- XNS: Clients Cannot Connect to Server over PSN

XNS: Clients Cannot Connect to Servers over Router

Symptom: Clients cannot make connections to XNS servers across a router. Clients might be able to connect to servers on their directly connected networks.

Table 14-1 outlines the problems that might cause this symptom and describes solutions to those problems.

Table 14-1   *XNS: Clients Cannot Connect to Servers over Router*

Possible Problem	Solution	
Router interface is down	**Step 1**	Use the **show interfaces** exec command to check the status of the router interfaces.
	Step 2	If the status line indicates that an interface that should be up is "administratively down," use the **no shutdown** interface configuration command on the interface.
	Step 3	If the status line indicates that the interface or line protocol is in any other state, refer to the chapter that discusses your media type.
Hardware or media problem	For information on troubleshooting hardware problems, see the chapter that discusses your media type. For information on troubleshooting media problems, see Chapter 15, "Troubleshooting Serial Lines."	
XNS routing is not enabled on router	**Step 1**	Use the **show running-config** privileged exec command to view the router configuration. Check whether XNS routing is enabled on the router.
	Step 2	If XNS routing is not enabled, add the **xns routing** router configuration command and related commands as necessary.
		Example:
		This example starts XNS routing and assigns XNS network numbers to the physical networks connected to two of the router's Ethernet interfaces:
		``` xns routing interface ethernet 0 xns network 20 interface ethernet 1 xns network 21 ```
		For more information on configuring XNS routing, see the *Network Protocols Configuration Guide, Part 2*.
Mismatched router network number	If the network number specified on the router is different from that configured on XNS servers, RIP[1] is not able to forward traffic correctly.	
	Step 1	Check the network numbers of network servers. The local XNS server administrator provides the server network numbers.
	Step 2	Use the **show xns interface** exec command to obtain the network number specified on the server side of the router.
	Step 3	Compare the network numbers. If they do not match, reconfigure the router or the server, as appropriate, with the correct network number. To reconfigure the router, use the following command:

continues

Table 14-1 *XNS: Clients Cannot Connect to Servers over Router (Continued)*

Possible Problem	Solution
Mismatched router network number *(continued)*	**xns network** *number*

The argument *number* is the network number, in decimal format. Every XNS interface in a system must have a unique XNS network number.

Example:

This example starts XNS routing and assigns XNS network numbers to the physical networks connected to two of the router's Ethernet interfaces:

```
xns routing
interface ethernet 0
xns network 20
interface ethernet 1
xns network 21
```

Step 4   If the network numbers match, check the router interface on the client side and make sure that the assigned network number is unique with respect to all network numbers in the XNS internetwork.

Misconfigured access list

Step 1   Use the **show xns access-list** privileged exec command on routers in the path from source to destination. This command shows whether there are access lists configured on the router.

Step 2   Disable all access lists that are configured on the router using the **no xns access-group** command.

Step 3   Test the connection from the client to the server to see whether connections are now possible. If the connection is successful, an access list is blocking traffic.

Step 4   To isolate the problem access list, apply one access list statement at a time until you can no longer create connections.

Step 5   When the problem list is identified, alter it so that necessary traffic is allowed to pass. Configure explicit **permit** statements for traffic that you want to be forwarded by the router.

Step 6   If problems persist, continue testing for problem access lists on all routers in the path from source to destination.

Table 14-1   *XNS: Clients Cannot Connect to Servers over Router (Continued)*

Possible Problem	Solution
Backdoor bridge between segments	**Step 1** Use the **show xns traffic exec** command to determine whether the bad hop count field is incrementing. The XNS network updates by default occur every 30 seconds: ``` C4000#show xns traffic Rec: 3968 total, 0 format errors, 0 checksum errors, 0 bad hop count, 3968 local destination, 0 multicast [...] ``` **Step 2** If this counter is increasing, use a network analyzer to look for packet loops on suspect segments. Look for routing updates. If a backdoor bridge exists, you will probably see hop counts that increment up to 15, at which point the route disappears. The route reappears unpredictably. **Step 3** Use a network analyzer to examine the traffic on each segment. Look for known remote network numbers that appear on the local network. That is, look for packets from a remote network whose source address is not the source address of the router. The backdoor is located on the segment on which a packet from a remote network appears whose source address is not the source address of a local router. To prevent XNS routing updates from being learned from the interface connected to the same segment as the backdoor bridge, you can use the **xns input-network-filter** command. **Example:** In the following example, **access list 476** controls which networks are added to the routing table when RIP packets are received on Ethernet interface 1. Network 16 is the only network whose information will be added to the routing table. Routing updates for all other networks are implicitly denied and are not added to the routing table: ``` access-list 476 permit 16 interface ethernet 1 xns input-network-filter 476 ```

[1]RIP = Routing Information Protocol

XNS: XNS Broadcast Packets Not Forwarded by Router

Symptom: XNS servers do not respond to broadcast requests from clients.

Table 14-2 outlines the problems that might cause this symptom and describes solutions to those problems.

Table 14-2   *XNS: XNS Broadcast Packets Not Forwarded by Router*

Possible Problem	Solution
Missing or misconfigured **xns helper-address** command	**Caution:** Because debugging output is assigned high priority in the CPU process, it can render the system unusable. For this reason, use **debug** commands only to troubleshoot specific problems or during troubleshooting sessions with Cisco technical support staff. Moreover, it is best to use **debug** commands during periods of lower network traffic and fewer users. Debugging during these periods decreases the likelihood that increased **debug** command processing overhead will affect system use.

Step 1   Enable the **debug xns packet** privileged exec command and check the output for XNS packets that have an unknown type *xx* specification.

Step 2   Use the **show running-config** privileged exec command to view the router configuration. Check the configuration of the client-side interface to see whether an **xns helper-address** interface configuration command entry is present.

Step 3   If the **xns helper-address** command is not present, add it to the client-side interface.

Syntax:

xns helper-address *network.host*

Syntax Description:

- *network*—Network on which the target XNS server resides. This is a 32-bit decimal number.

- *host*—Host number of the target XNS server. This is a 48-bit hexadecimal value represented as a dotted triplet of four-digit hexadecimal numbers (xxxx.xxxx.xxxx). The host must be directly connected to one of the router's directly attached networks. The number FFFF.FFFF.FFFF indicates all hosts on the specified network.

Example:

In the following example, the server at address 0000.0c00.23fe receives all broadcasts on network 51:

```
xns helper-address 51.0000.0c00.23fe
```

Step 4   If the command is present, make sure the MAC address specified in this command is a type of broadcast.

Following is an example of an all-nets broadcast:

```
interface ethernet 0
xns helper-address -1.ffff.ffff.ffff
```

Table 14-2 *XNS: XNS Broadcast Packets Not Forwarded by Router (Continued)*

Possible Problem	Solution
Missing or misconfigured **xns helper-address** command *(continued)*	The helper address specification differs depending on the network configuration. For more information, refer to the Cisco IOS *Network Protocols Configuration Guide, Part 2,* and *Network Protocols Command Reference, Part 2.*
Missing **xns forward-protocol** router configuration command	**Caution:** Because debugging output is assigned high priority in the CPU process, it can render the system unusable. For this reason, use **debug** commands only to troubleshoot specific problems or during troubleshooting sessions with Cisco technical support staff. Moreover, it is best to use **debug** commands during periods of lower network traffic and fewer users. Debugging during these periods decreases the likelihood that increased **debug** command processing overhead will affect system use.
	Step 1 Enable the **debug xns packet privileged** exec command and check the output for XNS packets that have an unknown type *xx* specification.
	Step 2 Use the **show running-config privileged** exec command to view the router configuration. Look for an **xns forward-protocol** global configuration command entry.
	Step 3 If the **xns forward-protocol** command is not present, add it as appropriate.
	Syntax:
	xns *forward-protocol* **protocol**
	Syntax Description:
	• **protocol**—Number of an XNS protocol, in decimal. See the documentation accompanying your host's XNS implementation for a list of protocol numbers.
Misconfigured access list	**Step 1** Use the **show access-lists** command to check whether there are access lists configured on the router.
	Step 2 Disable any access lists that are enabled on the router.
	Step 3 Test the connection to see whether connections are now possible. If the connection is successful, an access list is blocking traffic.
	Step 4 Enable access lists one at a time until connections are no longer possible.
	Step 5 Alter the problem list so traffic can pass. Configure explicit **permit** statements for traffic that you want to be forwarded by the router.
	Step 6 If problems persist, continue testing for problem access lists on all routers in the path from source to destination.

XNS: Clients Cannot Connect to Server over PSN

Symptom: Clients cannot connect to servers across a PSN. Clients can communicate with servers located on the local network.

Table 14-3 outlines the problems that might cause this symptom and describes solutions to those problems.

Table 14-3   *XNS: Clients Cannot Connect to Server over PSN*

Possible Problem		Solution
Address mapping error	Step 1	Use the **show running-config** privileged exec command to view the configuration of the router.
	Step 2	If you are running X.25, make sure **x25 map xns** interface configuration commands are properly configured. Make sure MAC addresses and X.121 addresses are correctly specified.
	Step 3	If you are running Frame Relay, make sure **frame-relay map xns** interface configuration commands are properly configured. Make sure MAC addresses and DLCIs[1] are correctly specified.
Mismatched router network number	Step 1	Check the network numbers of network servers. This information will be provided by the local XNS server administration staff.
	Step 2	Check the network number specified on the server side of the router.
	Step 3	Compare the network numbers. If they do not match, reconfigure the router or servers as appropriate, with the correct network number.
	Step 4	If the network numbers match, check the router interface on the client side and make sure the assigned network number is unique with respect to all network numbers in the XNS internetwork.
Encapsulation mismatch	Step 1	Use the **show interfaces** exec command to determine the encapsulation type being used (such as **encapsulation x25**).
	Step 2	If an encapsulation command is not present, the default is HDLC[2] encapsulation. For PSN interconnection, you must explicitly specify an encapsulation type. To set the encapsulation method used by the interface, use the **encapsulation** interface configuration command.
		Syntax:
		encapsulation *encapsulation-type*

Table 14-3   *XNS: Clients Cannot Connect to Server over PSN (Continued)*

Possible Problem	Solution
Encapsulation mismatch *(continued)*	**Syntax Description:** • *encapsulation-type*—One of the following keywords: • **atm-dxi**—Asynchronous Transfer Mode-Data Exchange Interface. • **bstun**—Block Serial Tunnel. • **frame-relay**—Frame Relay (for serial interface). • **hdlc**—HDLC protocol for serial interface. This encapsulation method provides the synchronous framing and error detection functions of HDLC without windowing or retransmission. • **lapb**—X.25 LAPB DTE operation (for serial interface). • **ppp**—PPP[3] (for serial interface). • **sdlc**—IBM serial SNA.[4] • **sdlc-primary**—IBM serial SNA (for primary serial interface). • **sdlc-secondary**—IBM serial SNA (for secondary serial interface). • **smds**—SMDS[5] (for serial interface).

[1]DLCI = data link connection identifiers

[2]HDLC = High-Level Data Link Control

[3]PPP = Point-to-Point Protocol

[4]SNA = Systems Network Architecture

[5]SMDS = Switched Multimegabit Data Services

PART **IV**

Troubleshooting Serial Lines and WAN Connections

## CHAPTER 15

Troubleshooting Serial Lines

This chapter presents general troubleshooting information and a discussion of tools and techniques for troubleshooting serial connections. The chapter consists of the following sections:

- Troubleshooting Using the **show interfaces serial** Command
- Using the **show controllers** Command
- Using **debug** Commands
- Using Extended **ping** Tests
- Troubleshooting Clocking Problems
- Adjusting Buffers
- Special Serial Line Tests
- Detailed Information on the **show interfaces serial** Command
- Troubleshooting T1 Problems
- Troubleshooting E1 Problems

Troubleshooting Using the show interfaces serial Command

The output of the **show interfaces serial** exec command displays information specific to serial interfaces. Figure 15-1 shows the output of the **show interfaces serial** exec command for a High-Level Data Link Control (HDLC) serial interface.

This section describes how to use the **show interfaces serial** command to diagnose serial line connectivity problems in a wide-area network (WAN) environment. The following sections describe some of the important fields of the command output.

Other fields shown in the display are described in detail in the section "Detailed Information on the **show interfaces serial** Command," later in this chapter.

Serial Lines: show interfaces serial Status Line Conditions

You can identify five possible problem states in the interface status line of the **show interfaces serial** display (see Figure 15-1):

- Serial x is down, line protocol is down
- Serial x is up, line protocol is down
- Serial x is up, line protocol is up (looped)
- Serial x is up, line protocol is down (disabled)
- Serial x is administratively down, line protocol is down

Figure 15-1 *Output of the HDLC show interface serial Command*

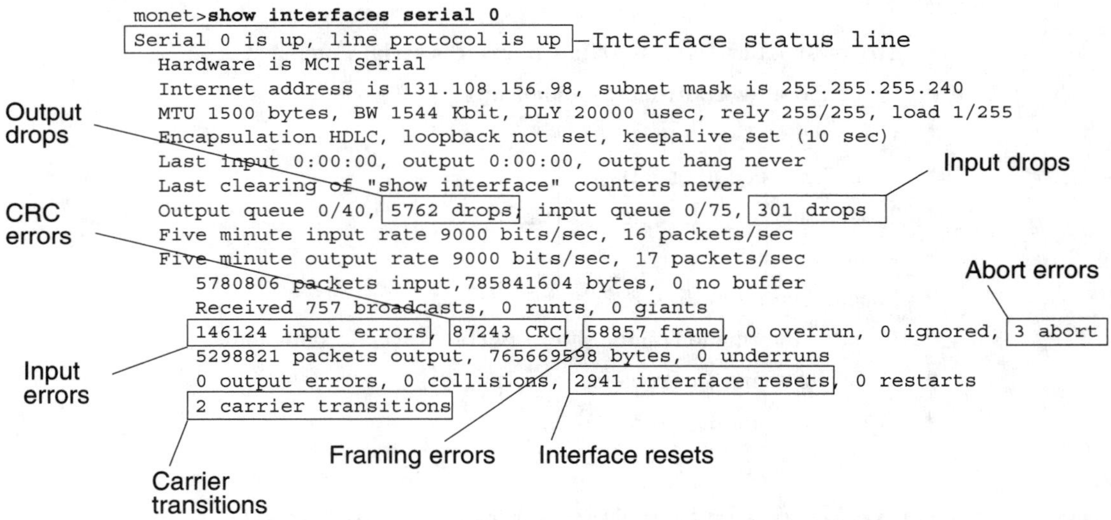

```
monet>show interfaces serial 0
  Serial 0 is up, line protocol is up  —Interface status line
    Hardware is MCI Serial
    Internet address is 131.108.156.98, subnet mask is 255.255.255.240
    MTU 1500 bytes, BW 1544 Kbit, DLY 20000 usec, rely 255/255, load 1/255
    Encapsulation HDLC, loopback not set, keepalive set (10 sec)
    Last input 0:00:00, output 0:00:00, output hang never
    Last clearing of "show interface" counters never
    Output queue 0/40, 5762 drops, input queue 0/75, 301 drops
    Five minute input rate 9000 bits/sec, 16 packets/sec
    Five minute output rate 9000 bits/sec, 17 packets/sec
      5780806 packets input,785841604 bytes, 0 no buffer
      Received 757 broadcasts, 0 runts, 0 giants
      146124 input errors, 87243 CRC, 58857 frame, 0 overrun, 0 ignored, 3 abort
      5298821 packets output, 765669598 bytes, 0 underruns
      0 output errors, 0 collisions, 2941 interface resets, 0 restarts
      2 carrier transitions
```

Output drops

CRC errors

Input errors

Carrier transitions

Framing errors

Interface resets

Input drops

Abort errors

Table 15-1 shows the interface status conditions, possible problems associated with the conditions, and solutions to those problems.

Table 15-1 *Serial Lines:* **show interfaces serial** *Status Line Conditions*

Status Line Condition	Possible Problem	Solution
Serial x is up, line protocol is up	—	This is the proper status line condition. No action is required.

Table 15-1   *Serial Lines:* **show interfaces serial** *Status Line Conditions (Continued)*

Status Line Condition	Possible Problem	Solution	
Serial *x* is down, line protocol is down (DTE[1] mode)	The router is not sensing a CD[2] signal (that is, the CD is not active). A telephone company problem has occurred—line is down or is not connected to CSU[3]/ DSU[4]. Cabling is faulty or incorrect. Hardware failure has occurred (CSU/DSU).	Step 1	Check the LEDs on the CSU/DSU to see whether the CD is active, or insert a breakout box on the line to check for the CD signal.
		Step 2	Verify that you are using the proper cable and interface (see your hardware installation documentation).
		Step 3	Insert a breakout box and check all control leads.
		Step 4	Contact your leased-line or other carrier service to see whether there is a problem.
		Step 5	Swap faulty parts.
		Step 6	If you suspect faulty router hardware, change the serial line to another port. If the connection comes up, the previously connected interface has a problem.
Serial *x* is up, line protocol is down (DTE mode)	A local or remote router is misconfigured. Keepalives are not being sent by the remote router. A leased-line or other carrier service problem has occurred (noisy line or misconfigured or failed switch). A timing problem has occurred on the cable (SCTE[5] not set on CSU/ DSU). A local or remote CSU/ DSU has failed. Router hardware (local or remote) has failed.	Step 1	Put the modem, CSU, or DSU in local loopback mode and use the **show interfaces serial** command to determine whether the line protocol comes up. If the line protocol comes up, a telephone company problem or a failed remote router is the likely problem.
		Step 2	If the problem appears to be on the remote end, repeat Step 1 on the remote modem, CSU, or DSU.
		Step 3	Verify all cabling. Make certain that the cable is attached to the correct interface, the correct CSU/DSU, and the correct telephone company network termination point. Use the **show controllers** exec command to determine which cable is attached to which interface.
		Step 4	Enable the **debug serial interface** exec command.

continues

Table 15-1 *Serial Lines:* **show interfaces serial** *Status Line Conditions (Continued)*

Status Line Condition	Possible Problem	Solution
Serial *x* is up, line protocol is down (DTE mode) *(continued)*		**Caution:** Because debugging output is assigned high priority in the CPU process, it can render the system unusable. For this reason, use **debug** commands only to troubleshoot specific problems or during troubleshooting sessions with Cisco technical support staff. Moreover, it is best to use **debug** commands during periods of lower network traffic and fewer users. Debugging during these periods decreases the likelihood that increased **debug** command processing overhead will affect system use.
		Step 5 If the line protocol does not come up in local loopback mode, and if the output of the **debug serial interface** exec command shows that the keepalive counter is not incrementing, a router hardware problem is likely. Swap router interface hardware.
		Step 6 If the line protocol comes up and the keepalive counter increments, the problem is *not* in the local router. Troubleshoot the serial line, as described in the sections "Troubleshooting Clocking Problems" and "CSU and DSU Loopback Tests," later in this chapter.
		Step 7 If you suspect faulty router hardware, change the serial line to an unused port. If the connection comes up, the previously connected interface has a problem.
Serial *x* is up, line protocol is down (DCE[6] mode)	The **clockrate** interface configuration command is missing. The DTE device does not support or is not set up for SCTE mode (terminal timing). The remote CSU or DSU has failed.	**Step 1** Add the **clockrate** interface configuration command on the serial interface. **Syntax:** **clock rate** *bps* **Syntax Description:** • *bps*—Desired clock rate in bits per second: 1200, 2400, 4800, 9600, 19200, 38400, 56000, 64000, 72000, 125000, 148000, 250000, 500000, 800000, 1000000, 1300000, 2000000, 4000000, or 8000000.

Table 15-1   *Serial Lines:* **show interfaces serial** *Status Line Conditions (Continued)*

Status Line Condition	Possible Problem	Solution	
Serial *x* is up, line protocol is down (DCE mode) *(continued)*	The **clockrate** interface configuration command is missing. The DTE device does not support or is not set up for SCTE mode (terminal timing). The remote CSU or DSU has failed.	Step 2	Set the DTE device to SCTE modem if possible. If your CSU/DSU does not support SCTE, you might have to disable SCTE on the Cisco router interface. Refer to the section "Inverting the Transmit Clock," later in this chapter.
		Step 3	Verify that the correct cable is being used.
		Step 4	If the line protocol is still down, there is a possible hardware failure or cabling problem. Insert a breakout box and observe leads.
		Step 5	Replace faulty parts, as necessary.
Serial *x* is up, line protocol is up (looped)	A loop exists in the circuit. The sequence number in the keepalive packet changes to a random number when a loop is initially detected. If the same random number is returned over the link, a loop exists.	Step 1	Use the **show running-config** privileged exec command to look for any **loopback** interface configuration command entries.
		Step 2	If you find a **loopback** interface configuration command entry, use the **no loopback** interface configuration command to remove the loop.
		Step 3	If you do not find the **loopback** interface configuration command, examine the CSU/DSU to determine whether they are configured in manual loopback mode. If they are, disable manual loopback.
		Step 4	Reset the CSU or DSU, and inspect the line status. If the line protocol comes up, no other action is needed.
		Step 5	If the CSU or DSU is not configured in manual loopback mode, contact the leased-line or other carrier service for line troubleshooting assistance.
Serial *x* is up, line protocol is down (disabled)	A high error rate has occurred due to a telephone company service problem. A CSU or DSU hardware problem has occurred. Router hardware (interface) is bad.	Step 1	Troubleshoot the line with a serial analyzer and breakout box. Look for toggling CTS[7] and DSR[8] signals.
		Step 2	Loop CSU/DSU (DTE loop). If the problem continues, it is likely that there is a hardware problem. If the problem does not continue, it is likely that there is a telephone company problem.
		Step 3	Swap out bad hardware, as required (CSU, DSU, switch, local or remote router).

continues

Table 15-1 *Serial Lines:* **show interfaces serial** *Status Line Conditions (Continued)*

Status Line Condition	Possible Problem	Solution	
Serial *x* is administratively down, line protocol is down	The router configuration includes the **shutdown** interface configuration command. A duplicate IP address exists.	Step 1	Check the router configuration for the **shutdown** command.
		Step 2	Use the **no shutdown** interface configuration command to remove the **shutdown** command.
		Step 3	Verify that there are no identical IP addresses using the **show running-config** privileged exec command or the **show interfaces** exec command.
		Step 4	If there are duplicate addresses, resolve the conflict by changing one of the IP addresses.

[1]DTE = data terminal equipment
[2]CD = carrier detect
[3]CSU = channel service unit
[4]DSU = digital service unit
[5]SCTE = serial clock transmit external
[6]DCE = data circuit-terminating equipment or data communications equipment
[7]CTS = clear-to-send
[8]DSR = data-set ready

Serial Lines: Increasing Output Drops on Serial Link

Output drops appear in the output of the **show interfaces serial** command (refer to Figure 15-1) when the system is attempting to hand off a packet to a transmit buffer but no buffers are available.

Symptom: Increasing output drops on serial link

Table 15-2 outlines the possible problem that might cause this symptom and describes solutions to that problem.

Table 15-2 *Serial Lines: Increasing Output Drops on Serial Link*

Possible Problem	Solution	
Input rate to serial interface exceeds bandwidth available on serial link	Step 1	Minimize periodic broadcast traffic, such as routing and SAP[1] updates, by using access lists or by other means. For example, to increase the delay between SAP updates, use the **ipx sap-interval** interface configuration command.

Table 15-2   *Serial Lines: Increasing Output Drops on Serial Link (Continued)*

Possible Problem	Solution	
Input rate to serial interface exceeds bandwidth available on serial link *(continued)*	**Step 2**	Increase the output hold queue size in small increments (for instance, 25 percent), using the **hold-queue out** interface configuration command.
	Step 3	On affected interfaces, turn off fast switching for heavily used protocols. For example, to turn off IP fast switching, enter the **no ip route-cache** interface configuration command. For the command syntax for other protocols, consult the Cisco IOS configuration guides and command references.
	Step 4	Implement priority queuing on slower serial links by configuring priority lists. For information on configuring priority lists, see the Cisco IOS configuration guides and command references.
		Note: Output drops are acceptable under certain conditions. For instance, if a link is known to be overused (with no way to remedy the situation), it is often considered preferable to drop packets than to hold them. This is true for protocols that support flow control and can retransmit data (such as TCP/IP and Novell IPX[2]). However, some protocols, such as DECnet and local-area transport, are sensitive to dropped packets and accommodate retransmission poorly, if at all.

[1]SAP = Service Advertising Protocol

[2]IPX = Internetwork Packet Exchange

Serial Lines: Increasing Input Drops on Serial Link

Input drops appear in the output of the **show interfaces serial** exec command (refer to Figure 15-1) when too many packets from that interface are still being processed in the system.

Symptom: Increasing number of input drops on serial link

Table 15-3 outlines the possible problem that might cause this symptom and describes solutions to that problem.

Table 15-3   *Serial Lines: Increasing Input Drops on Serial Link*

Possible Problem	Solution
Input rate exceeds the capacity of the router, or input queues exceed the size of output queues	**Note**: Input drop problems are typically seen when traffic is being routed between faster interfaces (such as Ethernet, Token Ring, and FDDI[1]) and serial interfaces. When traffic is light, there is no problem. As traffic rates increase, backups start occurring. Routers drop packets during these congested periods.

continues

Table 15-3   *Serial Lines: Increasing Input Drops on Serial Link (Continued)*

Possible Problem	Solution	
Input rate exceeds the capacity of the router, or input queues exceed the size of output queues *(continued)*	**Step 1**	Increase the output queue size on common destination interfaces for the interface that is dropping packets. Use the **hold-queue** *number* **out** interface configuration command. Increase these queues by small increments (for instance, 25 percent) until you no longer see drops in the **show interfaces** output. The default output hold queue limit is 100 packets.
	Step 2	Reduce the input queue size, using the **hold-queue** *number* **in** interface configuration command, to force input drops to become output drops. Output drops have less impact on the performance of the router than do input drops. The default input hold queue is 75 packets.

[1]FDDI = Fiber Distributed Data Interface

Serial Lines: Increasing Input Errors in Excess of 1 Percent of Total Interface Traffic

If input errors appear in the **show interfaces serial** output (refer to Figure 15-1), there are several possible sources of those errors. The most likely sources are summarized in Table 15-4.

NOTE   Any input error value for cyclic redundancy check (CRC) errors, framing errors, or aborts above 1 percent of the total interface traffic suggests some kind of link problem that should be isolated and repaired.

Symptom: Increasing number of input errors in excess of 1 percent of total interface traffic

Table 15-4   *Serial Lines: Increasing Input Errors in Excess of 1 Percent of Total Interface Traffic*

Possible Problem	Solution	
The following problems can result in this symptom: • Faulty telephone company equipment • Noisy serial line • Incorrect clocking configuration (SCTE not set)	**Note:** Cisco strongly recommends against the use of data converters when you are connecting a router to a WAN or a serial network.	
	Step 1	Use a serial analyzer to isolate the source of the input errors. If you detect errors, there likely is a hardware problem or a clock mismatch in a device that is external to the router.

Table 15-4 *Serial Lines: Increasing Input Errors in Excess of 1 Percent of Total Interface Traffic (Continued)*

Possible Problem	Solution	
• Incorrect cable or cable that is too long • Bad cable or connection • Bad CSU or DSU • Bad router hardware • Data converter or other device being used between router and DSU	**Step 2**	Use the loopback and **ping** tests to isolate the specific problem source. For more information, see the sections "Using Extended ping Tests" and "CSU and DSU Loopback Tests," later in this chapter.
	Step 3	Look for patterns. For example, if errors occur at a consistent interval, they could be related to a periodic function, such as the sending of routing updates.

Serial Lines: Troubleshooting Serial Line Input Errors

Table 15-5 describes the various types of input errors displayed by the **show interfaces serial** command (see Figure 15-1), possible problems that might be causing the errors, and solutions to those problems.

Table 15-5 *Serial Lines: Troubleshooting Serial Line Input Errors*

Input Error Type (Field Name)	Possible Problem	Solution	
CRC errors (CRC)	CRC errors occur when the CRC calculation does not pass (indicating that data is corrupted) for one of the following reasons: • The serial line is noisy. • The serial cable is too long, or the cable from the CSU/DSU to the router is not shielded • SCTE mode is not enabled on DSU.	**Step 1**	Ensure that the line is clean enough for transmission requirements. Shield the cable, if necessary.
		Step 2	Make sure that the cable is within the recommended length (no more than 50 feet [15.24 meters], or 25 feet [7.62 meters] for a T1 link).
		Step 3	Ensure that all devices are properly configured for a common line clock. Set SCTE on the local and remote DSU. If your CSU/DSU does not support SCTE, see the section "Inverting the Transmit Clock," later in this chapter.
		Step 4	Make certain that the local and remote CSU/DSU are configured for the same framing and coding scheme as that used by the leased-line or other carrier service (for example, ESF/B8ZS).

continues

Table 15-5 *Serial Lines: Troubleshooting Serial Line Input Errors (Continued)*

Input Error Type (Field Name)	Possible Problem	Solution	
CRC errors (CRC) *(continued)*	• The CSU line clock is incorrectly configured. • A ones density problem has occurred on the T1 link (incorrect framing or coding specification).	**Step 5**	Contact your leased-line or other carrier service, and have it perform integrity tests on the line.
Framing errors (frame)	A framing error occurs when a packet does not end on an 8-bit byte boundary for one of the following reasons: • The serial line is noisy • The cable is improperly designed; the serial cable is too long; the cable from the CSU or DSU to the router is not shielded. • SCTE mode is not enabled on the DSU; the CSU line clock is incorrectly configured; one of the clocks is configured for local clocking. • A ones density problem has occurred on the T1 link (incorrect framing or coding specification).	**Step 1**	Ensure that the line is clean enough for transmission requirements. Shield the cable, if necessary. Make certain that you are using the correct cable.
		Step 2	Make sure that the cable is within the recommended length (no more than 50 feet [15.24 meters], or 25 feet [7.62 meters] for a T1 link).
		Step 3	Ensure that all devices are properly configured to use a common line clock. Set SCTE on the local and remote DSU. If your CSU/DSU does not support SCTE, see the section "Inverting the Transmit Clock," later in this chapter.
		Step 4	Make certain that the local and remote CSU/DSU is configured for the same framing and coding scheme as that used by the leased-line or other carrier service (for example, ESF[1]/B8ZS[2]).
		Step 5	Contact your leased-line or other carrier service, and have it perform integrity tests on the line.

Table 15-5   *Serial Lines: Troubleshooting Serial Line Input Errors (Continued)*

Input Error Type (Field Name)	Possible Problem	Solution	
Aborted transmission (abort)	Aborts indicate an illegal sequence of 1 bit (more than seven in a row)	**Step 1**	Ensure that all devices are properly configured to use a common line clock. Set SCTE on the local and remote DSU. If your CSU/DSU does not support SCTE, see the section "Inverting the Transmit Clock," later in this chapter.
	The following are possible reasons for this to occur:		
	• SCTE mode is not enabled on DSU.	**Step 2**	Shield the cable, if necessary. Make certain that the cable is within the recommended length (no more than 50 feet [15.24 meters], or 25 feet [7.62 meters] for a T1 link). Ensure that all connections are good.
	• The CSU line clock is incorrectly configured.	**Step 3**	Check the hardware at both ends of the link. Swap faulty equipment, as necessary.
	• The serial cable is too long, or the cable from the CSU or DSU to the router is not shielded.	**Step 4**	Lower data rates and determine whether aborts decrease.
		Step 5	Use local and remote loopback tests to determine where aborts are occurring (see the section "Special Serial Line Tests," later in this chapter).
	• A ones density problem has occurred on the T1 link (incorrect framing or coding specification).	**Step 6**	Contact your leased-line or other carrier service, and have it perform integrity tests on the line.
	• A packet terminated in middle of transmission (typical cause is an interface reset or a framing error).		
	• A hardware problem has occurred (bad circuit, bad CSU/DSU, or bad sending interface on remote router).		

[1]ESF = Extended Superframe Format

[2]B8ZS = binary eight-zero substitution

Serial Lines: Increasing Interface Resets on Serial Link

Interface resets that appear in the output of the **show interfaces serial** exec command (see Figure 15-1) are the result of missed keepalive packets.

Symptom: Increasing interface resets on serial link

Table 15-6 outlines the possible problems that might cause this symptom and describes solutions to those problems.

Table 15-6   *Serial Lines: Increasing Interface Resets on Serial Link*

Possible Problem	Solution
The following problems can result in this symptom: • Congestion on link (typically associated with output drops) • Bad line causing CD transitions • Possible hardware problem at the CSU, DSU, or switch	When interface resets are occurring, examine other fields of the **show interfaces serial** command output to determine the source of the problem. Assuming that an increase in interface resets is being recorded, examine the following fields: **Step 1** If there is a high number of output drops in the **show interfaces serial** output, see the section "Serial Lines: Increasing Output Drops on Serial Link," earlier in this chapter. **Step 2** Check the Carrier Transitions field in the **show interfaces serial** display. If carrier transitions are high while interface resets are being registered, the problem is likely to be a bad link or a bad CSU or DSU. Contact your leased-line or carrier service, and swap faulty equipment, as necessary. **Step 3** Examine the Input Errors field in the **show interfaces serial** display. If input errors are high while interface resets are increasing, the problem is probably a bad link or a bad CSU/DSU. Contact your leased-line or other carrier service, and swap faulty equipment, as necessary.

Serial Lines: Increasing Carrier Transitions Count on Serial Link

Carrier transitions appear in the output of the **show interfaces serial** exec command whenever there is an interruption in the carrier signal (such as an interface reset at the remote end of a link).

Symptom: Increasing carrier transitions count on serial link

Table 15-7 outlines the possible problems that might cause this symptom and describes solutions to those problems.

Table 15-7   *Serial Lines: Increasing Carrier Transitions Count on Serial Link*

Possible Problem	Solution	
The following problems can result in this symptom: • Line interruptions due to an external source (such as physical separation of cabling, red or yellow T1 alarms, or lightning striking somewhere along the network) • Faulty switch, DSU, or router hardware	**Step 1**	Check hardware at both ends of the link (attach a breakout box or a serial analyzer, and test to determine the source of problems).
	Step 2	If an analyzer or breakout box is incapable of identifying any external problems, check the router hardware.
	Step 3	Swap faulty equipment, as necessary.

Using the show controllers Command

The **show controllers** exec command is another important diagnostic tool when troubleshooting serial lines. The command syntax varies, depending on platform:

- For serial interfaces on Cisco 7000 series routers, use the **show controllers cbus** exec command.

- For Cisco access products, use the **show controllers** exec command.

- For the AGS, CGS, and MGS, use the **show controllers mci** exec command.

Figure 15-2 shows the output from the **show controllers cbus** exec command. This command is used on Cisco 7000 series routers with the Fast Serial Interface Processor (FSIP) card. Check the command output to make certain that the cable to the channel service unit/digital service unit (CSU/DSU) is attached to the proper interface. You can also check the microcode version to see whether it is current.

Figure 15-2 show controllers cbus *Command Output*

```
Harold>show controllers cbus
Switch Processor 5, hardware version 11.1, microcode version 10.7        Microcode
Microcode loaded from system                                             version
512 Kbytes of main memory, 128 Kbytes cache memory
4 256 byte buffers, 4 1024 byte buffers, 312 1520 byte buffers           Interface and
1024 byte system buffer                                                  attached cable
Restarts: 0 line down, 0 hung output, 0 controller error                 information
FSIP 0, hardware version 1.0, microcode version 175.0
Microcode loaded from system
Interface 0 - Serial 0/0, electrical interface is Universal (cable unattached)
22 buffer RX queue threshold, 23 buffer TX queue limit, buffer size 1520
TX queue length is 0
ift 0001, rql 12, tq 0000 0000, tql 23
Transmitter delay is 0 microseconds
Interface 1 - Serial 0/1, electrical interface is Universal (cable unattached)
22 buffer RX queue threshold, 23 buffer TX queue limit, buffer size 1520
TX queue length is 0
ift 0001, rql 12, tq 0000 0000, tql 23
Transmitter delay is 0 microseconds
Interface 2 - Serial 0/2, electrical interface is Universal (cable unattached)
22 buffer RX queue threshold, 23 buffer TX queue limit, buffer size 1520
TX queue length is 0
ift 0001, rql 12, tq 0000 0000, tql 23
Transmitter delay is 0 microseconds
Interface 3 - Serial 0/3, electrical interface is Universal (cable unattached)
22 buffer RX queue threshold, 23 buffer TX queue limit, buffer size 1520
TX queue length is 0
ift 0001, rql 12, tq 0000 0000, tql 23
Transmitter delay is 0 microseconds
```

On access products such as the Cisco 2000, Cisco 2500, Cisco 3000, and Cisco 4000 series access servers and routers, use the **show controllers** exec command. Figure 15-3 shows the **show controllers** command output from the Basic Rate Interface (BRI) and serial interfaces on a Cisco 2503 access server. (Note that some output is not shown.)

The **show controllers** output indicates the state of the interface channels and whether a cable is attached to the interface. In Figure 15-3, serial interface 0 has an RS-232 DTE cable attached. Serial interface 1 has no cable attached.

Figure 15-4 shows the output of the **show controllers mci** command. This command is used on AGS, CGS, and MGS routers only. If the electrical interface is displayed as UNKNOWN (instead of V.35, EIA/TIA-449, or some other electrical interface type), an improperly connected cable is the likely problem. A bad applique or a problem with the internal wiring of the card is also possible. If the electrical interface is unknown, the corresponding display for the **show interfaces serial** exec command will show that the interface and line protocol are down.

Figure 15-3 **show controllers** *Command Output*

```
Maude>show controllers
BRI unit 0
D Chan Info:
Layer 1 is DEACTIVATED
```
D channel is
deactivated

```
[. . .]
0 missed datagrams, 0 overruns, 0 bad frame addresses
0 bad datagram encapsulations, 0 memory errors
0 transmitter underruns
```

```
B1 Chan Info:
Layer 1 is DEACTIVATED
```
B channel 1 is
deactivated

```
[. . .]
0 missed datagrams, 0 overruns, 0 bad frame addresses
0 bad datagram encapsulations, 0 memory errors
0 transmitter underruns

B2 Chan Info:

[. . .]
LANCE unit 0, idb 0x9515C, ds 0x96F00, regaddr = 0x2130000, reset_mask 0x2
IB at 0x40163F4: mode=0x0000, mcfilter 0000/0000/0000/0000
station address 0000.0c0a.28a7  default station address 0000.0c0a.28a7
buffer size 1524

[. . .]
0 missed datagrams, 0 overruns, 0 late collisions, 0 lost carrier events
0 transmitter underruns, 0 excessive collisions,  0 tdr, 0 babbles
0 memory errors, 0 spurious initialization done interrupts
0 no enp status, 0 buffer errors, 0 overflow errors
0 one_col, 0 more_col, 3 deferred, 0 tx_buff
0 throttled, 0 enabled
Lance csr0 = 0x73
```

```
HD unit 0, idb = 0x98D28, driver structure at 0x9AAD0
buffer size 1524 │ HD unit 0, RS-232 DTE cable │
```
Attached cable on
serial interface 0

```
[. . .]
0 missed datagrams, 0 overruns, 0 bad frame addresses
0 bad datagram encapsulations, 0 memory errors
0 transmitter underruns
```

```
HD unit 1, idb = 0x9C1B8, driver structure at 0x9DF60
buffer size 1524 │ HD unit 1, No DCE cable │
```
No attached cable on
serial interface 1

```
[. . .]
0 missed datagrams, 0 overruns, 0 bad frame addresses
0 bad datagram encapsulations, 0 memory errors
0 transmitter underruns
```

Figure 15-4 **show controllers mci** *Command Output*

Electrical interface identified as type
UNKNOWN, suggesting a hardware
failure or improperly connected cable.

```
MCI 1, controller type 1.1, microcode version 1.8
  128 Kbytes of main memory, 4 Kbytes cache memory
16 system TX buffers, largest buffer size 1520
  Restarts: 0 line down, 0 hung output, 0 controller error
  Interface 0 is Ethernet1, station address 0000.0c00.3b09
    22 total RX buffers, 9 buffer TX queue limit, buffer size 1520
    Transmitter delay is 0 microseconds
  Interface 1 is Serial2, electrical interface is UNKNOWN
    22 total RX buffers, 9 buffer TX queue limit, buffer size 1520
    Transmitter delay is 0 microseconds
    High speed synchronous serial interface
  Interface 3 is Serial3, electrical interface is V.35 DTE
    22 total RX buffers, 9 buffer TX queue limit, buffer size 1520
    Transmitter delay is 0 microseconds
    High speed synchronous serial interface
```

Using debug Commands

The output of the various **debug** privileged exec commands provides diagnostic information relating to protocol status and network activity for many internetworking events.

CAUTION   Because debugging output is assigned high priority in the CPU process, it can render the system unusable. For this reason, use **debug** commands only to troubleshoot specific problems or during troubleshooting sessions with Cisco technical support staff. Moreover, it is best to use **debug** commands during periods of lower network traffic and fewer users. Debugging during these periods decreases the likelihood that increased **debug** command processing overhead will affect system use. When you finish using a **debug** command, remember to disable it with its specific **no debug** command or with the **no debug all** command.

Following are some **debug** commands that are useful when troubleshooting serial and WAN problems. More information about the function and output of each of these commands is provided in the *Debug Command Reference* publication:

- **debug serial interface**—Verifies whether HDLC keepalive packets are incrementing. If they are not, a possible timing problem exists on the interface card or in the network.

- **debug x25 events**—Detects X.25 events, such as the opening and closing of switched virtual circuits (SVCs). The resulting cause and diagnostic information is included with the event report.

- **debug lapb**—Outputs Link Access Procedure, Balanced (LAPB) or Level 2 X.25 information.

- **debug arp**—Indicates whether the router is sending information about or learning about routers (with ARP packets) on the other side of the WAN cloud. Use this command when some nodes on a TCP/IP network are responding, but others are not.

- **debug frame-relay lmi**—Obtains Local Management Interface (LMI) information useful for determining whether a Frame Relay switch and a router are sending and receiving LMI packets.

- **debug frame-relay events**—Determines whether exchanges are occurring between a router and a Frame Relay switch.

- **debug ppp negotiation**—Shows Point-to-Point Protocol (PPP) packets transmitted during PPP startup, where PPP options are negotiated.

- **debug ppp packet**—Shows PPP packets being sent and received. This command displays low-level packet dumps.

- **debug ppp errors**—Shows PPP errors (such as illegal or malformed frames) associated with PPP connection negotiation and operation.

- **debug ppp chap**—Shows PPP Challenge Handshake Authentication Protocol (CHAP) and Password Authentication Protocol (PAP) packet exchanges.

- **debug serial packet**—Shows Switched Multimegabit Data Service (SMDS) packets being sent and received. This display also prints error messages to indicate why a packet was not sent or was received erroneously. For SMDS, the command dumps the entire SMDS header and some payload data when an SMDS packet is transmitted or received.

Using Extended ping Tests

The **ping** command is a useful test available on Cisco internetworking devices as well as on many host systems. In TCP/IP, this diagnostic tool is also known as an Internet Control Message Protocol (ICMP) echo request.

NOTE	The **ping** command is particularly useful when high levels of input errors are being registered in the **show interfaces serial** display. See Figure 15-1.

Cisco internetworking devices provide a mechanism to automate the sending of many **ping** packets in sequence. Figure 15-5 illustrates the menu used to specify extended **ping** options. This example specifies 20 successive **pings**. However, when testing the components on your serial line, you should specify a much larger number, such as 1000 **pings**. Also increase the datagram size to a larger number, such as 1500.

Figure 15-5 *Extended* **ping** *Specification Menu*

```
Betelgeuse# ping
Protocol [ip]:
Target IP address: 129.44.12.7
Repeat count [5]: 20                            ping count
Datagram size [100]: 64                         specification
Timeout in seconds [2]:
Extended commands [n]: yes                      Extended commands
Source address:                                 selected option
Type of service [0]:
Set DF bit in IP header? [no]:
Validate reply data? [no]:
Data pattern [0xABCD]: 0xffff                    Data pattern
Loose, Strict, Record, Timestamp, Verbose[none]:   specification
Sweep range of sizes [n]:
Type escape sequence to abort.
Sending 20, 64-byte ICMP Echos to  129.44.12.7, timeout is 2 seconds:
Packet has data pattern 0xFFFF
!!!!!!!!!!!!!!!!!!!!!
Success rate is 100 percent, round-trip min/avg/max = 1/3/4 ms
```

In general, perform serial line **ping** tests as follows:

Step 1   Put the CSU or DSU into local loopback mode.

Step 2   Configure the extended **ping** command to send different data patterns and packet sizes. Figure 15-6 and Figure 15-7 illustrate two useful **ping** tests, an all-zeros 1500-byte **ping** and an all-ones 1500-byte **ping**, respectively.

Step 3   Examine the **show interfaces serial** command output (see Figure 15-1) and determine whether input errors have increased. If input errors have not increased, the local hardware (DSU, cable, router interface card) is probably in good condition.

Assuming that this test sequence was prompted by the appearance of a large number of CRC and framing errors, a clocking problem is likely. Check the CSU or DSU for a timing problem. See the section "Troubleshooting Clocking Problems," next.

Step 4   If you determine that the clocking configuration is correct and is operating properly, put the CSU or DSU into remote loopback mode.

Step 5   Repeat the **ping** test and look for changes in the input error statistics.

Step 6   If input errors increase, there is a problem either in the serial line or on the CSU/DSU. Contact the WAN service provider and swap the CSU or DSU. If problems persist, contact your technical support representative.

Figure 15-6   *All-Zeros 1500-Byte* **ping** *Test*

```
yowzers#ping
Protocol [ip]:
Target IP address: 192.169.51.22
Repeat count [5]: 100
Datagram size [100]: 1500
Timeout in seconds [2]:
Extended commands [n]: y
Source address: 192.169.51.14
Type of service [0]:
Set DF bit in IP header? [no]:
Validate reply data? [no]:
Data pattern [0xABCD]: 0x0000
Loose, Strict, Record, Timestamp, Verbose[none]:
Sweep range of sizes [n]:
Type escape sequence to abort.
Sending 100, 1500-byte ICMP Echos to 192.169.51.22, timeout is 2 seconds:
Packet has data pattern 0x0000
!!!!!!!!!!!!!!!!!!!!!!!!!!!!!!!!!!!!!!!!!!!!!!!!!!!!!!!!!!!!!!!!!!!!!!!!
!!!!!!!!!!!!!!!!!!!!!!!!!!!!!!!!!
Success rate is 100 percent (100/100), round-trip min/avg/max = 4/6/8 ms
yowzers#
```

1500 byte packet size — Datagram size [100]: **1500**

All zeros ping — Data pattern [0xABCD]: **0x0000**

Figure 15-7 *All-Ones 1500-Byte* **ping** *Test*

```
                    zounds#ping
                    Protocol [ip]:
                    Target IP address: 192.169.51.22
                    Repeat count [5]: 100
1500 byte  ──────┤  Datagram size [100]: 1500
packet size         Timeout in seconds [2]:
                    Extended commands [n]: y
                    Source address: 192.169.51.14
                    Type of service [0]:
                    Set DF bit in IP header? [no]:
                    Validate reply data? [no]:
All ones   ──────┤  Data pattern [0xABCD]: 0xffff
ping                Loose, Strict, Record, Timestamp, Verbose[none]:
                    Sweep range of sizes [n]:
                    Type escape sequence to abort.
                    Sending 100, 1500-byte ICMP Echos to 192.169.51.22, timeout is 2 seconds:
                    Packet has data pattern 0xFFFF
                    !!!!!!!!!!!!!!!!!!!!!!!!!!!!!!!!!!!!!!!!!!!!!!!!!!!!!!!!!!!!!!!!!!!!!!!!!!!
                    !!!!!!!!!!!!!!!!!!!!!!!!!!!!!!!!
                    Success rate is 100 percent (100/100), round-trip min/avg/max = 4/6/8 ms
                    zounds#
```

Troubleshooting Clocking Problems

Clocking conflicts in serial connections can lead either to chronic loss of connection service or to degraded performance. This section discusses the important aspects of clocking problems: clocking problem causes, how to detect clocking problems, how to isolate clocking problems, and clocking problem solutions.

Clocking Overview

The CSU/DSU derives the data clock from the data that passes through it. To recover the clock, the CSU/DSU hardware *must* receive at least one 1-bit value for every 8 bits of data that pass through it; this is known as *ones density*. Maintaining ones density allows the hardware to recover the data clock reliably.

Newer T1 implementations commonly use Extended Superframe Format (ESF) framing with binary eight-zero substitution (B8ZS) coding. B8ZS provides a scheme by which a special code is substituted whenever eight consecutive zeros are sent through the serial link. This code is then interpreted at the remote end of the connection. This technique guarantees ones density independent of the data stream.

Older T1 implementations use D4 (also known as Superframe Format [SF]) framing and Alternate Mark Inversion (AMI) coding. AMI does not utilize a coding scheme like B8ZS. This restricts the type of data that can be transmitted because ones density is not maintained independent of the data stream.

Another important element in serial communications is serial clock transmit external (SCTE) terminal timing. SCTE is the clock echoed back from the data terminal equipment (DTE) device (for example, a router) to the data communications equipment (DCE) device (for example, the CSU/DSU).

When the DCE device uses SCTE instead of its internal clock to sample data from the DTE, it can better sample the data without error even if there is a phase shift in the cable between the CSU/DSU and the router. Using SCTE is highly recommended for serial transmissions faster than 64 kbps. If your CSU/DSU does not support SCTE, see the section "Inverting the Transmit Clock," later in this chapter.

Clocking Problem Causes

In general, clocking problems in serial WAN interconnections can be attributed to one of the following causes:

- Incorrect DSU configuration
- Incorrect CSU configuration
- Cables out of specification (longer than 50 feet [15.24 meters] or unshielded)
- Noisy or poor patch panel connections
- Several cables connected in a row

Detecting Clocking Problems

To detect clocking conflicts on a serial interface, look for input errors as follows:

Step 1 Use the **show interfaces serial** exec command on the routers at both ends of the link.

Step 2 Examine the command output for CRC, framing errors, and aborts.

Step 3 If either of these steps indicates errors exceeding an approximate range of 0.5 percent to 2.0 percent of traffic on the interface, clocking problems are likely to exist somewhere in the WAN.

Step 4 Isolate the source of the clocking conflicts, as outlined in the following section, "Isolating Clocking Problems."

Step 5 Bypass or repair any faulty patch panels.

Isolating Clocking Problems

After you determine that clocking conflicts are the most likely cause of input errors, use the following procedure to isolate the source of those errors:

Step 1 Perform a series of **ping** tests and loopback tests (both local and remote), as described in the section "CSU and DSU Loopback Tests," earlier in this chapter.

Step 2 Determine which end of the connection is the source of the problem, or whether the problem is in the line. In local loopback mode, run different patterns and sizes in the **ping** tests (for example, use 1500-byte datagrams). Using a single pattern and packet size may not force errors to materialize, particularly when a serial cable to the router or CSU/DSU is the problem.

Step 3 Use the **show interfaces serial** exec command, and determine whether input errors counts are increasing and where they are accumulating.

If input errors are accumulating on both ends of the connection, clocking of the CSU is the most likely problem.

If only one end is experiencing input errors, there is probably a DSU clocking or cabling problem.

Aborts on one end suggest that the other end is sending bad information or that there is a line problem.

NOTE   Always refer to the **show interfaces serial** command output (see Figure 15-1). Log any changes in error counts, or note if the error count does not change.

Clocking Problem Solutions

Table 15-8 outlines suggested remedies for clocking problems, based on the source of the problem.

Table 15-8   *Serial Lines: Clocking Problems and Solutions*

Possible Problem	Solution	
Incorrect CSU configuration	**Step 1**	Determine whether the CSUs at both ends agree on the clock source (local or line).
	Step 2	If the CSUs do not agree, configure them so that they do agree (usually the line is the source).
	Step 3	Check the LBO[1] setting on the CSU to ensure that the impedance matches that of the physical line. For information on configuring your CSU, consult your CSU hardware documentation.

Table 15-8 *Serial Lines: Clocking Problems and Solutions (Continued)*

Possible Problem	Solution	
Incorrect DSU configuration	**Step 1**	Determine whether the DSUs at both ends have SCTE mode enabled.
	Step 2	If SCTE is not enabled on both ends of the connection, enable it.
		(For any interface that is connected to a line of 128 kbps or faster, SCTE *must* be enabled. If your DSU does not support SCTE, see the section "Inverting the Transmit Clock," later in this chapter.)
	Step 3	Make sure that ones density is maintained. This requires that the DSU use the same framing and coding schemes (for example, ESF and B8ZS) used by the leased-line or other carrier service.
		Check with your leased-line provider for information on its framing and coding schemes.
	Step 4	If your carrier service uses AMI coding, either invert the transmit clock on both sides of the link, or run the DSU in bit-stuff mode. For information on configuring your DSU, consult your DSU hardware documentation.
Cable to router out of specification	If the cable is longer than 50 feet (15.24 meters), use a shorter cable.	
	If the cable is unshielded, replace it with shielded cable.	

[1]LBO = line build out

Inverting the Transmit Clock

If you are attempting serial connections at speeds greater than 64 kbps with a CSU/DSU that does not support SCTE, you might have to invert the transmit clock on the router. Inverting the transmit clock compensates for phase shifts between the data and clock signals.

The specific command used to invert the transmit clock varies between platforms. On a Cisco 7000 series router, enter the **invert-transmit-clock** interface configuration command. For Cisco 4000 series routers, use the **dte-invert-txc** interface configuration command.

To ensure that you are using the correct command syntax for your router, refer to the user guide for your router or access server and to the Cisco IOS configuration guides and command references.

NOTE On older platforms, inverting the transmit clock might require that you move a physical jumper.

Adjusting Buffers

Excessively high bandwidth utilization greater than 70 percent results in reduced overall performance and can cause intermittent failures. For example, DECnet file transmissions might be failing because of packets being dropped somewhere in the network.

If the situation is bad enough, you *must* increase the bandwidth of the link. However, increasing the bandwidth might not be necessary or immediately practical. One way to resolve marginal serial line overutilization problems is to control how the router uses data buffers.

CAUTION   In general, do *not* adjust system buffers unless you are working closely with a Cisco technical support representative. You can severely affect the performance of your hardware and your network if you incorrectly adjust the system buffers on your router.

Use one of the following three options to control how buffers are used:

* Adjust parameters associated with system buffers.
* Specify the number of packets held in input or output queues (hold queues).
* Prioritize how traffic is queued for transmission (priority output queuing).

The configuration commands associated with these options are described in the Cisco IOS configuration guides and command references.

The following section focuses on identifying situations in which these options are likely to apply and defining how you can use these options to help resolve connectivity and performance problems in serial/WAN interconnections.

Tuning System Buffers

There are two general buffer types on Cisco routers: *hardware buffers* and *system buffers*. Only the system buffers are directly configurable by system administrators. The hardware buffers are specifically used as the receive and transmit buffers associated with each interface and (in the absence of any special configuration) are dynamically managed by the system software itself.

The system buffers are associated with the main system memory and are allocated to different-size memory blocks. A useful command for determining the status of your system buffers is the **show buffers** exec command. Figure 15-8 shows the output from the **show buffers** command.

Figure 15-8 **show buffers** *Command Output*

```
Cookie-Monster>show buffers
Buffer elements:
    401 in free list (500 max allowed)
    87777499 hits, 0 misses, 0 created
Small buffers, 104 bytes (total 120, permanent 120):
    114 in free list (20 min, 250 max allowed)
    70005538 hits, 6 misses, 2 trims, 2 created
Middle buffers, 600 bytes (total 90, permanent 90):
    88 in free list (10 min, 200 max allowed)
    25696696 hits, 27 misses, 27 trims, 27 created
Big buffers, 1524 bytes (total 90, permanent 90):
    90 in free list (5 min, 300 max allowed)
    8214530 hits, 15 misses, 366 trims, 366 created          Trims
Large buffers, 5024 bytes (total 5, permanent 5):
    5 in free list (0 min, 30 max allowed)                    Created
    15017 hits, 12 misses, 16354 trims, 16354 created
Huge buffers, 18024 bytes (total 3, permanent 0):
    2 in free list (0 min, 4 max allowed)
    297582 hits, 17 misses, 30 trims, 33 created
```

`0 failures (0 no memory)` Failures

In the **show buffers** output, the following is true:

- **total** identifies the total number of buffers in the pool, including used and unused buffers.

- **permanent** identifies the permanent number of allocated buffers in the pool. These buffers are always in the pool and cannot be trimmed away.

- **in free list** identifies the number of buffers currently in the pool that are available for use.

- **min** identifies the minimum number of buffers that the route processor (RP) should attempt to keep in the free list:

    — The **min** parameter is used to anticipate demand for buffers from the pool at any given time.

    — If the number of buffers in the free list falls below the **min** value, the RP attempts to create more buffers for that pool.

- **max allowed** identifies the maximum number of buffers allowed in the free list:

    — The **max allowed** parameter prevents a pool from monopolizing buffers that it doesn't need anymore, and frees this memory back to the system for further use.

    — If the number of buffers in the free list is greater than the **max allowed** value, the RP should attempt to trim buffers from the pool.

- **hits** identifies the number of buffers that have been requested from the pool. The hits counter provides a mechanism for determining which pool must meet the highest demand for buffers.

- **misses** identifies the number of times that a buffer has been requested and that the RP detected that additional buffers were required. (In other words, the number of buffers in the free list has dropped below **min**.) The misses counter represents the number of times that the RP has been forced to create additional buffers.

- **trims** identifies the number of buffers that the RP has trimmed from the pool when the number of buffers in the free list exceeded the number of **max allowed** buffers.

- **created** identifies the number of buffers that has been created in the pool. The RP creates buffers when demand for buffers has increased until the number of buffers in the free list is less than **min** buffers or a miss occurs because of zero buffers in the free list.

- **failures** identifies the number of failures to grant a buffer to a requester even after attempting to create an additional buffer. The number of failures represents the number of packets that have been dropped due to buffer shortage.

- **no memory** identifies the number of failures caused by insufficient memory to create additional buffers.

The **show buffers** command output in Figure 15-8 indicates high numbers in the Trims and Created fields for large buffers. If you are receiving high numbers in these fields, you can increase your serial link performance by increasing the **max free** value configured for your system buffers. **trims** identifies the number of buffers that the RP has trimmed from the pool when the number of buffers in free list exceeded the number of **max allowed** buffers.

Use the **buffers max free** *number* global configuration command to increase the number of free system buffers. The value that you configure should be approximately 150 percent of the figure indicated in the total field of the **show buffers** command output. Repeat this process until the **show buffers** output no longer indicates trims and created buffers.

If the **show buffers** command output shows a large number of failures in the (**no memory**) field (see the last line of output in Figure 15-8), you must reduce the usage of the system buffers or increase the amount of shared or main memory (physical RAM) on the router. Call your technical support representative for assistance.

Implementing Hold Queue Limits

Hold queues are buffers used by each router interface to store outgoing or incoming packets. Use the **hold-queue** interface configuration command to increase the number of data packets queued before the router will drop packets. Increase these queues by small increments (for instance, 25 percent) until you no longer see drops in the **show interfaces** output. The default output hold queue limit is 100 packets.

NOTE   The **hold-queue** command is used for process-switched packets and periodic updates generated by the router.

Use the **hold-queue** command to prevent packets from being dropped and to improve serial link performance under the following conditions:

- You have an application that cannot tolerate drops, and the protocol is capable of tolerating longer delays. DECnet is an example of a protocol that meets both criteria. Local-area transport (LAT) does not meet this criteria because it does not tolerate delays.
- The interface is very slow (bandwidth is low or anticipated utilization is likely to sporadically exceed available bandwidth).

NOTE   When you increase the number specified for an output hold queue, you might need to increase the number of system buffers. The value used depends on the size of the packets associated with the traffic anticipated for the network.

Using Priority Queuing to Reduce Bottlenecks

Priority queuing is a list-based control mechanism that allows traffic to be prioritized on an interface-by-interface basis. Priority queuing involves two steps:

Step 1   Create a priority list by protocol type and level of priority.

Step 2   Assign the priority list to a specific interface.

Both of these steps use versions of the **priority-list** global configuration command. In addition, further traffic control can be applied by referencing **access-list** global configuration commands from **priority-list** specifications. For examples of defining priority lists and for details about command syntax associated with priority queuing, refer to the Cisco IOS configuration guides and command references.

NOTE   Priority queuing automatically creates four hold queues of varying size. This overrides any hold queue specification included in your configuration.

Use priority queuing to prevent packets from being dropped and to improve serial link performance under the following conditions:

- When the interface is slow, a variety of traffic types are being transmitted, and you want to improve terminal traffic performance

- If you have a serial link that is intermittently experiencing very heavy loads (such as file transfers occurring at specific times), and priority queuing will help select which types of traffic should be discarded at high traffic periods

In general, start with the default number of queues when implementing priority queues. After enabling priority queuing, monitor output drops with the **show interfaces serial** exec command. If you notice that output drops are occurring in the traffic queue that you have specified to be high priority, increase the number of packets that can be queued (using the **queue-limit** keyword option of the **priority-list** global configuration command). The default **queue-limit** arguments are 20 packets for the high-priority queue, 40 for medium, 60 for normal, and 80 for low.

NOTE   When bridging Digital Equipment Corporation (Digital) LAT traffic, the router must drop very few packets, or LAT sessions can terminate unexpectedly. A high-priority queue depth of about 100 (specified with the **queue-limit** keyword) is a typical working value when your router is dropping output packets and the serial lines are subjected to about 50 percent bandwidth utilization. If the router is dropping packets and is at 100 percent utilization, you need another line.

Another tool to relieve congestion when bridging Digital LAT is LAT compression. You can implement LAT compression with the interface configuration command **bridge-group** *group* **lat-compression**.

Special Serial Line Tests

In addition to the basic diagnostic capabilities available on routers, a variety of supplemental tools and techniques can be used to determine the conditions of cables, switching equipment, modems, hosts, and remote internetworking hardware. For more information, consult the documentation for your CSU, DSU, serial analyzer, or other equipment.

CSU and DSU Loopback Tests

If the output of the **show interfaces serial** exec command indicates that the serial line is up but the line protocol is down, use the CSU/DSU loopback tests to determine the source of the problem. Perform the local loop test first, and then perform the remote test. Figure 15-9 illustrates the basic topology of the CSU/DSU local and remote loopback tests.

Figure 15-9 *CSU/DSU Local and Remote Loopback Tests*

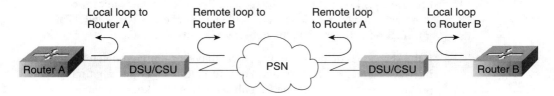

NOTE	These tests are generic in nature and assume attachment of the internetworking system to a CSU or DSU. However, the tests are essentially the same for attachment to a multiplexer with built-in CSU/DSU functionality. Because there is no concept of a loopback in X.25 or Frame Relay packet-switched network (PSN) environments, loopback tests do not apply to X.25 and Frame Relay networks.

CSU and DSU Local Loopback Tests for HDLC or PPP Links

Following is a general procedure for performing loopback tests in conjunction with built-in system diagnostic capabilities:

Step 1 Place the CSU/DSU in local loop mode (refer to your vendor documentation). In local loop mode, the use of the line clock (from the T1 service) is terminated, and the DSU is forced to use the local clock.

Step 2 Use the **show interfaces serial** exec command to determine whether the line status changes from "line protocol is down" to "line protocol is up (looped)," or whether it remains down.

Step 3 If the line protocol comes up when the CSU or DSU is in local loopback mode, this suggests that the problem is occurring on the remote end of the serial connection. If the status line does not change state, there is a possible problem in the router, connecting cable, or CSU/DSU.

Step 4 If the problem appears to be local, use the **debug serial interface** privileged exec command.

Step 5 Take the CSU/DSU out of local loop mode. When the line protocol is down, the **debug serial interface** command output will indicate that keepalive counters are not incrementing.

Step 6 Place the CSU/DSU in local loop mode again. This should cause the keepalive packets to begin to increment. Specifically, the values for mineseen and yourseen keepalives will increment every 10 seconds. This information will appear in the **debug serial interface** output.

If the keepalives do not increment, there may be a timing problem on the interface card or on the network. For information on correcting timing problems, refer to the section "Troubleshooting Clocking Problems," earlier in this chapter.

Step 7 Check the local router and CSU/DSU hardware, and any attached cables. Make certain that the cables are within the recommended lengths (no more than 50 feet [15.24 meters], or 25 feet [7.62 meters] for a T1 link). Make certain that the cables are attached to the proper ports. Swap faulty equipment, as necessary.

Figure 15-10 shows the output from the **debug serial interface** command for an HDLC serial connection, with missed keepalives causing the line to go down and the interface to reset.

Figure 15-10 **debug serial interface** *Command Output*

```
router# debug serial interface

Serial1: HDLC myseq 636119, mineseen 636119, yourseen 515032, line up
Serial1: HDLC myseq 636120, mineseen 636120, yourseen 515033, line up
Serial1: HDLC myseq 636121, mineseen 636121, yourseen 515034, line up
Serial1: HDLC myseq 636122, mineseen 636122, yourseen 515035, line up
Serial1: HDLC myseq 636123, mineseen 636123, yourseen 515036, line up
Serial1: HDLC myseq 636124, mineseen 636124, yourseen 515037, line up
Serial1: HDLC myseq 636125, mineseen 636125, yourseen 515038, line up
Serial1: HDLC myseq 636126, mineseen 636126, yourseen 515039, line up
Serial1: HDLC myseq 636127, mineseen 636127, yourseen 515040, line up
Serial1: HDLC myseq 636128, mineseen 636127, yourseen 515041, line up
Serial1: HDLC myseq 636129, mineseen 636129, yourseen 515042, line up

Serial1: HDLC myseq 636130, mineseen 636130, yourseen 515043, line up
Serial1: HDLC myseq 636131, mineseen 636130, yourseen 515044, line up
Serial1: HDLC myseq 636132, mineseen 636130, yourseen 515045, line up
Serial1: HDLC myseq 636133, mineseen 636130, yourseen 515046, line down
```

1 missed keepalive

3 missed keepalives

Line goes down, interface resets

CSU and DSU Remote Loopback Tests for HDLC or PPP Links

If you determine that the local hardware is functioning properly, but you still encounter problems when attempting to establish connections over the serial link, try using the remote loopback test to isolate the problem's cause.

NOTE	This remote loopback test assumes that HDLC encapsulation is being used and that the preceding local loop test was performed immediately before this test.

The following are the steps required to perform loopback testing:

Step 1 Put the remote CSU or DSU into remote loopback mode (refer to the vendor documentation).

Step 2 Using the **show interfaces serial** exec command, determine whether the line protocol remains up, with the status line indicating "Serial *x* is up, line protocol is up (looped)," or goes down, with the status line indicating "line protocol is down."

Step 3 If the line protocol remains up (looped), the problem is probably at the remote end of the serial connection (between the remote CSU/DSU and the remote router). Perform both local and remote tests at the remote end to isolate the problem source.

Step 4 If the line status changes to "line protocol is down" when remote loopback mode is activated, make certain that ones density is being properly maintained. The CSU/DSU must be configured to use the same framing and coding schemes used by the leased-line or other carrier service (for example, ESF and B8ZS).

Step 5 If problems persist, contact your WAN network manager or the WAN service organization.

Detailed Information on the show interfaces serial Command

This section covers the **show interfaces serial** command's parameters, syntax description, sample output display, and field descriptions.

show interfaces serial

To display information about a serial interface, use the **show interfaces serial** privileged exec command:

> **show interfaces serial** [*number*] [**accounting**]
> **show interfaces serial** [*number* [*:channel-group*] [**accounting**] (Cisco 4000 series)
> **show interfaces serial** [*slot | port* [*:channel-group*]] [**accounting**] (Cisco 7500 series)

show interfaces serial [*type slot* | *port-adapter* | *port*] [**serial**] (ports on VIP cards in the Cisco 7500 series)

show interfaces serial [*type slot* | *port-adapter* | *port*] [*:t1-channel*] [**accounting** | **crb**] (CT3IP in Cisco 7500 series)

Syntax Description

- *Number*—(Optional) Port number.

- **accounting**—(Optional) Displays the number of packets of each protocol type that have been sent through the interface.

- *:channel-group*—(Optional) On the Cisco 4000 series with an NPM or a Cisco 7500 series with a MIP, specifies the T1 channel-group number in the range of 0 to 23, defined with the channel-group controller configuration command.

- *slot*—Refer to the appropriate hardware manual for slot information.

- *port*—Refer to the appropriate hardware manual for port information.

- *port-adapter*—Refer to the appropriate hardware manual for information about port adapter compatibility.

- *:t1-channel*—(Optional) For the CT3IP, the T1 channel is a number between 1 and 28.

    T1 channels on the CT3IP are numbered 1 to 28 rather than the more traditional zero-based scheme (0 to 27) used with other Cisco products. This is to ensure consistency with telco numbering schemes for T1 channels within channelized T3 equipment.

- **crb**—(Optional) Shows interface routing and bridging information.

Command Mode

Privileged exec

Usage Guidelines

This command first appeared in Cisco IOS Release 10.0 for the Cisco 4000 series. It first appeared in Cisco IOS Release 11.0 for the Cisco 7000 series, and it was modified in Cisco IOS Release 11.3 to include the CT3IP.

Sample Displays

The following is sample output from the **show interfaces** command for a synchronous serial interface:

```
Router# show interfaces serial
Serial 0 is up, line protocol is up
    Hardware is MCI Serial
    Internet address is 150.136.190.203, subnet mask is 255.255.255.0
    MTU 1500 bytes, BW 1544 Kbit, DLY 20000 usec, rely 255/255, load 1/255
    Encapsulation HDLC, loopback not set, keepalive set (10 sec)
    Last input 0:00:07, output 0:00:00, output hang never
    Output queue 0/40, 0 drops; input queue 0/75, 0 drops
    Five minute input rate 0 bits/sec, 0 packets/sec
    Five minute output rate 0 bits/sec, 0 packets/sec
        16263 packets input, 1347238 bytes, 0 no buffer
        Received 13983 broadcasts, 0 runts, 0 giants
        2 input errors, 0 CRC, 0 frame, 0 overrun, 0 ignored, 2 abort
 1 carrier transitions
        22146 packets output, 2383680 bytes, 0 underruns
        0 output errors, 0 collisions, 2 interface resets, 0 restarts
```

Table 15-9 describes significant fields shown in the output.

Table 15-9   *Show Interfaces Serial Field Descriptions*

Field	Description
Serial...is {*up* | *down*}...**is administratively down**	Indicates whether the interface hardware is currently active (whether carrier detect is present) or whether it has been taken down by an administrator.
line protocol is {*up* | *down*}	Indicates whether the software processes that handle the line protocol consider the line usable (that is, whether keepalives are successful), or whether it has been taken down by an administrator.
Hardware is	Specifies the hardware type.
Internet address is	Specifies the Internet address and subnet mask.
MTU	Specifies the maximum transmission unit of the interface.
BW	Indicates the value of the bandwidth parameter that has been configured for the interface (in kilobits per second). The bandwidth parameter is used to compute IGRP metrics only. If the interface is attached to a serial line with a line speed that does not match the default (1536 or 1544 for T1, and 56 for a standard synchronous serial line), use the **bandwidth** command to specify the correct line speed for this serial line.

continues

Table 15-9   *Show Interfaces Serial Field Descriptions (Continued)*

Field	Description
DLY	Gives the delay of the interface in microseconds.
rely	Expresses reliability of the interface as a fraction of 255 (255/255 is 100 percent reliability), calculated as an exponential average over 5 minutes.
load	Expresses load on the interface as a fraction of 255 (255/255 is completely saturated), calculated as an exponential average over five minutes.
Encapsulation	Gives the encapsulation method assigned to the interface.
loopback	Indicates whether loopback is set.
keepalive	Indicates whether keepalives are set.
Last input	Gives the number of hours, minutes, and seconds since the last packet was successfully received by an interface. Useful for knowing when a dead interface failed.
Last output	Gives the number of hours, minutes, and seconds since the last packet was successfully transmitted by an interface.
output hang	Gives the number of hours, minutes, and seconds (or never) since the interface was last reset because of a transmission that took too long. When the number of hours in any of the last fields exceeds 24, the number of days and hours is printed. If that field overflows, asterisks are printed.
Output queue, drops input queue, drops	Gives the number of packets in output and input queues. Each number is followed by a slash, the maximum size of the queue, and the number of packets because the queue is full.
5 minute input rate 5 minute output rate	Gives the average number of bits and packets transmitted per second in the past 5 minutes.
	The 5-minute input and output rates should be used only as an approximation of traffic per second during a given 5-minute period. These rates are exponentially weighted averages with a time constant of 5 minutes. A period of four time constants must pass before the average will be within 2 percent of the instantaneous rate of a uniform stream of traffic over that period.
packets input	Gives the total number of error-free packets received by the system.
bytes	Gives the total number of bytes, including data and MAC encapsulation, in the error-free packets received by the system.

Table 15-9   *Show Interfaces Serial Field Descriptions (Continued)*

Field	Description
no buffer	Gives the number of received packets discarded because there was no buffer space in the main system. Compare with ignored count. Broadcast storms on Ethernet networks and bursts of noise on serial lines are often responsible for no input buffer events.
Received...broadcasts	Gives the total number of broadcast or multicast packets received by the interface.
runts	Gives the number of packets that are discarded because they are smaller than the medium's minimum packet size.
Giants	Gives the number of packets that are discarded because they exceed the medium's maximum packet size.
input errors	Gives the total number of no buffer, runts, giants, CRCs, frame, overrun, ignored, and abort counts. Other input-related errors can also increment the count, so this sum might not balance with the other counts.
CRC	The Cyclic Redundancy Check (CRC) counter is incremented by the originating station or far-end device when the checksum calculated from the data received does not match the checksum from the transmitted data. On a serial link, CRCs usually indicate noise, gain hits, or other transmission problems on the data link.
frame	Gives the number of packets received incorrectly, having a CRC error and a noninteger number of octets. On a serial line, this is usually the result of noise or other transmission problems.
overrun	Gives the number of times that the serial receiver hardware was incapable of handing received data to a hardware buffer because the input rate exceeded the receiver's capability to handle the data.
ignored	Gives the number of received packets ignored by the interface because the interface hardware ran low on internal buffers. Broadcast storms and bursts of noise can cause the ignored count to be increased.
abort	Indicates an illegal sequence of 1 bit on a serial interface. This usually indicates a clocking problem between the serial interface and the data link equipment.
carrier transitions	Gives the number of times that the carrier detect signal of a serial interface has changed state. For example, if data carrier detect (DCD) goes down and comes up, the carrier transition counter will increment two times. This indicates modem or line problems if the carrier detect line is changing state often.

continues

Table 15-9 *Show Interfaces Serial Field Descriptions (Continued)*

Field	Description
packets output	Gives the total number of messages transmitted by the system.
bytes output	Gives the total number of bytes, including data and MAC encapsulation, transmitted by the system.
underruns	Gives the number of times that the transmitter has been running faster than the router can handle. This might never be reported on some interfaces.
output errors	Gives the sum of all errors that prevented the final transmission of datagrams out of the interface being examined. Note that this might not balance with the sum of the enumerated output errors because some datagrams can have more than one error, and others can have errors that do not fall into any of the specifically tabulated categories.
collisions	Gives the number of messages retransmitted because of an Ethernet collision. This usually is the result of an overextended LAN (Ethernet or transceiver cable too long, more than two repeaters between stations, or too many cascaded multiport transceivers). Some collisions are normal. However, if your collision rate climbs to around 4 percent or 5 percent, you should consider verifying that there is no faulty equipment on the segment, or moving some existing stations to a new segment. A packet that collides is counted only once in output packets.
interface resets	Gives the number of times that an interface has been completely reset. This can happen if packets queued for transmission were not sent within several seconds. On a serial line, this can be caused by a malfunctioning modem that is not supplying the transmit clock signal, or by a cable problem. If the system notices that the carrier detect line of a serial interface is up but the line protocol is down, it periodically resets the interface in an effort to restart it. Interface resets can also occur when an interface is looped back or shut down.
restarts	Gives the number of times that the controller was restarted because of errors.
alarm indications, remote alarms, rx LOF, rx LOS	Gives the number of CSU/DSU alarms, and the number of occurrences of receive loss of frame and receive loss of signal.
BER inactive, NELR inactive, FELR inactive	Shows the status of G.703-E1 counters for bit error rate (BER) alarm, near-end loop remote (NELR), and far-end loop remote (FELR). Note that you cannot set the NELR or FELR.

Troubleshooting T1 Problems

This section describes the techniques and procedures to troubleshoot T1 circuits for dial-in customers.

Troubleshooting Using the show controller t1 Command

The **show controller t1** exec command provides information to logically troubleshoot physical layer and data link layer problems. This section describes how to logically troubleshoot using the **show controller t1** command.

This command displays the controller status that is specific to the controller hardware. The information displayed is generally useful for diagnostic tasks performed by technical support personnel.

The NPM or MIP can query the port adapters to determine their current status. Issue a **show controller t1** command to display statistics about the T1 link.

If you specify a slot and port number, statistics for each 15-minute period will be displayed.

Most T1 errors are caused by misconfigured lines. Ensure that linecoding, framing, and clock source are configured according to what the service provider recommends.

show controller t1 Conditions

The t1 controller can be in three states:

- Administratively down
- Down
- Up

Is the Controller Administratively Down?

The controller is administratively down when it has been manually shut down. You should restart the controller to correct this error.

Step 1 Enter enable mode.

```
maui-nas-03>en
Password:
maui-nas-03#
```

Step 2 Enter global configuration mode.

```
maui-nas-03#configure terminal
Enter configuration commands, one per line.  End with CNTL/Z.
maui-nas-03(config)#
```

Step 3   Enter controller configuration mode.

```
maui-nas-03(config)#controller t1 0
maui-nas-03(config-controlle)#
```

Step 4   Restart the controller.

```
maui-nas-03(config-controlle)#shutdown
maui-nas-03(config-controlle)#no shutdown
```

Is the Line Up?

If the T1 controller and line are not up, check to see if you are seeing one of the following messages in the **show controller t1** exec output:

```
Receiver has loss of frame.
```

or

```
Receiver has loss of signal.
```

If Receiver Has Loss of Frame

Step 1   Check to see whether the framing format configured on the port matches the framing format of the line. You can check the framing format of the controller from the running configuration or the **show controller t1** command output.

To change the framing format, use the **framing {SF | ESF}** command in the controller configuration mode, as shown here:

```
maui-nas-03#configure terminal
Enter configuration commands, one per line.  End with CNTL/Z.

maui-nas-03(config)#controller t1 0
maui-nas-03(config-controlle)#framing esf
```

Step 2   Try the other framing format to see if the alarm clears.

Step 3   Change the line build out setting using the **cablelength {long | short}** command.

Line build out (LBO) compensates for the loss in decibels based on the distance from the device to the first repeater in the circuit. A longer distance from the device to the repeater requires that the signal strength on the circuit be boosted to compensate for loss over that distance.

To configure transmit and receive levels for a cable length (line build out) longer than 655 feet for a T1 trunk with a channel service unit (CSU) interface, use the **cablelength long** controller configuration command. To configure transmit attenuation for a cable length (line build out) of 655 feet or shorter for a T1 trunk with a DSX-1 interface, use the **cablelength short** controller configuration command.

Consult your service provider and the Cisco IOS command reference for details on buildout settings.

If this does not fix the problem, proceed to the next section.

If Receiver Has Loss of Signal

Step 1 Make sure that the cable between the interface port and the T1 service provider's equipment or T1 terminal equipment is connected correctly. Check to see if the cable is hooked up to the correct ports. Correct the cable connections, if necessary.

Step 2 Check cable integrity. Look for breaks or other physical abnormalities in the cable. Ensure that the pinouts are set correctly. If necessary, replace the cable.

Step 3 Check the cable connectors. A reversal of the transmit and receive pairs or an open receive pair can cause errors. Set the receive pair to lines 1 and 2; the transmit pair should be lines 4 and 5.

The pins on an RJ-48 jack are numbered from 1 through 8. Pin 1 is the leftmost pin when looking at the jack with the metal pins facing you. Refer to Figure 15-11.

Figure 15-11 *RJ-45 Cable*

87654321
RJ-45 connector

Step 4 Try using a rollover cable.

Run the **show controller t1** exec command after each step to see whether the controller exhibits any errors.

If the Line Is in Loopback Mode

Check to see whether the line is in loopback mode from the **show controller t1** output. A line should be in loopback mode only for testing purposes.

To turn off loopback, use the **no loopback** command in the controller configuration mode, as shown here:

```
maui-nas-03(config-controlle)#no loopback
```

If the Controller Displays Any Alarms

Check the **show controller** command output to see if there are alarms displayed by the controller.

We will now discuss various alarms and the procedure necessary to correct them.

Receive (RX) Alarm Indication Signal (AIS) (Blue)

A received alarm indication signal (AIS) means that an alarm is occurring on the line upstream of the equipment connected to the port. The AIS failure is declared when an AIS defect is detected at the input and still exists after the loss of frame failure is declared (caused by the unframed nature of the "all-ones" signal). The AIS failure is cleared when the loss of frame failure is cleared.

Step 1   Check to see whether the framing format configured on the port matches the framing format of the line. If not, change the framing format on the controller to match that of the line.

Step 2   Contact your service provider to check for misconfiguration within the telco.

Receive (Rx) Remote Alarm Indication (Yellow)

A received remote alarm indication means that the far-end equipment has a problem with the signal that it is receiving from its upstream equipment.

For SF links, the far-end alarm failure is declared when bit 6 of all the channels has been zero for at least 335 ms. The failure is cleared when bit 6 of at least one channel is not zero for a period usually less than 1 second and always less than 5 seconds. The far-end alarm failure is not declared for SF links when a loss of signal is detected.

For ESF links, the far-end alarm failure is declared if the yellow alarm signal pattern occurs in at least seven out of ten contiguous 16-bit pattern intervals. The failure is cleared if the yellow alarm signal pattern does not occur in ten contiguous 16-bit signal pattern intervals.

Step 1   Insert an external loopback cable into the port. To create a loopback plug, refer to the section "Performing Hardware Loopback Plug Test," later in this chapter.

Step 2 Check to see if there are any alarms. If you do not see any alarms, then the local hardware is probably in good condition. In that case, do the following:

— Check the cabling. Refer to the section "If Receiver Has Loss of Signal" for more information.

— Check the settings at the remote end, and verify that they match your port settings.

— If the problem persists, contact your service provider.

Step 3 Remove the loopback plug, and reconnect your T1 line

Step 4 Check the cabling. Refer to the section "Loss of Signal" for more information.

Step 5 Power-cycle the router.

Step 6 Connect the T1 line to a different port. Configure the port with the same settings as that of the line. If the problem does not persist, then the fault lies with the one port:

— Reconnect the T1 line to the original port.

— Proceed to the "Troubleshooting Error Events" section, later in this chapter.

If the problem persists, then do the following:

- Perform a hardware loop test, as described in the section "Performing Hardware Loopback Plug Test."
- Replace the T1 controller card.
- Proceed to "Troubleshooting Error Events," the next section.

Transmitter Sending Remote Alarm (Red)

A red alarm is declared when the CSU cannot synchronize with the framing pattern on the T1 line.

Step 1 Check to see whether the framing format configured on the port matches the framing format of the line. If not, change the framing format on the controller to match that of the line.

Step 2 Check the settings at the remote end, and verify that they match your port settings.

Step 3 Contact your service provider.

Transmit (Tx) Remote Alarm Indication (Yellow)

A transmitted remote alarm indication at the interface indicates that the interface has a problem with the signal it is receiving from the far-end equipment.

Step 1 Check the settings at the remote end, and verify that they match your port settings.

Step 2 A Tx RAI should be accompanied by some other alarm that indicates the nature of the problem that the T1 port/card is having with the signal from the far-end equipment.

Troubleshoot that condition to resolve the Tx RAI.

Transmit (Tx) AIS (Blue)

Step 1 Check to see whether the framing format configured on the port matches the framing format of the line. If not, correct the mismatch.

Step 2 Power-cycle the router.

Step 3 Connect the T1 line to a different port. Configure the port with the same settings as that of the line.

If the problem persists, then do the following:

- Perform a hardware loop test, as described in the section "Performing a Hardware Loop Test."
- Replace the T1 controller card.
- Proceed to the "Troubleshooting Error Events" section, next.

Troubleshooting Error Events

The **show controller t1** exec command provides error messages that can be used to troubleshoot problems. We will now discuss several error messages and how to correct the errors.

To see whether the error counters are increasing, execute the **show controller t1** command repeatedly. Note the values of the counters for the current interval.

Consult your service provider for framing and linecoding settings. A good rule of thumb is to use B8ZS linecoding with ESF framing and AMI linecoding with SF framing.

Slip Secs Counter Is Increasing

The presence of slips on a T1 line indicates a clocking problem. The T1 provider (telco) will provide the clocking that the customer premises equipment (CPE) will need to synchronize to.

Step 1   Verify that the clock source is derived from the network. This can be ascertained by looking for "Clock Source Is Line Primary."

Note: If there are multiple T1s into an access server, only one can be the primary, while the other T1s derive the clock from the primary. In that case, verify that the T1 line designated as the primary clock source is configured correctly.

Step 2   Set the T1 clock source correctly from the controller configuration mode.

```
maui-nas-03(config-controlle)#clock source line primary
```

Framing Loss Seconds Counter Is Increasing

Step 1   Check to see whether the framing format configured on the port matches the framing format of the line. You can check this by looking for "Framing is {ESF|SF}" in the show controller t1 output.

Step 2   To change the framing format, use the **framing {SF | ESF}** command in the controller configuration mode, as shown here:

```
maui-nas-03(config-controlle)#framing esf
```

Step 3   Change the line build out using the **cablelength {long | short}** command.

Consult your service provider and the Cisco IOS command reference for details on buildout settings.

Line Code Violations Are Increasing

Step 1   Check to see whether the linecoding configured on the port matches the framing format of the line. You can check this by looking for "Line Code is {B8ZS|AMI}" in the **show controller t1** output.

Step 2   To change the linecoding, use the **linecode {ami | b8zs}** command in the controller configuration mode, as shown here:

```
maui-nas-03(config-controlle)#linecode b8zs
```

Step 3   Change the line build out using the **cablelength {long | short}** command.

Consult your service provider and the Cisco IOS command reference for details on buildout settings.

Verify that isdn switchtype and pri-group Are Configured Correctly

Use the **show running-config** command to check if isdn switchtype and pri-group timeslots are configured correctly. Contact your service provider for correct values.

To change the isdn switchtype and pri-group, enter these lines:

```
maui-nas-03#configure terminal
maui-nas-03(config)#isdn switch-type primary-5ess
maui-nas-03(config)#controller t1 0
maui-nas-03(config-controlle)#pri-group timeslots 1-24
```

Verifying the Signaling Channel

If the error counters do not increase but the problem persists, verify that the signaling channel is up and configured correctly.

Step 1   Run the **show interface serial x:23** command, where x should be replaced by the interface number.

Step 2   Check to see if the interface is up. If the interface is not up, use the **no shutdown** command to bring the interface up.

```
maui-nas-03#config terminal
Enter configuration commands, one per line.  End with CNTL/Z.
maui-nas-03(config)#interface serial 0:23
maui-nas-03(config-if)#no shutdown
```

Step 3   Ensure that encapsulation is PPP. If the interface is not using PPP, then use the **encapsulation ppp** command in the interface configuration mode to correct it.

```
maui-nas-03(config-if)#encapsulation ppp
```

Step 4   Check to see whether loopback is set. Loopback should be set only for testing purposes. Use the **no loopback** command to remove loopbacks.

```
maui-nas-03(config-if)#no loopback
```

Step 5   Power-cycle the router.

Step 6   If the problem persists, contact your service provider or Cisco TAC.

Troubleshooting a PRI

Whenever troubleshooting a PRI, you need to check whether the T1 is running cleanly on both ends. If Layer 1 problems have been resolved, as described previously, we must look to Layer 2 and 3 problems.

Troubleshooting Using the show isdn status Command

The **show isdn status** command is used to display a snapshot of all ISDN interfaces. It displays the status of Layers 1, 2, and 3.

Step 1   Verify that Layer 1 is active.

The Layer 1 status should always say ACTIVE unless the T1 is down.

If **show isdn status** indicates that Layer 1 is DEACTIVATED, then there is a problem with the physical connectivity on the T1 line. Refer to the previous section "Is the Controller Administratively Down?"

Also verify that the T1 is not administratively down. Use the **no shutdown** command to bring up the T1 controller.

Step 2   Check whether Layer 2 state is MULTIPLE_FRAME_ESTABLISHED.

The desired Layer 2 State is MULTIPLE_FRAME_ESTABLISHED, which indicates that we are exchanging Layer 2 frames and have finished Layer 2 initialization.

If Layer 2 is not MULTIPLE_FRAME_ESTABLISHED, use the **show controller t1** exec command to diagnose the problem. Refer to the section "Troubleshooting Using the show controller t1 Command."

Because **show isdn status** is a snapshot of the current status, it is possible that Layer 2 is bouncing up and down despite indicating MULTIPLE_FRAME_ESTABLISHED. Use **debug isdn q921** to verify that Layer 2 is stable.

Using debug q921

The **debug isdn q921** command displays data link layer (Layer 2) access procedures that are taking place at the router on the D-channel.

Ensure that you are configured to view **debug** messages by using the logging console or terminal monitor command as necessary.

NOTE   In a production environment, verify that console logging is disabled. Enter the **show logging** command. If logging is enabled, the access server might intermittently freeze up as soon as the console port gets overloaded with log messages. Enter the **no logging** console command.

NOTE   If **debug isdn q921** is turned on and you do not receive any **debug** outputs, place a call or reset the controller to get **debug** outputs.

Step 1   Verify that Layer 2 is stable. You should observe the **debug** outputs for messages indicating that the service is not bouncing up and down. If you see the following types of debug outputs, the line is not stable:

```
Mar 20 10:06:07.882: %ISDN-6-LAYER2DOWN: Layer 2 for Interface Se0:23,
TEI 0 changed to down
Mar 20 10:06:09.882: %LINK-3-UPDOWN: Interface Serial0:23, changed
state to down
Mar 20 10:06:21.274: %DSX1-6-CLOCK_CHANGE: Controller 0  clock is now
selected as clock source
Mar 20 10:06:21.702: %ISDN-6-LAYER2UP: Layer 2 for Interface Se0:23, TEI
0 changed to up
Mar 20 10:06:22.494: %CONTROLLER-5-UPDOWN: Controller T1 0, changed
state to up
Mar 20 10:06:24.494: %LINK-3-UPDOWN: Interface Serial0:23, changed
state to up
```

If Layer 2 does not appear to be stable, refer to the section "Troubleshooting Error Events."

Step 2   Verify that you are seeing only SAPI messages in both transmit (TX) and receive (RX) sides.

```
Mar 20 10:06:52.505: ISDN Se0:23: TX -> RRf sapi = 0  tei = 0  nr = 0
Mar 20 10:06:52.505: ISDN Se0:23: RX <- RRf sapi = 0  tei = 0  nr = 0
Mar 20 10:07:22.505: ISDN Se0:23: TX -> RRp sapi = 0  tei = 0  nr = 0
Mar 20 10:07:22.509: ISDN Se0:23: RX <- RRp sapi = 0  tei = 0  nr = 0
Mar 20 10:07:22.509: ISDN Se0:23: TX -> RRf sapi = 0  tei = 0  nr = 0
Mar 20 10:07:22.509: ISDN Se0:23: RX <- RRf sapi = 0  tei = 0  nr = 0
```

Step 3   Verify that you are not seeing SABME messages, which indicates that Layer 2 is trying to reinitialize. This is usually seen when we are transmitting poll requests (RRp) and not getting a response from the switch (RRf), or vice versa. The following are example of SABME messages:

```
Mar 20 10:06:21.702: ISDN Se0:23: RX <- SABMEp sapi = 0  tei = 0
Mar 20 10:06:22.494: ISDN Se0:23: TX -> SABMEp sapi = 0  tei = 0
```

If you are seeing SABME messages, do the following:

— Use the **show running-config** command to check whether **isdn switchtype** and **pri-group timeslots** are configured correctly. Contact your service provider for correct values.

— To change the **isdn switchtype** and **pri-group**, enter these lines:

```
maui-nas-03#configure terminal
maui-nas-03(config)#isdn switch-type primary-5ess
maui-nas-03(config)#controller t1 0
maui-nas-03(config-controlle)#pri-group timeslots 1-24
```

Step 4 Verify that the D-channel is up using the **show interfaces serial x:23** command.

If the D-channel is not up, then use **no shutdown** command to bring it up:

```
maui-nas-03(config)#interface serial 0:23
maui-nas-03(config-if)#no shutdown
```

Step 5 Check to see whether encapsulation is PPP. If not, use the **encapsulation ppp** command to set encapsulation.

```
maui-nas-03(config-if)#encapsulation ppp
```

Step 6 Check to see whether the interface is in loopback mode. For normal operation, the interface should not be in loopback mode.

```
maui-nas-03(config-if)#no loopback
```

Step 7 Power-cycle the router.

Step 8 If the problem persists, contact your service provider or Cisco TAC.

Performing Hardware Loopback Plug Test

The hardware loopback plug test can be used to test whether the router has any faults. If a router passes a hardware loopback plug test, then the problem exists elsewhere on the line.

To create a loopback plug, follow these steps:

Step 1 Use wire cutters to cut a working RJ-45 or RJ-48 cable so that there are 5 inches of cable and the connector attached to it.

Step 2 Strip the wires.

Step 3 Twist the wires from pins 1 and 4 together.

Step 4 Twist the wires from pins 2 and 5 together.

Leave the rest of the wires alone.

The pins on an RJ-45/48 jack are numbered from 1 through 8. Pin 1 is the left-most pin when looking at the jack with the metal pins facing you.

Performing the Loopback Plug Test

Step 1 Insert the plug into the T1 port in question.

Step 2 Save your router configuration using the **write memory** command.

```
maui-nas-03#write memory
Building configuration...
[OK]
```

Step 3 Set the encapsulation to HDLC.

```
maui-nas-03#config terminal
Enter configuration commands, one per line.  End with CNTL/Z.
maui-nas-03(config)#interface serial 0
maui-nas-03(config-if)#enc
maui-nas-03(config-if)#encapsulation HDLC
maui-nas-03(config-if)#^Z
```

Step 4 Use the **show running-config** command to check whether the interface has an IP address.

If the interface does not have an IP address, obtain a unique address and assign it to the interface with a subnet mask of 255.255.255.0

```
maui-nas-03(config)#ip address 172.22.53.1 255.255.255.0
```

Step 5 Clear the interface counters using the **clear counters** command.

```
maui-nas-03#clear counters
Clear "show interface" counters on all interfaces [confirm]
maui-nas-03#
```

Step 6 Perform the extended **ping** test as described in the "Using Extended ping Tests" section, earlier in this chapter.

Troubleshooting E1 Problems

This section describes the techniques and procedures to troubleshoot E1 circuits for dial-in customers.

Troubleshooting Using the show controller e1 Command

The **show e1 controller** exec command provides information to logically troubleshoot physical layer and data link layer problems. This section describes how to logically troubleshoot using the **show controller e1** command.

This command displays the controller status that is specific to the controller hardware. The information displayed is generally useful for diagnostic tasks performed by technical support personnel only.

The NPM or MIP can query the port adapters to determine their current status. Issue a **show controller e1** command to display statistics about the E1 link.

If you specify a slot and port number, statistics for each 15-minute period will be displayed.

Most E1 errors are caused by misconfigured lines. Ensure that linecoding, framing, clock source, and line termination (balanced or unbalanced) are configured according to what the service provider recommended.

Show controller e1 Conditions

The E1 controller can be in three states:

- Administratively down
- Down
- Up

Is the Controller Administratively Down?

The controller is administratively down when it has been manually shut down. You should restart the controller to correct this error.

Step 1   Enter enable mode.

```
maui-nas-03>en
Password:
maui-nas-03#
```

Step 2   Enter global configuration mode.

```
maui-nas-03#configure terminal
Enter configuration commands, one per line.  End with CNTL/Z.
maui-nas-03(config)#
```

Step 3   Enter controller configuration mode.

```
maui-nas-03(config)#controller e1 0
maui-nas-03(config-controlle)#
```

Step 4   Restart the controller.

```
maui-nas-03(config-controlle)#shutdown
maui-nas-03(config-controlle)#no shutdown
```

Is the Line Up?

If the E1 line is not up, check to see that the line configuration is correct and matches the settings of the remote end.

Check the framing of the line and the remote end. For E1 lines, the framing is either CRC4 or noCRC4.

Check the linecoding of the line and the remote end. The linecoding is either AMI or HDB3.

Check whether the line termination is set for balanced or unbalanced (75 ohm or 120 ohm).

Consult your service provider for more information regarding the correct settings. Make any changes as necessary to both local or remote end devices.

If the E1 controller and line are not up, check to see whether you are seeing one of the following messages in the **show controller e1** exec output:

```
Receiver has loss of frame.
```
or
```
Receiver has loss of signal.
```

If Receiver Has Loss of Frame

Step 1   Check to see whether the framing format configured on the port matches the framing format of the line. You can check the framing format of the controller from the running configuration or the **show controller e1** command output.

To change the framing format, use the **framing {CRC4 | no CRC4}** command in the controller configuration mode, as shown here:

```
maui-nas-03#configure terminal
Enter configuration commands, one per line.  End with CNTL/Z.

maui-nas-03(config)#controller E1 0
maui-nas-03(config-controlle)#framing CRC4
```

Step 2   Try the other framing format to see if the alarm clears.

If this does not fix the problem, proceed to the receiver has loss of signal section below.

Step 3   Check the framing format on the remote end.

Step 4   Check the linecoding on the remote end.

If Receiver Has Loss of Signal

Step 1   Make sure that the cable between the interface port and the E1 service provider's equipment or E1 terminal equipment is connected correctly. Check to see whether the cable is hooked up to the correct ports. Correct the cable connections if necessary.

Step 2   Check cable integrity. Look for breaks or other physical abnormalities in the cable. Ensure that the pinouts are set correctly. If necessary, replace the cable.

Step 3   Check the cable connectors. A reversal of the transmit and receive pairs or an open receive pair can cause errors. Set the receive pair to lines 1 and 2; the transmit pair should be lines 4 and 5.

The pins on a RJ-48 jack are numbered from 1 through 8. Pin 1 is the leftmost pin when looking at the jack with the metal pins facing you. Refer to Figure 15-12 for more information.

Figure 15-12 *RJ-45 Cable*

87654321
RJ-45 connector

Step 4   Try using a rollover cable.

Step 5   Check to see whether there are far-end block errors. If so, the problem exists with the receive lead on the local end. Contact TAC for more assistance.

Run the **show controller e1** exec command after each step to check whether the controller exhibits any errors.

If the Line Is in Loopback Mode

Check to see whether the line is in loopback mode from the **show controller e1** output. A line should be in loopback mode only for testing purposes.

To turn off loopback, use the **no loopback** command in the controller configuration mode, as shown here:

```
maui-nas-03(config-controlle)#no loopback
```

If the Controller Displays Any Alarms

Check the **show controller** command output to see whether any alarms are displayed by the controller.

We will now discuss various alarms and the procedure necessary to correct them.

Receiver (Rx) Has Remote Alarm

A received remote alarm means that an alarm is occurring on the line upstream of the equipment connected to the port.

Step 1   Check to see whether the framing format configured on the port matches the framing format of the line. If not, change the framing format on the controller to match that of the line.

Step 2 Check the linecoding setting on the remote-end equipment. Contact your service provider for the correct settings. Correct any misconfigurations, as necessary.

Step 3 Insert an external loopback cable into the port. To create a loopback plug, refer to the section "Performing Hardware Loopback Plug Test," earlier in the chapter.

Step 4 Check to see whether there are any alarms. If you do not see any alarms, then the local hardware is probably in good condition. In that case, do the following:

— Check the cabling. Refer to the section "Loss of Signal" for more information.

— Check the settings at the remote end, and verify that they match your port settings.

— If the problem persists, contact your service provider.

Step 5 Remove the loopback plug and reconnect your E1 line.

Step 6 Check the cabling. Refer to the section "Loss of Signal" for more information.

Step 7 Power-cycle the router.

Step 8 Connect the E1 line to a different port. Configure the port with the same settings as that of the line. If the problem does not persist, then the fault lies with the port:

— Reconnect the E1 line to the original port.

— Proceed to the "Troubleshooting E1 Error Events" section.

If the problem persists, then do the following:

— Perform a hardware loop test, as described in the section "Performing a Hardware Loop Test,"

— Replace the E1 controller card.

— Proceed to the "Troubleshooting E1 Error Events" section.

Transmitter Sending Remote Alarm (Red)

A red alarm is declared when the CSU cannot synchronize with the framing pattern on the E1 line.

Step 1 Check to see whether the framing format configured on the port matches the framing format of the line. If not, change the framing format on the controller to match that of the line.

Step 2   Check the settings at the remote end, and verify that they match your port settings.

Step 3   Insert an external loopback cable into the port. To create a loopback plug, refer to the section "Performing Hardware Loopback Plug Test," earlier in the chapter.

Step 4   Check to see whether there are any alarms. If you do not see any alarms, then the local hardware is probably in good condition. In that case, do the following:

— Check the cabling. Refer to the section "Loss of Signal" for more information.

— If the problem persists, contact your service provider.

Step 5   Connect the E1 line to a different port. Configure the port with the same settings as that of the line. If the problem does not persist, then the fault lies with the port:

— Reconnect the E1 line to the original port.

— Proceed to the "Troubleshooting E1 Error Events" section.

If the problem persists, then do the following:

- Perform a hardware loop test, as described in the section "Performing a Hardware Loop Test."
- Replace the E1 controller card.
- Proceed to the "Troubleshooting E1 Error Events" section.
- Contact your service provider.

Troubleshooting E1 Error Events

The **show controller e1** exec command provides error messages that can be used to troubleshoot problems. We will now discuss several error messages and how to correct the errors.

To see whether the error counters are increasing, execute the **show controller e1** command repeatedly. Note the values of the counters for the current interval.

Consult your service provider for framing and linecoding settings.

Slip Secs Counter Is Increasing

The presence of slips on E1 lines indicates a clocking problem. The E1 provider (telco) will provide the clocking that the customer premises equipment (CPE) will need to synchronize to.

Step 1   Verify that the clock source is derived from the network. This can be ascertained by looking for "Clock Source is Line Primary."

Note   If there are multiple E1s into an access server, only one can be the primary, while the other E1s derive the clock from the primary. In that case, verify that the E1 line designated as the primary clock source is configured correctly.

Step 2   Set the E1 clock source correctly from the controller configuration mode.

```
maui-nas-03(config-controlle)#clock source line primary
```

Framing Loss Seconds Counter Is Increasing

Step 1   Check to see whether the framing format configured on the port matches the framing format of the line. You can check this by looking for "Framing is {CRC4|no CRC4}" in the **show controller e1** output.

Step 2   To change the framing format, use the **framing {CRC4 | no CRC4}** command in the controller configuration mode, as shown here:

```
maui-nas-03(config-controlle)#framing crc4
```

Line Code Violations Are Increasing

Step 1   Check to see whether the linecoding configured on the port matches the framing format of the line. You can check this by looking for "Line Code is {AMI/HDB3}" in the **show controller e1** output.

Step 2   To change the linecoding, use the **linecode {ami | hdb3}** command in the controller configuration mode, as shown here:

```
maui-nas-03(config-controlle)#linecode ami
```

Verifying That isdn switchtype and pri-group Are Configured Correctly

Use the **show running-config** command to check whether **isdn switchtype** and **pri-group timeslots** are configured correctly. Contact your service provider for correct values.

To change the **isdn switchtype** and **pri-group**, use these lines:

```
maui-nas-03#configure terminal
maui-nas-03(config)#isdn switch-type primary-net5
maui-nas-03(config)#controller e1 0
maui-nas-03(config-controlle)#pri-group timeslots 1-31
```

Verifying the Signaling Channel

If the error counters do not increase but the problem persists, verify that the signaling channel is up and configured correctly.

Step 1   Run the **show interface serial** x:**15** command, where x should be replaced by the interface number.

Step 2   Check to see whether the interface is up. If the interface is not up, use the **no shutdown** command to bring up the interface.

```
maui-nas-03#config terminal
Enter configuration commands, one per line.   End with CNTL/Z.
maui-nas-03(config)#interface serial 0:15
maui-nas-03(config-if)#no shutdown
```

Step 3   Ensure that encapsulation is PPP. If the interface is not using PPP, then use the **encapsulation ppp** command in the interface configuration mode to correct it.

```
maui-nas-03(config-if)#encapsulation ppp
```

Step 4   Check to see whether loopback is set. Loopback should be set only for testing purposes. Use the **no loopback** command to remove loopbacks.

```
maui-nas-03(config-if)#no loopback
```

Step 5   Power-cycle the router.

Step 6   If the problem persists, contact your service provider or Cisco TAC.

Troubleshooting a PRI

Whenever troubleshooting a PRI, you need to check whether the E1 is running cleanly on both ends. If Layer 1 problems have been resolved, as described previously, we must look to Layer 2 and 3 problems.

Troubleshooting Using the show isdn status Command

The **show isdn status** command is used to display a snapshot of all ISDN interfaces. It displays the status of Layers 1, 2, and 3.

Step 1 Verify that Layer 1 is active.

The Layer 1 status should always say ACTIVE unless the E1 is down.

If **show isdn status** indicates that Layer 1 is DEACTIVATED, then there is a problem with the physical connectivity on the E1 line. Refer to the section "Is the Controller Administratively Down?"

Also verify that the E1 is not administratively down. Use the **no shutdown** command to bring up the E1 controller.

Step 2 Check whether Layer 2 state is MULTIPLE_FRAME_ESTABLISHED.

The desired Layer 2 state is MULTIPLE_FRAME_ESTABLISHED, which indicates that the startup protocol between ISDN switch and end device has been established and that we are exchanging Layer 2 frames.

If Layer 2 is not MULTIPLE_FRAME_ESTABLISHED, use the **show controller E1** exec command to diagnose the problem. Refer to the previous section "Troubleshooting Using the show controller e1 Command," and the upcoming section "Troubleshooting E1 Error Events."

Because **show isdn status** is a snapshot of the current status, it is possible that Layer 2 is bouncing up and down despite indicating Mulitple_Frame_Established. Use **debug isdn q921** to verify that Layer 2 is stable.

Using debug q921

The **debug isdn q921** command displays data link layer (Layer 2) access procedures that are taking place at the router on the D-channel.

Ensure that you are configured to view **debug** messages by using the **logging console** or **terminal monitor** commands, as necessary.

NOTE In a production environment, verify that console logging is disabled. Enter the **show logging** command. If logging is enabled, the access server might intermitttently freeze up as soon as the console port gets overloaded with log messages. Enter the **no logging** console command.

NOTE	If **debug isdn q921** is turned on and you do not receive any **debug** outputs, place a call or reset the controller to get **debug** outputs.

Step 1 Verify that Layer 2 is stable. You should observe the **debug** outputs for messages indicating that the service is not bouncing up and down. If you see the following types of **debug** outputs, the line is not stable:

```
Mar 20 10:06:07.882: %ISDN-6-LAYER2DOWN: Layer 2 for Interface Se0:15,
TEI 0 changed to down
Mar 20 10:06:09.882: %LINK-3-UPDOWN: Interface Serial0:15, changed
state to down
Mar 20 10:06:21.274: %DSX1-6-CLOCK_CHANGE: Controller 0  clock is now
selected as clock source
Mar 20 10:06:21.702: %ISDN-6-LAYER2UP: Layer 2 for Interface Se0:15, TEI
0 changed to up
Mar 20 10:06:22.494: %CONTROLLER-5-UPDOWN: Controller E1 0, changed
state to up
Mar 20 10:06:24.494: %LINK-3-UPDOWN: Interface Serial0:15, changed
state to up
```

If Layer 2 does not appear to be stable refer to the "Troubleshooting Error Events" section, earlier in this chapter.

Step 2 Verify that you are seeing only SAPI messages in both transmit (TX) and receive (RX) sides.

```
Mar 20 10:06:52.505: ISDN Se0:15: TX -> RRf sapi = 0  tei = 0  nr = 0
Mar 20 10:06:52.505: ISDN Se0:15: RX <- RRf sapi = 0  tei = 0  nr = 0
Mar 20 10:07:22.505: ISDN Se0:15: TX -> RRp sapi = 0  tei = 0  nr = 0
Mar 20 10:07:22.509: ISDN Se0:15: RX <- RRp sapi = 0  tei = 0  nr = 0
Mar 20 10:07:22.509: ISDN Se0:15: TX -> RRf sapi = 0  tei = 0  nr = 0
Mar 20 10:07:22.509: ISDN Se0:15: RX <- RRf sapi = 0  tei = 0  nr = 0
```

Step 3 Verify that you are not seeing SABME messages, which indicates that Layer 2 is trying to reinitialize. This is usually seen when we are transmitting poll requests (RRp) and not getting a response from the switch (RRf), or vice versa. The following are examples of SABME messages. We should get a response from ISDN switch for our SABME messages (UA frame received):

```
Mar 20 10:06:21.702: ISDN Se0:15: RX <- SABMEp sapi = 0  tei = 0
Mar 20 10:06:22.494: ISDN Se0:15: TX -> SABMEp sapi = 0  tei = 0
```

If you are seeing SABME messages, do the following:

— Use the **show running-config** command to check whether **isdn switchtype** and **pri-group timeslots** are configured correctly. Contact your service provider for correct values.

— To change the **isdn switchtype** and **pri-group**, use these lines:

```
maui-nas-03#configure terminal
maui-nas-03(config)#isdn switch-type primary-net5
maui-nas-03(config)#controller e1 0
maui-nas-03(config-controlle)#pri-group timeslots 1-31
```

Step 4   Verify that the D-channel is up using the **show interfaces serial x:15** command.

If the D-channel is not up, then use **no shutdown** command to bring it up:

```
maui-nas-03(config)#interface serial 0:15
maui-nas-03(config-if)#no shutdown
```

Step 5   Check to see whether encapsulation is PPP. If not, use the **encapsulation ppp** command to set encapsulation.

```
maui-nas-03(config-if)#encapsulation ppp
```

Step 6   Check to see whether the interface is in loopback mode. For normal operation, the interface should not be in loopback mode.

```
maui-nas-03(config-if)#no loopback
```

Step 7   Power-cycle the router.

Step 8   If the problem persists, contact your service provider or Cisco TAC.

## CHAPTER 16

Troubleshooting Dialup Connections

This chapter introduces and explains some of the technologies used in dialup networks. Configuration tips and interpretations of some of the **show** commands, which are useful for verifying correct operation of the network, are found in this chapter as well. Actual troubleshooting will be found in Chapter 17, "Troubleshooting ISDN Connections."

This chapter focuses on four principal areas:

1   Modem Operations

  — Using the **modem autoconfigure** Command

  — Establishing a Reverse Telnet Session to a Modem

  — Using Rotary Groups

  — Interpreting **show line** Output

  — Gathering Modem Performance Information for Trend Analysis

2   ISDN Operations

  — Components

  — Services

  — Interpreting **show isdn status** Output

3   Dialer Operations

  — Dialer Maps

  — Dialer Profiles

4   PPP Operations

  — LCP

  — Authentication/AAA

  — NCP

Modem Operations

This section discusses issues related specifically to the setup, verification, and use of modems with Cisco routers.

Using the modem autoconfigure Command

If you are using Cisco Internetwork Operating System (Cisco IOS) Release 11.1 or later, you can configure your Cisco router to communicate with and configure your modem automatically.

Use the following procedure to configure a Cisco router to automatically attempt to discover what kind of modem is connected to the line and then to configure the modem:

1 To discover the type of modem attached to your router, use the **modem autoconfigure discovery** line configuration command.

2 When the modem is successfully discovered, configure the modem automatically using the **modem autoconfigure type** *modem-name* line configuration command.

If you want to display the list of modems for which the router has entries, use the **show modemcap** *modem-name*. If you want to change a modem value that was returned from the **show modemcap** command, use the **modemcap edit** *modem-name attribute value* line configuration command.

For complete information on the use of these commands, refer to the Cisco IOS documentation *Dial Solutions Configuration Guide* and *Dial Solutions Command Reference*.

NOTE   Do *not* put **&W** in the modemcap entry used for the autoconfigure. Having the NVRAM rewritten every time a modem autoconfigure is done will destroy the modem.

Establishing a Reverse Telnet Session to a Modem

For diagnostic purposes, or to initially configure the modem if you are running Cisco IOS Release 11.0 or earlier, you must establish a reverse Telnet session to configure a modem to communicate with a Cisco device. As long as you lock the speed of the data terminal equipment (DTE) of the modem (see Table 16-5 for information on locking the modem speed), the modem will always communicate with the access server or router at the desired speed. Be certain that the speed of the Cisco device is configured before issuing commands to the modem via a reverse Telnet session. (See Table 16-5 for information on configuring the speed of the access server or router.)

To configure the modem for a reverse Telnet session, use the line configuration command **transport input telnet**. To set up a rotary group (in this case on port 1), enter the line configuration command **rotary 1.** Placing these commands under the line configuration causes the IOS to allocate IP listeners for incoming connections at port ranges starting with the following base numbers:

2000	Telnet protocol
3000	Telnet protocol with rotary
4000	Raw TCP protocol
5000	Raw TCP protocol with rotary
6000	Telnet protocol, Binary Mode
7000	Telnet protocol, Binary Mode with rotary
9000	XRemote Protocol
10000	XRemote Protocol with rotary

To initiate a reverse Telnet session to your modem, perform the following steps:

Step 1 From your terminal, use the command **telnet** *ip-address* **20yy**, where *ip-address* is the IP address of any active, connected interface on the Cisco device, and **yy** is the line number to which the modem is connected. For example, the following command would connect you to the auxiliary port on a Cisco 2501 router with IP address 192.169.53.52: **telnet 192.169.53.52 2001**. Generally, a Telnet command of this kind can be issued from anywhere on the network that can **ping** the IP address in question.

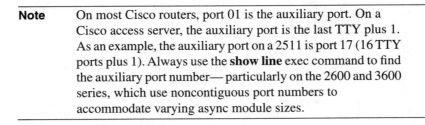

Note On most Cisco routers, port 01 is the auxiliary port. On a Cisco access server, the auxiliary port is the last TTY plus 1. As an example, the auxiliary port on a 2511 is port 17 (16 TTY ports plus 1). Always use the **show line** exec command to find the auxiliary port number— particularly on the 2600 and 3600 series, which use noncontiguous port numbers to accommodate varying async module sizes.

Step 2 If the connection is refused, it could indicate either that there is no listener at the specified address and port, or that someone is already connected to that port. Verify the address being connected to and the port number. Also make sure that the command **modem inout** or **modem DTR-active**, as well as **transport input all**, appears under the line configuration for the lines being reached. If using the rotary function, make sure that the command **rotary** *n* also appears in the line configuration (here, *n* is the number of the rotary group). To check whether someone is connected already, Telnet to the router and use the command **show line** *n*. Look for an asterisk to indicate that the line is in use. Make sure that CTS is high and that DSR is not. The command **clear line** *n* would be used to disconnect the current session on port number *n*. If the connection is still refused, the modem might be asserting carrier detect (CD) all the time. Disconnect the modem from the line, establish a reverse Telnet session, and then connect the modem.

Step 3   After successfully making the Telnet connection, enter **AT** and make sure that the modem replies with OK.

Step 4   If the modem is not responsive, refer to Table 16-1.

Table 16-1 outlines the problems that might cause a modem to router connectivity problem symptom and describes solutions to those problems.

Table 16-1   *Dialing: No Connectivity Between Modem and Router*

Possible Causes	Suggested Actions	
Modem control not enabled on the access server or router	**Step 1**	Use the **show line** exec command on the access server or router. The output for the auxiliary port should show **inout** or **RIisCD** in the Modem column. This indicates that modem control is enabled on the line of the access server or router.
	Step 2	Configure the line for modem control using the **modem inout** line configuration command. Modem control is now enabled on the access server.
		Example:
		The following example illustrates how to configure a line for both incoming and outgoing calls:
		``` line 5 modem inout ```
		Note: Be certain to use the **modem inout** command and not the **modem ri-is-cd** command while the connectivity of the modem is in question. The latter command allows the line to accept incoming calls only. Outgoing calls will be refused, making it impossible to establish a Telnet session with the modem to configure it. If you want to enable the **modem ri-is-cd** command, do so only after you are certain that the modem is functioning correctly.
Modem that could be misconfigured or have a hung session	**Step 1**	Enter **AT&FE1Q0** to return the modem to factory defaults, and make sure that the modem is set to echo characters and return output. The modem may have a hung session. Use **^U** to clear the line and **^Q** to open up the flow control (XON). Verify parity settings.

Table 16-1 *Dialing: No Connectivity Between Modem and Router (Continued)*

Possible Causes	Suggested Actions	
Incorrect cabling	**Step 1**	Check the cabling between the modem and the access server or router. Confirm that the modem is connected to the auxiliary port on the access server or router with a rolled RJ-45 cable and an MMOD DB-25 adapter. This cabling configuration is recommended and supported by Cisco for RJ-45 ports. (These connectors are typically labeled "Modem.")
	Step 2	Use the **show line** exec command to verify that the cabling is correct. See the explanation of the **show line** command output in the section "Using **debug** Commands" in Chapter 15, "Troubleshooting Serial Lines."
Hardware problem	**Step 1**	Verify that you are using the correct cabling and that all connections are good.
	Step 2	Check all hardware for damage, including cabling (broken wires), adapters (loose pins), access server ports, and modem.
	Step 3	See Chapter 3, "Troubleshooting Hardware and Booting Problems," for more information on hardware troubleshooting.

Using Rotary Groups

For some applications, the modems on a given router need to be shared by a group of users. The Cisco Dialout Utility would be a good example of this application. The general idea is to have one port for users to connect into that will connect them to whichever modem happens to be available. To add an async line to a rotary group, simply enter **rotary *n***, where *n* is the number of the rotary group in the configuration for the async line. For example, the following line configuration would allow users to connect to the rotary group by (referencing the previous example) **telnet 192.169.53.52 3001** for normal Telnet:

```
line 1 16
  modem InOut
  transport input all
  rotary 1
  speed 115200
  flowcontrol hardware
```

Alternatives include ports 5001 for Raw TCP, 7001 for binary Telnet (which Cisco Dialout Utility uses), and 10001 for Xremote connections.

NOTE To verify the configuration of the Cisco Dialout Utility, double-click the Dialout Utility icon at the bottom right of the screen and press the More button. Next, press the Configure Ports button. Make sure that the port is in the 7000 range if using rotary groups and the 6000 range if the Dialout Utility is targeting an individual modem. Enabling modem logging on the PC is also suggested for troubleshooting. This is done by selecting the following sequence: Start, Control Panel, Modems (choose your Cisco Dialout modem), Properties, Connection, Advanced, Record a Log File.

Interpreting show line Output

The output from the **show line** *line-number* exec command is useful when troubleshooting a modem-to-access server or router connection. Figure 16-1 shows the output from the **show line** command.

Figure 16-1 *show line Command Output*

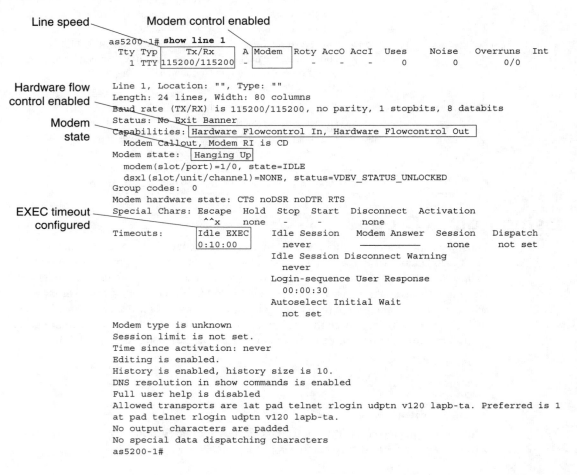

When connectivity problems occur, important output appears in the Modem State and the Modem Hardware State fields.

NOTE	The Modem Hardware State field does not appear in the **show line** output for every platform. In certain cases, the indications for signal states will be shown in the Modem State Field instead.

Table 16-2 shows typical Modem State and Modem Hardware State strings from the output of the **show line** command, and explains the meaning of each state.

Table 16-2 *Modem and Modem Hardware States in **show line** Output*

Modem State	Modem Hardware State	Meaning
Idle	CTS noDSR DTR RTS	These are the proper modem states for connections between an access server or router and a modem (when there is no incoming call). Output of any other kind generally indicates a problem.
Ready	—	If the modem state is ready instead of idle, there are three possibilities: • Modem control is not configured on the access server or router. Configure the access server or router with the **modem inout** line configuration command. • A session exists on the line. Use the **show users** exec command and use the **clear line** privileged exec command to stop the session, if desired. • DSR is high. There are two possible reasons for this: — **Cabling problems**—If your connector uses DB-25 pin 6 and has no pin 8, you must move the pin from 6 to 8 or get the appropriate connector. — **Modem configured for DCD always high**—The modem should be reconfigured to have DCD high only on CD[1]. This is usually done with the **&C1** modem command, but check your modem documentation for the exact syntax for your modem.

continues

Table 16-2 *Modem and Modem Hardware States in* **show line** *Output (Continued)*

Modem State	Modem Hardware State	Meaning
Ready *(continued)*	—	If your software does not support modem control, you must configure the access server line to which the modem is connected with the **no exec** line configuration command. Clear the line with the **clear line** privileged exec command, initiate a reverse Telnet session with the modem, and reconfigure the modem so that DCD is high only on CD.
		End the Telnet session by entering **disconnect**, and reconfigure the access server line with the **exec** line configuration command.
Ready	noCTS noDSR DTR RTS	There are four possibilities for the noCTS string appearing in the Modem Hardware State field:
		• The modem is turned off.
		• The modem is not properly connected to the access server. Check the cabling connections from the modem to the access server.
		• Cabling is incorrect (either rolled MDCE, or straight MDTE, but without the pins moved). See Table 16-1 for information on the recommended cabling configuration.
		• The modem is not configured for hardware flow control. Disable hardware flow control on the access server with the **no flowcontrol hardware** line configuration command, and then enable hardware flow control on the modem via a reverse Telnet session. (Consult your modem documentation, and see the section "Establishing a Reverse Telnet Session to a Modem," earlier in this chapter.)
		Re-enable hardware flow control on the access server with the **flowcontrol hardware** line configuration command.

Table 16-2   *Modem and Modem Hardware States in* **show line** *Output (Continued)*

Modem State	Modem Hardware State	Meaning
Ready	CTS DSR DTR RTS	There are two possibilities for the presence of the DSR string instead of the noDSR string in the Modem hardware state field:
		• Incorrect cabling (either rolled MDCE, or straight MDTE, but without the pins moved). See Table 16-1 for information on the recommended cabling configuration.
		• The modem is configured for DCD always high. Reconfigure the modem so that DCD is high only on CD. This is usually done with the **&C1** modem command, but check your modem documentation for the exact syntax for your modem.
		Configure the access server line to which the modem is connected with the **no exec** line configuration command. Clear the line with the **clear line** privileged exec command, initiate a reverse Telnet session with the modem, and reconfigure the modem so that DCD is high only on CD.
		End the Telnet session by entering **disconnect**. Reconfigure the access server line with the **exec** line configuration command.
Ready	CTS* DSR* DTR RTS[2]	If this string appears in the Modem Hardware State field, modem control is probably not enabled on the access server. Use the **modem inout** line configuration command to enable modem control on the line.
		See Table 16-1 for more information on configuring modem control on an access server or router line.

[1]CD = carrier detect.

[2]An * next to a signal indicates one of two things: The signal has changed within the past few seconds, or the signal is not being used by the modem control method selected.

Gathering Modem Performance Information

This section explains ways to gather performance data on MICA digital modems found in the Cisco AS5x00 family of access servers. The data can be used for trend analysis and is useful in troubleshooting performance problems that might be encountered. When looking at the numbers presented here, bear in mind that perfection is not possible in the real world. The modem call success rate (CSR) possible will be a function of the quality of the circuits, the client modem user base, and the set of modulations being used. A typical CSR percentage for V.34 calls is 95 percent. V.90 calls can be expected to connect successfully 92 percent of the time. Premature drops are likely to happen 10 percent of the time.

The tools used to gain an overall view of modem behavior on the access server are:

- **show modem**
- **show modem summary**
- **show modem connect-speeds**
- **show modem call-stats**

If troubleshooting an individual modem connection or gathering data for trend analysis, the following information will be useful:

```
debug modem csm
modem call-record terse
show modem op (MICA) / AT@E1 (Microcom) while connected
show modem log  - for the session of interest after disconnect.
ANI (caller's number)
Time of day
Client modem hardware / firmware revision
Interesting info from client (after disconnect)-ATI6, ATI11, AT&V, AT&V1, etc.
An audio record (.wav file) of the trainup attempt from the client modem
```

The commands will be explained further in the following sections, and some common trends will be discussed.

show modem/show modem summary

The **show modem** command gives a view of individual modems. From these numbers, the health of individual modems can be viewed.

```
router# show modem
  Codes:
  * - Modem has an active call
  C - Call in setup
  T - Back-to-Back test in progress
  R - Modem is being Reset
  p - Download request is pending and modem cannot be used for taking calls
  D - Download in progress
  B - Modem is marked bad and cannot be used for taking calls
  b - Modem is either busied out or shut-down
  d - DSP software download is required for achieving K56flex connections
  ! - Upgrade request is pending
                Inc calls      Out calls      Busied  Failed  No        Succ
       Mdm  Usage  Succ  Fail   Succ  Fail   Out     Dial    Answer    Pct.
     * 1/0   17%    74    3      0     0      0       0       0         96%
     * 1/1   15%    80    4      0     0      0       1       1         95%
     * 1/2   15%    82    0      0     0      0       0       0         100%
       1/3   21%    62    1      0     0      0       0       0         98%
       1/4   21%    49    5      0     0      0       0       0         90%
     * 1/5   18%    65    3      0     0      0       0       0         95%
```

To see the aggregate numbers for all the modems on the router, use the **show modem summary** command.

```
router#show modem summary
            Incoming calls       Outgoing calls      Busied  Failed  No   Succ
   Usage  Succ  Fail  Avail   Succ   Fail  Avail    Out     Dial   Ans  Pct.
    0%    6297   185    64      0      0     0        0       0     0    97%
```

Table 16-3 provides descriptions of the various **show modem** fields.

Table 16-3   **show modem** *Fields*

Fields	Descriptions
Incoming and Outgoing Calls	Calls dialing into and out of the modem.
	• **Usage**—Percentage of the total system uptime that all the modems are in use
	• **Succ**—Total calls successfully connected
	• **Fail**—Total calls that did not successfully connect
	• **Avail**—Total modems available for use in the system
Busied Out	Total number of times that the modems were taken out of service with the **modem busy** command or the **modem shutdown** command
Failed Dial	Total number of attempts that the modems did not hang up or that there was no dial tone
No Ans	Total number of times that call ringing was detected, but the calls were not answered by a modem
Succ Pct.	Successful connection percentage of total available modems

show modem call-stats

The **show modem call-stats** command offers a view of past performance for the modems. This is useful in trend analysis and can help the administrator to identify possible problems.

```
compress  retrain lostCarr  rmtLink  trainup hostDrop wdogTimr inacTout
   Mdm    #   %    #   %    #   %    #   %    #   %    #   %    #   %    #   %
   Total  9        41       271      3277     7        2114     0        0
```

Table 16-4 provides descriptions of the most common **show modem** call-stats fields.

Table 16-4   **show modem call-stats** *Fields*

rmtLink	This shows that error correction was in effect and that the call was hung up by the client system attached to the remote modem.
hostDrop	This shows that the call was hung up by the IOS host system. Some common reasons include: idle timeout, a circuit clear from the telco, or a PPP LCP termreq from the client. The best way to tell the reason for the hang up is by using **show modem call-record terse** or AAA accounting.

The other disconnect reasons should add up to less than 10 percent of the total.

show modem connect-speeds

As a way for an access server's administrator to maintain a watch on the user community's connection speeds, the **show modem connect** command allows the admin to see how many people are getting each rate of speed. This is useful in trend analysis.

```
router>show modem connect 33600 0
  Mdm   26400   28000   28800   29333   30667   31200   32000   33333   33600 TotCnt
  Tot     614       0    1053       0       0    1682       0       0     822   6304

router>show modem connect 56000 0
  Mdm   48000   49333   50000   50666   52000   53333   54000   54666   56000 TotCnt
  Tot     178     308      68      97      86      16       0       0       0   6304
```

Expect to see a healthy distribution of V.34 speeds. There should be a peak at 26.4 if the T1s use channel associated signaling (CAS). For ISDN (PRI) T1s, the peak should be at 31.2. Also, look for a smattering of K56Flex, V.90 speeds. If there are no V.90 connections, there may be a network topology problem.

modem call-record terse (11.3AA/12.0T)

Rather than an exec command, this is a configuration command placed at the system level of the access server in question. When a user disconnects, a message similar to the following will be displayed:

```
*May 31 18:11:09.558: %CALLRECORD-3-MICA_TERSE_CALL_REC: DS0 slot/contr/chan=2/0/
18, slot/port=1/29, call_id=378, userid=cisco, ip=0.0.0.0, calling=5205554099,
called=4085553932, std=V.90, prot=LAP-M, comp=V.42bis both, init-rx/tx b-
rate=26400/41333, finl-rx/tx brate=28800/41333, rbs=0, d-pad=6.0   dB, retr=1, sq=4,
snr=29, rx/tx chars=93501/94046,
bad=5, rx/tx ec=1612/732, bad=0, time=337, finl-state=Steady, disc(radius)=Lost
Carrier/Lost Carrier, disc(modem)=A220 Rx (line to host) data flushing - not OK/EC
condition - locally detected/received
DISC frame -- normal LAPM termination
```

show modem operational-status

The exec command **show modem operational-status** shows the current (or last) parameters pertaining to the modem's connection.

The documentation entry for this command is found in the *Cisco IOS Release 12.0 Dial Solutions Command Reference*. **show modem operational-status** is only for MICA modems. The equivalent command for Microcom modems is **modem at-mode / AT@E1**. Use the **modem at-mode <slot>/<port>** command to connect to the modem, and issue the **AT@E1** command. Complete documentation for the **modem at-mode** command can be found in the *Cisco AS5300 Software Configuration Guide*, and documentation for the **AT@E1** command is in the *AT Command Set and Register Summary for Microcom Modem Modules Command Reference*.

Use these two steps to find out what modems a user is coming in on.

Step 1   Issue the command **show user** and look for the TTY that they are connected into.

Step 2   Use the command **show line** and look for the modem slot/port numbers.

Gathering Client-Side Performance Data

For trend analysis, it's very important to gather client-side performance data. Good information to get includes this:

- Client hardware model/firmware version (attainable with the command ATI3I7 on the client's modem).
- Client-reported disconnect reasons (use ATI6 or AT&V1).
- Other information available on the client end, including the PC's modemlog.txt and ppplog.txt. The PC won't generate these files unless configured to do so.

Analyze the Performance Data

When you have collected and understood the performance data for your modem system, it's time to look at any remaining patterns/components that may have room for improvement.

Problems with Particular Server Modems

Use **show modem** or **show modem call-stats**, and look for any modems with abnormally high rates of trainup failure or bad disconnect rates. If adjacent pairs of modems are having problems, the problem is likely a hung or dead DSP. Use **copy flash modem** to the affected HMM to recover. Make sure that the modems are running the latest version of portware.

Verify that all modems are correctly configured. To make sure that the modems are correctly configured, use the configuration command **modem autoconfigure type <mica/ microcom_server>** in the line configuration. To make sure that the modems are being autoconfigured whenever a call is hung up, use the exec command **debug confmodem**. In some cases, it may require a reverse Telnet to fix modems that are badly misconfigured.

Problems with Particular DS0s

Bad DS0s are rare but possible. To find out if one is present, use the command **show controller t1 call-counters**. Look for any DS0s with abnormally high TotalCalls and abnormally low TotalDuration. To target suspected DS0s, it is sometimes necessary to take out of service other DS0s with the configuration command **isdn service dsl, ds0 busyout** under the serial interface for the T1. The output from **show controller t1 call-counters** look like this:

```
TimeSlot    Type    TotalCalls    TotalDuration
    1       pri        873        1w6d
    2       pri        753        2w2d
    3       pri        4444       00:05:22
```

Obviously, time slot 3 is the suspect channel in this case.

A Few of the More Common Trends Seen by Cisco's TAC

The following are some of the more commonly seen problems. Each problem's telltale signs are listed.

1 Bad Circuit Paths

If . . .

— Long-distance calls have problems, but local ones do not (or vice versa)

— Calls at certain times of day have problems

— Calls from specific remote exchanges have problems

Then . . .

You might be getting bad circuit paths through the Public Switched Telephone Network.

2 Long distance doesn't work well or at all, but local calls work fine.

If . . .

Long distance calls are bad but local calls are good.

Then . . .

— Double-check to make sure that the digital line connects into a digital switch, not a channel bank

— Check with telcos to examine the circuit paths used for long distance

3 Some calling areas have problems

If . . .

Calls from specific geographical regions/exchanges tend to have problems

Then . . .

Learn the network topology from the telco. If multiple analog-to-digital conversions (caused by nonintegrated SLCs or analog switches) are used to serve an area, V.90/K56flex modem connects will be impossible, and V.34 may be somewhat degraded.

ISDN Operations

Integrated Services Digital Network (ISDN) refers to a set of digital services that is available to end users. ISDN involves the digitization of the telephone network so that voice, data, text, graphics, music, video, and other source material can be provided to end users from a single end-user terminal over existing telephone wiring. Proponents of ISDN imagine a worldwide network much like the present telephone network, but with digital transmission and a variety of new services.

ISDN is an effort to standardize subscriber services, user/network interfaces, and network and internetwork capabilities. Standardizing subscriber services attempts to ensure a level of international compatibility. Standardizing the user/network interface stimulates development and marketing of these interfaces by third-party manufacturers. Standardizing network and internetwork capabilities helps achieve the goal of worldwide connectivity by ensuring that ISDN networks easily communicate with one another.

ISDN applications include high-speed image applications (such as Group IV facsimile), additional telephone lines in homes to serve the telecommuting industry, high-speed file transfer, and videoconferencing. Voice, of course, will also be a popular application for ISDN.

Many carriers are beginning to offer ISDN under tariff. In North America, large local exchange carriers (LECs) are beginning to provide ISDN service as an alternative to the T1 connections (digital carrier facilities provided by telephone companies) that currently carry bulk wide-area telephone service (WATS) services.

ISDN Components

ISDN components include terminals, terminal adapters (TAs), network-termination devices, line-termination equipment, and exchange-termination equipment. ISDN terminals come in two types. Specialized ISDN terminals are referred to as terminal equipment type 1 (TE1). Non-ISDN terminals such as DTE that predate the ISDN standards are referred to as terminal equipment type 2 (TE2). TE1s connect to the ISDN network through a four-wire, twisted-pair digital link. TE2s connect to the ISDN network through a terminal adapter. The ISDN TA can be either a standalone device or a board inside the TE2. If the TE2 is implemented as a standalone device, it connects to the TA via a standard physical layer interface. Examples include EIA/TIA-232-C (formerly RS-232-C), V.24, and V.35.

Beyond the TE1 and TE2 devices, the next connection point in the ISDN network is the network termination type 1 (NT1) or network termination type 2 (NT2) device. These are network-termination devices that connect the four-wire subscriber wiring to the conventional two-wire local loop. In North America, the NT1 is a customer premises equipment (CPE) device. In most other parts of the world, the NT1 is part of the network provided by the carrier. The NT2 is a more complicated device, typically found in digital private branch exchanges (PBXs), that performs Layer 2 and 3 protocol functions and concentration services. An NT1/2 device also exists; it is a single device that combines the functions of an NT1 and an NT2.

A number of reference points are specified in ISDN. These reference points define logical interfaces between functional groupings such as TAs and NT1s. ISDN reference points include the following:

- **R**—The reference point between non-ISDN equipment and a TA.
- **S**—The reference point between user terminals and the NT2.
- **T**—The reference point between NT1 and NT2 devices.
- **U**—The reference point between NT1 devices and line-termination equipment in the carrier network. The U reference point is relevant only in North America, where the NT1 function is not provided by the carrier network U.

A sample ISDN configuration is shown in Example 16-1. This example shows three devices attached to an ISDN switch at the central office. Two of these devices are ISDN-compatible, so they can be attached through an S reference point to NT2 devices. The third device (a standard, non-ISDN telephone) attaches through the R reference point to a TA. Any of these devices could also attach to an NT1/2 device, which would replace both the NT1 and the NT2. And, although they are not shown, similar user stations are attached to the far-right ISDN switch.

Example 16-1 *A Sample ISDN Configuration*

```
2503B#show running-config
Building configuration...

Current configuration:
!
version 11.1
service timestamps debug datetime msec
service udp-small-servers
service tcp-small-servers
!
hostname 2503B
!
!
username 2503A password 7 0822455D0A16
ip subnet-zero
isdn switch-type basic-5ess
!
interface Ethernet0
 ip address 172.16.141.11 255.255.255.192
!
interface Serial0
 no ip address
```

Example 16-1 *A Sample ISDN Configuration (Continued)*

```
 shutdown
!
interface Serial1
 no ip address
 shutdown
!
interface BRI0
 description phone#5553754
 ip address 172.16.20.2 255.255.255.0
 encapsulation ppp
 dialer idle-timeout 300
 dialer map ip 172.16.20.1 name 2503A broadcast 5553759
 dialer-group 1
 ppp authentication chap
!
no ip classless
!
dialer-list 1 protocol ip permit
!
line con 0
line aux 0
line vty 0 4
!
end

2503B#
```

ISDN Services

The ISDN Basic Rate Interface (BRI) service offers two B channels and one D channel (2B+D). BRI B-channel service operates at 64 kbps and is meant to carry user data; BRI D-channel service operates at 16 kbps and is meant to carry control and signaling information, although it can support user data transmission under certain circumstances. The D-channel signaling protocol comprises Layers 1 through 3 of the OSI reference model. BRI also provides for framing control and other overhead, bringing its total bit rate to 192 kbps. The BRI physical layer specification is International Telecommunication Union–Telecommunications Standards Sector (ITU-T; formerly the Consultative Committee for International Telegraph and Telephone [CCITT]) I.430.

ISDN Primary Rate Interface (PRI) service offers 23 B channels and one D channel in North America and Japan, yielding a total bit rate of 1.544 Mbps (the PRI D channel runs at 64 kbps). ISDN PRI in Europe, Australia, and other parts of the world provides 30 B plus one 64-kbps D channel and a total interface rate of 2.048 Mbps. The PRI physical layer specification is ITU-T I.431.

Layer 1

ISDN physical layer (Layer 1) frame formats differ depending on whether the frame is outbound (from terminal to network) or inbound (from network to terminal). Both physical layer interfaces are shown in Figure 16-2.

Figure 16-2 *ISDN Physical Layer Frame Formats*

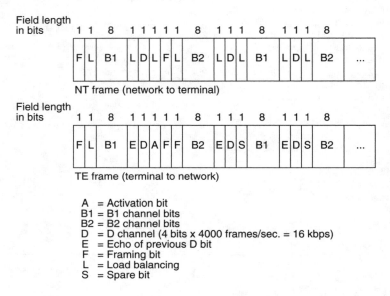

The frames are 48 bits long, of which 36 bits represent data. The bits of an ISDN physical layer frame are used as follows:

- **F**—Provides synchronization
- **L**—Adjusts the average bit value
- **E**—Is used for contention resolution when several terminals on a passive bus contend for a channel
- **A**—Activates devices
- **S**—Is unassigned
- **B1, B2, and D**—Is used for user data

Multiple ISDN user devices can be physically attached to one circuit. In this configuration, collisions can result if two terminals transmit simultaneously. ISDN, therefore, provides features to determine link contention. When an NT receives a D bit from the TE, it echoes back the bit in the next E-bit position. The TE expects the next E bit to be the same as its last transmitted D bit.

Terminals cannot transmit into the D channel unless they first detect a specific number of ones (indicating "no signal") corresponding to a pre-established priority. If the TE detects a bit in the echo channel that is different from its D bits, it must stop transmitting immediately. This simple technique ensures that only one terminal can transmit its D message at one time. After successful D message transmission, the terminal has its priority reduced by being required to detect more continuous ones before transmitting. Terminals cannot raise their priority until all other devices on the same line have had an opportunity to send a D message. Telephone connections have higher priority than all other services, and signaling information has a higher priority than nonsignaling information.

Layer 2

Layer 2 of the ISDN signaling protocol is Link Access Procedure on the D channel, also known as LAPD. LAPD is similar to High-Level Data Link Control (HDLC) and Link Access Procedure, Balanced (LAPB). As the expansion of the LAPD abbreviation indicates, it is used across the D channel to ensure that control and signaling information flows and is received properly. The LAPD frame format (see Figure 16-3) is very similar to that of HDLC; like HDLC, LAPD uses supervisory, information, and unnumbered frames. The LAPD protocol is formally specified in ITU-T Q.920 and ITU-T Q.921.

Figure 16-3 *LAPD Frame Format*

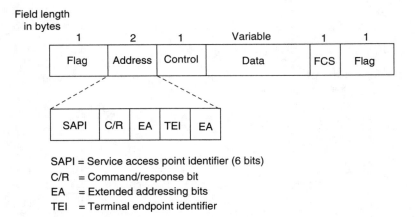

SAPI = Service access point identifier (6 bits)
C/R = Command/response bit
EA   = Extended addressing bits
TEI = Terminal endpoint identifier

The LAPD Flag and Control fields are identical to those of HDLC. The LAPD Address field can be either 1 or 2 bytes long. If the extended address bit of the first byte is set, the address is 1 byte; if it is not set, the address is 2 bytes. The first Address field byte contains the service access point identifier (SAPI), which identifies the portal at which LAPD services are provided to Layer 3. The C/R bit indicates whether the frame contains a command or a response. The Terminal Endpoint Identifier (TEI) field identifies either a single terminal or multiple terminals. A TEI of all ones indicates a broadcast.

Layer 3

Two Layer 3 specifications are used for ISDN signaling: ITU-T (formerly CCITT) I.450 (also known as ITU-T Q.930) and ITU-T I.451 (also known as ITU-T Q.931). Together, these protocols support user-to-user, circuit-switched, and packet-switched connections. A variety of call establishment, call termination, information, and miscellaneous messages are specified, including SETUP, CONNECT, RELEASE, USER INFORMATION, CANCEL, STATUS, and DISCONNECT. These messages are functionally similar to those provided by the X.25 protocol (see Chapter 19, "Troubleshooting X.25 Connections," for more information). Figure 16-4, from ITU-T I.451, shows the typical stages of an ISDN circuit-switched call.

Figure 16-4 *ISDN Circuit-Switched Call Stages*

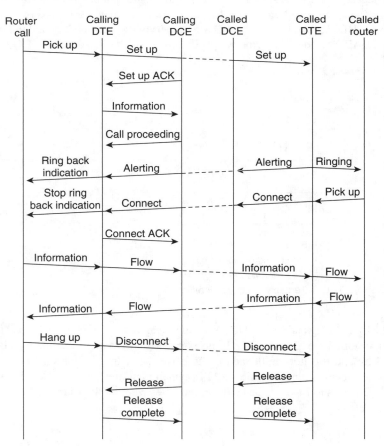

Interpreting show isdn status Output

To find out what the current condition of the ISDN connection is between the router and the telco switch, use the command **show isdn status**. The two kinds of interfaces that are supported by this command are the Basic Rate Interface (BRI) and the Primary Rate Interface (PRI) (Tables 16-5 and 16-6).

```
3620-2#show isdn status
Global ISDN Switchtype = basic-ni
ISDN BRI0/0 interface
        dsl 0, interface ISDN Switchtype = basic-ni
    Layer 1 Status:
        ACTIVE
    Layer 2 Status:
        TEI = 88, Ces = 1, SAPI = 0, State = MULTIPLE_FRAME_ESTABLISHED
        TEI = 97, Ces = 2, SAPI = 0, State = MULTIPLE_FRAME_ESTABLISHED
    Spid Status:
        TEI 88, ces = 1, state = 5(init)
            spid1 configured, no LDN, spid1 sent, spid1 valid
            Endpoint ID Info: epsf = 0, usid = 0, tid = 1
        TEI 97, ces = 2, state = 5(init)
            spid2 configured, no LDN, spid2 sent, spid2 valid
            Endpoint ID Info: epsf = 0, usid = 1, tid = 1
    Layer 3 Status:
        0 Active Layer 3 Call(s)
    Activated dsl 0 CCBs = 0
    The Free Channel Mask:  0x80000003
```

Table 16-5 show isdn status *for BRI*

Field	Significance
Layer 1 Status: DEACTIVATED	This indicates that the BRI interface is not seeing a signal on the line. There are five possibilities. • The BRI interface is shut down. Either check the configuration for the command **shutdown** under the BRI interface, or look for an administratively down indication from the **show interface** command. Use the configuration utility, and enter **no shutdown** under the BRI interface. Type the command **clear interface bri** at the exec prompt to make sure that the BRI interface is restarted. • Cabling is bad. Make sure that you use a straight-through RJ-45 cable. To check the cable, hold the RJ-45 cable ends side by side. If the pins are in the same order, the cable is straight-through. If the order of the pins is reversed, the cable is rolled. Verify that the correct cable is in place and is working.

continues

Table 16-5 show isdn status *for BRI (Continued)*

Field	Significance
Layer 1 Status: DEACTIVATED (continued)	• The ISDN BRI port of a router might require an NT1 device. In ISDN, NT1 is a device that provides the interface between the customer premises equipment and central office switching equipment. If the router does not have an internal NT1, obtain and connect an NT1 to the BRI port. Make sure that the BRI or terminal adapter is attached to the S/T port of the NT1. Refer to the manufacturer's documentation to verify correct operation of the external NT1.
	• The line might not be functioning. Contact the carrier to confirm operation of the connection and to verify the switch type settings.
	• Make sure that the router is functioning correctly. If there is faulty or malfunctioning hardware, replace as necessary.
Layer 2 Status: State = TEI_ASSIGNED	Check the switchtype setting and SPIDS. The Interface Specific ISDN switch setting will override the Global switch setting. The SPID status will indicate whether the switch accepted the SPIDS with Valid or Invalid.
	Contact your service provider to verify the setting configured on the router.
	To change the SPID settings, use the **isdn spid***n* interface configuration command, where *n* is either 1 or 2, depending on the channel in question. Use the **no** form of this command to remove the specified SPID.
	`isdn spidn spid-number [ldn]` `no isdn spidn spid-number [ldn]`
	Syntax description:
	• spid-number—Number identifying the service to which you have subscribed. This value is assigned by the ISDN service provider and is usually a 10-digit telephone number with additional digits.
	• ldn—(Optional) Local directory number (LDN), which is a seven-digit number assigned by the service provider. The switch in the incoming setup message delivers this information. If you do not include the local directory, access to the switch is permitted, but the other B channels may not be capable of receiving incoming calls.
	To see the Layer 2 negotiations between the switch and the router, use the privileged exec command **debug isdn q921**. The **q921** debugs are documented in the *Debug Command Reference*. **debug** commands rely heavily on CPU resources, so caution should be used when employing them.

```
5200-1# show isdn status
Global ISDN Switchtype = primary-5ess
ISDN Serial0:23 interface
        dsl 0, interface ISDN Switchtype = primary-5ess
    Layer 1 Status:
        ACTIVE
    Layer 2 Status:
        TEI = 0, Ces = 1, SAPI = 0, State = MULTIPLE_FRAME_ESTABLISHED
    Layer 3 Status:
        0 Active Layer 3 Call(s)
    Activated dsl 0 CCBs = 0
    The Free Channel Mask:  0x807FFFFF
    Total Allocated ISDN CCBs = 0
5200-1#
```

If the **show isdn status** command does not work or does not show the PRI, try using the **show isdn service** command. Make sure that the **pri-group** command appears in the configuration under the T1/E1 controller in the configuration. If the command is not present, configure the controller with the **pri-group** command.

Following is an example of a configuration for a Cisco router with a channelized T1 card:

```
controller t1 0
framing esf
line code b8zs
pri-group timeslots 1-24
```

Table 16-6 details the fields for the **show isdn status** command.

Table 16-6   **show isdn status** *for PRI*

Field	Significance
Layer 1 Status: DEACTIVATED	This indicates that the PRI interface is not seeing T1/E1 framing on the line. There are several possibilities.
	• The PRI interface is shut down. Either check the configuration for the command **shutdown** under the serial0:23 interface, or look for an administratively down indication from the **show interface** command. Use the configuration utility and enter **no shutdown** under the interface in question. Type the command **clear controller T1/E1** *n* at the exec prompt to make sure that the PRI interface is restarted.
	• Cabling is bad. Make sure that you use a straight-through RJ-45 cable. To check the cable, hold the RJ-45 cable ends side by side. If the pins are in the same order, the cable is straight-through. If the order of the pins is reversed, the cable is rolled. Verify that the correct cable is in place and is working.
	• The line might not be functioning. Contact the carrier to confirm operation of the connection and to verify the switch type settings.
	• Make sure that the router is functioning correctly. If there is faulty or malfunctioning hardware, replace as necessary.

continues

Table 16-6   **show isdn status** *for PRI (Continued)*

Field	Significance
Layer 2 Status: State = TEI_ASSIGNED	Check the switchtype setting and check. The Interface Specific ISDN switch setting will override the Global switch setting. Verify that the T1/E1 is configured to match the provider's switch. (T1/E1 problems are discussed in Chapter 15.)
	To see the Layer 2 negotiations between the switch and the router, use the privileged exec command **debug isdn q921**. The **q921** debugs are documented in the *Debug Command Reference*. **debug** commands rely heavily on CPU resources, so caution should be used when employing them.
Number of Calls/Call Control Blocks in Use/ Total Allocated ISDN Call Control Blocks	These numbers indicate how many calls are in progress, and the number of resources that are allocated to support those calls. If the number of allocated CCBs is higher than the number of CCBs being used, it could indicate a problem in releasing CCBs. Make sure that there are available CCBs for incoming calls.

Dial-on-Demand Routing: Dialer Interface Operations

Dial-on-demand routing (DDR) is a method of providing WAN connectivity on an economical as-needed basis, either as a primary link or as backup for a nondial serial link.

A *dialer interface* is defined as any router interface capable of placing or receiving a call. This generic term should be distinguished from the term *Dialer interface* (with a capital D), which refers to a logical interface configured to control one or more physical interfaces of a router and which is seen in a router configuration as interface Dialer X. From this point forward, unless otherwise stated, we will be using the term *dialer* in its generic sense.

Dialer interface configuration comes in two flavors: dialer map-based (sometimes referred to as legacy DDR) and dialer profiles. Which method you use depends on the circumstances under which you need dial connectivity. Dialer map-based DDR was first introduced in IOS version 9.0, and dialer profiles were introduced in IOS version 11.2.

Triggering a Dial

At its heart, DDR is just an extension of routing wherein *interesting packets* are routed to a dialer interface, triggering a dial attempt. We will attempt here to explain the concepts involved in defining interesting traffic, and to explain the routing used for DDR connections.

Interesting Packets

Interesting is the term used to describe packets or traffic that either will trigger a dial attempt or, if a dial link is already active, will reset the idle timer on the dialer interface. For a packet to be considered interesting, it must have these characteristics:

- The packet must meet the "permit" criteria defined by an access list.
- The access list must be referenced by a dialer list, or the packet must be of a protocol which is universally permitted by the **dialer-list** command.
- The dialer list must be associated with a dialer interface by use of a **dialer-group** command.

By default, no packets are considered to be interesting. Interesting packet definitions must be explicitly declared in a router or access server configuration.

Dialer Group

In the configuration of each dialer interface on the router or access server, there must be a **dialer-group** command. If the **dialer-group** command is not present, there is no logical link between the interesting packet definitions and the interface. The command syntax is as follows:

```
dialer-group [group number]
```

The **group-number** is the number of the dialer access group to which the specific interface belongs. This access group is defined with the **dialer-list** command. Acceptable values are nonzero, positive integers between 1 and 10.

An interface can be associated with a single dialer access group only; multiple dialer-group assignment is not allowed. A second dialer access group assignment will override the first. A dialer access group is defined with the **dialer-group** command. The **dialer-list** command associates an access list with a dialer access group.

Packets that match the dialer group specified trigger a connection request.

The destination address of the packet is evaluated against the access list specified in the associated **dialer-list** command. If it passes, either a call is initiated (if no connection has already been established) or the idle timer is reset (if a call is currently connected).

Dialer List

The **dialer-list** global configuration command is used to define a DDR diaier list to control dialing by protocol, or by a combination of protocol and access list. Interesting packets are those that match the protocol level **permit** or which are permitted by the **list** in the **dialer-list** command:

```
dialer-list dialer-group protocol protocol-name {permit | deny | list access-list-
number | access-group}
```

- dialer-group is the number of a dialer access group identified in any **dialer-group** interface configuration command.

- protocol-name is one of the following protocol keywords: appletalk, bridge, clns, clns_es, clns_is, decnet, decnet_router-L1, decnet_router-L2, decnet_node, ip, ipx, vines, or xns.

- permit permits access to an entire protocol.

- deny denies access to an entire protocol.

- list specifies that an access list will be used for defining a granularity finer than an entire protocol.

- access-list-number specifies the number of the access list the dialer-list is using to decide what is interesting traffic. Access list numbers can be specified for any standard or extended access lists, including DECnet, Banyan VINES, IP, Novell IPX, XNS, and bridging types. See Table 16-7 for the supported access list types and numbers.

- access-group filters list name used in the **clns filter-set** and **clns access-group** commands.

Table 16-7 *Access List Numbering by Protocol*

Access List Type	Access List Number Range (Decimal)
AppleTalk	600 to 699
Banyan VINES (standard)	1 to 100
Banyan VINES (extended)	101 to 200
DECnet	300 to 399
IP (standard)	1 to 99
IP (extended)	100 to 199
Novell IPX (standard)	800 to 899
Novell IPX (extended)	900 to 999
Transparent Bridging	200 to 299
XNS	500 to 599

Access List

For each networking protocol that is to be sent across the dial connection, an *access list* may be configured. For purposes of cost control, it is usually desirable to configure an access list to prevent certain traffic—such as routing updates—from bringing up or keeping up a connection. Note that when we create access lists for the purpose of defining interesting and uninteresting traffic, we are not declaring that uninteresting packets cannot cross the dial link—only that they will not reset the idle timer, nor will they bring up a connection on their own. As long as the dial connection is up, uninteresting packets will still be allowed to flow across the link.

For example, a router running EIGRP as its routing protocol can have an access list configured to declare EIGRP packets uninteresting and all other IP traffic interesting:

```
access-list 101 deny eigrp any any
access-list 101 permit ip any any
```

Access lists can be configured for all protocols that might cross the dial link. Remember that for any protocol, the default behavior in the absence of an access list permit statement is to deny all traffic. If there is no access list and if there is no **dialer-list** command permitting the protocol, then that protocol will be uninteresting. In actual practice, if there is no dialer list for a protocol, those packets will not flow across the link at all.

Example: Putting It All Together

With all the elements in place, it is possible to examine the complete process by which the "interesting" status of a packet is determined. In this example, IP and IPX are the protocols that may cross the dial link, but the user wants to prevent broadcasts and routing updates from initiating a call or keeping the link up.

```
!
interface async 1
 dialer-group 7
!
access-list 121 deny eigrp any any
access-list 121 deny ip any host 255.255.255.255
access-list 121 permit ip any any
access-list 903 deny -1 FFFFFFFF 0 FFFFFFFF 452
access-list 903 deny -1 FFFFFFFF 0 FFFFFFFF 453
access-list 903 deny -1 FFFFFFFF 0 FFFFFFFF 457
access-list 903 permit -1
!
dialer-list 7 protocol ip list 121
dialer-list 7 protocol ipx list 903
!
```

If a packet to be considered *interesting* when sent across interface async 1, it must first be permitted by the **access-list 121** statements. In this case, EIGRP packets are denied, as are any other broadcast packets, while all other IP traffic is permitted. Remember that this does not prevent EIGRP packets from transiting the link—only that they will not reset the idle timer or initiate a dial attempt.

Similarly, **access-list 903** declares IPX RIP, SAPs, and GNS requests to be uninteresting, while all other IPX traffic is interesting. Without these **deny** statements, the dial connection would likely never come down and a very large phone bill would result because packets of these types constantly flow across an IPX network.

With **dialer-group 7** configured on the async interface, we know that **dialer-list 7** is needed to tie the interesting traffic filters (that is, access lists) to the interface. One **dialer-list** statement is required (and *only* one can be configured) for each protocol, making sure that the dialer list number is the same as the dialer group number on the interface.

Again, it is important to remember that **deny** statements in the access lists configured for defining interesting traffic will *not* prevent the denied packets from crossing the link.

Using the command **debug dialer**, you can see the activity that triggers a dial attempt:

```
Dialing cause: Async1: ip (s=172.16.1.111 d=172.16.2.22)
```

Here we see that IP traffic with a source address of 172.16.1.111 and a destination address of 172.16.2.22 has triggered a dial attempt on interface Async1.

Routing

Now that interesting packets have been defined, they must be routed properly for a call to be initiated. The routing process depends on two things: routing table entries, and an "up" interface to which to route packets.

Interfaces—up/up (Spoofing)

For packets to be routed to and through and interface, that interface must be up/up, as seen in a **show interfaces** output:

```
Montecito# show interfaces ethernet 0
Ethernet0 is up, line protocol is up
  Hardware is Lance, address is . . .
```

What about a dialer interface that is not connected? If the protocol is not up and running on the interface, the implication is that the interface itself will not be up; routes that rely on that interface will be flushed from the routing table, and traffic will not be routed to that interface. The result would be that no calls would be initiated by the interface.

To counter this possibility, any interface that is configured as a dialer interface (for example, a Serial or Async interface with the command **dialer in-band** or **dialer dtr**) or that, by its nature, is a dialer interface (BRIs and PRIs), will be in a state of up/up (spoofing):

```
Montecito# show interfaces bri 0
BRI0 is up, line protocol is up (spoofing)
  Hardware is BRI
  Internet address is . . .
```

In other words, the interface pretends to be up/up so that associated routes will remain in force and so that packets can be routed to the interface.

In some circumstances, a dialer interface will not be up/up (spoofing). The **show interface** output may show it as being administratively down:

```
Montecito# show interfaces bri 0
BRI0 is administratively down, line protocol is down
  Hardware is BRI
  Internet address is . . .
```

Administratively down merely means that the interface has been configured with the command **shutdown**. This is the default state of any router interface when the router is booted for the very first time. To remedy this, use the interface configuration command **no shutdown**.

The interface may also be seen to be in standby mode:

```
Montecito# show interfaces bri 0
BRI0 is standby mode, line protocol is down
  Hardware is BRI
  Internet address is . . .
```

This state indicates that the interface has been configured as the backup for another interface. When a connection requires redundancy in case of failure, a dialer interface can be set up as the backup. This is accomplished by adding the following commands to the primary connection's interface:

```
backup interface [interface]
backup delay [enable-delay] [disable-delay]
```

After the **backup interface** command has been configured, the interface used as the backup will be put into standby mode until the primary interface goes to a state of **down/down.** At that time, the dialer interface configured as a backup will go to a state of up/up (spoofing) pending a dial event.

Static Routes and Floating Static Routes

The surest way to route packets to a dialer interface is with static routing. These routes are manually entered into the configuration of the router or access server with this command:

```
ip route prefix mask {address | interface} [distance]
```

- prefix—IP route prefix for the destination.
- mask—Prefix mask for the destination.
- address—IP address of the next hop that can be used to reach the destination network.
- interface—Network interface to use for outbound traffic.
- distance—(Optional) An administrative distance. This argument is used in *floating static routes.*

Static routes are used in situations in which the dial link is the only connection to the remote site. A static route has an administrative distance value of 1, which makes it preferred over dynamic routes to the same destination.

On the other hand, floating static routes—that is, static routes with a predefined administrative distance—are typically used in backup DDR scenarios, in which a dynamic routing protocol such as RIP or EIGRP is used to route packets across the primary link. If a normal static route were to be used, its administrative distance of 1 would make it preferable to either EIGRP (75) or RIP (120), causing packets to be routed across the dial line even if the primary were up and capable of passing traffic. However, if the static route is configured with an administrative distance higher than that of any of the dynamic routing protocols in use on the router, the floating static route will be used only in the absence of a better route—one with a lower administrative distance.

If backup DDR is being invoked by use of the **backup interface** command, the situation is somewhat different. Because the dialer interface remains in standby mode while the primary is up, either a static route or a floating static route may be configured, and the dialer interface will not attempt to connect until after the primary interface goes down/down.

For a given connection, the number of static (or floating static) routes necessary is a function of the addressing on the dialer interfaces. In cases in which the two dialer interfaces (one on each of the two routers) share a common network or subnet, typically only one static route is required, pointing to the remote local-area network using the address of the remote router's dialer interface as the next-hop address.

Examples

Example 1:

Dial is the only connection, with numbered interfaces, as shown in Figure 16-5. One route is sufficient.

Figure 16-5 *Dial Using Numbered Interfaces*

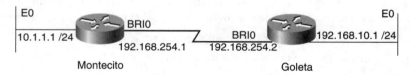

Montecito:

```
ip route 192.168.10.0 255.255.255.0 172.16.20.2
Goleta:
ip route 10.1.1.0 255.255.255.0 172.16.20.1
```

Example 2:

Dial is the only connection, with unnumbered interfaces, as shown in Figure 16-6. This can be configured with just one route, but it is common to configure two routes: a host route to the LAN interface on the remote router, and a route to the remote LAN via the remote LAN interface. This is done to prevent mapping problems from Layer 3 to Layer 2, which can result in encapsulation failures.

This method is also used if the dialer interfaces on the two devices are numbered, but not in the same network or subnet.

Figure 16-6 *Dial Using Unnumbered Interfaces*

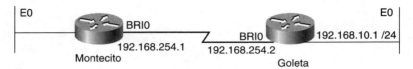

Montecito:

```
ip route 192.168.10.0 255.255.255.0 192.168.10.1
ip route 192.168.10.1 255.255.255.255 BRI0
```

Goleta:

```
ip route 10.1.1.0 255.255.255.0 10.1.1.1
ip route 10.1.1.1 255.255.255.255 BRI0
```

Example 3:

Dial is a backup connection, using numbered interfaces, as shown in Figure 16-7. One floating static route is required.

Figure 16-7 *Backup Using Numbered Interfaces*

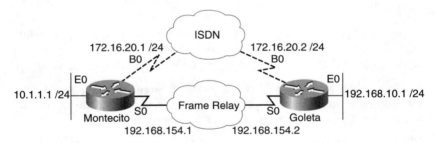

Montecito:

```
ip route 192.168.10.0 255.255.255.0 172.16.20.2 200
```

Goleta:

```
ip route 10.1.1.0 255.255.255.0 172.16.20.1 200
```

Example 4:

Dial is a backup connection using unnumbered interfaces, as shown in Figure 16-8. As in Example 2, this method is also used if the dialer interfaces on the two devices are numbered, but not in the same network or subnet.

Figure 16-8 *Backup Using Unnumbered Interfaces*

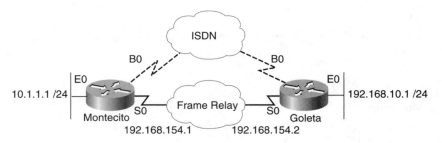

Montecito:

```
ip route 192.168.10.0 255.255.255.0 192.168.10.1 200
ip route 192.168.10.1 255.255.255.255 BRI0 200
```

Goleta:

```
ip route 10.1.1.0 255.255.255.0 10.1.1.1 200
ip route 10.1.1.1 255.255.255.255 BRI0 200
```

Dialer Maps

Dialer map-based (or legacy) DDR is powerful and comprehensive, but its limitations affect scaling and extensibility. Dialer map-based DDR is based on a static binding between the per-destination call specification and the physical interface configuration.

However, dialer map-based DDR also has many strengths. It supports Frame Relay, ISO CLNS, LAPB, snapshot routing, and all routed protocols that are supported on Cisco routers. By default, dialer map-based DDR supports fast switching.

When configuring an interface for outbound calling, one dialer map must be configured for each remote destination and for each different called number at the remote destination. For instance, if a multilink PPP connection is the goal when dialing from an ISDN BRI into another ISDN BRI interface that has a different local directory number for each of its B channels, one dialer map is needed for each of the remote numbers:

```
!
interface bri 0
 dialer map ip 172.16.20.1 name Montecito broadcast 5551234
 dialer map ip 172.16.20.1 name Montecito broadcast 5554321
!
```

The order in which dialer maps are configured can be important. If two or more dialer map commands refer to the same remote address, the router or access server will try them one after another, *in order,* until a successful connection is established.

NOTE	IOS can dynamically build dialer maps on a router receiving a call. The dialer map is built based on the authenticated username and the negotiated IP address of the caller. Dynamic dialer maps can be seen only in the output of the command **show dialer map**, and will not appear in the running configuration of the router or access server.

Command Syntax

To configure a serial interface or an ISDN interface to call one or multiple sites, or to receive calls from multiple sites, use a form of the **dialer map** interface configuration command; all options are shown in the first form of the command. Table 16-8 lists the dialer map syntax descriptions. To delete a particular dialer map entry, use a **no** form of this command:

```
dialer map protocol next-hop-address [name hostname] [spc] [speed 56 ¦ 64]
[broadcast] [modem-script modem-regexp] [system-script system-regexp] [dial-
string[:isdn-subaddress]]
```

To configure a serial interface or ISDN interface to place a call to multiple sites and to authenticate calls from multiple sites, use the second form of the **dialer map** command:

```
dialer map protocol next-hop-address [name hostname] [spc] [speed 56 ¦ 64]
[broadcast] [dial-string[:isdn-subaddress]]
```

To configure a serial interface or ISDN interface to support bridging, use the third form of the command:

```
dialer map bridge [name hostname] [spc] [broadcast] [dial-string[:isdn-subaddress]]
```

To configure an asynchronous interface to place a call to a single site that requires a system script or that has no assigned modem script, or to multiple sites on a single line, on multiple lines, or on a dialer rotary group, use the fourth form of the **dialer map** command:

```
dialer map protocol next-hop-address [name hostname] [broadcast] [modem-script
modem-regexp] [system-script system-regexp] [dial-string]
```

Table 16-8   *Syntax Description*

protocol	Consists of protocol keywords; one of the following: **appletalk**, **bridge**, **clns**, **decnet**, **ip**, **ipx**, **novell**, **snapshot**, **vines**, and **xns**.
next-hop-address	Gives the protocol address used to match against addresses to which packets are destined. This argument is not used with the **bridge** protocol keyword.
name	(Optional) Indicates the remote system with which the local router or access server communicates. Used for authenticating the remote system on incoming calls.

continues

Table 16-8 *Syntax Description (Continued)*

hostname	(Optional) Gives the case-sensitive name or ID of the remote device (usually the host name). For routers with ISDN interfaces, if calling line identification—sometimes called *CLI*, but also known as *caller ID* and *automatic number identification* (ANI)—is provided, *hostname* can contain the number that the calling line ID provides.
spc	(Optional) Specifies a semipermanent connection between customer equipment and the exchange; used only in Germany for circuits between an ISDN BRI and a 1TR6 ISDN switch, and in Australia for circuits between an ISDN PRI and a TS-014 switch.
speed 56 | 64	(Optional) Specifies a keyword and value indicating the line speed in kilobits per second to use. Used for ISDN only. The default speed is 64 kbps.
broadcast	(Optional) Indicates that broadcasts should be forwarded to this protocol address.
modem-script	(Optional) Indicates the modem script to be used for the connection (for asynchronous interfaces).
modem-regexp	(Optional) Is a regular expression to which a modem script will be matched (for asynchronous interfaces).
system-script	(Optional) Indicates the system script to be used for the connection (for asynchronous interfaces).
system-regexp	(Optional) Is a regular expression to which a system script will be matched (for asynchronous interfaces).
dial-string:isdn-subaddress	(Optional) Is a telephone number sent to the dialing device when it recognizes packets with the specified next-hop address that matches the access lists defined, and the optional subaddress number used for ISDN multipoint connections. The dial string and ISDN subaddress, if used, must be the last item in the command line.

Dialer Profiles

NOTE Unlike the previous sections, in this section the term *dialer interface* refers to the configured interface, not to a physical interface on the router or access server.

The dialer profiles implementation of DDR, introduced in IOS version 11.2, is based on a separation between logical and physical interface configuration. Dialer profiles also enable the logical and physical configurations to be bound together dynamically on a per-call basis.

The dialer profiles methodology is advantageous when you want to share an interface (ISDN, asynchronous, or synchronous serial) to place or receive calls, when you want to change any configuration on a per-user basis (except encapsulation in the first phase of dialer profiles), when you want to bridge to many destinations, and for avoiding split horizon problems.

Dialer profiles allow the configuration of physical interfaces to be separated from the logical configuration required for a call, and they also allow the logical and physical configurations to be bound together dynamically on a per-call basis.

A *dialer profile* consists of the following elements:

- A *dialer interface* (a logical entity) configuration including one or more dial strings (each of which is used to reach one destination subnetwork)
- A *dialer map class* that defines all the characteristics for any call to the specified dial string
- An ordered *dialer pool* of physical interfaces to be used by the dialer interface

All calls going to or from the same destination subnetwork use the same dialer profile.

A dialer interface configuration includes all settings needed to reach a specific destination subnetwork (and any networks reached through it). Multiple dial strings can be specified for the same dialer interface, each dial string being associated with a different dialer map-class. The dialer map class defines all the characteristics for any call to the specified dial string. For example, the map class for one destination might specify a 56-kbps ISDN speed; the map class for a different destination might specify a 64-kbps ISDN speed.

Each dialer interface uses a dialer pool, a pool of physical interfaces ordered on the basis of the priority assigned to each physical interface. A physical interface can belong to multiple dialer pools, with contention being resolved by priority. ISDN BRI and PRI interfaces can set a limit on the minimum and maximum number of B channels reserved by any dialer pools. A channel reserved by a dialer pool remains idle until traffic is directed to the pool.

When dialer profiles are used to configure DDR, a physical interface has no configuration settings except encapsulation and the dialer pools to which the interface belongs.

NOTE   The preceding paragraph has one exception: Commands that apply before authentication is complete must be configured on the physical (or BRI or PRI) interface, not on the dialer profile. Dialer profiles do not copy PPP authentication commands (or LCP commands) to the physical interface.

Figure 16-9 shows a typical application of dialer profiles. Router A has dialer interface 1 for dial-on-demand routing with subnetwork 1.1.1.0, and dialer interface 2 for dial-on-demand routing with subnetwork 2.2.2.0. The IP address for dialer interface 1 is its address as a node in network 1.1.1.0; at the same time, that IP address serves as the IP address of the physical interfaces used by the dialer interface 1. Similarly, the IP address for dialer interface 2 is its address as a node in network 2.2.2.0.

Figure 16-9 *Typical Dialer Profiles Application*

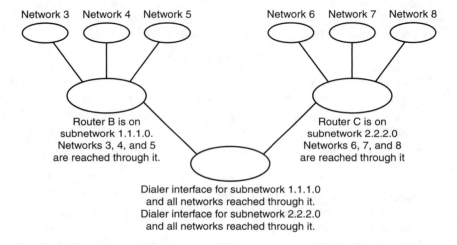

A dialer interface uses only one dialer pool. A physical interface, however, can be a member of one or many dialer pools, and a dialer pool can have several physical interfaces as members.

Figure 16-10 illustrates the relationships among the concepts of dialer interface, dialer pool, and physical interfaces. Dialer interface 0 uses dialer pool 2. Physical interface BRI 1 belongs to dialer pool 2 and has a specific priority in the pool. Physical interface BRI 2 also belongs to dialer pool 2. Because contention is resolved on the basis of priority levels of the physical interfaces in the pool, BRI 1 and BRI 2 must be assigned different priorities in the pool. Perhaps BRI 1 is assigned priority 100, and BRI 2 is assigned priority 50 in dialer pool 2 (a priority of 50 is higher than a priority of 100). BRI 2 has a higher priority in the pool, and its calls will be placed first.

Figure 16-10 *Relationships Among Dialer Interfaces, Dialer Pools, and Physical Interfaces*

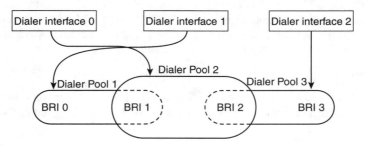

Dialer profile configuration steps:

Step	Purpose	Command
1	Create a dialer interface	**interface dialer number**
2	Specify the IP address and mask of the dialer interface as a node in the destination network to be called	**ip address** *address mask*
3	Specify PPP encapsulation	**encapsulation ppp**
4	Specify the remote router CHAP authentication name	**dialer remote-name** *username*
5	Specify the remote destination to call and the map class that defines characteristics for calls to this destination	**dialer string** *dial-string* **class** *class-name*
6	Specify the dialing pool to use for calls to this destination	**dialer pool** *number*
7	Assign the dialer interface to a dialer group	**dialer-group** *group-number*
8	Specify an access list by list number or by protocol and list number to define the "interesting" packets that can trigger a call	**dialer-list** *dialer-group* **protocol** *protocol-name* {**permit** | **deny** | **list** *access-list-number*}

PPP Operations

The Point-to-Point Protocol (PPP) is by far the most common link-layer transport protocol, having completely usurped SLIP as the protocol of choice for dial (and, in many cases, nondial) synchronous and asynchronous serial connections. PPP was originally defined in

1989 by Request For Comments 1134 (RFC 1134), which has since been made obsolete by a series of RFCs culminating (as of this writing) in RFC 1661. Numerous RFCs also define elements of the protocol, such as RFC 1990 ("The PPP Multilink Protocol"), RFC 2125 ("The PPP Bandwidth Allocation Protocol"), and many others. An online repository of RFCs can be found at ftp://ftp.cisco.com/pub/rfc/RFC/.

Perhaps the best definition of just what PPP is can be found in RFC 1661, which states:

- The Point-to-Point Protocol (PPP) provides a standard method for transporting multiprotocol datagrams over point-to-point links. PPP is comprised of three main components:

    1 A method for encapsulating multiprotocol datagrams

    2 A Link Control Protocol (LCP) for establishing, configuring, and testing the data-link connection

    3 A family of Network Control Protocols (NCPs) for establishing and configuring different network layer protocols

Phases of PPP Negotiation

PPP negotiation consists of three phases: Link Control Protocol (LCP), authentication, and Network Control Protocol (NCP). Each proceeds in order following the establishment of the async or ISDN connection.

Link Control Protocol

PPP does not follow a client/server model—all connections are peer-to-peer so that, although there is a caller and a receiver, both ends of the point-to-point connection must agree on the negotiated protocols and parameters.

When negotiation begins, each of the peers that want to establish a PPP connection must send a configure request (seen in **debug ppp negotiation** and referred to hereafter as CONFREQ). Included in the CONFREQ are any options that are not the link default; these often include Maximum Receive Unit, Async Control Character Map, Authentication Protocol, and the Magic Number. Also seen often are the options that deal with multilink PPP.

There are three possible responses to any CONFREQ:

- A configure-acknowledge (CONFACK) must be issued if the peer recognizes the options and agrees to the values seen in the CONFREQ.

- A configure-reject (CONFREJ) must be sent if any of the options in the CONFREQ are not recognized (for instance, some vendor-specific options), or if the values for any of the options have been explicitly disallowed in the configuration of the peer.

- A configure-negative-acknowledge (CONFNAK) must be sent if all the options in the CONFREQ are recognized, but any of the values are not acceptable to the peer.

The two peers will continue to exchange CONFREQs, CONFREJs, and CONFNAKs until each sends a CONFACK, until the dial connection is broken, or until one or both of the peers deems the negotiation to be not completable.

Authentication

With LCP negotiation successfully completed, and an AUTHTYPE agreed upon, the next step is authentication. Authentication, while not mandatory per RFC 1661, is *highly* recommended on all dial connections; in some instances, it is a requirement for proper operation, with dialer profiles being a case in point.

The two principal types of authentication in PPP are the Password Authentication Protocol (PAP) and the Challenge Handshake Authentication Protocol (CHAP), defined by RFC 1334 and updated by RFC 1994. PAP is the simpler of the two, but it is less secure because the plain-text password is sent across the dial connection. CHAP, on the other hand, is more secure because the plain-text password is not ever sent across the dial connection.

This leads to a good question: Why should PAP ever be used? Two reasons frequently seen by Cisco TAC engineers are these:

- The existence of large installed bases of client applications that do not support CHAP
- Incompatibilities between different vendor implementations of CHAP

When discussing authentication, it is helpful to use the terms *requester* and *authenticator* to distinguish the roles played by the devices at either end of the connection, although either peer can act in either role. *Requester* describes the device that requests network access and supplies authentication information; the *authenticator* verifies the validity of the authentication information and either allows or disallows the connection. It is common for both peers to act in both roles when a DDR connection is being made between routers.

PAP

PAP is fairly simple. After successful completion of the LCP negotiation, the requester repeatedly sends its username/password combination across the link until the authenticator responds with an acknowledgment or until the link is broken. The authenticator may disconnect the link if it determines that the username/password combination is not valid.

CHAP

CHAP is somewhat more complicated. The authenticator sends a *challenge* to the requester, which then responds with a value. This value is calculated by using a "one-way hash" function to hash the challenge and the CHAP password together. The resulting value is sent to the authenticator along with the requester's CHAP host name (which may be different from its actual host name) in a *response* message.

The authenticator reads the host name in the response message, looks up the expected password for that host name, and then calculates the value that it ought to expect the requester to have sent in its *response* by performing the same hash function that the requester performed. If the resulting values match, the authentication is successful. Failure should lead to a disconnect.

AAA

As part of authentication, use may be made of an authentication, authorization, and accounting (AAA, or triple-A) service such as TACACS+ or RADIUS. AAA is not a replacement for PAP or CHAP, but it is a mechanism for accomplishing them.

Network Control Protocol

Assuming successful authentication, the NCP phase begins. As in LCP, the peers exchange CONFREQs, CONFREJs, CONFNAKs, and CONFACKs, although in this phase of negotiation, the elements being negotiated have to do with higher-layer protocols—IP, IPX, bridging, CDP, and so on. One or more of these protocols may be negotiated. Because it is the most commonly used, and because other protocols operate in much the same fashion, Internet Protocol Control Protocol (IPCP), defined in RFC 1332, will be the focus of this discussion. Other pertinent RFCs include (but are not limited to) the following:

- RFC 1552 (IPX Control Protocol)
- RFC 1378 (AppleTalk Control Protocol)
- RFC 1638 (Bridging Control Protocol)[1]
- RFC 1762 ("DECnet Control Protocol")
- RFC 1763 ("VINES Control Protocol")

In addition, Cisco Discovery Protocol Control Protocol (CDPCP) may be negotiated during NCP, although this is not common—many Cisco TAC engineers advise that the command **no cdp enable** be configured on any and all dialer interfaces to prevent CDP packets from keeping a call up indefinitely.

The key element negotiated in IPCP is each peer's address. Each of the peers is in one of two possible states: either it has an IP address, or it does not.[2] If the peer already has an address, it will send that address in a CONFREQ to the other peer. If the address is

---

[1]Note that Cisco IOS does not support Bridging on asynchronous interfaces.

[2]Interfaces configured using *ip unnumbered [interface name]* are considered to have an IP address. They use the IP address of the interface named in the configuration command.

acceptable to the other peer, a CONFACK will be returned. If the address is not acceptable, the reply will be a CONFNAK containing an address for the peer to use.

If the peer has no address, it will send a CONFREQ with the address 0.0.0.0—this tells the other peer to assign an address, which is accomplished by sending a CONFNAK with the proper address.

Other options may be negotiated in IPCP. Commonly seen are the primary and secondary addresses for Domain Name Server and NetBIOS Name Server, as described in informational RFC 1877. Also commonly seen is the IP Compression Protocol (RFC 1332).

Alternate PPP Methodologies

PPP offers great flexibility in the manner in which it can be used. The following methodologies describe how to connect multiple links between two or more devices, and how to scale PPP for large numbers of inbound connections.

Multilink PPP

The Multilink Point-to-Point Protocol (MLP) feature provides load-balancing functionality over multiple WAN links, while providing multivendor interoperability, packet fragmentation and proper sequencing, and load calculation on both inbound and outbound traffic. Cisco's implementation of multilink PPP supports the fragmentation and packet sequencing specifications in RFC 1717.

Multilink PPP allows packets to be fragmented and for the fragments to be sent at the same time over multiple point-to-point links to the same remote address. The multiple links come up in response to a dialer load threshold that you define. The load can be calculated on inbound traffic, outbound traffic, or either, as needed for the traffic between the specific sites. MLP provides bandwidth on demand and reduces transmission latency across WAN links.

Multilink PPP is designed to work over single or multiple interfaces of the following types that are configured to support both dial-on-demand rotary groups and PPP encapsulation:

- Asynchronous serial interfaces
- Basic Rate Interfaces (BRIs)
- Primary Rate Interfaces (PRIs)

Configuration

To configure multilink PPP on asynchronous interfaces, you configure the asynchronous interfaces to support DDR and PPP encapsulation, and then you configure a dialer interface to support PPP encapsulation, bandwidth on demand, and multilink PPP. At some point, however, adding more asynchronous interfaces does not improve performance, With the default MTU size, multilink PPP should support three asynchronous interfaces using V.34 modems. However, packets might be dropped occasionally if the MTU is small or large bursts of short frames occur.

To enable multilink PPP on a single ISDN BRI or PRI interface, you are not required to define a dialer rotary group separately because ISDN interfaces are dialer rotary groups, by default. If you do not use PPP authentication procedures, your telephone service must pass caller ID information.

A load threshold number is required. For an example of configuring multilink PPP on a single ISDN BRI interface, see the next section, "Example of Multilink PPP on One ISDN Interface."

When multilink PPP is configured, and if you want a multilink bundle to be connected indefinitely, use the **dialer idle-timeout** command to set a very high idle timer. (The **dialer-load threshold 1** command does not keep a multilink bundle of *n* links connected indefinitely, and the **dialer-load threshold 2** command does not keep a multilink bundle of two links connected indefinitely.)

To enable multilink PPP on multiple ISDN BRI or PRI interfaces, you set up a dialer rotary interface and configure it for multilink PPP. Then you configure the BRIs separately and add them each to the same rotary group. See the "Example of Multilink PPP on Multiple ISDN Interfaces," next.

Example of Multilink PPP on One ISDN Interface

The following example enables multilink PPP on the BRI interface 0. Because an ISDN interface is a rotary group by default, when one BRI is configured, no dialer rotary group configuration is required.

```
interface bri 0
ip address 171.1.1.7 255.255.255.0
 encapsulation ppp
 dialer idle-timeout 30
 dialer load-threshold 40 either
 dialer map ip 172.16.20.2 name Goleta 5551212
 dialer-group 1
 ppp authentication pap
 ppp multilink
```

Example of Multilink PPP on Multiple ISDN Interfaces

The following example configures multiple ISDN BRIs to belong to the same dialer rotary group for multilink PPP. The **dialer rotary-group** command is used to assign each of the

ISDN BRIs to that dialer rotary group—number 0, in this case—which must match the number of the dialer interface.

```
interface BRI0
 no ip address
 encapsulation ppp
 dialer rotary-group 0
!
interface BRI1
 no ip address
 encapsulation ppp
 dialer rotary-group 0
!
interface Dialer0
 ip address 172.16.20.1 255.255.255.0
 encapsulation ppp
 dialer in-band
 dialer idle-timeout 500
 dialer map ip 172.16.20.2 name Goleta broadcast 5551212
 dialer load-threshold 30 either
 dialer-group 1
 ppp authentication chap
 ppp multilink
```

Multichassis Multilink PPP

Multilink PPP provides the capability of splitting and recombining packets to a single end system across a logical pipe (also called a *bundle*) formed by multiple links. Multilink PPP provides bandwidth on demand and reduces transmission latency across WAN links.

Multichassis multilink PPP (MMP), on the other hand, provides the additional capability for links to terminate at multiple routers with different remote addresses. MMP can also handle both analog and digital traffic.

This functionality is intended for situations in which there are large pools of dial-in users, where a single access server cannot provide enough dial-in ports. MMP allows companies to provide a single dialup number to its users and to apply the same solution to analog and digital calls. This feature enables Internet service providers, for example, to allocate a single ISDN rotary number to several ISDN PRIs across several routers.

For a complete description of the MMP commands referenced herein, refer to the *Cisco Dial Solutions Command Reference*. To locate documentation of other commands that appear in this chapter, use the command reference master index or search online.

MMP is supported on the Cisco 7500, 4500, and 2500 series platforms, and on synchronous serial, asynchronous serial, ISDN BRI, ISDN PRI, and dialer interfaces.

MMP does not require reconfiguration of telephone company switches.

Configuration

Routers or access servers are configured to belong to groups of peers, called *stack groups*. All members of the stack group are peers; stack groups do not need a permanent lead router. Any stack group member can answer calls coming from a single access number, which is usually an ISDN PRI hunt group. Calls can come in from remote user devices, such as routers, modems, ISDN terminal adapters, or PC cards.

When a connection is established with one member of a stack group, that member owns the call. If a second call comes in from the same client and a different router answers the call, the router establishes a tunnel and forwards all packets belonging to the call to the router that owns the call. Establishing a tunnel and forwarding calls through it to the router that owns the call is sometimes called *projecting the PPP link to the call master.*

If a more powerful router is available, it can be configured as a member of the stack group, and the other stack group members can establish tunnels and forward all calls to it. In such a case, the other stack group members are just answering calls and forwarding traffic to the more powerful offload router.

NOTE   High-latency WAN lines between stack group members can make stack group operation inefficient.

MMP call handling, bidding, and Layer 2 forwarding operations in the stack group proceed as follows, as shown in Figure 16-11:

1   When the first call comes in to the stack group, Router A answers.

2   In the bidding, Router A wins because it already has the call. Router A becomes the *call master* for that session with the remote device. (Router A might also be called the *host to the master bundle interface*.)

3   When the remote device that initiated the call needs more bandwidth, it makes a second multilink PPP call to the group.

4   When the second call comes in, Router D answers it and informs the stack group. Router A wins the bidding because it already is handling the session with that remote device.

5   Router D establishes a tunnel to Router A and forwards the raw PPP data to Router A.

6   Router A reassembles and resequences the packets.

7   If more calls come in to Router D and they, too, belong to Router A, the tunnel between A and D enlarges to handle the added traffic. Router D does not establish an additional tunnel to A.

8 If more calls come in and are answered by any other router, that router also establishes
a tunnel to A and forwards the raw PPP data.

9 The reassembled data is passed on the corporate network as if it had all come through
one physical link.

Figure 16-11 *Typical Multichassis Multilink PPP Scenario*

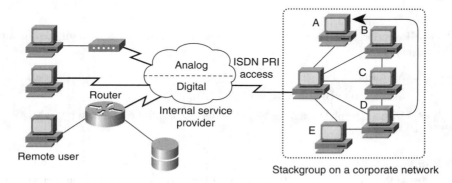

In contrast to the previous figure, Figure 16-12 features an offload router. Access servers
that belong to a stack group answer calls, establish tunnels, and forward calls to a Cisco
4700 router that wins the bidding and is the call master for all the calls. The Cisco 4700
reassembles and resequences all the packets coming in through the stack group.

Figure 16-12 *Multichassis Multilink PPP with an Offload Router as a Stack Group Member*

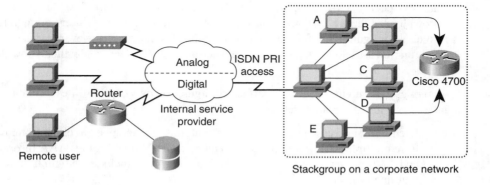

NOTE	You can build stack groups using different access server, switching, and router platforms. However, universal access servers such as the Cisco AS5200 should not be combined with ISDN-only access servers such as the 4x00 platform. Because calls from the central office are allocated in an arbitrary way, this combination could result in an analog call being delivered to a digital-only access server, which would not be capable of handling the call.

MMP support on a group of routers requires that each router be configured to support the following:

- Multilink PPP
- Stack Group Bidding Protocol (SGBP)
- Virtual template used for cloning interface configuration to support MMP

Virtual Profiles

Virtual Profiles is a unique Point-to-Point Protocol (PPP) application that can create and configure a virtual access interface dynamically when a dial-in call is received, and can tear down the interface dynamically when the call ends. Virtual Profiles works with straightforward PPP and with multilink PPP (MLP).

The configuration information for a Virtual Profiles virtual access interface can come from a virtual template interface or from user-specific configuration stored on an authentication, authorization, and accounting (AAA) server, or both.

The user-specific AAA configuration used by Virtual Profiles is *interface* configuration and is downloaded during LCP negotiations. Another feature, called per-user configuration, also uses configuration information gained from a AAA server. However, per-user configuration uses network configuration (such as access lists and route filters) downloaded during NCP negotiations.

Two rules govern virtual access interface configuration by Virtual Profiles virtual template interfaces and AAA configurations:

- Each virtual access application can have at most one template to clone from, but can have multiple AAA configurations to clone from (Virtual Profiles AAA information and AAA per-user configuration, which in turn might include configuration for multiple protocols).
- When Virtual Profiles is configured by virtual template, its template has higher priority than any other virtual template.

This feature runs on all Cisco IOS platforms that support MLP.

For a complete description of the commands mentioned in this section, refer to the "Virtual Profiles Commands" chapter in the *Dial Solutions Command Reference* in the Cisco IOS documentation set. To locate documentation of other commands that appear in this chapter, you can use the command reference master index or search online.

Background Information

This section presents background information about Virtual Profiles to help you understand this application before you start to configure it.

- **Restrictions**—We recommend that unnumbered addresses be used in virtual template interfaces to ensure that duplicate network addresses are not created on virtual access interfaces.

- **Prerequisites**—Use of user-specific AAA interface configuration information with Virtual Profiles requires the router to be configured for AAA and requires the AAA server to have user-specific interface configuration AV pairs. The relevant AV pairs (on a RADIUS server) begin as follows:

  ```
  cisco-avpair = "lcp:interface-config=...",
  ```

  The information that follows the equals sign (=), could be any Cisco IOS interface configuration command. For example, the line might be the following:

  ```
  cisco-avpair = "lcp:interface-config=ip address 200.200.200.200
  255.255.255.0",
  ```

  Use of a virtual template interface with Virtual Profiles requires a virtual template to be defined specifically for Virtual Profiles.

- **Interoperability with other Cisco dial features**— The Cisco IOS Virtual Profiles feature interoperates with Cisco DDR, multilink PPP (MLP), and dialers such as ISDN.

DDR Configuration of Physical Interfaces   Virtual Profiles fully interoperates with physical interfaces in the following DDR configuration states when no other virtual access interface application is configured:

- **Dialer profiles are configured for the interface**—The dialer profile is used instead of the Virtual Profiles configuration.

- **DDR is not configured on the interface**—Virtual Profiles overrides the current configuration.

- **Legacy DDR is configured on the interface**—Virtual Profiles overrides the current configuration.

NOTE	If a dialer interface is used (including any ISDN dialer), its configuration is used on the physical interface instead of the Virtual Profiles configuration.

Multilink PPP Effect on Virtual Access Interface Configuration   As shown in Table 16-9, exactly how a virtual access interface will be configured depends three factors:

- Whether Virtual Profiles is configured by Virtual Template, by AAA, by both, or by neither. These states are shown as "VP VT only," "VP AAA only," "VP VT and VP AAA," and "No VP at all," respectively, in Table 16-9.
- The presence or absence of a dialer interface.
- The presence or absence of MLP. The column label "MLP" is a stand-in for any virtual access feature that supports MLP and clones from a virtual template interface.

In Table 16-9, "(Multilink VT)" means that a virtual template interface is cloned *if* one is defined for MLP or a virtual access feature that uses MLP.

Table 16-9   *Virtual Profiles Configuration Cloning Sequence*

Virtual Profiles Configuration	MLP No Dialer	MLP Dialer	No MLP No Dialer	No MLP Dialer
VP VT only	VP VT	VP VT	VP VT	VP VT
VP AAA only	(Multilink VT) VP AAA	(Multilink VT) VP AAA	VP AAA	VP AAA
VP VT and VP AAA	VP VT VP AAA	VP VT VP AAA	VP VT VP AAA	VP VT VP AAA
No VP at all	(Multilink VT)[1]	Dialer[2]	No virtual access interface is created.	No virtual access interface is created.

[1]The Multilink bundle virtual access interface is created and uses the default settings for MLP or the relevant virtual access feature that uses MLP.

[2]The Multilink bundle virtual access interface is created and cloned from the dialer interface configuration.

The order of items in any cell of the table is important. Where VP VT is shown above VP AAA, it means that first the Virtual Profiles virtual template is cloned on the interface, and then the AAA interface configuration for the user is applied to it. The user-specific AAA interface configuration adds to the configuration and overrides any conflicting physical interface or virtual template configuration commands.

Interoperability with Other Features That Use Virtual Templates (Q10)   Virtual Profiles also interoperates with virtual access applications that clone a virtual template interface. Each virtual access application can have at most one template to clone from, but it can clone from multiple AAA configurations.

The interaction between Virtual Profiles and other virtual template applications is as follows:

- If Virtual Profiles is enabled and a virtual template is defined for it, the Virtual Profiles virtual template is used.

- If Virtual Profiles is configured by AAA alone (no virtual template is defined for Virtual Profiles), the virtual template for another virtual access application (VPDN, for example) can be cloned onto the virtual access interface.

- A virtual template, if any, is cloned to a virtual access interface before the Virtual Profiles AAA configuration or AAA per-user configuration. AAA per-user configuration, if used, is applied last.

Terminology

The following new or uncommon terms are used here:

- **AV pair**—A configuration parameter on an AAA server; part of the user configuration that the AAA server sends to the router in response to user-specific authorization requests. The router interprets each AV pair as a Cisco IOS router configuration command and applies the AV pairs in order. In this chapter, the term *AV pair* refers to an interface configuration parameter on a RADIUS server.

  An interface configuration AV pair for Virtual Profiles can take a form such as this:

  ```
  cisco-avpair = "lcp:interface-config=ip address 1.1.1.1 255.255.255.0",
  ```

- **Cloning**—Creating and configuring a virtual access interface by applying configuration commands from a specific virtual template. The virtual template is the source of the generic user information and router-dependent information. The result of cloning is a virtual access interface configured with all the commands in the template.

- **Virtual access interface**—Instance of a unique virtual interface that is created dynamically and exists temporarily. Virtual access interfaces can be created and configured differently by different applications, such as Virtual Profiles and virtual private dialup networks.

- **Virtual template interface**—Generic interface configuration for certain users or for a certain purpose, plus router-dependent information. This takes the form of a list of Cisco IOS interface commands to be applied to the virtual interface as needed.

- **Virtual profile**—Instance of a unique virtual access interface created dynamically when certain users call in, and torn down dynamically when the call disconnects. A specific user's virtual profile can be configured by a virtual template interface, a user-specific interface configuration stored on an AAA server, or both a virtual template interface and a user-specific interface configuration from AAA.

Configuration of a virtual access interface begins with a virtual template interface (if any), followed by application of user-specific configuration for the particular user's dial-in session (if any).

Annotated Example of PPP Negotiation

In Figure 16-13, a **ping** brings up an ISDN link between routers Montecito and Goleta. Note that although there is no timestamping in this example, it is usually recommended that you use the global configuration command **service timestamps debug datetime msec**.

Figure 16-13 *Router-ISDN-Router*

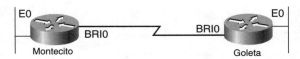

These debugs are taken from Montecito; the debugging on Goleta would look much the same.

NOTE   Your debugs may appear in a different format. This output is the older PPP debugging output format prior to the modifications introduced in IOS version 11.2(8). See Chapter 17 for an example of PPP debugging in newer versions of IOS.

Example 16-2 shows the debug and ping information for the ISDN link between Montecito and Goleta.

Example 16-2 *Montecito pings Goleta*

```
Montecito#show debugging
PPP:
  PPP authentication debugging is on
  PPP protocol negotiation debugging is on
A: Montecito#ping 172.16.20.2

Type escape sequence to abort.
Sending 5, 100-byte ICMP Echoes to 172.16.20.2, timeout is 2 seconds:

B: %LINK-3-UPDOWN: Interface BRI0: B-Channel 1, changed state to up
C: ppp: sending CONFREQ, type = 3 (CI_AUTHTYPE), value = C223/5
C: ppp: sending CONFREQ, type = 5 (CI_MAGICNUMBER), value = 29EBD1A7
D: PPP BRI0: B-Channel 1: received config for type = 0x3 (AUTHTYPE) value = 0xC223
digest = 0x5 acked
D: PPP BRI0: B-Channel 1: received config for type = 0x5 (MAGICNUMBER) value =
0x28FC9083 acked
```

Example 16-2 *Montecito pings Goleta*

```
E: PPP BRI0: B-Channel 1: state = ACKsent fsm_rconfack(0xC021): rcvd id 0x65
F: ppp: config ACK received, type = 3 (CI_AUTHTYPE), value = C223
F: ppp: config ACK received, type = 5 (CI_MAGICNUMBER), value = 29EBD1A7
G: PPP BRI0: B-Channel 1: Send CHAP challenge id=1 to remote
H: PPP BRI0: B-Channel 1: CHAP challenge from Goleta
J: PPP BRI0: B-Channel 1: CHAP response id=1 received from Goleta
K: PPP BRI0: B-Channel 1: Send CHAP success id=1 to remote
L: PPP BRI0: B-Channel 1: remote passed CHAP authentication.
M: PPP BRI0: B-Channel 1: Passed CHAP authentication with remote.
N: ipcp: sending CONFREQ, type = 3 (CI_ADDRESS), Address = 172.16.20.1
P: ppp BRI0: B-Channel 1: Negotiate IP address: her address 172.16.20.2 (ACK)
Q: ppp: ipcp_reqci: returning CONFACK.
R: PPP BRI0: B-Channel 1: state = ACKsent fsm_rconfack(0x8021): rcvd id 0x25
S: ipcp: config ACK received, type = 3 (CI_ADDRESS), Address = 172.16.20.1
T: BRI0: install route to 172.16.20.2
U: %LINEPROTO-5-UPDOWN: Line protocol on Interface BRI0: B-Channel 1, changed state
to up
```

A—Traffic is generated in order to initiate a dial attempt.

B—The connection is established (ISDN debugs are not used in this example).

Begin LCP:

C—Montecito sends LCP configuration requests for AUTHTYPE and for MAGICNUMBER.

D—Goleta sends its CONFREQs. If the value for MAGICNUMBER is the same as the value sent by Montecito, there is a strong probability that the line is looped.

E—This indicates that Montecito has sent acknowledgments to Goleta's CONFREQs.

F—Montecito receives CONFACKs from Goleta.

Begin authentication phase:

G, H—Montecito and Goleta challenge each other for authentication.

J—Goleta responds to the challenge.

K, L—Goleta successfully passes authentication.

M—Goleta sends a message to Montecito, saying that authentication was successful.

NCP negotiation begins:

N, P—Each router sends its configured IP address in a CONFREQ.

Q, R—Montecito sends a CONFACK to Goleta's CONFREQ . . .

S— . . . and vice versa.

T, U—A route is installed from Montecito to Goleta, and the protocol on the interface changes to "up," indicating that the NCP negotiations have completed successfully.

Before Calling Cisco Systems's TAC Team

Before calling Cisco Systems's Technical Assistance Center (TAC), make sure that you have read through this chapter and completed the actions suggested for your system's problem.

Additionally, do the following and document the results so that we can better assist you:

For all problems, collect the output of **show running-config** and **show version**. Ensure that the command **service timestamps debug datetime msec** is in the configuration.

For DDR problems, collect the following:

* **show dialer map**
* **debug dialer**
* **debug ppp negotiation**
* **debug ppp authentication**

If ISDN is involved, collect the following:

* **show isdn status**
* **debug isdn q931**
* **debug isdn events**

If modems are involved, collect the following:

* **show lines**
* **show line** [*x*]
* **show modem** (if integrated modems are involved)
* **show modem version** (if integrated modems are involved)
* **debug modem**
* **debug modem csm** (if integrated modems are involved)
* **debug chat** (if a DDR scenario)

If T1s or PRIs are involved, collect the following:

* show controller t1

Additional Sources

* Cisco IOS Dial Solutions Guide
* The TAC Technology Support Pages: www.cisco.com/tac/

## CHAPTER 17

Troubleshooting ISDN Connections

Introduction

Dialup is simply the application of the Public Switched Telephone Network (PSTN) to carry data on behalf of the end user. It involves customer premises equipment (CPE) sending the telephone switch a phone number to direct a connection to. The Cisco 3600, AS5200, AS5300, and AS5800 are all examples of routers that have the capability to run a PRI along with banks of digital modems. The AS2511, on the other hand, is an example of a router that communicates with external modems.

Since the time of the last *Internetworking Troubleshooting Handbook*, the carrier market has grown significantly, and there has been a demand for higher modem densities. The answer to this need was a higher degree of interoperation with the telco equipment and the development of the digital modem. This type of modem is capable of direct digital access to the PSTN. This has allowed the development of faster CPE modems that can take advantage of the clarity of signal that the digital modems enjoy. The fact that digital modems connecting into the PSTN through a PRI or BRI can transmit data at greater than 53K using the V.90 communication standard attests to the success of the idea.

The first Cisco access servers were the Cisco 2509 and Cisco 2511. The 2509 could support 8 incoming connections using external modems, and the 2511 could support 16. The AS5200 was introduced with 2 PRIs and could support 48 users using digital modems, which represented a major leap forward in technology. Modem densities have increased steadily, with the AS5300 supporting four and then eight PRIs. Recently, the AS5800 was introduced to fill the needs of carrier class installations that needed to handle dozens of incoming T1s and hundreds of user connections.

A few outdated technologies bear mentioning in a historical discussion of dialer technology. 56K flex is an older (pre-V.90) 56K modem standard that was proposed by Rockwell. Cisco supports version 1.1 of the 56K flex standard on its internal modems, but the company recommends migrating the CPE modems to V.90 as soon as possible. Another outdated technology is the AS5100, which was a joint venture between Cisco and a modem manufacturer. Created as a way to increase modem density through the use of quad modem cards, the AS5100 involved a group of 2511s built as cards that inserted into a backplane shared by quad modem cards and a dual T1 card.

Troubleshooting Incoming Calls

Troubleshooting an incoming call starts at the bottom—the physical layer—and works up the protocol stack. The general flow of reasoning looks for the following (a "yes" answer advances to the next question):

- Do we see the call arrive?
- Does the receiving end answer the call?
- Does the call complete?
- Is data passing across the link?
- Is the session established? (PPP or terminal)

For modem connections, a data call looks the same as a terminal session coming in until the end, when the data call goes to negotiate PPP.

For incoming calls involving digital modems, first make sure that the underlying ISDN or CAS is receiving the call. If you are using an external modem, you can skip the ISDN and CAS group sections.

Incoming ISDN Call Troubleshooting

Use the command **debug isdn q931** to watch the q931 signaling messages go back and forth while the router negotiates the ISDN connection. Here's an example output from a successful connection:

```
Router# debug isdn q931
RX <- SETUP pd = 8 callref = 0x06
  Bearer Capability i = 0x8890
  Channel ID i = 0x89
  Calling Party Number i = 0x0083, `5551234'
TX -> CONNECT pd = 8 callref = 0x86
RX <- CONNECT_ACK pd = 8 callref = 0x06
```

The SETUP message indicates that a connection is being initiated by the remote end. The call reference numbers are maintained as a pair. In this case, the call reference number for the incoming side of the connection is 0x06, while the call reference number of the outbound side of the connection is 0x86. The bearer capability (often referred to as the bearercap) tells the router what kind of call is coming in. In this case, the connection is type 0x8890. That value indicates "ISDN speed 64 kbps." If the bearercap had been 0x8090A2, it would have indicated "Speech/voice call u-law."

If no setup message was seen coming in, verify the correct number (try calling it manually, if it is voice-provisioned) and check the status of the ISDN interface (see Chapter 16, "Troubleshooting Dialup Connections"). If all that checks out, make sure that the call originator is making the correct call. Contact the telco to trace the call to see where it's being sent. If the connection is a long-distance one, try a different long-distance carrier using a 1010 long-distance code.

If the call coming in is an async modem call, make sure that the line is provisioned to allow voice calls.

NOTE   BRI async modem calling is a feature of 3600 routers running 12.0(3)T or later. It requires a recent hardware revision of the BRI interface network module. WIC modules do not support async modem calling.

If the call arrived but did not complete, look for a cause code (see Table 17-10). A successful completion is shown by a connect-ack being issued.

If this is an async modem call, move forward to the "Incoming Modem Call Troubleshooting" section.

At this point, the ISDN call is connected, but no data has been seen coming across the link. Use the command **debug ppp negotiate** to see whether any PPP traffic is coming across the line. If not, there may be a speed mismatch. To determine whether this is the case, use the **show running-config** privileged exec command to view the router configuration. Check the **dialer map** interface configuration command entries in the local and remote router. These entries should look similar to the following:

```
dialer map ip 131.108.2.5 speed 56 name C4000
```

For dialer profiles, a map class must be defined to set the speed. Note that, by default, ISDN interfaces attempt to use 64K communications speeds on each channel.

For detailed information on configuring dialer maps and profiles, refer to the *Cisco IOS Dial Solutions Configuration Guide*, *Dial Solutions Command Reference*, and *Dial Solutions Quick Configuration Guide*.

Getting valid PPP packets indicates that the link is up and working. Proceed to the section "Troubleshooting PPP."

Incoming CAS Call Troubleshooting

To troubleshoot the CAS group serving connectivity to the modems, use the commands **debug modem**, **debug modem csm**, and **debug cas**.

NOTE   The **debug cas** command first appeared in 12.0(7)T for the AS5200 and AS5300. Earlier versions of IOS use a system-level configuration command **service internal**, along with the exec command **modem-mgmt debug rbs**. Debugging this information on an AS5800 requires connecting to the trunk card itself.

The first thing to look for is if the telco switch went off-hook to signal the incoming call. If not, verify the number being called by attaching a phone to the originating side's phone line and then calling the number. If the call comes in, the problem is in the originating CPE. If the call still does not show up on the CAS, check the T1 (per Chapter 15, "Troubleshooting Serial Lines"). A good debug to use in this instance is **debug serial interfaces.**

The following shows a good connection using **debug modem CSM**:

```
Router# debug modem csm
CSM_MODEM_ALLOCATE: slot 1 and port 0 is allocated.
MODEM_REPORT(0001): DEV_INCALL at slot 1 and port 0
CSM_PROC_IDLE: CSM_EVENT_ISDN_CALL at slot 1, port 0
CSM_RING_INDICATION_PROC: RI is on
CSM_RING_INDICATION_PROC: RI is off
CSM_PROC_IC1_RING: CSM_EVENT_MODEM_OFFHOOK at slot 1, port 0
MODEM_REPORT(0001): DEV_CONNECTED at slot 1 and port 0
CSM_PROC_IC2_WAIT_FOR_CARRIER: CSM_EVENT_ISDN_CONNECTED at slot 1, port 0
```

If this code is seen, then the call was directed to a modem. Proceed to the "Incoming Modem Call Troubleshooting" section.

Incoming Modem Call Troubleshooting

The debugs used in troubleshooting incoming modem calls are listed here:

> **debug modem**
> **debug modem csm** (for integrated digital modems)

These other debugs are used in conjunction to indicate the new call coming in:

> **debug isdn q931**
> **debug cas**

Assuming that the call reaches the modem, the modem must pick up the call.

Tips for Debugging External Modems

To facilitate debugging on an external modem connected to a TTY line, turn up the speaker volume—it helps make some problems more apparent.

When the originating modem calls, does the receiving modem ring? If not, verify the number and try a manual call from the remote site. Try using a regular phone on the receiving end as well. Replace cables and hardware as needed.

Async Modem Call Pickup

If an external modem is not answering, check the cabling between the modem and the access server or router. Confirm that the modem is connected to the TTY or auxiliary port on the router with a rolled RJ-45 cable and an MMOD DB-25 adapter. This cabling configuration is recommended and supported by Cisco for RJ-45 ports. (These connectors are typically labeled "Modem.")

The most common types of RJ-45 cabling are straight, rolled, and crossover. If you hold the two ends of an RJ-45 cable side by side, you'll see eight colored strips, or pins, at each end. If the order of the colored pins is the same at each end, then the cable is straight. If the order of the colors is reversed at each end, then the cable is rolled. The cable is a crossover cable if colors indicate the following:

```
RJ45 to RJ45 crossover cable
     RJ45                      RJ45
        5 ----------------- 2

        2 ----------------- 5

        4 ----------------- 1

        1 ----------------- 4
```

To make sure that the signaling is okay, use the **show line** command outlined in Chapter 16.

Cabling issues aside, an external modem must be initialized to autoanswer. Check the remote modem to see whether it is set to autoanswer. Usually, an AA indicator light is on when autoanswer is set. Set the remote modem to autoanswer if it is not already set. To find out how to verify and change the modem's settings, refer to your modem documentation. Use a reverse telnet (See Chapter 16) to initialize the modem.

Digital (Integrated) Modem Call Pickup

On an external modem, it is clear whether the call is getting answered, but internal modems require a manual call to the receiving number. Listen for the answer back tone (ABT). If no ABT is heard, check the configuration for two things:

- Make sure that the command **isdn incoming-voice modem** exists under any ISDN interfaces handling incoming modem connections.

- Under the line configuration for the modem's TTY, make sure that the command **modem inout** exists.

It is also possible that an internal modem was not allocated by the Call Switching Module (CSM) to handle the incoming call. This problem can be caused by modem or resource pools being configured for too few incoming connections, or the access server my simply be out of modems. Check the availability of modems, and adjust the modem pool or resource pool manager settings appropriately. If a modem was allocated and the configuration shows **modem inout,** gather debugs and contact Cisco for assistance.

Modem Trainup

A successful trainup is indicated by the receiving modem raising DSR. Trainup failures can indicate a circuit problem or modem incompatibility.

If you really want to get to the bottom of an individual modem problem, you'll want to get your hands to the AT prompt at the originating modem, while it's attached to the POTS line of interest. If you're calling into a digital modem in a Cisco access server, be prepared to record a .wav file of the trainup "music," or Digital Impairment Learning (DIL) sequence. The DIL is the musical score (PCM sequence) that the originating V.90 analog modem tells the receiving digital modem to play back. The sequence allows the analog modem to discern any digital impairment in the circuit (such as multiple D/A conversions, a-law/u-law, robbed bits, and digital pads). If you don't hear the DIL, the modems did not negotiate V.90 in V.8/V.8bis (that is, a modem compatibility issue has arisen). If you *do* hear the DIL, but then you hear a retrain in V.34, the analog modem has decided, on the basis of the DIL playback, that V.90 was infeasible.

Does the music have noise in it? If so, then clean up the circuit.

Does the client give up quickly, without running V.34 training? Perhaps it doesn't know what to do when it hears V.8bis. Try disabling V.8bis (hence, 56K flex) on the server (if acceptable), getting new client firmware, or swapping out the client modem. Alternately, the dialing end could insert five commas at the end of the dial string. This delays the calling modem's listening and causes the V.8bis tone from the receiving server to time out without affecting the client modem. Five commas in the dial string is a ballpark estimate, though, so you might need to adjust this to allow for local conditions.

Session Establishment

At this point in the sequence, the modems are connected and trained up. Now it's time to find out whether any traffic is coming across properly.

If the line receiving the call is configured with **autoselect ppp** and the async interface is configured with **async mode interactive**, use the command **debug modem** to verify the autoselect process. As traffic comes in over the async link, the access server examines the traffic to determine whether the traffic is character-based or packet-based. Depending on the determination, the access server then either starts a PPP session or goes no farther than having an exec session on the line.

This is a normal autoselect sequence with inbound PPP LCP packets:

```
*Mar  1 21:34:56.958: TTY1: DSR came up
*Mar  1 21:34:56.962: tty1: Modem: IDLE->READY
*Mar  1 21:34:56.970: TTY1: EXEC creation
*Mar  1 21:34:56.978: TTY1: set timer type 10, 30 seconds
*Mar  1 21:34:59.722: TTY1: Autoselect(2) sample 7E              Note 1
*Mar  1 21:34:59.726: TTY1: Autoselect(2) sample 7EFF
*Mar  1 21:34:59.730: TTY1: Autoselect(2) sample 7EFF7D
*Mar  1 21:34:59.730: TTY1: Autoselect(2) sample 7EFF7D23
```

```
*Mar  1 21:34:59.734: TTY1 Autoselect cmd: ppp negotiate       Note 2
*Mar  1 21:34:59.746: TTY1: EXEC creation
*Mar  1 21:34:59.746: TTY1: create timer type 1, 600 seconds
*Mar  1 21:34:59.794: TTY1: destroy timer type 1 (OK)
*Mar  1 21:34:59.794: TTY1: destroy timer type 0
*Mar  1 21:35:01.798: %LINK-3-UPDOWN: Interface Async1, changed state to up    Note 3
```

Note 1: The inbound traffic is displayed in hexadecimal format, based on the bits coming in over the line, regardless of whether the bits are ASCII characters or elements of a packet. The bits represented in this example are correct for an LCP packet. Anything different would be either a malformed packet or character traffic.

Note 2: Having determined that the inbound traffic is actually an LCP packet, the access server triggers the PPP negotiation process.

Note 3: The async interface changes state to up, and the PPP negotiation (not shown) commences.

If the call is a PPP session, and if **async mode dedicated** is configured on the async interface, use the command **debug ppp negotiation** to see whether any configuration request packets (the debugs will show them as CONFREQ) are coming from the remote end. If PPP packets are seen to be both inbound and outbound, proceed to the section "PPP Debugging." Otherwise, connect in from the call-originating end with a character-mode (or "exec") session (that is, a non-PPP session).

NOTE   If the receiving end has the setting **async modem dedicated** under the async interface, an exec dial-in will see nothing but what appears to be random ASCII garbage. To allow a terminal session and still have PPP capability, use the async interface configuration command **async mode interactive**. Under the associated line's configuration, use the command **autoselect ppp**.

If the modems connect with a terminal session and no data comes across, check the causes shown in Table 17-1.

Table 17-1   *Modem Cannot Send or Receive Data*

Possible Causes	Suggested Actions	
Modem speed setting is not locked	**Step 1**	Use the **show line** exec command on the access server or router. The output for the auxiliary port should indicate the currently configured Tx and Rx speeds.
	Step 2	If the line is not configured to the correct speed, use the **speed** line configuration command to set the line speed on the access server or router line. Set the value to the highest speed in common between the modem and the access server or router port.

continues

Table 17-1 *Modem Cannot Send or Receive Data (Continued)*

Possible Causes	Suggested Actions
Modem speed setting is not locked *(continued)*	To set the terminal baud rate, use the **speed** line configuration command. This command sets both the transmit (to terminal) and receive (from terminal) speeds.

Syntax:

speed *bps*

Syntax Description:

- *bps*—Baud rate in bits per second (bps). The default is 9600 bps.

Example:

The following example sets lines 1 and 2 on a Cisco 2509 access server to 115200 bps:

```
line 1 2
 speed 115200
```

Note: If you cannot use flow control for some reason, limit the line speed to 9600 bps. Faster speeds likely will result in lost data.

Step 3   Use the **show line** exec command again, and confirm that the line speed is set to the desired value.

Step 4   When you are certain that the access server or router line is configured for the desired speed, initiate a reverse Telnet session to the modem via that line. For more information, see the section "Establishing a Reverse Telnet Session to a Modem," in Chapter 16.

Step 5   Use a modem command string that includes the lock DTE speed command for your modem. See your modem documentation for exact configuration command syntax.

Note: The modem AT command to lock DTE speed, which might also be referred to as *port rate adjust* or *buffered mode*, is often related to the way in which the modem handles error correction. This command varies widely from one modem to another.

Locking the modem speed ensures that the modem always communicates with the Cisco access server or router at the speed configured on the Cisco auxiliary port. If this command is not used, the modem reverts to the speed of the data link (the telephone line) instead of communicating at the speed configured on the access server.

Table 17-1   *Modem Cannot Send or Receive Data (Continued)*

Possible Causes	Suggested Actions
Hardware flow control is not configured on the local or remote modem or router	**Step 1** Use the **show line** *aux-line-number* exec command, and look for the following in the Capabilities field (see the section "Interpreting Show Line Output" in Chapter 16): `Capabilities: Hardware Flowcontrol In, Hardware Flowcontrol Out` If there is no mention of hardware flow control in this field, hardware flow control is not enabled on the line. Hardware flow control for access server-to-modem connections is recommended. For an explanation of the output of the **show line** command, see the section "Using **debug** Commands," earlier in this chapter. **Step 2** Configure hardware flow control on the line using the **flowcontrol hardware** line configuration command. To set the method of data flow control between the terminal or other serial device and the router, use the **flowcontrol** line configuration command. Use the **no** form of this command to disable flow control. **Syntax:** **flowcontrol** {**none** I **software** [**lock**] [**in** I **out**] I **hardware** [**in** I **out**]} **Syntax description:** • **none**—Turns off flow control. • **software**—Sets software flow control. An optional keyword specifies the direction: **in** causes the Cisco IOS software to listen to flow control from the attached device, and **out** causes the software to send flow control information to the attached device. If you do not specify a direction, both are assumed. • **lock**—Makes it impossible to turn off flow control from the remote host when the connected device needs software flow control. This option applies to connections using the Telnet or rlogin protocols. • **hardware**—Sets hardware flow control. An optional keyword specifies the direction: **in** causes the software to listen to flow control from the attached device, and **out** causes the software to send flow control information to the attached device. If you do not specify a direction, both are assumed. For more information about hardware flow control, see the hardware manual that was shipped with your router.

continues

Table 17-1   *Modem Cannot Send or Receive Data (Continued)*

Possible Causes	Suggested Actions	
Hardware flow control is not configured on the local or remote modem or router *(continued)*		**Example:** The following example sets hardware flow control on line 7: ``` line 7 flowcontrol hardware ``` **Note:** If you cannot use flow control for some reason, limit the line speed to 9600 bps. Faster speeds likely will result in lost data.
	Step 3	After enabling hardware flow control on the access server or router line, initiate a reverse Telnet session to the modem via that line. For more information, see the section "Establishing a Reverse Telnet Session to a Modem."
	Step 4	Use a modem command string that includes the **RTS/CTS Flow** command for your modem. This command ensures that the modem is using the same method of flow control (that is, hardware flow control) as the Cisco access server or router. See your modem documentation for exact configuration command syntax.
dialer map commands are misconfigured	**Step 1**	Use the **show running-config** privileged exec command to view the router configuration. Check the **dialer map** command entries to see whether the **broadcast** keyword is specified.
	Step 2	If the keyword is missing, add it to the configuration. **Syntax:** **dialer map** *protocol next-hop-address* [**name** *hostname*] [**broadcast**] [*dial-string*] **Syntax description:** • *protocol*—The protocol subject to mapping. Options include IP, IPX[1], bridge, and snapshot. • *next-hop-address*—The protocol address of the opposite site's async interface. • **name** *hostname*—A required parameter used in PPP authentication. It is the name of the remote site for which the dialer map is created. The name is case-sensitive and must match the host name of the remote router. • **broadcast**—An optional keyword that broadcast packets (such as IP RIP or IPX RIP/SAP updates) to be forwarded to the remote destination. In static routing sample configurations, routing updates are not desired and the **broadcast** keyword is omitted.

Table 17-1   *Modem Cannot Send or Receive Data (Continued)*

Possible Causes	Suggested Actions	
dialer map commands are misconfigured *(continued)*		• *dial-string*—The remote site's phone number. Any access codes (for example, 9 to get out of an office; international dialing codes; and area codes) must be included.
	Step 3	Make sure that **dialer map** commands specify the correct next-hop addresses.
	Step 4	If the next-hop address is incorrect, change it using the **dialer map** command.
	Step 5	Make sure that all other options in **dialer map** commands are correctly specified for the protocol that you are using.
		For detailed information on configuring dialer maps, refer to the Cisco IOS *Wide-Area Networking Configuration Guide* and *Wide-Area Networking Command Reference*.
A problem has occurred with the dialing modem	Make sure that the dialing modem is operational and is securely connected to the correct port. See whether another modem works when connected to the same port.	

Debugging an incoming exec session generally falls into a few main categories. Possible causes and suggested actions can be found in Tables 17-2 through 17-5.

- Dialup client receives no exec prompt
- Dialup session sees "garbage"
- Dialup session ends up in an existing session
- Dialup receiving modem does not disconnect properly

Table 17-2   *Dialup Client Receives No exec Prompt*

Possible Causes	Suggested Actions	
Autoselect is enabled on the line	Attempt to access exec mode by issuing a carriage return.	
Line is configured with the **no exec** command	Step 1	Use the **show line** exec command to view the status of the appropriate line.
		Check the Capabilities field to see whether it include "exec suppressed." If this is the case, the **no exec** line configuration command is enabled.
	Step 2	Configure the **exec** line configuration command on the line to allow exec sessions to be initiated. This command has no arguments or keywords.
		Example:
		The following example turns on the exec on line 7:
		`line 7` `exec`

continues

Table 17-2   *Dialup Client Receives No exec Prompt (Continued)*

Possible Causes	Suggested Actions

Flow control is not enabled, is enabled only on one device (either DTE or DCE), or is misconfigured	**Step 1** Use the **show line** *aux-line-number* exec command, and look for the following in the Capabilities field (see the section "Interpreting Show Line Output" in Chapter 16):
	
	 `Capabilities: Hardware Flowcontrol In, Hardware`
	 `Flowcontrol Out`
	
	 If there is no mention of hardware flow control in this field, hardware flow control is not enabled on the line. Hardware flow control for access server-to-modem connections is recommended.

	Step 2 Configure hardware flow control on the line using the **flowcontrol hardware** line configuration command.
	
	 Example:
	
	 The following example sets hardware flow control on line 7:
	
	 `line 7`
	 ` flowcontrol hardware`

	NOTE If you cannot use flow control for some reason, limit the line speed to 9600 bps. Faster speeds likely will result in lost data.
	Step 3 After enabling hardware flow control on the access server or router line, initiate a reverse Telnet session to the modem via that line. For more information, see the section "Establishing a Reverse Telnet Session to a Modem," earlier in this chapter.
	Step 4 Use a modem command string that includes the **RTS/CTS Flow** command for your modem. This command ensures that the modem is using the same method of flow control (that is, hardware flow control) as the Cisco access server or router. See your modem documentation for exact configuration command syntax. Figure 16-1 shows the hardware flow control command string for a Hayes-compatible modem.
Modem speed setting is not locked	**Step 1** Use the **show line** exec command on the access server or router. The output for the auxiliary port should indicate the currently configured Tx and Rx speeds. For an explanation of the output of the **show** line command, see the section "Using **debug** Commands," earlier in this chapter.
	Step 2 If the line is not configured to the correct speed, use the **speed** line configuration command to set the line speed on the access server or router line. Set the value to the highest speed in common between the modem and the access server or router port.

Table 17-2   *Dialup Client Receives No exec Prompt (Continued)*

Possible Causes	Suggested Actions
Modem speed setting is not locked *(continued)*	To set the terminal baud rate, use the **speed** line configuration command. This command sets both the transmit (to terminal) and receive (from terminal) speeds. **Syntax:** **speed** *bps* **Syntax description:** • *bps*—Baud rate in bits per second (bps). The default is 9600 bps. **Example:** The following example sets lines 1 and 2 on a Cisco 2509 access server to 115200 bps: ``` line 1 2 speed 115200 ``` **NOTE** If you cannot use flow control for some reason, limit the line speed to 9600 bps. Faster speeds likely will result in lost data. **Step 3** Use the **show line** exec command again, and confirm that the line speed is set to the desired value. **Step 4** When you are certain that the access server or router line is configured for the desired speed, initiate a reverse Telnet session to the modem via that line. For more information, see the section "Establishing a Reverse Telnet Session to a Modem," earlier in this chapter. **Step 5** Use a modem command string that includes the lock DTE speed command for your modem. See your modem documentation for exact configuration command syntax. **Note:** The lock DTE speed command, which might also be referred to as port rate adjust or buffered mode, is often related to the way in which the modem handles error correction. This command varies widely from one modem to another. Locking the modem speed ensures that the modem always communicates with the Cisco access server or router at the speed configured on the Cisco auxiliary port. If this command is not used, the modem reverts to the speed of the data link (the telephone line) instead of communicating at the speed configured on the access server.

continues

Table 17-3   *Dialup Sessions Sees "Garbage"*

Possible Causes	Suggested Actions	
Modem speed setting is not locked	**Step 1**	Use the **show line** exec command on the access server or router. The output for the auxiliary port should indicate the currently configured Tx and Rx speeds.
	Step 2	If the line is not configured to the correct speed, use the **speed** line configuration command to set the line speed on the access server or router line. Set the value to the highest speed in common between the modem and the access server or router port.

To set the terminal baud rate, use the **speed** line configuration command. This command sets both the transmit (to terminal) and receive (from terminal) speeds.

Syntax:

speed *bps*

Syntax description:

- *bps*—Baud rate in bits per second (bps). The default is 9600 bps.

Example:

The following example sets lines 1 and 2 on a Cisco 2509 access server to 115200 bps:

```
line 1 2
 speed 115200
```

NOTE   If you cannot use flow control for some reason, limit the line speed to 9600 bps. Faster speeds likely will result in lost data.

Step 3   Use the **show line** exec command again, and confirm that the line speed is set to the desired value.

Step 4   When you are certain that the access server or router line is configured for the desired speed, initiate a reverse Telnet session to the modem via that line. For more information, see the section "Establishing a Reverse Telnet Session to a Modem," earlier in this chapter.

Step 5   Use a modem command string that includes the lock DTE speed command for your modem. See your modem documentation for exact configuration command syntax.

Note: The **lock** DTE speed command, which might also be referred to as *port rate adjust* or *buffered mode*, is often related to the way in which the modem handles error correction. This command varies widely from one modem to another.

Table 17-3   *Dialup Sessions Sees "Garbage" (Continued)*

Possible Causes	Suggested Actions
Modem speed setting is not locked *(continued)*	Locking the modem speed ensures that the modem always communicates with the Cisco access server or router at the speed configured on the Cisco auxiliary port. If this command is not used, the modem reverts to the speed of the data link (the telephone line) instead of communicating at the speed configured on the access server.

Symptom: Remote dial-in session ends up in an already existing session initiated by another user. That is, instead of getting a login prompt, a dial-in user sees a session established by another user (which might be a UNIX command prompt, a text editor session, and so forth).

Table 17-4   *Dialup Session Ends Up in Existing Session*

Possible Causes	Suggested Actions	
Modem configured for DCD is always high	**Step 1**	The modem should be reconfigured to have DCD high only on CD. This is usually accomplished by using the **&C1** modem command string, but check your modem documentation for the exact syntax for your modem.
	Step 2	You might have to configure the access server line to which the modem is connected with the **no exec** line configuration command. Clear the line with the **clear line** privileged exec command, initiate a reverse Telnet session with the modem, and reconfigure the modem so that DCD is high only on CD.
	Step 3	End the Telnet session by entering **disconnect**, and reconfigure the access server line with the **exec** line configuration command.
Modem control is not enabled on the access server or router	**Step 1**	Use the **show line** exec command on the access server or router. The output for the auxiliary port should **show inout** or **RIisCD** in the Modem column. This indicates that modem control is enabled on the line of the access server or router.
	Step 2	Configure the line for modem control using the **modem inout** line configuration command. Modem control is now enabled on the access server.
		Note: Be certain to use the **modem inout** command instead of the **modem ri-is-cd** command while the connectivity of the modem is in question. The latter command allows the line to accept incoming calls only. Outgoing calls will be refused, making it impossible to establish a Telnet session with the modem to configure it. If you want to enable the **modem ri-is-cd** command, do so only after you are certain that the modem is functioning correctly.

continues

Table 17-4 *Dialup Session Ends Up in Existing Session (Continued)*

Possible Causes	Suggested Actions	
Cabling is incorrect	Step 1	Check the cabling between the modem and the access server or router. Confirm that the modem is connected to the auxiliary port on the access server or router with a rolled RJ-45 cable and an MMOD DB-25 adapter. This cabling configuration is recommended and supported by Cisco for RJ-45 ports. (These connectors are typically labeled "Modem.")
		Two types of RJ-45 cabling are commonly encountered when connecting a modem: straight and rolled. If you hold the two ends of an RJ-45 cable side by side, you'll see eight colored strips, or pins, at each end. If the order of the colored pins is the same at each end, then the cable is straight. If the order of the colors is reversed at each end, then the cable is rolled.
		The rolled cable (CAB-500RJ) is standard with Cisco's 2500/CS500.
	Step 2	Use the **show line** exec command to verify that the cabling is correct.

Table 17-5 *Dialup Receiving Modem Does Not Disconnect Properly*

Possible Causes	Suggested Actions	
Modem is not sensing DTR	Enter the **Hangup DTR** modem command string. This command tells the modem to drop the carrier when the DTR signal is no longer being received.	
	On a Hayes-compatible modem, the **&D3** string is commonly used to configure **Hangup DTR** on the modem. For the exact syntax of this command, see the documentation for your modem.	
Modem control is not enabled on the router or access server	Step 1	Use the **show line** exec command on the access server or router. The output for the auxiliary port should show **inout** or **RIisCD** in the Modem column. This indicates that modem control is enabled on the line of the access server or router.
	Step 2	Configure the line for modem control using the **modem inout** line configuration command. Modem control is now enabled on the access server.

Table 17-5 *Dialup Receiving Modem Does Not Disconnect Properly (Continued)*

Possible Causes	Suggested Actions
Modem control is not enabled on the router or access server *(continued)*	**Note:** Be certain to use the **modem inout** command instead of the **modem dialin** command while the connectivity of the modem is in question. The latter command allows the line to accept incoming calls only. Outgoing calls will be refused, making it impossible to establish a Telnet session with the modem to configure it. If you want to enable the **modem dialin** command, do so only after you are certain that the modem is functioning correctly.

Troubleshooting Outbound Calls

The troubleshooting approach for incoming calls starts at the bottom, but troubleshooting an outbound connection starts at the top. Outbound connection troubleshooting goes along these lines (a "yes" answer to the question gets to the next question):

- Does dial-on-demand routing initiate a call?
- If this is an async modem, do the chat scripts issue the expected commands?
- Does the call make it out to the PSTN?
- Does the remote end answer the call?
- Does the call complete?
- Is data passing over the link?
- Is the session established? (PPP or terminal)

Verifying Dialer Operation

To see whether the dialer is trying to make a call to its remote destination, use the command **debug dialer events**. More detailed information can be gained from **debug dialer packet**, but the **debug dialer packet** command is resource-intensive and should not be used on a busy system that has multiple dialer interfaces operating.

The following line of **debug** dialer events output for an IP packet lists the name of the DDR interface and the source and destination addresses of the packet:

```
Dialing cause: Async1: ip (s=172.16.1.111 d=172.16.2.22)
```

If this does not occur, the most common reason is improper configuration, either of the interesting traffic definitions, the state of the dialer interface, or the routing (Table 17-6).

Table 17-6   *Traffic Does Not Initiate a Dial Attempt*

Possible Causes	Suggested Actions	
Missing or incorrect "interesting traffic" definitions	**Step 1**	Using the command **show running-config**, ensure that the interface is configured with a dialer group and that there is a global level dialer list configured with a matching number.
	Step 2	Ensure that the **dialer-list** command is configured to permit either an entire protocol or to permit traffic matching an access list.
	Step 3	Verify that the access list declares packets going across the link to be interesting. One useful test is to use the privileged exec command **debug ip packet [list number]** using the number of the pertinent access list, and then attempt to **ping** or otherwise send traffic across the link. If the interesting traffic filters have been properly defined, you will see the packets in the **debug** output. If there is no **debug** output from this test, then the access list is not matching the packets.
Interface state	Using the command **show interfaces [*interface name*]**, ensure that the interface is in the state "up/up (spoofing)."	
Interface in "standby" mode	Another (primary) interface on the router has been configured to use the dialer interface as a backup interface. Furthermore, the primary interface is not in a state of "down/down," which is required to bring the dialer interface out of standby mode. Also, a *backup delay* must be configured on the primary interface, or the **backup interface** command will never be enforced.	
	To check that the dialer interface will change from standby to up/up (spoofing), it is usually necessary to pull the cable from the primary interface. Simply shutting down the primary interface with the configuration command **shutdown** will not put the primary interface into down/down, but instead will put it into administratively down, which is not the same thing.	
	In addition, if the primary connection is via Frame Relay, the Frame Relay configuration must be done on a point-to-point serial subinterface, and the telco must be passing the "active" bit, a practice also known as "end-to-end LMI."	
Interface that is "administratively down"	The dialer interface has been configured with the command **shutdown**. This is also the default state of any interface when a Cisco router is booted for the very first time. Use the interface configuration command **no shutdown** to remove this impediment.	

Table 17-6   *Traffic Does Not Initiate a Dial Attempt (Continued)*

Possible Causes	Suggested Actions
Incorrect routing	Issue the exec command **show ip route [*a.b.c.d*]**, where *a.b.c.d* is the address of the dialer interface of the remote router. (If **ip unnumbered** is used on the remote router, use the address of the interface listed in the **ip unnumbered** command.)
	The output should show a route to the remote address via the dialer interface. If there is no route, ensure that static or floating static routes have been configured by examining the output of **show running-config**.
	If there is a route via an interface other than the dialer interface, the implication is that DDR is being used as a backup. Examine the router configuration to make sure that static or floating static routes have been configured. The surest way to test the routing in this case is to disable the primary connection and then execute the **show ip route [*a.b.c.d*]** command to verify that the proper route has been installed in the routing table.
	Note: If you attempt this during live network operations, a dial event may be triggered. This sort of testing is best accomplished during scheduled maintenance cycles.

Placing the Call

If the routing and the interesting traffic filters are correct, a call should be initiated. This can be seen by using **debug dialer events**:

```
Async1 DDR: Dialing cause ip (s=10.0.0.1, d=10.0.0.2)
Async1 DDR: Attempting to dial 5551212
```

If the dialing cause is seen but no attempt is made to dial, the usual reason is a misconfigured dialer map or dialer profile (Table 17-7).

Table 17-7   *Call Not Placed*

Possible Problem	Suggested Actions
Misconfigured dialer map	Use the command **show running-config** to ensure that the dialing interface is configured with at least one **dialer map** statement that points to the protocol address and called number of the remote site.
Misconfigured dialer profile	Use the command **show running-config** to ensure that the dialer interface is configured with a **dialer pool X** command and that a dialer interface on the router is configured with a matching **dialer pool—member X**. If dialer profiles are not properly configured, you may see a **debug** message such as "Dialer1: Can't place call, no dialer pool set."
	Make sure that a dialer string is configured.

Async Outbound Calling—Verify Chat Script Operation

If the outbound call is a modem call, a chat script must execute for the call to proceed. For dialer map-based DDR, the chat script is invoked by the **modem-script** parameter in a dialer map command. If the DDR is dialer profile-based, this is accomplished by the command **script dialer,** configured on the TTY line. Both uses rely on a chat script existing in the router's global configuration, such as this, for example:

```
chat-script callout AT OK atdt\T TIMEOUT 60 CONNECT \c
```

In either event, the command to view the chat script activity is **debug chat**. If the dial string (such as phone number) used in the **dialer map** or **dialer string** command were 5551212, the debug output would look like this:

```
CHAT1: Attempting async line dialer script
CHAT1: Dialing using Modem script: callout & System script: none
CHAT1: process started
CHAT1: Asserting DTR
CHAT1: Chat script callout started
CHAT1: Sending string: AT
CHAT1: Expecting string: OK
CHAT1: Completed match for expect: OK
CHAT1: Sending string: atdt5551212
CHAT1: Expecting string: CONNECT
CHAT1: Completed match for expect: CONNECT
CHAT1: Chat script callout finished, status = Success
```

Chat script problems can be broken into three categories:

- Configuration error
- Modem failure
- Connection failure

Table 17-8 shows chat script failures and suggested actions.

Table 17-8   *Chat Script Failure*

Output from debug chat Shows:	Suggested Action
No matching chat script found for [number]	A chat script has not been configured. Add one.
Chat script dialout finished, status = Connection timed out; remote host not responding	The modem is not responding to the chat script. Verify communication with the modem (see Table 16-2 in Chapter 16).
Timeout expecting: CONNECT	**Possibility 1**: The local modem is not actually placing the call. Verify that the modem can place a call by using reverse Telnet to the modem and manually initiating a dial.
	Possibility 2: The remote modem is not answering. Test this by dialing the remote modem with an ordinary POTS telephone.

Table 17-8 *Chat Script Failure (Continued)*

Output from debug chat Shows:	Suggested Action
Timeout expecting: CONNECT *(continued)*	**Possibility 3**: The number being dialed is incorrect. Verify the number by dialing it manually, and correct the configuration, if necessary.
	Possibility 4: The modem trainup is taking too long or the TIMEOUT value is too low. If the local modem is external, turn up the modem speaker volume and listen to the trainup tones. If the trainup is abruptly cut off, try increasing the TIMEOUT value in the **chat-script** command. If the TIMEOUT is already 60 seconds or more, see the section "Modem Trainup," earlier in this chapter.

ISDN Outbound Calling

The first thing to check at the first suspicion of an ISDN failure, either on a BRI or a PRI, is the output from **show isdn status**. The key things to note are that Layer 1 should be Active and Layer 2 should be in a state of MULTIPLE_FRAME_ESTABLISHED. See the section "Interpreting **show isdn status** Output," in Chapter 16, for information on reading this output and for corrective measures.

For outbound ISDN calls, **debug isdn q931** and **debug isdn events** are the best tools to use. Fortunately, debugging outbound calls is very similar to debugging incoming calls. A normal successful call might look like this:

```
*Mar 20 21:07:45.025: ISDN BR0: Event: Call to 5553759 at 64 Kb/s
*Mar 20 21:07:45.033: ISDN BR0: TX -> SETUP pd = 8  callref = 0x2C
*Mar 20 21:07:45.037:          Bearer Capability i = 0x8890
*Mar 20 21:07:45.041:          Channel ID i = 0x83
*Mar 20 21:07:45.041:          Keypad Facility i = 0x35353533373539
*Mar 20 21:07:45.141: ISDN BR0: RX <-  CALL_PROC pd = 8  callref = 0xAC
*Mar 20 21:07:45.145:          Channel ID i = 0x89
*Mar 20 21:07:45.157: ISDN BR0: received HOST_PROCEEDING
        Channel ID i = 0x0101
*Mar 20 21:07:45.161:   --------------------
        Channel ID i = 0x89
*Mar 20 21:07:45.313: ISDN BR0: RX <-  CONNECT pd = 8  callref = 0xAC
*Mar 20 21:07:45.325: ISDN BR0: received HOST_CONNECT
```

Note that the CONNECT message is the key indicator of success. If a CONNECT is not received, you may see a DISCONNECT or a RELEASE_COMP ("release complete") message followed by a cause code:

```
*Mar 20 22:11:03.212: ISDN BR0: RX <-  RELEASE_COMP pd = 8  callref = 0x8F
*Mar 20 22:11:03.216:          Cause i = 0x8295 - Call rejected
```

The cause value indicates two things. The second byte of the 4- or 6-byte value indicates from where in the end-to-end call path the DISCONNECT or RELEASE_COMP was received. This can help you to localize the problem. The third and fourth bytes indicate the actual reason for the failure. See the tables that follow for the meanings of the different values.

Note: If you see this line, the likely reason is a higher-protocol failure:

```
Cause i = 0x8090 - Normal call clearing
```

PPP authentication failure is a typical reason. Turn on **debug ppp negotiation** and **debug ppp authentication** before assuming that the connection failure is necessarily an ISDN problem.

Cause Code Fields

Table 17-9 lists the ISDN cause code fields that display in the following format within the **debug** commands:

```
i=0x y1 y2 z1 z2 [a1 a2]
```

Table 17-9 *ISDN Cause Code Fields*

Field	Value—Description
0x	The values that follow are in hexadecimal.
y1	8-ITU-T standard coding.
y2	0-User
	1-Private network serving local user
	2-Public network serving local user
	3-Transit network
	4-Public network serving remote user
	5-Private network serving remote user
	7-International network
	A-Network beyond internetworking point
z1	Class (the more significant hexadecimal number) of cause value. Refer to Table 17-10 for detailed information about possible values.
z2	Value (the less significant hexadecimal number) of cause value. Refer to Table 17-10 for detailed information about possible values.
a1	(Optional) Diagnostic field that is always 8.
a2	(Optional) Diagnostic field that is one of the following values:
	0-Unknown
	1-Permanent
	2-Transient

Cause Values

Table 17-10 lists descriptions of some of the most commonly seen cause values of the cause information element—the third and fourth bytes of the cause code.

Table 17-10 *ISDN Cause Values*

Hex Value	Cause	Explanation
81	Unallocated (unassigned) number	The ISDN number was sent to the switch in the correct format; however, the number is not assigned to any destination equipment.
90	Normal call clearing	Normal call clearing has occurred.
91	User busy	The called system acknowledges the connection request but is incapable of accepting the call because all B channels are in use.
92	No user responding	The connection cannot be completed because the destination does not respond to the call.
93	No answer from user (user alerted)	The destination responds to the connection request but fails to complete the connection within the prescribed time. The problem is at the remote end of the connection.
95	Call rejected	The destination is capable of accepting the call, but it rejected the call for an unknown reason.
9C	Invalid number format	The connection could not be established because the destination address was presented in an unrecognizable format or because the destination address was incomplete.
9F	Normal, unspecified	This reports the occurrence of a normal event when no standard cause applies. No action is required.
A2	No circuit/channel available	The connection cannot be established because no appropriate channel is available to take the call.
A6	Network out of order	The destination cannot be reached because the network is not functioning correctly, and the condition might last for an extended period of time. An immediate reconnect attempt will probably be unsuccessful.
AC	Requested circuit/channel not available	The remote equipment cannot provide the requested channel for an unknown reason. This might be a temporary problem.
B2	Requested facility not subscribed	The remote equipment supports the requested supplementary service by subscription only. This is frequently a reference to long-distance service.

continues

Table 17-10 *ISDN Cause Values (Continued)*

Hex Value	Cause	Explanation
B9	Bearer capability not authorized	The user requested a bearer capability that the network provides, but the user is not authorized to use it. This might be a subscription problem.
D8	Incompatible destination	This indicates that an attempt was made to connect to non-ISDN equipment—for example, to an analog line.
E0	Mandatory information element missing	The receiving equipment received a message that did not include one of the mandatory information elements. This is usually the result of a D-channel error. If this error occurs systematically, report it to your ISDN service provider.
E4	Invalid information element contents	The remote equipment received a message that includes invalid information in the information element. This is usually the result of a D-channel error.

For more complete information about ISDN codes and values, refer to the "ISDN Switch Codes and Values" chapter in the *Cisco IOS Debug Command Reference* for your version of IOS, in print or online at www.cisco.com/univercd/home/home.htm.

CAS Outbound Calling

For outbound calling via CAS T1 or E1 and integrated digital modems, much of the troubleshooting is similar to other DDR troubleshooting. (The same holds true for outbound integrated modem calls over a PRI line.) The unique features involved in making a call in this manner require special debugging in the event of a call failure.

As for other DDR situations, you must ensure that a call attempt is demanded—**debug dialer events** is useful for this (see the section "Verifying Dialer Operation," earlier in this chapter).

Before a call can be placed, a modem must be allocated for the call. To view this process and the subsequent call use the following **debug** commands:

> **debug modem**
> **debug modem csm**
> **debug cas**

Note: The **debug cas** command first appeared in IOS version 12.0(7)T for the AS5200 and AS5300. Earlier versions of IOS use a system-level configuration command **service internal** along with the exec command **modem-mgmt debug rbs**:

Turning On the Debugs

```
router#conf t
Enter configuration commands, one per line.  End with CNTL/Z.
router(config)#service internal
router(config)#^Z

router#modem-mgmt csm ?
  debug-rbs      enable rbs debugging
  no-debug-rbs   disable rbs debugging

router#modem-mgmt csm debug-rbs
router#
neat msg at slot 0: debug-rbs is on
neat msg at slot 0: special debug-rbs is on
```

Turning Off the Debugs

```
router#
router#modem-mgmt csm no-debug-rbs
neat msg at slot 0: debug-rbs is off
```

Debugging this information on an AS5800 requires connecting to the trunk card itself.

The following is an example of a normal outbound call over a CAS T1 provisioned and configured for FXS-Ground-Start:

```
Mica Modem(1/0): Rcvd Dial String(5551111) [Modem receives digits from chat script]
CSM_PROC_IDLE: CSM_EVENT_MODEM_OFFHOOK at slot 1, port 0
CSM_RX_CAS_EVENT_FROM_NEAT:(A003):  EVENT_CHANNEL_LOCK at slot 1 and port 0
CSM_PROC_OC4_DIALING: CSM_EVENT_DSX0_BCHAN_ASSIGNED at slot 1, port 0
Mica Modem(1/0): Configure(0x1)
Mica Modem(1/0): Configure(0x2)
Mica Modem(1/0): Configure(0x5)
Mica Modem(1/0): Call Setup

neat msg at slot 0: (0/2): Tx RING_GROUND
Mica Modem(1/0): State Transition to Call Setup

neat msg at slot 0: (0/2): Rx TIP_GROUND_NORING [Telco switch goes OFFHOOK]
CSM_RX_CAS_EVENT_FROM_NEAT:(A003):  EVENT_START_TX_TONE at slot 1 and port 0
CSM_PROC_OC5_WAIT_FOR_CARRIER: CSM_EVENT_DSX0_START_TX_TONE at slot 1, port 0

neat msg at slot 0: (0/2): Tx LOOP_CLOSURE [Now the router goes OFFHOOK]

Mica Modem(1/0): Rcvd Tone detected(2)
Mica Modem(1/0): Generate digits:called_party_num=5551111 len=8
Mica Modem(1/0): Rcvd Digits Generated
CSM_PROC_OC5_WAIT_FOR_CARRIER: CSM_EVENT_ADDR_INFO_COLLECTED at slot 1, port 0
CSM_RX_CAS_EVENT_FROM_NEAT:(A003):  EVENT_CHANNEL_CONNECTED at slot 1 and port 0
CSM_PROC_OC5_WAIT_FOR_CARRIER: CSM_EVENT_DSX0_CONNECTED at slot 1, port 0
Mica Modem(1/0): Link Initiate
Mica Modem(1/0): State Transition to Connect
Mica Modem(1/0): State Transition to Link
Mica Modem(1/0): State Transition to Trainup
Mica Modem(1/0): State Transition to EC Negotiating
Mica Modem(1/0): State Transition to Steady State
Mica Modem(1/0): State Transition to Steady State Speedshifting
Mica Modem(1/0): State Transition to Steady State
```

debugs for T1s and E1s with other signaling types are similar.

Getting to this point in the debugging indicates that the calling and answering modems have trained and connected and that higher-layer protocols can begin to negotiate. If a modem is properly allocated for the outbound call, but the connection fails to get this far, the T1 must be examined. See Chapter 15 for T1 troubleshooting.

Troubleshooting PPP

Troubleshooting the PPP portion of a connection begins when you have established that the dial connection, ISDN or async, successfully establishes.

It is important to understand what a successful **debug** PPP sequence looks like before you troubleshoot PPP negotiation. In this way, comparing a faulty PPP **debug** session against a successfully completed **debug** PPP sequence saves you time and effort.

Following is an example of a successful PPP sequence. See Table 17-11 for a detailed description of the output fields.

```
Montecito#
Mar 13 10:57:13.415: %LINK-3-UPDOWN: Interface Async1, changed state to up
Mar 13 10:57:15.415: As1 LCP: O CONFREQ [ACKrcvd] id 2 len 25
Mar 13 10:57:15.415: As1 LCP:    ACCM 0x000A0000 (0x0206000A0000)
Mar 13 10:57:15.415: As1 LCP:    AuthProto CHAP (0x0305C22305)
Mar 13 10:57:15.415: As1 LCP:    MagicNumber 0x1084F0A2 (0x05061084F0A2)
Mar 13 10:57:15.415: As1 LCP:    PFC (0x0702)
Mar 13 10:57:15.415: As1 LCP:    ACFC (0x0802)
Mar 13 10:57:15.543: As1 LCP: I CONFACK [REQsent] id 2 len 25
Mar 13 10:57:15.543: As1 LCP:    ACCM 0x000A0000 (0x0206000A0000)
Mar 13 10:57:15.543: As1 LCP:    AuthProto CHAP (0x0305C22305)
Mar 13 10:57:15.543: As1 LCP:    MagicNumber 0x1084F0A2 (0x05061084F0A2)
Mar 13 10:57:15.543: As1 LCP:    PFC (0x0702)
Mar 13 10:57:15.547: As1 LCP:    ACFC (0x0802)
Mar 13 10:57:16.919: As1 LCP: I CONFREQ [ACKrcvd] id 4 len 23
Mar 13 10:57:16.919: As1 LCP:    ACCM 0x000A0000 (0x0206000A0000)
Mar 13 10:57:16.919: As1 LCP:    MagicNumber 0x001327B0 (0x0506001327B0)
Mar 13 10:57:16.919: As1 LCP:    PFC (0x0702)
Mar 13 10:57:16.919: As1 LCP:    ACFC (0x0802)
Mar 13 10:57:16.919: As1 LCP:    Callback 6  (0x0D0306)
Mar 13 10:57:16.919: As1 LCP: O CONFREJ [ACKrcvd] id 4 len 7
<SMALL>Mar 13 10:57:16.919: As1 LCP:    Callback 6  (0x0D0306)</SMALL>
Mar 13 10:57:17.047: As1 LCP: I CONFREQ [ACKrcvd] id 5 len 20
<SMALL>Mar 13 10:57:17.047: As1 LCP:    ACCM 0x000A0000 (0x0206000A0000)</SMALL>
<SMALL>Mar 13 10:57:17.047: As1 LCP:    MagicNumber 0x001327B0 (0x0506001327B0)</SMALL>
<SMALL>Mar 13 10:57:17.047: As1 LCP:    PFC (0x0702)</SMALL>
<SMALL>Mar 13 10:57:17.047: As1 LCP:    ACFC (0x0802)</SMALL>
Mar 13 10:57:17.047: As1 LCP: O CONFACK [ACKrcvd] id 5 len 20
Mar 13 10:57:17.047: As1 LCP:    ACCM 0x000A0000 (0x0206000A0000)
Mar 13 10:57:17.047: As1 LCP:    MagicNumber 0x001327B0 (0x0506001327B0)
Mar 13 10:57:17.047: As1 LCP:    PFC (0x0702)
Mar 13 10:57:17.047: As1 LCP:    ACFC (0x0802)
Mar 13 10:57:17.047: As1 LCP: State is Open
Mar 13 10:57:17.047: As1 PPP: Phase is AUTHENTICATING, by this end
Mar 13 10:57:17.047: As1 CHAP: O CHALLENGE id 1 len 28 from "Montecito"
```

```
Mar 13 10:57:17.191: As1 CHAP: I RESPONSE id 1 len 30 from "Goleta"
Mar 13 10:57:17.191: As1 CHAP: O SUCCESS id 1 len 4
Mar 13 10:57:17.191: As1 PPP: Phase is UP
<SMALL>Mar 13 10:57:17.191: As1 IPCP: O CONFREQ [Closed] id 1 len 10</SMALL>
<SMALL>Mar 13 10:57:17.191: As1 IPCP:    Address 172.22.66.23 (0x0306AC164217)</SMALL>
<SMALL>Mar 13 10:57:17.303: As1 IPCP: I CONFREQ [REQsent] id 1 len 40</SMALL>
Mar 13 10:57:17.303: As1 IPCP:    CompressType VJ 15 slots CompressSlotID (0x0206002D0F01)
Mar 13 10:57:17.303: As1 IPCP:    Address 0.0.0.0 (0x030600000000)
Mar 13 10:57:17.303: As1 IPCP:    PrimaryDNS 0.0.0.0 (0x810600000000)
Mar 13 10:57:17.303: As1 IPCP:    PrimaryWINS 0.0.0.0 (0x820600000000)
Mar 13 10:57:17.303: As1 IPCP:    SecondaryDNS 0.0.0.0 (0x830600000000)
Mar 13 10:57:17.303: As1 IPCP:    SecondaryWINS 0.0.0.0 (0x840600000000)
Mar 13 10:57:17.303: As1 IPCP: O CONFREJ [REQsent] id 1 len 22
Mar 13 10:57:17.303: As1 IPCP:    CompressType VJ 15 slots CompressSlotID (0x0206002D0F01)
Mar 13 10:57:17.303: As1 IPCP:    PrimaryWINS 0.0.0.0 (0x820600000000)
Mar 13 10:57:17.303: As1 IPCP:    SecondaryWINS 0.0.0.0 (0x840600000000)
Mar 13 10:57:17.319: As1 CCP: I CONFREQ [Not negotiated] id 1 len 15
Mar 13 10:57:17.319: As1 CCP:    MS-PPC supported bits 0x00000001 (0x120600000001)
Mar 13 10:57:17.319: As1 CCP:    Stacker history 1 check mode EXTENDED (0x1105000104)
Mar 13 10:57:17.319: As1 LCP: O PROTREJ [Open] id 3 len 21 protocol CCP
Mar 13 10:57:17.319: As1 LCP:    (0x80FD0101000F1206000000000111050001)
Mar 13 10:57:17.319: As1 LCP:    (0x04)
Mar 13 10:57:17.319: As1 IPCP: I CONFACK [REQsent] id 1 len 10
Mar 13 10:57:17.319: As1 IPCP:    Address 172.22.66.23 (0x0306AC164217)
Mar 13 10:57:18.191: %LINEPROTO-5-UPDOWN: Line protocol on Interface Async1, changed state to up
Mar 13 10:57:19.191: As1 IPCP: TIMEout: State ACKrcvd
Mar 13 10:57:19.191: As1 IPCP: O CONFREQ [ACKrcvd] id 2 len 10
Mar 13 10:57:19.191: As1 IPCP:    Address 172.22.66.23 (0x0306AC164217)
Mar 13 10:57:19.315: As1 IPCP: I CONFACK [REQsent] id 2 len 10
Mar 13 10:57:19.315: As1 IPCP:    Address 172.22.66.23 (0x0306AC164217)
Mar 13 10:57:20.307: As1 IPCP: I CONFREQ [ACKrcvd] id 2 len 34
Mar 13 10:57:20.307: As1 IPCP:    Address 0.0.0.0 (0x030600000000)
Mar 13 10:57:20.307: As1 IPCP:    PrimaryDNS 0.0.0.0 (0x810600000000)
Mar 13 10:57:20.307: As1 IPCP:    PrimaryWINS 0.0.0.0 (0x820600000000)
Mar 13 10:57:20.307: As1 IPCP:    SecondaryDNS 0.0.0.0 (0x830600000000)
Mar 13 10:57:20.307: As1 IPCP:    SecondaryWINS 0.0.0.0 (0x840600000000)
Mar 13 10:57:20.307: As1 IPCP: O CONFREJ [ACKrcvd] id 2 len 16
Mar 13 10:57:20.307: As1 IPCP:    PrimaryWINS 0.0.0.0 (0x820600000000)
Mar 13 10:57:20.307: As1 IPCP:    SecondaryWINS 0.0.0.0 (0x840600000000)
Mar 13 10:57:20.419: As1 IPCP: I CONFREQ [ACKrcvd] id 3 len 22
Mar 13 10:57:20.419: As1 IPCP:    Address 0.0.0.0 (0x030600000000)
Mar 13 10:57:20.419: As1 IPCP:    PrimaryDNS 0.0.0.0 (0x810600000000)
Mar 13 10:57:20.419: As1 IPCP:    SecondaryDNS 0.0.0.0 (0x830600000000)
Mar 13 10:57:20.419: As1 IPCP: O CONFNAK [ACKrcvd] id 3 len 22
Mar 13 10:57:20.419: As1 IPCP:    Address 10.1.1.1 (0x03060A010101)
Mar 13 10:57:20.419: As1 IPCP:    PrimaryDNS 171.68.10.70 (0x8106AB440A46)
Mar 13 10:57:20.419: As1 IPCP:    SecondaryDNS 171.68.10.140 (0x8306AB440A8C)
Mar 13 10:57:20.543: As1 IPCP: I CONFREQ [ACKrcvd] id 4 len 22
Mar 13 10:57:20.543: As1 IPCP:    Address 10.1.1.1 (0x03060A010101)
Mar 13 10:57:20.547: As1 IPCP:    PrimaryDNS 171.68.10.70 (0x8106AB440A46)
Mar 13 10:57:20.547: As1 IPCP:    SecondaryDNS 171.68.10.140 (0x8306AB440A8C)
Mar 13 10:57:20.547: As1 IPCP: O CONFACK [ACKrcvd] id 4 len 22
Mar 13 10:57:20.547: As1 IPCP:    Address 10.1.1.1 (0x03060A010101)
Mar 13 10:57:20.547: As1 IPCP:    PrimaryDNS 171.68.10.70 (0x8106AB440A46)
Mar 13 10:57:20.547: As1 IPCP:    SecondaryDNS 171.68.10.140 (0x8306AB440A8C)
Mar 13 10:57:20.547: As1 IPCP: State is Open
Mar 13 10:57:20.551: As1 IPCP: Install route to 10.1.1.1
```

Note that your debugs may appear in a different format. This output is the newer PPP debugging output format, which was modified in IOS version 11.2(8). See Chapter 16 for an example of PPP debugging with the older versions of IOS.

Table 17-11 *PPP LCP Negotiation Details*

Time Stamp	Description
10:57:15.415	Outgoing configuration request (O CONFREQ). The NAS sends an outgoing PPP configuration request packet to the client.
10:57:15.543	Incoming configuration acknowledgment (I CONFACK). The client acknowledges Montecito's PPP request.
10:57:16.919	Incoming configuration request (I CONFREQ). The client wants to negotiate the callback protocol.
10:57:16.919	Outgoing configuration reject (O CONFREJ). The NAS rejects the callback option.
10:57:17.047	Incoming configuration request (I CONFREQ). The client requests a new set of options. Notice that Microsoft Callback is not requested this time.
10:57:17.047	Outgoing configuration acknowledgment (O CONFACK). The NAS accepts the new set of options.
10:57:17.047	PPP LCP negotiation is completed successfully (LCP: State is Open). Both sides have acknowledged (CONFACK) the other side's configuration request (CONFREQ).
10:57:17.047 to 10:57:17.191	PPP authentication is completed successfully. After LCP negotiates, authentication starts. Authentication must take place before any network protocols, such as IP, are delivered. Both sides authenticate with the method negotiated during LCP. Montecito is authenticating the client using CHAP.
10:57:20.551	The state is open for IP Control Protocol (IPCP). A route is negotiated and installed for the IPCP peer, which is assigned IP address 1.1.1.1.

Link Control Protocol

Two types of problems are typically encountered during LCP negotiation. The first occurs when one peer makes configuration requests that the other peer cannot or will not acknowledge. Although this is a frequent occurrence, it can be a problem if the requester insists on the parameter. A typical example is when negotiating AUTHTYPE. For instance, many access servers are configured to accept only CHAP for authentication. If the caller is configured to do only PAP authentication, CONFREQs and CONFNAKs will be exchanged until one peer drops the connection.

```
BR0:1 LCP: I CONFREQ [ACKrcvd] id 66 len 14
BR0:1 LCP:    AuthProto PAP (0x0304C023)
BR0:1 LCP:    MagicNumber 0xBC6B9F91 (0x0506BC6B9F91)
```

```
BR0:1 LCP: O CONFNAK [ACKrcvd] id 66 len 9
BR0:1 LCP:     AuthProto CHAP (0x0305C22305)
BR0:1 LCP: I CONFREQ [ACKrcvd] id 67 len 14
BR0:1 LCP:     AuthProto PAP (0x0304C023)
BR0:1 LCP:     MagicNumber 0xBC6B9F91 (0x0506BC6B9F91)
BR0:1 LCP: O CONFNAK [ACKrcvd] id 67 len 9
BR0:1 LCP:     AuthProto CHAP (0x0305C22305)
BR0:1 LCP: I CONFREQ [ACKrcvd] id 68 len 14
BR0:1 LCP:     AuthProto PAP (0x0304C023)
BR0:1 LCP:     MagicNumber 0xBC6B9F91 (0x0506BC6B9F91)
BR0:1 LCP: O CONFNAK [ACKrcvd] id 68 len 9
BR0:1 LCP:     AuthProto CHAP (0x0305C22305)
```

. . . and so on.

The second type of problem seen in LCP is when *only* outbound CONFREQs are seen on one or both peers, as in the example that follows. This is usually the result of what is referred to as a *speed mismatch* at the lower layer. This condition can occur in either async or ISDN DDR.

LCP failure example:

```
Jun 10 19:57:59.768: As5 PPP: Phase is ESTABLISHING, Active Open
Jun 10 19:57:59.768: As5 LCP: O CONFREQ [Closed] id 64 len 25
Jun 10 19:57:59.768: As5 LCP: ACCM 0x000A0000 (0x0206000A0000)
Jun 10 19:57:59.768: As5 LCP: AuthProto CHAP (0x0305C22305)
Jun 10 19:57:59.768: As5 LCP: MagicNumber 0x5779D9D2 (0x05065779D9D2)
Jun 10 19:57:59.768: As5 LCP: PFC (0x0702)
Jun 10 19:57:59.768: As5 LCP: ACFC (0x0802)
Jun 10 19:58:01.768: As5 LCP: TIMEout: State REQsent
Jun 10 19:58:01.768: As5 LCP: O CONFREQ [REQsent] id 65 len 25
Jun 10 19:58:01.768: As5 LCP: ACCM 0x000A0000 (0x0206000A0000)
Jun 10 19:58:01.768: As5 LCP: AuthProto CHAP (0x0305C22305)
Jun 10 19:58:01.768: As5 LCP: MagicNumber 0x5779D9D2 (0x05065779D9D2)
Jun 10 19:58:01.768: As5 LCP: PFC (0x0702)
Jun 10 19:58:01.768: As5 LCP: ACFC (0x0802).
Jun 10 19:58:03.768: As5 LCP: TIMEout: State REQsent
Jun 10 19:58:03.768: As5 LCP: O CONFREQ [REQsent] id 66 len 25
Jun 10 19:58:03.768: As5 LCP: ACCM 0x000A0000 (0x0206000A0000)
Jun 10 19:58:03.768: As5 LCP: AuthProto CHAP (0x0305C22305)
Jun 10 19:58:03.768: As5 LCP: MagicNumber 0x5779D9D2 (0x05065779D9D2)
Jun 10 19:58:03.768: As5 LCP: PFC (0x0702)
Jun 10 19:58:03.768: As5 LCP: ACF.C (0x0802)
Jun 10 19:58:05.768: As5 LCP: TIMEout: State REQsent
Jun 10 19:58:05.768: As5 LCP: O CONFREQ [REQsent] id 67 len 25
```

This repeats every 2 seconds until this occurs:

```
Jun 10 19:58:19.768: As5 LCP: O CONFREQ [REQsent] id 74 len 25
Jun 10 19:58:19.768: As5 LCP: ACCM 0x000A0000 (0x0206000A0000)
Jun 10 19:58:19.768: As5 LCP: AuthProto CHAP (0x0305C22305)
Jun 10 19:58:19.768: As5 LCP: MagicNumber 0x5779D9D2 (0x05065779D9D2)
Jun 10 19:58:19.768: As5 LCP: PFC (0x0702)
Jun 10 19:58:19.768: As5 LCP: ACFC (0x0802)
Jun 10 19:58:21.768: As5 LCP: TIMEout: State REQsent
Jun 10 19:58:21.768: TTY5: Async Int reset: Dropping DTR
```

If the connection is asynchronous, the probable cause is a speed mismatch between the router and its modem, usually as a result of having failed to lock the DTE speed of the modem to the configured speed of the TTY line. The problem may be found on either or both of the peers; both should be checked. (See Table 17-1.)

If the symptoms are seen when the connection is over ISDN, the problem likely is that one peer is connecting at 56K, while the other is at 64K. Although this condition is rare, it does happen; the problem could be one or both peers, or possibly the telco itself. Use **debug isdn q931** and examine the SETUP messages on each of the peers. The bearer capability sent from one peer should match the bearer capability seen in the SETUP message received on the other peer. As a possible remedy, you can configure the dialing speed, 56K or 64K, in either the interface-level command **dialer map** or in the command **dialer isdn speed** configured under a map class.

```
*Mar 20 21:07:45.033: ISDN BR0: TX ->  SETUP pd = 8  callref = 0x2C
*Mar 20 21:07:45.037:          Bearer Capability i = 0x8890
*Mar 20 21:07:45.041:          Channel ID i = 0x83
*Mar 20 21:07:45.041:          Keypad Facility i = 0x35353533373539
```

This situation is one that may warrant a call to the Cisco TAC. Collect the following outputs from both peers before calling the TAC:

> **show running-config**
> **show version**
> **debug isdn q931**
> **debug isdn events**
> **debug ppp negotiation**

Authentication

Failed authentication is the single most common reason for a PPP failure. Misconfigured or mismatched usernames and passwords create error messages in **debug** output.

The following example shows that the username Goleta does not have permission to dial in to the NAS, which does not have a local username configured for this user. To fix the problem, use the **username** *name* **password** *password* command to add the username Goleta to the NAS's local AAA database:

```
Mar 13 11:01:42.399: As2 LCP: State is Open
Mar 13 11:01:42.399: As2 PPP: Phase is AUTHENTICATING, by this end
Mar 13 11:01:42.399: As2 CHAP: O CHALLENGE id 1 len 28 from "Montecito"
Mar 13 11:01:42.539: As2 CHAP: I RESPONSE id 1 len 30 from "Goleta"
Mar 13 11:01:42.539: As2 CHAP: Unable to validate Response.  Username Goleta not found
Mar 13 11:01:42.539: As2 CHAP: O FAILURE id 1 len 26 msg is "Authentication failure"
Mar 13 11:01:42.539: As2 PPP: Phase is TERMINATING
```

The following example shows that the username Goleta is configured on the NAS. However, the password comparison failed. To fix this problem, use the **username** *name* **password** *password* command to specify the correct login password for Goleta:

```
Mar 13 11:04:06.843: As3 LCP: State is Open
Mar 13 11:04:06.843: As3 PPP: Phase is AUTHENTICATING, by this end
Mar 13 11:04:06.843: As3 CHAP: O CHALLENGE id 1 len 28 from "Montecito"
Mar 13 11:04:06.987: As3 CHAP: I RESPONSE id 1 len 30 from "Goleta"
Mar 13 11:04:06.987: As3 CHAP: O FAILURE id 1 len 25 msg is "MD/DES compare failed"
Mar 13 11:04:06.987: As3 PPP: Phase is TERMINATING
```

Network Control Protocol

After the peers have successfully performed whatever authentication is required, the negotiation moves into the NCP phase. If both peers are properly configured, the NCP negotiation might look like the following example, which shows a client PC dialing into and negotiating with a NAS:

```
solvang# show debug
      Generic IP:
      IP peer address activity debugging is on
      PPP:
      PPP protocol negotiation debugging is on

*Mar  1 21:35:04.186: As4 PPP: Phase is UP
*Mar  1 21:35:04.190: As4 IPCP: O CONFREQ [Not negotiated] id 1 len 10
*Mar  1 21:35:04.194: As4 IPCP:    Address 10.1.2.1 (0x03060A010201)
*Mar  1 21:35:04.282: As4 IPCP: I CONFREQ [REQsent] id 1 len 28
*Mar  1 21:35:04.282: As4 IPCP:    CompressType VJ 15 slots CompressSlotID
(0x0206002D0F01)
*Mar  1 21:35:04.286: As4 IPCP:    Address 0.0.0.0 (0x030600000000)
*Mar  1 21:35:04.290: As4 IPCP:    PrimaryDNS 0.0.0.0 (0x810600000000)
*Mar  1 21:35:04.298: As4 IPCP:    SecondaryDNS 0.0.0.0 (0x830600000000)
*Mar  1 21:35:04.306: As4 IPCP: O CONFREJ [REQsent] id 1 len 10
*Mar  1 21:35:04.310: As4 IPCP:    CompressType VJ 15 slots CompressSlotID
(0x0206002D0F01)
*Mar  1 21:35:04.314: As4 CCP: I CONFREQ [Not negotiated] id 1 len 15
*Mar  1 21:35:04.318: As4 CCP:    MS-PPC supported bits 0x00000001 (0x120600000001)
*Mar  1 21:35:04.318: As4 CCP:    Stacker history 1 check mode EXTENDED (0x1105000104)
*Mar  1 21:35:04.322: As4 LCP: O PROTREJ [Open] id 3 len 21 protocol CCP
*Mar  1 21:35:04.326: As4 LCP:    (0x80FD0101000F12060000000111050001)
*Mar  1 21:35:04.330: As4 LCP:    (0x04)
*Mar  1 21:35:04.334: As4 IPCP: I CONFACK [REQsent] id 1 len 10
*Mar  1 21:35:04.338: As4 IPCP:    Address 10.1.2.1 (0x03060A010201)
*Mar  1 21:35:05.186: %LINEPROTO-5-UPDOWN: Line protocol on Interface Async4,
changed state to up
*Mar  1 21:35:07.274: As4 IPCP: I CONFREQ [ACKrcvd] id 2 len 22
*Mar  1 21:35:07.278: As4 IPCP:    Address 0.0.0.0 (0x030600000000)
*Mar  1 21:35:07.282: As4 IPCP:    PrimaryDNS 0.0.0.0 (0x810600000000)
*Mar  1 21:35:07.286: As4 IPCP:    SecondaryDNS 0.0.0.0 (0x830600000000)
*Mar  1 21:35:07.294: As4 IPCP: O CONFNAK [ACKrcvd] id 2 len 22
*Mar  1 21:35:07.298: As4 IPCP:    Address 10.1.2.2 (0x03060A010202)
*Mar  1 21:35:07.302: As4 IPCP:    PrimaryDNS 10.2.2.3 (0x81060A020203)
*Mar  1 21:35:07.310: As4 IPCP:    SecondaryDNS 10.2.3.1 (0x83060A020301)
*Mar  1 21:35:07.426: As4 IPCP: I CONFREQ [ACKrcvd] id 3 len 22
*Mar  1 21:35:07.430: As4 IPCP:    Address 10.1.2.2 (0x03060A010202)
*Mar  1 21:35:07.434: As4 IPCP:    PrimaryDNS 10.2.2.3 (0x81060A020203)
*Mar  1 21:35:07.442: As4 IPCP:    SecondaryDNS 10.2.3.1 (0x83060A020301)
*Mar  1 21:35:07.446: ip_get_pool: As4: validate address = 10.1.2.2
*Mar  1 21:35:07.450: ip_get_pool: As4: using pool default
*Mar  1 21:35:07.450: ip_get_pool: As4: returning address = 10.1.2.2
*Mar  1 21:35:07.454: set_ip_peer_addr: As4: address = 10.1.2.2 (3) is redundant
*Mar  1 21:35:07.458: As4 IPCP: O CONFACK [ACKrcvd] id 3 len 22
*Mar  1 21:35:07.462: As4 IPCP:    Address 10.1.2.2 (0x03060A010202)
*Mar  1 21:35:07.466: As4 IPCP:    PrimaryDNS 10.2.2.3 (0x81060A020203)
*Mar  1 21:35:07.474: As4 IPCP:    SecondaryDNS 10.2.3.1 (0x83060A020301)
*Mar  1 21:35:07.478: As4 IPCP: State is Open
*Mar  1 21:35:07.490: As4 IPCP: Install route to 10.1.2.2
```

Table 17-12 *PPP NCP Negotiation Details*

Time Stamp	Description
21:35:04.190	Outgoing configuration request (O CONFREQ). The NAS sends an outgoing PPP configuration request packet containing its IP address to the peer.
21:35:04.282	Incoming CONFREQ. The peer requests to do VJ header compression and needs an IP address for itself, as well as addresses of the primary and secondary DNS servers.
21:35:04.306	Outbound Config-Reject (CONFREJ). VJ header compression is rejected.
21:35:04.314 to 21:35:04.330	The peer sends a request to do Compression Control Protocol; the entire protocol is rejected by the NAS by means of a PROTREJ message. The peer should not (and does not) attempt to retry CCP.
21:35:04.334	The peer acknowledges the IP address of the NAS with a CONFACK.
21:35:07.274	Incoming CONFREQ. The peer no longer requests to do VJ header compression, but it still needs an IP address for itself, as well as addresses of the primary and secondary DNS servers.
21:35:07.294	The NAS sends a CONFNAK containing the address that it wants the peer to use, along with addresses of the primary and secondary DNS servers.
21:35:07.426	The peer sends the addresses back to the NAS—in effect, an attempt to confirm that the addresses were properly received.
21:35:07.458	The NAS acknowledges the addresses with a CONFACK.
21:35:07.478	Each side of the connection has issued a CONFACK, so negotiation is finished. The command **show interfaces Async4** on the NAS will show "IPCP: Open."
21:35:07.490	A host route to the remote peer is installed in the NAS's routing table.

It should be noted that it is possible for the peers to simultaneously negotiate more than one Layer 3 protocol. It is not uncommon, for instance, to see IP and IPX being negotiated. It is also possible for one protocol to successfully negotiate while the other fails to do so.

Any problems that occur during NCP negotiation can typically be traced to the configurations of the negotiating peers. If PPP negotiation fails during the NCP phase, take the steps outlined in Table 17-13.

Table 17-13 *Troubleshooting NCP*

Task	Steps
Verify interface protocol configuration.	Examine the output of the privileged exec command **show running-config**. Verify that the interface is configured to support the protocol that you want to run over the connection.

Table 17-13 *Troubleshooting NCP (Continued)*

Task	Steps
Verify interface address.	Confirm that the interface in question has an address configured. If your are using **ip unnumbered [*interface-name*]** or **ipx ppp-client loopback [*number*]**, ensure that the referenced interface is configured with an address.
Verify client address availability.	If the NAS is supposed to issue an IP address to the caller, ensure that such an address is available. The IP address to be handed out to the caller can be derived in several ways:

• **Configured locally on the interface**—Check the interface configuration for the command **peer default ip address a.b.c.d.** In practice, this method should be used only on interfaces that accept a connections from a single caller, such as on an async (*not* a group-async) interface.

• **From an address pool locally configured on the NAS**—The interface should have the command **peer default ip address pool [*pool-name*]**. In addition, the pool must be defined at the system level with the command **ip local pool [*pool-name*] [*first-address*] [*last-address*]**. The range of addresses defined in the pool should be large enough to accommodate as many simultaneously connected callers as the NAS is capable of. (QQ17)

• **With QQ17**—The range of address cannot be greater than the maximum amount of simultaneous connection that can be handled on the routing platform, but it can be less.

• **From a DHCP server**—The NAS interface must be configured with the command **peer default ip address dhcp**. Furthermore, the NAS must be configured to point to a DHCP server with the global configuration command **ip dhcp-server [*address*]**.

• **Via AAA**—If you are using TACACS+ or RADIUS for authorization, the AAA server can be configured to hand a specific IP address to a given caller every time that caller connects.

| Verify server address configuration. | To return the configured addresses of domain name servers or Windows NT servers in response to BOOTP requests, ensure that the global-level commands **async-bootp dns-server [*address*]** and **async-bootp nbns-server [*address*]** are configured. |

Note that although the command **async-bootp subnet-mask [*mask*]** can be configured on the NAS, the subnet mask will *not* be negotiated between the NAS and a PPP dial-in client PC. Because of the nature of point-to-point connections, the client automatically uses the IP address of the NAS (learned during IPCP negotiation) as the default gateway. The subnet mask is not needed in that point-to-point environment. The PC knows that if the destination address does not match the local address, the packet should be forwarded to the default gateway (NAS), which is always reached via the PPP link.

Before Calling Cisco Systems' TAC Team

Before calling Cisco Systems' Technical Assistance Center (TAC), make sure that you have read through this chapter and completed the actions suggested for your system's problem.

Additionally, do the following and document the results so that the TAC can better assist you:

- For all problems, collect the output of **show running-config** and **show version**. Ensure that the command **service timestamps debug datetime msec** is in the configuration.
- For DDR problems, collect the following:
  - **show dialer map**
  - **debug dialer**
  - **debug ppp negotiation**
  - **debug ppp authentication**
- If ISDN is involved, collect the following:
  - **show isdn status**
  - **debug isdn q931**
  - **debug isdn events**
- If modems are involved, collect the following:
  - **show lines**
  - **show line** [*x*]
  - **show modem** (if integrated modems are involved)
  - **show modem version** (if integrated modems are involved)
  - **debug modem**
  - **debug modem csm** (if integrated modems are involved)
  - **debug chat** (if a DDR scenario)
- If T1s or PRIs are involved, collect:
  - **show controller t1**

Additional Sources

- Cisco IOS Dial Solutions Guide
- The TAC Technology Support Pages: www.cisco.com/tac/

## CHAPTER 18

Troubleshooting Frame Relay Connections

Frame Relay was originally conceived as a protocol for use over ISDN interfaces. Initial proposals to this effect were submitted to the International Telecommunication Union Telecommunication Standardization Sector (ITU-T), formerly the Consultative Committee for International Telegraph and Telephone (CCITT), in 1984. Work on Frame Relay was also undertaken in the American National Standards Institute (ANSI)–accredited T1S1 standards committee in the United States.

A major development in Frame Relay's history occurred in 1990 when Cisco Systems, StrataCom, Northern Telecom, and Digital Equipment Corporation formed a consortium to focus Frame Relay technology development and to accelerate the introduction of interoperable Frame Relay products. This consortium developed a specification conforming to the basic Frame Relay protocol being discussed in T1S1 and ITU-T, but it extended it with features that provide additional capabilities for complex internetworking environments. These Frame Relay extensions are referred to collectively as the Local Management Interface (LMI).

Frame Relay Technology Basics

Frame Relay provides a packet-switching data communications capability that is used across the interface between user devices (for example, routers, bridges, and host machines) and network equipment (for example, switching nodes). User devices are often referred to as data terminal equipment (DTE), whereas network equipment that interfaces to DTE is often referred to as data circuit-terminating equipment (DCE). The network providing the Frame Relay interface can be either a carrier-provided public network or a network of privately owned equipment serving a single enterprise.

As an interface to a network, Frame Relay is the same type of protocol as X.25 (see Chapter 19, "Troubleshooting X.25 Connections"). However, Frame Relay differs significantly from X.25 in its functionality and format. In particular, Frame Relay is a more streamlined protocol, facilitating higher performance and greater efficiency.

As an interface between user and network equipment, Frame Relay provides a means for statistically multiplexing many logical data conversations (referred to as *virtual circuits*) over a single physical transmission link. This contrasts with systems that use time-division multiplexing (TDM) techniques for supporting multiple data streams. Frame Relay's statistical multiplexing provides more flexible and efficient use of available bandwidth. It can be used without TDM techniques or on top of channels provided by TDM systems.

Another important characteristic of Frame Relay is that it exploits the recent advances in wide-area network (WAN) transmission technology. Earlier WAN protocols such as X.25 were developed when analog transmission systems and copper media were predominant. These links are much less reliable than the fiber media/digital transmission links available today. Over links such as these, link-layer protocols can forgo time-consuming error correction algorithms, leaving these to be performed at higher protocol layers. Greater performance and efficiency is therefore possible without sacrificing data integrity. Frame Relay is designed with this approach in mind. It includes a cyclic redundancy check (CRC) algorithm for detecting corrupted bits (so that the data can be discarded), but it does not include any protocol mechanisms for correcting bad data (for example, by retransmitting it at this level of protocol).

Another difference between Frame Relay and X.25 is the absence of explicit, per-virtual-circuit flow control in Frame Relay. Now that many upper-layer protocols are effectively executing their own flow control algorithms, the need for this functionality at the link layer has diminished. Frame Relay, therefore, does not include explicit flow control procedures that duplicate those in higher layers. Instead, very simple congestion notification mechanisms are provided to allow a network to inform a user device that the network resources are close to a congested state. This notification can alert higher-layer protocols that flow control may be needed.

Current Frame Relay standards address permanent virtual circuits (PVCs) that are administratively configured and managed in a Frame Relay network. Another type, switched virtual circuits (SVCs), has also been proposed. The Integrated Services Digital Network (ISDN) signaling protocol is proposed as the means by which DTE and DCE can communicate to establish, terminate, and manage SVCs dynamically.

LMI Extensions

In addition to the basic Frame Relay protocol functions for transferring data, the consortium Frame Relay specification includes LMI extensions that make supporting large, complex internetworks easier. Some LMI extensions are referred to as "common" and are expected to be implemented by everyone who adopts the specification. Other LMI functions are referred to as "optional." A summary of the LMI extensions follows:

- **Virtual circuit status messages (common)**—Provide communication and synchronization between the network and the user device, periodically reporting the existence of new PVCs and the deletion of already existing PVCs, and generally provide information about PVC integrity. Virtual circuit status messages prevent the sending of data into black holes—that is, over PVCs that no longer exist.

- **Multicasting (optional)**—Allows a sender to transmit a single frame but have it delivered by the network to multiple recipients. Thus, multicasting supports the efficient conveyance of routing protocol messages and address resolution procedures that typically must be sent to many destinations simultaneously.

- **Global addressing (optional)**—Gives connection identifiers global rather than local significance, allowing them to be used to identify a specific interface to the Frame Relay network. Global addressing makes the Frame Relay network resemble a local-area network (LAN) in terms of addressing; Address Resolution Protocols, therefore, perform over Frame Relay exactly as they do over a LAN.

- **Simple flow control (optional)**—Provides for an XON/XOFF flow control mechanism that applies to the entire Frame Relay interface. It is intended for devices whose higher layers cannot use the congestion notification bits and that need some level of flow control.

Frame Format

The Frame Relay frame is shown in Figure 18-1. The Flags fields delimit the beginning and end of the frame. Following the leading Flags field are 2 bytes of address information. Ten bits of these 2 bytes make up the actual circuit ID (called the DLCI, for data link connection identifier).

Figure 18-1 *The Frame Relay Frame*

The 10-bit DLCI value is the heart of the Frame Relay header. It identifies the logical connection that is multiplexed into the physical channel. In the basic (not extended by the LMI) mode of addressing, DLCIs have local significance; that is, the end devices at two different ends of a connection may use a different DLCI to refer to that same connection. Figure 18-2 provides an example of the use of DLCIs in nonextended Frame Relay addressing.

Figure 18-2 *Frame Relay Addressing*

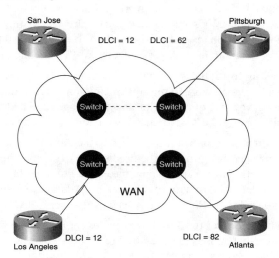

In Figure 18-2, assume two PVCs, one between Atlanta and Los Angeles, and one between San Jose and Pittsburgh. Los Angeles uses DLCI 12 to refer to its PVC with Atlanta, whereas Atlanta refers to the same PVC as DLCI 82. Similarly, San Jose uses DLCI 12 to refer to its PVC with Pittsburgh. The network uses internal proprietary mechanisms to keep the two locally significant PVC identifiers distinct.

At the end of each DLCI byte is an extended address (EA) bit. If this bit is 1, the current byte is the last DLCI byte. All implementations currently use a 2-byte DLCI, but the presence of the EA bits means that longer DLCIs may be agreed on and used in the future.

The bit marked C/R following the most significant DLCI byte is currently not used.

Finally, 3 bits in the 2-byte DLCI provide congestion control. The forward explicit congestion notification (FECN) bit is set by the Frame Relay network in a frame to tell the DTE receiving the frame that congestion was experienced in the path from source to destination. The backward explicit congestion notification (BECN) bit is set by the Frame Relay network in frames traveling in the opposite direction from frames encountering a congested path. The notion behind both of these bits is that the FECN or BECN indication can be promoted to a higher-level protocol that can take flow control action as appropriate. (FECN bits are useful to higher-layer protocols that use receiver-controlled flow control, whereas BECN bits are significant to those that depend on emitter-controlled flow control.)

The discard eligibility (DE) bit is set by the DTE to tell the Frame Relay network that a frame has lower importance than other frames and should be discarded before other frames if the network becomes short of resources. Thus, it represents a very simple priority mechanism. This bit is usually set only when the network is congested.

LMI Message Format

The previous section described the basic Frame Relay protocol format for carrying user data frames. The consortium Frame Relay specification also includes the LMI procedures. LMI messages are sent in frames distinguished by an LMI-specific DLCI (defined in the consortium specification as DLCI = 1023). The LMI message format is shown in Figure 18-3.

Figure 18-3 *The LMI Message Format*

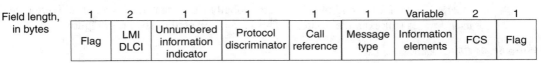

Field length, in bytes	1	2	1	1	1	1	Variable	2	1
	Flag	LMI DLCI	Unnumbered information indicator	Protocol discriminator	Call reference	Message type	Information elements	FCS	Flag

In LMI messages, the basic protocol header is the same as in normal data frames. The actual LMI message begins with 4 mandatory bytes, followed by a variable number of information elements (IEs). The format and encoding of LMI messages is based on the ANSI T1S1 standard.

The first of the mandatory bytes (the *unnumbered information indicator*) has the same format as the Link Access Procedure, Balanced (LAPB) unnumbered information (UI) frame indicator with the poll/final bit set to 0. (For more information about LAPB, see Chapter 19.) The next byte is referred to as the *protocol discriminator*, which is set to a value that indicates LMI. The third mandatory byte (the *call reference*) is always filled with zeros.

The final mandatory byte is the Message Type field. Two message types have been defined. Status-enquiry messages allow the user device to inquire about network status. Status messages respond to status-enquiry messages. Keepalives (messages sent through a connection to ensure that both sides will continue to regard the connection as active) and PVC status messages are examples of these messages and are the common LMI features that are expected to be a part of every implementation that conforms to the consortium specification.

Together, status and status-enquiry messages help verify the integrity of logical and physical links. This information is critical in a routing environment because routing algorithms make decisions based on link integrity.

Following the Message Type field is some number of IEs. Each IE consists of a single-byte IE identifier, an IE Length field, and 1 or more bytes containing actual data.

Global Addressing

In addition to the common LMI features, several optional LMI extensions are extremely useful in an internetworking environment. The first important optional LMI extension is global addressing. As noted previously, the basic (nonextended) Frame Relay specification supports only values of the DLCI field that identify PVCs with local significance. In this case, no addresses identify network interfaces or nodes attached to these interfaces. Because these addresses do not exist, they cannot be discovered by traditional address resolution and discovery techniques. This means that with normal Frame Relay addressing, static maps must be created to tell routers which DLCIs to use to find a remote device and its associated internetwork address.

The global addressing extension permits node identifiers. With this extension, the values inserted in the DLCI field of a frame are globally significant addresses of individual end-user devices (for example, routers). This is implemented as shown in Figure 18-4.

Figure 18-4 *Global Addressing Exchange*

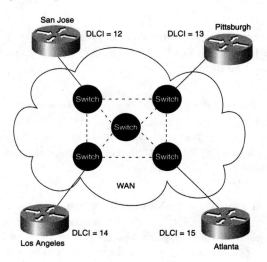

In Figure 18-4, note that each interface has its own identifier. Suppose that Pittsburgh must send a frame to San Jose. The identifier for San Jose is 12, so Pittsburgh places the value 12 in the DLCI field and sends the frame into the Frame Relay network. At the exit point, the DLCI field contents are changed by the network to 13 to reflect the source node of the frame. Each router interface has a distinct value as its node identifier, so individual devices can be distinguished. This permits adaptive routing in complex environments.

Global addressing provides significant benefits in a large, complex internetwork. The Frame Relay network now appears to the routers on its periphery like any LAN. No changes to higher-layer protocols are needed to take full advantage of their capabilities.

Multicasting

Multicasting is another valuable optional LMI feature. Multicast groups are designated by a series of four reserved DLCI values (1019 to 1022). Frames sent by a device using one of these reserved DLCIs are replicated by the network and sent to all exit points in the designated set. The multicasting extension also defines LMI messages that notify user devices of the addition, deletion, and presence of multicast groups.

In networks that take advantage of dynamic routing, routing information must be exchanged among many routers. Routing messages can be sent efficiently by using frames with a multicast DLCI. This allows messages to be sent to specific groups of routers.

Frame Relay Configuration

When implementing Frame Relay—and, specifically, LMI—in an internetwork, the LMI type must be consistent across all points between the end devices. The three LMI types that can be used are ANSI, Cisco, and Q.933A. The current Internetworking Operating System (IOS) on Cisco routers autosenses the LMI type from the frame switch to which it is attached.

Another important setting to consider when looking at Frame Relay networks is the initial encapsulation type used when the protocol is activated on an interface. This setting must be consistent between end devices on the internetwork. If you are connecting Cisco-only devices, Cisco encapsulation may be used. This is the default encapsulation type on Cisco routers. If you are connecting to hardware from other vendors, IETF encapsulation should be used.

Network Implementation

Frame Relay can be used as an interface to either a publicly available carrier-provided service or to a network of privately owned equipment. A typical means of private network implementation is to equip traditional T1 multiplexers with Frame Relay interfaces for data devices, as well as non-Frame Relay interfaces for other applications such as voice and video/teleconferencing. Figure 18-5 shows this configuration.

Figure 18-5 *A Hybrid Frame Relay Network*

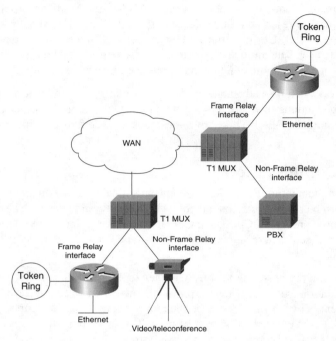

A public Frame Relay service is deployed by putting Frame Relay switching equipment in the central offices of a telecommunications carrier. In this case, users can realize economic benefits from traffic-sensitive charging rates and are relieved from the work necessary to administer and maintain the network equipment and service.

In either type of network, the lines that connect user devices to the network equipment can operate at a speed selected from a broad range of data rates. Speeds between 56 kbps and 2 Mbps are typical, although Frame Relay can support lower and higher speeds.

Whether in a public or private network, the support of Frame Relay interfaces to user devices does not necessarily dictate that the Frame Relay protocol is used between the network devices. No standards for interconnecting equipment inside a Frame Relay network currently exist. Thus, traditional circuit-switching, packet-switching, or a hybrid approach combining these technologies can be used.

Troubleshooting Frame Relay

This section discusses troubleshooting procedures for connectivity problems related to Frame Relay links. It describes specific Frame Relay symptoms, the problems that are likely to cause each symptom, and the solutions to those problems.

The following sections cover the most common network issues in Frame Relay networks:

- Frame Relay: Frame Relay Link Is Down
- Frame Relay: Cannot **ping** Remote Router
- Frame Relay: Cannot **ping** End to End

Frame Relay: Frame Relay Link Is Down

Symptom: Connections over a Frame Relay link fail. The output of the **show interfaces serial** exec command shows that the interface and line protocol are down, or that the interface is up and the line protocol is down.

Table 18-1 outlines the problems that might cause this symptom and describes solutions to those problems.

Table 18-1   *Frame Relay: Frame Relay Link Is Down*

Possible Problem	Solution
A cabling, hardware, or carrier problem has occurred.	Perform these steps for the local and remote router:
	Step 1 Use the **show interfaces serial** command to see whether the interface and line protocol are up.
	Step 2 If the interface and line protocol are down, check the cable to make sure that it is a DTE[1] serial cable. Make sure that cables are securely attached.
	Step 3 If the cable is correct, try moving it to a different port. If that port works, then the first port is defective. Replace either the card or the router.
	Step 4 If the cable doesn't work on the second port, try replacing the cable. If it still doesn't work, there might be a problem with the DCE[2]. Contact your carrier about the problem.
	For detailed information on troubleshooting serial lines, refer to Chapter 15, "Troubleshooting Serial Lines."

continues

Table 18-1 *Frame Relay: Frame Relay Link Is Down (Continued)*

Possible Problem	Solution	
An LMI[3] type mismatch has occurred.	**Step 1**	Use the **show interfaces serial** command to check the state of the interface.
	Step 2	If the output shows that the interface is up but the line protocol is down, use the **show frame-relay lmi** exec command to see which LMI type is configured on the Frame Relay interface.
	Step 3	Make sure that the LMI type is the same for all devices in the path from source to destination. Use the **frame-relay lmi-type** {**ansi**	**cisco**	**q933a**} interface configuration command to change the LMI type on the router.
Keepalives are not being sent.	**Step 1**	Enter the **show interfaces** command to find out whether keepalives are configured. If you see a line that says "keepalives not set," keepalives are not configured.
	Step 2	Use the **keepalive** *seconds* interface configuration command to configure keepalives. The default value for this command is 10 seconds.
Encapsulation mismatch has occurred.	**Step 1**	When connecting Cisco devices with non-Cisco devices, you must use IETF[4] encapsulation on both devices. Check the encapsulation type on the Cisco device with the **show frame-relay map** exec command.
	Step 2	If the Cisco device is not using IETF encapsulation, use **the encapsulation frame-relay ietf** interface configuration command to configure IETF encapsulation on the Cisco Frame Relay interface.
		For information on viewing or changing the configuration of the non-Cisco device, refer to the vendor documentation.
The DLCI[5] is inactive or has been deleted.	**Step 1**	Use the **show frame-relay pvc** exec command to view the status of the interface's PVC.
	Step 2	If the output shows that the PVC[6] is inactive or deleted, there is a problem along the path to the remote router. Check the remote router or contact your carrier to check the status of the PVC.

Table 18-1 *Frame Relay: Frame Relay Link Is Down (Continued)*

Possible Problem	Solution	
The DLCI is assigned to the wrong subinterface.	**Step 1**	Use the **show frame-relay pvc** privileged exec command to check the assigned DLCIs. Make sure that the correct DLCIs are assigned to the correct subinterface. If the DLCI is incorrect, use the **no frame-relay map interface-dlci** command to delete the incorrect DLCI number entry under the interface. Use the **frame-relay map interface-dlci** interface configuration command to define the mapping between an address and the correct DLCI used to connect to the address.

Syntax:

frame-relay map *protocol protocol-address dlci* [*broadcast*] [*ietf* | *cisco*]

Syntax description:

- *protocol*—Supported protocols: AppleTalk, DECnet, IP, XNS, IPX, and VINES.
- *protocol-address*—Address for the protocol.
- *dlci*—DLCI number for the interface.
- *broadcast*—(Optional) Broadcasts should be forwarded to this address when multicast is not enabled.
- *ietf*—(Optional) IETF form of Frame Relay encapsulation. Use when the communication server is connected to another vendor's equipment across a Frame Relay network.
- *cisco*—(Optional) Cisco encapsulation method.

Example:

The following example maps IP address 131.108.123.1 to DLCI 100:

```
interface serial 0
frame-relay map ip 131.108.123.1 100 broadcast
```

Step 2 If the DLCIs appear to be correct, shut down the main interface using the **shutdown** interface configuration command, and then bring the interface back up using the **no shutdown** command.

[1]DTE = data terminal equipment

[2]DCE = data circuit-terminating equipment

[3]LMI = Local Management Interface

[4]IETF = Internet Engineering Task Force

[5]DLCI = Data link connection identifier

[6]PVC = permanent virtual circuit

Frame Relay: Cannot ping Remote Router

Symptom: Attempts to **ping** the remote router across a Frame Relay connection fail.

Table 18-2 outlines the problems that might cause this symptom and describes solutions to those problems.

Table 18-2   *Frame Relay: Cannot* **ping** *Remote Router*

Possible Problem	Solution	
Encapsulation mismatch has occurred.	Step 1	When connecting Cisco devices with non-Cisco devices, you must use IETF encapsulation on both devices. Check the encapsulation type on the Cisco device with the **show frame-relay map** exec command.
	Step 2	If the Cisco device is not using IETF encapsulation, use the **encapsulation frame-relay ietf** interface configuration command to configure IETF encapsulation on the Cisco Frame Relay interface.
		For information on viewing or changing the configuration of the non-Cisco device, refer to the vendor documentation.
DLCI is inactive or has been deleted.	Step 1	Use the **show frame-relay pvc** exec command to view the status of the interface's PVC.
	Step 2	If the output shows that the PVC is inactive or deleted, there is a problem along the path to the remote router. Check the remote router, or contact your carrier to check the status of the PVC.
DLCI is assigned to the wrong subinterface.	Step 1	Use the **show frame-relay pvc** privileged exec command to check the assigned DLCIs. Make sure that the correct DLCIs are assigned to the correct subinterfaces.
	Step 2	If the DLCIs appear to be correct, shut down the main interface using the **shutdown** interface configuration command, and then bring the interface back up using the **no shutdown** command.
An access list was misconfigured.	Step 1	Use the **show access-list** privileged exec command to see whether there are access lists configured on the router.
	Step 2	If there are access lists configured, test connectivity by disabling access lists using the **no access-group** global configuration command. Check whether connectivity is restored.
	Step 3	If connections work, re-enable access lists one at a time, checking connections after enabling each access list.
	Step 4	If enabling an access list blocks connections, make sure that the access list does not deny necessary traffic. Make sure to configure explicit **permit** statements for any traffic that you want to pass.
	Step 5	Continue testing access lists until all access lists are restored and connections still work.

Table 18-2   *Frame Relay: Cannot* **ping** *Remote Router (Continued)*

Possible Problem	Solution
The **frame-relay map** command is missing.	**Step 1** Use the **show frame-relay map** privileged exec command to see whether an address map is configured for the DLCI.
	Step 2 If you do not see an address map for the DLCI, enter the **clear frame-relay-inarp** privileged exec command and then use the **show frame-relay map** command again to see whether there is now a map to the DLCI.
	Step 3 If there is no map to the DLCI, add a static address map. Use the **frame-relay map** interface configuration command.

Syntax:

- **frame-relay map** *protocol protocol-address dlci [broadcast] [ietf | cisco]*

Syntax Description:

- *protocol*—Supported protocols: AppleTalk, DECnet, IP, XNS, IPX, and VINES.

- *protocol-address*—Address for the protocol.

- *dlci*—DLCI number for the interface.

- *broadcast*—(Optional) Broadcasts should be forwarded to this address when multicast is not enabled.

- *ietf*—(Optional) IETF form of Frame Relay encapsulation. Use when the communication server is connected to another vendor's equipment across a Frame Relay network.

- *cisco*—(Optional) Cisco encapsulation method.

Example:

The following example maps IP address 131.108.123.1 to DLCI 100:

```
interface serial 0
frame-relay map ip 131.108.123.1 100 broadcast
```

Step 4 Make sure that the DLCIs and next-hop addresses specified in **frame-relay map** commands are correct. The specified protocol address should be in the same network as your local Frame Relay interface.

For complete information on configuring Frame Relay address maps, refer to the Cisco IOS *Wide-Area Networking Configuration Guide.*

continues

Table 18-2 *Frame Relay: Cannot* **ping** *Remote Router (Continued)*

Possible Problem	Solution
No **broadcast** keyword is found in **frame-relay map** statements.	**Step 1** Use the **show running-config** privileged exec command on local and remote routers to view the router configuration. Check **frame-relay map** command entries to see whether the **broadcast** keyword is specified.
	Step 2 If the keyword is not specified, add the **broadcast** keyword to all **frame-relay map** commands.

Syntax:

frame-relay map *protocol protocol-address dlci* [*broadcast*] [*ietf* | *cisco*]

Syntax Description:

- *protocol*—Supported protocols: AppleTalk, DECnet, IP, XNS, IPX, and VINES.
- *protocol-address*—Address for the protocol.
- *dlci*—DLCI number for the interface.
- *broadcast*—(Optional) Broadcasts should be forwarded to this address when multicast is not enabled.
- *ietf*—(Optional) IETF form of Frame Relay encapsulation. Use when the communication server is connected to another vendor's equipment across a Frame Relay network.
- *cisco*—(Optional) Cisco encapsulation method.

Example:

The following example maps IP address 131.108.123.1 to DLCI 100:

```
interface serial 0
frame-relay map ip 131.108.123.1 100 broadcast
```

Note: By default, the **broadcast** keyword is added to dynamic maps learned via Inverse ARP[1].

[1]ARP = Address Resolution Protocol

Frame Relay: Cannot ping End to End

Symptom: Attempts to **ping** devices on a remote network across a Frame Relay connection fail.

Table 18-3 outlines the problems that might cause this symptom and describes solutions to those problems.

Table 18-3   *Frame Relay: Cannot* **ping** *End to End*

Possible Problem	Solution
Split horizon problem	In a hub-and-spoke Frame Relay environment, you must configure subinterfaces to avoid problems with split horizon. For detailed information on configuring subinterfaces, refer to the Cisco IOS *Wide-Area Networking Configuration Guide* and *Wide-Area Networking Command Reference.* Frame Relay subinterfaces provide a mechanism for supporting partially meshed Frame Relay networks. Most protocols assume transitivity on a logical network; that is, if station A can talk to station B, and station B can talk to station C, then station A should be capable of talking to station C directly. Transitivity is true on LANs, but not on Frame Relay networks, unless A is directly connected to C. Additionally, certain protocols such as AppleTalk and transparent bridging cannot be supported on partially meshed networks because they require *split horizon*, in which a packet received on an interface cannot be transmitted out the same interface even if the packet is received and transmitted on different virtual circuits. Configuring Frame Relay subinterfaces ensures that a single physical interface is treated as multiple virtual interfaces. This capability enables us to overcome split horizon rules. Packets received on one virtual interface can now be forwarded out another virtual interface, even if they are configured on the same physical interface. Subinterfaces address the limitations of Frame Relay networks by providing a way to subdivide a partially meshed Frame Relay network into a number of smaller, fully meshed (or point-to-point) subnetworks. Each subnetwork is assigned its own network number and appears to the protocols as if it is reachable through a separate interface. (Note that point-to-point subinterfaces can be unnumbered for use with IP, reducing the addressing burden that might otherwise result.)
No default gateway on workstation	**Step 1** From the local workstation or server, try to **ping** the remote workstation or server. Make several attempts to **ping** the remote device if the first **ping** is unsuccessful. **Step 2** If all your attempts fail, check whether the local workstation or server can **ping** the local router's Frame Relay interface. **Step 3** If you are unable to **ping** the local interface, check the local workstation or server to see whether it is configured with a default gateway specification. **Step 4** If no default gateway is specified, configure the device with a default gateway. The default gateway should be the address of the local router's LAN interface. For information on viewing or changing the workstation or server's default gateway specification, refer to the vendor documentation.

## CHAPTER 19

Troubleshooting X.25 Connections

In the 1970s, a set of protocols was needed to provide users with wide-area network (WAN) connectivity across public data networks (PDNs). PDNs such as TYMNET had achieved remarkable success, but it was felt that protocol standardization would increase subscriptions to PDNs by providing improved equipment compatibility and lower cost. The result of the ensuing development effort was a group of protocols, the most popular of which is X.25.

X.25 was developed by the common carriers (telephone companies, essentially) rather than any single commercial enterprise. The specification, therefore, designed to work well regardless of a user's system type or manufacturer. Users contract with the common carriers to use their packet-switched networks (PSNs) and are charged based on PSN use. Services offered (and charges levied) are regulated by the Federal Communications Commission (FCC).

One of X.25's unique attributes is its international nature. X.25 and related protocols are administered by an agency of the United Nations called the International Telecommunications Union (ITU). The ITU Telecommunication Standardization Sector (ITU-T; formerly CCITT, the Consultative Committee for International Telegraph and Telephone) is the ITU committee responsible for voice and data communications. ITU-T members include the FCC, the European Postal Telephone and Telegraph organizations, the common carriers, and many computer and data communications companies. As a result, X.25 is truly a global standard.

X.25 Technology Basics

X.25 defines a telephone network for data communications. To begin communication, one computer calls another to request a communication session. The called computer can accept or refuse the connection. If the call is accepted, the two systems can begin full-duplex information transfer. Either side can terminate the connection at any time.

The X.25 specification defines a point-to-point interaction between data terminal equipment (DTE) and data circuit-terminating equipment (DCE). DTEs (terminals and hosts in the user's facilities) connect to DCEs (modems, packet switches, and other ports into the PDN, generally located in the carrier's facilities), which connect to packet-switching exchanges (PSEs, or switches) and other DCEs inside a PSN and, ultimately, to another DTE. The relationship between the entities in an X.25 network is shown in Figure 19-1.

Figure 19-1   *The X.25 Model*

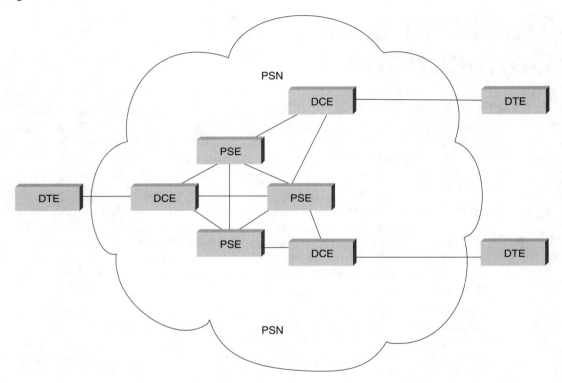

A DTE can be a terminal that does not implement the complete X.25 functionality. A DTE is connected to a DCE through a translation device called a packet assembler/disassembler (PAD). The operation of the terminal-to-PAD interface, the services offered by the PAD, and the interaction between the PAD and the host are defined by ITU-T Recommendations X.28, X.3, and X.29, respectively.

The X.25 specification maps to Layers 1 through 3 of the OSI reference model. Layer 3 X.25 describes packet formats and packet exchange procedures between peer Layer 3 entities. Layer 2 X.25 is implemented by Link Access Procedure, Balanced (LAPB). LAPB defines packet framing for the DTE/DCE link. Layer 1 X.25 defines the electrical and mechanical procedures for activating and deactivating the physical medium connecting the DTE and the DCE. This relationship is shown in Figure 19-2. Note that Layers 2 and 3 are also referred to as the ISO standards ISO 7776 (LAPB) and ISO 8208 (X.25 packet layer).

Figure 19-2 *X.25 and the OSI Reference Model*

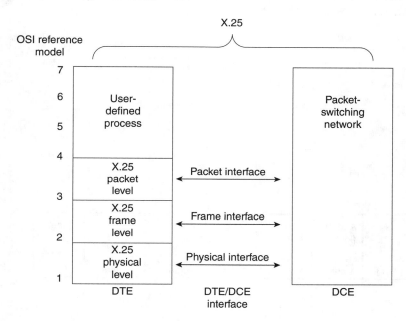

End-to-end communication between DTEs is accomplished through a bidirectional association called a *virtual circuit*. Virtual circuits permit communication between distinct network elements through any number of intermediate nodes without the dedication of portions of the physical medium that characterizes physical circuits. Virtual circuits can be either permanent or switched (temporary). Permanent virtual circuits (PVCs) are typically used for the most often used data transfers, whereas switched virtual circuits (SVCs) are used for sporadic data transfers. Layer 3 X.25 is concerned with end-to-end communication involving both PVCs and SVCs.

When a virtual circuit is established, the DTE sends a packet to the other end of the connection by sending it to the DCE using the proper virtual circuit. The DCE looks at the virtual circuit number to determine how to route the packet through the X.25 network. The Layer 3 X.25 protocol multiplexes among all the DTEs served by the DCE on the destination side of the network, and the packet is delivered to the destination DTE.

X.25 Frame Format

An X.25 frame is composed of a series of fields, as shown in Figure 19-3. Layer 3 X.25 fields make up an X.25 packet and include a header and user data. Layer 2 X.25 (LAPB) fields include frame-level control and addressing fields, the embedded Layer 3 packet, and a frame check sequence (FCS).

Figure 19-3 *LAPB Structure*

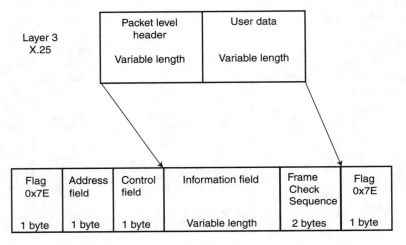

Note: Information and confirmation of field lengths and content were obtained from the following publications: *Internetworking* by Mark A. Miller, P.E., published by M&T Books, 1991. The second book is *Data and Computer Communications* by William Stallings, published by Prentice Hall, 1994.

Layer 3

The Layer 3 X.25 header is made up of a general format identifier (GFI), a logical channel identifier (LCI), and a packet type identifier (PTI). The GFI is a 4-bit field that indicates the general format of the packet header. The LCI is a 12-bit field that identifies the virtual circuit. The LCI is locally significant at the DTE/DCE interface. In other words, the PDN connects two logical channels, each with an independent LCI, on two DTE/DCE interfaces to establish a virtual circuit. The PTI field identifies 1 of X.25's 17 packet types.

Addressing fields in call setup packets provide source and destination DTE addresses. These are used to establish the virtual circuits that constitute X.25 communication. ITU-T Recommendation X.121 specifies the source and destination address formats. X.121 addresses (also referred to as international data numbers, or IDNs) vary in length and can be up to 14 decimal digits long. Byte four in the call setup packet specifies the source DTE and destination DTE address lengths. The first four digits of an IDN are called the *data network identification code* (DNIC). The DNIC is divided into two parts, with the first three digits specifying the country and the last digit specifying the PSN itself. The remaining digits are called the national terminal number (NTN) and are used to identify the specific DTE on the PSN. The X.121 address format is shown in Figure 19-4.

Figure 19-4 *The X.121 Address Format*

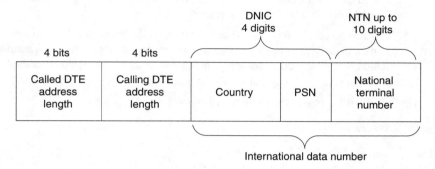

The addressing fields that make up the X.121 address are necessary only when an SVC is used, and then only during call setup. After the call is established, the PSN uses the LCI field of the data packet header to specify the particular virtual circuit to the remote DTE.

Layer 3 X.25 uses three virtual circuit operational procedures: call setup, data transfer, and call clearing. Execution of these procedures depends on the virtual circuit type being used. For a PVC, Layer 3 X.25 is always in data transfer mode because the circuit has been permanently established. If an SVC is used, all three procedures are used.

Packets are used to transfer data. Layer 3 X.25 segments and reassembles user messages if they are too long for the maximum packet size of the circuit. Each data packet is given a sequence number, so error and flow control can occur across the DTE/DCE interface.

Layer 2

Layer 2 X.25 is implemented by LAPB, which allows each side (the DTE and the DCE) to initiate communication with the other. During information transfer, LAPB checks that the frames arrive at the receiver in the correct sequence and free of errors.

As with similar link layer protocols, LAPB uses three frame format types:

- **Information (I) frames**—These frames carry upper-layer information and some control information (necessary for full-duplex operations). Send and receive sequence numbers and the poll final (P/F) bit perform flow control and error recovery. The send sequence number refers to the number of the current frame. The receive sequence number records the number of the frame to be received next. In full-duplex conversation, both the sender and the receiver keep send and receive sequence numbers. The poll bit is used to force a final bit message in response; this is used for error detection and recovery.

- **Supervisory (S) frames**—These frames provide control information. They request and suspend transmission, report on status, and acknowledge the receipt of I frames. They do not have an information field.

- **Unnumbered (U) frames**—These frames, as the name suggests, are not sequenced. They are used for control purposes. For example, they can initiate a connection using standard or extended windowing (module 8 versus 128), disconnect the link, report a protocol error, or carry out similar functions.

The LAPB frame is shown in Figure 19-5.

Figure 19-5   *The LAPB Frame*

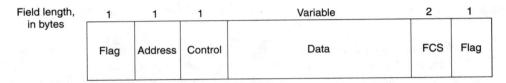

The fields of an LAPB frame are as follows:

- **Flag**—Delimits the LAPB frame. Bit stuffing is used to ensure that the flag pattern does not occur within the body of the frame.

- **Address**—Indicates whether the frame carries a command or a response.

- **Control**—Provides further qualifications of command and response frames, and also indicates the frame format (I, S, or U), frame function (for example, receiver ready or disconnect), and the send/receive sequence number.

- **Data**—Carries upper-layer data. Its size and format vary, depending on the Layer 3 packet type. The maximum length of this field is set by agreement between a PSN administrator and the subscriber at subscription time.

- **FCS**—Ensures the integrity of the transmitted data.

Layer 1

Layer 1 X.25 uses the X.21 bis physical layer protocol, which is roughly equivalent to EIA/TIA-232-C (formerly RS-232-C). X.21 bis was derived from ITU-T Recommendations V.24 and V.28, which identify the interchange circuits and electrical characteristics, respectively, of a DTE-to-DCE interface. X.21 bis supports point-to-point connections, speeds up to 19.2 kbps, and synchronous, full-duplex transmission over four-wire media. The maximum distance between DTE and DCE is 15 meters.

Troubleshooting X.25

This section presents troubleshooting information relating to X.25 connectivity. The "Using the **show interfaces serial** Command" section discusses the use of the **show interfaces serial** command in an X.25 environment and describes some of the key fields of the command output.

The remaining sections describe specific X.25 symptoms, the problems that are likely to cause each symptom, and the solutions to those problems.

Using the show interfaces serial Command

This section describes the information provided by the **show interfaces serial** exec command in an X.25 environment. For additional information about the output of the **show interfaces serial** exec command, refer to Chapter 15, "Troubleshooting Serial Lines," and the Cisco IOS *Configuration Fundamentals Command Reference*.

The **show interfaces serial** command provides important information useful for identifying problems in X.25 internetworks. The following fields provide especially important information:

- **REJs**—Number of rejects
- **SABMs**—Number of set asynchronous balance mode requests
- **RNRs**—Number of receiver not ready events
- **FRMRs**—Number of protocol frame errors
- **RESTARTs**—Number of restarts
- **DISCs**—Number of disconnects

All but the RESTARTs count are LAPB events. Because X.25 requires a stable data link, LAPB problems commonly cause an X.25 restart event that implicitly clears all virtual connections. If unexplained X.25 restarts occur, examine the underlying LAPB connection for problems. Use the **debug lapb** exec command to display all traffic for interfaces using LAPB encapsulation. The no form of this command disables debugging output:

```
[no] debug lapb
```

The **[no] debug lapb** command displays information on the X.25 Layer 2 protocol. It is useful to users who are familiar with LAPB. You can use the **debug lapb** command to determine why X.25 interfaces or LAPB connections are going up and down. It is also useful for identifying link problems, as evidenced when the **show interfaces** command displays a large number of rejects or frame errors over the X.25 link.

CAUTION	Exercise care when using **debug** commands. Many **debug** commands are processor-intensive and can cause serious network problems (such as degraded performance or loss of connectivity) if they are enabled on an already heavily loaded router. When you finish using a **debug** command, remember to disable it with its specific **no debug** command (or use the **no debug all** command to turn off all debugging).

Figure 19-6 shows the output of the X.25 version of the **show interfaces serial** exec command and indicates the important fields.

Figure 19-6 *Output from the X.25 Version of the show interfaces serial Command*

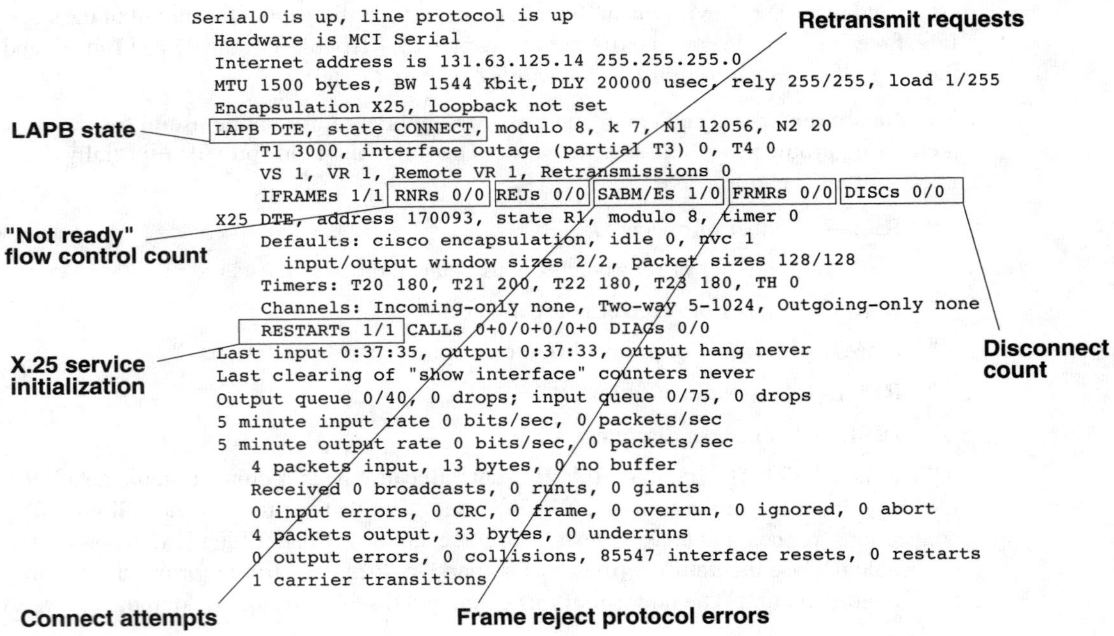

```
Serial0 is up, line protocol is up
  Hardware is MCI Serial                          Retransmit requests
  Internet address is 131.63.125.14 255.255.255.0
  MTU 1500 bytes, BW 1544 Kbit, DLY 20000 usec, rely 255/255, load 1/255
  Encapsulation X25, loopback not set
  LAPB DTE, state CONNECT, modulo 8, k 7, N1 12056, N2 20
    T1 3000, interface outage (partial T3) 0, T4 0
    VS 1, VR 1, Remote VR 1, Retransmissions 0
    IFRAMEs 1/1 RNRs 0/0 REJs 0/0 SABM/Es 1/0 FRMRs 0/0 DISCs 0/0
  X25 DTE, address 170093, state R1, modulo 8, timer 0
    Defaults: cisco encapsulation, idle 0, nvc 1
      input/output window sizes 2/2, packet sizes 128/128
    Timers: T20 180, T21 200, T22 180, T23 180, TH 0
    Channels: Incoming-only none, Two-way 5-1024, Outgoing-only none
    RESTARTs 1/1 CALLs 0+0/0+0/0+0 DIAGs 0/0
  Last input 0:37:35, output 0:37:33, output hang never
  Last clearing of "show interface" counters never
  Output queue 0/40, 0 drops; input queue 0/75, 0 drops
  5 minute input rate 0 bits/sec, 0 packets/sec
  5 minute output rate 0 bits/sec, 0 packets/sec
    4 packets input, 13 bytes, 0 no buffer
    Received 0 broadcasts, 0 runts, 0 giants
    0 input errors, 0 CRC, 0 frame, 0 overrun, 0 ignored, 0 abort
    4 packets output, 33 bytes, 0 underruns
    0 output errors, 0 collisions, 85547 interface resets, 0 restarts
    1 carrier transitions
```

Callouts in figure: **LAPB state**, **"Not ready" flow control count**, **X.25 service initialization**, **Connect attempts**, **Frame reject protocol errors**, **Retransmit requests**, **Disconnect count**

X.25: No Connections over X.25 Link

Symptom: Connections over an X.25 link fail.

Table 19-1 outlines the problems that might cause this symptom and describes solutions to those problems.

Table 19-1   *X.25: No Connections over X.25 Link*

Possible Problem	Solution	
Link is down.	Use the **show interfaces serial** exec command to determine whether the link is down. If the link is down, refer to Chapter 15.	
Cabling is incorrect, or the router hardware is bad.	**Step 1**	Use the **show interfaces serial** exec command to determine the status of the interface.
	Step 2	If the interface is down, refer to Chapter 15. If the interface is up but the line protocol is down, check the LAPB[1] state in the output of the **show interfaces serial** command.
	Step 3	If the LAPB state is not CONNECT, use the **debug lapb** privileged exec command (or attach a serial analyzer) to look for SABMs being sent and for UA[2] packets being sent in reply to SABMs[3]. If UAs are not being sent, one of the other possible problems described in this table is the likely cause.
		Caution: Exercise care when using **debug** commands. Many **debug** commands are processor-intensive and can cause serious network problems (such as degraded performance or loss of connectivity) if they are enabled on an already heavily loaded router. When you finish using a **debug** command, remember to disable it with its specific **no debug** command (or use the **no debug all** command to turn off all debugging).
		Use **debug** commands to isolate problems, not to monitor normal network operation. Because the high processor overhead of **debug** commands can disrupt router operation, you should use **debug** commands only when you are looking for specific types of traffic or problems and have narrowed your problems to a likely subset of causes.
	Step 4	If the **show interfaces serial** exec command indicates that the interface and line protocol are up but no connections can be made, there is probably a router or switch misconfiguration. Refer to the other possible problems outlined in this table.
	Step 5	Check all cabling and hardware for damage or wear. Replace cabling or hardware as required. For more information, refer to Chapter 3, "Troubleshooting Hardware and Booting Problems."
Protocol parameters are misconfigured.	**Step 1**	Enable the **debug lapb** privileged exec command and look for SABMs being sent. If no SABMs are being sent, disable the **debug lapb** command and enable the **debug x25 events** privileged exec command.
	Step 2	Look for RESTART messages (for PVCs[4]) or CLEAR REQUESTS with nonzero cause codes (for SVCs[5]).

continues

Table 19-1   *X.25: No Connections over X.25 Link (Continued)*

Possible Problem	Solution	
Protocol parameters are misconfigured. *(continued)*	**Step 1**	Enable the **debug lapb** privileged exec command and look for SABMs being sent. If no SABMs are being sent, disable the **debug lapb** command and enable the **debug x25 events** privileged exec command.
	Step 2	Look for RESTART messages (for PVCs[6]) or CLEAR REQUESTS with nonzero cause codes (for SVCs[7]).
		To interpret X.25 cause and diagnostic codes provided in the **debug x25 events** output, refer to the *Debug Command Reference*.
	Step 3	Verify that all critical LAPB parameters (modulo, T1, N1, N2, and k) and the critical X.25 parameters (modulo, X.121 addresses, SVC ranges, PVC definitions, and default window and packet sizes) match the parameters required by the service provider.
The x25 map command is misconfigured.	**Step 1**	Use the **show running-config** privileged exec command to view the router configuration. Look for x25 map interface configuration command entries.
	Step 2	Make sure that **x25 map** commands specify the correct address mappings.
		To retract a prior mapping, use the **no** form of the x25 map command with the appropriate network protocol(s) and X.121 address argument:
		`no x25 map protocol address x121-address`
		To set up the LAN protocols-to-remote host mapping, use the x25 map interface configuration command:
		`x25 map protocol address [protocol2 address2[...[protocol9 address9]]] x121-address [option]`
		Syntax Description:
		• *protocol*—Protocol type, entered by keyword. Supported protocols are entered by keyword. As many as nine protocol and address pairs can be specified in one command line.
		• *address*—Protocol address.
		• *x121-address*—X.121 address of the remote host.
		• *option*—(Optional) Additional functionality that can be specified for originated calls.

Table 19-1   *X.25: No Connections over X.25 Link (Continued)*

Possible Problem	Solution	
The x25 map command is misconfigured. *(continued)*	**Step 3**	Ensure that all router X.25 configuration options match the settings of attached switches. Reconfigure the router or switch as necessary.
	Step 4	Enable the **debug x25 events** command and look for RESTART messages (for PVCs) or CLEAR REQUESTs with nonzero cause codes (for SVCs).
		To interpret X.25 cause and diagnostic codes provided in the **debug x25 events** output, refer to the *Debug Command Reference*.

[1]LAPB = Link Access Procedure, Balanced

[2]UA = Unnumbered acknowledgment

[3]SAMB = Set Asynchronous Balance Mode

[4]PVC = permanent virtual circuit

[5]SVC = switched virtual circuit

[6]PVC = permanent virtual circuit

[7]SVC = switched virtual circuit

X.25: Excess Serial Errors on X.25 Link

Symptom: The output of the **show interfaces serial** command shows REJs, RNRs, FRMRs, RESTARTs, or DISCs in excess of 0.5 percent of information frames (IFRAMEs).

NOTE   If any of these fields are increasing and represent more than 0.5 percent of the number of IFRAMEs, there is probably a problem somewhere in the X.25 network. There should always be at least one SABM. However, if there are more than 10, the packet switch probably is not responding.

Table 19-2 outlines the problem that might cause this symptom and describes solutions to that problem.

Table 19-2   *X.25: Excess Serial Errors on X.25 Link*

Possible Problem	Solution	
Incorrect cabling or bad router hardware	**Step 1**	Use the **show interfaces serial** exec command to determine the status of the interface.
	Step 2	If the interface is down, refer to Chapter 15. If the interface is up but the line protocol is down, check the LAPB state in the output of the **show interfaces serial** command.
	Step 3	If the LAPB state is not CONNECT, use the **debug lapb** privileged exec command (or attach a serial analyzer) to look for SABMs being sent and for UA packets being sent in reply to SABMs.
	Step 4	If the **show interfaces serial** exec command indicates that the interface and line protocol are up but no connections can be made, there is probably a router or switch misconfiguration.
	Step 5	Check all cabling and hardware for damage or wear. Replace cabling or hardware as required. For more information, refer to Chapter 3.

PART V

Troubleshooting Bridging and Switching Environments

## CHAPTER 20

Troubleshooting Transparent Bridging Environments

Transparent bridges were first developed at Digital Equipment Corporation (Digital) in the early 1980s and are now very popular in Ethernet/IEEE 802.3 networks.

- This chapter first defines a transparent bridge as a learning bridge that implements a Spanning Tree. A deeper description of the Spanning-Tree Protocol is included.

- Cisco devices implementing transparent bridging previously were split in two categories: routers running IOS, and the Catalyst range of switches, running specific software. This is not the case anymore, however, because several Catalyst products are now based on the IOS. This chapter introduces the different bridging techniques available on IOS devices. For Catalyst software specific configuration and troubleshooting, refer to Chapter 23, "Troubleshooting ATM LAN Environments."

- Finally, this chapter introduces some troubleshooting steps classified by symptoms of potential problems that typically occur in network implementations featuring transparent bridging.

Transparent Bridging Technology Basics

Transparent bridges are so named because their presence and operation are transparent to network hosts. When transparent bridges are powered on, they learn the network's topology by analyzing the source address of incoming frames from all attached networks. For example, if a bridge sees a frame arrive on line 1 from Host A, the bridge concludes that Host A can be reached through the network connected to line 1. Through this process, transparent bridges build a table such as the one in Table 20-1.

Table 20-1   *A Transparent Bridging Table*

Host Address	Network Number
0000.0000.0001	1
0000.b07e.ee0e	7
. . .	
0050.50e1.9b80	4
0060.b0d9.2e3d	2
0000.0c8c.7088	1
. . .	

The bridge uses its table as the basis for traffic forwarding. When a frame is received on one of the bridge interfaces, the bridge looks up the frame's destination address in its internal table. If the table contains an association between the destination address and any of the bridge's ports aside from the one on which the frame was received, the frame is forwarded out the indicated port. If no association is found, the frame is flooded to all ports except the inbound port. Broadcasts and multicasts are also flooded in this way.

Transparent bridges successfully isolate intrasegment traffic, thereby reducing the traffic seen on each individual segment. This usually improves network response times as seen by the user. The extent to which traffic is reduced and response times are improved depends on the volume of intersegment traffic relative to the total traffic, as well as the volume of broadcast and multicast traffic.

Bridging Loops

Without a bridge-to-bridge protocol, the transparent bridge algorithm fails when there are multiple paths of bridges and local-area networks (LANs) between any two LANs in the internetwork. Figure 20-1 illustrates such a bridging loop.

Figure 20-1 *Inaccurate Forwarding and Learning in Transparent Bridging Environments*

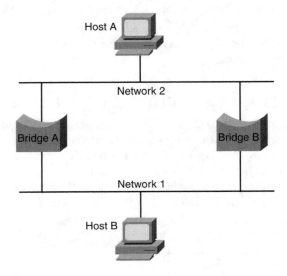

Suppose that Host A sends a frame to Host B. Both bridges receive the frame and correctly conclude that Host A is on Network 2. Unfortunately, after Host B receives two copies of Host A's frame, both bridges again receive the frame on their Network 1 interfaces because all hosts receive all messages on broadcast LANs. In some cases, the bridges then change their internal tables to indicate that Host A is on Network 1. If this is the case, when Host

B replies to Host A's frame, both bridges receive and subsequently drop the replies because their tables indicate that the destination (Host A) is on the same network segment as the frame's source.

In addition to basic connectivity problems such as the one just described, the proliferation of broadcast messages in networks with loops represents a potentially serious network problem. Referring again to Figure 20-1, assume that Host A's initial frame is a broadcast. Both bridges will forward the frames endlessly, using all available network bandwidth, and blocking the transmission of other packets on both segments.

A topology with loops such as that shown in Figure 20-2 can be useful as well as potentially harmful. A loop implies the existence of multiple paths through the internetwork. A network with multiple paths from source to destination can increase overall network fault tolerance through improved topological flexibility.

The Spanning-Tree Algorithm

The Spanning-Tree Algorithm (STA) was developed by Digital, a key Ethernet vendor, to preserve the benefits of loops while eliminating their problems. Digital's algorithm was subsequently revised by the IEEE 802 committee and was published in the IEEE 802.1d specification. The Digital algorithm and the IEEE 802.1d algorithm are not the same, nor are they compatible.

The STA designates a loop-free subset of the network's topology by placing those bridge ports that, if active, would create loops into a standby (blocking) condition. Blocking bridge ports can be activated in the event of primary link failure, providing a new path through the internetwork.

The STA uses a conclusion from graph theory as a basis for constructing a loop-free subset of the network's topology. Graph theory states the following: "For any connected graph consisting of nodes and edges connecting pairs of nodes, there is a Spanning Tree of edges that maintains the connectivity of the graph but contains no loops."

Figure 20-2 illustrates how the STA eliminates loops. The STA calls for each bridge to be assigned a unique identifier. Typically, this identifier is one of the bridge's Media Access Control (MAC) addresses, plus a priority. Each port in every bridge is also assigned a unique (within that bridge) identifier (typically, its own MAC address). Finally, each bridge port is associated with a path cost. The path cost represents the cost of transmitting a frame onto a LAN through that port. In Figure 20-3, path costs are noted on the lines emanating from each bridge. Path costs are usually default values, but network administrators can assign them manually.

Figure 20-2 *A Transparent Bridge Network Before STA Is Run*

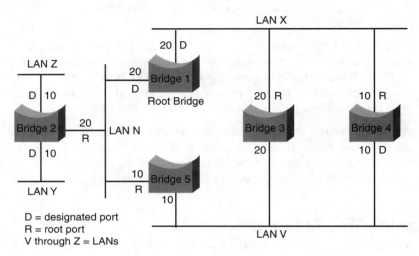

The first activity in Spanning Tree computation is the selection of the root bridge, which is the bridge with the lowest-value bridge identifier. In Figure 20-2, the root bridge is Bridge 1. Next, the root port on all other bridges is determined. A bridge's root port is the port through which the root bridge can be reached with the least aggregate path cost. The value of the least aggregate path cost to the root is called the *root path cost*.

Finally, designated bridges and their designated ports are determined. A designated bridge is the bridge on each LAN that provides the minimum root path cost. A LAN's designated bridge is the only bridge allowed to forward frames to and from the LAN for which it is the designated bridge. A LAN's designated port is the port that connects it to the designated bridge.

In some cases, two or more bridges can have the same root path cost. For example, in Figure 20-3, Bridges 4 and 5 can both reach Bridge 1 (the root bridge) with a path cost of 10. In this case, the bridge identifiers are used again, this time to determine the designated bridges. Bridge 4's LAN V port is selected over Bridge 5's LAN V port.

Using this process, all but one of the bridges directly connected to each LAN are eliminated, thereby removing all two-LAN loops. The STA also eliminates loops involving more than two LANs, while still preserving connectivity. Figure 20-3 shows the results of applying the STA to the network shown in Figure 20-2. Figure 20-3 shows the tree topology more clearly. Comparing this figure to the pre-Spanning Tree figure shows that the STA has placed both Bridge 3 and Bridge 5's ports to LAN V in standby mode.

Figure 20-3 *A Transparent Bridge Network After STA Is Run*

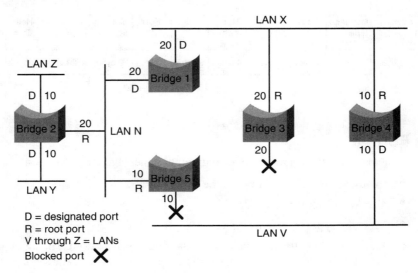

The Spanning Tree calculation occurs when the bridge is powered up and whenever a topology change is detected. The calculation requires communication between the Spanning Tree bridges, which is accomplished through configuration messages (sometimes called *bridge protocol data units*, or BPDUs). Configuration messages contain information identifying the bridge that is presumed to be the root (root identifier) and the distance from the sending bridge to the root bridge (root path cost). Configuration messages also contain the bridge and port identifier of the sending bridge and the age of information contained in the configuration message.

Bridges exchange configuration messages at regular intervals (typically 1 to 4 seconds). If a bridge fails (causing a topology change), neighboring bridges soon detect the lack of configuration messages and initiate a Spanning Tree recalculation.

All transparent bridge topology decisions are made locally. Configuration messages are exchanged between neighboring bridges. There is no central authority on network topology or administration.

Frame Format

Transparent bridges exchange configuration messages and topology change messages. Configuration messages are sent between bridges to establish a network topology. Topology change messages are sent after a topology change has been detected to indicate that the STA should be rerun.

The IEEE 802.1d configuration message format is shown in Figure 20-4.

Figure 20-4 *The Transparent Bridge Configuration*

Protocol identifier	Version	Message type	Flags	Root ID	Root path cost	Bridge ID	Port ID	Message age	Maximum age	Hello time	Forward delay
2 bytes	1 byte	1 byte	1 byte	8 bytes	4 bytes	8 bytes	2 bytes	2 bytes	2 bytes	2 bytes	2 bytes

Message Format

The fields of the transparent bridge configuration message are as follows:

- **Protocol identifier**—Contains the value 0.
- **Version**—Contains the value 0.
- **Message type**—Contains the value 0.
- **Flag**—A 1-byte field, of which only the first 2 bits are used. The topology change (TC) bit signals a topology change. The topology change acknowledgment (TCA) bit is set to acknowledge receipt of a configuration message with the TC bit set.
- **Root ID**—Identifies the root bridge by listing its 2-byte priority followed by its 6-byte ID.
- **Root path cost**—Contains the cost of the path from the bridge sending the configuration message to the root bridge.
- **Bridge ID**—Identifies the priority and ID of the bridge sending the message.
- **Port ID**—Identifies the port from which the configuration message was sent. This field allows loops created by multiply attached bridges to be detected and dealt with.
- **Message age**—Specifies the amount of time since the root sent the configuration message on which the current configuration message is based.
- **Maximum age**—Indicates when the current configuration message should be deleted.
- **Hello time**—Provides the time period between root bridge configuration messages.
- **Forward delay**—Provides the length of time that bridges should wait before transitioning to a new state after a topology change. If a bridge transitions too soon, not all network links may be ready to change their state, and loops can result.

Topological change messages consist of only 4 bytes. They include a Protocol Identifier field, which contains the value 0; a Version field, which contains the value 0; and a Message Type field, which contains the value 128.

Different IOS Bridging Techniques

Cisco routers have three different ways of implementing bridging:

- **Default behavior**—Prior to IRB and the CRB features (see later), you could bridge or route a protocol only on a platform basis. That is, if the **ip route** command was used, for example, then IP routing was done on all interfaces. In this situation, IP could not be bridged on any of the router's interfaces.

- **Concurrent routing and bridging (CRB)**—With CRB, you can determine whether to bridge or route a protocol on an interface basis. That is, you can route a given protocol on some interfaces and bridge the same protocol on bridge group interfaces within the same router. The router can then be both a router and a bridge for a given protocol, but there cannot be any kind of communication between routing-defined interfaces and bridge group interfaces. For a given protocol, the router can be logically considered as different independent devices: one router and one or more bridges, as shown in Figure 20-5.

Figure 20-5 *The Router Can Be Logically Considered as Different Independent Devices*

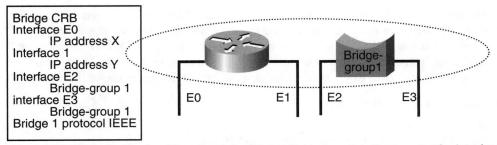

```
Bridge CRB
Interface E0
        IP address X
Interface 1
        IP address Y
Interface E2
        Bridge-group 1
interface E3
        Bridge-group 1
Bridge 1 protocol IEEE
```

EO   E1   E2   E3

Bridge-group1

In this configuration for the IP protocol, the Cisco device is acting like a router for interfaces E0 and E1 and is acting like a bridge for interfaces E2 and E3. Note that there is no communication possible between the two functions (a host connected on E0 would never be able to reach a host connected on E2 through the router with this configuration).

- **Integrated routing and bridging (IRB)**—IRB provides the capability to route between a bridge group and a routed interface using a concept called Bridge-Group Virtual Interface (BVI). Because bridging is in the data link layer and routing is in the network layer, they have different protocol configuration models. With IP, for example, bridge-group interfaces belong to the same network and have a collective IP network address, while each routed interface represents a distinct network and has its own IP network address. The concept of Bridge-Group Virtual Interface was created to enable these interfaces to exchange packets for a given protocol. Conceptually, the Cisco router looks like a router connected to one or more bridge groups, as shown in Figure 20-6.

Figure 20-6 *The Bridge-Group Virtual Interface Brings Routing to Bridge Group 1*

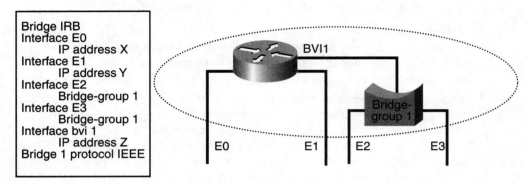

```
Bridge IRB
Interface E0
      IP address X
Interface E1
      IP address Y
Interface E2
      Bridge-group 1
Interface E3
      Bridge-group 1
Interface bvi 1
      IP address Z
Bridge 1 protocol IEEE
```

The Bridge-Group Virtual Interface brings routing to bridge-group1. One can assign an IP address to the whole bridge group and routed communication is now possible between a host connected to E0 and a host connected to E2, for instance.

The BVI is a virtual interface within the router that acts like a normal routed interface that represents the corresponding bridge group to routed interfaces within the router. The interface number of the BVI is the number of the bridge group that this virtual interface represents. The number is the link between this BVI and the bridge group. The sample principle applies to the Route Switch Module in a Catalyst Switch, as shown in Figure 20-7.

Figure 20-7 *Route Switch Module in a Catalyst Switch*

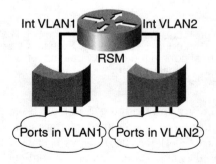

The IRB concept is also used (but hidden) on the Catalyst Route Switch Module (RSM). The VLAN interfaces are virtual interfaces connecting different bridge groups (the VLANs).

Troubleshooting Transparent Bridging

This section presents troubleshooting information for connectivity problems in transparent bridging internetworks. It describes specific transparent bridging symptoms, the problems that are likely to cause each symptom, and the solutions to those problems.

<table>
<tr><td>NOTE</td><td>Problems associated with source-route bridging (SRB), translational bridging, and source-route transparent (SRT) bridging are addressed in Chapter 10, "Troubleshooting IBM."</td></tr>
</table>

To do an efficient troubleshooting of your bridged network, you should get a basic knowledge of its design, especially when a Spanning Tree is involved.

Try to have the following available:

- The topology map of the bridged network
- The location of the root bridge
- The location of the redundant link (and blocked ports)

When you are troubleshooting connectivity issues, try to narrow down the problem to a minimum number of hosts (ideally only a client and a server).

The following sections describe the most common network problems in transparent bridged networks:

- Transparent Bridging: No Connectivity
- Transparent Bridging: Unstable Spanning Tree
- Transparent Bridging: Sessions Terminate Unexpectedly
- Transparent Bridging: Looping and Broadcast Storms Occur

Transparent Bridging: No Connectivity

Symptom: Client cannot connect to hosts across a transparently bridged network.

Table 20-2 outlines the problems that might cause this symptom and describes solutions to those problems.

Table 20-2 *Transparent Bridging: No Connectivity*

Possible Causes	Suggested Actions	
Hardware or media problem has occurred	Step 1	Use the **show bridge** exec command to see whether there is a connectivity problem. If there is, the output will not show any MAC[1] addresses in the bridging table.
	Step 2	Use the **show interfaces** exec command to determine whether the interface and line protocol are up.
	Step 3	If the interface is down, troubleshoot the hardware or the media. Refer to Chapter 3, "Troubleshooting Hardware and Booting Problems."
	Step 4	If the line protocol is down, check the physical connection between the interface and the network. Make sure that the connection is secure and that cables are not damaged.
		If the line protocol is up but input and output packet counters are not incrementing, check the media and host connectivity. Refer to the media troubleshooting chapter that covers the media type used in your network.
Host is down	Step 1	Use the **show bridge** exec command on bridges to make sure that the bridging table includes the MAC addresses of attached end nodes.
		The bridging table comprises the source and destination MAC addresses of hosts and is populated when packets from a source or destination pass through the bridge.
	Step 2	If any expected end nodes are missing, check the status of the nodes to verify that they are connected and properly configured.
	Step 3	Reinitialize or reconfigure end nodes as necessary, and re-examine the bridging table using the **show bridge** command.
Bridging path is broken	Step 1	Identify the path that packets should take between end nodes. If there is a router on this path, split the troubleshooting in two parts: node1-router and router-node2.
	Step 2	Connect to each bridge on the path, and check the status of the ports that are used on the path between end nodes, just as described in the previous discussion on a hardware or media problem.
	Step 3	Using the **show bridge** command, check that the MAC address of the nodes are learned on the correct ports. If not, there may be instability on your Spanning Tree topology. (See Table 20-2.)
	Step 4	Check the state of the ports using the **show span** command. If the ports that should transmit traffic between the end nodes are not in the forwarding state, the topology of your tree may have changed unexpectedly. (See Table 20-3.)

Table 20-2   *Transparent Bridging: No Connectivity (Continued)*

Possible Causes	Suggested Actions	
Bridging filters are misconfigured	**Step 1**	Use the **show running-config** privileged exec command to determine whether bridge filters are configured.
	Step 2	Disable bridge filters on suspect interfaces, and determine whether connectivity returns.
	Step 3	If connectivity does not return, the filter is not the problem. If connectivity is restored after removing filters, one or more bad filters are causing the connectivity problem.
	Step 4	If multiple filters or filters using access lists with multiple statements exist, apply each filter individually to identify the problem filter. Check the configuration for input and output LSAP[2] and TYPE filters, which can be used simultaneously to block different protocols. For example, LSAP (F0F0) can be used to block NetBIOS, and TYPE (6004) can be used to block local-area transport.
	Step 5	Modify any filters or access lists that are blocking traffic. Continue testing filters until all filters are enabled and connections still work.
Input and output queues are full	Excessive multicast or broadcast traffic can cause input and output queues to overflow, resulting in dropped packets.	
	Step 1	Use the **show interfaces** command to look for input and output drops. Drops suggest excessive traffic over the media. If the current number of packets on the input queue is consistently at or greater than 80 percent of the current size of the input queue, the size of the input queue may require tuning to accommodate the incoming packet rate. Even if the current number of packets on the input queue never seems to approach the size of the input queue, bursts of packets may still be overflowing the queue.
	Step 2	Reduce broadcast and multicast traffic on attached networks by implementing bridging filters, or segment the network using more internetworking devices.
	Step 3	If the connection is a serial link, increase bandwidth, apply priority queuing, increase the hold queue size, or modify the system buffer size. For more information, refer to Chapter 15, "Troubleshooting Serial Lines."

[1]MAC = Media Access Control

[2]LSAP = link services access point

Transparent Bridging: Unstable Spanning Tree

Symptom: Transient loss of connectivity between hosts. Several hosts are affected at the same time.

Table 20-3 outlines the problems that might cause this symptom and describes solutions to those problems.

Table 20-3   *Transparent Bridging: Unstable Spanning Tree*

Possible Causes	Suggested Actions	
Link flapping	**Step 1**	Use **show span** command to check whether the number of topology changes is steadily increasing.
	Step 2	If so, check the link between your bridges, using the **show interface** command. If you cannot find a link flapping between two bridges this way, use the **debug spantree event** privileged exec command on your bridges.
		This will log all changes related to Spanning Tree; in a stable topology, there should not be any. The only links to track are the ones connecting bridging devices—a transition on a link to an end station should have no impact on the network.
		Caution: Exercise caution when using the **debug spantree event** command. Because debugging output is assigned high priority in the CPU process, it can render the system unusable. For this reason, use **debug** commands only to troubleshoot specific problems or during troubleshooting sessions with Cisco technical support staff. Moreover, it is best to use **debug** commands during periods of lower network traffic and fewer users. Debugging during these periods decreases the likelihood that increased **debug** command processing overhead will affect system use.
Root bridge that keeps changing/ multiple bridges that claim to be the root	**Step 1**	Check the consistency of the root bridge information all over the bridged network using the **show span** commands on the different bridges.
	Step 2	If several bridges are claiming to be the root, check that you are running the same Spanning-Tree Protocol on every bridge (see the entry "Spanning-Tree Algorithm mismatch," in Table 20-5).
	Step 3	Use the **bridge <group> priority <number>** command on root bridge to force the desired bridge to become the root. The lower the priority, the more likely the bridge is to become the root.
	Step 4	Check the diameter of your network. With standard Spanning Tree settings, there should never be more that seven bridging hops between two hosts.

Table 20-3 *Transparent Bridging: Unstable Spanning Tree (Continued)*

Possible Causes	Suggested Actions	
Hellos not being exchanged	Step 1	Check whether bridges are communicating with one another. Use a network analyzer or the **debug spantree tree** privileged exec command to see whether Spanning Tree hello frames are being exchanged.
		Caution: Exercise caution when using the **debug spantree tree** command. Because debugging output is assigned high priority in the CPU process, it can render the system unusable. For this reason, use **debug** commands only to troubleshoot specific problems or during troubleshooting sessions with Cisco technical support staff. Moreover, it is best to use **debug** commands during periods of lower network traffic and fewer users. Debugging during these periods decreases the likelihood that increased **debug** command processing overhead will affect system use.
	Step 2	If hellos are not being exchanged, check the physical connections and software configuration on bridges.

Transparent Bridging: Sessions Terminate Unexpectedly

Symptom: Connections in a transparently bridged environment are successfully established, but sessions sometimes terminate abruptly.

Table 20-4 outlines the problems that might cause this symptom and describes solutions to those problems.

Table 20-4 *Transparent Bridging: Sessions Terminate Unexpectedly*

Possible Causes	Suggested Actions	
Excessive retransmissions	Step 1	Use a network analyzer to look for host retransmissions.
	Step 2	If you see retransmissions on slow serial lines, increase the transmission timers on the host. For information on configuring your hosts, refer to the vendor documentation. For information on troubleshooting serial lines, refer to Chapter 15.
		If you see retransmissions on high-speed LAN media, check for packets sent and received in order, or dropped by any intermediate device such as a bridge or a switch. Troubleshoot the LAN media as appropriate. For more information, refer to the media troubleshooting chapter that covers the media type used in your network.
	Step 3	Use a network analyzer to determine whether the number of retransmissions subsides.
Excessive delay over serial link	Increase bandwidth, apply priority queuing, increase the hold queue size, or modify the system buffer size. For more information, refer to Chapter 15.	

Transparent Bridging: Looping and Broadcast Storms Occur

Symptom: Packet looping and broadcast storms occur in transparent bridging environments. End stations are forced into excessive retransmission, causing sessions to time out or drop.

NOTE Packet loops are typically caused by network design problems or hardware issues.

Table 20-4 outlines the problems that might cause this symptom and describes solutions to those problems.

Bridging loops are the worst-case scenario in a bridged network because they will potentially impact every user. In case of emergency, the best way of recovering quickly connectivity is to disable manually all the interfaces providing a redundant path in the network. Unfortunately, the cause of the bridging loop will be very difficult to identify afterward, if you do so. Try the actions recommended in Table 20-5 first, if possible.

Table 20-5   *Transparent Bridging: Looping and Broadcast Storms Occur*

Possible Causes	Suggested Actions	
No Spanning Tree implemented	Step 1	Examine a topology map of your internetwork to check for possible loops.
	Step 2	Eliminate any loops that exist, or make sure that the appropriate links are in backup mode.
	Step 3	If broadcast storms and packet loops persist, use the **show interfaces** exec command to obtain input and output packet count statistics. If these counters increment at an abnormally high rate (with respect to your normal traffic loads), a loop is probably still present in the network.
	Step 4	Implement a Spanning-Tree Algorithm to prevent loops.
Spanning-Tree Algorithm mismatch	Step 1	Use the **show span** exec command on each bridge to determine which Spanning-Tree Algorithm is being used.
	Step 2	Make sure that all bridges are running the same Spanning-Tree Algorithm (either DEC or IEEE).[1] Use of both DEC and IEEE Spanning-Tree Algorithms may be needed in the network for some very specific configuration (generally involving IRB). If the mismatch in the Spanning-Tree Protocol is not intended, you should reconfigure bridges as appropriate so that all bridges use the same Spanning-Tree Algorithm.
	Note: The DEC and IEEE Spanning-Tree Algorithms are incompatible.	

Table 20-5   *Transparent Bridging: Looping and Broadcast Storms Occur (Continued)*

Possible Causes	Suggested Actions	
Multiple bridging domains incorrectly configured	Step 1	Use the **show span** exec command on bridges to ensure that all domain group numbers match for given bridging domains.
	Step 2	If multiple domain groups are configured for the bridge, ensure that all domain specifications are assigned correctly. Use the **bridge <group> domain <domain-number>** global configuration command to make any necessary changes.
	Step 3	Make sure that no loops exist between bridging domains. An interdomain bridging environment does not provide loop prevention based on Spanning Tree. Each domain has its own Spanning Tree, which is independent of the Spanning Tree in another domain.
Link error (unidirectional link), duplex mismatch, high level of error on a port		Loops occur when a port that should block moves to the forwarding state. A port needs to receive BPDUs from a neighbor bridge to stay in a blocking state. Any error that lead to BPDUs being lost can then be the cause of a bridging loop.
	Step 1	Identify blocking ports from your network diagram.
	Step 2	Check the status of the ports that should be blocking in your bridged network, using the **show interface** and **show bridge** exec commands.
	Step 3	If you find a supposedly blocked port that is currently forwarding (or about to forward, in learning or listening state), you have found the real source of the problem. Check where this port is receiving BPDUs. If not, there is probably an issue on the link connected to this port (check then link errors, duplex setting, and so on). If the port is still receiving BPDUs, go to the bridge that you expect to be designated for this LAN. From there, check all the links on the path toward the root. You will find an issue on one of these links (provided that your initial network diagram was correct).

[1]IEEE = Institute of Electrical and Electronic Engineers

Before Calling Cisco Systems' TAC Team

Try to collect as much information as you can on the topology of your network, when stable.

The minimal data to collect is this:

- The physical topology of the network
- The expected location of the root bridge (and the backup root bridge)
- The location of blocked ports

Additional Sources

Books

- Clark, K., and K. Hamilton. *Cisco LAN Switching.* Indianapolis: Cisco Press, 1999.
- Perlman, Radia. *Interconnections, Bridges and Routers.* Boston: Addison-Wesley, 1998.

URLs

Transparent bridging documentation: www.cisco.com/univercd/cc/td/doc/product/software/ios120/12cgcr/ibm_c/bcprt1/bctb.htm

Technology support pages on CCO: www.cisco.com/tac (Look for the LAN part in the Technology Home Page section.)

## CHAPTER 21

Troubleshooting ATM LAN Emulation Networks

This chapter introduces general troubleshooting techniques related to LAN Emulation (LANE) networks.

We will first briefly introduce LANE as it was conceived: a LAN technology aimed at emulating a legacy Ethernet network over ATM. We will then cover troubleshooting of the most common problems using this technology:

- Troubleshooting LANE Clients not coming up
- Troubleshooting LANE connectivity (after LANE Clients are up)

Introduction

LANE is a standard defined by the ATM Forum that provides ATM-attached stations the same capabilities that they normally obtain from legacy Ethernet LANs. As the name suggests, the function of the LANE protocol is to emulate a LAN on top of an ATM network. By making an ATM interface look like one or more separate Ethernet interfaces, LANE enables LAN users to take advantage of ATM's benefits without requiring modifications to end-station hardware or software.

ATM is a connection-oriented service that establishes connections between source and destination devices. LAN-based protocols, on the other hand, are connectionless and use broadcasts so that source devices can find one or more destination devices. The primary purpose of LANE, then, is to provide the same services that a broadcast medium such as Ethernet does.

The LANE protocol resolves MAC addresses to ATM addresses so that LANE end systems can set up direct connections between themselves and then can forward data. The LANE protocol can be deployed in two types of ATM-attached equipment:

- Hosts or routers with ATM network interface cards (NICs). ATM NICs implement the LANE protocol and interface to the ATM network while presenting the current Ethernet service interface to the higher-level protocol drivers. The network layer protocols continue to communicate as if they were on an Ethernet by using known procedures. However, they are capable of taking advantage of most of the advanced services of the ATM network.

- The second class of network device that implements LANE consists of ATM-attached LAN switches and routers. These devices, together with directly attached ATM hosts equipped with ATM NICs, are used to provide a virtual LAN service in which ports are assigned to particular virtual LANs, independent of physical location.

The LANE specification defines several components that enable the protocol to provide the broadcast and address resolution services required to emulate traditional LANs:

- **LAN Emulation Client (LEC)**—An entity such as a workstation, LAN switch, or router that performs data forwarding and receiving, address resolution, and other control functions for a single endpoint in a single emulated LAN. The LEC provides a standard LAN service to any higher layers that interface to it. A router or switch can have multiple resident LECs, each connecting with different emulated LANs. The LANE client registers its MAC and ATM address with the LES.

- **LAN Emulation Server (LES)**—A server that provides a registration facility for clients to join the emulated LAN. Among other things, the LES handles LAN Emulation Address Resolution Protocol (LE_ARP) requests and maintains a list or lookup table of LAN destination MAC addresses. Each emulated LAN must have a LES.

- **Broadcast-and-Unknown Server (BUS)**—A server that floods unknown destination traffic and that forwards multicast and broadcast traffic to clients within an emulated LAN. Each emulated LAN (ELAN) must have a BUS.

Note   In Cisco's LANE implementation, the LES and the BUS are combined.

- **LAN Emulation Configuration Server (LECS)**—A server that assigns individual clients to particular emulated LANs by directing them to the LES that corresponds to the emulated LAN. The LECS can enforce security by restricting ELAN membership to certain LECs based on their MAC addresses. The LECS component, however, is optional in LANE—a client can contact directly the LES to join an emulated LAN.

Troubleshooting a LAN Emulation Network

Though not very complex in theory, the different configurations necessary to implement a LANE network include a lot of long ATM addresses. It becomes easy to insert a typo that will cause the whole setup to fail. Very often, then, troubleshooting a LANE network simply means to have it work! For this reason, this part is split in two sections:

- The "Troubleshooting LECs Not Coming Up" section deals with initial configuration issues when it is a matter of bringing up a LEC.

- When the initial connection of the LECs is established, the second part, Table 21-2, goes deeper into the troubleshooting of the live network.

Troubleshooting LECs Not Coming Up

The flowchart shown in Figure 21-1 explains which section to use in this section. Issue a **show lane client** exec command on the device hosting the LEC. Use the field Last Fail Reason, and jump to the corresponding section in next table (the **show lane client** command is fully described in the section "Understanding the show lane client Output," later in this chapter). If you could not solve your issue by simply following the flowchart, refer to the entry "If None of This Works," in Table 21-1.

Figure 21-1 *Flowchart Explaining How to Troubleshoot a LEC Not Coming Up*

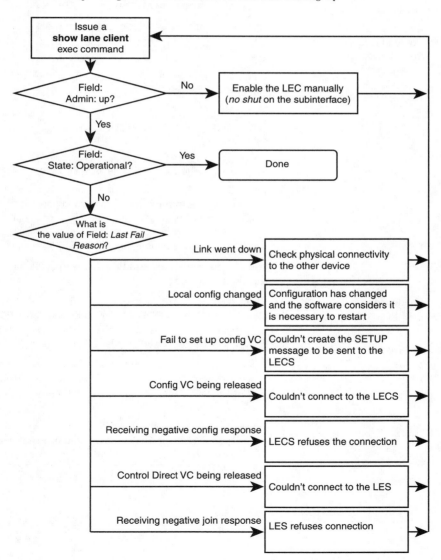

Table 21-1 *Troubleshooting LECs Not Coming Up*

Possible Problem	Solution	
Cannot connect to the LECS (config vc being released): Couldn't get our prefix *Or* Fail to set up config VC: Couldn't create a SETUP message to be sent to the LECS	Step 1	Enter the **show lane default** command. Check that full ATM addresses are showing up in the output. When the prefix is acquired correctly, you will typically see something like this: ``` ok#sh lane default interface ATM2/0: LANE Client: 47.00918100000001604799FD01.0050A219F038.** LANE Server: 47.00918100000001604799FD01.0050A219F039.** LANE Bus: 47.00918100000001604799FD01.0050A219F03A.** LANE Config Server: 47.00918100000001604799FD01.0050A219F03B.00 note: ** is the subinterface number byte in hex ``` If not, ". . ." is appearing at the beginning of each address. The output will then look like this: ``` notok#sh lane default interface ATM1/0: LANE Client: ...00000C409820.** LANE Server: ...00000C409821.** LANE Bus: ...00000C409822.** LANE Config Server: ...00000C409823.00 note: ** is the subinterface number byte in hex ```
	Step 2	Check that the ILMI PVC is configured on your ATM interface. You should have **atm pvc <x> 0 16 ilmi** in your configuration (where *x* represents the PVC number—be careful that the VPI may be different from 0). Check also that the PVC used for signaling is also configured: *atm pvc <x> 0 5 qsaal*.
	Step 3	Use the command **show atm ilmi-status** to check that the ILMI state is up and normal.
Cannot connect to the LECS (config vc being released): Incorrect LECS address	Step 1	Check the LECS ATM address given on the output of **show lane client**. If it is 47.0079000000000000000000000.00A03E000001.00 but you didn't want to use this well-known address, it is probably because the device couldn't get the LECS address via ILMI. • If the remote ATM switch is not a Cisco device, be careful—some vendors don't support LECS address advertising via ILMI. In that case, you can use the well-known address on the LECS, for instance. • Check on the ATM switch where the client is connected if the LECS address is specified with the command **atm lecs-address-default**.

Table 21-1 *Troubleshooting LECs Not Coming Up (Continued)*

Possible Problem	Solution	
Cannot connect to the LECS (config vc being released): Incorrect LECS address *(continued)*	**Step 2**	If you hard-coded the LECS ATM address in your configuration, or if you have a valid LECS ATM address that differs from the well-known address in **show lane client**, go to the device hosting the LECS. Use the **show lane config** command to compare the LECS address with the one that you see at the client, and check that the server is up and running.
The LECS refuses the connection (receiving negative config response)	**Step 1**	Check your configuration for the type (Ethernet/Token Ring) and the name of the ELAN that you are trying to join. Connect to the device hosting the LECS, and check whether the name and type of the ELAN match.
	Step 2	Check whether the LES could connect to the LECS. On the device hosting the LES, use the command **show lane server**, and check that the LECS is *connected*. To connect to the LECS, the LES needs the same information that a simple client would. Refer to the previous entry "Cannot Connect to the LECS."
Couldn't connect to the LES (Control Direct VC being released)	**Step 1**	If you hard-coded the LES address into the configuration, check on the machine hosting the LES server that its address exactly matches the one that you configured.
	Step 2	On the device that hosts the LECS, check that the LECS database entry for this ELAN is set with the right LES address. To know this, go to the device hosting the LES and type **show lane default**.
The LES refuses the connection (receiving negative join response)	**Step 1**	If the ELAN to which you are trying to connect is restricted, and if you connect to the LES directly bypassing the LECS, this could be a security issue. Check the LANE database configuration on the LECS to be sure that it includes the ATM address of the client attempting to connect.
	Step 2	If you configured on the same subinterface a LEC and a LES, and you also specified the ATM address for the LES with the command **lane server-atm-address**, the LEC might be trying to contact a backup LES (which refuses the connection). The reason is that the LEC is also using the **lane server-atm-address** command to decide which LES to contact. It then unconditionally contacts the local LES that may currently be the backup. The easy way of fixing this is to configure the LES on a different subinterface.

continues

Table 21-1   *Troubleshooting LECs Not Coming Up (Continued)*

Possible Problem	Solution
If none of this works	A simple configuration problem can, in fact, hide a much deeper issue with the network itself. Enable **debug lane client all** on your machine, and go to the section " LANE Client Connection Example, with debug lane client all Enabled " to compare to the output of a successful connection." Exercise caution when using **debug lane client all**. Because debugging output is assigned high priority in the CPU process, it can render the system unusable. It is best to use **debug** commands during periods of lower network traffic and fewer users. You should avoid sending verbose debugging output to the console (use the **logging console info** command). Instead, send the **debug** output to the logging buffer using the command **logging buffer <buffer-size> debug**.

Table 21-2   *Troubleshooting LANE Connectivity When LECs Are Up*

Possible Problem	Solution	
The LE_ARP cannot be completed.	**Step 1**	Locate an IP address to which you do not have connectivity (that is, an address that you cannot ping).
	Step 2	Write down its real MAC address. This information can be obtained from the station itself.
	Step 3	Check that indeed there is no mapping between this MAC address and an ATM destination address. You can check this with **show lane le-arp**. Refer to the section "Understanding the LE_ARP Process," later in this chapter.
	Step 4	Likely, there is no connectivity with the destination LEC. Check that the destination LEC is indeed "UP, operational." Refer to the next possible problem, regarding an ELAN split in two parts.
Using SSRP redundancy, the ELAN is split in two parts.	This happens when two clients seem to be up in the same ELAN. In reality, however, they connect to different LES. There is a big connectivity problem in the network. A part of the LECs went down and contacted the backup LECS/LES/BUS. As a result, both LECs are up but cannot communicate.	
	Step 1	Locate two LANE clients between which you do not have connectivity. Those lane clients are "UP, Operational."
	Step 2	Issue a **show lane client name <elanname>** command on both clients.
	Step 3	Check the ATM address in the line with type direct. If the ATM address is different in the two displays, then you do have two separated ELANs. This means that one LES was not reachable on one ELAN and that the backup LES was contacted.

Table 21-2   *Troubleshooting LANE Connectivity When LECs Are Up (Continued)*

Possible Problem	Solution
Using SSRP redundancy, the ELAN is split in two parts. *(continued)*	**Step 4** In the LECS database, locate the LES with the highest priority (which is the one listed first in the database). Then find the client that contacted a backup address and could not establish contact with the primary LES. There must be a serious physical issue between this LEC and the primary LES.
Using HSRP, a problem has occurred with the default gateway.	Connectivity seems to work fine, but several users report problems to ping the default gateway several times a day. Each outage is several minutes long. The default gateway is an HSRP virtual IP address. When this happens, third-party devices are often used to connect those users to the ATM network. **Step 1** The first recommendation is to upgrade all devices to the latest release. **Step 2** Another strongly recommended action is to force the usage of the real MAC address on the default gateway. This can be done in configuration interface on the router: `RouterName(config-if)#`**`standby use-bia`** Here, **use-bia** means to use the *burned-in address*, not the virtual MAC address. The burned-in address can be seen on the router via the **show interface** command on the router.
A problem with shaped VP tunnels has occurred.	Sometimes two remote ATM campus networks are linked with a shaped VP tunnel. The network designer must make sure that enough bandwidth is reserved on the link. If the traffic between the two campus site goes above the VP limit, some cells will be discarded, resulting in frames being lost. Generally speaking, when it comes to such a design, routing between the sites is *strongly* recommended. Troubleshooting this is often tricky. Refer to Chapter 22, "Troubleshooting ATM PVCs in a WAN Environment," for more information. The troubleshooting procedures are the same.
An ATM signaling issue has occurred.	This can be considered as advanced. Connectivity is broken between two LANE clients. They are both "UP, Operational." Even though the **le-arp** entry is there, the data direct VCC is not established. **Step 1** Locate two LANE Clients between which connectivity is broken. **Step 2** Check that the **le-arp** entries are both complete and point to the right ATM address. **Step 3** Check that indeed no data direct is established between the LANE Clients. You can check this via **show lane client**. There is no VC with the type of data.

continues

Table 21-2 *Troubleshooting LANE Connectivity When LECs Are Up (Continued)*

Possible Problem	Solution	
An ATM signaling issue has occurred. *(continued)*	**Step 4**	Enable **debug atm sig-error** and **debug atm errors**. Check that when you try to ping, you see an ATM signaling error appearing. Look for "cause code" messages.
	Step 5	Those problems are usually seen in a multivendor environment. If Steps 1 through 4 didn't help, upgrade all devices to the latest release.

Annex: Commands and Examples

In this section, we'll give examples of the most common ebug and show commands used when troubleshooting LANE.

LANE Client Connection Example, with debug lane client all Enabled

Figure 21-2 shows VCs required for LANE to work.

Figure 21-2 *Example of VCs Required for LANE to Work*

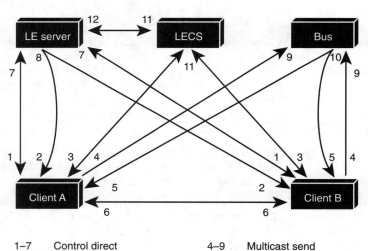

1–7	Control direct	4–9	Multicast send
2–8	Control distribute	5–10	Multicast forward
3–11	Configure direct (client)	6–6	Data direct
		11–12	Configure direct (server)

This is the sequence of events that needs to happen for LEC to come up from LEC's perspective, which is shown in **debug lane client all**:

1 Configure direct (3–11)

2 Control direct (1–7)

3 Control distribute (2–8)

4 Multicast send (4–9)

5 Multicast forward (5–10)

6 Data direct (6–6), LEC to LEC, is not shown in this **debug** output

ATM Addresses Used in This debug Output

The ATM addresses of the LECS/LES/BUS/LEC used in this example are shown below.

```
LECS    47.00918100000000603E899601.00E01E2EE8B3.00
LES     47.00918100000000603E899601.00E01E2EE8B1.01
BUS     47.00918100000000603E899601.00E01E2EE8B2.01
LEC     47.00918100000000603E899601.00E01E2EE8B0.01
ELAN Name    Elan1
```

Address Registration via ILMI

The LEC first registers its ATM address with the ATM network.

```
LEC ATM0.1: action A_REGISTER_ADDR
LEC ATM0.1: predicate PRED_LEC_NSAP TRUE
LEC ATM0.1: state IDLE event LEC_LOCAL_ACTIVATE => REGISTER_ADDR
LEC ATM0.1: action A_POST_LISTEN
LEC ATM0.1: sending LISTEN
LEC ATM0.1: listen on 47.00918100000000603E899601.00E01E2EE8B0.01
LEC ATM0.1: state REGISTER_ADDR event LEC_CTL_ILMI_SET_RSP_POS => POSTING_LISTEN
LEC ATM0.1: received LISTEN
LEC ATM0.1: action A_ACTIVATE_LEC
LEC ATM0.1: predicate PRED_CTL_DIRECT_NSAP FALSE
LEC ATM0.1: predicate PRED_LECS_NSAP FALSE
LEC ATM0.1: state POSTING_LISTEN event LEC_SIG_LISTEN_POS => GET_LECS_ADDR
LEC ATM0.1: action A_ALLOC_LECS_ADDR
LEC ATM0.1: state GET_LECS_ADDR event LEC_CTL_ILMI_SET_RSP_POS => GET_LECS_ADDR
```

Connecting to LECS (Configure Direct)

The LEC sets up a connection to LECS (bidirectional point-to-point VC) to find the ATM address of the LES for its ELAN. When this is done, this VC to the LECS is released.

The LEC finds the LECS ATM address by using three methods, in this order:

1 Using hard-coded ATM address

2 Getting the LECS via ILMI VPI=0, VCI=16 (not supported by some vendors)

3 Fixing the address defined by the ATM Forum:
(47.007900000000000000000000.00A03E000001.00)

Using the same VCC, the LECS returns the ATM address of the LES for the LEC ELAN.

In this debug output, the LEC is getting LECS address via ILMI:

```
LEC ATM0.1: action A_SEND_LECS_SETUP
LEC ATM0.1: sending SETUP
LEC ATM0.1:    callid              0x40518C04
LEC ATM0.1:    called party        47.00918100000000603E899601.00E01E2EE8B3.00   LECS
address
LEC ATM0.1:    calling_party       47.00918100000000603E899601.00E01E2EE8B0.01   LEC
address
LEC ATM0.1: state GET_LECS_ADDR event LEC_CTL_ILMI_SET_RSP_NEG => LECS_CONNECT

LEC ATM0.1: received CONNECT
LEC ATM0.1:    callid              0x40518C04
LEC ATM0.1:    vcd                 884
LEC ATM0.1: action A_SEND_CFG_REQ
LEC ATM0.1: sending LANE_CONFIG_REQ on VCD 884
LEC ATM0.1:    SRC MAC address     00e0.1e2e.e8b0       LEC's MAC address
LEC ATM0.1:    SRC ATM address     47.00918100000000603E899601.00E01E2EE8B0.01
LEC ATM0.1:    LAN Type   1
LEC ATM0.1:    Frame size      1
LEC ATM0.1:    LAN Name  elan1       elan LEC is trying to join
LEC ATM0.1:    LAN Name size       5
LEC ATM0.1: state LECS_CONNECT event LEC_SIG_CONNECT => GET_LES_ADDR
LEC ATM0.1: received LANE_CONFIG_RSP on VCD 884
LEC ATM0.1:    SRC MAC address     00e0.1e2e.e8b0
LEC ATM0.1:    SRC ATM address     47.00918100000000603E899601.00E01E2EE8B0.01
LEC ATM0.1:    LAN Type   1
LEC ATM0.1:    Frame size      1
LEC ATM0.1:    LAN Name  elan1
LEC ATM0.1:    LAN Name size       5

LEC ATM0.1: action A_PROCESS_CFG_RSP
LEC ATM0.1: sending RELEASE
LEC ATM0.1:    callid              0x40518C04
LEC ATM0.1:    cause code          31

LEC ATM0.1: state GET_LES_ADDR event LEC_CTL_CONFIG_RSP_POS => LECS_RELEASE
LEC ATM0.1: received RELEASE_COMPLETE
LEC ATM0.1:    callid              0x40518C04
LEC ATM0.1:    cause code          16
```

Connecting to LES (Control Direct) and Back from LES (Control Distribute)

In the next step, the LEC establishes a VC to the LES (called the control direct). It then waits for the LES to add itself to the multipoint VC between the LES and all LECs (called the control distribute).

- The LEC sets up a connection to the LES for its ELAN (bidirectional point-to-point VC).

- The LES maintains a VC (server configure) to the LECS (not shown in debug because it is not a LEC action) to verify whether the LEC is allowed to join the ELAN. Notice that the join request contains the LEC MAC address, its ATM address, and the name of the ELAN.

- If allowed, the LES adds the LEC to the unidirectional point-to-multipoint control distribute VC and confirms the join over the control direct VC.

```
LEC ATM0.1: action A_SEND_LES_SETUP
LEC ATM0.1: sending SETUP          Control Direct (LEC to LES)
LEC ATM0.1:    callid              0x40518E74
LEC ATM0.1:    called party        47.00918100000000603E899601.00E01E2EE8B1.01   LES
address
LEC ATM0.1:    calling_party       47.00918100000000603E899601.00E01E2EE8B0.01   LEC
address

LEC ATM0.1: state LECS_RELEASE event LEC_SIG_RELEASE_COMP => CTL_DIRECT_CONN

LEC ATM0.1: received CONNECT
LEC ATM0.1:    callid              0x40518E74
LEC ATM0.1:    vcd                 889

LEC ATM0.1: action A_SEND_JOIN_REQ
LEC ATM0.1: sending LANE_JOIN_REQ on VCD 889
LEC ATM0.1:    Status              0
LEC ATM0.1:    LECID               0
LEC ATM0.1:    SRC MAC address     00e0.1e2e.e8b0
LEC ATM0.1:    SRC ATM address     47.00918100000000603E899601.00E01E2EE8B0.01
LEC ATM0.1:    LAN Type  1
LEC ATM0.1:    Frame size          1
LEC ATM0.1:    LAN Name  elan1
LEC ATM0.1:    LAN Name size       5

LEC ATM0.1: state CTL_DIRECT_CONN event LEC_SIG_CONNECT => JOIN_CTL_DIST_CONN

LEC ATM0.1: received SETUP          Control Distribute (LES to LEC)
LEC ATM0.1:    callid              0x404DC0A8
LEC ATM0.1:    called party        47.00918100000000603E899601.00E01E2EE8B0.01
LEC ATM0.1:    calling_party       47.00918100000000603E899601.00E01E2EE8B1.01

LEC ATM0.1: action A_PROCESS_CTL_DIST_SETUP
LEC ATM0.1: sending CONNECT
LEC ATM0.1:    callid              0x404DC0A8
LEC ATM0.1:    vcd                 890

LEC ATM0.1: state JOIN_CTL_DIST_CONN event LEC_SIG_SETUP => JOIN

LEC ATM0.1: received CONNECT_ACK

LEC ATM0.1: state JOIN event LEC_SIG_CONNECT_ACK => JOIN

LEC ATM0.1: received LANE_JOIN_RSP on VCD 889
LEC ATM0.1:    Status              0
LEC ATM0.1:    LECID               1
LEC ATM0.1:    SRC MAC address     00e0.1e2e.e8b0
LEC ATM0.1:    SRC ATM address     47.00918100000000603E899601.00E01E2EE8B0.01
LEC ATM0.1:    LAN Type  1
LEC ATM0.1:    Frame size          1
LEC ATM0.1:    LAN Name  elan1
LEC ATM0.1:    LAN Name size       5
```

Obtaining BUS Address

In the next step, the LEC establishes a VC to the BUS (called the multicast send). It then waits for the BUS to add itself to the multipoint VC between the BUS and all LECs (called the multicast forward).

- The LEC sends an LE_ARP request for the broadcast address (all ones) to the LES.
- The LES returns an LE_ARP response with the ATM address of the BUS.
- The LEC then sets up the multicast send VC to the BUS.
- The BUS adds the LEC to the multicast forward VC.

```
LEC ATM0.1: action A_PROCESS_JOIN_RSP_SEND_REQ
LEC ATM0.1: sending LANE_ARP_REQ on VCD 889
LEC ATM0.1:    SRC MAC address       00e0.1e2e.e8b0
LEC ATM0.1:    SRC ATM address       47.00918100000000603E899601.00E01E2EE8B0.01 LES
address
LEC ATM0.1:    TARGET MAC address  ffff.ffff.ffff                        Broadcast
address
LEC ATM0.1:    TARGET ATM address  00.000000000000000000000000.000000000000.00 NSAP
address is empty

LEC ATM0.1: state JOIN event LEC_CTL_JOIN_RSP_POS => GET_BUS_ADDR

LEC ATM0.1: received LANE_ARP_RSP on VCD 890
LEC ATM0.1:    SRC MAC address       00e0.1e2e.e8b0
LEC ATM0.1:    SRC ATM address       47.00918100000000603E899601.00E01E2EE8B0.01
LEC ATM0.1:    TARGET MAC address  ffff.ffff.ffff
LEC ATM0.1:    TARGET ATM address  47.00918100000000603E899601.00E01E2EE8B2.01 BUS
address is filled in

LEC ATM0.1: action A_SEND_BUS_SETUP
LEC ATM0.1: predicate PRED_MCAST_SEND_NSAP FALSE

LEC ATM0.1: sending SETUP        Mulitcast Send (LEC to BUS)
LEC ATM0.1:    callid            0x40506F14
LEC ATM0.1:    called party      47.00918100000000603E899601.00E01E2EE8B2.01
LEC ATM0.1:    calling_party     47.00918100000000603E899601.00E01E2EE8B0.01

LEC ATM0.1: state GET_BUS_ADDR event LEC_CTL_ARP_RSP => MCAST_SEND_FORWARD_CONN

LEC ATM0.1: received CONNECT
LEC ATM0.1:    callid            0x40506F14
LEC ATM0.1:    vcd               893

LEC ATM0.1: action A_PROCESS_BUS_CONNECT

LEC ATM0.1: state MCAST_SEND_FORWARD_CONN event LEC_SIG_CONNECT =>
MCAST_FORWARD_CONN

LEC ATM0.1: received SETUP        Mulitcast Forward (BUS to LEC)
LEC ATM0.1:    callid            0x4051B580
LEC ATM0.1:    called party      47.00918100000000603E899601.00E01E2EE8B0.01
LEC ATM0.1:    calling_party     47.00918100000000603E899601.00E01E2EE8B2.01

LEC ATM0.1: action A_SEND_BUS_CONNECT

LEC ATM0.1: sending CONNECT
LEC ATM0.1:    callid            0x4051B580
LEC ATM0.1:    vcd               894
```

```
LEC ATM0.1: state MCAST_FORWARD_CONN event LEC_SIG_SETUP => ACTIVE
LEC ATM0.1: received CONNECT_ACK
LEC ATM0.1: action A_PROCESS_CONNECT_ACK
LEC ATM0.1: state ACTIVE event LEC_SIG_CONNECT_ACK => ACTIVE
```

LANE Client Is Operational

After all these steps have been completed, the LEC is UP and Operational. We can see this using the following command:

```
Cat5000_LANE>#show lane client
LE Client ATM0.1  ELAN name: elan1  Admin: up  State: operational
Client ID: 1                        LEC up for 10 minutes 0 second
Join Attempt: 759
HW Address: 00e0.1e2e.e8b0   Type: ethernet        Max Frame Size: 1516
           VLANID: 100
ATM Address: 47.00918100000000603E899601.00E01E2EE8B0.01

    VCD  rxFrames  txFrames  Type      ATM Address
      0         0         0  configure 47.00918100000000603E899601.00E01E2EE8B3.00
    889         1         2  direct    47.00918100000000603E899601.00E01E2EE8B1.01
    890         4         0  distribute47.00918100000000603E899601.00E01E2EE8B1.01
    893         0       317  send      47.00918100000000603E899601.00E01E2EE8B2.01
    894         9         0  forward   47.00918100000000603E899601.00E01E2EE8B2.01
```

Understanding the show lane client Output

This command is by far the most important when it comes to LANE troubleshooting. On the TAC page, the Output Interpreter will decode the output for you. We will describe the most important fields here.

Let's focus on the following output:

```
Gambrinus#sh lane client
LE Client ATM2/0/0  ELAN name: default  Admin: up  State: operational
Client ID: 2                            LEC up for 15 minutes 39 seconds
ELAN ID: 1
Join Attempt: 691
Last Fail Reason: Control Direct VC being released
HW Address: 0060.4750.8402   Type: ethernet        Max Frame Size: 1516
ATM Address: 47.009181000000006047508401.006047508402.00

    VCD  rxFrames  txFrames  Type       ATM Address
      0         0         0  configure  47.009181000000006047508401.006047508405.00
    256         1        10  direct     47.009181000000006047508401.000000000002.01
    257       476         0  distribute 47.009181000000006047508401.000000000002.01
    258         0        56  send       47.009181000000006047508401.000000000003.01
    259         2         0  forward    47.009181000000006047508401.000000000003.01
    263         1        18  data       47.009181000000006047508401.006047508402.00
```

1 LE Client ATM2/0/0 ELAN name: default Admin: up State: operational

We can see that the client is administratively up and is operational. As we've seen earlier in this chapter, this is the right state; it is up and running.

2 Client ID: 2 LEC up for 15 minutes, 39 seconds

The only thing to keep in mind here is that the LEC is up for only 15 minutes. Is this normal? Did a maintenance action happen 15 minutes ago?

3 Join Attempt: 691

Although scary, this does not necessarily indicate that the LEC went down 691 times. The LECS/LES was perhaps unreachable for a long amount of time.

4 Last Fail Reason: Control Direct VC being released

This precious field indicates that the last reason for which the LEC could not reach the "UP/Operational" state was because it could not reach the LES

5 ATM Address: 47.00918100000000006047508401.006047508402.0

This is interesting only when we check other LECs' **sh lane client** to find that the remote side of a data direct is this station.

6 0 0 0 configure 47.00918100000000006047508401.006047508405.00

This line gives detail on the connection to the LECS; this VCC is called the configure direct, as the Type field suggests. The VCD number is 0 because the connection is torn down, per the spec.

7 256 1 10 direct 47.00918100000000006047508401.000000000002.01

This line gives details on the connection to the LES; this VCC is called the control direct, as suggested by the Type field.

8 257 476 0 distribute 47.00918100000000006047508401.000000000002.01

This line gives details on the connection from the LES to all LECs. It is called the control distribute. We can see that the LES address is the same for the control direct and control distribute, as it should be.

9 258 0 56 send 47.00918100000000006047508401.000000000003.01

This line gives details on the connection to the BUS. It is called multicast send, as the Type field suggests.

10 259 2 0 forward 47.00918100000000006047508401.000000000003.01

This line gives details on the connection from the BUS to all LECs. It is called multicast forward. We can see that the BUS address is the same for the multicast send and multicast forward.

11 263 1 18 data 47.00918100000000006047508401.006047508402.00

The remaining lines give details on each data direct VCC. Refer to the section "Understanding the LE_ARP Process" for more details.

Understanding the LE_ARP Process

The LAN Emulation Address Resolution Protocol is one of the most important in LANE. When a LEC must forward a unicast frame (that is, a frame with the destination MAC address set to the real MAC address), it should not forward it to the BUS.

Practically, it will try to create a mapping between this destination MAC address and the ATM address of the LEC to be contacted to reach this station. The LEC can be a LANE module, a router, or a directly attached station. This process is called LE_ARP. Waiting for this process to complete, the source LEC will forward the traffic to the BUS as unknown traffic.

Let's examine this in details. Say that we have the following topology:

```
IP station-----(ethernet connection)-----catalyst----(ATM lane module)------ls1010
10.200.10.61
```

As you can see, the LANE Client is up and operational:

```
Gambrinus#sh lane client
LE Client ATM2/0/0  ELAN name: default  Admin: up  State: operational
Client ID: 2                LEC up for 12 minutes 26 seconds
ELAN ID: 1
Join Attempt: 10
Last Fail Reason: Control Direct VC being released
HW Address: 0060.4750.8402   Type: ethernet          Max Frame Size: 1516
ATM Address: 47.009181000000006047508401.006047508402.00

  VCD  rxFrames  txFrames  Type      ATM Address
    0         0         0  configure 47.009181000000006047508401.006047508405.00
   94        15       109  direct    47.009181000000006047508401.000000000002.01
   95      1015         0  distribute 47.009181000000006047508401.000000000002.01
   96         0       202  send      47.009181000000006047508401.000000000003.01
   97       105         0  forward   47.009181000000006047508401.000000000003.01
```

Say that we want to contact the station 10.200.10.62:

```
Gambrinus#ping 10.200.10.62
```

From the user point of view, it works, and nothing special can be seen:

```
Type escape sequence to abort.
Sending 5, 100-byte ICMP Echos to 10.200.10.62, timeout is 2 seconds:
!!!!!
Success rate is 100 percent (5/5), round-trip min/avg/max = 4/5/8 ms
```

If we enabled **debug lane client packet**, we would have seen the details of the process. That is, the LEC sends an LE_ARP request to the LES and waits for the response with the ATM address to be used.

```
<snip>
*Mar 22 02:32:46.499: LEC ATM2/0/0: sending LANE_ARP_REQ on VCD 94
*Mar 22 02:32:46.499: LEC ATM2/0/0:   LECID              2
*Mar 22 02:32:46.499: LEC ATM2/0/0:   SRC MAC address    0060.4750.8402
*Mar 22 02:32:46.499: LEC ATM2/0/0:   SRC ATM address    47.0091810000000060470
*Mar 22 02:32:46.499: LEC ATM2/0/0:   TARGET MAC address 00e0.b012.17ff
*Mar 22 02:32:46.499: LEC ATM2/0/0:   TARGET ATM address 00.00000000000000000000
*Mar 22 02:32:46.499: LEC ATM2/0/0:   Flags              0x0
*Mar 22 02:32:46.499: LEC ATM2/0/0:   num of TLVs        0
<snip>
```

```
*Mar 22 02:32:46.515: LEC ATM2/0/0: received LANE_ARP_RSP on VCD 95
*Mar 22 02:32:46.515: LEC ATM2/0/0:   LECID              2
*Mar 22 02:32:46.515: LEC ATM2/0/0:   SRC MAC address    00e0.b012.17ff
*Mar 22 02:32:46.515: LEC ATM2/0/0:   SRC ATM address    47.0091810000000060471
*Mar 22 02:32:46.515: LEC ATM2/0/0:   TARGET MAC address 0060.4750.8402
*Mar 22 02:32:46.515: LEC ATM2/0/0:   TARGET ATM address 47.0091810000000060470
*Mar 22 02:32:46.515: LEC ATM2/0/0:   Flags              0x0
*Mar 22 02:32:46.515: LEC ATM2/0/0:   num of TLVs        0
<snip>
```

When the LEC receives the reply, it sets up a virtual channel connection (VCC) directly to this ATM address. This VCC is called data direct VCC. Any frame that needs to be sent to this destination MAC address will be forwarded on this VCC.

To ensure that no frame is left on the delivery path through the BUS when the data direct VCC becomes active, a mechanism called FLUSH is used. Still with **debug lane client packet**, we can see more details of the FLUSH process.

```
*Mar 22 02:32:46.627: LEC ATM2/0/0: sending LANE_FLUSH_REQ on VCD 96
<snip>
*Mar 22 02:32:46.633: LEC ATM2/0/0: received LANE_FLUSH_RSP on VCD 95
```

The result of the LE_ARP process is saved and can be checked:

```
Gambrinus#sh lane le-arp
Active le-arp entries: 1

Hardware Addr    ATM Address                                      VCD  Interface
00e0.b012.17ff   47.009181000000006047508401.000000000001.01  100  ATM2/0/0
```

If we check the ARP table on the source IP station, we can see that the right MAC address was taken in account.

```
<snip>
Gambrinus#sh arp
Protocol  Address          Age (min)  Hardware Addr  Type   Interface
Internet  10.200.10.62            20  00e0.b012.17ff ARPA   ATM2/0/0
<snip>
```

And, most interesting, the output of **show lane client** has changed. You can see that there is a new VCC and that traffic is flowing on it. It remains up as long as there is traffic over it. The default timeout is 300 seconds without activity.

```
Gambrinus#sh lane client
LE Client ATM2/0/0  ELAN name: default  Admin: up  State: operational
Client ID: 2                    LEC up for 13 minutes 15 seconds
ELAN ID: 1
Join Attempt: 10
Last Fail Reason: Control Direct VC being released
HW Address: 0060.4750.8402   Type: ethernet           Max Frame Size: 1516
ATM Address: 47.009181000000006047508401.006047508402.00

VCD  rxFrames  txFrames  Type      ATM Address
  0         0         0  configure 47.009181000000006047508401.006047508405.00
 94        15       115  direct    47.009181000000006047508401.000000000002.01
 95      1384         0  distribute 47.009181000000006047508401.000000000002.01
 96         0       232  send      47.009181000000006047508401.000000000003.01
 97       112         0  forward   47.009181000000006047508401.000000000003.01
 99         1         2  data      47.009181000000006047508401.000000000001.01
```

Additional Commands

The following show commands are the most useful for troubleshooting LANE.

- **show lane**
- **show lane client**
- **show lane server**
- **show lane config**
- **show lane default**
- **show atm ilmi-status**

Before Calling Cisco Systems' TAC Team

Before calling the Cisco Systems Technical Assistance Center (TAC), make sure that you have read through this chapter and completed the actions suggested for your system's problem.

Additionally, do the following and document the results so that we can better assist you:

- If the problem is that a LANE Client cannot reach the "UP, operational" state (that is, the LANE Client is down or cannot join the ELAN), locate which service (LES, LECS, BUS) is preventing the LEC to go up.
- Create a map of your network clearly indicating the location of the LECS/LES/BUS.
- Take the output of **show lane** on every key device. That is where the active LECS/LES/BUS elements are and where the LANE Clients giving problems are.
- If you are using a VP tunnel to a remote site, provide the contract details for this VP.

Additional Sources of Information

- *Cisco LAN Switching (CCIE Professional Development)*, Cisco Press
- www.cisco.com/tac (check the ATM section in the Technology Home Page)
- www.atmforum.com/ (includes a lot of standards that can be downloaded for free)
- www.techfest.com/networking
- www.protocols.com/
- cell-relay.indiana.edu/
- news:comp.dcom/cell-relay (archived in http:// cell-relay.indiana.edu/)

## CHAPTER 22

Troubleshooting ATM PVCs in a WAN Environment

This chapter describes how to troubleshoot ATM problems that are seen when transporting L2 frames/L3 packets over a WAN backbone. The following topics will be reviewed:

- How are frames or packets segmented into ATM cells?
- What are the important **show** commands, and how do you interpret them?
- How can you detect and troubleshoot incorrect shaping or policing?

Introduction

Asynchronous Transfer Mode (ATM) is a technology that was defined by the ITU-T (formerly known as the CCITT) in the early 1990s. The related standards describe a transport technology in which information is carried in small, fixed-length data units called *cells*.

In an ATM network, a clear distinction can be made between the devices supporting the applications, called end systems (ES), and the devices that are only relaying the cells. We will call these relaying devices intermediate systems (IS) or ATM switches. Examples of end systems are routers or LAN Emulation (LANE) modules. Examples of IS are ls1010, 8540MSR, and BPX. An ATM network can therefore be represented as shown in Figure 22-1.

Figure 22-1 *ATM Network Representation*

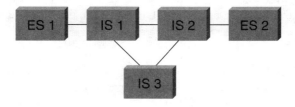

Among many other things, ATM defines how to segment and reassemble different types of information. ATM can transport video, voice, and data. Proper quality of service (QoS) is reserved and guaranteed by the ATM network. Because any type of information can be segmented into cells via the related standard, ATM is a flexible tool. Therefore, it can be used in many environments. We will categorize those areas in two main ones:

- A LAN switched environment, in which LAN Emulation (LANE) is most commonly used. Typically, there is little QoS in this dynamic environment. (ATM connections are built and torn down on demand.)

- A WAN environment, in which we have two players:

    — The telco, which typically offers very precise quality of service in a static environment. This ATM network is made of ATM switches. Because a telco offers an ATM service, we will call him an ATM service provider.

    — The enterprise, which asks for an ATM service from the ATM service provider.

This chapter focuses solely on the last type of ATM connections, in an enterprise environment. End systems in such an environment are routers 99 percent of the time. Therefore, we will use only the word *router* in the rest of this document. Those routers will exchange packets (see the following note). We will use IP as our reference protocol, so all explanations are valid for other Layer 3 protocols such as IPX and ATALK. As such, from the enterprise point of view, the network is represented in Figure 22-2.

Figure 22-2 *Network from the Enterprise Point of View*

Router 1   ATM cloud   Router 2

NOTE Because ATM is a flexible tool, we can segment pretty much any type of information into cells. We often talk about packets or frames, Layer 3 or Layer 2 data units. Clearly, we could use the term *protocol data unit*, which would allow us to discuss very generally whatever layer is involved, in sync with the OSI specification. For the sake of clarity, we will talk about packets, however, and you will understand frames, if necessary.

There must be a traffic contract on the quality of service that will be respected by the enterprise routers and the ATM service provider. Initially, it looks quite simple, with only two devices in the picture and an ATM provider's cloud that is simply not visible from the enterprise point of view. Unfortunately, the problems in this environment are not trivial precisely because you do not have full visibility of the ATM provider's equipment.

Understanding the Segmentation and Reassembly for AAL5 Frames

AAL here refers to the ATM Adaptation Layer. As the name suggests, it adapts user information (data, voice, video, and so on) to a format that can be easily divided into ATM cells. The process for AAL5 is described in Figure 22-3.

Figure 22-3 *AAL5 Process*

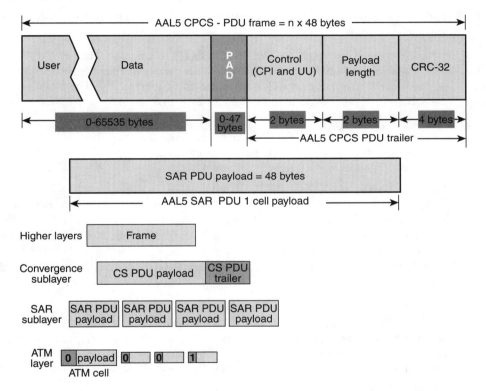

At the destination router, the reverse process is being applied. The destination router can easily find which cell is the end of the AAL5 packet with a special bit set to 1 in the cell header.

The whole process is usually implemented in hardware and works efficiently. For now, let's focus on what can go wrong. Two main problems that can arise are described here:

- One or more cells are corrupted at the destination by either the transmitter or a device in the ATM network. The only field in the cell that performs a type of cyclic redundancy check (CRC) is the Header Checksum field (HEC). As the name suggests, it checks only the cell header.

- One or more cells could be discarded in the provider's network.

Let's examine the impact of those two problems at the destination router and determine how we can detect them:

- If one cell is corrupted, the number of cells is still the same. The CPCS-PDU frame is reassembled with the correct size. The router checks whether the length field is indeed correct. But, because one cell is corrupted, the whole frame will be trivially corrupted. Therefore, the CRC field of the AAL5 CPCS-PDU frame will be different from the one that was originally sent.

- If one cell is missing at destination, both the size and the CRC will be different from the ones that are contained in the CPCS-PDU frame.

NOTE   You will see that the CRC error counter of the show interface is equal to the number of input error. On some end systems, such as the LANE modules of the Catalyst 5000, only the input error counter increases. Focusing on the input errors is then recommended. As a rule of thumb, if you are not running a recent release, checking the output of **sh controller** is also recommended because it gives more physical details on the counters of the ATM card itself.

Whatever the real problem is, a wrong CRC will be detected at the destination. The administrator of the routers can detect this by checking the interface statistics. One CRC error results in an increment of input error counter by 1 (see the previous note). The command **show interface atm (module/port)** illustrates this behavior:

```
Medina#sh int atm 3/0
ATM3/0 is up, line protocol is up
  Hardware is ENHANCED ATM PA
  MTU 4470 bytes, sub MTU 4470, BW 149760 Kbit, DLY 80 usec,
     reliability 255/255, txload 1/255, rxload 1/255
  Encapsulation ATM, loopback not set
  Keepalive not supported
  Encapsulation(s): AAL5
  4096 maximum active VCs, 2 current VCCs
  VC idle disconnect time: 300 seconds  Signalling vc = 1, vpi = 0, vci = 5
  UNI Version = 4.0, Link Side = user
  0 carrier transitions
  Last input 00:00:07, output 00:00:07, output hang never
  Last clearing of "show interface" counters never
  Input queue: 0/75/0 (size/max/drops); Total output drops: 0
  Queueing strategy: Per VC Queueing
```

```
5 minute input rate 0 bits/sec, 0 packets/sec
5 minute output rate 0 bits/sec, 0 packets/sec
    104 packets input, 2704 bytes, 0 no buffer
    Received 0 broadcasts, 0 runts, 0 giants, 0 throttles
    32 input errors, 32 CRC, 0 frame, 0 overrun, 0 ignored, 0 abort
    106 packets output, 2353 bytes, 0 underruns
    0 output errors, 0 collisions, 1 interface resets
    0 output buffer failures, 0 output buffers swapped out
```

If the router has been configured for multiple PVCs, then relying only on the interface global counter might not be very adequate. The input error counter might show that the traffic for multiple PVCs. In this scenario, using the **sh atm pvc** *vpi/vci* counters is recommended:

```
Medina#sh atm pvc 0/36
ATM3/0.1: VCD: 4, VPI: 0, VCI: 36
VBR-NRT, PeakRate: 2000, Average Rate: 1000, Burst Cells: 32
AAL5-LLC/SNAP, etype:0x0, Flags: 0x20, VCmode: 0x0
OAM frequency: 0 second(s), OAM retry frequency: 1 second(s), OAM retry frequen)
OAM up retry count: 3, OAM down retry count: 5
OAM Loopback status: OAM Disabled
OAM VC state: Not Managed
ILMI VC state: Not Managed
InARP frequency: 15 minutes(s)
Transmit priority 2
InPkts: 24972, OutPkts: 25032, InBytes: 6778670, OutBytes: 6751812
InPRoc: 24972, OutPRoc: 25219, Broadcasts: 0
InFast: 0, OutFast: 0, InAS: 0, OutAS: 0
InPktDrops: 0, OutPktDrops: 0
CrcErrors: 0, SarTimeOuts: 0, OverSizedSDUs: 0
OAM cells received: 0
F5 InEndloop: 0, F5 InSegloop: 0, F5 InAIS: 0, F5 InRDI: 0
F4 InEndloop: 0, F4 InSegloop: 0, F4 InAIS: 0, F4 InRDI: 0
OAM cells sent: 0
F5 OutEndloop: 0, F5 OutSegloop: 0, F5 OutRDI: 0
F4 OutEndloop: 0, F4 OutSegloop: 0, F4 OutRDI: 0
OAM cell drops: 0
Status: UP
```

In this output (see the accompanying note), the CRC error counter indicates the number of CRC errors of the CPCS-PDU frame. Both commands were typed on the same router; because no CrcErrors can be seen on the display of statistics for PVC 0/36, we can assume that the input errors of the **sh int** were due to another PVC.

NOTE	The output of **sh atm pvc** might vary depending on the card functionality and code feature. The example shown on this page uses the PA-A3 with 12.1 IOS code version.

As a last remark, *one* input error does not always mean *one* packet loss. The cell discarded by the ATM provider could be the last one of the frame; therefore, the cell discarded had this special bit set to 1. The only way for the destination to find the frame boundaries is to check this bit. As a result, the destination router concatenates at reassembly time all cells that it receives until it finds a cell with this bit set to 1. If the last cell of a frame is discarded, two CPCS-PDU frames will be lost and will result in only one CRC and length error.

Understanding the Basics of Traffic Shaping and Policing

Two basic terms will be used in this chapter: *traffic shaping* and *policing*. *Traffic shaping* refers to an action done by the source of the ATM traffic. *Policing* refers to actions done by the ATM switches, usually at the provider's side.

Traffic shaping is the action of adapting the cell flow to a specific traffic contract. This is illustrated in Figure 22-4.

Figure 22-4 *Traffic Shaping—Adapting the Cell Flow to a Specific Traffic Contract*

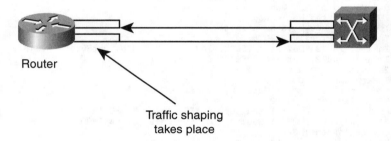

Policing is the action of checking whether the cell flow respects a specific traffic contract. This is illustrated in Figure 22-5.

Figure 22-5 *Policing—Checking Whether the Cell Flow Respects a Specific Traffic Contract*

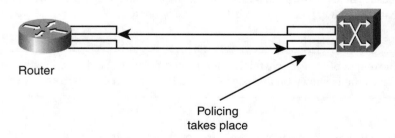

These figures are not implying that traffic shaping and policing refer to a common contract and use a similar algorithm. Misconfigured policing or shaping often leads to cells being discarded by the policer. It also happens that even though shaping and policing are both set to the same values, policing starts discarding cells. This is usually the result of a poor shaper or a misbehaving policer.

Understanding Variable Bit Rate Nonreal Time (VBR-NRT)

This chapter provides only an introduction to traffic shaping. If needed, more details can be found in the Traffic Management specification available on the ATM Forum web site.

In ATM, traffic shaping works by inserting equal times between the cells. For example, if an OC-3/STM-1 connection is 155 Mbps, only about 149 Mbps can be used for forwarding ATM cells. (SONET/SDH has approximately 3 percent of overhead.) As a result, the max rate is 353.208 cells (353.208 × 53 × 8 bits can fit in the OC-3c/STM-1 frames payload in a second). If a user requests a connection of 74.5 Mbps (half the line rate), equal spaces of 2.83 usec will be inserted between each cell. 2.83 usec is the time needed to send one cell at OC3c/STM-1 (1/353.208 sec). Because we requested half the line rate, we can send one cell, wait an equal amount of time, and then start over again.

Now that we've described the generic approach, let's focus briefly on the most classic traffic requested, variable bit-rate traffic (VBR) shaping as shown in Figure 22-6.

Figure 22-6 *Variable Bit-rate Traffic Shaping*

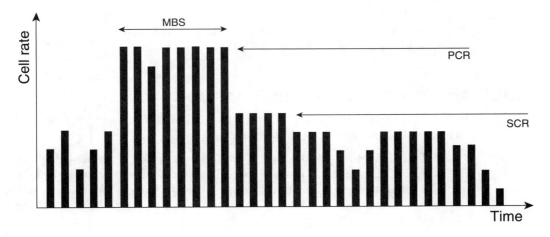

VBR traffic shaping is an effective approach for a bursty network. Parameters used are peak cell rate (PCR), sustainable cell rate (SCR), and maximum burst size (MBS). When a traffic contract has been agreed upon, the ATM network guarantees the transmission of cells within the VBR parameters. The number of cells allowed to exceed SCR is set by MBS and bound by the PCR.

The three traffic contract parameters are defined below:

- **PCR**—Maximum rate at which the source can send cells.
- **SCR**—Bound on the long-term average cell rate.
- **MBS**—Maximum number of cells that can be sent above SCR at PCR.

Creating a Mapping Between a Destination Address and PVC

A common source of problems is the incorrect configuration of the ATM mapping. Basically, after configuring the PVC itself, you must instruct the router on which PVC needs to be used to reach a specific destination. You have three ways to ensure the right mapping:

- If you put the PVC on a point-to-point subinterface, the router will assume that there is only one point-to-point PVC configured on the subinterface. Therefore, any IP packet with a destination IP address in the same subnet will be forwarded on this VC. This is the simplest way to configure the mapping and is therefore the recommended version.
- If you put the PVC in a point-to-multipoint subinterface or the main interface, you will have to create a static mapping. Refer to the "Command Mode" section for a configuration example.
- You can use Inverse ARP to create the mapping automatically. Refer to the documentation for configuration guidelines.

Troubleshooting Connectivity Issues

The user can often have the feeling that part of the information is being lost between the two routers. The most common symptoms are these:

- TCP connections are slow because of cells being discarded in the ATM cloud. This results in IP packets being discarded and in a high number of retransmissions. TCP itself believes that this is because of congestion and will try to lower its transmitting window, resulting in a very slow TCP connection. Of course, this affects all TCP-based protocols, including Telnet and FTP.
- Large IP packets tend to fail, but small packets cross the ATM network with no problem. This is again because of cells being discarded.

Let's concentrate on this second symptom, to help us detect the problem. Say that for every 100 cells transmitted back to back by the source router, the cloud will discard the last one because of policing. This means that if a **ping** has a data part of 100 bytes, 3 ATM cells will be needed to send it (because 3×48 bytes will be needed to contain the ICMP echo request). In practice, this means that the 33 first **ping**s will succeed (more precisely, the first 99 cells will be seen within contract by the provider), but the 34th one will fail because one of its cells will be discarded.

Assuming that we keep the same setup and use 1500-byte packets instead of small ICMP echos (**ping**s), we will need 32 cells to transmit each large packet ($32 \times 48 = 1536$ bytes, the smallest multiple of 48 above the packet size). If the network discards 1 cell out of 100, about one packet out of three or four will be discarded. Raising the packet size is then a simple and efficient way to prove that you have a policing issue.

In practice, you can generate large **ping**s from the router itself:

```
Medina#ping
Protocol [ip]:
Target IP address: 10.2.1.2
Repeat count [5]: 100
Datagram size [100]: 1500
Timeout in seconds [2]: 2
Extended commands [n]:
Sweep range of sizes [n]:
Type escape sequence to abort.
Sending 100, 1500-byte ICMP Echos to 10.2.1.2, timeout is 2 seconds:
!!!.!!.!!!.!!.!!!.!!.!!!.!!.!!!.!!.!!!.!!.!!!.!!.!!!.!!.!!!.!!.!!!.!!.!!!.!
!.!!!.!!.!!!.!!.!
Success rate is 72 percent (72/100)
```

If the real problem is related to policing, doing the same test with larger packets will generate a totally different result:

```
Medina#ping
Protocol [ip]:
Target IP address: 10.2.1.2
Repeat count [5]: 100
Datagram size [100]: 3000
Timeout in seconds [2]: 2
Extended commands [n]:
Sweep range of sizes [n]:
Type escape sequence to abort.
Sending 100, 3000-byte ICMP Echos to 10.2.1.2, timeout is 2 seconds:
!.!.!..!.!.!..!.!..!.!...!..!.!.!..!.!.!.!.!.!.!..!.!...!..!.!..!.!.!..!.!.!..!.!.
.!.!..!.!.!.!..!..!
Success rate is 42 percent (42/100)
```

If, after running those tests, you conclude that you are suffering from a policing issue, contact your ATM provider immediately and check the following points:

- Is the provider indeed discarding cells? The provider *must* be capable of telling you this.

- If so, for what specific reason is this happening? The answer will usually be policing, but sometimes the network is simply congested.

If the reason is policing, then what are the traffic parameters? Do they match with the settings on the router?

If the router and the provider do use the same traffic parameters, then there is a real problem. In other words, either the router is not shaping well or the provider is not policing accurately. If this happens, refer to the documentation of the ATM card for known limitations, and check for known bugs. Also keep in mind that no two implementations of traffic shaping give exactly the same resulting traffic; small variations can be accepted, but it should always generate only a negligible amount of traffic loss.

Some traffic analyzers on the market can check the traffic compliance according to a given set of traffic parameters. Among them, the most classic are from GN Nettest and HP. Those devices can determine whether the traffic from the router is shaped accurately.

If you find that a Cisco router is not shaping accurately and you cannot find any documented bug or card limitation, it is wise to open a case with the TAC.

Troubleshooting PVC Total Connectivity Failure

The previous section focused on a partial packet loss. We will now focus on total connectivity loss (Table 22-1).

Table 22-1   *Total Connectivity Loss Between Two ATM-Attached Routers*

Possible Problem	Solution
The PVC is broken inside the provider's cloud.	This is the most common problem. If the provider has a big problem inside its ATM cloud, the signal coming from the provider's equipment will still be good. As a result, the router's interface will still be up/up. At the same time, any cell sent by the router will be accepted by the provider but will never reach the destination.
	Usually, calling the provider will give a quick answer. But, because the interface is not going down, the Layer 3 route will not be removed by the routing table, and alternative or backup routes cannot be used.[1] The best solution in this environment is to enable OAM management to automate the process. Refer to the WAN configuration guide on CCO.
	You can prove that the ATM card is okay by using loopbacks. Refer to the solution of the next problem in this table.
One of the interfaces is down/down.	**Step 1** Locate one ATM interface in down/down state. Ensure that it is not administratively down (that is, that the interface or subinterface has not been shut down).
	Step 2 Check that the framing and scrambling are correctly configured.
	The framing can be checked via **sh atm int atm** and must be agreed upon with the provider. It can be configured via **atm framing xxx** in interface configuration mode.

Table 22-1   *Total Connectivity Loss Between Two ATM-Attached Routers (Continued)*

One of the interfaces is down/down. *(continued)*		The scrambling is important in DS-3. It can be configured via **atm ds3-scramble** or **atm e3-scramble** in interface configuration mode.
	Step 3	Check the quality of the cable.
	Step 4	Look for evidence of physical error in **show controller** of the ATM device as well as **show atm pvc** output. Check the PVC status. Check that you are not receiving AIS, for example.
	Step 5	If the physical side seems okay and you see the outgoing traffic counters growing, check that you are actually forwarding traffic out of the interface by loopbacking the physical interface. You have two ways to do this: • Physically loop back the Tx to the Rx. • Use the possibilities of the ATM card to help you on this. In configuration interface mode, enter: **Sevilla(config-if)#loopback diagnostic** When the loopback is in place, the interface must come back up/up if the hardware is not faulty.
	Step 6	When you have defined the loopback, try to **ping** yourself. If the card is behaving well, you should be able do it. Make sure that you have the right mapping defined.
There is a Layer 3 routing problem.	**Step 1**	Both interfaces are up/up. Check the appropriate routing table (in the case of IP, **show ip route**). Enter **show ip route a.b.c.d**, where **a.b.c.d** is the destination IP address that you cannot reach. This IP address is reachable only via the ATM PVC.
	Step 2	Check that the peer router (the router on the other side of the PVC) is reachable.
	Step 3	If the peer router is a reachable neighbor and the routing table does not point to the ATM subinterface where the PVC is defined for a given route, your problem likely is a routing problem; refer to Chapter 7, "Troubleshooting TCP/IP."

There is a mismatch in the mapping of Layer 3 address of the peer router.		There is no automatic mapping between a PVC and the Layer 3 address of the router reachable via the PVC.
		
		This can be checked via the command **sh atm map**:
		
		`Ema#sh atm map`
		`Map list test : PERMANENT`
		`ip 164.48.227.142 maps to VC 140`

[1]Show controller output is specific to each ATM card. Often, valuable information can be deduced from this output, but no generic description can be given.

Important Commands

This section explains the differences between the old syntax and the new one. By old syntax, we mean the use of **sh atm vc** and **atm pvc**. By new syntax (available as from 11.3T), we mean **sh atm pvc** and **pvc**.

PVC

Use the **pvc** interface configuration command to do one or more of the following (the full description can be found in the command reference):

- Create an ATM PVC on a main interface or subinterface.
- Assign a name to an ATM PVC.
- Specify ILMI, QSAAL, or SMDS protocols to be used on this PVC.
- Enter interface-atm-pvc configuration mode.

Command Mode

The following section will describe how a basic configuration can be done and mention the most important show commands to be used for troubleshooting ATM PVCs in a WAN environment.

Sample Display

A simple configuration of a VBR-nrt PVC is provided in the following text. Note that per subinterface configuration display is supported since 12.0T.

```
Medina#sh running-config int atm 3/0.1
Building configuration...

Current configuration:
!
interface ATM3/0.1 multipoint
 ip address 10.2.1.1 255.255.255.252
 no ip directed-broadcast
 pvc 0/36
  protocol ip 10.2.1.1 broadcast
  protocol ip 10.2.1.2 broadcast
  vbr-nrt 2000 1000 32
  encapsulation aal5snap
 !
end
```

Its status can be checked via **sh atm pvc 0/36**, as shown previously, or with the earlier command **show atm vc**.

```
Medina#sh atm vc
                VCD /                                     Peak  Avg/Min Burst
Interface       Name      VPI   VCI  Type   Encaps   SC   Kbps  Kbps    Cells  Sts
3/0             1         0     5    PVC    SAAL     UBR  149760                UP
3/0             2         0     16   PVC    ILMI     UBR  149760                UP
3/0.1           4         0     36   PVC    SNAP     VBR    2000  1000    32    UP
Once you located the right VCD number, you can display the VC statistics:

Medina#sh atm vc 4
ATM3/0.1: VCD: 4, VPI: 0, VCI: 36
VBR-NRT, PeakRate: 2000, Average Rate: 1000, Burst Cells: 32
AAL5-LLC/SNAP, etype:0x0, Flags: 0x20, VCmode: 0x0
OAM frequency: 0 second(s)
InARP frequency: 15 minutes(s)
Transmit priority 2
InPkts: 24972, OutPkts: 25137, InBytes: 6778670, OutBytes: 6985152
InPRoc: 24972, OutPRoc: 25419, Broadcasts: 0
InFast: 0, OutFast: 0, InAS: 0, OutAS: 0
InPktDrops: 0, OutPktDrops: 0
CrcErrors: 0, SarTimeOuts: 0, OverSizedSDUs: 0
OAM cells received: 0
OAM cells sent: 0
Status: UP
```

The reader can compare the new **sh atm pvc** command and the old **show atm vc** command. Using the new command is definitely recommended.

The mapping has been configured as this is a point-to-multipoint interface, and can be checked via:

```
Medina#sh atm map
Map list ATM3/0.1pvc4 : PERMANENT
ip 10.2.1.1 maps to VC 4, VPI 0, VCI 36, ATM3/0.1
        , broadcast
ip 10.2.1.2 maps to VC 4, VPI 0, VCI 36, ATM3/0.1
        , broadcast
```

The user can see that the subinterface type is multipoint, as such, a mapping was required. In the case of point-to-point subinterface, the protocol line in the PVC configuration can be skipped since the router will assume that all IP packets with destination in the same subnet need to be forwarded to the PVC. Inverse ARP can be configured in the PVC configuration as well to automate the mapping process.

atm pvc

If the user is running 11.3 (non-T train) or earlier, the PVC configuration command is not yet available, so the old syntax must be used. As you can see, the whole PVC configuration is done in only one line, seriously limiting the configuration possibilities. (The full description can be found in the command reference.)

Command Mode

The following section will describe how a basic configuration can be done when the router is running an IOS software version earlier than 11.3T and mention the most important show commands to be used for troubleshooting ATM PVCs in a WAN environment.

Sample Display

A simple configuration of a VBR-nrt PVC is provided in the following text. Note that per subinterface configuration display is supported since 12.0T.

```
Medina#sh run interface atm 3/0.1
Building configuration...

Current configuration:
!
interface ATM3/0.1 multipoint
 no ip directed-broadcast
 map-group MyMap
 atm pvc 4 0 36 aal5snap 2000 1000 32
end
```

This assumes that we have a map list definition matching the map group name, as shown in this partial configuration:

```
<snip>
!
map-list MyMap
 ip 10.2.1.1 atm-vc 4 broadcast
 ip 10.2.1.2 atm-vc 4 broadcast
<snip>
```

We can check the mapping with the same command as for the new syntax:

```
Medina#sh atm map
Map list MyMap : PERMANENT
ip 10.2.1.1 maps to VC 4
        , broadcast
ip 10.2.1.2 maps to VC 4
        , broadcast
```

Again, you will see that the new syntax is easier and clearer.

Before Calling Cisco Systems TAC Team

Before calling Cisco Systems's Technical Assistance Center (TAC), make sure that you have read through this chapter and completed the actions suggested for your system's problem.

Additionally, do the following and document the results so that we can better assist you:

- Do a **show tech** of both routers, to help the CSE in understanding the router behavior.

- Do a **sh atm pvc** on both routers and a **sh atm pvc** *vpi/vci* of the PVC that gives problem, to help the CSE in understanding the problem.
- Explain the ATM provider point-of-view on the problem, especially if the provider believes that the problem is on the router.

Additional Sources

- http://cell-relay.indiana.edu/
- http://www.atmforum.com/ (You can download a lot of standards for free.)
- http://www.itu.int/ (You will need registered access.)
- http://www.protocols.com/
- http://www.techfest.com/networking/
- news:comp.dcom.cell-relay (This is archived in the site http://www.techfest.com/networking/.)

Summary

- Compare configuring PVCs on point-to-point and point-to-multipoint subinterfaces.
- Configure a router and a switch with mismatching shaping and policing. Check with a **ping** test that the traffic sent by the router is indeed policed incorrectly.
- Configure OAM management to have the subinterface going down upon PVC failure.
- Compare configuring a PVC with the old and the new syntax, and check the main reasons for moving to the new syntax.
- Compare checking the PVC status/statistics with the old command **sh atm vc** and the new command **show atm pvc**. Check the enhancements done in the new syntax.

## CHAPTER 23

Troubleshooting LAN Switching Environments

The sections in this chapter describe common LAN switch features and offer solutions to some of the most common LAN switching problems. The following items will be covered:

- LAN Switching Introduction
- General Switch Troubleshooting Suggestions
- Troubleshooting Port Connectivity Problems
- Troubleshooting Ethernet 10/100-Mb Half-/Full-Duplex Autonegotiation
- ISL Trunking on Catalyst 5000 and 6000 Family Switches
- Example of Configuring and Troubleshooting Ethernet 10/100-Mb Autonegotiation
- Configuring EtherChannel Switch-to-Switch on Catalyst 4000/5000/6000 Switches
- Using PortFast and Other Commands to Fix End-Station Startup Connectivity Problems
- Configuring and Troubleshooting IP Multilayer Switching
- Troubleshooting Spanning Tree Protocol and Related Design Considerations

LAN Switching Introduction

If you are new to LAN switching, then the following sections will take you through some of the main concepts related to switches. One of the prerequisites to troubleshooting any device is to know the rules under which it operates. Switches have become much more complex over the last few years as they have gained popularity and sophistication. The next few paragraphs describe some of the key concepts to know about switches.

Hubs and Switches

Because of the great demand placed on local-area networks, we have seen a shift from a shared-bandwidth network, using hubs and coaxial cable, to a dedicated bandwidth network, using switches. A hub allows multiple devices to be connected to the same network segment. The devices on that segment share the bandwidth with each other. If it is a 10-Mb hub and six devices are connected to six different ports on the hub, all six devices would share the 10 Mb of bandwidth with each other. A 100-Mb hub would share 100 Mb of bandwidth among the connected devices. In terms of the OSI model, a hub would be considered a Layer 1 (physical layer) device. It hears an electrical signal on the wire and passes it along to the other ports.

A switch can physically replace a hub in your network. A switch allows multiple devices to be connected to the same network, just like a hub does, but this is where the similarity ends. A switch allows each connected device to have dedicated bandwidth instead of shared bandwidth. The bandwidth between the switch and the device is reserved for communication to and from that device alone. Six devices connected to six different ports on a 10-Mb switch would each have 10 Mb of bandwidth to work with, instead of sharing that bandwidth with the other devices. A switch can greatly increase the available bandwidth in your network, which can lead to improved network performance.

Bridges and Switches

A basic switch would be considered a Layer 2 device. When we use the word *layer*, we are referring to the seven-layer OSI model. A switch does not just pass electrical signals along, like a hub does; instead, it assembles the signals into a frame (Layer 2) and then decides what to do with the frame. A switch determines what to do with a frame by borrowing an algorithm from another common networking device, a transparent bridge. Logically, a switch acts just like a transparent bridge would, but it can handle frames much faster than a transparent bridge (because of special hardware and architecture). When a switch decides where the frame should be sent, it passes the frame out the appropriate port (or ports). You can think of a switch as a device creating instantaneous connections between various ports, on a frame-by-frame basis.

VLANs

Because the switch decides on a frame-by-frame basis which ports should exchange data, it is a natural extension to put logic inside the switch to allow it to select ports for special groupings. This grouping of ports is called a virtual local-area network (VLAN). The switch makes sure that traffic from one group of ports never gets sent to other groups of ports (which would be routing). These port groups (VLANs) can each be considered an individual LAN segment.

VLANs are also described as being broadcast domains. This is because of the transparent bridging algorithm, which says that broadcast packets (packets destined for the "all devices" address) should be sent out all ports that are in the same group (that is, in the same VLAN). Therefore, all ports that are in the same VLAN are also in the same broadcast domain.

Transparent Bridging Algorithm

The transparent bridging algorithm and the Spanning-Tree Protocol are covered in more detail elsewhere (see Chapter 20, "Troubleshooting Transparent Bridging Environments"). When a switch receives a frame, it must decide what to do with that frame. It could ignore the frame, it could pass the frame out one other port, or it could pass the frame out many other ports.

To know what to do with the frame, the switch learns the location of all devices on the segment. This location information is placed in a CAM table (Content Addressable Memory, named for the type of memory used to store these tables). The CAM table shows, for each device, the device's MAC address, out which port that MAC address can be found, and which VLAN this port is associated with. The switch continually does this *learning* process as frames are received into the switch. The switch's CAM table is continually being updated.

This information in the CAM table is used to decide how a received frame should be handled. To decide where to send a frame, the switch looks at the *destination* MAC address in a received frame and then looks up that destination MAC address in the CAM table. The CAM table shows which port the frame should be sent out for that frame to reach the specified destination MAC address.

These are the basic rules that a switch will use in carrying out the frame forwarding responsibility:

If the destination MAC address is found in the CAM table, then the switch will send the frame out the port that is associated with that destination MAC address in the CAM table. This is called *forwarding*.

If the associated port to send the frame out is the same port on which the frame originally came in, then there is no need to send the frame back out that same port, and the frame is ignored. This is called *filtering*.

If the destination MAC address is not in the CAM table (the address is unknown), then the switch will send the frame out *all* other ports that are in the *same* VLAN as the received frame. This is called *flooding*. It will not flood the frame out the same port on which the frame was received.

If the destination MAC address of the received frame is the broadcast address (FFFF.FFFF.FFFF), then the frame is sent out all ports that are in the same VLAN as the received frame. This is also called *flooding*. The frame will not be sent out the same port on which the frame it was received.

Spanning-Tree Protocol

As we have seen, the transparent bridging algorithm floods unknown and broadcast frames out all the ports that are in the same VLAN as the received frame. This causes a potential problem. If the network devices running this algorithm are connected in a physical loop, then flooded frames (such as broadcasts) will be passed from switch to switch, around and around the loop forever. Depending on the physical connections involved, the frames may actually multiply exponentially as a result of the flooding algorithm, which can cause serious network problems.

There is a benefit to having a physical loop in your network: It can provide redundancy. If one link fails, there is still another way for the traffic to reach its destination. To allow the benefits derived from redundancy, without breaking the network because of flooding, a protocol called the Spanning-Tree Protocol was created. It was standardized in the IEEE 802.1d specification.

The purpose of the Spanning-Tree Protocol is to identify and temporarily block the loops in a network segment or VLAN. The switches run the Spanning-Tree Protocol, which involves electing a root bridge or switch. The other switches measure their distance from the root switch. If there is more than one way to get to the root switch, then there is a loop. The switches follow the algorithm to determine which ports should be blocked to break the loop. STP is dynamic; if a link in the segment fails, then ports that were originally blocking may possibly be changed to forwarding mode.

Trunking

Trunking is a mechanism that is most often used to allow multiple VLANs to function independently across multiple switches. Routers and servers may use trunking as well, which allows them to live simultaneously on multiple VLANs. If your network has only one VLAN in it, then you may never need trunking; if your network has more than one VLAN, however, you will probably want to take advantage of the benefits of trunking.

A port on a switch normally belongs to only one VLAN; any traffic received or sent on this port is assumed to belong to the configured VLAN. A trunk port, on the other hand, is a port that can be configured to send and receive traffic for many VLANs. It accomplishes this by attaching VLAN information to each frame, a process called "tagging" the frame. Also, trunking must be active on both sides of the link; the other side must be expecting frames that include VLAN information for proper communication to occur.

Different methods of trunking exist, depending on the media being used. Trunking methods for Fast Ethernet or Gigabit Ethernet are Inter-Switch Link (ISL) or 802.1q. Trunking over ATM uses LANE. Trunking over FDDI uses 802.10.

EtherChannel

EtherChannel is a technique that can be used when you have multiple connections to the same device. Instead of having each link function independently, EtherChannel groups the ports together to work as one unit. It distributes traffic across all the links and provides redundancy in case one or more links fail. EtherChannel settings must be the same on both sides of the links involved in the channel. Normally, the Spanning-Tree Protocol would block all these parallel connections between devices because they are loops; however, EtherChannel runs "underneath" Spanning-Tree Protocol so that the protocol thinks that all the ports within a given EtherChannel are only a single port.

Multilayer Switching

Multilayer switching (MLS) refers to the capability of a switch to forward frames based on information in the Layer 3 (and sometimes Layer 4) header. This usually applies to IP packets, but now it also can occur for IPX packets. The switch learns how to handle these packets by communicating with one or more routers. Using a simplified explanation, the switch watches how the router processes a packet, and then the switch takes over processing future packets in this same flow. Traditionally, switches have been much faster at switching frames than routers, so to have them offload traffic from the router can result in significant speed improvements. If something changes in the network, the router can tell the switch to erase its Layer 3 cache and build it from scratch again as the situation evolves. The protocol used to communicate with the routers is called Multilayer Switching Protocol (MLSP).

How to Learn About These Features

These are just some of the basic features that switches support. More are being added every day. It is important to understand how your switches work, which features you are using, and how those features should work. One of the best places to learn this information about Cisco switches is on Cisco's web site.

Go to www.cisco.com; under the section "Service & Support," select Technical Documents. From here, select Documentation Home Page to find documentation sets for all Cisco products. The "Multilayer LAN Switches" link will lead you to documentation for all Cisco LAN switches. To learn about the features of a switch, read the "Software Configuration Guide" for the particular release of software that you use. The software configuration guides give you background information about what the feature does and what commands to use to configure it on your switch. All this information is free on the web; you do not even need an account for this documentation because it is available to anyone. Some of these configuration guides can be read in an afternoon and are well worth the time spent.

Another part of Cisco's web site is populated by Cisco's Technical Assistance Center (TAC). It is filled with information designed to help you implement, maintain, and troubleshoot your network. Go to the TAC web site at: www.cisco.com/tac; from here, you can select Products Home Page to get detailed support information organized by specific products, or you can go to the Technologies Home Page to get support information on technology (Fast Ethernet, Spanning-Tree Protocol, trunking, and so on). TAC documents and online tools specific to LAN Technologies are here: www.cisco.com/warp/customer/473/. Some of the material on the TAC web site, and, in particular, the online tools, are accessible only to users with a Cisco support contract.

General Switch Troubleshooting Suggestions

Many ways exist by which to troubleshoot a switch. As the features of switches grow, the possible things that can break also increase. If you develop an approach or test plan for troubleshooting, you will be better off in the long run than if you just try a hit-and-miss approach. Here are some general suggestions for making your troubleshooting more effective:

- Take the time to become familiar with normal switch operation. Cisco's web site has a tremendous amount of technical information describing how Cisco switches work, as mentioned in the previous section. The configuration guides, in particular, are very helpful. Many cases opened with Cisco's Technical Assistance Center (TAC) are solved with information from the product configuration guides.

- For the more complex situations, have an accurate physical and logical map of your network. A physical map shows how the devices and cables are connected. A logical map shows what segments (VLANs) exist in your network and which routers provide routing services to these segments. A spanning-tree map is highly useful for troubleshooting complex issues. Because of a switch's capability to create different segments by implementing VLANs, the physical connections alone do not tell the whole story; you must know how the switches are configured to determine which segments (VLANs) exist and to know how they are logically connected.

- Have a plan. Some problems and solutions are obvious; some are not. The symptoms that you see in your network may be the result of problems in another area or layer. Before jumping to conclusions, try to verify in a structured way what is working and what is not. Because networks can be complex, it is helpful to isolate possible problem domains. One way of doing this is by using the OSI seven-layer model. For example, check the physical connections involved (Layer 1), check connectivity issues within the VLAN (Layer 2), check connectivity issues across different VLANs (Layer 3), and so on. Assuming a correct configuration on the switch, many of the problems that you encounter will be related to physical layer issues (physical ports and cabling). Today, switches are involved in Layer 3 and Layer 4 issues, incorporating intelligence to switch packets based on information derived from routers, or by actually having routers living inside the switch (Layer 3 or Layer 4 switching).

- Do not assume that a component is working without checking it first. This can save you a lot of wasted time. For example, if a PC is not capable of logging into a server across your network, many things could be wrong. Don't skip the basic things and assume that something works—someone might have changed something without telling you. It takes only a minute to check some of the basic things (for example, that the ports involved are connected to the right place and are active), which could save you many wasted hours.

Troubleshooting Port Connectivity Problems

If the port doesn't work, nothing works! Ports are the foundation of your switching network. Some ports have special significance because of their location in the network and the amount of traffic that they carry. These ports would include connections to other switches, routers, and servers. These ports can be more complicated to troubleshoot because they often take advantage of special features such as trunking and EtherChannel. The rest of the ports are significant as well because they connect the actual users of the network.

Many things can cause a port to be nonfunctional: hardware issues, configuration issues, and traffic issues. Let's look at these categories a little deeper.

Hardware Issues

This section discusses issues related to general hardware requirements, copper, and fiber.

General

Port functionality requires two working ports connected by a working cable (assuming that it is of the correct type). Most Cisco switches default to having a port in notconnect state, which means that it is currently not connected to anything but is willing to connect. If you connect a good cable to two switch ports in the notconnect state, the link light should become green for both ports, and the port status should be "connected," which means that the port is up as far as Layer 1 is concerned. The following paragraphs point out items to check if Layer 1 is not up.

Check the port status for both ports involved. Make sure that neither port involved in the link is shut down. The administrator could have manually shut down one or both ports.

Software inside the switch could have shut down the port because of configuration error conditions (we will expand on this later). If one side is shut down and the other is not, the status on the enabled side will be notconnect (because it does not sense a neighbor on the other side of the wire). The status on the shut-down side would say something like "disable" or "errDisable" (depending on what actually shut down the port). The link will not come up unless both ports are enabled.

When you hook up a good cable (again, assuming that it is of the correct type) between two enabled ports, both ports should show a green link light within a few seconds. Also, the port state should show "connected" in the command-line interface (CLI). At this point, if you do not have link, your problem is limited to three things: the port on one side, the port on the other side, or the cable in the middle. In some cases, other devices are involved: media converters (fiber-to-copper, and so on), or, on Gigabit links, you may have gigabit interface connectors (GBICs). Still, this is a reasonably limited area to search.

Media converters can add noise to a connection or weaken the signal if they are not functioning correctly. They also add extra connectors that can cause problems, so this is another component to debug.

Check for loose connections. Sometimes a cable appears to be seated in the jack, but it actually isn't; unplug the cable and re-insert it. You should also look for dirt or broken or missing pins. Do this for both ports involved in the connection.

The cable could be plugged into the wrong port, which commonly happens. Make sure that both ends of the cable are plugged into the ports where you really want them.

You also can have a link on one side and not on the other. Check both sides for link. A single broken wire can cause this type of problem.

A link light does not guarantee that the cable is fully functional. It may have encountered physical stress that causes it to be functional at a marginal level. Usually you will notice this if the port has lots of packet errors.

To determine whether the cable is the problem, swap it with a known good cable. Don't just swap it with any other cable; make sure that you swap it with a cable that you know is good and is of the correct type.

If this is a very long cable run (underground, across a large campus, for example), then it would be nice to have a sophisticated cable tester. If you do not have a cable tester, you might consider the following:

- Trying different ports to see if they come up using this long cable
- Connecting the port in question to another port in the same switch, just to see if the port will link up locally
- Temporarily relocating the switches near each other so that you can try out a known good cable

Copper

Make sure that you have the correct cable for the type of connection you are making. Category 3 cable can be used for 10 MB UTP connections, but Category 5 should be used for 10/100 connections.

A straight-through RJ-45 cable is used for end stations, routers, or servers to connect to a switch or hub. An Ethernet crossover cable is used for switch-to-switch or hub-to-switch connections. Below is the pin-out for an Ethernet crossover cable. Maximum distances for Ethernet or Fast Ethernet copper wires are 100 meters. A good general rule of thumb is that when crossing an OSI layer, such as between a switch and a router, use a straight-through cable; when connecting two devices in the same OSI layer, such as between two routers or two switches, use a crossover cable. For purposes of this rule only, treat a workstation like a router.

Figure 23-1 shows the pinouts required for a switch-to-switch crossover cable.

Figure 23-1 *Illustration of the Pinouts Required for a Switch-to-Switch Crossover Cable*

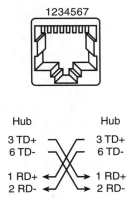

Fiber

For fiber, make sure that you have the correct cable for the distances involved and the type of fiber ports being used (single mode, multimode). Make sure that the ports being connected are both single-mode or both multimode ports. Single-mode fiber generally reaches 10 km, and multimode fiber can usually reach 2 km, but the special case of 100BaseFX multimode used in half-duplex mode can go only 400 meters.

For fiber connections, make sure that the transmit lead of one port is connected to the receive lead of the other port, and vice versa; transmit-to-transmit and receive-to-receive will not work.

For gigabit connections, GBICs must be matched on each side of the connection. There are different types of GBICs, depending on the cable and distances involved: short wavelength (SX), long wavelength/long haul (LX/LH), and extended distance (ZX). An SX GBIC needs to connect with an SX GBIC; an SX GBIC will not link with an LX GBIC. Also, some gigabit connections require conditioning cables, depending on the lengths involved. Refer to the GBIC installation notes (for examples, see www.cisco.com/univercd/cc/td/doc/product/lan/cat5000/cnfg_nts/ethernet/5399_01.htm).

If your gigabit link will not come up, check to make sure that the flow control and port negotiation settings are consistent on both sides of the link. There could be incompatibilities in the implementation of these features if the switches being connected are from different vendors. If in doubt, turn off these features on both switches.

Configuration Issues

Another cause of port connectivity issues is incorrect software configuration of the switch. If a port has a solid orange light, it means that software inside the switch shut down the port, either by way of the user interface or by internal processes.

Make sure that the administrator has not shut down the ports involved (as mentioned earlier). The administrator could have manually shut down the port on one side of the link. This link will not come up until you re-enable the port; check the port status.

Some switches, such as the Catalyst 4000/5000/6000, may shut down the port if software processes inside the switch detect an error. When you look at the port status, it will read "errDisable." You must fix the configuration problem and then manually take the port out of errDisable state. Some newer software versions—CatOS 5.4(1) and later—have the capability to automatically re-enable a port after a configurable amount of time spent in the errDisable state. Some of the causes for this errDisable state are listed here:

- **EtherChannel misconfiguration**—If one side is configured for EtherChannel and the other is not, it can cause the spanning-tree process to shut down the port on the side configured for EtherChannel. If you try to configure EtherChannel but the ports involved do not have the same settings (speed, duplex, trunking mode, and so on) as their neighbor ports across the link, then it could cause the errDisable state. It is best to set each side for the EtherChannel desirable mode if you want to use EtherChannel. The section "Configuring EtherChannel Switch-to-Switch Connections on Catalyst 4000/5000/6000 Switches" talks in depth about configuring EtherChannel.

- **Duplex mismatch**—If the switch port receives a lot of late collisions, this usually indicates a duplex mismatch problem. There are other causes for late collisions—such as a bad NIC or cable segments that are too long—but the most common reason today is a duplex mismatch. The full-duplex side thinks that it can send whenever it wants to, but the half-duplex side expects packets only at certain times, not at any time.

- **BPDU port guard**—Some newer versions of switch software can monitor whether PortFast is enabled on a port. A port using PortFast should be connected to an end station, not to devices that generate spanning-tree packets called BPDUs. If the switch notices a BPDU coming into a port that has PortFast enabled, it will put the port in errDisable mode.

- **Unidirectional Link Detection**—Unidirectional Link Detection (UDLD) is a protocol on some new versions of software that discovers whether communication over a link is one-way only. A broken fiber cable or other cabling/port issues could cause this one-way only communication. These partially functional links can cause problems when the switches involved do not know that the link is partially broken. Spanning-tree loops can occur with this problem. UDLD can be configured to put a port in errDisable state when it detects a unidirectional link.

- **Native VLAN mismatch**—Before a port has trunking turned on, it belongs to a single VLAN. When trunking is turned on, the port can carry traffic for many VLANs. The port will still remember the VLAN that it was in before trunking was turned on, which is called the native VLAN. The native VLAN is central to 802.1q trunking. If the native VLAN on each end of the link does not match, a port will go into the errDisable state.

- **Other**—Any process within the switch that recognizes a problem with the port can place it in the errDisable state.

Another cause of inactive ports occurs when the VLAN to which the ports belong disappears. Each port in a switch belongs to a VLAN. If that VLAN is deleted, then the port will become inactive. Some switches show a steady orange light on each port in which this has happened. If you come to work one day and see hundreds of orange lights, don't panic; it could be that all the ports belonged to the same VLAN and someone accidentally deleted the VLAN to which the ports belong. When you add the VLAN back into the VLAN table, the ports will become active again because a port remembers its assigned VLAN.

If you have a link and the ports show that they are connected, but you cannot communicate with another device, this can be particularly perplexing. It usually indicates a problem above the physical layer: Layer 2 or Layer 3. Try the actions suggested in the next paragraphs.

Check the trunking mode on each side of the link. Make sure that both sides are in the same mode. If you turn the trunking mode to on (as opposed to auto or desirable) for one port, and the other port has the trunking mode set to off, the ports will not be capable of communicating. Trunking changes the formatting of the packet; the ports must be in agreement as to what format they are using on the link, or they will not understand each other.

Make sure that all devices are in the same VLAN. If they are not in the same VLAN, then a router must be configured to allow the devices to communicate.

Make sure that your Layer 3 addressing is correctly configured.

Traffic Issues

In this section, we describe some of the things you can learn by looking at a port's traffic information. Most switches have some way to track the packets going in and out of a port. Commands that generate this type of output on the Catalyst 4000/5000/6000 switches are **show port** and **show mac**. Output from these commands on the 4000/5000/6000 switches is described in the switch command references.

Some of these port traffic fields show how much data is being transmitted and received on the port. Other fields show how many error frames are being encountered on the port. If you have a large amount of alignment errors, FCS errors, or late collisions, this may indicate a duplex mismatch on the wire. Other causes for these types of errors may be bad network interface cards or cable problems. If you have a large number of deferred frames, it is a sign that your segment has too much traffic; the switch is not capable of sending enough traffic on the wire to empty its buffers. Consider removing some devices to another segment.

Switch Hardware Failure

If you have tried everything you can think of and the port will not work, there might be faulty hardware.

Sometimes ports are damaged by electrostatic discharge (ESD). You may or may not see any indication of this.

Look at the power-on self-test (POST) results from the switch to see whether any failures are indicated for any part of the switch.

If you see behavior that can be considered "strange," this could indicate hardware problems, but it could also indicate software problems. It is usually easier to reload the software than it is to get new hardware. Try working with the switch software first.

The operating system might have a bug. Loading a newer operating system could fix this. You can research known bugs by reading the release notes for the version of code that you are using or by using Cisco's Bug Navigator tool (www.cisco.com/support/bugtools).

The operating system could have somehow become corrupted. Reloading the same version of the operating system could fix the problem.

If the status light on the switch is flashing orange, this usually means that there is some kind of hardware problem with the port or the module or the switch. The same thing is true if the port or module status indicates "faulty."

Before exchanging the switch hardware, you might try a few things:

- Reseat the module in the switch. If you do this with the power on, make sure that the module is hot-swappable. If in doubt, turn off the switch before reseating the module, or refer to the hardware installation guide. If the port is built into the switch, ignore this step.

- Reboot the switch. Sometimes this causes the problem to disappear; this is a workaround, not a fix.

- Check the switch software. If this is a new installation, remember that some components may work with only certain releases of software. Check the release notes or the hardware installation and configuration guide for the component you are installing.

- If you are reasonably certain that you have a hardware problem, then replace the faulty component.

Troubleshooting Ethernet 10/100-Mb Half-/Full-Duplex Autonegotiation

This section presents general troubleshooting information and a discussion of techniques for troubleshooting Ethernet autonegotiation.

- This section shows how to determine the current behavior of a link. It goes on to show how users can control the behavior, and it also explains situations when autonegotiation will fail.

- Many different Cisco Catalyst switches and Cisco routers support autonegotiation. This section focuses on autonegotiation between Catalyst 5000 switches. However, the concepts explained here can be applied to the other types of devices.

Introduction

Autonegotiation is an optional function of the IEEE 802.3u Fast Ethernet standard that enables devices to automatically exchange information over a link about speed and duplex capabilities.

Autonegotiation is targeted at ports, which are allocated to areas where transient users or devices connect to a network. For example, many companies provide shared offices or cubes for account managers and system engineers to use when they are in the office rather than on the road. Each office or cube will have an Ethernet port permanently connected to the office's network. Because it may not be possible to ensure that every user has either a 10-Mb, a 100-Mb Ethernet, or a 10/100-Mb card in their laptops, the switch ports that handle these connections must be capable of negotiating their speed and duplex mode. The alternative would be to provide both a 10-Mb and a 100-Mb port in each office or cube and then label them accordingly.

Autonegotiation should not be used for ports that support network infrastructure devices such as switches and routers, or other nontransient end systems such as servers and printers. Although autonegotiation for speed and duplex is normally the default behavior on switch ports that are capable of it, ports connected to fixed devices should always be configured for the correct behavior rather than allowed to negotiate it. This eliminates any potential negotiation issues and ensures that you always know exactly how the ports should be operating. For example, a 10/100BaseTX Ethernet switch-to-switch link that has been configured for 100 Mb full-duplex will operate only at that speed and mode. There is no possibility for the ports to downgrade the link to a slower speed during a port reset or a switch reset. If the ports cannot operate as configured, they should stop passing any traffic. On the other hand, a switch-to-switch link that has been allowed to negotiate its behavior could end up operating at 10 Mb half-duplex. A nonfunctional link is usually easier to discover than a link that is operational but not operating at the expected speed or mode.

One of the most common causes of performance issues on 10/100-Mb Ethernet links is one port on the link operating at half-duplex mode while the other port is operating at full-duplex mode. This occasionally happens when one or both ports on a link are reset and the autonegotiation process doesn't result in the same configuration for both link partners. It also happens when users reconfigure one side of a link and forget to reconfigure the other side. Many performance-related support calls will be avoided by creating a policy that requires ports for all nontransient devices to be configured for their required behavior and enforcing the policy with adequate change control measures.

Troubleshooting Ethernet Autonegotiation Between Network Infrastructure Devices

Figure 23-2 show the process you should follow in troubleshooting Ethernet autonegotiation between network infrastructure devices.

Figure 23-2 *Troubleshooting Ethernet Autonegotiation*

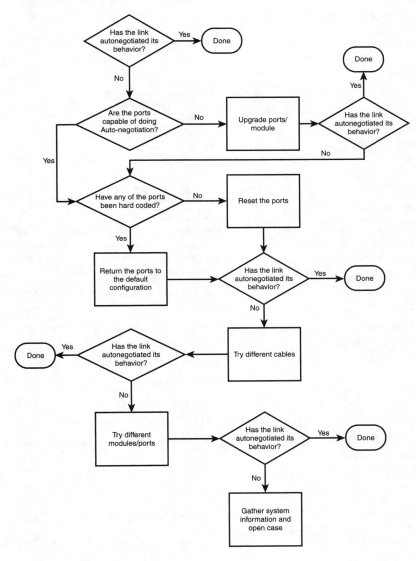

Procedures and Scenarios

Figure 23-3 shows a scenario using Cat 5k to Cat 5k, using Fast Ethernet.

Figure 23-3 *Scenario 1: Cat 5K to Cat 5K, Using Fast Ethernet*

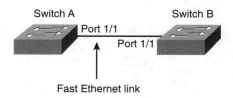

Table 23-1 *Autonegotiation Connectivity Issues*

Possible Problem	Solution	
Was the current behavior of the link autonegotiated?	**Step 1**	Use the **show port mod_num/port_num** command to determine the current behavior of the link. If both link partners (interfaces at either end of the link) have an "a-" prefix on their Duplex and Speed status fields, autonegotiation was probably successful.
Autonegotiation is not supported.	**Step 1**	Issue the **show port capabilities mod_num/port_num** command to verify that your modules support autonegotiation.
Autonegotiation is not working on Catalyst switches.	**Step 1**	Use the **set port speed mod_num/port_num auto** command on a Catalyst to configure autonegotiation.
	Step 2	Try different ports or modules.
	Step 3	Try resetting the ports.
	Step 4	Try different patch cables.
	Step 5	Turn the devices off and back on again.
Autonegotiation is not working on Cisco routers.	**Step 1**	Issue the correct IOS command to enable autonegotiation (if available).
	Step 2	Try different interfaces.
	Step 3	Try resetting the interfaces.
	Step 4	Try different patch cables.
	Step 5	Turn the devices off and back on again.

Example of Configuring and Troubleshooting Ethernet 10/100-Mb Autonegotiation

This section walks you through examining the behavior of a 10/100-Mb Ethernet port that supports autonegotiation. It will also show how to make changes to its default behavior and how to restore it to the default behavior.

Tasks That Will Be Performed

In this section, you'll perform these tasks:

- Examine the capabilities of the ports.
- Configure autonegotiation for port 1/1 on both switches.
- Determine whether the speed and duplex mode are set to autonegotiate.
- Change the speed on port 1/1 in Switch A to 10 Mb.
- Understand the meaning of the "a-" prefix on the Duplex and Speed status fields.
- View the duplex status of port 1/1 on Switch B.
- Understand the duplex mismatch error.
- Understand the spanning-tree error messages.
- Change the duplex mode to half on port 1/1 on Switch A.
- Set the duplex mode and speed of port 1/1 on Switch B.
- Restore the default duplex mode and speed to ports 1/1 on both switches.
- View the changes of the port status on both switches.

The following steps are performed on the console of a Catalyst 5K switch.

Step 1   The **show port capabilities 1/1** command displays the capabilities of a Ethernet 10/100BaseTX 1/1 port on Switch A.

Enter this command for both of the ports that you are troubleshooting. Both ports must support the speed and duplex capabilities shown here if they are supposed to be using autonegotiation.

The *italic* text in the output shows where the information on the speed and duplex mode capabilities will be found.

```
Switch-A> (enable) show port capabilities 1/1
Model WS-X5530
Port 1/1
Type 10/100BaseTX
Speed auto,10,100
Duplex half,full
```

Step 2 Autonegotiation is configured for both speed and duplex mode on port 1/1 of both switches by entering the **set port speed 1/1 auto** command (auto is the default for ports that support autonegotiation).

```
Switch-A> (enable) set port speed 1/1 auto
Port(s) 1/1 speed set to auto detect.
Switch-A (enable)
```

Note   The **set port speed {mod_num/port_num} auto** command also sets the duplex mode to auto. There is no **set port duplex {mod_num/port_num} auto** command.

Step 3 The **show port 1/1** command below displays the status of ports 1/1 on switches A and B.

```
Switch-A> (enable) show port 1/1
Port  Name               Status      Vlan        Level  Duplex Speed Type
----- ------------------ ----------- ----------- ------ ------ ----- ------------
 1/1                     connected   1           normal a-full a-100 10/100BaseTX
Switch-B> (enable) show port 1/1
Port  Name               Status      Vlan        Level  Duplex Speed Type
----- ------------------ ----------- ----------- ------ ------ ----- -----------
 1/1                     connected   1           normal a-full a-100 10/100BaseTX
```

The *italic* text in this output shows where the information on the current status of a port can be found. Note that most of the normal output from the **show port {mod_num/port_num}** command has been omitted.

The "a-" prefixes on the "full" and "100" indicate that this port has not been hard-coded (configured) for a specific duplex mode or speed. Therefore, it is willing to autonegotiate its duplex mode and speed if the device it is connected to (its link partner) is also willing to autonegotiate its duplex mode and speed.

Also note that the status shows "connected" on both ports, which means that a link pulse has been detected from the other port. The status can show "connected" even if duplex has been incorrectly negotiated or misconfigured.

Step 4   To demonstrate what happens when one link partner is autonegotiating and the other link partner is not, the speed on port 1/1 in Switch A will be set to 10 Mb by using the **set port speed 1/1 10** command.

```
Switch-A> (enable) set port speed 1/1 10
Port(s) 1/1 speed set to 10Mbps.
Switch-A> (enable)
```

Note   Hard-coding the speed on a port disables all autonegotiation functionality on the port for speed and duplex.

When a port has been configured for a speed, its duplex mode will automatically be configured for the mode that it had previously negotiated—in this case, full duplex. Therefore, entering the **set port speed 1/1 10** command caused the duplex mode on port 1/1 to be configured as if the command **set port duplex 1/1 full** had also been entered. This is explained in the next step.

Step 5   Now you must understand the meaning of the "a-" prefix in the Duplex and Speed status fields.

The absence of the "a-" prefix in the status fields of the output from the **show port 1/1** command on Switch A shows that the duplex mode is now configured for full-duplex operation, and the speed is now configured for 10 Mb.

```
Switch-A> (enable) show port 1/1
Port  Name               Status     Vlan       Level  Duplex Speed Type
----- ------------------ ---------- ---------- ------ ------ ----- ------------
 1/1                     connected  1          normal full   10    10/100BaseTX
```

Step 6   The **show port 1/1** command on Switch B indicates that the port is now operating at half-duplex and 10 Mb.

```
Switch-B> (enable) show port 1/1
Port  Name               Status     Vlan       Level  Duplex Speed Type
----- ------------------ ---------- ---------- ------ ------ ----- ------------
 1/1                     connected  1          normal a-half a-10 10/100BaseTX
```

This step shows that it is possible for a link partner to detect the speed at which the other link partner is operating, even though the other link partner is not configured for autonegotiation. Sensing the type of electrical signal that is arriving to see if it is 10 Mb or 100 Mb does this. This is how Switch B determined that port 1/1 should be operating at 10 Mb.

It is not possible to detect the correct duplex mode in the same way that the correct speed can be detected. In this case, where Switch B's 1/1 port is configured for autonegotiation and Switch A's is not, Switch B's 1/1 port was forced to select the default duplex mode. On Catalyst Ethernet ports, the default mode is autonegotiate and, if autonegotiation fails, then is half-duplex.

This example also shows that a link can be successfully connected when there is a mismatch in the duplex modes. Port 1/1 on Switch A is configured for full-duplex operation, while port 1/1 on Switch B has defaulted to half-duplex operation. To avoid this, always configure both link partners.

The "a-" prefix on the Duplex and Speed status fields does not always mean that the current behavior was negotiated. Sometimes it means only that the port has not been configured for a speed or duplex mode.

The previous output from Switch B shows the Duplex field as "a-half" and the Speed field as "a-10," which indicates that the port is operating at 10 Mb in half-duplex mode. In this example, however, the link partner on this port (port 1/1 on Switch A) is configured for full-duplex mode and 10 Mb. Therefore, it was not possible for port 1/1 on Switch B to have autonegotiated its current behavior. This proves that the "a-" prefix indicates only a willingness to perform autonegotiation, not that autonegotiation actually took place.

Step 7   The following message about a duplex mode mismatch is displayed on Switch A after the speed on port 1/1 was changed to 10 Mb. The mismatch was caused by Switch B's 1/1 port defaulting to half-duplex mode because it sensed that its link partner was no longer performing autonegotiation.

```
%CDP-4-DUPLEXMISMATCH:Full/half duplex mismatch detected o1
```

It is important to note that this message is created by the Cisco Discovery Protocol (CDP), not the 802.3 autonegotiation protocol. CDP can report problems that it discovers, but it typically doesn't automatically fix them.

A duplex mismatch may or may not result in an error message. Another indication of a duplex mismatch is rapidly increasing FCS and alignment errors on the half-duplex side, and "runts" on the full-duplex port (as seen in a **sh port {mod_num/port_num}**).

Step 8   In addition to the duplex mismatch error message, you may also see the following spanning-tree messages when you change the speed on a link. A discussion of the Spanning-Tree Protocol is beyond the scope of this document; see the section found later in this chapter "Troubleshooting Spanning-Tree Protocol and Related Design Considerations," for more information.

```
%PAGP-5-PORTFROMSTP:Port 1/1 left bridge port 1/1
%PAGP-5-PORTTOSTP:Port 1/1 joined bridge port 1/1
```

Step 9   To demonstrate what happens when the duplex mode has been configured, the mode on port 1/1 in Switch A will be set to half-duplex mode using the **set port duplex 1/1 half** command.

```
Switch-A> (enable) set port duplex 1/1 half
Port(s) 1/1 set to half-duplex.
Switch-A> (enable)
```

The **show port 1/1** command shows the change in the duplex mode on this port.

```
Switch-A> (enable) sh port 1/1
Port  Name               Status     Vlan       Level  Duplex Speed Type
----- ------------------ ---------- ---------- ------ ------ ----- ------------
 1/1                     connected  1          normal half   10    10/100BaseTX
```

At this point, ports 1/1 on both switches are operating at half-duplex mode. Port 1/1 on Switch B, however, is still configured to autonegotiate, as shown in the following output of the **show port 1/1** command.

```
Switch-B> (enable) show port 1/1
Port  Name               Status     Vlan       Level  Duplex Speed Type
----- ------------------ ---------- ---------- ------ ------ ----- ------------
 1/1                     connected  1          normal a-half a-10  10/100BaseTX
```

The next step shows how to configure the duplex mode on port 1/1 in Switch B to half-duplex mode. This is in keeping with the recommended policy of always configuring both link partners in the same way.

Step 10 To implement the policy of always configuring both link partners for the same behavior, this step now sets the duplex mode to half-duplex and the speed to 10 on port 1/1 in Switch B.

Here is the output of entering the **set port duplex 1/1 half** command on Switch B:

```
Switch-B> (enable) set port duplex 1/1 half
Port 1/1 is in auto-sensing mode.
Switch-B> (enable)
```

The **set port duplex 1/1 half** command failed because this command won't work if autonegotiation is enabled. This also means that this command will not disable autonegotiation. Autonegotiation can be disabled only by using the **set port speed {mod_num/port_num {10 | 100}}** command.

Here is the output of entering the **set port speed 1/1 10** command on Switch B:

```
Switch-B> (enable) set port speed 1/1 10
Port(s) 1/1 speed set to 10 Mbps.
Switch-B> (enable)
```

Now the **set port duplex 1/1 half** command on Switch B will work:

```
Switch-A> (enable) set port duplex 1/1 half
Port(s) 1/1 set to half-duplex.
Switch-A> (enable)
```

The **show port 1/1** command on Switch B shows that the ports is now configured for half-duplex mode and 10 Mb.

```
Switch-B> (enable) show port 1/1
Port  Name               Status     Vlan       Level  Duplex Speed Type
----- ------------------ ---------- ---------- ------ ------ ----- -----------
 1/1                     connected  1          normal half   10    10/100BaseTX
```

Note   The **set port duplex {mod_num/port_num {half | full }}** command is dependent on the **set port speed {mod_num/ port_num {10 | 100 }}** command. In other words, you must set the speed before you can set the duplex mode.

Step 11 Configure ports 1/1 on both switches to autonegotiate with the **set port speed 1/1 auto** command.

```
Switch-A> (enable) set port speed 1/1 auto
Port(s) 1/1 speed set to auto detect.
Switch-A> (enable)
```

Note   When a port's duplex mode has been configured to something other than auto, the only way to configure the port to autosense its duplex mode is to issue the **set port speed {mod_num/port_num} auto** command. There is no **set port duplex {mod_num/port_num} auto** command. In other words, issuing the **set port speed {mod_num/port_num} auto** command has the effect of resetting both port speed sensing and duplex mode sensing to auto.

Step 12 Examine the status of ports 1/1 on both switches by using the **show port 1/1** command.

```
Switch-A> (enable) show port 1/1
Port  Name               Status     Vlan        Level  Duplex Speed Type
----- ------------------ ---------- ----------  ------ ------ ----- ------------
 1/1                     connected  1           normal a-full a-100 10/100BaseTX
Switch-B> (enable) show port 1/1
Port  Name               Status     Vlan        Level  Duplex Speed Type
----- ------------------ ---------- ----------  ------ ------ ----- ------------
 1/1                     connected  1           normal a-full a-100 10/100BaseTX
```

Both ports are now set to their default behavior of autonegotiation. Both ports have negotiated full-duplex mode and 100 Mb.

Before Calling Cisco Systems' TAC Team

Before calling Cisco Systems' Technical Assistance Center (TAC), make sure that you have read through this chapter and completed the actions suggested for your system's problem.

Additionally, do the following and document the results so that we can better assist you:

- Capture the output of **show version** from all the affected devices.
- Capture the output of **show port mod_num/port_num** from all the affected ports.
- Capture the output of **show port mod_num/port_num capabilities** from all the affected ports.

Additional Sources

- IEEE web site: www.ieee.org/

ISL Trunking on Catalyst 5000 and 6000 Family Switches

This section illustrates how to create a switch-to-switch Inter-Switch Link (ISL) trunk. Trunk ports enable connections between switches to carry traffic from more than one virtual local-area network (VLAN). Without trunking, a link between two switches can carry only traffic from one VLAN.

- This section shows how to determine the current behavior of a link. It goes on to show how users can control the behavior, and it also explains situations when autonegotiation will fail.

- Many different Cisco Catalyst switches and Cisco routers support autonegotiation. This section focuses on autonegotiation between Catalyst 5000 switches. However, the concepts explained here can be applied to the other types of devices.

Introduction

Trunking is not required in very simple switched networks with only one VLAN (broadcast domain). In most LANs, a small portion of traffic is made up of special protocols used for managing the network (Cisco Discovery Protocol, Virtual Trunking Protocol, Dynamic Trunking Protocol, Spanning-Tree Protocol, and Port Aggregation Protocol, to name a few examples). The management VLAN (VLAN 1) is also used when you **ping** or Telnet directly to or from the switch (this VLAN and the IP address of the switch are defined by configuring the sc0 interface, explained later). In a multi-VLAN environment, many network administrators advocate restricting this management traffic to its own VLAN, normally VLAN 1. User traffic is then configured to flow in VLANs other than this default VLAN.

ISL (Cisco proprietary) is one of two possible trunking protocols for Ethernet. The other protocol is the IEEE 802.1q standard.

Troubleshooting ISL Trunking on Catalyst 5000 and 6000 Family Switches

This section will walk the reader through some basic ISL trunking scenarios. The reader will learn basic ISL trunking configuration and troubleshooting skills (Figure 23-4).

Figure 23-4 *Troubleshooting ISL Trunking on Catalyst 5000 and 6000 Family Switches*

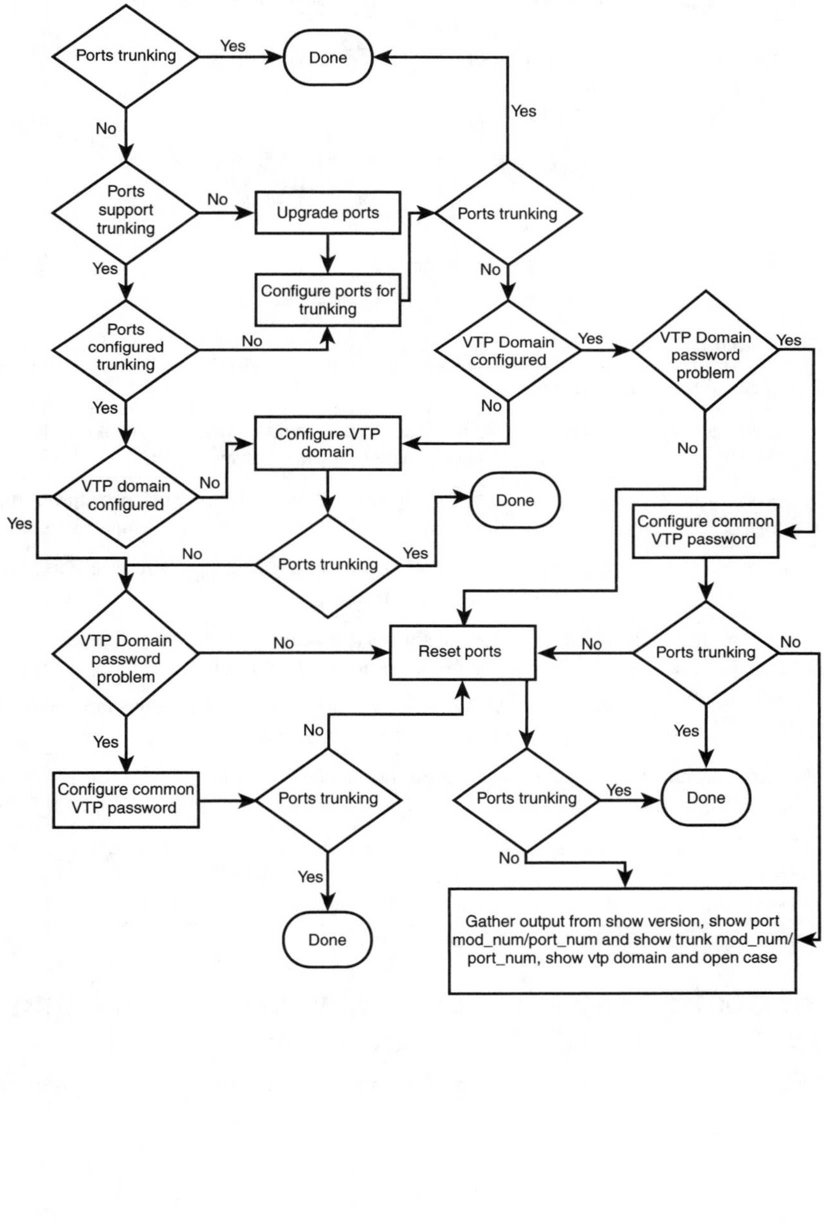

Procedures and/or Scenarios

Scenario: Cat 5K to Cat 5K, using Fast Ethernet for ISL trunking (Figure 23-5).

Figure 23-5 *Cat 5K to Cat 5K, Using Fast Ethernet for ISL Trunking*

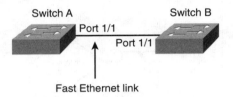

Table 23-2 *ISL Trunking Issues*

Possible Problem	Solution	
Are the ports trunking?	**Step 1**	Use the **show trunk mod_num/port_num** command to determine whether the ports are trunking.
Trunking is not supported.	**Step 1**	Issue the **show port capabilities mod_num/port_num** command to verify that your modules support trunking.
Trunking is not configured.	**Step 1**	Use the **set trunk mod_num/port_num desirable** on a Catalyst to configure trunking.
Verify that the VTP domain name has been configured.	**Step 1**	Use the **show vtp domain** command to determine whether a domain name has been configured. All switches in a domain must have the same name. The name is case-sensitive.
VTP domain name is not configured.	**Step 1**	Set **vtp domain domain_name**.
A VTP domain password problem has occurred.	**Step 1**	Use the **show vtp domain** command to determine whether a password has been established. All switches must have the same password. The passwords are case-sensitive.

Example of Configuring and Troubleshooting ISL Trunking on Catalyst 5000 and 6000 Family Switches

This section walks you through configuring and troubleshooting ISL trunking.

Tasks That Will Be Performed

In this section, you will perform these tasks:

- Verify ISL support on the ports.
- Connect the switches.
- Verify that the ports are operational.
- Assign IP addresses to the management ports.
- Verify that the switches are not trunking over their link.
- Ping from switch to switch.
- Create a VLAN 2 in each switch.
- Move the management interface (sc0) to VLAN 2.
- Verify that you cannot **ping** from switch to switch.
- Configure the same VTP domain name in each switch.
- Enable trunking between the switches.
- Verify that the switches are trunking over their link.
- Ping from switch to switch.

Step-by-Step

The following steps are performed on the console of a Catalyst 5K switch.

Step 1 Make certain that the ports you have decided to use support ISL trunking. Several types of Ethernet interfaces support ISL trunking. 10BaseT (common Ethernet) ports do not support trunking; most 100BaseT (Fast Ethernet) ports do.

Use the **show port capabilities {module_number}|{module_number/ port_number}** command on both switches to determine whether the ports that you are using support ISL. In this example, note that the port designator 1/1 has been specified at the end of the command. This limits the response to the information directly applicable to port 1/1.

```
Switch-A> show port capabilities 1/1
Model                 WS-X5530
Port                  1/1
Type                  10/100BaseTX
Speed                 auto,10,100
Duplex                half,full
Trunk encap type      ISL
Trunk mode            on,off,desirable,auto,nonegotiate
Channel               1/1-2
```

```
Broadcast suppression    percentage(0-100)
Flow control             no
Security                 yes
Membership               static,dynamic
Fast start               yes
QOS                      n/a
Rewrite                  no
UDLD                     Not capable
Switch-A>
```

Step 2 Connect the two switch ports using the Ethernet crossover cable. In this example, Switch A's 1/1 port is connected to Switch B's 1/1 port.

Step 3 Verify that the ports are operational by entering the **show port 1/1** command on Switch A. You should see that the status shows "connected."

```
Switch-A> (enable) show port 1/1
Port  Name              Status     Vlan       Level  Duplex Speed Type
----- ----------------- ---------- ---------- ------ ------ ----- ------------
1/1                     connected  1          normal a-full a-100 10/100BaseTX


Switch-A> (enable)
```

Step 4 Use the **set interface sc0 172.16.84.17 255.255.255.0 172.16.84.255** command on Switch A and the **set interface sc0 172.16.84.18 255.255.255.0 172.16.84.255** command on Switch B to assign IP addresses from the same subnet to the management ports on both switches. The VLAN for sc0 (the management VLAN) must also be specified in this command if it is different than the default of VLAN 1.

```
Switch-A> (enable) set int sc0 172.16.84.17 255.255.255.0 172.16.84.255
Interface sc0 IP address, netmask, and broadcast set.
Switch-A> (enable)
```

Step 5 Verify that the link between switches A and B is not trunking by entering the **show trunk 1/1** command on Switch A.

```
Switch-A> (enable) show trunk 1/1
Port     Mode        Encapsulation  Status        Native vlan
-------- ----------- -------------- ------------- -----------
 1/1     auto        isl            not-trunking  1


Port     Vlans allowed on trunk
-------- -----------------------------------------------------------------------
 1/1     1-1005


Port     Vlans allowed and active in management domain
-------- -----------------------------------------------------------------------
 1/1     1
```

```
Port      Vlans in spanning tree forwarding state and not pruned
--------  ----------------------------------------------------------------
 1/1      1
Switch-A> (enable)
```

NOTE   The term **Native vlan** in the output indicates the VLAN in which this port will be placed when it is not in trunking mode. If the port is instead configured for 802.1q trunking, **Native vlan** also indicates the VLAN for whose frames will be untagged; all others will be tagged (conversely, with ISL trunking, every data frame is tagged with the appropriate VLAN identifier).

The trunking status should read "not-trunking" because the default mode for the Dynamic Trunking Protocol (DTP) is Auto. DTP is the strategic replacement for Dynamic ISL (DISL) because it incorporates support for 802.1q trunking negotiation. DTP is available as of version 4.x Catalyst software and certain hardware modules. The following bullets describe the five different states for which DTP can be configured.

— **Auto**—The port listens for DTP frames from the neighboring switch. If the neighboring switch indicates that it would like to be a trunk, or if it is a trunk, then Auto state creates the trunk with the neighboring switch. Auto does not propagate any intent to become an trunk; it depends solely on the neighboring switch to make the trunking decision.

— **Desirable**—DTP is spoken to the neighboring switch. This communicates to the neighboring switch that it is capable of being an ISL trunk and would like the neighboring switch to also be an ISL trunk.

— **On**—DTP is spoken to the neighboring switch. This automatically enables ISL trunking on its port, regardless of the state of its neighboring switch. It remains an ISL trunk unless it receives an ISL packet that explicitly disables the ISL trunk.

— **Nonegotiate**—DTP is not spoken to the neighboring switch. This automatically enables ISL trunking on its port, regardless of the state of its neighboring switch.

— **Off**—ISL is not allowed on this port, regardless of the DTP mode configured on the other switch.

On an individual trunk link, Cisco generally recommends configuring desirable trunking mode on the port nearest the network core, and auto trunking mode on the other side of the link. To hard-code trunking to be enabled, set the trunking mode on both sides to on; you will need to manually set the VLANs to be forwarded across the trunk link (use the full **set trunk** command) and ensure that the trunk settings are consistent on either side.

Step 6 **ping** Switch B from Switch A to verify that the switches can talk to each other over the link.

```
Switch-A> ping 172.16.84.18
172.16.84.18 is alive
Switch-A>
```

Step 7 Create VLAN 2 in Switch A by entering the **set vlan 2** command on Switch A. Switch B will learn about VLAN 2 after the DTP domain is established in Step 11.

```
Switch-A> (enable) set vlan 2
Vlan 2 configuration successful
Switch-A> (enable)
```

Step 8 Move the management interface in switches A and B to VLAN 2, which you created previously. Use the **set interface sc0 2** command to do this. The following output shows this being done on Switch A.

```
Switch-A> (enable) set int sc0 2
Interface sc0 vlan set.
Switch-A> (enable)
```

Use the **show interface** command to view the change that you just made. The following output shows this being done on Switch A.

```
Switch-A> (enable) sh int
sl0: flags=51<UP,POINTOPOINT,RUNNING>
        slip 0.0.0.0 dest 0.0.0.0
sc0: flags=63<UP,BROADCAST,RUNNING>
        vlan 2 inet 172.16.84.17 netmask 255.255.255.0 broadcast
172.16.84.255
Switch-A> (enable)
```

Step 9 Attempt to **ping** Switch B from Switch A. This should fail because the management ports are now in VLAN 2, while the link between the switches is in VLAN 1.

```
Switch-A> (enable) ping 172.16.84.18
no answer from 172.16.84.18
Switch-A> (enable)
```

Step 10 Establish the same VTP domain, named Cookbook, for both switches by entering the **set vtp domain Cookbook** command on both switches.

```
Switch-A> (enable) set vtp domain Cookbook
VTP domain Cookbook modified
Switch-A> (enable)
```

Step 11 Turn on trunking between the switches by configuring port 1/1 on Switch A for desirable mode by entering the **set trunk 1/1desirable** command on Switch A. Switch B will place its 1/1 port into trunking mode after the DTP negotiation between the two switches is complete.

```
Switch-A> (enable) set trunk 1/1 desirable
Port(s) 1/1 trunk mode set to desirable.
Switch-A> (enable)
```

You should see the following message as ISL becomes active:

```
1999 Aug 10 15:33:10 %DTP-5-TRUNKPORTON:Port 1/1 has become isl trunk
```

Possible Combinations of DTP Configurations

Table 23-3 shows the 15 possible unique combinations of DTP modes and indicates whether they will result in an active bidirectional trunk. Although it is theoretically possible to trunk in one direction on a link and not the other, it is not recommended.

Table 23-3   *The Fifteen Possible Unique Combinations of DTP Modes*

Switch A Port 1/1	Switch B Port 1/1	ISL Trunk Status
DTP Mode Auto	DTP Mode Auto	Not-trunking
DTP Mode Desirable	DTP Mode Auto	Trunking
DTP Mode ON	DTP Mode Auto	Trunking
DTP Mode Nonegotiate	DTP Mode Auto	Not-trunking
DTP Mode Off	DTP Mode Auto	Not-trunking
DTP Mode Desirable	DTP Mode Desirable	Trunking
DTP Mode On	DTP Mode Desirable	Not-trunking
DTP Mode Nonegotiate	DTP Mode Desirable	Not-trunking
DTP Mode Off	DTP Mode Desirable	Not-trunking
DTP Mode On	DTP Mode On	Trunking

continues

Table 23-3   *The Fifteen Possible Unique Combinations of DTP Modes (Continued)*

Switch A Port 1/1	Switch B Port 1/1	ISL Trunk Status
DTP Mode Nonegotiate	DTP Mode On	Trunking
DTP Mode Off	DTP Mode On	Not-trunking
DTP Mode Nonegotiate	DTP Mode Nonegotiate	Trunking
DTP Mode Off	DTP Mode Nonegotiate	Not-trunking
DTP Mode Off	DTP Mode Off	Not-trunking

Before Calling Cisco Systems' TAC Team

Before calling Cisco Systems's Technical Assistance Center (TAC), make sure that you have read through this chapter and completed the actions suggested for your system's problem.

Additionally, do the following and document the results so that we can better assist you:

- Capture the output of **show version** from all the affected switches.
- Capture the output of **show vtp domain** from all the affected switches.
- Capture the output of **show trunk mod_num/port_num** from all the affected ports.
- Capture the output of **show port mod_num/port_num capabilities** from all the affected ports.

Configuring EtherChannel Switch-to-Switch Connections on Catalyst 4000/5000/6000 Switches

EtherChannel allows multiple physical Fast Ethernet or Gigabit Ethernet links to be combined into one logical channel. This allows load-sharing of traffic among the links in the channel, as well as redundancy in case one or more links in the channel fail. EtherChannel can be used to interconnect LAN switches, routers, servers, and clients via unshielded twisted-pair (UTP) wiring or single-mode and multimode fiber.

EtherChannel is an easy way to aggregate bandwidth between critical networking devices. On the Catalyst 5000, a channel can be created from two ports, making it a 200-Mbps link (400 Mbps full-duplex), or four ports, making it a 400-Mbps link (800 Mbps full-duplex). Some cards and platforms also support Gigabit EtherChannel and have the capability to use from two to eight ports in an EtherChannel. The concept is the same, no matter what speeds or number of links are involved. Normally, the Spanning-Tree Protocol would consider these redundant links between two devices to be loops and would cause the redundant links to be in blocking mode, effectively making these links inactive (providing only backup capabilities in case the main link fails). When using IOS 3.1.1 or greater, Spanning-Tree

Protocol treats the channel as one big link, so all the ports in the channel can be active at the same time.

This section takes you through the steps for configuring EtherChannel between two Catalyst 5000 switches and shows you the results of the commands as they are executed. Catalyst 4000 and 6000 switches could have been used in the scenarios presented in this document to obtain the same results. For the Catalyst 2900XL and 1900/2820, the command syntax is different, but the EtherChannel concepts are the same.

EtherChannel may be configured manually by typing in the appropriate commands, or it may be configured automatically by having the switch negotiate the channel with the other side using the Port Aggregation Protocol (PAgP). It is recommended to use PAgP desirable mode to configure EtherChannel whenever possible because manually configuring EtherChannel can create some complications. This section gives examples of configuring EtherChannel manually and examples of configuring EtherChannel by using PAgP. Also included is how to troubleshoot EtherChannel and how to use trunking with EtherChannel. In this chapter, the terms *EtherChannel*, *Fast EtherChannel*, *Gigabit EtherChannel*, and *channel* will all refer to EtherChannel.

Contents

The following topics will be covered in this section:

- Tasks for manually configuring EtherChannel
- Verifying the EtherChannel configuration
- Using PAgP to automatically configure EtherChannel (preferred method)
- Trunking and EtherChannel
- Troubleshooting EtherChannel
- Commands used in this section

Figure 23-6 illustrates our test environment. The configuration of the switches has been cleared using the **clear config all** command. Then the prompt was changed using **set system name**. An IP address and mask were assigned to the switch for management purposes using **set int sc0 172.16.84.6 255.255.255.0** for Switch A and **set int sc0 172.16.84.17 255.255.255.0** for Switch B. A default gateway was assigned to both switches using **set ip route default 172.16.84.1**.

The switch configurations were cleared so that we could start from the default conditions. The switches were given names so that we can identify them from the prompt on the command line. The IP addresses were assigned so that we can **ping** between the switches for testing. The default gateway was not used.

Figure 23-6 *Test Environment*

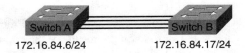

172.16.84.6/24   172.16.84.17/24

Many of the commands display more output than is needed for our discussion. Extraneous output will be deleted.

Tasks for Manually Configuring EtherChannel

The following tasks will be performed to manually configure EtherChannel:

- Show the IOS version and modules that we are using in this chapter.
- Verify that EtherChannel is supported on the ports.
- Verify that the ports are connected and operational.
- Verify that the ports to be grouped have the same settings.
- Identify valid port groups.
- Create the channel.

Step-by-Step

The following steps will be done from the console of Switch-A and Switch-B:

Step 1 The **show version** command displays the software version that the switch is running. The **show module** command lists which modules are installed in the switch.

```
Switch-A show version
WS-C5505 Software, Version McpSW: 4.5(1) NmpSW: 4.5(1)
Copyright (c) 1995-1999 by Cisco Systems
...

Switch-A show module
Mod Module-Name       Ports Module-Type           Model     Serial-Num Status
--- ----------------- ----- --------------------- --------- ---------- -------
1                     0     Supervisor III        WS-X5530  006841805  ok
2                     24    10/100BaseTX Ethernet WS-X5225R 012785227  ok
...
```

Step 2   Verify that EtherChannel is supported on the ports. The **show port capabilities** command appears in versions 4.x and greater. If you have an IOS earlier than 4.x, you must skip this step. Not every Fast Ethernet module supports EtherChannel. Some of the original EtherChannel modules have "Fast EtherChannel" written on the bottom-left corner of the module (as you face it in the switch), which tells you that the feature is supported. However, this convention was abandoned on later modules. The modules in this test do not have "Fast EtherChannel" printed on them, but they do support the feature.

```
Switch-A show port capabilities
Model                WS-X5225R
Port                 2/1
Type                 10/100BaseTX
Speed                auto,10,100
Duplex               half,full
Trunk encap type     802.1Q,ISL
Trunk mode           on,off,desirable,auto,nonegotiate
Channel              2/1-2,2/1-4
Broadcast suppression  percentage(0-100)
Flow control         receive-(off,on),send-(off,on)
Security             yes
Membership           static,dynamic
Fast start           yes
Rewrite              yes
Switch-B show port capabilities
Model                WS-X5234
Port                 2/1
Type                 10/100BaseTX
Speed                auto,10,100
Duplex               half,full
Trunk encap type     802.1Q,ISL
Trunk mode           on,off,desirable,auto,nonegotiate
Channel              2/1-2,2/1-4
Broadcast suppression  percentage(0-100)
Flow control         receive-(off,on),send-(off,on)
Security             yes
Membership           static,dynamic
Fast start           yes
Rewrite              no
```

A port that does not support EtherChannel would look like this:

```
Switch show port capabilities
Model                     WS-X5213A
Port                      2/1
Type                      10/100BaseTX
Speed                     10,100,auto
Duplex                    half,full
Trunk encap type          ISL
Trunk mode                on,off,desirable,auto,nonegotiate
Channel                   no
Broadcast suppression     pps(0-150000)
Flow control              no
Security                  yes
Membership                static,dynamic
Fast start                yes
```

Step 3   Verify that the ports are connected and operational. Before connecting the cables, the port status is as follows:

```
Switch-A show port
Port  Name               Status       Vlan        Level  Duplex Speed Type
----- ------------------ ----------   ----------   ------ ------ ----- ------------
 2/1                     notconnect 1              normal  auto  auto 10/100BaseTX
 2/2                     notconnect 1              normal  auto  auto 10/100BaseTX
 2/3                     notconnect 1              normal  auto  auto 10/100BaseTX
 2/4                     notconnect 1              normal  auto  auto 10/100BaseTX
```

After connecting the cables between the two switches, the status is as follows:

```
1999 Dec 14 20:32:44 %PAGP-5-PORTTOSTP:Port 2/1 joined bridge port 2/1
1999 Dec 14 20:32:44 %PAGP-5-PORTTOSTP:Port 2/2 joined bridge port 2/2
1999 Dec 14 20:32:44 %PAGP-5-PORTTOSTP:Port 2/3 joined bridge port 2/3
1999 Dec 14 20:32:44 %PAGP-5-PORTTOSTP:Port 2/4 joined bridge port 2/4
```

```
Switch-A show port
Port  Name               Status       Vlan        Level  Duplex Speed Type
----- ------------------ ----------   ----------   ------ ------ ----- ------------
 2/1                     connected  1              normal a-full a-100 10/100BaseTX
 2/2                     connected  1              normal a-full a-100 10/100BaseTX
 2/3                     connected  1              normal a-full a-100 10/100BaseTX
 2/4                     connected  1              normal a-full a-100 10/100BaseTX
```

```
Switch-B show port
Port  Name                 Status      Vlan      Level  Duplex Speed Type
----- -------------------- ---------- ----------  ------ ------ ----- ------------
2/1                        connected  1           normal a-full a-100 10/100BaseTX
2/2                        connected  1           normal a-full a-100 10/100BaseTX
2/3                        connected  1           normal a-full a-100 10/100BaseTX
2/4                        connected  1           normal a-full a-100 10/100BaseTX
```

Because the switch configurations were cleared before starting this test, the ports are in their default conditions. They are all in vlan1, and their speed and duplex are set to auto. After connecting the cables, they negotiate to a speed of 100 Mbps and full-duplex mode. The status is connected, so we can **ping** the other switch.

```
Switch-A ping 172.16.84.17
172.16.84.17 is alive
```

In your network, you may want to set the speeds manually to 100 Mbps and full-duplex mode instead of relying on autonegotiation because you will probably want your ports to always run at the fastest speed. For a discussion of autonegotiation, see the section "Troubleshooting Ethernet 10-/100-Mb Half-/Full-Duplex Autonegotiation."

Step 4   Verify that the ports to be grouped have the same settings. This is an important point and will be covered in more detail in the troubleshooting section. If the command to set up EtherChannel doesn't work, it is usually because the ports involved in the channel have differing configurations. This includes the ports on the other side of the link as well as the local ports. In our case, because the switch configurations were cleared before starting this test, the ports are in their default conditions. They are all in VLAN1, their speed and duplex are set to auto, and all spanning-tree parameters for each port are set the same. We saw from the previous output that after the cables are connected, the ports negotiate to a speed of 100 Mbps and full-duplex mode. Because Spanning-Tree Protocol runs for each VLAN, it is easier to just configure the channel and respond to error messages than to try to check every spanning-tree field for consistency for each port and VLAN in the channel.

Step 5 Identify valid port groups. On the Catalyst 5000, only certain ports can be put together into a channel. These restrictive dependencies do not apply to all platforms. The ports in a channel on a Catalyst 5000 must be contiguous. Notice from the **show port capabilities** command that for port 2/1, the possible combinations are these:

```
Switch-A show port capabilities
Model                    WS-X5225R
Port                     2/1
...
Channel                  2/1-2,2/1-4
```

Notice that this port can be a part of a group of two (2/1-2) or part of a group of four (2/1-4). An Ethernet Bundling Controller (EBC) on the module causes these configuration limitations. Let's look at another port.

```
Switch-A show port capabilities 2/3
Model                    WS-X5225R
Port                     2/3
...
Channel                  2/3-4,2/1-4
```

This port can be grouped into a group of two ports (2/3-4) or into a group of four (2/1-4).

NOTE Depending on the hardware, there might be additional restrictions. On certain modules (WS-X5201 and WS-X5203), you cannot form an EtherChannel with the last two ports in a "port group" unless the first two ports in the group already form an EtherChannel. A port group is a group of ports that are allowed to form an EtherChannel (2/1-4 is a port group in the previous example). For example, if you are creating separate EtherChannels with only *two* ports in a channel, you cannot assign ports 2/3-4 to a channel until you have first configured ports 2/1-2 to a channel, for the modules that have this restriction. Likewise, before configuring ports 2/6-7, you must configure ports 2/5-6. This restriction does not occur on the modules used for this document (WS-X5225R, WS-X5234).

Because we are configuring a group of four ports (2/1-4), this is within the approved grouping. We would not be able to assign a group of four to ports 2/3-6. This is a group of contiguous ports, but they do not start on the approved boundary, as shown by the **show port capabilities** command (valid groups would be ports 1-4, 5-8, 9-12, 13-16, 17-20, and 21-24).

Step 6   Create the channel. To create the channel, use the command **set port channel <mod/port on** for each switch. We recommend turning off the ports on one side of the channel using the **set port disable** command before turning on EtherChannel manually. This will avoid possible problems with Spanning-Tree Protocol during the configuration process. Spanning-Tree Protocol could shut down some ports (with a port status of errdisable) if one side is configured as a channel before the other side can be configured as a channel. Because of this possibility, it is much easier to create EtherChannels using PAgP, which we will cover in the section " Using PAgP to Configure EtherChannel " coming up later in this chapter. To avoid this situation when configuring EtherChannel manually, we will disable the ports on Switch A, configure the channel on Switch A, configure the channel on Switch B, and *then* re-enable the ports on Switch A.

First verify that channeling is off.

```
Switch-A (enable) show port channel
No ports channelling
Switch-B (enable) show port channel
No ports channelling
```

Now disable the ports on Switch A until both switches have been configured for EtherChannel so that Spanning-Tree Protocol will not generate errors and shut down the ports.

```
Switch-A (enable) set port disable 2/1-4
Ports 2/1-4 disabled.
[output from SwitchA upon disabling ports]
1999 Dec 15 00:06:40 %PAGP-5-PORTFROMSTP:Port 2/1 left bridg1
1999 Dec 15 00:06:40 %PAGP-5-PORTFROMSTP:Port 2/2 left bridge port 2/2
1999 Dec 15 00:06:40 %PAGP-5-PORTFROMSTP:Port 2/3 left bridge port 2/3
1999 Dec 15 00:06:40 %PAGP-5-PORTFROMSTP:Port 2/4 left bridge port 2/4
```

Turn the channel mode to on for Switch A.

```
Switch-A (enable) set port channel 2/1-4 on
Port(s) 2/1-4 channel mode set to on.
```

Check the status of the channel. Notice that the channel mode has been set to on, but the status of the ports is disabled (because we disabled them earlier). The channel is not operational at this point, but it will become operational when the ports are enabled.

```
Switch-A (enable) show port channel
Port  Status      Channel    Channel      Neighbor                   Neighbor
                  mode       status       device                     port
----- ---------- --------- ----------- ------------------------- ----------
 2/1  disabled    on         channel
 2/2  disabled    on         channel
 2/3  disabled    on         channel
 2/4  disabled    on         channel
----- ---------- --------- ----------- ------------------------- ----------
```

Because Switch A ports were (temporarily) disabled, Switch B ports no longer have a connection. The following message is displayed on Switch B's console when Switch A ports were disabled.

```
Switch-B (enable)
2000 Jan 13 22:30:03 %PAGP-5-PORTFROMSTP:Port 2/1 left bridge port 2/1
2000 Jan 13 22:30:04 %PAGP-5-PORTFROMSTP:Port 2/2 left bridge port 2/2
2000 Jan 13 22:30:04 %PAGP-5-PORTFROMSTP:Port 2/3 left bridge port 2/3
2000 Jan 13 22:30:04 %PAGP-5-PORTFROMSTP:Port 2/4 left bridge port 2/4
```

Turn on the channel for Switch B.

```
Switch-B (enable) set port channel 2/1-4 on
Port(s) 2/1-4 channel mode set to on.
```

Verify that channel mode is on for Switch B.

```
Switch-B (enable) show port channel
Port  Status      Channel    Channel      Neighbor                   Neighbor
                  mode       status       device                     port
----- ---------- --------- ----------- ------------------------- ----------
 2/1  notconnect  on         channel
 2/2  notconnect  on         channel
 2/3  notconnect  on         channel
 2/4  notconnect  on         channel
----- ---------- --------- ----------- ------------------------- ----------
```

Notice that the channel mode for Switch B is on, but the status of the ports is notconnect. That is because Switch A ports are still disabled.

Finally, the last step is to enable the ports on Switch A.

```
Switch-A (enable) set port enable 2/1-4
Ports 2/1-4 enabled.
1999 Dec 15 00:08:40 %PAGP-5-PORTTOSTP:Port 2/1 joined bridge port 2/1-4
1999 Dec 15 00:08:40 %PAGP-5-PORTTOSTP:Port 2/2 joined bridge port 2/1-4
1999 Dec 15 00:08:40 %PAGP-5-PORTTOSTP:Port 2/3 joined bridge port 2/1-4
1999 Dec 15 00:08:40 %PAGP-5-PORTTOSTP:Port 2/4 joined bridge port 2/1-4
```

Verifying the EtherChannel Configuration

To verify that the channel is set up properly, use the **show port channel** command.

```
Switch-A (enable) show port channel
Port   Status      Channel     Channel     Neighbor                          Neighbor
                   mode        status      device                            port
-----  ----------  ----------  ----------  -----------------------------     ----------
2/1    connected   on          channel     WS-C5505      066509957(Sw        2/1
2/2    connected   on          channel     WS-C5505      066509957(Sw        2/2
2/3    connected   on          channel     WS-C5505      066509957(Sw        2/3
2/4    connected   on          channel     WS-C5505      066509957(Sw        2/4
-----  ----------  ----------  ----------  -----------------------------     ----------


Switch-B (enable) show port channel
Port   Status      Channel     Channel     Neighbor                          Neighbor
                   mode        status      device                            port
-----  ----------  ----------  ----------  -----------------------------     ----------
2/1    connected   on          channel     WS-C5505      066507453(Sw        2/1
2/2    connected   on          channel     WS-C5505      066507453(Sw        2/2
2/3    connected   on          channel     WS-C5505      066507453(Sw        2/3
2/4    connected   on          channel     WS-C5505      066507453(Sw        2/4
-----  ----------  ----------  ----------  -----------------------------     ----------
```

Spanning-Tree Protocol is shown to treat the ports as one logical port in the following command. In the following output, when the port is listed as 2/1-4, this means that Spanning-Tree Protocol is treating ports 2/1, 2/2, 2/3, and 2/4 as one port.

```
Switch-A (enable) show spantree
VLAN 1
Spanning tree enabled
Spanning tree type           ieee

Designated Root              00-10-0d-b2-8c-00
Designated Root Priority     32768
Designated Root Cost         8
Designated Root Port         2/1-4
Root Max Age   20 sec     Hello Time 2  sec    Forward Delay 15 sec

Bridge ID MAC ADDR           00-90-92-b0-84-00
Bridge ID Priority           32768
Bridge Max Age 20 sec     Hello Time 2  sec    Forward Delay 15 sec

Port       Vlan  Port-State    Cost    Priority  Fast-Start  Group-Method
---------  ----  ------------  -----   --------  ----------  ------------
2/1-4      1     forwarding       8         32   disabled    channel
```

EtherChannel can be implemented with different ways of distributing the traffic across the ports in a channel. The EtherChannel specification does not dictate how the traffic should be distributed across the links in a channel. The Catalyst 5000 uses the last bit or the last 2 bits (depending on how many links are in the channel) of the source and destination MAC addresses in the frame to determine which port in the channel to use. You should see similar amounts of traffic on each of the ports in the channel, assuming that traffic is generated by a normal distribution of MAC addresses on one side of the channel. To verify that traffic is going over all the ports in the channel, you can use the **show mac** command. If your ports were active before configuring EtherChannel, then you may reset the traffic counters to zero by the **clear counters** command. Then the traffic values will represent how EtherChannel has distributed the traffic.

In our test environment, we did not get a real-world distribution because no workstations, servers, or routers are generating traffic. The only devices generating traffic are the switches themselves. We issued some **ping**s from Switch A to Switch B, and you can tell from the following output that the unicast traffic is using the first port in the channel. The Receive information in this case (Rcv-Unicast) shows how Switch B distributed the traffic across the channel to Switch A. A little lower in the output, the Transmit information (Xmit-Unicast) shows how Switch A distributed the traffic across the channel to Switch B. We also see here that a small amount of switch-generated multicast traffic (Dynamic ISL, CDP) goes out all four ports. The broadcast packets are ARP queries (for the default gateway, which doesn't exist in our lab here). If we had workstations sending packets through the switch to a destination on the other side of the channel, we would expect to see traffic going over each of the four links in the channel. You can monitor the packet distribution in your own network using the **show mac** command.

```
Switch-A (enable) clear counters
This command will reset all MAC and port counters reported in CLI and SNMP.
Do you want to continue (y/n) [n]? y
MAC and Port counters cleared.
Switch-A (enable) show mac
```

Port	Rcv-Unicast	Rcv-Multicast	Rcv-Broadcast
2/1	9	320	183
2/2	0	51	0
2/3	0	47	0
2/4	0	47	0
(...)			

Port	Xmit-Unicast	Xmit-Multicast	Xmit-Broadcast
2/1	8	47	184
2/2	0	47	0
2/3	0	47	0
2/4	0	47	0
(...)			

Port	Rcv-Octet	Xmit-Octet
2/1	35176	17443
2/2	5304	4851
2/3	5048	4851
2/4	5048	4851
(...)		

```
Last-Time-Cleared
-------------------------
Wed Dec 15 1999, 01:05:33
```

Using PAgP to Automatically Configure EtherChannel (Preferred Method)

The Port Aggregation Protocol (PAgP) facilitates the automatic creation of EtherChannel links by exchanging packets between channel-capable ports. The protocol learns the capabilities of port groups dynamically and informs the neighboring ports.

When PAgP identifies correctly paired channel-capable links, it groups the ports into a channel. The channel is then added to the spanning tree as a single bridge port. A given outbound broadcast or multicast packet is transmitted out one port in the channel only, not out every port in the channel. In addition, outbound broadcast and multicast packets transmitted on one port in a channel are blocked from returning on any other port of the channel.

Four user-configurable channel modes exist: on, off, auto, and desirable. PAgP packets are exchanged only between ports in auto and desirable modes. Ports configured in on or off modes do not exchange PAgP packets. The recommended settings for switches that you want to form and EtherChannel is to have both switches set to desirable mode. This gives the most robust behavior in case one side encounters error situations or must be reset. The default mode of the channel is auto.

Both the auto and desirable modes allow ports to negotiate with connected ports to determine whether they can form a channel, based on criteria such as port speed, trunking state, native VLAN, and so on.

Ports can form an EtherChannel when they are in different channel modes, as long as the modes are compatible. For example:

- A port in desirable mode can form an EtherChannel successfully with another port that is in desirable or auto mode.

- A port in auto mode can form an EtherChannel with another port in desirable mode.

- A port in auto mode cannot form an EtherChannel with another port that is also in auto mode because neither port will initiate negotiation.

- A port in on mode can form a channel only with a port in on mode because ports in on mode do not exchange PAgP packets.

- A port in off mode will not form a channel with any port.

When using EtherChannel, if a "SPANTREE-2: Channel misconfig—*x/x-x* will be disabled" or similar syslog message is displayed, it indicates a mismatch of EtherChannel modes on the connected ports. We recommend that you correct the configuration and re-enable the ports by entering the **set port enable** command. Valid EtherChannel configurations include these:

Port Channel Mode	Valid Neighbor Port Channel Mode(s)
Desirable	Desirable or auto
Auto (default)[1]	Desirable or auto
On	On
Off	Off

[1]If both the local and neighbor ports are in auto mode, an EtherChannel bundle will not form.

Table 23-4 is a summary of all the possible channeling mode scenarios. Some of these combinations may cause the Spanning-Tree Protocol to put the ports on the channeling side into errdisable state (that is, shut them down).

Table 23-4 *Summary of All Possible Channeling Mode Scenarios*

Switch A Channel Mode	Switch B Channel Mode	Channel State
On	On	Channel
On	Off	Not Channel (errdisable)
On	Auto	Not Channel (errdisable)
On	Desirable	Not Channel (errdisable)
Off	On	Not Channel (errdisable)
Off	Off	Not Channel
Off	Auto	Not Channel
Off	Desirable	Not Channel
Auto	On	Not Channel (errdisable)
Auto	Off	Not Channel
Auto	Auto	Not Channel
Auto	Desirable	Channel
Desirable	On	Not Channel (errdisable)
Desirable	Off	Not Channel
Desirable	Auto	Channel
Desirable	Desirable	Channel

We turned off the channel from the previous example using the following command on Switch A and Switch B:

```
Switch-A (enable) set port channel 2/1-4 auto
Port(s) 2/1-4 channel mode set to auto.
```

The default channel mode for a port that is capable of channeling is auto. To verify this, enter the following command:

```
Switch-A (enable) show port channel 2/1
Port   Status      Channel     Channel     Neighbor                    Neighbor
                   mode        status      device                      port
-----  ----------  ----------  ----------  --------------------------  ----------
 2/1   connected   auto        not channel
```

The previous command also shows that currently the ports are not channeling. Another way to verify the channel state is as follows:

```
Switch-A (enable) show port channel
No ports channelling
Switch-B (enable) show port channel
No ports channelling
```

To make the channel work with PAgP is really very simple. At this point, both switches are set to auto mode, which means that they will channel if a connected port sends a PAgP request to channel. Setting Switch A to desirable causes Switch A to send PAgP packets to the other switch, asking it to channel.

```
Switch-A (enable) set port channel 2/1-4 desirable
Port(s) 2/1-4 channel mode set to desirable.
1999 Dec 15 22:03:18 %PAGP-5-PORTFROMSTP:Port 2/1 left bridg1
1999 Dec 15 22:03:18 %PAGP-5-PORTFROMSTP:Port 2/2 left bridge port 2/2
1999 Dec 15 22:03:18 %PAGP-5-PORTFROMSTP:Port 2/3 left bridge port 2/3
1999 Dec 15 22:03:18 %PAGP-5-PORTFROMSTP:Port 2/4 left bridge port 2/4
1999 Dec 15 22:03:19 %PAGP-5-PORTFROMSTP:Port 2/2 left bridge port 2/2
1999 Dec 15 22:03:19 %PAGP-5-PORTFROMSTP:Port 2/3 left bridge port 2/3
1999 Dec 15 22:03:20 %PAGP-5-PORTFROMSTP:Port 2/4 left bridge port 2/4
1999 Dec 15 22:03:23 %PAGP-5-PORTTOSTP:Port 2/1 joined bridge port 2/1-4
1999 Dec 15 22:03:23 %PAGP-5-PORTTOSTP:Port 2/2 joined bridge port 2/1-4
1999 Dec 15 22:03:23 %PAGP-5-PORTTOSTP:Port 2/3 joined bridge port 2/1-4
1999 Dec 15 22:03:24 %PAGP-5-PORTTOSTP:Port 2/4 joined bridge port 2/1-4
```

To view the channel, do as follows:

```
Switch-A (enable) show port channel
Port  Status     Channel    Channel    Neighbor                      Neighbor
                 mode       status     device                        port
----- ---------- ---------- ---------- ----------------------------- ----------
 2/1  connected  desirable  channel    WS-C5505   066509957(Sw  2/1
 2/2  connected  desirable  channel    WS-C5505   066509957(Sw  2/2
 2/3  connected  desirable  channel    WS-C5505   066509957(Sw  2/3
 2/4  connected  desirable  channel    WS-C5505   066509957(Sw  2/4
----- ---------- ---------- ---------- ----------------------------- ----------
```

Because Switch B was in auto mode, it responded to the PAgP packets and created a channel with Switch A.

```
Switch-B (enable)
2000 Jan 14 20:26:41 %PAGP-5-PORTFROMSTP:Port 2/1 left bridg1
2000 Jan 14 20:26:41 %PAGP-5-PORTFROMSTP:Port 2/2 left bridge port 2/2
2000 Jan 14 20:26:41 %PAGP-5-PORTFROMSTP:Port 2/3 left bridge port 2/3
2000 Jan 14 20:26:41 %PAGP-5-PORTFROMSTP:Port 2/4 left bridge port 2/4
2000 Jan 14 20:26:45 %PAGP-5-PORTFROMSTP:Port 2/2 left bridge port 2/2
2000 Jan 14 20:26:45 %PAGP-5-PORTFROMSTP:Port 2/3 left bridge port 2/3
2000 Jan 14 20:26:45 %PAGP-5-PORTFROMSTP:Port 2/4 left bridge port 2/4
2000 Jan 14 20:26:47 %PAGP-5-PORTTOSTP:Port 2/1 joined bridge port 2/1-4
2000 Jan 14 20:26:47 %PAGP-5-PORTTOSTP:Port 2/2 joined bridge port 2/1-4
2000 Jan 14 20:26:47 %PAGP-5-PORTTOSTP:Port 2/3 joined bridge port 2/1-4
2000 Jan 14 20:26:48 %PAGP-5-PORTTOSTP:Port 2/4 joined bridge port 2/1-4
```

```
Switch-B (enable) show port channel
Port  Status       Channel   Channel      Neighbor                           Neighbor
                   mode      status       device                             port
----- ----------   --------- ----------   -------------------------------    ----------
2/1   connected    auto      channel      WS-C5505  066507453(Sw  2/1
2/2   connected    auto      channel      WS-C5505  066507453(Sw  2/2
2/3   connected    auto      channel      WS-C5505  066507453(Sw  2/3
2/4   connected    auto      channel      WS-C5505  066507453(Sw  2/4
----- ----------   --------- ----------   -------------------------------    ----------
```

NOTE   It is recommended to set both sides of the channel to desirable so that both sides will try to initiate the channel in case one side drops out. Setting the EtherChannel ports on Switch B to desirable mode, even though the channel is currently active and in auto mode, poses no problem. The command is as follows:

```
Switch-B (enable) set port channel 2/1-4 desirable
Port(s) 2/1-4 channel mode set to desirable.

Switch-B (enable) show port channel
Port  Status       Channel   Channel      Neighbor                           Neighbor
                   mode      status       device                             port
----- ----------   --------- ----------   -------------------------------    ----------
2/1   connected    desirable channel      WS-C5505  066507453(Sw  2/1
2/2   connected    desirable channel      WS-C5505  066507453(Sw  2/2
2/3   connected    desirable channel      WS-C5505  066507453(Sw  2/3
2/4   connected    desirable channel      WS-C5505  066507453(Sw  2/4
----- ----------   --------- ----------   -------------------------------    ----------
```

Now if Switch A drops out for some reason, or if new hardware replaces Switch A, then Switch B will try to re-establish the channel. If the new equipment cannot channel, then Switch B will treat its ports 2/1-4 as normal nonchanneling ports. This is one of the benefits of using the desirable mode. If the channel was configured by using the PAgP on mode and one side of the connection has an error of some kind or a reset, it could cause an errdisable state (shutdown) on the other side. With PAgP set in desirable mode on each side. The channel will stabilize and renegotiate the EtherChannel connection.

Trunking and EtherChannel

EtherChannel is independent of trunking. You can turn trunking on, or you can leave trunking off. You also can turn on trunking for all the ports before creating the channel, or you can turn it on after creating the channel (as we will do here). As far as EtherChannel is concerned, it does not matter; trunking and EtherChannel are completely separate features. What does matter is that all the ports involved are in the same mode: Either they are all trunking before you configure the channel, or they are all not trunking before you configure the channel. All the ports must be in the same trunking state before creating the channel.

After a channel is formed, whatever is changed on one port is also changed for the other ports in the channel. The modules used in this test bed can do ISL or 802.1q trunking. By default, the modules are set to auto trunking and negotiate mode, which means that they will trunk if the other side asks them to trunk, and they will negotiate whether to use the ISL or 802.1q method for trunking. If they are not asked to trunk, they will work as normal nontrunking ports.

```
Switch-A (enable) show trunk 2
Port      Mode         Encapsulation  Status        Native vlan
--------  -----------  -------------  ------------  -----------
  2/1     auto         negotiate      not-trunking  1
  2/2     auto         negotiate      not-trunking  1
  2/3     auto         negotiate      not-trunking  1
  2/4     auto         negotiate      not-trunking  1
```

There are a number of different ways to turn on trunking. For this example, we will set Switch A to desirable. Switch A is already set to negotiate. The combination desirable/ negotiate will cause Switch A to ask Switch B to trunk and to negotiate the type of trunking to do (ISL or 802.1q). Because Switch B defaults to autonegotiate, Switch B will respond to Switch A's request. The following results occur:

```
Switch-A (enable) set trunk 2/1 desirable
Port(s) 2/1-4 trunk mode set to desirable.
Switch-A (enable)
1999 Dec 18 20:46:25 %DTP-5-TRUNKPORTON:Port 2/1 has become isl trunk
1999 Dec 18 20:46:25 %DTP-5-TRUNKPORTON:Port 2/2 has become isl trunk
1999 Dec 18 20:46:25 %PAGP-5-PORTFROMSTP:Port 2/1 left bridge port 2/1-4
1999 Dec 18 20:46:25 %PAGP-5-PORTFROMSTP:Port 2/2 left bridge port 2/1-4
1999 Dec 18 20:46:25 %DTP-5-TRUNKPORTON:Port 2/3 has become isl trunk
1999 Dec 18 20:46:26 %PAGP-5-PORTFROMSTP:Port 2/3 left bridge port 2/1-4
1999 Dec 18 20:46:26 %DTP-5-TRUNKPORTON:Port 2/4 has become isl trunk
1999 Dec 18 20:46:26 %PAGP-5-PORTFROMSTP:Port 2/4 left bridge port 2/1-4
1999 Dec 18 20:46:28 %PAGP-5-PORTTOSTP:Port 2/1 joined bridge port 2/1-4
1999 Dec 18 20:46:29 %PAGP-5-PORTTOSTP:Port 2/2 joined bridge port 2/1-4
1999 Dec 18 20:46:29 %PAGP-5-PORTTOSTP:Port 2/3 joined bridge port 2/1-4
1999 Dec 18 20:46:29 %PAGP-5-PORTTOSTP:Port 2/4 joined bridge port 2/1-4

Switch-A (enable) show trunk 2
Port      Mode         Encapsulation  Status        Native vlan
--------  -----------  -------------  ------------  -----------
  2/1     desirable    n-isl          trunking      1
  2/2     desirable    n-isl          trunking      1
  2/3     desirable    n-isl          trunking      1
  2/4     desirable    n-isl          trunking      1
```

The trunk mode was set to desirable. The result was that trunking mode was negotiated with the neighbor switch, and both decided on ISL (*n-isl*). The current status now is *trunking*. The following shows what happened on Switch B because of the command issued on Switch A.

```
Switch-B (enable)
2000 Jan 17 19:09:52 %DTP-5-TRUNKPORTON:Port 2/1 has become isl trunk
2000 Jan 17 19:09:52 %DTP-5-TRUNKPORTON:Port 2/2 has become isl trunk
2000 Jan 17 19:09:52 %PAGP-5-PORTFROMSTP:Port 2/1 left bridge port 2/1-4
2000 Jan 17 19:09:52 %DTP-5-TRUNKPORTON:Port 2/3 has become isl trunk
2000 Jan 17 19:09:52 %PAGP-5-PORTFROMSTP:Port 2/2 left bridge port 2/1-4
2000 Jan 17 19:09:53 %DTP-5-TRUNKPORTON:Port 2/4 has become isl trunk
2000 Jan 17 19:09:53 %PAGP-5-PORTFROMSTP:Port 2/3 left bridge port 2/1-4
2000 Jan 17 19:09:53 %PAGP-5-PORTFROMSTP:Port 2/4 left bridge port 2/1-4
2000 Jan 17 19:09:55 %PAGP-5-PORTTOSTP:Port 2/1 joined bridge port 2/1-4
2000 Jan 17 19:09:55 %PAGP-5-PORTTOSTP:Port 2/2 joined bridge port 2/1-4
2000 Jan 17 19:09:55 %PAGP-5-PORTTOSTP:Port 2/3 joined bridge port 2/1-4
2000 Jan 17 19:09:55 %PAGP-5-PORTTOSTP:Port 2/4 joined bridge port 2/1-4

Switch-B (enable) show trunk 2
Port      Mode          Encapsulation   Status        Native vlan
--------  -----------   -------------   -----------   -----------
  2/1     auto          n-isl           trunking      1
  2/2     auto          n-isl           trunking      1
  2/3     auto          n-isl           trunking      1
  2/4     auto          n-isl           trunking      1
```

Notice that all four ports (2/1-4) became trunking even though we specifically change only one port (2/1) to desirable. This is an example of how changing one port in the channel affects all the ports.

Troubleshooting EtherChannel

The challenges for EtherChannel can be divided into two main areas: troubleshooting during the configuration phase, and troubleshooting during the execution phase. Configuration errors usually occur because of mismatched parameters on the ports involved (different speeds, different duplex, different spanning-tree port values, and so on). But you can also generate errors during the configuration by setting the channel on one side to on and waiting too long before configuring the channel on the other side. This causes spanning tree loops, which generate an error and shut down the port.

When an error is encountered while configuring EtherChannel, be sure to check the status of the ports after correcting the EtherChannel error situation. If the port status is errdisable, the ports have been shut down by the software, and they will not come on again until you enter the **set port enable** command.

NOTE   If the port status becomes errdisable, you must specifically enable the ports using the **set port enable** command for the ports to become active. Currently, you can correct all the EtherChannel issues, but the ports will not come up or form a channel until they are enabled again. Future versions of the operating system may periodically check whether errdisable ports should be enabled.

For the following tests, we will turn off trunking and EtherChannel. The following topics will be covered:

- Setting mismatched parameters
- Waiting too long before configuring the other side
- Correcting errdisable state
- Showing what happens when a link breaks and is restored

Setting Mismatched Parameters

This section examines an example of mismatched parameters. We will set port 2/4 in VLAN 2 while the other ports are still in VLAN 1. To create a new VLAN, we must assign a VTP domain for the switch and then create the VLAN.

```
Switch-A (enable) show port channel
No ports channelling


Switch-A (enable) show port
Port  Name               Status     Vlan       Level  Duplex Speed Type
----- ------------------ ---------- ---------- ------ ------ ----- ------------
 2/1                     connected  1          normal a-full a-100 10/100BaseTX
 2/2                     connected  1          normal a-full a-100 10/100BaseTX
 2/3                     connected  1          normal a-full a-100 10/100BaseTX
 2/4                     connected  1          normal a-full a-100 10/100BaseTX

Switch-A (enable) set vlan 2
Cannot add/modify VLANs on a VTP server without a domain name.

Switch-A (enable) set vtp domain testDomain
VTP domain testDomain modified

Switch-A (enable) set vlan 2 name vlan2
Vlan 2 configuration successful

Switch-A (enable) set vlan 2 2/4
VLAN 2 modified.
VLAN 1 modified.
VLAN  Mod/Ports
----  ----------------------
2     2/4

Switch-A (enable)
1999 Dec 19 00:19:34 %PAGP-5-PORTFROMSTP:Port 2/4 left bridg4

Switch-A (enable) show port
Port  Name               Status     Vlan       Level  Duplex Speed Type
----- ------------------ ---------- ---------- ------ ------ ----- ------------
 2/1                     connected  1          normal a-full a-100 10/100BaseTX
 2/2                     connected  1          normal a-full a-100 10/100BaseTX
 2/3                     connected  1          normal a-full a-100 10/100BaseTX
 2/4                     connected  2          normal a-full a-100 10/100BaseTX

Switch-A (enable) set port channel 2/1-4 desirable
Port(s) 2/1-4 channel mode set to desirable.
```

```
Switch-A (enable)
1999 Dec 19 00:20:19 %PAGP-5-PORTFROMSTP:Port 2/1 left bridge port 2/1
1999 Dec 19 00:20:19 %PAGP-5-PORTFROMSTP:Port 2/2 left bridge port 2/2
1999 Dec 19 00:20:19 %PAGP-5-PORTFROMSTP:Port 2/3 left bridge port 2/3
1999 Dec 19 00:20:20 %PAGP-5-PORTFROMSTP:Port 2/4 left bridge port 2/4
1999 Dec 19 00:20:20 %PAGP-5-PORTFROMSTP:Port 2/2 left bridge port 2/2
1999 Dec 19 00:20:22 %PAGP-5-PORTFROMSTP:Port 2/3 left bridge port 2/3
1999 Dec 19 00:20:22 %PAGP-5-PORTFROMSTP:Port 2/4 left bridge port 2/4
1999 Dec 19 00:20:24 %PAGP-5-PORTTOSTP:Port 2/1 joined bridge port 2/1-2
1999 Dec 19 00:20:25 %PAGP-5-PORTTOSTP:Port 2/2 joined bridge port 2/1-2
1999 Dec 19 00:20:25 %PAGP-5-PORTTOSTP:Port 2/3 joined bridge port 2/3
1999 Dec 19 00:20:25 %PAGP-5-PORTTOSTP:Port 2/4 joined bridge port 2/4


Switch-A (enable) show port channel
Port  Status     Channel    Channel    Neighbor                    Neighbor
                 mode       status     device                      port
----- ---------- ---------- ---------- ------------------------- ----------
 2/1  connected  desirable  channel    WS-C5505  066509957(Sw  2/1
 2/2  connected  desirable  channel    WS-C5505  066509957(Sw  2/2
----- ---------- ---------- ---------- ------------------------- ----------
```

Notice that the channel formed only between ports 2/1 and 2/2. Ports 2/3 and 2/4 were left out because port 2/4 was in a different VLAN. There was no error message; PAgP just did what it could to make the channel work. You need to watch the results when you create the channel to make sure that it did what you wanted it to do.

Now let's set the channel manually to on with port 2/4 in a different VLAN and see what happens. First, we will set the channel mode back to auto to tear down the existing channel, and then we will set the channel manually to on.

```
Switch-A (enable) set port channel 2/1-4 auto
Port(s) 2/1-4 channel mode set to auto.
Switch-A (enable)
1999 Dec 19 00:26:08 %PAGP-5-PORTFROMSTP:Port 2/1 left bridge port 2/1-2
1999 Dec 19 00:26:08 %PAGP-5-PORTFROMSTP:Port 2/2 left bridge port 2/1-2
1999 Dec 19 00:26:08 %PAGP-5-PORTFROMSTP:Port 2/3 left bridge port 2/3
1999 Dec 19 00:26:08 %PAGP-5-PORTFROMSTP:Port 2/4 left bridge port 2/4
1999 Dec 19 00:26:18 %PAGP-5-PORTTOSTP:Port 2/1 joined bridge port 2/1
1999 Dec 19 00:26:19 %PAGP-5-PORTTOSTP:Port 2/2 joined bridge port 2/2
1999 Dec 19 00:26:19 %PAGP-5-PORTTOSTP:Port 2/3 joined bridge port 2/3
1999 Dec 19 00:26:19 %PAGP-5-PORTTOSTP:Port 2/4 joined bridge port 2/4

Switch-A (enable) show port channel
No ports channelling

Switch-A (enable) set port channel 2/1-4 on
Mismatch in vlan number.
Failed to set port(s) 2/1-4 channel mode to on.

Switch-A (enable) show port channel
No ports channelling
```

On Switch B, we can turn on the channel—notice that it indicates that the ports are channeling fine, but we know that Switch A is not configured correctly.

```
Switch-B (enable) show port channel
No ports channelling
```

```
Switch-B (enable) show port
Port  Name               Status      Vlan       Level  Duplex Speed Type
----- ------------------ ----------- ---------- ------ ------ ----- ------------
 2/1                     connected   1          normal a-full a-100 10/100BaseTX
 2/2                     connected   1          normal a-full a-100 10/100BaseTX
 2/3                     connected   1          normal a-full a-100 10/100BaseTX
 2/4                     connected   1          normal a-full a-100 10/100BaseTX

Switch-B (enable) set port channel 2/1-4 on
Port(s) 2/1-4 channel mode set to on.

Switch-B (enable)
2000 Jan 17 22:54:59 %PAGP-5-PORTFROMSTP:Port 2/1 left bridge port 2/1
2000 Jan 17 22:54:59 %PAGP-5-PORTFROMSTP:Port 2/2 left bridge port 2/2
2000 Jan 17 22:54:59 %PAGP-5-PORTFROMSTP:Port 2/3 left bridge port 2/3
2000 Jan 17 22:54:59 %PAGP-5-PORTFROMSTP:Port 2/4 left bridge port 2/4
2000 Jan 17 22:55:00 %PAGP-5-PORTTOSTP:Port 2/1 joined bridge port 2/1-4
2000 Jan 17 22:55:00 %PAGP-5-PORTTOSTP:Port 2/2 joined bridge port 2/1-4
2000 Jan 17 22:55:00 %PAGP-5-PORTTOSTP:Port 2/3 joined bridge port 2/1-4
2000 Jan 17 22:55:00 %PAGP-5-PORTTOSTP:Port 2/4 joined bridge port 2/1-4

Switch-B (enable) show port channel
Port  Status     Channel    Channel    Neighbor                    Neighbor
                 mode       status     device                      port
----- ---------- ---------- ---------- --------------------------- ----------
 2/1  connected  on         channel    WS-C5505   066507453(Sw     2/1
 2/2  connected  on         channel    WS-C5505   066507453(Sw     2/2
 2/3  connected  on         channel    WS-C5505   066507453(Sw     2/3
 2/4  connected  on         channel    WS-C5505   066507453(Sw     2/4
----- ---------- ---------- ---------- --------------------------- ----------
```

This makes it clear that you must check both sides of the channel when manually configuring the channel to make sure that both sides are up, not just one side. The previous output shows that Switch B is set for a channel, but Switch A is not channeling because it has one port that is in the wrong vlan.

Waiting Too Long Before Configuring the Other Side

In our situation, Switch B has EtherChannel turned on, but Switch A does not have EtherChannel turned on because it has a VLAN configuration error (ports 2/1-3 are in VLAN 1, and port 2/4 is in VLAN 2). Here is what happens when one side of a EtherChannel is set to on while the other side is still in auto mode: After a few minutes, Switch B shut down its ports because of a spanning-tree loop detection. This is because Switch B ports 2/1-4 all act like one big port, while Switch A ports 2/1-4 are all totally independent ports. A broadcast sent from Switch B to Switch A on port 2/1 will be sent back to Switch B on ports 2/2, 2/3, and 2/4 because Switch A treats these ports as independent ports. This is why Switch B thinks there is a spanning-tree loop. Notice that the ports on Switch B are now disabled and have a status of errdisable.

```
Switch-B (enable)
2000 Jan 17 22:55:48 %SPANTREE-2-CHNMISCFG: STP loop - channel 2/1-4 is disabled in vlan 1.
2000 Jan 17 22:55:49 %PAGP-5-PORTFROMSTP:Port 2/1 left bridge port 2/1-4
2000 Jan 17 22:56:01 %PAGP-5-PORTFROMSTP:Port 2/2 left bridge port 2/1-4
2000 Jan 17 22:56:13 %PAGP-5-PORTFROMSTP:Port 2/3 left bridge port 2/1-4
2000 Jan 17 22:56:36 %PAGP-5-PORTFROMSTP:Port 2/4 left bridge port 2/1-4
```

```
Switch-B (enable) show port channel
Port  Status      Channel   Channel   Neighbor                  Neighbor
                  mode      status    device                    port
----- ----------  --------- --------- ------------------------- ----------
 2/1  errdisable  on        channel
 2/2  errdisable  on        channel
 2/3  errdisable  on        channel
 2/4  errdisable  on        channel
----- ----------  --------- --------- ------------------------- ----------
Switch-B (enable) show port
Port  Name                Status     Vlan         Level  Duplex Speed Type
----- ------------------- ---------- ----------- ------- ------ ----- -----------
 2/1                      errdisable 1            normal  auto   auto 10/100BaseTX
 2/2                      errdisable 1            normal  auto   auto 10/100BaseTX
 2/3                      errdisable 1            normal  auto   auto 10/100BaseTX
 2/4                      errdisable 1            normal  auto   auto 10/100BaseTX
```

Correcting errdisable State

Sometimes when you try to configure EtherChannel but the ports are not configured the same, it will cause the ports on one side of the channel to be shut down. The link lights will be yellow on the port. You can tell this by the console by typing **show port**. The ports will be listed as errdisable. To recover from this, you should fix the mismatched parameters on the ports involved and then re-enable the ports. Just note that this re-enabling of the ports is a separate step that must be done for the ports to become functional again.

In our example, we know that Switch A had a VLAN mismatch, so we will go to Switch A and put port 2/4 back into VLAN 1. Then we will turn on the channel for ports 2/1-4. Switch A will not show that it's connected until we re-enable Switch B ports. Then when we have fixed Switch A and put it in channeling mode, we will go back to Switch B and re-enable the ports.

```
Switch-A (enable) set vlan 1 2/4
VLAN 1 modified.
VLAN 2 modified.
VLAN  Mod/Ports
----  -----------------------
1     2/1-24

Switch-A (enable) set port channel 2/1-4 on
Port(s) 2/1-4 channel mode set to on.
Switch-A (enable) sh port channel
Port  Status      Channel   Channel   Neighbor                  Neighbor
                  mode      status    device                    port
----- ----------  --------- --------- ------------------------- ----------
 2/1  notconnect  on        channel
 2/2  notconnect  on        channel
 2/3  notconnect  on        channel
 2/4  notconnect  on        channel
----- ----------  --------- --------- ------------------------- ----------
```

```
Switch-B (enable) show port channel
Port  Status      Channel   Channel     Neighbor                 Neighbor
                  mode      status      device                   port
----- ---------   --------- ----------- ------------------------ ----------
 2/1  errdisable  on        channel
 2/2  errdisable  on        channel
 2/3  errdisable  on        channel
 2/4  errdisable  on        channel
----- ---------   --------- ----------- ------------------------ ----------

Switch-B (enable) set port enable 2/1-4
Ports 2/1-4 enabled.
Switch-B (enable) 2000 Jan 17 23:15:22 %PAGP-5-PORTTOSTP:Port 2/1 joined bridg4
2000 Jan 17 23:15:22 %PAGP-5-PORTTOSTP:Port 2/2 joined bridge port 2/1-4
2000 Jan 17 23:15:22 %PAGP-5-PORTTOSTP:Port 2/3 joined bridge port 2/1-4
2000 Jan 17 23:15:22 %PAGP-5-PORTTOSTP:Port 2/4 joined bridge port 2/1-4

Switch-B (enable) show port channel
Port  Status      Channel   Channel     Neighbor                 Neighbor
                  mode      status      device                   port
----- ---------   --------- ----------- ------------------------ ----------
 2/1  connected   on        channel
 2/2  connected   on        channel
 2/3  connected   on        channel
 2/4  connected   on        channel
----- ---------   --------- ----------- ------------------------ ----------
```

Showing What Happens When a Link Breaks and Is Restored

When a port in the channel goes down, then any packets that would normally be sent on that port are shifted over to the next port in the channel. You can verify that this is happening by using the **show mac** command. In our test bed, we will have Switch A send **ping** packets to Switch B to see which link the traffic is using. First we will clear the counters and then use **show mac**, send three **ping**s, and use **show mac** again to look at which channel the **ping** responses were received on.

```
Switch-A (enable) clear counters
This command will reset all MAC and port counters reported in CLI and SNMP.
Do you want to continue (y/n) [n]? y
MAC and Port counters cleared.

Switch-A (enable) show port channel
Port  Status      Channel   Channel     Neighbor                 Neighbor
                  mode      status      device                   port
----- ---------   --------- ----------- ------------------------ ----------
 2/1  connected   on        channel     WS-C5505  066509957(Sw   2/1
 2/2  connected   on        channel     WS-C5505  066509957(Sw   2/2
 2/3  connected   on        channel     WS-C5505  066509957(Sw   2/3
 2/4  connected   on        channel     WS-C5505  066509957(Sw   2/4
----- ---------   --------- ----------- ------------------------ ----------

Switch-A (enable) show mac
```

```
Port      Rcv-Unicast          Rcv-Multicast        Rcv-Broadcast
--------  -------------------- -------------------- --------------------
 2/1                         0                   18                    0
 2/2                         0                    2                    0
 2/3                         0                    2                    0
 2/4                         0                    2                    0
Switch-A (enable) ping 172.16.84.17
172.16.84.17 is alive
Switch-A (enable) ping 172.16.84.17
172.16.84.17 is alive
Switch-A (enable) ping 172.16.84.17
172.16.84.17 is alive
Switch-A (enable) show mac

Port      Rcv-Unicast          Rcv-Multicast        Rcv-Broadcast
--------  -------------------- -------------------- --------------------
 2/1                         3                   24                    0
 2/2                         0                    2                    0
 2/3                         0                    2                    0
 2/4                         0                    2                    0
```

Now at this point, we have received the **ping** responses on port 3/1, so when Switch B console sends a response to Switch A, the EtherChannel uses port 2/1. Now we will shut down port 2/1 on Switch B. From Switch A, we will issue another **ping** and see what channel the response comes back on. (Switch A is sending on the same port to which Switch B is connected. We just show the received packets from Switch B because the transmit packets are farther down in the **show mac** display.)

```
1999 Dec 19 01:30:23 %PAGP-5-PORTFROMSTP:Port 2/1 left bridge port 2/1-4

Switch-A (enable) ping 172.16.84.17
172.16.84.17 is alive
Switch-A (enable) show mac

Port      Rcv-Unicast          Rcv-Multicast        Rcv-Broadcast
--------  -------------------- -------------------- --------------------
 2/1                         3                   37                    0
 2/2                         1                   27                    0
 2/3                         0                    7                    0
 2/4                         0                    7                    0
```

Notice that now that port 2/1 is disabled, EtherChannel automatically uses the next port in the channel, 2/2. Now we re-enable port 2/1 and wait for it to join the bridge group; then we issue two more **ping**s.

```
1999 Dec 19 01:31:33 %PAGP-5-PORTTOSTP:Port 2/1 joined bridge port 2/1-4

Switch-A (enable) ping 172.16.84.17
172.16.84.17 is alive
Switch-A (enable) ping 172.16.84.17
172.16.84.17 is alive
Switch-A (enable) show mac

Port      Rcv-Unicast          Rcv-Multicast        Rcv-Broadcast
--------  -------------------- -------------------- --------------------
 2/1                         5                   50                    0
 2/2                         1                   49                    0
 2/3                         0                   12                    0
 2/4                         0                   12                    0
```

Note that these **ping**s are sent from port 2/1, so when the link comes back up, EtherChannel will again add it to the bundle and use it. All this is done transparently to the user.

Commands Used in This Section

Commands to use for setting the configuration include these:

- **set port channel on**—To turn on the EtherChannel feature
- **set port channel auto**—To reset the ports to their default mode of auto
- **set port channel desirable**—To send PAgP packets to the other side requesting that a channel be created
- **set port enable**—To enable the ports after **set port disable** or after an errdisable state
- **set port disable**—To disable a port while other configuration settings are being made
- **set trunk desirable**—To turn on trunking by causing this port to send a request to the other switch that this be a trunk link and, if the port is set to negotiate (the default setting), to negotiate the type of trunking to use on the link (ISL or 802.1q)

Commands to use for verifying the configuration include these:

- **show version**—To display what version of software the switch is running
- **show module**—To display which modules are installed in the switch
- **show port capabilities**—To determine whether the ports that we want to use have the capability to do EtherChannel
- **show port**—To determine the status of the port (notconnect, connected) and the speed and duplex settings
- **ping**—To test connectivity to the other switch
- **show port channel**—To see the current status of the EtherChannel bundle
- **show port channel** *mod/port*—To give a more detailed view of the channel status of a single port
- **show spantree**—To verify that the Spanning-Tree Protocol looked at the channel as one link
- **show trunk**—To see the trunking status of ports

Commands to use for troubleshooting the configuration include these:

- **show port channel**—To see the current status of the EtherChannel bundle
- **show port**—To determine the status of the port (notconnect, connected) and the speed and duplex settings
- **clear counters**—To reset the switch packet counters to zero. The counters are visible with the **show mac** command

- **show mac**—To view packets received and sent by the switch
- **ping**—To test connectivity to the other switch and generate traffic that shows up with the **show mac** command

Using PortFast and Other Commands to Fix End-Station Startup Connectivity Problems

If you have workstations connected to switches that either are incapable of logging into your network domain (NT or Novell) or are incapable of getting a DHCP address, then you may want to try the suggestions listed in this document before exploring other avenues. The suggestions are relatively easy to implement and are very often the cause of workstation connectivity problems encountered during the workstation's initialization/startup phase.

With more customers deploying switching to the desktop and replacing their shared hubs with switches, we often see problems introduced in client/server environments because of this initial delay. The biggest problem that we see is that Windows 95/98/NT, Novell, VINES, IBM NetworkStation/IBM Thin Clients, and AppleTalk clients cannot connect to their servers. If the software on these devices is not persistent during the startup procedure, *they will give up trying to connect to their server before the switch has even allowed traffic to pass through.*

| NOTE | This initial connectivity delay often manifests itself as errors that appear when you first boot up a workstation. The following are several examples of error messages and errors that you might see: |

- A Microsoft networking client displays "No Domain Controllers Available."
- DHCP reports, "No DHCP Servers Available."
- A Novell IPX networking workstation does not have the "Novell Login Screen" upon bootup.
- An AppleTalk networking client displays "Access to your AppleTalk network has been interrupted. To re-establish your connection, open and close the AppleTalk control panel." It is also possible that the AppleTalk client's Chooser application either will not display a zone list or will display an incomplete zone list.

The initial connectivity delay is also frequently seen in a switched environment in which a network administrator updates software or drivers. In this case, a vendor may optimize the drivers so that network initialization procedures happen earlier in the client's startup process (before the switch is ready to process the packets).

With the various features that are now included in some switches, it can take close to a minute for a switch to begin servicing a newly connected workstation. This delay would affect the workstation every time that it is turned on or rebooted. The four main features that cause this delay are listed here:

- Spanning-Tree Protocol
- EtherChannel negotiation
- Trunking negotiation
- Link speed/duplex negotiation between the switch and the workstation

These four features are listed in order of causing the most delay (Spanning-Tree Protocol) to causing the least delay (speed/duplex negotiation). A workstation connected to a switch usually does not cause spanning-tree loops, usually does not need EtherChannel, and usually does not need to negotiate a trunking method. (Disabling link speed/detection negotiation can also reduce port delay, if you need to optimize your startup time as much as possible.)

This section shows how to implement startup speed-optimization commands on three Catalyst switch platforms. In the timing sections, we show how the switch port delay is reduced and by how much.

Contents

The following topics will be covered in this section:

- Background
- How to reduce startup delay on the Catalyst 4000/5000/6000 switch
- Timing tests on the Catalyst 5000
- How to reduce startup delay on the Catalyst 2900XL/3500XL switch
- Timing tests on the Catalyst 2900XL
- How to reduce startup delay on the Catalyst 1900/2800 switch
- Timing tests on the Catalyst 1900
- An additional benefit to PortFast

The terms *workstation*, *end station*, and *server* are all used interchangeably in this section to refer to any device directly connected to a switch by a single NIC card. These terms may also refer to devices with multiple NIC cards in which the NIC card is used only for redundancy—in other words, the workstation or server is not configured to act as a bridge; it just has multiple NIC cards for redundancy.

NOTE   Some server NIC cards support trunking or EtherChannel. In some situations, the server needs to live on several VLANs at the same time (trunking), or the server needs more bandwidth on the link connecting it to the switch (EtherChannel). In these cases, you would *not* turn off PagP, and you would *not* turn off trunking. Also, these devices are rarely turned off or reset. The instructions in this chapter do not apply to these type of devices.

Background

This section covers four features that some switches have that cause initial delays when a device is connected to a switch. Usually a workstation will either not cause the spanning-tree problem (loops), or not need the feature (PAgP, DTP), so the delay is unnecessary.

Spanning Tree

If you have recently started moving from a hub environment to a switch environment, these connectivity problems may show up because a switch works much differently than a hub. A switch provides connectivity at the data link layer, not at the physical layer. The switch must use a bridging algorithm to decide whether packets received on a port need to be transmitted out other ports. The bridging algorithm is susceptible to physical loops in the network topology. Because of this susceptibility to loops, switches run a protocol called the *Spanning-Tree Protocol* that causes loops to be eliminated in the topology. Running this protocol causes all ports that are included in the spanning-tree process to become active much slower than they otherwise would because the protocol detects and blocks loops. A bridged network having physical loops, without spanning tree, will break. So, in spite of the time involved, the Spanning-Tree Protocol is a good thing. The spanning-tree process running on Catalyst switches is an industry-standard specification (IEEE 802.1d).

After a port on the switch has a link and joins the bridge group, it will run Spanning-Tree Protocol on that port. A port running a spanning tree can have one of five states: blocking, listening, learning, forwarding, and disabled. The Spanning-Tree Protocol dictates that the port starts out blocking and then immediately moves through the listening and learning phases. By default, it will spend approximately 15 seconds listening and 15 seconds learning.

During the listening state, the switch is trying to determine where it fits in the spanning-tree topology. It especially wants to know whether this port is part of a physical loop. If it is part of a loop, then this port may be chosen to go into blocking mode. Blocking mode means that the port won't send or receive user data for the sake of eliminating loops. If the port is not part of a loop, it will proceed to the learning state, which involves learning which MAC addresses live off this port. This whole spanning-tree initialization process takes about 30 seconds.

If you are connecting a workstation or a server with a single NIC card to a switch port, this connection *cannot* create a physical loop. These connections are considered leaf nodes. There is no reason to make the workstation wait 30 seconds while the switch checks for loops when the workstation cannot cause a loop. So, Cisco added a feature called PortFast, or Fast-Start, which means that the spanning tree for this port will assume that the port is not part of a loop and will immediately move to the forwarding state, without going through the blocking, listening, or learning states. This can save a lot of time. This command *does not* turn off the spanning tree. It just makes the spanning tree on the selected port skip a few (unnecessary in this circumstance) steps in the beginning.

NOTE	The PortFast feature should *never* be used on switch ports that connect to other *switches, hubs,* or *routers*. These connections may cause physical loops, and it is very important that the spanning-tree process go through the full initialization procedure in these situations. A spanning-tree loop can bring your network down. If PortFast is turned on for a port that *is* part of a physical loop, it can cause a window of time in which packets could possibly be continuously forwarded (and even multiply) in such a way that the network can't recover. In later Catalyst operating system software (5.4(1)), a feature called PortFast BPDU-Guard detects the reception of BPDUs on ports having PortFast enabled. Because this should never happen, BPDU-Guard puts the port into errDisable state.

EtherChannel

Another feature that a switch may have is called EtherChannel (or Fast EtherChannel, or Gigabit EtherChannel). This feature allows multiple links between the same two devices to work as if they were one fast link, with traffic load balanced among the links. A switch can form these bundles automatically with a neighbor using a protocol called Port Aggregation Protocol (PAgP). Switch ports that can run PAgP usually default to a passive mode called auto, which means that they are *willing* to form a bundle if the neighbor device across the link asks them to. Running the protocol in auto mode can cause a port to delay for up to 15 seconds before passing control to the spanning-tree algorithm (PAgP runs on a port before spanning tree does). There is no reason to have PAgP running on a port connected to a workstation. Setting the switch port PAgP mode to off will eliminate this delay.

Trunking

Another switch feature is the capability of a port to form a trunk. A trunk is configured between two devices when they need to carry traffic from multiple VLANs. A VLAN is something that switches create to make a group of workstations appear to be on their own segment or broadcast domain. Trunk ports make these VLANs extend across multiple switches so that a single VLAN can cover an entire campus. They do this by adding tags to the packets, indicating which VLAN the packet belongs to.

Different types of trunking protocols exist. If a port can become a trunk, then it may also have the capability to trunk automatically and, in some cases, even negotiate what type of trunking to use on the port. This capability to negotiate the trunking method with the other device is called Dynamic Trunking Protocol (DTP); the precursor to DTP is a protocol called Dynamic ISL (DISL). If these protocols are running, they can delay a port on the switch becoming active.

Usually a port connected to a workstation belongs to only one VLAN and therefore does not need to trunk. If a port has the capability to negotiate the formation of a trunk, it will usually default to the auto mode. If the port is changed to a trunking mode of off, it will further reduce the delay of a switch port becoming active.

Speed and Duplex Negotiation

Just turning on PortFast and turning off PAgP (if present) is usually enough to solve the problem, but if you need to eliminate every possible second, you could also set the port speed and duplex manually on the switch if it is a multispeed port (10/100). Autonegotiation is a nice feature, but turning it off could save you 2 seconds on a Catalyst 5000 (it does not help much on the 2800 or 2900XL).

There can be complications, though, if you turn off autonegotiation on the switch but leave it active on the workstation. Because the switch will not negotiate with the client, the client might not choose the same duplex setting that the switch is using. See the section "Troubleshooting Ethernet 10-/100-Mb Half-/Full-Duplex Autonegotiation," earlier in this chapter, for additional information on the caveats of autonegotiation.

How to Reduce Startup Delay on the Catalyst 4000/5000/6000 Switch

The following five commands show how to turn on PortFast, turn off PAgP negotiation, turn off trunking negotiation (DISL, DTP), and turn off speed/duplex negotiation. The **set spantree portfast** command can be done on a range of ports at once (**set spantree portfast 2/1-12 enable**). Usually **set port channel** must be turned off using a valid group of channel-capable ports. In the case that follows, module 2 has the capability to channel with ports 2/1-2 or with ports 2/1-4, so either of these groups of ports would have been valid to use.

NOTE   Version 5.2 of Cat OS for Catalyst 4000/5000 has a new command called **set port host,** which is a macro that combines the commands **set spantree portfast, set portchannel off**, **set trunk off** into one command.

Configuration

Use the following commands to reduce startup delay on the Catalyst 4000/5000/6000 switches.

```
Switch-A (enable) set spantree portfast 2/1 enable

Warning: Spantree port fast start should only be enabled on ports connected
to a single host.  Connecting hubs, concentrators, switches, bridges, etc. to
a fast start port can cause temporary spanning tree loops.  Use with caution.

Spantree port 2/1 fast start enabled.
Switch-A (enable) set port channel 2/1-2 off
Port(s) 2/1-2 channel mode set to off.

Switch-A (enable) set trunk 2/1 off
Port(s) 2/1 trunk mode set to off.
```

The changes to the configuration will be automatically saved to NVRAM.

Verification

The version of the switch software used in this document is 4.5(1). For the full output of **show version** and **show module,** refer to the section "Timing Tests with and Without DTP, PAgP, and PortFast on a Catalyst 5000," later in this chapter.

```
Switch-A (enable) show version
WS-C5505 Software, Version McpSW: 4.5(1) NmpSW: 4.5(1)
```

The following command shows how to view the current state of a port with regard to spanning tree. Currently the port is in the spanning tree forwarding state (sending and receiving packets), and the Fast-Start column shows that PortFast is currently disabled. In other words, the port will take at least 30 seconds to move to the forwarding state whenever it initializes.

```
Switch-A (enable) show port spantree 2/1

Port     Vlan Port-State    Cost  Priority Fast-Start Group-Method
-------- ---- ------------- ----- -------- ---------- ------------
 2/1      1   forwarding      19        32 disabled
```

Now we will enable PortFast on this switch port. The switch warns us that this command should be used only on ports that are connected to a single host (a workstation, server, and so on) and are never to be used on ports connected to other hubs or switches. The reason that we enable PortFast is so the port will start forwarding immediately. We can do this because a workstation or server will not cause a network loop, so why waste time checking? But another hub or switch could cause a loop, and we want to always go through the normal listening and learning stages when connecting to these types of devices.

```
Switch-A (enable) set spantree portfast 2/1 enable

Warning: Spantree port fast start should only be enabled on ports connected to a
single host.  Connecting hubs, concentrators, switches, bridges, etc. to
a fast start port can cause temporary spanning tree loops.  Use with caution.

Spantree port 2/1 fast start enabled.
```

To verify that PortFast is enabled for this port, use the following command:

```
Switch-A (enable) show port spantree 2/1

Port    Vlan  Port-State     Cost   Priority  Fast-Start  Group-Method
------- ----  -------------  -----  --------  ----------  ------------
 2/1     1    forwarding       19        32   enabled
```

Another way to view the PortFast settings for one or more ports is to view the spanning-tree information for a specific VLAN. Later, in the section "Timing Tests with and Without DTP, PAgP, and PortFast on a Catalyst 5000," we show how to have the switch report each stage of spanning tree that it moves through in real time. The output that follows also shows the forward delay time (15 seconds), which is how long the spanning tree will be in the listening state and how long it will be in the learning state for each port in the VLAN.

```
Switch-A (enable) show spantree 1
VLAN 1
Spanning tree enabled
Spanning tree type          ieee

Designated Root             00-e0-4f-94-b5-00
Designated Root Priority    8189
Designated Root Cost        19
Designated Root Port        2/24
Root Max Age   20 sec   Hello Time 2  sec   Forward Delay 15 sec

Bridge ID MAC ADDR          00-90-92-b0-84-00
Bridge ID Priority          32768
Bridge Max Age 20 sec   Hello Time 2  sec   Forward Delay 15 sec

Port    Vlan  Port-State     Cost   Priority  Fast-Start  Group-Method
------- ----  -------------  -----  --------  ----------  ------------
 2/1     1    forwarding       19        32   enabled
...
```

To verify that PAgP is off, use the **show port channel** command, which follows. Be sure to specify the module number (2, in this case) so that the command will show you the channel mode even if there is no channel formed. If we do **show port channel** with no channels formed, it just says "no ports channeling." We want to go further and see the current channel mode.

```
Switch-A (enable) show port channel
No ports channeling

Switch-A (enable) show port channel 2
Port  Status      Channel   Channel    Neighbor                  Neighbor
                  mode      status     device                    port
----- ----------  --------  ---------- ------------------------- ----------
 2/1  notconnect  auto      not channel
 2/2  notconnect  auto      not channel
...
Switch-A (enable) set port channel 2/1-2 off
Port(s) 2/1-2 channel mode set to off.
```

```
Switch-A (enable) show port channel 2
Port  Status      Channel   Channel     Neighbor                    Neighbor
                  mode      status      device                      port
----- ----------  --------- ----------- ------------------------    ----------
 2/1  connected   off       not channel
 2/2  connected   off       not channel
...
```

To verify that trunking negotiation is off, use the **set trunk off** command. We show the default state here. Then we turn trunking to off and show the resulting state. We specify module number 2 so that we can see the current channel mode for the ports in this module.

```
Switch-A (enable) show trunk 2
Port     Mode          Encapsulation   Status         Native vlan
-------- ------------  -------------   ------------   -----------
 2/1     auto          negotiate       not-trunking   1
 2/2     auto          negotiate       not-trunking   1
...

Switch-A (enable) set trunk 2/1-2 off
Port(s) 2/1-2 trunk mode set to off.

Switch-A (enable) show trunk 2
Port     Mode          Encapsulation   Status         Native vlan
-------- ------------  -------------   ------------   -----------
 2/1     off           negotiate       not-trunking   1
 2/2     off           negotiate       not-trunking   1
...
```

We do not show an example here of turning off speed/duplex autonegotiation by manually setting the speed and duplex on the switch; it should not be necessary except in the rarest of cases. We give an example of how to do this in Step 10 of the next section, if you feel that it will be necessary for your situation.

Timing Tests with and Without DTP, PAgP, and PortFast on a Catalyst 5000

The following test shows what happens with switch port initialization timing as the various commands are applied. The default settings of the port are used first to give a benchmark. They have PortFast disabled, PAgP (EtherChannel) mode set to auto (it will channel if asked to channel), and the trunking mode (DTP) set to auto (it will trunk if asked to trunk). The test then proceeds to turn on PortFast and measure the time, then to turn off PAgP and measure the time, and then to turn off trunking and measure the time. Finally, we turn off autonegotiation and measure the time. All these tests will be done on a Catalyst 5000 with a 10/100 Fast Ethernet card that supports DTP and PAgP.

NOTE	Turning on PortFast is not the same thing as turning off the Spanning-Tree Protocol (as noted earlier in the document). With PortFast on, the Spanning-Tree Protocol is still running on the port; it just skips blocking, listening, and learning, and goes immediately to the forwarding state. Turning off the Spanning-Tree Protocol is not recommended because it affects the entire VLAN and can leave the network vulnerable to physical topology loops, which can cause serious network problems.

Step 1   Show the switch IOS version and configuration (**show version**, **show module**).

```
Switch-A (enable) show version
WS-C5505 Software, Version McpSW: 4.5(1) NmpSW: 4.5(1)
Copyright (c) 1995-1999 by Cisco Systems
NMP S/W compiled on Mar 29 1999, 16:09:01
MCP S/W compiled on Mar 29 1999, 16:06:50

System Bootstrap Version: 3.1.2

Hardware Version: 1.0  Model: WS-C5505  Serial #: 066507453

Mod Port Model       Serial #  Versions
--- ---- ----------  --------- -----------------------------------------
1   0    WS-X5530    006841805 Hw : 1.3
                               Fw : 3.1.2

                               Fw1: 3.1(2)
                               Sw : 4.5(1)
2   24   WS-X5225R   012785227 Hw : 3.2
                               Fw : 4.3(1)
                               Sw : 4.5(1)

        DRAM                    FLASH                   NVRAM
Module Total   Used    Free    Total   Used    Free    Total Used  Free
------ ------- ------- ------- ------- ------- ------- ----- ----- -----
1      32640K  13648K  18992K  8192K   4118K   4074K   512K  119K  393K

Uptime is 28 days, 18 hours, 54 minutes

Switch-A (enable) show module
Mod Module-Name        Ports Module-Type            Model     Serial-Num Status
--- ------------------ ----- ---------------------- --------- ---------- -------
1                      0     Supervisor III         WS-X5530  006841805 ok
2                      24    10/100BaseTX Ethernet  WS-X5225R 012785227 ok
```

```
Mod MAC-Address(es)                          Hw     Fw         Sw
--- -------------------------------------- ------ ---------- ----------------
1   00-90-92-b0-84-00 to 00-90-92-b0-87-ff 1.3    3.1.2      4.5(1)
2   00-50-0f-b2-e2-60 to 00-50-0f-b2-e2-77 3.2    4.3(1)     4.5(1)


Mod Sub-Type Sub-Model  Sub-Serial Sub-Hw
--- -------- ---------- ---------- ------
1   NFFC     WS-F5521   0008728786 1.0
```

> **Step 2** Set logging for spanning-tree to the most verbose (**set logging level spantree 7**). The following is the default logging level (2) for spanning tree, which means that only critical situations will be reported.

```
Switch-A (enable) show logging

Logging buffer size:           500
        timestamp option:      enabled
Logging history size:          1
Logging console:               enabled
Logging server:                disabled
        server facility:       LOCAL7
        server severity:       warnings(4)


Facility                Default Severity          Current Session Severity
------------            ---------------------     -----------------------
...
spantree                2                         2
...
0(emergencies)          1(alerts)                 2(critical)
3(errors)               4(warnings)               5(notifications)
6(information)          7(debugging)
```

We are going to change the level for the spanning-tree to 7 (**debug**) so we can see the spanning-tree states change on the port. This configuration change lasts only for the terminal session, and then it goes back to normal.

```
Switch-A (enable) set logging level spantree 7
System logging facility <spantree for this session set to severity
7(debugging)

Switch-A (enable) show logging
...
```

Facility	Default Severity	Current Session Severity
...		
spantree	2	7
...		

Step 3   Start with the port on the catalyst shut down.

```
Switch-A (enable) set port disable 2/1
Port 2/1 disabled.
```

Step 4   Now we will check the time and enable the port. We want to see how long it stays in each state.

```
Switch-A (enable) show time
Fri Feb 25 2000, 12:20:17
Switch-A (enable) set port enable 2/1
Port 2/1 enabled.
Switch-A (enable)
2000 Feb 25 12:20:39 %PAGP-5-PORTTOSTP:Port 2/1 joined bridge port 2/1
2000 Feb 25 12:20:39 %SPANTREE-6-PORTBLK: port 2/1 state in vlan 1
changed to blocking.
2000 Feb 25 12:20:39 %SPANTREE-6-PORTLISTEN: port 2/1 state in vlane 1
changed to Listening.
2000 Feb 25 12:20:53 %SPANTREE-6-PORTLEARN: port 2/1 state in vlan 1
changed to Learning.
2000 Feb 25 12:21:08 %SPANTREE-6-PORTFWD: port 2/1 state in vlan 1
changed to forwarding.
```

Notice from the previous output that it took about 22 seconds (20:17 to 20:39) for the port to begin the spanning-tree blocking stage. This time was spent negotiating the link and doing DTP and PAgP stuff. When we started blocking, we are in the spanning-tree realm. From blocking, it went immediately to listening (20:39 to 20:39). From listening to learning took approximately 14 seconds (20:39 to 20:53).

From learning to forwarding took 15 seconds (20:53 to 21:08). So, the total time before the port actually became functional for traffic was about 51 seconds (20:17 to 21:08).

NOTE   Technically, the listening and learning stages should both be 15 seconds, which is how the forward delay parameter is set for this VLAN. The learning stage probably is closer to 15 seconds than 14 seconds if we had more accurate measurements. None of the measurements here are perfectly accurate—we are just trying to give a feel for how long things take.

Step 5   We know from the previous output and from the **show spantree** command that the spanning tree is active on this port. Let us look at other things that could slow the port reaching the forwarding state. The **show port capabilities** command shows that this port has the capability to trunk and to create an EtherChannel. The **show trunk** command indicates that this port is in auto mode and that it is set to negotiate the type of trunking to use (ISL or 802.1q, negotiated through Dynamic Trunking Protocol [DTP]).

```
Switch-A (enable) show port capabilities 2/1
Model                   WS-X5225R
Port                    2/1
Type                    10/100BaseTX

Speed                   auto,10,100
Duplex                  half,full
Trunk encap type        802.1Q,ISL
Trunk mode              on,off,desirable,auto,nonegotiate
Channel                 2/1-2,2/1-4
Broadcast suppression   percentage(0-100)
Flow control            receive-(off,on),send-(off,on)
Security                yes
Membership              static,dynamic
Fast start              yes
Rewrite                 yes
Switch-A (enable) show trunk 2/1
Port      Mode         Encapsulation   Status         Native vlan
--------  -----------  -------------   -----------    -----------
  2/1     auto         negotiate       not-trunking   1
...
```

Step 6   First, we will enable PortFast on the port. Trunking negotiation (DTP) is still in auto mode, and EtherChannel (PAgP) is still in auto mode.

```
Switch-A (enable) set port disable 2/1
Port 2/1 disabled.

Switch-A (enable) set spantree portfast 2/1 enable

Warning: Spantree port fast start should only be enabled on ports connected
to a single host.  Connecting hubs, concentrators, switches, bridges, etc. to
a fast start port can cause temporary spanning-tree loops.  Use with caution.

Spantree port 2/1 fast start enabled.

Switch-A (enable) show time
```

```
Fri Feb 25 2000, 13:45:23
Switch-A (enable) set port enable 2/1
Port 2/1 enabled.
Switch-A (enable)
Switch-A (enable)
2000 Feb 25 13:45:43 %PAGP-5-PORTTOSTP:Port 2/1 joined bridgeport 2/1
2000 Feb 25 13:45:44 %SPANTREE-6-PORTFWD: port 2/1 state in vlan 1 change to forwarding.
```

Now we have a total time of 21 seconds! It takes 20 seconds before it joins the bridge group (45:23 to 45:43). But then, because PortFast is enabled, it only takes 1 second until STP starts forwarding (instead of 30 seconds). We saved 29 seconds by enabling PortFast. Let's see if we can reduce the delay further.

Step 7 Now we will turn off PAgP mode. We can see from the **show port channel** command that the PAgP mode is set to auto, which means that it will channel if asked to by a neighbor speaking PAgP. You must turn off channeling for at least a group of two ports; you cannot do it for just an individual port.

```
Switch-A (enable) show port channel 2/1
Port  Status      Channel   Channel   Neighbor                  Neighbor
                  mode      status    device                    port
----- ---------- --------- --------- ------------------------- ----------
 2/1  connected  auto      not channel

Switch-A (enable) set port channel 2/1-2 off
Port(s) 2/1-2 channel mode set to off.
```

Step 8 Now let's shut down the port and repeat the test.

```
Switch-A (enable) set port disable 2/1
Port 2/1 disabled.

Switch-A (enable) show time
Fri Feb 25 2000, 13:56:23
Switch-A (enable) set port enable 2/1
Port 2/1 enabled.
Switch-A (enable)
2000 Feb 25 13:56:32 %PAGP-5-PORTTOSTP:Port 2/1 joined bridgeport 2/1
2000 Feb 25 13:56:32 %SPANTREE-6-PORTFWD: port 2/1 state in vlan 1
changed to forwarding.
```

Notice here that now it takes only 9 seconds to reach the forwarding state (56:23 to 56:32) instead of 21 seconds, as in the previous test. Turning PAgP from auto to off in this test saved about 12 seconds.

Step 9   Let's turn trunking to off (instead of auto) and see how that affects the time that it takes for the port to reach forwarding state. We will again turn the port off and then on, and record the time.

```
Switch-A (enable) set trunk 2/1 off
Port(s) 2/1 trunk mode set to off.
Switch-A (enable) set port disable 2/1
Port 2/1 disabled.
```

Start the test with trunking set to off (instead of auto).

```
Switch-A (enable) show time
Fri Feb 25 2000, 14:00:19
Switch-A (enable) set port enable 2/1
Port 2/1 enabled.
Switch-A (enable)
2000 Feb 25 14:00:22 %PAGP-5-PORTTOSTP:Port 2/1 joined bridge port 2/1
2000 Feb 25 14:00:23 %SPANTREE-6-PORTFWD: port 2/1 state in vlan 1
change for forwarding.
```

We saved a few seconds at the beginning because it took only 4 seconds to reach the spanning-tree forwarding state (00:19 to 00:22). We saved about 5 seconds by changing the trunking mode from auto to off.

Step 10   (Optional). If the switch port initialization time was the problem, it should be solved by now. But if you have to shave a few more seconds off the time, you could set the port the speed and duplex manually instead of using autonegotiation.

Setting the speed and duplex manually on our side requires that you set the speed and duplex on the other side as well. This is because setting the port speed and duplex disables autonegotiation on the port, and the connecting device will not see autonegotiation parameters. The connecting device will connect only at half-duplex mode, and the resulting duplex mismatch results in poor performance and port errors. Remember, if you set speed and duplex on one side, you must set speed and duplex on the connecting device as well to avoid these problems.

To view the port status after setting the speed and duplex, use the **show port** command.

```
Switch-A (enable) set port speed 2/1 100
Port(s) 2/1 speed set to 100 Mbps.
Switch-A (enable) set port duplex 2/1 full
Port(s) 2/1 set to full-duplex.
Switch-A (enable) show port
Port  Name                 Status      Vlan        Level  Duplex Speed Type
----- -------------------- ----------  ----------  ------ ------ ----- ------------
 2/1                       connected   1           normal   full    100 10/100BaseTX
...
```

The timing results are as follows:

```
Switch-A (enable) show time
Fri Feb 25 2000, 140528 Eastern
Switch-A (enable) set port enable 2/1
Port 2/1 enabled.
Switch-A (enable)
2000 Feb 25 140529 Eastern -0500 %PAGP-5-PORTTOSTP:Port 2/1 joined bridgeport 2/1
2000 Feb 25 140530 Eastern -0500 %SPANTREE-6-PORTFWD: port 2/1 state in vlan 1 changed to
forwarding.
```

The final result gives a time of 2 seconds (0528 to 0530).

Step 11 We did another visually timed test (watching our watches) by starting a continuous **ping** (**ping -t**) directed to the switch on a PC attached to the switch. We then disconnected the cable from the switch. The **ping**s started failing. Then we reconnected the cable to the switch and checked our watches to see how long it took for the switch to respond to the **ping**s from the PC. It took about 5 or 6 seconds with autonegotiation for speed and duplex turned on, and about 4 seconds with autonegotiation for speed and duplex turned off.

A lot of variables are involved in this test (PC initialization, PC software, switch console port responding to requests, and so on), but we just wanted to get some feel for how long it would take to get a response from the PCs point of view. All the tests were from the switches' internal debug message point of view.

How to Reduce Startup Delay on the Catalyst 2900XL/3500XL Switch

The 2900XL and 3500XL models can be configured from a web browser, by SNMP, or by the command-line interface (CLI). We will use the CLI. The following is an example of viewing the spanning-tree state of a port, turning on PortFast and then verifying that it is on. The 2900XL/3500XL *does* support EtherChannel and trunking, but it *does not* support dynamic EtherChannel creation (PAgP) or dynamic trunk negotiation (DTP) in the version that we tested (11.2[8.2]SA6), so we have no need to turn them off in this test. Also, after turning on PortFast, the elapsed time for the port to come up is already less than 1 second, so there is not much point in trying to change speed/duplex negotiation settings to speed things up. We hope that 1 second will be fast enough! By default, PortFast is off on the switch ports. The commands to turn on PortFast are discussed next.

Configuration

The following commands will help you reduce startup delay on the Catalyst 2900XL and 3500XL platforms:

```
2900XL#conf t
2900XL(config)#interface fastEthernet 0/1
2900XL(config-if)#spanning-tree portfast
2900XL(config-if)#exit
2900XL(config)#exit
2900XL#copy run start
```

This platform is like the router IOS; you must save the configuration (**copy run start**) if you want it to be permanently saved.

Verification

To verify that PortFast is enabled, use this command:

```
2900XL#show spanning-tree interface fastEthernet 0/1
Interface Fa0/1 (port 13) in Spanning tree 1 is FORWARDING
    Port path cost 19, Port priority 128
    Designated root has priority 8192, address 0010.0db1.7800
    Designated bridge has priority 32768, address 0050.8039.ec40
    Designated port is 13, path cost 19
    Timers: message age 0, forward delay 0, hold 0
    BPDU: sent 2105, received 1
    The port is in the portfast mode
```

Or, just look at the switch configuration.

```
2900XL#show running-config
Building configuration...

Current configuration:
!
version 11.2
...
!
interface VLAN1
 ip address 172.16.84.5 255.255.255.0
 no ip route-cache
!
interface FastEthernet0/1
 spanning-tree portfast
!
interface FastEthernet0/2
!
...
```

Timing Tests on the Catalyst 2900XL

The following steps show how to measure the effect of using PortFast on the 2900XL switch:

Step 1 The 11.2(8.2)SA6 version of software was used on the 2900XL for the following tests.

```
Switch#show version
Cisco Internetwork Operating System Software
IOS (tm) C2900XL Software (C2900XL-C3H2S-M), Version 11.2(8.2)SA6, MAINTENANCE INTERIM
SOFTWARE
Copyright (c) 1986-1999 by cisco Systems, Inc.
Compiled Wed 23-Jun-99 16:25 by boba
Image text-base: 0x00003000, data-base: 0x00259AEC

ROM: Bootstrap program is C2900XL boot loader

Switch uptime is 1 week, 4 days, 22 hours, 5 minutes
System restarted by power-on
System image file is "flash:c2900XL-c3h2s-mz-112.8.2-SA6.bin", booted via console

cisco WS-C2924-XL (PowerPC403GA) processor (revision 0x11) with 8192K/1024K bytes of memory.
Processor board ID 0x0E, with hardware revision 0x01
Last reset from power-on

Processor is running Enterprise Edition Software
Cluster command switch capable
Cluster member switch capable
24 Ethernet/IEEE 802.3 interface(s)

32K bytes of flash-simulated non-volatile configuration memory.
Base ethernet MAC Address: 00:50:80:39:EC:40
Motherboard assembly number: 73-3382-04
Power supply part number: 34-0834-01
Motherboard serial number: FAA02499G7X
Model number: WS-C2924-XL-EN
System serial number: FAA0250U03P
Configuration register is 0xF
```

Step 2 We want the switch to tell us what is happening and when it is happening, so we enter the following commands:

```
2900XL(config)#service timestamps debug uptime
2900XL(config)#service timestamps log uptime
2900XL#debug spantree events
Spanning Tree event debugging is on
2900XL#show debug
```

```
                    General spanning tree:
                       Spanning Tree event debugging is on
```

Step 3   Then we shut down the port in question.

```
2900XL#conf t
Enter configuration commands, one per line.  End with CNTL/Z.
2900XL(config)#interface fastEthernet 0/1
2900XL(config-if)#shut
2900XL(config-if)#
00:31:28: ST: sent Topology Change Notice on FastEthernet0/6
00:31:28: ST: FastEthernet0/1 - blocking
00:31:28: %LINK-5-CHANGED: Interface FastEthernet0/1, changed state to administratively down
00:31:28: %LINEPROTO-5-UPDOWN: Line protocol on Interface FastEthernet0/1, changed state to
down
2900XL(config-if)#exit
2900XL(config)#exit
2900XL#
```

Step 4   At this point, we paste the following commands from the Clipboard into the switch. These commands show the time on the 2900XL and turn the port back on:

```
show clock
conf t
int f0/1
no shut
```

Step 5   By default, PortFast is off. You can confirm it two ways: The first way is that the **show spanning-tree interface** command would not mention PortFast; the second way is to look at the running config, where you would not see the **spanning-tree portfast** command under the interface.

```
2900XL#show spanning-tree interface fastEthernet 0/1
Interface Fa0/1 (port 13) in Spanning tree 1 is FORWARDING
   Port path cost 19, Port priority 128
   Designated root has priority 8192, address 0010.0db1.7800
   Designated bridge has priority 32768, address 0050.8039.ec40
   Designated port is 13, path cost 19
   Timers: message age 0, forward delay 0, hold 0
   BPDU: sent 887, received 1
[Note: there is no message about being in portfast mode is in this spot...]

2900XL#show running-config
Building configuration...
...
!
```

```
interface FastEthernet0/1
[Note: there is no spanning-tree portfast command under this interface...]
!
...
```

Step 6   Here is the first timing test with PortFast off:

```
2900XL#show clock
*00:27:27.632 UTC Mon Mar 1 1993
2900XL#conf t
Enter configuration commands, one per line.  End with CNTL/Z.
2900XL(config)#int f0/1
2900XL(config-if)#no shut
2900XL(config-if)#
00:27:27: ST: FastEthernet0/1 - listening
00:27:27: %LINK-3-UPDOWN: Interface FastEthernet0/1, changed state to up
00:27:28: %LINEPROTO-5-UPDOWN: Line protocol on Interface FastEthernet0/1, changed state to up
00:27:42: ST: FastEthernet0/1 - learning
00:27:57: ST: sent Topology Change Notice on FastEthernet0/6
00:27:57: ST: FastEthernet0/1 - forwarding
```

Total time from shutdown until the port started forwarding was 30 seconds (27:27 to 27:57).

Step 7   To turn on PortFast, do the following:

```
2900XL#conf t
Enter configuration commands, one per line.  End with CNTL/Z.
2900XL(config)#interface fastEthernet 0/1
2900XL(config-if)#spanning-tree portfast
2900XL(config-if)#exit
2900XL(config)#exit
2900XL#
```

To verify that PortFast is enabled, use the **show spanning-tree interface** command. Notice that at the end of the command output, it says that PortFast is enabled.

```
2900XL#show spanning-tree interface fastEthernet 0/1
Interface Fa0/1 (port 13) in Spanning tree 1 is FORWARDING
   Port path cost 19, Port priority 128
   Designated root has priority 8192, address 0010.0db1.7800
   Designated bridge has priority 32768, address 0050.8039.ec40
   Designated port is 13, path cost 19
   Timers: message age 0, forward delay 0, hold 0
   BPDU: sent 1001, received 1
   The port is in the portfast mode
```

You can also see that PortFast is enabled in the configuration output:

```
2900XL#sh  ru
Building configuration...
...
interface FastEthernet0/1
 spanning-tree portfast
...
```

Step 8   Now let's do the timing test with PortFast enabled.

```
2900XL#show clock
*00:23:45.139 UTC Mon Mar 1 1993
2900XL#conf t
Enter configuration commands, one per line.  End with CNTL/Z.
2900XL(config)#int f0/1
2900XL(config-if)#no shut
2900XL(config-if)#
00:23:45: ST: FastEthernet0/1 -jump to forwarding from blocking
00:23:45: %LINK-3-UPDOWN: Interface FastEthernet0/1, changed state to up
00:23:45: %LINEPROTO-5-UPDOWN: Line protocol on Interface FastEthernet0/1, changed state to up
```

In this case, the total time was less than 1 second. If port initialization delay on the switch was the problem, then PortFast should solve it.

Remember, the switch does not currently support trunk negotiation, so we do not need to turn it off. Nor does it support PAgP for trunking, so we do not need to turn it off either. The switch does support autonegotiation of speed and duplex, but because the delay is so small, this would not be a reason to turn it off.

Step 9   We also did the **ping** test (just like Step 11 from the Catalyst 5000 example) from a workstation to the switch. It took about 5 to 6 seconds for the response to come from the switch whether autonegotiation for speed and duplex was on or off.

How to Reduce Startup Delay on the Catalyst 1900/2800 Switch

The 1900/2820 switches call PortFast by another name—they call it "spantree start-forwarding." For the version of software we are running to do our tests (V8.01.05), the switches default to having PortFast *enabled* on the Ethernet (10-Mbps) ports, and PortFast *disabled* on the Fast Ethernet (uplink) ports. So, when you use **show run** to view the configuration, if an Ethernet port says nothing about PortFast, then PortFast is enabled. If it says **no spantree start-forwarding** in the configuration, then PortFast is disabled. On a Fast Ethernet (100-Mbps) port, the opposite is true: For a Fast Ethernet port, PortFast is on only if the port shows **spantree start-forwarding** in the configuration.

Configuration

Here is an example of setting PortFast on a Fast Ethernet port. These examples use Enterprise edition software, version 8. The 1900 automatically saves the configuration after changes have been made. Remember, you would not want PortFast enabled on any port that connects to another switch or hub—only if the port attaches to an end station. The configuration is saved automatically to NVRAM.

```
1900#show version
Cisco Catalyst 1900/2820 Enterprise Edition Software
Version V8.01.05
Copyright (c) Cisco Systems, Inc.  1993-1998
1900 uptime is 0day(s) 01hour(s) 10minute(s) 42second(s)
cisco Catalyst 1900 (486sxl) processor with 2048K/1024K bytes of memory
Hardware board revision is 5
Upgrade Status: No upgrade currently in progress.
Config File Status: No configuration upload/download is in progress
27 Fixed Ethernet/IEEE 802.3 interface(s)
Base Ethernet Address: 00-50-50-E1-A4-80
1900#conf t
Enter configuration commands, one per line.  End with CNTL/Z
1900(config)#interface FastEthernet 0/26
1900(config-if)#spantree start-forwarding
1900(config-if)#exit
1900(config)#exit
1900#
```

Verification

One way to verify that PortFast is on is to look at the configuration. Remember, a Fast Ethernet port must say that it is on. An Ethernet port has PortFast enabled unless the configuration shows that it is off. In the configuration that follows, interface Ethernet 0/1 has PortFast turned off (you can see the command to turn it off), interface Ethernet 0/2 has PortFast on (you see nothing, which means that it is on), and interface Fast Ethernet 0/26 (port A in the menu system) has PortFast on (you can see the command to turn it on).

```
1900#show running-config
Building configuration...
...
!
interface Ethernet 0/1

  no spantree start-forwarding
!
interface Ethernet 0/2

!
...
!
interface FastEthernet 0/26
  spantree start-forwarding
!
```

The easiest way to view the PortFast status is through the menu system. If you select (P) for Port Configuration from the main menu and then select a port, the output will tell you whether port fast mode is enabled. The following output is for port Fast Ethernet 0/26 (which is port "A" on this switch).

```
Catalyst 1900 - Port A Configuration

Built-in 100Base-FX
802.1d STP State:  Blocking    Forward Transitions:  0

---------------------- Settings ---------------------------------------
[D] Description/name of port
[S] Status of port                            Suspended-no-linkbeat
[I] Port priority (spanning tree)             128 (80 hex)
[C] Path cost (spanning tree)                 10
[H] Port fast mode (spanning tree)            Enabled
[E] Enhanced congestion control               Disabled
[F] Full duplex / Flow control                Half duplex

---------------------- Related Menus ----------------------------------
[A] Port addressing            [V] View port statistics
[N] Next port                  [G] Goto port
[P] Previous port              [X] Exit to Main Menu

Enter Selection:
```

Timing Tests on the Catalyst 1900

The timing values are harder to verify on a 1900/2820 because of the lack of debugging tools, so we just started a **ping** from a PC connected to the switch directed to the switch itself. We disconnected and then reconnected the cable, and recorded how long it took for the switch to respond to the **ping** with PortFast on and with PortFast off. For an Ethernet port with PortFast on (the default state), the PC received a response within 5 to 6 seconds. With PortFast off, the PC received a response in 34 to 35 seconds.

An Additional Benefit to PortFast

There is another spanning-tree-related benefit to using PortFast in your network. Every time a link becomes active and moves to the forwarding state in spanning tree, the switch will send a special spanning-tree packet called a Topology Change Notification (TCN). The TCN notification is passed up to the root of the spanning tree, where it is propagated to all the switches in the VLAN. This causes all the switches to age out their table of MAC addresses using the forward delay parameter, which is usually set to 15 seconds. So, every time a workstation joins the bridge group, the MAC addresses on all the switches will be aged out after 15 seconds instead of the normal 300 seconds.

When a workstation becomes active, it does not really change the topology to any significant degree, so as far as all the switches in the VLAN are concerned, it is unnecessary for them to have to go through the fast aging TCN period. If you turn on PortFast, the switch will not send TCN packets when a port becomes active.

Commands to Use for Verifying That the Configuration Is Working

For the 4000/5000/6000 series, use these commands to verify the configuration:

- **show port spantree 2/1**—To see whether "Fast-Start" (PortFast) is enabled or disabled
- **show spantree 1**—To see all ports in VLAN 1 and to determine whether they have "Fast-Start" enabled
- **show port channel**—To see whether you have any active channels
- **show port channel 2**—To see the channel mode (auto, off, and so on) for each port on module 2
- **show trunk 2**—To see the trunk mode (auto, off, and so on) for each port on module 2
- **show port**—To see the status (connected, notconnect, and so on), speed, and duplex mode for all ports on the switch

For the 2900XL/3500XL series, use these commands:

- **show spanning-tree interface FastEthernet 0/1**—To see whether PortFast is enabled on this port (No mention of PortFast means that it is not enabled.)
- **show running-config**—If a port shows the command **spanning-tree portfast,** then PortFast is enabled

For the 1900/2800 series, use this command:

- **show running-config**—To see the current settings (some commands are invisible when they represent the default settings of the switch)

Use the menu system to view the port status screen.

Commands to Use for Troubleshooting the Configuration

For the 4000/5000/6000 series, use these commands in troubleshooting:

- **show port spantree 2/1**—To see whether "Fast-Start" (PortFast) is enabled or disabled

- **show spantree 1**—To see all ports in VLAN 1 and to determine whether they have "Fast-Start" enabled
- **show port channel**—To see whether you have any active channels
- **show port channel 2**—To see the channel mode (auto, off, and so on) for each port on module 2
- **show trunk 2**—To see the trunk mode (auto, off, and so on) for each port on module 2
- **show port**—To see the status (connected, notconnect, and so on), speed, and duplex mode for all ports on the switch
- **show logging**—To see what type of messages will generate logging output
- **set logging level spantree 7**—To set the switch to log the spanning tree port states in real time on the console
- **set port disable 2/1**—To turn off the port in software (like **shutdown** on the router)
- **set port enable 2/1**—To turn on the port in software (like **no shutdown** on the router)
- **show time**—To show the current time in seconds (used at the beginning of a timing test)
- **show port capabilities**—To see what features are implemented on the port
- **set trunk 2/1 off**—To set the trunking mode to off (to speed port initialization time)
- **set port channel 2/1-2 off**—To set the EtherChannel (PAgP) mode to off (to speed port initialization time)
- **set port speed 2/1 100**—To set the port to 100 Mbps and to turn off autonegotiation
- **set port duplex 2/1 full**—To set the port duplex to full

For the 2900XL/3500XL series, use these commands:

- **service timestamps debug uptime**—To show the time with the debug messages
- **service timestamps log uptime**—To show the time with the logging messages
- **debug spantree events**—So that we can see when the port moves through the spanning tree stages
- **show clock**—To see the current time (for the timing tests)
- **show spanning-tree interface FastEthernet 0/1**—To see whether PortFast is enabled on this port (No mention of PortFast means that it is not enabled.)
- **shut**—To turn off a port from software
- **no shut**—To turn on a port from software

For the 1900/2800 series, use this command:

- **show running-config**—To see the current settings (Some commands are invisible when they represent the default settings of the switch.)

Configuring and Troubleshooting IP Multilayer Switching

This document outlines basic troubleshooting of Multilayer Switching (MLS) for IP. This feature has become a highly desired method of accelerating routing performance through the use of dedicated application-specific integrated circuits (ASICs). Traditional routing is done through a central CPU and software; MLS offloads a significant portion of routing (packet rewrite) to hardware and thus has also been termed *switching*. *MLS* and *Layer 3 switching* are equivalent terms. The NetFlow feature of IOS is distinct and is not covered in this document. MLS also includes support for IPX (IPX MLS) and multicasting (MMLS), but this document will exclusively concentrate on basic MLS IP troubleshooting.

Introduction

As greater demands are placed on networks, the need for greater performance increases. More PCs are being connected to LANs, WANs, and the Internet, and their users require fast access to databases, files/web pages, networked applications, other PCs, and streaming video. To keep connections quick and reliable, networks must be capable of rapidly adjusting to changes and failures and finding the best path, all while remaining as invisible as possible to end users. End users who experience rapid information flow between their PC and server with minimal network slowness are happy ones. Determining the best path is the primary function of routing protocols, and this can be a CPU-intensive process; thus, a significant performance increase is gained by offloading a portion of this function to switching hardware. This is the point of the MLS feature.

There are three major components of MLS: Two of them are the MLS-RP and the MLS-SE. The MLS-RP is the MLS-enabled router, performing the traditional function of routing between subnets/VLANs. The MLS-SE is an MLS-enabled switch, which normally requires a router to route between subnets/VLANs but, with special hardware and software, can handle rewriting of the packet. When a packet transverses a routed interface, nondata portions of the packet are changed (rewritten) as it is carried to its destination, hop by hop.

Confusion can arise here because it seems that a Layer 2 device is taking on a Layer 3 task; actually, the switch is only rewriting Layer 3 information and is "switching" between subnets/VLANs—the router is still responsible for standards-based route calculations and best-path determination. Much of this confusion can be avoided by mentally keeping the routing and switching functions separate, especially when, as is commonly the case, they are contained within the same chassis (as with an internal MLS-RP). Think of MLS as a much more advanced form of route caching, with the cache kept separate from the router on a switch. Both the MLS-RP and the MLS-SE, along with respective hardware and software minimums, are required for MLS.

The MLS-RP can be internal (installed in a switch chassis) or external (connected via a cable to a trunk port on the switch). Examples of internal MLS-RPs are the Route-Switch Module (RSM) and the Route-Switch Feature Card (RSFC), which are installed in a slot or supervisor of a Catalyst 5xxx family member, respectively; the same applies to the Multilayer Switch Feature Card (MSFC) for the Catalyst 6xxx family. Examples of external MLS-RPs include any member of the Cisco 7500, 7200, 4700, 4500, or 3600 series routers. In general, to support the MLS IP feature, all MLS-RPs require a minimum IOS version in the 11.3WA or 12.0WA trains; consult release documentation for specifics. Also, *MLS must be enabled* for a router to be an MLS-RP.

The MLS-SE is a switch with special hardware. For a member of the Catalyst 5xxx family, MLS requires that the supervisor have a NetFlow Feature Card (NFFC) installed; the Supervisor IIG and IIIG have one by default. In addition, a bare minimum of Catalyst OS 4.1.1 software is required. Note that the 4.x train has "gone General Deployment (GD)"— that is, passed rigorous end-user criteria and field-experience targets for stability—so check Cisco's web site for the latest releases. IP MLS is supported and automatically enabled for Catalyst 6xxx hardware and software with the MSFC/PFC (other routers have MLS disabled by default). Note that IPX MLS and MLS for multicasting may have different hardware and software (IOS and Catalyst OS) requirements. More Cisco platforms do/will support the MLS feature. Also, *MLS must be enabled* for a switch to be an MLS-SE.

The third major component of MLS is the Multilayer Switching Protocol (MLSP). Because understanding the basics of MLSP gets at the heart of MLS and is essential to performing effective MLS troubleshooting, we will describe MLSP here more in detail. MLSP is utilized by the MLS-RP and the MLS-SE to communicate with one another—tasks include enabling MLS; installing, updating, or deleting flows (cache information); and managing and exporting flow statistics (NetFlow Data Export is covered in other documentation). MLSP also allows the MLS-SE to learn the Media Access Control (MAC, Layer 2) addresses of the MLS-enabled router interfaces, check the flowmask of the MLS-RP (explained later in this chapter), and confirm that the MLS-RP is operational. The MLS-RP sends out multicast "hello" packets every 15 seconds using MLSP; if three of these intervals are missed, then the MLS-SE recognizes that the MLS-RP has failed or that connectivity to it has been lost.

Figure 23-7 illustrates three essentials that must be completed (using MLSP) for a shortcut to be created: the candidate, enabler, and caching steps. The MLS-SE checks for a cached MLS entry; if MLS cache entry and packet information match (a hit), the packet's header is rewritten locally on the switch (a shortcut, or bypassing of the router) instead of being sent on to the router, as would normally happen. Packets that do not match and that are sent on to the MLS-RP are *candidate packets*—that is, there is a possibility of switching them locally.

After passing the candidate packet through the MLS flowmask (explained later in Step 7) and rewriting the information contained in the packet's header (the data portion is not touched), the router sends it toward the next hop along the destination path. The packet is now called an *enabler packet*. If the packet returns to the same MLS-SE from which it left, an MLS shortcut is created and placed into the MLS cache. Rewriting for that packet and all similar packets that follow (called a flow) is now done locally by switch hardware instead of by router software. *The same MLS-SE must see both the candidate and the enabler packets for a particular flow for an MLS shortcut to be created.* (This is why network topology is important to MLS.) Remember, the point of MLS is to allow the communication path between two devices in different VLANs, connected off the same switch, to bypass the router and thus enhance network performance.

Figure 23-7 *The Three Essentials That Must Be Completed (Using MLSP) for a Shortcut to Be Created: the Candidate, Enabler, and Caching Steps*

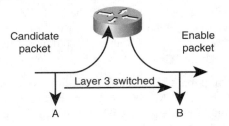

By using the flowmask (essentially an access list), the administrator can adjust the degree of similarity of these packets, and thus adjust the scope of the flows: destination address; destination and source addresses; or destination, source, and Layer 4 information. Note that the first packet of a flow always passes through the router; from then on it is locally switched. Each flow is unidirectional—communication between PCs, for example, requires the setup and use of *two* shortcuts. The main purpose of MLSP is to set up, create, and maintain these shortcuts.

These three components (the MLS-RP, the MLS-SE, and the MLSP) free up vital router resources by allowing other network components to take on some of its functions. Depending on the topology and configuration, MLS provides a simple and highly effective method of increasing network performance in the LAN.

Troubleshooting IP MLS Technology

Figure 23-8 is a flow diagram for basic IP MLS troubleshooting. It is derived from the most common types of MLS-IP cases opened with the Technical Assistance Center (TAC) and faced by our customers and TAC engineers, up to the time that this document was created. MLS is a robust feature, and you should have no problems with it. However, if an issue does arise, the following should help you to resolve the types of IP MLS problems that you might likely face. A few essential assumptions have been made:

- That you are familiar with the basic configuration steps required to enable IP MLS on the router and switches, and that you have completed these steps. See the resources listed at the end of this document for excellent material.

- That IP routing is enabled on the MLS-RP (it is on by default). If the command **no ip routing** appears in the global configuration of a **show run**, it has been turned off, and IP MLS will not function.

- That IP connectivity exists between the MLS-RP and MLS-SE. You can **ping** the IP addresses of the router from the switch and look for exclamation points (called "bangs") to be displayed in return.

- That the MLS-RP interfaces are in an "up/up" state on the router. Type **show ip interface brief** on the router to confirm this.

WARNING   Whenever making configuration changes to a router intended to be permanent, remember to save those changes with a **copy running-config starting-config** (shortened versions of this command include **copy run start** and **wr mem**). Any configuration modifications will be lost if the router reloads or is reset. The RSM, RSFC, and MSFC are routers, not switches. In contrast, changes made at the switch prompt of a Catalyst 5xxx or 6xxx family member are automatically saved.

Figure 23-8 *Flow Diagram for Basic IP MLS Troubleshooting*

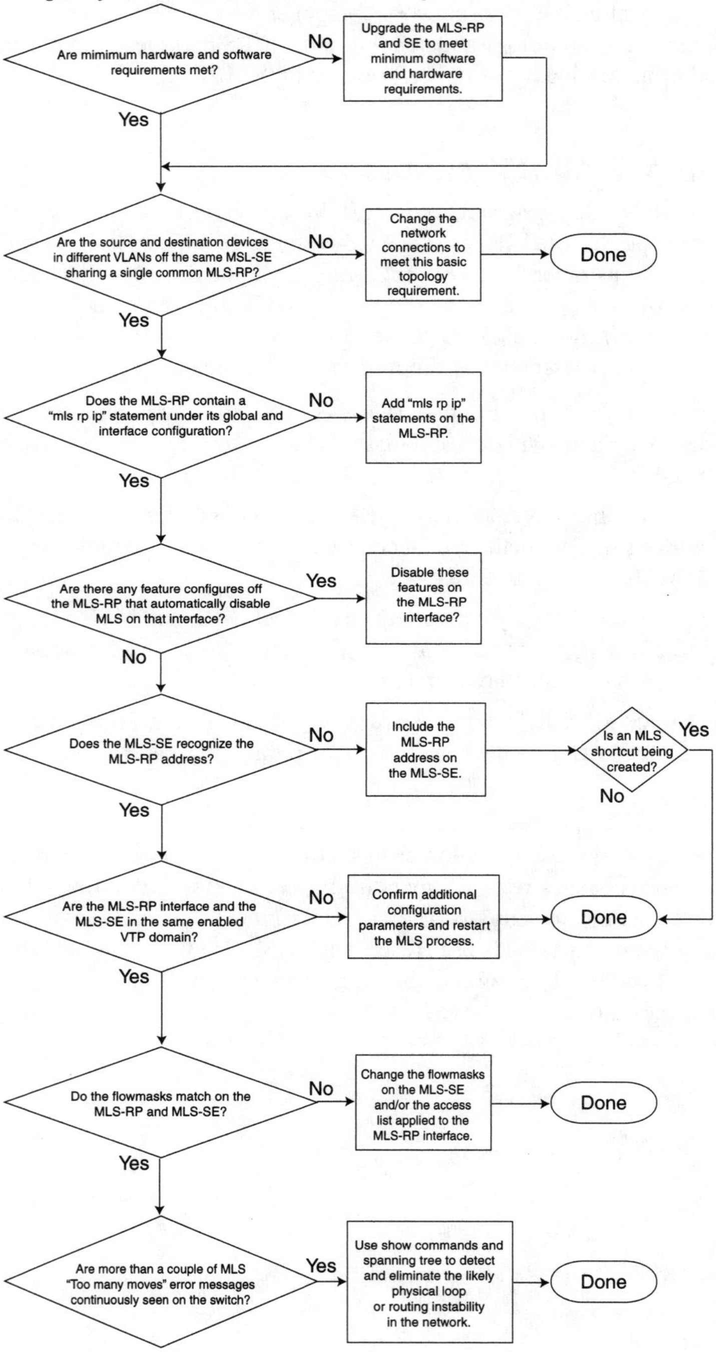

Step 1   Are minimum hardware and software requirements met?

Upgrade the MLS-RP and SE to meet minimum software and hardware requirements. For the MLS-RP, no additional hardware is required. Although MLS can be configured on nontrunked interfaces, the connection to the MLS-SE is generally through VLAN interfaces (as with an RSM) or support trunking (can be configured to carry multiple VLAN information by configuring ISL or 802.1q).

Also, remember that, as of publication time, only members of the 7500, 7200, 4700, 4500, and 3600 router families support MLS externally. Currently, only these external routers and the routers that fit into the Catalyst 5xxx or 6xxx switch families (such as the RSM and RSFC for the Catalyst 5xxx family, and the MSFC for the Catalyst 6xxx family) can be MLS-RPs. The MSFC requires the Policy Feature Card (PFC) as well, both installed on the Catalyst 6xx Supervisor. IP MLS is now a standard feature in IOS 12.0 and later router software. IOS software lower than IOS 12.0 generally requires a special train; for such IP MLS support, install the latest images in IOS 11.3 that have the letters "WA" in their filenames.

For the MLS-SE, a NetFlow Feature Card (NFFC) is required for a member of the Catalyst 5xxx family; this card is installed in the Supervisor module of the Catalyst switch and is included as standard hardware in newer Catalyst 5xxx series Supervisors (since 1999). The NFFC is not supported on the Supervisors I or II and is an option on early Supervisor IIIs. Also, a minimum of 4.1.1 CatOS is required for IP MLS. In contrast, for the Catalyst 6xxx family, the required hardware comes as standard equipment, and IP MLS has been supported since the first CatOS software release, 5.1.1 (in fact, IP MLS is an essential and default ingredient for its high performance). With new platforms and software being released that support IP MLS, it is important to check documentation and release notes, and to generally install the latest release in the lowest train that meets your feature requirements. Always check the release notes and consult with your local Cisco sales office for new MLS support and feature developments.

Commands to check the installed hardware and software are **show version** on the router, and **show module** on the switch.

Note   The Catalyst 6xxx family of switches does *not* support an external MLS-RP at this time. The MLS-RP must be an MSFC.

Step 2   Are the source and destination devices in different VLANs off the same MLS-SE, sharing a single common MLS-RP?

It is a basic topology requirement of MLS that the router have a path to each of the VLANs. Remember that the point of MLS is to create a shortcut between two VLANs so that the "routing" between the two end devices can be performed by the switch, thus freeing the router for other tasks. The switch is not actually routing; it is rewriting the frames so that it appears to the end devices that they are talking through the router. If the two devices are in the same VLAN, then the MLS-SE will switch the frame locally without utilizing MLS, as switches do in such a transparently bridged environment, and no MLS shortcut will be created. It is possible to have multiple switches and routers in the network, and even multiple switches along the flow path, but the path between the two end devices for which an MLS shortcut is desired must include a single MLS-RP in that VLAN for that path.

In other words, the flow from source to destination must cross a VLAN boundary on the same MLS-RP, and a candidate and enabler packet pair must be seen by the same MLS-SE for the MLS shortcut to be created. If these criteria are not met, then the packet will be routed normally without the use of MLS. See the documents suggested at the end of this chapter for diagrams and discussions regarding supported and unsupported network topologies.

Step 3   Does the MLS-RP contain an **mls rp ip** statement under *both* its global and interface configuration?

If one is not present, add **mls rp ip** statements appropriately on the MLS-RP. Except for routers for which IP MLS is automatically enabled (such as the Catalyst 6xxx MSFC), this is a required configuration step. For most MLS-RPs (routers configured for IP MLS), this statement must appear both in the global configuration and under the interface configuration.

Note   When configuring the MLS-RP, also remember to place the **mls rp management-interface** command under one of its IP MLS interfaces. This required step tells the MLS-RP out which interface it should send MLSP messages to communicate with the MLS-SE. Again, it is necessary to place this command under one interface only.

Step 4   Are any features configured on the MLS-RP that automatically disable MLS on that interface?

Several configuration options on the router are not compatible with MLS. These include IP accounting, encryption, compression, IP security, network address translation (NAT), and committed access rate (CAR). For further information, see links regarding IP MLS configuration included at the end of this chapter. Packets traversing a router interface configured with any of these features must be routed normally; no MLS shortcut will be created. For MLS to work, you must disable these features on the MLS-RP interface.

Another important feature that affects MLS is access lists, both input and output. Further information on this option is included in the discussion of flowmasks (Step 7).

Step 5   Does the MLS-SE recognize the MLS-RP address?

For MLS to function, the switch must recognize the router as an MLS-RP. Internal MLS-RPs (again, the RSM or RSFC in a Catalyst 5xxx family member, and the MSFC in a Catalyst 6xxx family member) are automatically recognized by the MLS-SE in which they are installed. For external MLS-RPs, you must explicitly inform the switch of the router's address. This address is not actually an IP address, although on external MLS-RPs it is chosen from the list of IP addresses configured on the router's interfaces; it is simply a router ID. In fact, for internal MLS-RPs, the MLS-ID is normally not even an IP address configured on the router. Because internal MLS-RPs are included automatically, it is commonly a loopback address (127.0.0.x). For MLS to function, include on the MLS-SE the MLS-ID found on the MLS-RP.

Use **show mls rp** on the router to find the MLS-ID, and then configure that ID on the switch using **the set mls include <*MLS-ID*>** command. This is a required configuration step when using external MLS-RPs.

WARNING   Changing the IP address of MLS-RP interfaces and then reloading the router may cause the MLS process on the router to choose a new MLS-ID. This new MLS-ID may be different from the MLS-ID that was manually included on the MLS-SE, which may cause MLS to cease functioning. This is not a software glitch, just an effect of the switch trying to communicate with a MLS-ID that is no longer valid. Be sure to include this new MLS-ID on the switch to get MLS working once again. You may have to disable/enable IP MLS as well.

Note	When the MLS-SE is not directly connected to the MLS-RP, the address that must be included on the MLS-SE may appear as the loopback address mentioned previously: a switch connected in between the MLS-SE and MLS-RP. You must include the MLS-ID even though the MLS-RP is internal. To the second switch, the MLS-RP appears as an *external* router because the MLS-RP and MLS-SE are not contained in the same chassis.

Step 6   Are the MLS-RP interface and the MLS-SE in the same enabled VTP domain?

MLS requires that MLS components, including the end stations, must be in the same Virtual Trunking Protocol (VTP) domain. VTP is a Layer 2 protocol used for managing VLANs on several Catalyst switches from a central switch; it allows an administrator to create or delete a VLAN on all switches in a domain without having to do so on every switch in that domain. The MLSP, which the MLS-SE and the MLS-RP use to communicate with one another, does not cross a VTP domain boundary. If the network administrator has VTP enabled on the switches (VTP is enabled on Catalyst 5xxx and 6xxx family members by default), use the **show vtp domain** command on the switch to learn in which VTP domain the MLS-SE has been placed. Except for the Catalyst 6xxx MSFC, on which MLS is essentially a plug-and-play feature, add, *in the following steps*, the VTP domain to each of the router's MLS interfaces. This will permit MLSP multicasts to move between the MLS-RP and MLS-SE, and therefore allow MLS to function.

In interface configuration mode of the MLS-RP, enter the following commands:

— **no mls rp ip**—Disable MLS on the affected MLS-RP interface before modifying the VTP domain.

— **mls rp vtp-domain < VTP domain name>**—The VTP domain name on each MLS-enabled interface must match that of the switch.

— **mls rp vlan-id <VLAN #>**—This is required only for non-ISL trunking, external MLS-RP interfaces.

— **mls rp management-interface**—Do this for only one interface on the MLS-RP. This required step tells the MLS-RP out which interface it should send MLSP messages.

— **mls rp ip**—Enable MLS once again on the interface of the MLS-RP.

To change the VTP domain name of the MLS-SE, use the following command at the switch CatOS enable prompt:

```
set vtp domain name <VTP domain name>
```

For MLS to work, be sure that VTP is enabled on the switch:

```
set vtp enable
```

Step 7 Do the flowmasks agree on the MLS-RP and MLS-SE?

A flowmask is a filter configured by a network administrator that is used by MLS to determine whether a shortcut should be created. Just like an access list, the more detailed the criteria you set up, the deeper into the packet the MLS process must look to verify whether the packet meets those criteria. To adjust the scope of MLS-created shortcuts, the flowmask can be made more or less specific; the flowmask is essentially a "tuning" device.

There are three types of IP MLS modes: destination-ip, destination-source-ip, and full-flow-ip. *Destination-ip* mode, the default, is in use when no access list is applied to the router's MLS-enabled interface. *Source-destination-ip* mode is in use when a standard access list is applied, and *full-flow-ip* is in effect for an extended access list. The MLS mode on the MLS-RP is implicitly determined by the type of access list applied to the interface. By contrast, the MLS mode on the MLS-SE is explicitly configured. By choosing the appropriate mode, you can thus configure MLS so that either only the destination address must match for an MLS shortcut to be created, or both source and destination must match, or even Layer 4 information such as TCP/UDP port numbers must match.

The MLS mode is configurable on both the MLS-RP and the MLS-SE, and in general they must match. However, if either source-destination-ip or full-flow-ip MLS modes are deemed to be required, it is best to configure it on the router by applying the appropriate access list. MLS will always choose the most specific mask, giving the flowmask configured on the MLS-RP precedence over the one found on the MLS-SE. *Be careful* if you change the MLS mode of the switch from the default destination-ip: You should make sure that it matches the MLS mode on the router for MLS to work. For source-destination-ip and full-flow-ip modes, remember to apply the access list to the appropriate router interface. With no access list applied, even if configured, the MLS mode simply will be destination-ip, the default.

WARNING   Whenever the flowmask is changed, whether on the MLS-RP or on the MLS-SE, all cached MLS flows are purged, and the MLS process is restarted. A purge also can occur when applying the command **clear ip route-cache** on the router. Applying the global router configuration command **no ip routing**, which turns off IP routing and essentially transforms the router into a transparent bridge, will cause a purge and disable MLS (remember, routing is a prerequisite of MLS). Each of these may temporarily—but seriously—affect router performance in a production network because the router will experience a spike in its load until the new shortcuts are created: After all, it must now handle all the flows that were just previously being processed by the switch.

Note   Especially with a member of the Catalyst 5000 family as the MLS-SE, it is best to avoid the very wide use of flowmasks that are configured with Layer 4 information. By forcing the router to peer so deeply into every packet on the interface, much of the intended benefits of MLS are bypassed. This is much less of an issue when utilizing a Catalyst 6xxx family member as the MLS-SE because the switch ports themselves can recognize Layer 4 information.

Note   Until recently, MLS did not support flowmasks configured inbound on an MLS-RP interface, only outbound. Now, by using the **mls rp ip input-acl** command in addition to normal MLS-RP configuration commands on a router interface, an inbound flowmask is supported.

Step 8   Are more than a couple of MLS "Too many moves" error messages continuously seen on the switch?

As the previous note mentions, changing a flowmask, clearing the route cache, or globally turning off IP routing will cause a cache purge. Other circumstances can also cause full or many single entry purges, and cause MLS to complain of "Too many moves." There are several forms of this message, but each contains these three words. Aside from what has already been mentioned, the most common cause of this error occurs when the switch learns multiple identical Ethernet Media Access Control

(MAC) address within the same VLAN; Ethernet standards do not allow for identical MAC addresses within the same VLAN. If you see this message infrequently, or just a few times in a row, there is no cause for concern. MLS is a robust feature, and the message may be simply caused by normal network events, such as a PC connection being moved between ports, for example. If you see this message continuously for several minutes, however, it is likely a symptom of a more serious issue.

When such a situation arises, its root cause is commonly the presence of two devices with the same MAC address actually connected to a VLAN, or a physical loop within the VLAN (or multiple VLANs, if bridging across these broadcast domains). Use spanning-tree troubleshooting covered in the section "Troubleshooting Spanning-Tree Protocol and Related Design Considerations" found later in this chapter and the hint that follows to find the loop and eliminate it. Also, any rapid topology changes can cause temporary network (and MLS) instability (flapping router interfaces, a bad NIC, and so on).

TIP	Use the **show mls notification** and **show looktable** commands on the switch to point you in the right direction of the duplicate MAC address or physical loop. The first will provide a TA value; the command **show looktable <TA value>** will return a possible MAC address that may be traced to the root of the problem.

Commands or Screen Captures

For descriptions and detailed examples of IP MLS router and switch commands, refer to the excellent documentation listed under the "Additional Sources" section.

Before Calling Cisco Systems' TAC Team

Before calling Cisco Systems's Technical Assistance Center (TAC), make sure you that have read through this chapter and completed the actions suggested for your system's problem.

Additionally, do the following and document the results so that we can better assist you:

- Capture the output of **show module** from all the affected switches.
- Capture the output of **show vtp domain** from all the affected switches.

- Capture the output of **show trunk <mod_num/port_num>** from all the affected ports.

- Capture the output of **show port <mod_num/port_num> capabilities** from all the affected ports.

- Capture the output of **show tech-support** from the MLS-RP.

- Capture the output of **show mls rp** on the MLS-RP and both **show mls** and **sh mls include** on the MLS-SEs.

- The output of additional commands may be necessary, depending on the nature of the issue.

A clear network topology and dial-in or Telnet access also help considerably in effective problem resolution.

Troubleshooting Spanning-Tree Protocol and Related Design Considerations

NOTE   The text in this section comes directly from the Cisco web site www.cisco.com/warp/customer/473/16.html.

The primary function of the Spanning-Tree Algorithm (STA) is to cut loops created by redundant links in bridged networks. The Spanning-Tree Protocol (STP) operates at Layer 2 of the OSI model and, by the means of bridge protocol data units (BPDUs) exchanged between bridges, elects the ports that will eventually forward or block traffic. This protocol can fail in some specific cases, and troubleshooting the resulting situation can be very difficult, depending on the design of the network. We can even say that in this particular area, the most important part of the troubleshooting is done before the problem occurs.

This section is not intended to be a complete LAN design guide, but just a list of recommendations that will help in implementing a safe network as far as bridging is concerned. Assuming knowledge of the protocol itself, we will introduce the following topics:

- The reasons that can cause the STP to fail

- What information to look for to identify the source of the problem

- What kind of design minimizes spanning-tree risks and is easy to troubleshoot

Spanning-Tree Protocol Failure

A failure in the STA generally leads to a bridging loop (not a spanning-tree loop because you don't need STP to have a loop). Most customers calling the TAC for spanning-tree problems suspect a bug, but experience proves that it is seldom the case. Even if the software is at stake, a bridging loop in an STP environment necessarily comes from a port that should block but that is forwarding traffic.

What can cause a blocked port to go to forwarding? Let's first recall why a port ends up in a blocking state. Each LAN has a single designated bridge. This bridge is responsible for the connectivity of the LAN toward the root bridge.

In Figure 23-9, Bridge B has been elected as the designated bridge, and Bridge C is blocking because it is only providing an alternate path to the root. Why is Bridget C blocking, not Bridge B? This is determined practically by the BPDUs that B and C exchange on the LAN. Here, Bridget B had a better BPDU than Bridge C. Bridge B keeps sending BPDUs advertising its superiority over the other bridges on this LAN. If Bridge C fails to receive these BPDUs for a certain period of time (called the max age—20 seconds, by default), it would start a transition to the forwarding mode.

Figure 23-9 *Blocked Port on Bridge C Keeps Receiving BPDUs from Bridge B*

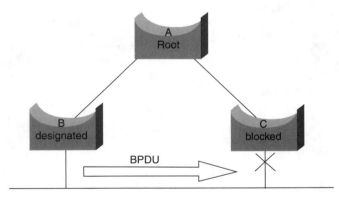

Important note: A port must keep receiving superior BPDUs to stay in blocking mode.

The following subsections list the different situations that can lead the STA to fail. Most of these failures are, in fact, related to a massive loss of BPDUs, causing blocked ports to transition to forwarding mode.

Duplex Mismatch

Duplex mismatch on a point-to-point link is a very common configuration error. This occurs especially when one side of the link is hard-coded as full duplex. If you leave the other side in autonegotiation mode, it will end up in half-duplex mode (a port with duplex hard-coded does not negotiate anymore).

The worst-case scenario is when a bridge sending BPDUs is configured for half-duplex operation on a link, whereas its peer is configured for full-duplex mode. In Figure 23-10, the duplex mismatch on the link between bridges A and B can easily lead to a bridging loop. Because Bridge B is configured for full-duplex operation, it does not perform carrier sense when accessing the link. Bridge B will then start sending frames even if Bridge A is already using the link. This is a problem for Bridge A, which detects a collision and runs the back-off algorithm before attempting another transmission of its frame. The result is that, if there is enough traffic from B to A, every single packet (including the BPDUs) sent by Bridge A will be deferred or collisioned and eventually dropped. From an STP point of view, because it does not receive BPDUs from Bridge A anymore, Bridge B has lost its root. This leads Bridge B to unblock its port to Bridge C, hence creating the loop.

Figure 23-10 *Bridging Loop Created by a Duplex Mismatch*

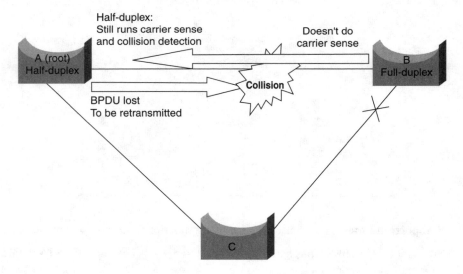

Unidirectional Link

This is a very frequent cause for a bridging loop. Unidirectional links are often caused by a failure not detected on a fiber link, for instance, or a problem with a transceiver. Anything that can lead a link to stay up while providing a one-way communication is very dangerous as far as STP is concerned. The example shown in Figure 23-11 is very straightforward.

Figure 23-11 *Bridging Loop in a Unidirectional Link Scenario*

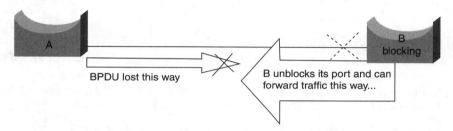

Here, let's suppose that the link between bridges A and B is unidirectional and drops traffic from A to B while transmitting traffic from B to A. Suppose that Bridge B should be blocking. We already mentioned that a port can block only if it receives BPDUs from a bridge that has a better priority. In this case, all these BPDUs coming from Bridge A are lost, and Bridge B eventually forwards traffic, creating a loop. Note that, in this case, if the failure exists at startup, the STP will not converge correctly. This means that rebooting the bridges will have absolutely no effect (whereas it could temporarily help in the previous case).

Cisco introduced the UDLD protocol on high-end switches. This feature is capable of detecting wrong cabling or unidirectional links on Layer 2 and automatically breaks resulting loops by disabling some ports. It is really worth running wherever possible in a bridged environment.

Packet Corruption

Packet corruption can also lead to the same kind of failure. If a link is experiencing a high rate of physical errors, a certain number of consecutive BPDUs could be lost, leading a blocking port to transition to forwarding. This case is rather seldom because STP default parameters are very conservative. The blocking port would need to miss its BPDUs for 50 seconds before transitioning to forwarding, and a single BPDU successfully transmitted would break the loop. This case specially occurs when STP parameters have been adjusted without care (max age reduced, for instance).

Resource Errors

Even on high-end switches that perform most of their switching functions in hardware using specialized Asics, STP is implemented in software. This means that if the CPU of the bridge is overutilized for any reason, it is possible that it lacks resources to send out BPDUs. The STA is generally not very processor-intensive and has priority over other processes. You will see in the upcoming section "Look for Resource Errors" that there are some guidelines that govern the number of instances of STP that a particular platform can handle.

PortFast Configuration Error

PortFast is a feature that you typically will want to enable for a port connected to a host. When the link comes up on this port, the first stages of the STA are skipped and the port directly transitions to the forwarding mode. This can obviously be dangerous when not used correctly. Loops occurs then when moving a cable and *should* be transient only.

In Figure 23-12, Bridge A is a bridge with port p1 already forwarding and port p2 configured for PortFast. Bridge B is a hub. As soon as the second cable is plugged into Bridge A, p2 goes to forwarding and creates a loop between p1 and p2. This will stop as soon as p1 or p2 receives a BPDU that will put one of these two ports in blocking modes. The problem with that kind of transient loop is that if the looping traffic is very intensive, the bridge may have trouble successfully sending the BPDU that will stop the loop. This can delay the convergence considerably. The latest high-end Catalyst software implements a feature called BPDU guard that will even disable the port if it is configured for PortFast and receives a BPDU.

Figure 23-12 *Transient Bridging Loop Because of a Wrong PortFast Configuration*

Cable connected

Transient loop:
p1 and p2 forwarding

p2 has received a BPDU
that immediately
blocked it

Awkward STP Parameter Tuning and Diameter Issues

We already saw that an aggressive value for the max age parameter and the forward-delay could lead to a very unstable STP. The loss of some BPDUs can then cause a loop to appear. Another issue, not very well known, is related to the diameter of the bridged network. The conservative default values for the STP impose a maximum network diameter of 7. This means that two distinct bridges in the network should not be more than seven bridges away the one to the other. Part of this restriction comes from the Age field BPDUs carry: When a BPDU is propagated from the root bridge toward the leaves of the tree, the Age field is incremented each time that it goes though a bridge. Eventually, when the Age field of a BPDU goes beyond the max age, it is discarded. Typically, this will occur if the root is too far away from some bridges of the network. This issue will affect convergence of the spanning tree.

Software Errors

As mentioned in the introduction to this chapter, the STP is one of the very first features that was implemented in Cisco products. You can expect this feature to be very stable. Only interaction with new features, such as EtherChanneling, caused STP to fail in some very specific cases that have been addressed now. A software bug can be anything, so there is no way of really describing the issue that it could introduce. Let's simply state again that the most dangerous situation would be to ignore some BPDUs or, generally speaking, having a blocking port transitioning to forwarding.

Troubleshooting a Failure

Unfortunately, there is no systematic procedure to troubleshoot an STP issue. This section instead looks like a checklist, recapitulating some of the actions available to you. Most of the indications given here apply to bridging loop troubleshooting. Other failures of the STP leading to a loss of connectivity can be identified using a more conventional way, by exploring the path taken by traffic experiencing a problem.

Note that most of these troubleshooting steps assume connectivity to the different devices of the bridge network. This means having console access. During a bridging loop, for example, you will probably not be able to Telnet.

Use the Diagram of the Network

You need to know some basic things about your network before troubleshooting a bridging loop.

You need to know at least the following:

- The topology of the bridged network

- Where the root bridge is located
- Where the blocked ports (and the redundant links) are located

This knowledge is essential at least for two reasons:

- How could you know what to fix in the network if you don't know how it should look when it is working?
- Most of the troubleshooting steps are simply using **show** commands to try to identify error conditions. Knowledge of the network helps you focus on the critical ports on the key devices.

Identify a Bridging Loop

It used to be that a broadcast storm could have the same effect on the network. Nowadays, with high-speed links and devices providing switching at hardware level, it is nearly impossible that, for instance, a single server brings down a network by broadcasting. The real way of identifying a bridging loop for sure is to capture the traffic on a saturated link and to check that you see similar packets multiple times.

But practically, if all users in a certain bridging domain have connectivity issues at the same time, you can already suspect a bridging loop.

Check the port utilization on your devices and look for abnormal values. See the "Check Port Utilization" upcoming section for additional information.

On the Catalyst switches running a CatOS, you can easily check the overall backplane usage using the **show system** command. This command is very useful because it not only gives you the current usage of the switch backplane, but it also specifies the peak usage (and its date). An unusual peak utilization shows you whether there has ever been a bridging loop on this device.

Restore Connectivity Quickly and Be Ready for Another Time

Bridging loops have extremely severe consequences on a bridged network. Administrators generally don't have time to look for the reason of the loop and prefer to restore connectivity as soon as possible. If you do this, you will not find the real cause of the issue and need to be ready for the next time that it occurs.

Break the Loop Disabling Ports

The easy way out of a bridging loop is to disable manually every single port that is providing redundancy in the network. If you have been able to identify a part of the network that is more affected, start disabling ports in this area. Even better, if possible, start by disabling ports that should be blocking. Each time you disable a port, check if connectivity is restored in the network as if you are hit by a bridging loop—its effect should stop immediately after you break it. Knowing which disabled port stopped the loop, you can be sure that the failure was located on a redundant path where this port was located. If this port should have been blocking, you have probably found the link on which the failure appeared.

Log STP Events on Devices Hosting Blocked Ports

If you couldn't precisely identify the source of the problem—or, for instance, if the problem is only transient—enable the logging of the STP event on the bridges and switches of the network experiencing the failure. If you want to limit the number of devices to configure, enable this logging at least on devices hosting blocked ports because this is always the transition of a blocked port that creates a loop.

- **IOS**—Enter the exec command **debug spantree events** to enable STP debugging information being generated. Use the **general config mode** command logging buffered to capture this debug information in the device's buffers.

- **CatOS**—The command **set logging level spantree 7 default** increases the default level of STP-related event to debugging. Be sure that you are logging a maximum amount of messages in the switch's buffers using the **set logging buffer 500** command.

You can also try to send this output to a syslog device. Unfortunately, when a bridging loop occurs, you seldom can keep connectivity to a syslog server.

Check Ports

As mentioned before, the critical ports to be investigated first are the blocking ports. The next section gives a list of what you can look for on the different ports, with a quick description of the commands to enter for both IOS-based machines and CatOS-based switches.

Check That Blocked Ports Receive BPDUs

Especially on blocked ports and root ports, check that you keep receiving BPDUs periodically. Several issues can lead to a port not receiving packets/BPDUs:

- If you are running an IOS release 12.0 or greater, the command **show spanning-tree bridge-group #.** has a field named BPDU that will show you the number of BPDUs that you received for each interface. Issuing the command once or twice more will quickly tell you if the device is receiving BPDUs.

- If you don't have the field BPDU on the output of the **show spanning-tree** command, then the easiest way to checking whether you are receiving BPDUs is to simply enable STP debug with the **debug spantree tree** command.

   For CatOS, the **show mac <module/port>** command will tell you the number of multicast packets that a specific port receives. But the simplest is to use **show spantree statistic <modele#/port#> <vlan#>**. This command displays the exact number of configuration BPDUs received for the specified port on the specified VLAN (a port can belong to several VLANs, if trunking). See the section "An Additional CatOS Command," later in this chapter, for more information.

Check for Duplex Mismatch

To look for a duplex mismatch, you obviously have to check each side of the point-to-point link.

- **IOS**—Simply use the **show interface** command to check the speed and duplex status of the specified port.

- **CatOS**—The very first lines of the output of **show port <module#/port#>** will give you the speed and duplex for which the port is configured.

Check Port Utilization

We have seen that an interface overloaded can fail to transmit vital BPDUs. A very loaded link is also an indication of a possible bridging loop.

- **IOS**—Use the command **show interface** to determine an interface utilization. Several fields will help you here (Load, Packets Input/Output, and so on).

- **CatOS**—The command used to display statistics about packets received and sent on a port is **show mac <modele#/port#>**. The command **show top** automatically evaluates the port utilization over a 30-second period of time and displays the result classified by percentage bandwidth utilization (other options are available). Also, the **show system** command gives an indication on the backplane utilization, even if it does not point to a specific port.

Check Packet Corruption

IOS—Look for increasing figures in the input errors fields of the **show interface** command.

CatOS—The command **show port <modele#/port#>** gives you some details with the Aling-Err, FCS-Err, Xmit-Err, Rcv-Err, and Undersize fields. You will get even more detailed statistics using the **show counters <modele#/port#>** command.

An Additional CatOS Command

The Catalyst-specific software is richer than the IOS as far as STP troubleshooting is concerned. The command **show spantree statistics <modele#/port#> <vlan#>** gives very accurate information on a specific port. On suspected ports, run this command and pay special attention to the fields:

- **Forward trans count**—This counter remembers how many times a port transitions from learning to forwarding. In a stable topology, this counter should always show 1. This counter is reset to 0 if the corresponding port is going down and up. So, if the value is higher than 1, it means that the transition that this port experienced is the result of a STP recalculation, not of a direct link failure.

- **Max age expiry count**—This counter tracks the number of times that the max age expired on this link. Basically, a port expecting BPDUs will wait for the max age (default 20 seconds) before considering its designated bridge as lost. Each time this event occurs, the counter is incremented. When the value is not zero, you know that, for whatever reason, the designated bridge for this LAN is unstable or has problems transmitting its BPDUs.

Look for Resource Errors

We have seen that a high CPU utilization can be dangerous for a system running the STA. Here is how to check that the device is not running short of CPU resource:

- **IOS**—Use the **show processes cpu** command. Check that the CPU utilization is not getting too close to 100 percent.

- **CatOS**—Look for the field RsrcErrors (resource error) in the output of **show inband** (on some supervisors, this command is hidden under the name **show biga**). Basically, this counter is incremented when the processor was too overloaded to perform some of its tasks. There is a limitation on the number of different instances of STP that a supervisor engine can handle. Check the release notes of the software that you are running for this.

The following is a summary of the restrictions that apply to the Catalyst 4000/5000/6000 series:

Ensure that the total number of logical ports across all instances of STP for different VLANs does not exceed the maximum number supported for each supervisor engine type and memory configuration. You can use the **show spantree summary** command and this formula to compute the sum of logical ports on the switch:

(number of non-ATM trunks × number of active VLANs on that trunk)
+ 2*(number of ATM trunks × number of active VLANs on that trunk)
+ number of nontrunking ports.

The sum of all logical ports, as calculated with this formula, should be less than or equal to:

For the Catalyst 4000 series:

- 1500 for the Catalyst 4000 family Supervisor Engine I and II

For the Catalyst 5000 series:

- 200 for Supervisor Engine I (with 8-MB DRAM)
- 400 for Supervisor Engine I (with 20-MB DRAM)
- 1500 for Supervisor Engine II and III F
- 1800 for Supervisor Engine II G and III G
- 4000 for Supervisor Engine III

For the Catalyst 6000 series:

- 4000 for Supervisor

Disable Unneeded Features

Troubleshooting is a matter of identifying what is currently wrong in the network. In this regard, disabling as many features as possible helps to simplify the network structure and eases the identification of the problem. EtherChanneling, for instance, is an advanced feature that needs STP to logically bundle several different links into a single one. It makes sense to disable this feature during a troubleshooting period. Again, this is just an example, but generally, going to a configuration as simple as possible reduces the troubleshooting effort.

Useful Commands

This section lists useful commands for the Catalyst IOS and the Catalyst OS.

Catalyst IOS Commands

show interface

show spanning-tree

show bridge

show processes cpu

debug spantree

logging buffered

Catalyst OS Commands

show port

show mac

show spantree

show spantree statistics

show spantree blockedports

show spantree summary

show top

show inband/show biga

show system

show counters

set spantree root [secondary]

set spantree uplinkfast

set logging level

set logging buffered

Designing STP to Avoid Trouble

We have seen that the spanning tree can fail in some few circumstances and that troubleshooting the related issues can be quite difficult in a live network. This part introduces some guidelines to reduce the risks associated with the spanning tree.

Know Where the Root Is

It sounds trivial, but very often the information is not available at troubleshooting time. Don't leave the STP to decide which bridge will be root. Depending on the design of the network, you should be able to identify for each VLAN which switch is well suited to be root. Generally, it is good to choose a powerful bridge in the middle of the network. Putting the root bridge in the center of the network, directly connected to the servers and routers, generally reduces the average distance from the clients to the servers and routers.

In Figure 23-13, you can clearly see that if Bridge B is the root, the link from A to C will be blocked on A or C. In this case, hosts connected to switch B can access the server and the router in two hops, and hosts connected to Bridge C in three hops. That makes an average of 2.5 hops.

If Bridge A is the root, the router and the server are reachable in two hops for both hosts connected on B and C. The average distance to them is now two hops.

Figure 23-13 *Root Bridge Location Is Important*

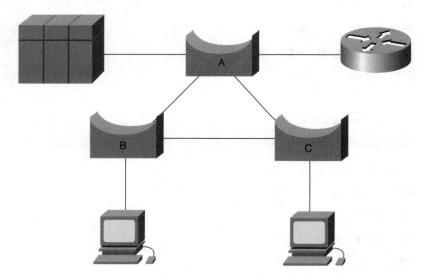

This example is obvious, but it is the same kind of reasoning that is needed in more complex topologies.

Important note: For each VLAN, hard-code the root bridge and the backup root bridge by reducing the value of the STP priority parameter (or using the **set spantree root** macro).

Know Where Redundancy Is

Plan the way that your redundant links are organized. Here again, forget about the plug-and-play feature of the STP. Decide which ports will be blocking by turning the cost parameter of the STP. Hopefully, this is usually not necessary if you have a hierarchical design and a well-located root bridge.

NOTE   For each VLAN, know which ports should be blocking in the stable network. Have a network diagram that clearly shows each physical loop in the network and which blocked ports break the loops.

In case of accidental bridging loops, knowing exactly where the redundant links are helps you identify the loop and its cause. Knowing where the blocked ports should be also help you to find where the error is coming from (by simple comparison).

Minimize the Number of Blocked Ports

The only critical action taken by STP is blocking ports. A single blocking port transitioning to forwarding by error can meltdown a big part of the network. A good way to limit the risk implied by the use of the STP is to reduce the number of blocked ports as much as possible.

Prune VLANs That Are Not Used

You don't need more than two redundant links between two nodes in a bridged network. However, a configuration like that shown in Figure 23-14 frequently appears.

Figure 23-14   *Typical Network Design with VLANs Spanning Too Many Links*

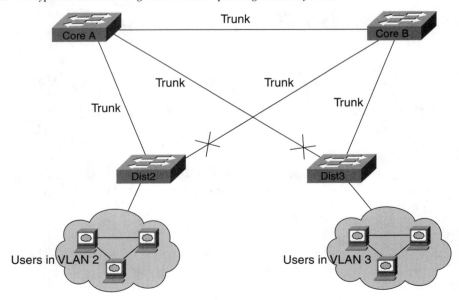

This is a very common design. Distribution switches are dual-attached to two core switches. Users connected on distribution switches are in only a subset of the VLANs available in the network (here, users connected on Dist2 are all in VLAN 2; Dist3 connects only users in VLAN 3). By default, trunks carry all the VLANs defined in the VTP domain. Now only is Dist2 receiving unnecessary broadcast and multicast traffic for VLAN 3, but it is also blocking one of its ports for VLAN 3. The result is that there are three redundant paths between Core A and Core B. This means more blocked ports and increased chances for a loop.

Important note: Prune any VLAN not needed off your trunks.

VTP pruning can help doing this, but that kind of plug-and-play feature is not really needed in the core of the network.

Let's take the same example as previously shown in Figure 23-14. This time, we just use an access VLAN to connect the distribution switches to the core, as shown in Figure 23-15.

Figure 23-15 *Pruning VLANs Already Reduces the Number of Blocked Ports and Avoids Unnecessary Flooding*

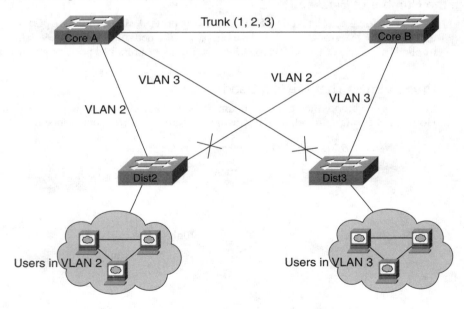

In this design, we have only one port blocked per VLAN. Note also that with this design, it is possible to remove all redundant links in just one step by shutting down Core A or Core B.

Use Layer 3 Switching

Layer 3 switching means approximately routing at the speed of switching. A router performs two main functions:

1 It builds a forwarding table, generally exchanging information with its peers by the way of routing protocols.

2 It receives packets and forwards them to the correct interface based on their destination address.

High-end Cisco Layer 3 switches now can perform this second function, at the same speed as Layer 2 switching function. There is no speed penalty in introducing a routing hop and creating an additional segmentation of the network. Figure 23-16 illustrates this, using the same diagram structure.

Figure 23-16 *Layer 3 Switching Makes a Design with No Blocking Port Possible*

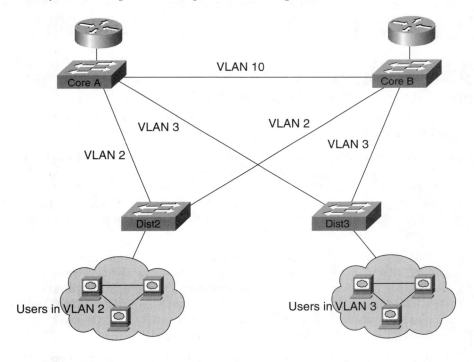

In Figure 23-16, Core A and Core B are now some Layer 3 switches. Note that we are not bridging any more VLAN 2 and VLAN 3 between Core A and Core B; thus, we no longer have a loop to cut by the ways of the STP.

- Redundancy is still there, relying on Layer 3 routing protocols (and ensuring a reconvergence even faster that with STP).

- There is no longer any single port blocked by the STP. This removes all the potential for a bridging loop.

- There is no speed penalty because leaving the VLAN via Layer 3 switching is as fast as bridging inside the VLAN.

The only drawback is that migrating to that kind of design generally implies a rework of the addressing scheme.

Keep STP Even If It Is Not Needed

Even if you have succeeded in removing all the blocked ports of your network, and even if you don't have any physical redundancy, it is safer to keep STP enabled. STP is generally not too processor-intensive (and, anyway, CPU is not involved in packet switching in most Cisco switches), and the few BPDUs sent on each link do not significantly reduce the available bandwidth. On the other end, a bridged network without STP can melt down in a fraction of second if an operator makes an error on a patch panel, for instance. Generally, disabling the STP in a bridged network is not worth the risk.

Keep Traffic Off the Administrative VLAN, and Avoid Having a Single VLAN Spanning the Entire Network

Keeping traffic of the administration VLAN and avoiding having a single VLAN spanning the entire network are related points.

A Cisco switch typically has a single IP address bound to a VLAN (which is often called the administrative VLAN). In this VLAN, the switch is behaving like a generic IP host. In particular, every single broadcast/multicast packet will be forwarded to the CPU. Having a high rate of broadcast/multicast on the administrative VLAN can hit the CPU and impact its capability to process vital BPDUs. Therefore, it is always a good idea to keep user traffic off the administrative VLAN.

Until recently, in a Cisco implementation, there was no way to remove VLAN 1 from a trunk. This VLAN is generally used as an administrative VLAN, where all switches are accessible in the same IP subnet. Although useful, this may be dangerous because a bridging loop on VLAN 1 will affect all trunks and will probably bring the whole network down. Of course, the same problem exists whatever the VLAN is. If possible, try to segment the bridging domains using high-speed Layer 3 switches.

As of version 5.4, the CatOS software allows the clearing of VLAN 1 on trunks (in fact, VLAN 1 still exists but blocks traffic, thus preventing any loop possibility).

Avoid Tuning STP Parameters

Take special care if you plan to change STP timers from their default values. (Another option is to use CatOS macros.) Trying to get faster reconvergence from this, for instance, is very dangerous because it has implications on the diameter of the network and the stability of the STP. The only parameters that you may want to change are the bridge priority (to select the root bridge) and the port cost or priority (to control redundancy and load balancing).

Cisco Catalyst software provides you with macros that will finely tune most important STP parameters for you:

- The **set spantree root [secondary]** command macro decreases the bridge priority so that it becomes root (or alternate root). You have an additional option that helps you tune the STP timers by specifying the diameter of your network. Even when correctly done, timer tuning does not significantly improve the convergence time (specially compared to features such as uplink fast or backbone fast, or a good Layer 3 switching design) and introduces some instability risks in the network. That kind of tuning must be updated each time a device is added into the network. It is better to keep the conservative default values, familiar to network engineers.

- The **set spantree uplinkfast** command increases the switch priority so that it cannot be root. You typically want to use this command on a distribution switch, at least dually attached to some core switches. Read the uplink fast feature documentation to learn more about the impact of this command.

Configure UDLD When Possible

In case of a unidirectional link occurring on a link with a blocked port, you have a 50 percent chance of a bridging loop. This is the most dangerous possibility of STP failure because the algorithm is not capable of handling this situation. The latest Catalyst software implements the Uni-Directional Link Detection (UDLD) feature that helps to detect this dangerous condition. This works on point-to-point links between Cisco devices only.

Additional Sources

For further information, including step-by-step configuration materials and full command examples for both the IP MLS-RP and the MLS-SE, you are highly encouraged to view the following (log in to maximize the amount of material that you can view):

- The Technical Assistance Center (TAC) web site, on Cisco Connection Online (CCO), at www.cisco.com/tac

- The MLS Technology Pages, off the CCO TAC web site, at www.cisco.com/cgi-bin/Support/PSP/psp_view.pl?p=Internetworking:Multi-layer_Switching

- For MLS supported and unsupported network topologies, at www.cisco.com/univercd/cc/td/doc/product/lan/cat5000/rel_5_2/layer3/mls.htm#xtocid1101958

- The Layer 3 Switching Software Configuration Guide, at www.cisco.com/univercd/cc/td/doc/product/lan/cat5000/rel_5_2/layer3/index.htm

- The Catalyst 5xxx release notes, at www.cisco.com/univercd/cc/td/doc/product/lan/cat5000/c5krn/index.htm

- The Catalyst 6xxx release notes, at www.cisco.com/univercd/cc/td/doc/product/lan/cat6000/relnotes/index.htm

PART **VI**

Troubleshooting Other Internetwork Problems

## CHAPTER 24

Troubleshooting
CiscoWorks 2000

Objectives

The main objective of this chapter is to present troubleshooting information for problems commonly encountered when installing and using CiscoWorks 2000 (RME 2.2 and CWSI 2.4). It contains the following sections:

- Introduction to the Network Management Products Family CiscoWorks 2000
- Troubleshooting Information for CiscoWorks 2000 Installation and Setup
- Methods for Evaluating and Troubleshooting RME Problems
- Information for Troubleshooting CiscoWorks for Switched Internetworking (CWSI) Campus
- Troubleshooting Information for Applications Included in CWSI Campus (VlanDirector, AtmDirector, TrafficDirector, and CiscoView)

Introduction

CiscoWorks 2000 is a family of management products that combines the best of enterprise router and switch management functionality with easy-to-access deployment of web-based technologies. CiscoWorks 2000 offers a new model of network-management solutions for large, fast-changing enterprise networks. Resource Manager Essentials and CWSI Campus make up the foundation of the CiscoWorks 2000 family, This new generation of management tools leverages the power of the Internet to bring network-accessible knowledge to the management process, and to give users standard web-browser access to management functionality. The CiscoWorks 2000 products integrate switch and router management, provide management application integration via the browser-based Cisco Management Connection, and share common services between functional modules.

Cisco delivered its first Internet-based product when it shipped Resource Manager in 1997, and it integrated several separate applications into a single suite called CiscoWorks for switched Internetworks (CWSI). CiscoWorks 2000 takes these products a step further. Cisco has added management functionality that crosses switches and routers, has dramatically increased web-accessible features, and has integrated existing products onto a common management foundation to leverage a single set of background services.

CWSI Campus offers sophisticated traffic management, ATM management, VLAN management, and device configuration to CiscoWorks 2000. It complements the Resource Manager Essentials automated software upgrade, inventory, and configuration management features. The two applications share some back-end processes, which allows Resource Manager Essentials to run on a standalone basis but requires that CWSI Campus be installed with Resource Manager Essentials as a base to build upon.

The network-management product CiscoWorks Classic was replaced by CiscoWorks 2000 Resource Manager Essentials. For those who want to know the details of migrating from CiscoWorks Classic to Essentials, please refer to the CCO link, at www.cisco.com/univercd/cc/td/doc/product/rtrmgmt/cw2000/cw2000e/rme_ltu/ug_appb. htm. CiscoWorks 2000 has four different versions that correspond to four different operating system flavors: CW2000 on NT, CW 2000 on Solaris, CW 2000 on HPUX, and CW 2000 on AIX. In this chapter, if not specifically pointed out, the troubleshooting information should apply to all flavors of CW 2000.

Troubleshooting Information for CiscoWorks 2000 Installation and Setup

The following subsections are presented in this section:

- Required Server Software Installation Troubleshooting
- Essentials Troubleshooting Tools
- Logging in After Upgrading
- Checking Files and Directories After Installation
- Understanding Installation Error Messages
- Accessing the Essentials Server
- Setting Up the Browser
- Adding and Importing Device Information
- Gathering Server Information
- Essentials Daemon Manager and CWSI Campus
- Cannot Log in to AniServer
- Testing Connection to the Database

Required Server Software Installation Troubleshooting

CiscoWorks 2000 for Windows NT version's installation requires Windows NT 4.0 Option Pack components be installed. If you did not install one of the following required components of the Windows NT 4.0 Option Pack during initial installation, you can install them later:

- Internet Service manager
- Microsoft Management Console
- Windows Scripting Host

To install one or more of these components after initial installation, follow these steps:

Step 1   Select Start; Program; Windows NT 4.0 Option Pack; Windows NT 4.0 Option Pack setup. The Windows NT 4.0 Option Pack Setup dialog box appears.

Step 2   Click Next. A dialog box appears in which you can select Add/Remove or Remove All Installation program options.

Step 3   Select Add/Remove. The Select Components dialog box appears.

Step 4   Select the missing required components.

Step 5   Click Next. The Completing Installation dialog box appears.

Step 6   Click Finish to complete the installation.

Essentials Troubleshooting Tools

Essentials provides several troubleshooting options that are accessible from the navigation tree. To access these tools, select Admin; Troubleshooting.

1   **Collecting server information**—You can gather troubleshooting information about the status of the server using the Collect Server Info option. To collect server information, follow these steps:

Step 1   Select Admin; Troubleshooting; Collect Server Info. The Collect Server Info dialog box appears.

Step 2   Select a report from the Reports history list.

Step 3   Click Display. The report displays, showing information such as the product database, the operating system, and disk utilization statistics.

Step 4   To create a new report, click Create. The new report appears in the Reports history list.

Note: It might take up to 5 minutes to collect the information.

Step 5   To delete reports, select them from the Reports history list, and then click Delete.

2 **Viewing process failures**—You can check for potential failures of the back-end server processes using the Process Failures option. The Process Failures table provides you with only two possible states for the failure.

3 **Failed to run**—The process exited or sent a failed message.

4 **Administrator has shut down the server**—The administrator or another program has shut down the process.

To view process failures, follow these steps:

Step 1 Select Admin; Troubleshooting; Process Failures. Table 24-1 describes the columns that the Process Failures table displays.

Table 24-1 *Viewing Process Failures*

Column	Description
Process Name	Name of the process.
State	Process status: "Failed to run" or "Administrator has shut down this server."
Pid	Process ID. A unique key by which the operating system identifies all running programs.
RC	Return code. "0" indicates normal program operation. Any other number typically represents an error. Refer to the error log.
Signo	Signal number. "0" indicates normal program operation. Any other number is the last signal delivered to the program before it terminated.
Start Time	Time and date that the process was started.
Stop Time	Time and date that the process was stopped.
Core	"Not applicable" means that the program is running normally. "CORE FILE CREATED" means that the program is not running normally and that the operating system has created a file called a core file. The core file contains important data about the process failures.
Information	Reason for the failure. "Not applicable" means that the program is not running normally.

Step 2 Click any process name to see details. The Process Details table appears. Click Back to return to the Process Failures table.

Step 3 Click any process state to see the System Log. The System Log appears. Click Back to return to the Process Failures table.

Step 4 Click Update at any time to refresh the fields.

5 **Collecting self-test information**—You can rerun self-tests and generate a report with the results using the SelfTest option. To collect self-test information, follow these steps:

Step 1 Select Admin Troubleshooting SelfTest. The Server Selftest Info dialog box appears.

Step 2 Click Run Tests to rerun self-tests and generate a report. The tests are run and a report appears in the Reports history list.

Note: It might take up to 5 minutes to run the tests.

Step 3 Select the report from the Reports history list.

Step 4 Click Display. The report is displayed, showing whether the tests passed or failed.

Step 5 You can delete reports by selecting them from the Reports history list and then clicking Delete.

Logging in After Upgrading

After upgrading from Cisco Resource Manager 1.1 to Essentials 2.1, or from Essentials 2.0 to Essentials 2.1, or from Essential 2.1 to Essential 2.2, you might need to clear your browser cache to log into Essentials.

If the Login Manager dialog box on the Essentials desktop does not appear correctly when you attempt to log in for the first time after upgrading, clear your browser cache as follows, and then re-enter the Essentials server URL in your browser.

For Microsoft Internet Explorer, follow these steps:

Step 1 Select View Internet Options. The Internet Options dialog box appears.

Step 2 Select the General tab.

Step 3 Click Delete Files.

For Netscape Navigator, follow these steps:

Step 1 Select Edit Preferences. The Preferences dialog box appears.

Step 2 Select Advanced Cache.

Step 3 Click Clear Memory Cache, and then click OK in the Memory Cache dialog box.

Step 4 Click Clear Disk Cache, and then click OK in the Disk Cache dialog box.

Checking Files and Directories After Installation

If you encountered problems while installing Essentials, make sure that the following directories are installed in the right directories.

For CW 2000 installation on NT, the following directories should be installed in the C:\Program Files\CSCOpx directory (or the directory that you specified for the installation):

- bin
- cgi-bin (programs run by the web server)
- collect
- conf (configuration files)
- etc (Essentials system files)
- example (sample import files)
- htdocs (web server files)
- lib
- man
- objects (Essentials subsystems)
- selftest
- www
- upgrade (MIB upgrades)
- setup (setup information)
- shared (system files)
- temp (temporary files)
- tftpboot (files exported by tftpboot)
- dbupgrade
- files
- log (log files)
- proxy (temporary files)

The Essentials installation tool installed the following directories in the C:\Program Files\CSCOpx\objects directory (or the directory that you specified for the installation):

- availability (availability)
- cmf (Common Management Framework)
- config (configuration management)
- data (syslog analysis configuration files)

- db (Essentials database)
- inventory (inventory)
- mngconnection (Management Connection)
- perl5 (Essentials perl interpreter and libraries)
- proxy (proxy server information)
- share (shared program files)
- swim (Software Management)
- sysloga (syslog analysis)
- web (web server process and utilities)

For CW 2000 installation on Solaris, HPUX and AIX, make sure that the following directories have been installed in the /opt/CSCOpx/, /opt/CSCOpx/, and /usr/CSCOpx/ directories, respectively:

- bin
- cgi-bin (programs run by the web server)
- collect
- conf (configuration files)
- etc (Essentials system files)
- example (sample import files)
- htdocs (web server files)
- lib
- man
- objects (Essentials subsystems)
- selftest
- www

Also, the Essentials installation tool installed the following directories in the /opt/CSCOpx/objects, /opt/CSCOpx/objects, and /usr/CSCOpx/objects directories, respectively on Solaris, HPUX, and AIX:

- availability (availability)
- cmf (Common Management Framework)
- config (configuration management)
- data (syslog analysis configuration files)
- db (Essentials database)
- dmgt (daemon management)

- inventory (inventory)
- mngconnect (Management Connection)
- perl (Essentials perl interpreter and libraries)
- share (shared program files)
- swim (Software Management)
- tcltk (web administration)
- util (utility programs and scripts)
- web (web server process and utilities)

NOTE   There are no config (configuration management) or util (utility programs and scripts) directories on AIX.

In addition, the following files should have been added to the /etc directory on Solaris:

- rc2.d/K90dmgtd
- init.d/dmgtd
- rc3.d/S10dmgtd
- rc.config.d/CiscoRMCtrl

On HPUX, the following files should be added:

- /sbin/rc2.d/K90dmgtd
- /sbin/init.d/dmgtd
- /sbin/rc3.d/S10dmgtd
- /eetc/rc.config.d/CiscoRMCtrl

On AIX, the file rc.dmgtd should be added in the /etc directory.

Understanding Installation Error Messages

After verifying that the correct files are installed, check the c:\rme_in001.log file (or the log file with the highest number, such as rme_in003.log) for installation errors on NT, or check the /var/tmp/ciscoinstall.log file for installation errors on Solaris, HPUX, and AIX. You might find the following types of messages:

- Information messages, which give you important details

- Warning messages, which indicate that something might be wrong with a particular process, but the process will complete
- Error messages, which indicate that a particular process could not complete

Table 24-2 shows error messages that might occur during installation on NT and describes the reasons for the errors.

Table 24-2 *Installation Error Messages on NT*

Error Message	Reason for Error	User Action
Administrator privileges are needed to install or uninstall this package. Please log in as administrator and try again.	The user is not logged on to Windows NT with administrator privileges.	Log on to Windows NT with administrator privileges, and try installing again.
Decompression failed on <*file*. The error was for <error code per CompressGet.	If Essentials was downloaded, a transmission error might have occurred. Otherwise, the installation media is damaged.	Retry the download. If you install from product CD, check the media to make sure that it's not damaged.
General file transmission error. Please check your target location and try again. Error number: <error code>.	If Essentials was downloaded, a transmission error might have occurred.	Retry the download.
Unable to write <infoFile or Unable to create <infoFile.	A file write operation failed.	Run the file system checking utility, and then repeat the installation.
Cannot stop service <*servicename*>.	The Essentials installation (or reinstallation) tried to stop the service <*servicename*>, but the service did not stop.	Select Control Panel; Services, and try to stop the service <*servicename*> manually. Then proceed with (un)installing.
UseDLL failed for <*dll*>.	<*dll*> is supposed to be available at any time for any process, but NT failed to load it.	Check permissions on Windows NT System 32. If the <*dll*> is secure.dll, check the product installation media for errors or Reinstall Windows NT.
<*function*> failed: DLL function not found.	<*dll*> is supposed to be available at any time for any process, but NT failed to load it.	Check permissions on Windows NT System 32. If the <*dll*> is secure.dll, check the product installation media for errors or Reinstall Windows NT.
OpenFile failed: <*pathname*>.	A file open operation failed.	Run the file system checking utility. Then repeat the installation.

continues

Table 24-2   *Installation Error Messages on NT (Continued)*

Error Message	Reason for Error	User Action
ProtectFile failed: *<file>*: error. WWW admin security may be incomplete.	Setting the file permissions failed because the user might not be allowed to change them.	Log in as administrator. **Note:** If you are installing on a FAT file system, Essentials cannot provide file security.
Installing in root directory is not allowed. Please choose nonroot directory.	You attempted to install Essentials in the root directory of a drive (for example, c:\ or d:\), which is not supported.	Choose a nonroot directory in which to install Essentials.
Resource Manager Essentials can be installed only on NT Workstation or NT Server. It is not supported on PDC/BDC.	The installation program determined one of the following: Windows NT is not installed on the system. The system is configured as a primary domain controller (PDC) or a backup domain controller (BDC).	Install Essentials on a Windows NT 4.0 Workstation or Windows NT 4.0 Server system that is not configured as a PDC or a BDC.
You have less than 1 M free space on *<drive name>*. Please free up some space and try again.	There is insufficient drive space for temporary installation files.	Make more drive space available, and then rerun the installation program.
This program requires to run on Window NT.	You attempted to install on a system that does not have Windows NT 4.0 installed.	Install Essentials on a Windows NT 4.0 Workstation or Windows NT 4.0 Server system that is not configured as a PDC or a BDC.
Unable to determine the type of operating system. Resource Manager Essentials can be installed only on NT Workstation or NT Server.	The installation program could not determine which operating system is running on the system.	Install Essentials on a Windows NT 4.0 Workstation or Windows NT 4.0 Server system that is not configured as a PDC or a BDC.
Physical memory is <...>M Paging File Size is: <...>M(initial), <...>M(max). It is recommended that initial paging file size is bigger than physical memory and that max paging file size is at least twice bigger than physical memory.	The paging file size is smaller than recommended.	Finish the installation, and then increase the paging file size.

Table 24-2 *Installation Error Messages on NT (Continued)*

Error Message	Reason for Error	User Action
The Resource Manager Essentials installation found the IIS/PWS v2/v3. Internet Information Server 4.0 is required.	IIS or PWS version 2 or 3 is installed on the system, but version 4.0 is required.	Install IIS or PWS 4.0 and the other required Microsoft software. Then rerun the installation program. Refer to the Essentials installation manual for more information.
The Resource Manager Essentials installation could not find Windows Scripting Host. Windows Scripting Host is required for IIS 4.0.	The Windows scripting host is not installed on the system.	Install the Windows Scripting Host (and any other required components of the Windows NT 4.0 Option Pack). Then rerun the installation program.
Downgrade to FCS version is not supported. If you wish to revert to FCS, back up your data, then uninstall the current version and do a new install of this version. Exiting.	The installation program detected that some Essentials patches or upgrades are installed. In this case, you cannot downgrade to the FCS version of the product using the installation program.	To revert back to the FCS version of the product, follow these steps: **Step 1** Back up your Essentials data files. **Step 2** Uninstall Essentials. **Step 3** Install the FCS version of Essentials again. **Step 4** Restore the backed-up data.
There is not enough space available on the disk *<drive>*: This drive has <...> bytes in a cluster. Total required <...> clusters (<...> bytes), only <...> clusters (<...> bytes) available. Please free up some space and rerun installation.	There is insufficient disk space available on drive *<drive* to install the product.	Create additional free space on the drive, or install the product on a different drive.
INFO: You must now install Campus CWSI 2.3 to continue using CWSI.	No error is indicated; this is information only. This appears only if a previous version of CWSI is installed.	If you want to use CWSI Campus, you must install it after installing Essentials.
You must now install CWSI 2.3 if you want to use the Campus product. CWSI 2.1 will not work correctly with Essentials 2.1.	No error is indicated; this is information only. This appears only if a previous version of CWSI is installed.	If you want to use CWSI Campus, you must install it after installing Essentials.

continues

Table 24-2 *Installation Error Messages on NT (Continued)*

Error Message	Reason for Error	User Action
You have CWSI 2.1 installed and will need to upgrade to CWSI 2.3 when Resource Manager Essentials install completes to continue to use CWSI.	No error is indicated; this is information only. This appears only if a previous version of CWSI is installed.	If you have CWSI 2.1 installed, you need to upgrade to CWSI Campus 2.3 after installing Essentials to continue to use the CWSI/Campus product.
Cannot determine the local Administrators group.	The installation program cannot find one of the built-in Windows NT user groups. This prohibits the setup of Essentials security.	Check the Windows NT operating system. Reinstall Windows NT, if necessary, and then rerun the Essentials installation program.
Cannot determine the local Everyone group.	The installation program cannot find one of the built-in Windows NT user groups. This prohibits the setup of Essentials security.	Check the Windows NT operating system. Reinstall Windows NT, if necessary, and then rerun the Essentials installation program.
Failed to set file permissions.	The installation program is incapable of setting file permissions. These are most likely caused by the following: The account that you used to log into the system has insufficient permissions. The drive on which you are installing the product has a FAT file system.	Fix the cause of the permission setting problem, and then rerun the installation program.
Unable to uninstall Resource Manager Essentials because the following components are shared: CWSI 2.x. You need to uninstall these dependent applications then run the Resource Manager Essentials uninstallation again.	You cannot uninstall Essentials while CWSI or CWSI Campus is installed.	Uninstall CWSI or CWSI Campus from the system. Then you can uninstall Essentials.
FSSupportsACLs failed: <*OS error message*>.	You attempted to install on a non-NTFS file system. This prohibits Essentials from using file-level security.	Install Essentials on an NTFS file system if you want the file-level security enabled.

Table 24-2   *Installation Error Messages on NT (Continued)*

Error Message	Reason for Error	User Action
<...> is already running! Wait for it to finish and press the OK button below.	One of the installation subtasks is still running.	Wait for the installation subtask to finish running, and then click the OK button to proceed.
Unable to create/open log file.	The installation program was incapable of creating or opening the installation log file (located in the root directory of the drive on which you are installing, named rme_in*xxx*.log, where *xxx* is a sequential number start from 001).	Determine why the file could not be created or opened, fix the problem, and then rerun the installation program. Common causes of this problem include lack of disk space or write protection on the file.
Web Server Configuration Failed, see installation log.	The configuration of the web server failed.	Check the installation log file (rme_in*xxx*.log,) for more information.
		Try uninstalling the Windows NT 4.0 Option Pack, and then reinstall it and rerun the Essentials installation program.
Error creating user bin <... more info here>. See the troubleshooting section in user manual.	The installation program could not create the user account bin.	Fix the problem that caused the failure to create the user account bin, and then rerun the installation program.
Setup detected a previously installed version of CiscoWorks... Please uninstall the previous version and restart Setup.	The TrafficDirector application was installed after a CWSI/CWSI Campus installation.	Install the TrafficDirector application as part of the CWSI Campus installation.
INFO: ComponentError returned the following data transfer error... Setup will now abort. Media Name:... Component:... File Group:... File:... Error Number...	Some TrafficDirector applications are still running, so the files still in use cannot be installed or upgraded.	Ensure that all the TrafficDirector application windows and applications are closed, and ensure that all executables—including database processes—are stopped.

continues

Table 24-3 shows error messages that might occur during installation on UNIX and describes the reasons for the errors.

Table 24-3 *Installation Error Messages on Solaris, HPUX, and AIX*

Error Message	Reason for Error	User Action
<sub-package> did not install. (This message doesn't apply to AIX platform installation.)	The specified package did not install correctly.	Verify that you have enough disk space. and reinstall Essentials as explained in the *Installing Essentials* manual on CCO.
pkgchk *<pkg_name>* failed. (This message doesn't apply to AIX platform installation.)	The UNIX package validation tool (pkgchk) found a problem with the specified directory.	Reinstall Essentials.
WARNING: RAM in system is $RAM. $MIN_RAM recommended.	Your system has less than the recommended memory.	Add memory to your system.
WARNING: SWAP in system is less than 2x RAM.	Your system has less than the recommended swap space, which is two times the RAM.	Increase swap space.
ERROR: You must be root to run Unix install. Exiting.	You did not log in as root. The installation is terminated.	Log in as root and enter the correct root password.
Insufficient disk space in /var/adm.	/var/adm must have at least 5 MB of available disk space.	Make at least 5 MB of disk space available on /var/adm, and then run the installation program again.
Insufficient disk space in /var/tmp.	/var/tmp must have at least 1 MB of available disk space.	Make at least 1 MB of disk space available on /var/tmp, and then run the installation program again.
Insufficient disk space on any local volume.	The installation program requires a local volume with sufficient disk space on which to install the product.	Make at least 250 MB of disk space available on a local disk volume.
ERROR: The patch bos.libpthreads4.3.0.2 has to be installed for the product to work correctly. Install bos.libpthreads patch 4.3.0.2 and retry installation. Exiting. (This applies to the AIX platform only.)	The patch bos.libpthreads 4.3.0.2, which is required on AIX 4.3 systems, is not installed on the system.	Install the patch bos.libpthreads 4.3.0.2, and then rerun the installation program. Refer to the *Installing Essentials* manual on CCO for more information.

Table 24-3   *Installation Error Messages on Solaris, HPUX, and AIX (Continued)*

Error Message	Reason for Error	User Action
WARNING: The patch x1C.rte3.1.4.8 has to be installed for the product to work correctly. (This applies to the AIX platform only.)	The patch x1C.rte3.1.4.8 is not installed. This might cause Essentials to work incorrectly.	Complete the installation program, and then install the patch x1C.rte3.1.4.8. Refer to the *Installing Essentials* manual on CCO for more information.

Accessing the Essentials Server

The Essentials server uses the port 1741. Make sure that you enter the correct URL when accessing the server:

http://*server_name*:1741

Here, *server_name* is the name of the Essentials server.

If you still cannot access the server, enter the following command at a DOS prompt to make sure that your server is running:

```
ping server_name
```

If you get a message that the server is "alive" and get a proxy error when you try to connect to the server, make sure that the proxy is set up correctly. If your server is configured to use a proxy server outside the firewall (specified in Netscape Navigator under Options; Network Preferences; Proxies), you will get proxy errors if you have incorrectly configured the proxy to ignore requests to a certain machine, set of machines, or domain.

Your proxy is set up incorrectly if you encounter any of the following:

- You receive an error message that you are using a proxy outside the firewall.
- The proxy server recognizes www-int as an internal server, so it does not proxy requests to that server.
- You set up a new internal server, www-nms, but when you make a request to the proxy server, it does not recognize www-nms as an internal server and proxies the request.
- The proxy server outside the firewall tries to request data from a server inside the firewall, and the request is blocked.
- You get a "Connection Refused" error from the proxy server.

Setting Up the Browser

If the Essentials buttons do not work, you have not enabled Java and JavaScript. Enable Java and JavaScript as described in the *Installing Essentials* manual on CCO, in the "Configuring Client Systems" section. Ensure that your cache is *not* set to zero. If you experience browser problems, increase your cache settings, as explained in the same section in the *Installing Essentials* manual on CCO.

Do not resize the browser window while the desktop or main page is still loading. This can cause a Java error.

Adding and Importing Device Information

This subsection describes some problems that might occur when you attempt to add or import device information.

1   **Adding device information**—If you added a device using Admin; Inventory; Add Devices, and the Add/Import Status Summary dialog box shows that the device status has not changed from *pending* within 15 minutes, check the status of all processes to ensure that they are running normally, as explained in the following steps:

   Step 1   To view the latest device status information, in the Add/Import Status Summary dialog box (Admin; Inventory; Import Status), click Update.

   Step 2   To determine whether the DIServer process is running, select Admin; System Admin; Process Status. (The DIServer is the process responsible for validating devices and changing their status from pending.)

   Even if the DIServer process shows the state "Running Normally," it might be in an error state. You need to stop and restart it by following these steps:

   To stop the DIServer process, select Admin; System Admin; Stop Process. The Stop Process dialog box appears. Click the Process radio button.

   In the Process Name field, select DIServer and then click Finish.

   To restart the DIServer process, follow these steps:

   From the System Admin folder, click Start Processes. The Start Process dialog box appears.

   Click the Process radio button.

   In the Process Name field, select DIServer, and then click Finish.

Step 3   Return to the Add/Import Status Summary screen by selecting Inventory; Import Status, and then click Update. The device status should change to *managed* within a couple of minutes.

2 **Importing Device Information**—If you have difficulty importing device information, try the following solutions:

— Increase the SNMP timeout setting. Refer to the online help for more information.

— Verify that you have correct read community strings entered for the devices.

Gathering Server Information

Essentials contains a utility that can help you troubleshoot server problems. You can obtain information about the Essentials server in one of two ways:

Select Admin; Troubleshooting; Collect Server Info. The Collect Server Information dialog box appears. Click Display to collect information about the server. After the information has been collected, the dialog box tells you how to view the server information in your web browser.

From the server, enter the following command from the command window:

```
collect.info   filename.html
```

Here, *filename* is a filename of your choice.

If collect.info is not recognized as a command, add the following path name to your PATH system variable:

```
On NT:              C:\Program Files\CSCOpx\cgi-bin\admin\perl
On Solaris and HPUX:     /opt/CSCOpx/bin
On AIX:             /usr/CSCOpx/bin
```

On UNIX machines, the server information will be collected into the /var/tmp/px_status.info file. Send this file to Cisco via e-mail if directed to do so by your technical support representative.

Essentials Daemon Manager and CWSI Campus

CWSI Campus relies on the Essentials Daemon Manager. Therefore, the Essentials Daemon Manager must be running for CWSI Campus to run. If the Essentials Daemon Manager has stalled, you must stop and restart the Essentials Daemon Manager.

On Windows NT, to stop the Essentials Daemon Manager from the GUI, follow these steps:

Step 1   From the Windows NT menu, select Start; Settings; Control Panels.

Step 2   Double-click Services.

Step 3   In the dialog box, select Essentials Daemon Manager.

Step 4   Click Stop.

To restart the Essentials Daemon Manager from the GUI, follow these steps:

Step 1   From the Windows NT menu, select Start; Settings; Control Panels.

Step 2   Double-click Services.

Step 3   In the dialog box, select Essentials Daemon Manager.

Step 4   Click Start.

To stop and start the Essentials Daemon Manager from the command-line interface, follow these steps:

Step 1   Log in as administrator.

Step 2   Open a command prompt or shell window.

Step 3   Stop the server by entering the following command at the prompt:

```
net stop crmdmgtd
```
```
Start the server by entering the following command at the prompt:
```

Step 4   net start crmdmgtd

On a Solaris system, to stop and restart the Essentials Daemon Manager, follow these steps:

Step 1   Log in as root.

Step 2   Open a command prompt or shell window.

Step 3   Stop the server by entering the following command at the prompt:

```
# /etc/init.d/dmgtd stop
```

Step 4   Start the server by entering the following command at the prompt:

```
# /etc/init.d/dmgtd start
```

Cannot Log in to AniServer

If you have just restarted your computer and cannot log in to <Hostname>AniServer, the ANI server might not be ready to receive messages. Wait a few minutes, and then try to log in again.

If you still cannot log in, follow these steps:

Step 1   Open a command prompt or shell window.

Step 2 Check to see if the daemons are running using the command-line utility pdshow in C:\Program Files\CSCOpx\bin (on Windows NT), or /opt/CSCOpx/bin (on Solaris).

```
pdshow RmeOrb AniServer
```

This will show whether OSAgent and AniServer are running, and whether AniServer is connected to the database.

Step 3 Run osfind.

Set the OSAGENT_PORT environment variable to 42342. This is the port used by OSAgent in Essentials.

Set OSAGENT_PORT=42342 (on Windows NT)

```
# setenv OSAGENT_PORT 42342 (on Solaris)
```

Run osfind. This verifies whether AniServer has registered with the OSAgent. This tool is located in C:\Program Files\CSCOpx\lib\visigenics\bin (on Windows NT), or /opt/CSCOpx/lib/visigenics/bin (on Solaris).

If <Hostname>AniServer is registered with the OSAgent, verify that the name of <Hostname>AniServer in the login box is the same name as the name registered with OsAgent.

If <Hostname>AniServer is registered, retry to log in to CWSI Campus.

If <Hostname>AniServer is not registered, you must stop and restart CWSI Campus.

Step 4 Enter the following command to stop the CWSI Campus processes.

```
Stopcwsiserver
```

When the prompt returns, all daemons have been stopped.

Step 5 Enter the following command to start the CWSI Campus processes.

```
Startcwsiserver
```

Wait until the prompt returns.

Step 6 Run osfind.

If <Hostname>AniServer is registered, retry to log in to CWSI Campus.

If <Hostname>AniServer is not registered, continue to next step.

Step 7 Check to see if the <Hostname>AniServer was properly registered with the daemon manager during installation using the utility pdreg.

```
pdreg -1 AniServer
```

This verifies whether AniServer is registered with Essentials Daemon Manager.

If AniServer is registered with Essentials Daemon Manager but is not running, check the ani.log to see how far the initialization has proceeded.

If AniServer is not registered, the following error message appears:

```
ERROR AniServer is not a registered server name.
```

If AniServer is not registered with Essentials Daemon Manager, it will not be capable of initializing itself. Contact your Cisco TAC representative for additional assistance.

Testing Connection to the Database

You can run a utility to determine if you can connect to the CWSI Campus database. To run the utility, follow these steps:

Step 1 Locate the testdbconn utility in the <CWSIROOT>\bin directory, where <CWSIROOT> is the directory in which you installed CWSI Campus.

Step 2 Run the testdbconn utility.

If the program finishes and the prompt returns, the database connection is fine.

Methods for Evaluating and Troubleshooting RME Problems

Essentials provides you with methods for evaluating and troubleshooting problems.

The following sections are presented in this section:

- Error Message Format
- Process Status Features
- Troubleshooting a Process Problem

Error Message Format

Essentials displays two types of error messages:

- Interface error messages
- Back-end error messages stored in the syslog

Interface error messages are displayed in dialog boxes with descriptions of the probable causes and recommended corrective actions, if any.

Three types of interface error messages are available:

- **USER**—Indicates a user error or invalid input
- **SYSTEM**—Indicates a system failure
- **INTERNAL**—Indicates a product code issue

Some interface error messages include a Details button. Click Details for additional information and recommended corrective action. An informational dialog box appears.

Back-end error messages result from problems that occur in processes running on the Essentials server. Back-end error messages are stored in the syslog.

Refer to the appropriate Essentials installation guide for the location of the error message logs. Figure 24-1 shows the syslog error message format.

Figure 24-1 *Syslog Error Message Format*

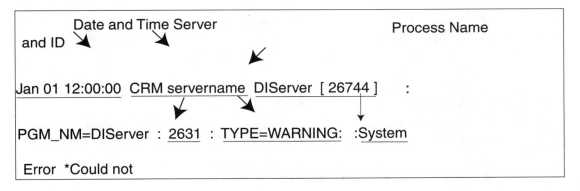

Process Status Features

Two interfaces are available for viewing and troubleshooting process problems:

- Essentials desktop (navigation tree)
- Command-line interface (CLI)

Use the Process Status, Start Process, and Stop Process System Admin options to view process status and troubleshoot process problems. Use the CLI for processes that cannot be monitored through the desktop interface (for example, syslogd).

Table 24-4 shows the process features available in the desktop interface and their command-line equivalents.

Table 24-4   *Process Features*

Essentials Desktop	Command-line Equivalents
Process Status	pdshow
Start Process	pdexec
Stop Process	pdterm

For a complete description of the desktop interface processes, refer to the RME online help.

Several events can cause a process to fail. For example, the database engine might fail for one of the following reasons:

- On UNIX systems, the database uses a small amount of space in the /tmp file system. If this space fills up, the database can no longer accept connections from client code and fails.
- The file system containing the database file is full.
- If an application process fails, examine your system to see whether either of these conditions or any others has occurred, and attempt to correct them.

Troubleshooting a Process Problem

The Process Failures table gives you information about potential process failures. It tells you that the process has failed or that an administrator has shut down the process.

If a process behaves in an unexpected way and you want to know the possible cause, to troubleshoot a process, perform the following steps:

Step 1   Select Admin; Troubleshooting; Process Failures.

Step 2   Click on the process name to display the Process Details table.

Step 3   Click Back to return to the Process Failures table.

Step 4   Click any process state to display the System Log.

Step 5   Click Back to return to the Process Failures table.

Step 6   Click Update at any time to refresh the fields.

Starting a Process

Scenario: You check process status and notice that the DbServer process in the Process Status table shows a state of "Failed to run." You attempt to restart the process.

For the desktop interface, to attempt a process restart using the navigation tree, perform the following steps:

Step 1 Select Admin; System Admin; Start Process.

The Start Process dialog box appears.

Step 2 Click Process, select DbServer in the Process Name drop-down list box, and then click Finish.

The Process Status table appears. If the status now reads "Running normally," you have solved the problem.

If the process is still not running normally, you may need collect more server and process information to further troubleshooting.

For the command-line interface, to restart a process using the CLI, perform the following steps:

Step 1 Enter **pdexec DbServer**.

Step 2 Enter **pdshow DbServer** again to see whether the process is operating properly.

If the process is operating properly, the following message appears:

```
Process= DbServer
State  = Running normally
          Pid    = 21473
          RC     = 0
          Signo  = 0
          Start  = 19:16:15 06/02/1999
          Stop   = Not applicable
          Core   = Not applicable
          Info   = Data server (dbeng50) invoked
```

If the process is still not running normally, check the error log for further troubleshooting.

Stopping a Process

Scenario: You want to back up all data that you have stored on your hard drive, so you shut down the DbServer process.

On the desktop interface, to stop the DbServer process using the navigation tree, perform the following steps:

Step 1   Select Admin; System Admin; Stop Process.

Step 2   The Stop Process dialog box appears.

Step 3   Click the Process radio button.

Step 4   Select DbServer from the Process Name drop-down list box, and then click Finish.

The process stops, and the Process Status table displays the message "Administrator has shut down this server."

On the command-line interface, to stop the DbServer process using the CLI, perform the following steps:

Step 1   Enter **pdterm DbServer**.

Step 2   Enter **pdshow DbServer**.

The following status message appears, showing that the process has been stopped.

```
Process= DbServer
State  = Administrator has shut down this server
Pid    = 0
RC     = 0
Signo  = 0
Start  = 19:16:15 06/02/97
Stop   = 11:27:05 06/03/97
Core   = Not applicable
Info   = Not applicable
```

Troubleshooting Suggestions

Table 24-5 lists troubleshooting suggestions. If the action items suggested do not resolve the error, check the release notes supporting your platform for possible workarounds.

Table 24-5   *Troubleshooting Suggestions*

Error Message	Possible Reasons	Actions
Admin: unable to log on to Essentials (Windows NT only)	An incompatible Microsoft Internet Information Server (IIS) is installed.	Check installation instructions, unload old Microsoft IIS, and then load the correct Microsoft IIS, if necessary.
Authorization required. Please log in with your username and password.	An incompatible browser is causing cookie failure (unable to retrieve cookie).	Refer to the installation documentation for supported version of Internet Explorer/Netscape Navigator software.

Table 24-5   *Troubleshooting Suggestions (Continued)*

Error Message	Possible Reasons	Actions	
Database: inaccessible. This can appear by Process status showing one of the following: ICServer not running DIServer not running AvLoader not running DbMonitor not running DbServer not running EssentialsOSG not running Alternatively, the error message "failed to get complete list of domains" could appear on an Add Device operation.	Server cannot connect to the database, which is corrupt or inaccessible.	**Step 1**	Log in to Essentials as admin.
		Step 2	Select Admin; Troubleshooting Process; Failures to get a list of Essentials backend processes that have failed.
		Step 3	Select Admin; Troubleshooting; Self Test.
		Step 4	Click Create to create a report.
		Step 5	Click Display to display the report.
		Step 6	Select Admin; Troubleshooting; Collect Server Info.
		Step 7	Click the Product Database Status link to get detailed database status.
Database: ODBC error with Essentials (Windows NT only)	The ODBC resource .dll and the ODBC driver manager are different versions.	Install ODBC from Windows NT CD (selecting SQL server).	
Device Configuration: archive cannot retrieve the configuration module for Catalyst devices.	Incorrect password was given when adding or importing the device.	Enter the correct Telnet and enable passwords for the Catalyst devices in the Essentials database. The configuration archive uses Telnet to gather module configurations for Catalyst devices. For the configuration archive to successfully gather the ATM and RSM module configurations, these modules must have the same Telnet passwords as that for the supervisors of the Catalyst 5000 Family of devices. See Essentials online help for more information on entering passwords.	

continues

Table 24-5 *Troubleshooting Suggestions (Continued)*

Error Message	Possible Reasons	Actions
Device Configuration: archive cannot retrieve the running configuration for a device.	Incorrect read and write community strings were given when adding or importing the device.	Enter the correct read and write community strings in the Essentials database. Change the order of the protocols used to retrieve the configuration. (The configuration archive downloads configurations from devices using three different transport protocols—TFTP, Telnet, and RCP, normally in that order). See Essentials online help for more information on setting the transport protocol order used for gathering configurations.
Device Configuration: archive cannot retrieve the startup configuration for a device.	Incorrect password was given when adding or importing the device.	Enter the correct Telnet and enable passwords for the device in the Essentials database. If the device is configured for TACACS authentication, add the TACACS username and password (not the Telnet password) in the Essentials database when you import the device. If the device is configured for local user authentication, add the local username and password in the Essentials database. If the device is configured for Telnet authentication, ensure that you use the Telnet password, enable password, enable secret (if configured), and local username and password (if configured). Do not enter either the local or TACACS username and password. See Essentials online help for more information on entering passwords and TACACS, local, and RCP information.
Device Configuration: "DNS hostname mismatch. *ip_address* unknown to DNS."	The device does not have the DNS server set up to resolve the host name.	Ensure that the DNS server recognizes the device hostname. Alternatively, specify the IP address instead of the hostname.

Table 24-5   *Troubleshooting Suggestions (Continued)*

Error Message	Possible Reasons	Actions
Device Configuration: server runtime error when running Tasks; Device Configuration or Admin; Device Configuration tasks.	CMLogger is not running.	**Step 1** Log in to Essentials as admin. **Step 2** Select Admin; System Admin; Start Process. **Step 3** Start the System. If the configuration tasks still fail, select Admin; Troubleshooting; Process Failures to get a list of Essentials back-end processes that have failed. **Step 4** Select Admin; Troubleshooting; Self Test. **Step 5** Click Create to create a report. **Step 6** Click Display to display the report. **Step 7** Select Admin; Troubleshooting; Collect Server Info. **Step 8** Click the Product Database Status link to get detailed database status.
Device Configuration: SNMP timeout prevents TFTP from retrieving the running configuration for a device.	SNMP did not allow sufficient time for the operation.	Increase the SNMP timeout by configuring SNMP retries and timeouts. See Essentials online help for more information on configuring system-wide SNMP timeouts and retries.
Display: applet cannot start: class browserServer not found (Solaris only).	The server name is not in the *httpd.conf* file.	Add the server name in the *httpd.conf* file.
Display: only right side of Essentials Window displayed.	Browser software is incompatible.	Refer to the installation documentation for supported Internet Explorer/Netscape Navigator software.
	Desktop is not registered in DNS.	Register the desktop in DNS.
Inventory: device import from local database fails (Solaris only).	User bin is not a member of the CiscoWorks group.	Add group membership before starting Essentials.

continues

Table 24-5 *Troubleshooting Suggestions (Continued)*

Error Message	Possible Reasons	Actions
	Name resolution is incorrect.	Correct the name resolution. If that is not possible, then remote import rules will be applied; add *.rhosts* to the *bin* home directory.
Inventory: device import fails from remote NMS.	Essentials and the remote NMS reside in different DNS domains.	Set up Essentials and remote NMS stations in the same DNS domains.
Inventory: device serial or router chassis numbers differ from those shown on outside labels.	Hardware reports get data from the user-defined optional serial number field when the device or router is added to the Essentials (or via Change Device Attributes), not from the SNMP variable chassis serial number. The manually changed serial number takes precedence over the external number.	No action is required, although you can manually change the serial number back to match the external number.
Inventory: device stays in a pending state.	The database is corrupt.	Stop Essentials. Install a backup database, if available; otherwise, install the basic database, *px.db,* over the corrupt database.
	DIServer is not running.	Check the process status. If DIServer is not running, restart it.
	A broadcast address has been imported and is being used for an SNMP write.	Suspend the device. Run the address validation tool on the device (Tools; Connectivity Tools; Validate Device Addresses) to ensure that a broadcast or network address is not being used.
Inventory: devices not importing.	An access list has been applied to the SNMP-server community configuration.	Add **permit** statements to the access lists on all routers.
	An SNMP timeout has occurred.	Increase SNMP slow timeout and retry values.

Table 24-5   *Troubleshooting Suggestions (Continued)*

Error Message	Possible Reasons	Actions
	Reverse DNS lookup failure occurred.	Add the device entry to the local hosts file.
	The device name is not configured in the DNS or *localhost* file.	Add the device entry to the DNS or local hosts file.
Inventory: cannot add device to database.	HP OpenView/SNMP has an old version of *wsnmp.dll* files.	Remove or rename HP OpenView version *wsnmp.dll* files.
Performance: Essentials running slow when importing device (Windows NT only).	Software is incompatible.	Refer to the installation documentation. Verify that correct SP and Microsoft IIS have been loaded. If necessary, unload and reload Essentials.
Printing: cannot print graphs in Essentials.	A browser print restriction has occurred.	To print an Essentials window, use the Print Screen or Capture Screen function on your machine.
Reports: browser hangs when running reports.	Browser software is incompatible.	Refer to installation documentation for supported browser software.
Software Management: approver cannot change scheduled time for Distribute Images jobs using Software Management.	Maker-checker is enforced on Distribute Images jobs.	When Distribute Images jobs require approval, Software Management doesn't allow the schedule time for the job to be changed from Browse Job Status dialog boxes. Create a new job and submit for approval.
Software Management: cannot Undo an Upgrade operation on Microcom and Catalyst devices.	Undo software upgrade not supported on device.	Check Supported Device Matrix in online help for supported devices and software releases and Software Management features.

continues

Table 24-5   *Troubleshooting Suggestions (Continued)*

Error Message	Possible Reasons	Actions
Software Management: Distribute Images and Image Import jobs fail on a device.	Defective software is running on the device.	Go to CCO and examine the software image. If the software image is not deferred, enable debugging and check the Enable Debugging check box (Admin; Software Management; Edit Preferences). Rerun the job, and then use the Mail or Copy Log file option to extract Software Management debugging information. Send the information to Cisco TAC or your customer support with a complete description of the problem.
Software Management: job remains in "pending" state after scheduled time.	Essentials server is not functioning, or has been powered off or rebooted before job schedule time arrives.	Software Management moves the job to error state 1 hour after the job schedule time. Do not alter the job while in "pending" state; the system will take care of it. If necessary, create another job.
Software Management: job remains in "running" state, and the Job Details report shows no progress on job.	Essentials server is not functioning, or has been powered off or rebooted while the job is running, causing the job to be abnormally terminated.	Software Management moves the job to error state one hour after the job schedule time. Do not alter the job while in "pending" state; the system will take care of it. If necessary, create another job.
Software Management: while adding modem images or CIP microcode images into the software management library, the image type is displayed as "Unknown." Software management cannot retrieve attributes from images.	Images for Cisco 3640 digital modems are not imported as AS5300 format files. The Microcom firmware image is not the combined firmware/DSP code. The CIP microcode version is older than 22.0.	Download a supported version of software/firmware from CCO. Check the Supported Device Matrix in online help for supported devices and software releases.

Table 24-5   *Troubleshooting Suggestions (Continued)*

Error Message	Possible Reasons	Actions
Software Management: cannot schedule Distribute Images and Image Import jobs.	The at service is not running or is incorrectly configured.	If Essentials is running on Window NT, use Control Panel; Services to check that the at service is running. If it is not, start it manually. If Essentials is running on Solaris, check that the /usr/bin/at command is present. Check that the at.deny file in /usr/lib/cron directory does not contain the bin username.
Software Management: Essentials cannot upload images from device.	Essentials needs read-write SNMP access to device.	Configure the read-write community string on the device.
Software Management: Mail or Copy Log File function does not mail log files (Windows NT only).	E-mail address is incorrect.	Use the correct e-mail address in the Mail or Copy Log File submenu.
Software Management: MICA/Microcom/CIP card: Software Management does not recognize the MICA/Microcom/CIP cards on AS5x00 or 7x00 device.	Devices are running an unsupported version of Cisco IOS System Software.	See the Supported Device Matrix in online help for supported devices and software releases.
Software Management: RCP is not being used to transfer software images between Essentials and devices.	The device does not support RCP protocol (only IOS devices support RCP). RCP is not properly configured on Essentials server.	Check whether your device is Cisco IOS-based. Make sure that RCP is defined as the preferred protocol. Make sure that the configuration (Admin; System Admin System Configuration) is properly configured with an RCP username. If Essentials is running on a Windows NT machine, verify that the CRMrsh service is running correctly on the Essentials server. (Verify this using Control Panel; Services.) If the service is "stopped," run it manually.

continues

Table 24-5 *Troubleshooting Suggestions (Continued)*

Error Message	Possible Reasons	Actions
Software Management: RCP is not being used to transfer software images between Essentials and devices. *(continued)*		Check the Event Viewer to make sure that the service has started properly. (Access Event Viewer from Administrative Tools group, and then view the application log by selecting Log Application.)
		If Essentials is running on Solaris, make sure that the home directory for RCP user account contains the .rhosts file and can be written to by the bin user.
Software Management: "Internal Error: Can't resolve address for proxy" message when invoking functions "Browse Bugs by Device" or "Locate Devices by Bugs."	A proxy or DNS is incorrectly set up.	Check the proxy URL in Admin; System Admin System Configuration.
		If you configure proxy using a host name, check the DNS configuration on the Essentials server.
		Check that proxy configuration is not set for login each time.
		If these actions do not solve the problem, run your browser on the server where Essentials is installed, configure the proxy in the browser, and check whether www.cisco.com is accessible.
Software Management: Schedule Synchronization Job report is not mailed (Windows NT only).	E-mail address is incorrect.	Correct the e-mail address in the Schedule Synchronization Job submenu.
	SMTP server is not configured.	Configure SMTP using Admin; System Admin; System Configuration.
Software Management: unable to download Cisco IOS (error 4151).	The /var/tmp file has insufficient space to accommodate IOS images.	Increase /var/tmp space.

Table 24-5   *Troubleshooting Suggestions (Continued)*

Error Message	Possible Reasons	Actions
Software Management: CCO Upgrade Analysis screen and Recommend Image Upgrade (from Distribute Images) screen time out.	The connection to CCO from the Essentials server is slow. The CCO server machine is down. CCO filters are not set with the right criteria.	These operations require access to CCO for image information. Make sure that the CCO server is up and running. Select the right filtering criteria, and retry the operation. Select a fewer number of devices, and retry the operation. If these actions do not solve the problem, check the proxy configuration, as described in Software Management.
Software Management: upgrade failure.	Software Management does not allow a direct upgrade from version 4.0 software to version 4.2 X.25 software on the Cisco 700 series.	Upgrade the device to version 4.1 first (any feature set), and then upgrade to version 4.2 X.25 software image.
Syslog Analyzer: filters not taking effect immediately after changing.	It takes about 5 minutes for filters to take effect.	If you need the filters to take effect immediately, you must restart the Syslog Analyzer collector.
Syslog Analyzer: no messages on any generated syslog report.	Network devices are not sending messages to Essentials server.	Examine the Syslog Analyzer Collector Status (Admin; Syslog Analysis; Collector Status). If numbers are all zero, then verify that network devices are sending messages to the Essentials server. Refer to online help for information on setting up a Cisco IOS/Catalyst device.
Syslog Analyzer: message source is given as "???" in /var/syslog_info (Solaris only.)	Solaris bug has occurred; syslogd cannot resolve the source address of the network device sending the message.	Add the name resolution for this device to DNS, /etc/hosts, or your naming service. Alternatively, install the Solaris patch 103291-02. This will change the "???" to an octal IP address in brackets ([171.69.219.72.1.2]). This allows the format to be parsed by Syslog Analyzer.

continues

Table 24-5 *Troubleshooting Suggestions (Continued)*

Error Message	Possible Reasons	Actions
Syslog Analyzer: syslog messages get appended to /var/log/syslog_info (Solaris) or to c:\Program Files\CSCOpx\log\syslog.log (Windows NT), but all Syslog Reports are empty.	Processes are not running properly.	Check whether Syslog Analyzer is running properly (Admin; System Admin; Process Status); if not, start it. Check that CMLogger, RmeOrb, and DBServer are running; if not, restart the system.
	A timestamp problem has occurred.	If the Messages Processed counter is not zero, check timestamps for a message in the syslog file. If there are two timestamps and the second timestamp is current, then the Syslog Analyzer uses the second timestamp. If the second timestamp is older than 7 days, the reports do not display it. If the Message Processed counter is zero and the Messages Filtered counter is not zero, then change the filters. If the Messages Processed and Messages Filtered counters are zero, but the Invalid Messages counter is not zero, contact Cisco TAC or your customer support.
Syslog Analyzer: remote collector not running properly when installed and started on non-Essentials machine.	Configuration parameters are incorrect.	Check the remote collector table for the name and status of the remote collector: Admin; Syslog Analysis; Collector Status. View SAEnvProperties.ini and check that the parameter BGSERVER is set to the hostname of the Essentials server. Perform a **ping** command using this host name to ensure that it is resolvable and reachable from this machine. On Windows NT, also ensure that the PORT parameter is set to 514.
Syslog Analyzer: remote collector— messages in syslog file, but not in reports.	An incorrect version of Java is running.	Install Java 1.1.5 or higher.

Table 24-5   *Troubleshooting Suggestions (Continued)*

Error Message	Possible Reasons	Actions
	The remote collector stopped.	On Solaris, check using the command **/usr/bin/ps -ef | grep java**.
		Restart using **sh /opt/CSCOsac/lib/sacStart.sh**.
	The remote collector is not installed correctly.	On Windows NT, use Control Panel; Services to verify this.
		If a Syslog_Collector is not listed, then reinstall it using SacNTService/install.
		If the collector is installed but is not running, start the remote collector from Control Panel; Services. (You must specify the properties file using the **-pr** option.)
Syslog Analyzer: logging is enabled in the IOS/Catalyst device to send messages to Essentials but is not working. Syslog Analyzer: logging is enabled in the IOS/Catalyst device to send messages to Essentials but is not working.	Messages sent to the Essentials server by network devices are logged by a process independent of the Syslog Analyzer. For Solaris, the logging process is syslogd. For Windows NT, it is the Essentials syslog service. The problem may be that the syslog daemons are not running properly.	Connect to the network device and generate a syslog message as follows: **Step 1** Telnet to the device and log in. The prompt changes to host>. **Step 2** Type **enale** and the enable password. The prompt changes to host#. **Step 3** Type **configure terminal**. You are now in configuration mode, and the prompt changes to host (config)#. **Step 4** Ensure that logging is enabled by entering **logging on**. **Step 5** Specify the IP address of the Essential server to receive the router syslog messages; for example, type **logging 123.45.255.90**. **Step 6** Type **end**. For Solaris, view the file pointed to by the line "local7.info" in the file /etc/syslog.conf (default /var/log/syslog_info). If this file does not exist, create one, and make sure that it is accessible by syslogd. For Windows NT, view the file in C:\Program Files \CSCOpx\log\syslog.log Send an HUP signal to syslogd (**kill -HUP `cat /etc/syslog.pid`**).

continues

Table 24-5 *Troubleshooting Suggestions (Continued)*

Error Message	Possible Reasons	Actions
Syslog Analyzer: logging is enabled in the IOS/Catalyst device to send messages to Essentials but is not working.		If the syslog message is not there, check that the syslog daemons are running properly. For Solaris, type **/usr/ucb/ps -aux	grep syslogd**. For Windows NT, go to Control Panel and ensure that Essentials syslog service is in "Started" state.
Syslog Analyzer: logging is enabled in the IOS/Catalyst device to send messages to Essentials but is not working. *(continued)*		
	The device might be configured incorrectly.	Ensure that the device is logging to the correct Essentials server. (Refer to the device system documentation for details on enabling syslog.)
Syslog Analyzer: the following error message is sent to the Windows NT Event Viewer when using remote NT Windows collector: "Could not start the Syslog Collector service on the *server_name* ERROR 0002: The system cannot find the file "specified" new messages not appearing in reports after changing syslog message file (defined using: Admin; Syslog Analysis; Change Storage Options).	Installation failure has occurred.	When installing on a remote Windows NT collector, use the command **SacNTService/install** (not SacNTService.exe/install).

Table 24-5   *Troubleshooting Suggestions (Continued)*

Error Message	Possible Reasons	Actions
Syslog Analyzer: the following error messages are sent to the Windows NT Event Viewer when using remote Windows NT collector: "Could not start the Syslog Collector service on the *server_name* ERROR 1067: The process terminated unexpectedly" and "SacNTService: The service cannot be started without the properties file specified, please specify the properties file you want to use."	Configuration failure has occurred.	After the SacNTService is installed on a remote Windows NT collector, it must be configured using Control Panel; Services. Ensure that the Startup Parameters field contains the location of the SaenvProperties.ini file (for example, -pr c:\\temp\\SaenvProperties.ini) (Remember to use \\ to separate the directory paths.)
Syslog Analyzer: new messages not appearing in reports after changing syslog message file (defined using: Admin; Syslog Analysis; Change Storage Options).	A new filename needs to be defined in configuration information.	On Windows NT, run the registry editor Regedit. Then go to: HKEY_LOCAL_SYSTEM System CurrentControlSet Services crmlog. Set Parameters to the name of the file for logging syslog messages. On Solaris, modify the /etc/syslog.conf file. (Refer to the Solaris man pages for more information.)
Syslog Analyzer: server runtime error when running Tasks Syslog Analyzer tasks.	CMLogger is not running.	**Step 1** Log in to Essential as admin. **Step 2** Select Admin; System Admin; Start Processes. **Step 3** Start the system. If the task still fails, select Admin; Troubleshooting; Process Failures to get a list of Essential back-end processes that have failed. **Step 4** Select Admin; Troubleshooting; Self Test.

continues

Table 24-5   *Troubleshooting Suggestions (Continued)*

Error Message	Possible Reasons	Actions
Syslog Analyzer: server runtime error when running Tasks Syslog Analyzer tasks. *(continued)*		**Step 5** Click Create to create a report. **Step 6** Click Display to display the report. **Step 7** Select Admin; Troubleshooting; Collect Server Info. **Step 8** Click the Product Database Status link to get detailed database status.
Syslog Analyzer: Unexpected Device Report (Tasks; Syslog Analysis; Unexpected Device Report) contains syslog messages that should not be in the Standard Report (Tasks; Syslog Analysis; Standard Report).	The Syslog Standard Device Report displays messages for all selected devices and dates. These devices must be managed by Essentials inventory. This error could arise if the device is not managed by Essentials inventory.	Add the device to inventory by selecting Admin; Inventory; Add Device. After adding the device, messages formerly in the Unexpected Device Report will not be transferred to the Standard Report, but new messages for the device will be displayed in the Standard Report.
	If the device is managed by Essentials inventory, it could be a name resolution problem. (Syslog analyzer uses all IP addresses associated with the device name to try to map it to a device managed by Essentials Inventory.)	Verify the device name-to-IP address mapping as follows: **Step 1** For Windows NT, view the syslog.log file in C:\Program Files\CSCOpx\log. For Solaris, view the syslog_info file in /var/log. **Step 2** Note the source of the syslog messages from the device (the source is the host name appearing immediately after the timestamp). **Step 3** Obtain a list of IP addresses (perform **nslookup** on the device name at the command prompt). **Step 4** Generate a detailed device report (Tasks; Inventory; Detailed Device Report) for the particular device. **Step 5** Check the Network Address column, and verify that the IP addresses returned from **nslookup** appear on the list.

Table 24-5   *Troubleshooting Suggestions (Continued)*

Error Message	Possible Reasons	Actions
		Step 6 If any IP addresses are not on the list, then the device name-to-IP address mapping is incorrect. Update the naming services (DNS, /etc/hosts, etc.) with the missing IP addresses.
System Configuration: server runtime error when running Admin; System Admin; Device Configuration task.	CMLogger is not running.	Same action steps as the previous row, which has "CMLogger is not running" as a possible reason.
"TFTP server on the device timed out" error appears during operation on Cisco 700 Series devices.	The TFTP client cannot be accessed on the Essentials server.	Check whether the TFTP client is available on the Essentials server. Solaris: /usr/bin/tftp Windows NT: nnt\system32\tftp.exe

Information for Troubleshooting CWSI (CiscoWorks for Switched Internetworking) Campus

The following subsections provide information to troubleshoot CWSI Campus:

- Understanding CWSI Campus Background Processes
- Starting CWSI Campus
- Improving CWSI Campus Performance
- Entering Valid Community Strings
- Working with Discovery
- Display Discrepancy Reports

Understanding CWSI Campus Background Processes

To use many of the troubleshooting techniques, you must first understand the background processes of CWSI Campus. Refer to the "Enabling trace or debug" and "Stopping and Starting CWSI Campus Processes" sections for information about understanding and working with the CWSI Campus background processes:

CWSI Campus includes the following major technology components that enhance the overall performance:

- A multithreaded discovery process for identifying network devices and accessing SNMP and RMON information

- An underlying database engine that offers increased performance and data storage without requiring external administration by network operators

- Object-oriented technology for interprocess communication between software components and databases

These background processes are described in Table 24-6. The server processes represent the processes controlled by the CWSI Campus software; these are the background processes for the client processes. The client processes require user input.

To verify that these processes are running, you can use the **pdshow** command from any command prompt. You also can use the Task Manager (on Windows NT) or **ps-** (on UNIX systems).

Table 24-6   *CWSI Campus Processes*

Process	Description	Type	pdshow	Task Manager or ps
Process Manager	This daemon manager starts and monitors many of the CWSI Campus processes, including ANI, RTPoller, Event Channel, and OSAgent. The Process Manager is one of the Essentials processes that monitors CWSI Campus.		dmgtd	
AniServer	ANI is a multithreaded Java program. It is installed as a daemon process and runs in the background, beginning as the workstation starts up. ANI is responsible for the discovery of the network, and it does all SNMP communication.	Server	AniServer	jre.exe
CWSI Campus Database	The database engine is responsible for checking all ANI information into the database. For ANI, this is a checkpoint only. ANI performs all its operations from the data stored in memory. The database stores user-entered information and allows ANI to quickly load its data model into memory upon a subsequent restart.	Server	DbCwsi (UNIX only)	dbeng50 (The Essentials database engine has the same name, so your system should be running two processes with this name.)

Table 24-6   *CWSI Campus Processes (Continued)*

Process	Description	Type	pdshow	Task Manager or ps
OSAgent	OSAgent is a Common Object Broker Architecture (CORBA) agent that passes messages between the AniServer and clients. All servers must register with the OsAgent, and all clients looking for service find it with the help of the OsAgent. The CWSI Campus login window is used to register the CWSI Campus client with OsAgent and to indicate that it is searching for an ANI named AniServer. The OSAgent is one of the Essentials processes that monitors CWSI Campus.	Server	RmeOrb	osagent
RTPoller	This process is used by the AtmDirector application for periodic polling of the network for status of devices and links.	Server	RTPoller	jre.exe
Event Channel	This process sends events to all servers and clients that have registered with it.	Server	EventChannel	jre.exe
CWSI Campus Client	This process downloads a complete picture of the topology so that selection and display are done locally. It receives events from ANI about changes in discovery or network status.	Client	—	—
UserTracking Client	This process provides a graphical user interface for the UserTracking application.	Client	—	—
VlanDirector Client	This process provides a graphical user interface for the VlanDirector application.	Client	—	—
Topology Client	This process displays network topology and is used as the primary starting point for other applications.	Client	—	—

continues

Table 24-6 *CWSI Campus Processes (Continued)*

Process	Description	Type	pdshow	Task Manager or ps
AtmDirector	This process links to the OSAgent and CWSI Campus database for some processing.	—		
CiscoView	This process links to the OSAgent to provide communication with devices on the CWSI Campus map and CiscoView.	—		
TrafficDirector	TrafficDirector does not link directly with any of the background processes. You can start TrafficDirector from the CWSI Campus map.	—		

Figure 24-2 illustrates the interactions of the CWSI Campus processes.

Figure 24-2 *CWSI Campus Architecture*

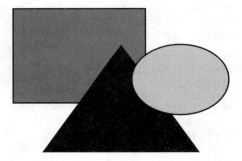

Enabling trace or debug

Some of the troubleshooting steps may require that you enable **trace** or **debug** in ANI to gather additional information. You also might be asked to enable **trace** or **debug** for particular subsystems of CWSI Campus when you contact your Cisco TAC representative for additional assistance.

To enable **trace** and **debug**, follow these steps:

Step 1 Open a command prompt or shell window.

Step 2 Enter **stopcwsiserver** to stop the CWSI Campus server processes.

Step 3 Start ANI and enable **trace** and **debug** by entering the following command:

> **`ani -trace`** `<subsystem>` **`-debug`** `<subsystem>` **`-logfile`** `<logfile name>`

> The troubleshooting instructions or the TAC representative will provide you with the appropriate subsystem name. You can enter any name for the log file, and the log file will appear in the `<CWSIROOT>` directory, where `<CWSIROOT>` is the directory in which you installed CWSI Campus.

Step 4 To stop the process, press Ctrl-C from the command prompt or shell window.

Step 5 Contact your Cisco TAC representatives, and provide them with this log file.

Stopping and Starting CWSI Campus Processes

The following command-line scripts control the CWSI Campus processes:

> **stopcwsiserver** stops the CWSI daemons.
> **startcwsiserver** starts the CWSI daemons.

To use these scripts, you must be signed in as the administrator on Windows NT or as root on UNIX operating systems. Open a command prompt or shell window. Enter **stopcwsiserver** to stop the CWSI Campus server processes. When the prompt returns, all the daemons have been stopped. To restart the processes, enter **startcwsiserver** and wait until the prompt returns.

Losing the Connection to EventChannel

If an error occurs stating that you have lost connection to EventChannel, follow these steps:

Step 1 From the command prompt or shell window, enter **pdshow AniServer** to determine whether AniServer is still running. If it is not running, continue with Step 3.

Step 2 Check the start and stop time to determine whether AniServer was restarted while CWSI Campus was running. If AniServer did go down without your knowledge, open the ani.log file to determine the cause.

Step 3 From the command prompt or shell window, enter **pdshow EventChannel** to determine whether EventChannel is running. If EventChannel is not running, continue with Step 5.

Step 4   Check the start and stop time to determine whether EventChannel was restarted while CWSI Campus was running. If AniServer had been restarted, EventChannel is reset, which terminates the connection between the CWSI Campus client and Event Channel.

Step 5   If either AniServer or EventChannel are not running, follow these steps:

— Exit CWSI Campus.

— Enter the **startcwsiserver** command.

— Start CWSI Campus.

Starting CWSI Campus

If you have difficulty starting the CWSI Campus applications, follow the tips in these subsections.

If you have just restarted your computer and cannot log in to <Hostname>AniServer, the ANI server might not be ready to receive messages. Wait a few minutes, and then try to log in again.

If you still cannot log in, refer to the previous section of "Troubleshooting Information for CiscoWorks 2000 Installation and Setup." That section includes detailed steps for resolving this error on Windows NT and UNIX systems.

Identifying a Corrupt Database

A corrupt database cannot be easily identified. In past versions of CWSI Campus, symptoms included a connection that hangs or intermittent hanging. However, these problems have been resolved. Currently, the only way to know definitively whether the database is corrupt is to look at the ani.log file. If many SQL exceptions and errors are present in the ani.log, the database may be corrupt.

Replacing a Corrupt Database

ANI cannot perform effectively with a corrupt database. If you determine that you have a corrupt database, you need to reinitialize a new database.

NOTE   If you have entered information into the UserTracking application, this information will be lost when you delete the corrupt database.

You can replace a corrupt database using two different methods:

- Running the scripts
- Replacing the corrupt database manually

These will be discussed next.

Running the Script

If you run the script to replace a corrupt database, the script automatically stops all CWSI Campus servers. After the database engine stops, the script then erases the old database, sets the correct permissions, and replaces the old database with an empty, reinitialized database. The script automatically restarts the CWSI Campus servers.

To use this script, follow these steps:

Step 1 Run the reinitdb script.

On Windows NT, select Run from the Start menu and enter **reinitdb**.

On UNIX systems, log in as root and run the reinitdb script located in the <CWSIROOT>/bin directory.

Step 2 Read the information that appears on the screen.

Step 3 Press any key to run the script, or press Ctrl-C to exit out of the script without running it.

Step 4 After the script finishes, wait a few minutes before starting CWSI Campus to allow time for the CWSI Campus servers to start up properly.

Replacing the Corrupt Database Manually

You should not need to manually replace a corrupt database because the script automatically performs all necessary steps for you. However, you can use this method if you want to retain a copy of your old database.

NOTE   If you are using CWSI Campus on a UNIX operating system, you may need to change the owner and group before replacing the database. When you copy the cwsi_ini.db file, it sets the owner and group to your current user. If you do not change it, CWSI Campus will not function properly. To prevent this, you must be sure that both the owner and the group are set to BIN.

To create a new database, follow these steps:

Step 1 Run the stopcwsiserver script.

Step 2 Locate the current database: <CWSIROOT>\db\data\cwsi.db.

Step 3 Back up the current database by renaming it. For example, you could name it cwsiold.db.

Step 4 Make a copy of the cwsi_ini.db file (which is also in the data directory).

Note	Do not delete or rename the original cwsi_ini.db file (which is also in the data directory).

Step 5 Rename the copy of cwsi_ini.db to cwsi.db. This is a fresh database file.

Step 6 Delete the cwsi.log file.

Step 7 Run the startcwsiserver script.

Using the Same Database on Multiple Workstations

You cannot install CWSI Campus on multiple workstations and allow them to share the database. Also, if you plan to install multiple copies of CWSI Campus on your network, you should change the name of the AniServer that each copy is accessing.

Using Multiple Copies of CWSI Campus

If you plan to install multiple copies of CWSI Campus on your network, you should be aware of how the CWSI Campus discovery process works in this environment.
The discovery process uses ANI, which runs as a server process and exchanges information with other CWSI Campus applications running as clients. Each AniServer is intended to manage a single domain. Therefore, if you install another copy of CWSI Campus configured with the same AniServer name (AniServer, by default) in your network, unpredictable behavior might result, depending on which AniServer the client chooses as its default AniServer.

Depending on the available system resources on your initial CWSI Campus system, using the wrong AniServer might result in poor system performance of all CWSI Campus systems that are accessing and using the resources of the default AniServer.

If you want to install another copy of CWSI Campus to manage another domain, you must manually configure your systems to run separate AniServer processes.

To configure your systems, follow these steps:

Step 1 Close all CWSI Campus applications.

Step 2 Run the stopcwsiserver script.

Step 3 Locate and open the ani.properties file with a text editor.

The ani.properties file is located in the <CWSIROOT>/etc/cwsi/ directory.

Step 4 Change the following line to rename the AniServer process running on your local workstation:

```
AniName = AniServer_Name
```

For example, if you just installed a Solaris version of CWSI Campus, you could rename the AniServer to SOLAniServer.

Step 5 After making these changes, save the file and close your text editor.

Step 6 Run the startcwsiserver script.

Improving CWSI Campus Performance

You can improve the performance of CWSI Campus by reducing the overhead on the CWSI Campus workstation. To reduce the CPU cycles required by CWSI Campus, follow these steps:

Step 1 Reduce the number of discovery threads. This process causes discovery to take less CPU power, but discovery will take longer. To change the discovery threads, follow these steps:

Note   The operation of ANI and CWSI campus clients depends on the information in the ani.properties file. An incorrect entry in this property file can cause CWSI Campus to operate incorrectly. Follow the instruction carefully, and do not attempt to edit other information.

— Run the stopcwsiserver script.

— Locate the ani.properties file in the CWSI directory.

— Locate the following line:

```
Discovery.threads=12.
```

— Change this line so that it now states:

`Discovery.threads=5.`

— Run the startcwsiserver script.

Step 2 In UserTracking, increase the VMPSMajor and VMPSMinor time schedules.

Step 3 Increase the discovery time scheduling interval.

Step 4 Change the discovery time scheduling interval to be fixed (once a day, twice a day) based on your need for timely information.

Step 5 Set up the system for high performance.

Install enough physical memory to handle CWSI Campus and any other programs that you run simultaneously. You should avoid using swapping.

Ensure a fast network connection; the connection should be better than a 10-MB shared media connection.

If you are using Windows NT, use ultra-fast wide SCSI drives. Also, place the swap file on its own partition, if possible, or ensure that it remains unfragmented.

Entering Valid Community Strings

To allow CWSI Campus to configure the devices in your network, you must ensure that the proper community strings are set. These sections will help you troubleshoot problems that you may experience.

Which Community Strings Are Valid?

When entering valid community strings, what determines whether these examples are invalid or valid?

Example 1: Invalid Community Strings Entry

172.26.1.*:sub1::::::sub1:

172.26.1.*:sub2::::::sub2:

Example 2: Valid Community Strings Entry

..*.*:sub1:::::::sub1:

172.26.1.*:sub2:::::::sub2:

The first example is invalid because you have assigned different community strings to the same nested address. CWSI Campus probably will overwrite the first entry with the second. However, unpredictable results are also possible.

The second example is valid because 172.26.1.* is an address nested in the *.*.*.* address.

What Happens If I Enter an Invalid Write Community String?

If you accidentally enter an invalid write community string, you will still be able to discover the network (provided that you entered a valid read-only community string). You will not be able to perform any write actions until you enter a valid read-write string.

Working with Discovery

If you have experienced difficulty interpreting your discovered network, follow the suggestions in this section for assistance with common problems.

Why Do Links Appear as Dashed Lines?

When a link between devices appears as a dashed line, it means that during the last discovery cycle, CWSI Campus was incapable of doing a complete discovery of one of the devices at either end of the link. This situation could happen if the link is inoperable for any reason, such as if the link was removed from the network.

The most likely explanation for these dashed lines is an SNMP timeout. SNMP typically has the lowest priority of the background processes for the Cisco device system. For example, SNMP can be affected if you create a new VLAN because a spanning-tree recalculation occurs, which takes precedence over SNMP.

You can lengthen the SNMP timeout for an individual device. To lengthen the timeout, follow these steps:

Step 1   Select Edit; SNMP Communities from the CWSI Campus map window.

Step 2   Enter the community string using this syntax:

```
target:read:UNUSED:timeout:retries:UNUSED:UNUSED:write:
```

The default timeout is 3 seconds.

Step 3   If individual devices are configured with different community strings, enter new lines for each device.

Any changes made to the community strings take effect immediately.

Why Do Devices Appear with a Red X?

Devices with a red X on them are not being discovered properly. For any device to be discovered by CWSI Campus, the following criteria must be met:

- CWSI Campus has the proper SNMP community strings.
- You should be able to **ping** the device.
- The device should be running an SNMP server.
- The device is visible through CDP or ILMI by its neighbors.
- The device can see its neighbors through CDP or ILMI.
- If the device has a **permit** list, you must include the IP address of the network management workstation.
- The software version on the device should support CDP or ILMI.

Why Do Devices Appear as an Empty Box with a Red X?

Devices appearing as a box with a red X signify that the device is reachable but is unknown to CWSI Campus. This icon is typically displayed for non-Cisco devices. It may also display if a new Cisco device has been released since the last release of CWSI Campus.

Why Does Discovery Take a Long Time?

Several factors determine how long a discovery will take, including the following:

- The number of devices that are unreachable
- The number of LANE objects to be read
- The number of threads allocated to do discovery

If you experience a slow discovery, follow these steps:

Step 1 Restrict discovery to only the VTP domains that you want to manage.

Step 2 Ensure that you have entered the appropriate community strings for your devices.

Step 3 Increase the number of threads available to discovery if you have many devices to discover. CWSI Campus allocates 12 threads to discovery. If you have many slow or unreachable devices, they can fill the thread pool and prevent other devices from being discovered.

Step 4 To change or increase discovery threads, follow these steps:

NOTE   The operation of ANI and CWSI Campus clients depends on the information in the ani.properties file. An incorrect entry in this property file can cause CWSI Campus to operate incorrectly. Follow the instructions carefully, and do not attempt to edit other information.

- — Run the stopcwsiserver script.
- — Locate the ani.properties file in the CWSI directory.
- — Locate the following line:

  `Discovery.threads=12`
- — Change the line so that it reads:

  `Discovery.threads=60.`
- — Run the startcwsiserver script.

How Can Discovery Be Disabled?

You cannot completely shut off discovery. CWSI Campus was built on a real-time data model that relies upon discovery data.

You can set the discovery interval to an extremely large number so that discovery occurs only when the ANI server starts or when you manually discover the network.

How Can Devices Be Deleted?

If CWSI Campus has discovered a device that you do not want displayed on the map, you cannot delete this device. The following solutions are available:

- Remove the links to the device, and drag the device icon to a remote portion of the map so that it does not appear in the main map window.

  This solution works well if the device is in your network, but you do not want to display it on the CWSI Campus map.

- Replace the CWSI Campus database and force an initial discovery.

  This solution works best for erroneously discovered devices that are not really in your network, or if you have removed a device since the initial discovery.

Why Does the ATM Network Appear as a Cloud?

If CWSI Campus cannot correlate the ATM link information, the ATM network appears as a ATM cloud on the CWSI Campus map. Possible causes and their solutions include these:

- ILMI is not active on the ATM network.
  - Verify that ILMI is active on the ATM devices in your network.
- Default ATM-VLAN has not been properly configured.
- You did not use an ATM device as a seed for discovery.
- ILMI is not returning the correct IP information.
  - ILMI does not automatically update when IP addresses are changed. Reset the LightStream 1010 ATM switch to clear out the ILMI table.
- The ILMI entries are not up-to-date between any given ATM link.
  - Verify that the ILMI entries are up-to-date and that they are consistent.
- Your LANE modules have older software image versions.
  - If any devices have one or more LANE modules and are running software image versions that are older than 3.2(7) or the 11.3(3a)WA4(5), the ATM network will not be discovered properly. Use software image versions 3.2(7) or 11.3(3a)WA4(6) or later.

Why Do Some Ethernet Links Not Include Speed?

On some devices (typically unknown devices), CWSI Campus can retrieve only the media table from the IF table RFC 1213 MIB ifType. In these cases, the link is displayed as Ethernet. For most devices, CWSI Campus reads the enterprise-specific MIBs, which contain more detailed port-type information. Therefore, 10 M and 100 M are displayed on the map.

Why Do the Wrong Devices or Connections Appear?

Make sure that your routers do not have the same sysName. Routers advertise sysName as their CDP cache identification, and CWSI Campus depends on CDP information for discovery. Therefore, if you have two or more devices with the same sysName, CWSI Campus displays unpredictable results.

You can also check the log file to see if a large number of duplicate devices has been discovered and rejected as duplicates.

Why Do Some Unknown Devices Appear with an OID As the Device Name?

Devices that are unsupported by CWSI Campus will not appear with a device name, but will appear with an Object Identifier (OID) instead. CWSI Campus attempts to map the OID to a Cisco product tree MIB. If the OID is under the CiscoProducts or workgroup tree, the OID appears as the device name.

Why Are Frame Relay CDP Links Not Discovered?

Some Frame Relay CDP links may not be discovered by CWSI Campus, even though their neighbors appear by using the **show cdp** command on the CLI. This is caused by an IOS bug in which point-to-multipoint Frame Relay WAN links do not appear in the SNMP list of CDP neighbors, even though they appear on the CLI.

Displaying Discrepancy Reports

Discrepancy reports enable you to discover inconsistencies in your network.

These subsections provide information about working with discrepancy reports.

You can display and print reports about inconsistencies in your network map:

Step 1   From the CWSI Map window, select Reports; Discrepancies.

The Discrepancy window opens.

Step 2   To print the discrepancy report, select File; Export.

The report is saved as a file. You can print the report from the program in which it has been saved.

Interpreting the Discrepancy Report

The discrepancy report displays information on inconsistencies or irregularities in your network.

Table 24-7 describes these irregularities that may appear in your report.

When interpreting the discrepancy report, keep in mind that configurations that you set up intentionally may appear as discrepancies. If you are aware that this is how you wanted to configure your network, then do not be overly concerned with the discrepancies.

Table 24-7 *Discrepancy Table*

Discrepancy	Meaning
Trunk VLANs mismatch	Different ends of a trunk specify different VLANs.
Native VLANs mismatch	Different ends of a single VLAN link specify different VLANs (native VLANs differ).
VLAN name conflict	VLANs with different ISL numbers have the same name in different domains.
VLAN index conflict	VLANs with different names have the same ISL number in different domains.
VLAN SAID conflict	Different SAID numbers are on the same VLAN in different domains.
LANE configuration server ATM address missing	LANE ATM addresses are not found on the ATM switch.
LANE client VLAN/ATM-VLAN misassociation	ATM-VLAN is associated with a VLAN with a different name.
LANE client with no ATM-VLAN	A LANE client has no ATM-VLANs.
LANE broadcast server with no ATM-VLAN	A LANE broadcast server has no ATM-VLAN.
Link duplex mismatch	Full-duplex and half-duplex are configured on either side of a link.
Link speed mismatch	A different link speed is set on either side of a link (for 10/100 ports or for any group of links).
Trunk VLAN protocol mismatch	Protocol encapsulation differs across a trunk (ISL versus 802.1Q).
Trunk/nontrunk mismatch	Trunking ports versus nontrunking ports are configured on either side of a link.
VTP disconnected domain	A link in a VTP domain is not set to trunk. There are devices in this domain that do not communicate through any trunk.
No VTP server in domain	There is no VTP server in the domain.
EtherChannel port spanning tree not disabled	Spanning tree is not supported with Catalyst software release 2.3 and lower. Therefore, you must disable spanning tree on switches with active VLANs that go across the Fast EtherChannel connections. For Catalyst software release 3.1 and higher, you can configure spanning tree on Fast EtherChannel links.

Customizing the Discrepancy Report

You can customize the Discrepancy Report to display only those discrepancies about which you want to be notified.

Step 1 From the CWSI Campus Map, select Options; Properties. The CWSI Properties window opens.

Step 2 In the Properties window, select Discrepancy. The discrepancies are displayed.

Step 3 Select only those discrepancies that you want displayed.

Troubleshooting Information for Applications Included in CWSI Campus

The following subsections are presented in this section:

- Troubleshooting VlanDirector
- Troubleshooting AtmDirector
- Troubleshooting TrafficDirector
- Troubleshooting CiscoView

Troubleshooting VlanDirector

Use the information provided here to help you troubleshoot problems with the VlanDirector application.

Does VTP Need To Be Enabled?

The VlanDirector application requires VTP to be enabled. For most predictable results, Cisco recommends having at least one switch configured as a VTP server, and the remaining switches configured as VTP clients.

If There Are Multiple VTP Servers in a VTP Domain, Which VTP Server Does VlanDirector Make the Changes To?

If the two VTP servers are in the same domain and are connected by VTP trunks, it does not matter which switch the VlanDirector application changes. VTP ensures that the information on all VTP servers and clients in a single VTP domain is coordinated and shares the same configuration.

If the servers are in different VTP domains, then they do not share VLAN states, and they are both known to the VlanDirector application. You must select the VTP domain in which you want to make the VLAN changes, and the corresponding VTP servers will reflect those changes.

If there are two servers with the same VTP domain that are not connected by trunks, the configurations managed by the two servers may diverge. This configuration is not supported by the VlanDirector application, and it creates a discrepancy.

Can VLANs in Different VTP Domains Have the Same Name?

You can have VLANs with the same name, provided that other characteristics, such as VLAN Index and SAID value, are also identical. Discrepancies occur when there are identically named VLANs with other attributes that are different (such as index and so on). If the two VLANs share identical definitions, no discrepancy is detected.

Can You Drag Ports from One VLAN to Another on VTP Transparent Switches?

Attempting to drag a port to a VLAN may or may not work, depending upon the definition of that particular VLAN on both the VTP server and the transparent switch. If the definitions are identical (including name, VLAN index, and so on), the dragging process will probably work fine. However, if the definitions are not identical, then the results are undefined: The process may or may not work. Therefore, to add VTP transparent switches to the same VLANs that are running on the VTP server, you must ensure that the VLAN definitions are consistent.

Will VlanDirector Display VLAN Information for a Switch That Is in Transparent Mode?

The VlanDirector application does not discover any VLANs configured on a switch in transparent mode. Thus, if the VLAN state of a transparent switch differs from the state reported by a server in the same domain, the VlanDirector application will not properly handle VLAN changes to the transparent switch.

Why Is the Switch Highlighted When Any VLAN Is Selected?

In the VlanDirector application, you can select a VLAN, and the switches associated with that VLAN are highlighted on the CWSI Campus map. You can also highlight a switch in the CWSI Campus map to indicate which VLANs are active on that switch. However, if the switch has trunks that carry all VLANs, then the switch will be highlighted, regardless which VLAN you select.

Why Is There a Lighting Bolt on the Port?

The lightning bolt on a port means that the port is part of a link (either a device-to-device link or a connection into a shared media).

The lightning bolt is used to differentiate between a port that is connected to another switch (linking) and a port that is configured as a user port. Cisco Discovery Protocol (CDP) has discovered a CDP peer out of this port.

The bolt indicates that you cannot manipulate the port for VLAN configuration by itself; you must configure it as part of its corresponding link. You do this by selecting the link from the CWSI Campus map and dragging the link to the appropriate VLAN.

Configuring LANE Services

The VlanDirector application enables you to configure LANE services. Tables 24-8 through 24-11 provide you with detailed troubleshooting information for resolving LANE configuration problems.

Table 24-8   *ATM-VLANs Missing in VlanDirector Names Window*

Probable Cause	Possible Solution
Devices do not have required software image versions.	Make sure that all devices are running the required software image version for LANE services. See the CWSI Campus release notes for the correct software image versions for your devices.
Incorrect read community strings were entered in CWSI Campus.	Verify that the SNMP community strings entered in CWSI Campus match the actual ones for all the devices on which LANE components are being configured. To check the community strings, select Edit; SNMP Communities from the CWSI Campus map. See the section "Preparing for Network Discovery" of the *Getting Started with CWSI Campus* publication if you need additional assistance entering the correct community strings.
No SNMP connectivity is on LANE devices.	Make sure that all LANE devices are reachable through SNMP.
SNMP timeouts are occurring on the devices.	Check the CWSI Campus map to see if devices appear with a red X on them. Increase the SNMP timeout for the devices, and rediscover the devices or network. To lengthen the timeout, select Edit; SNMP Communities from the CWSI Campus map window. See the section "Preparing for Network Discovery" of the *Getting Started with CWSI Campus* publication if you need additional assistance entering the SNMP timeout.

continues

Table 24-8 *ATM-VLANs Missing in VlanDirector Names Window (Continued)*

Probable Cause	Possible Solution
LANE servers on devices do not have enough memory.	If the configuration server resides on a Catalyst 5000 series switch, verify that the device has at least 16 MB of memory.
The configuration servers cannot be discovered.	Verify that the master configuration server has been discovered by selecting Edit; Configure Config Server from the VlanDirector Names window. Cisco does not recommend using more than one master configuration server in an ATM fabric. If there are multiple master configuration servers, CWSI Campus will randomly select one of them to use for discovery, and the others will be ignored.
| The LE servers cannot be discovered. | You should have at least one active LE server for each ATM-VLAN.<br><br>The configuration server database should reflect the correct master ship state of the LE servers.<br><br>Use the CLI to check the configuration server database. A valid configuration server database is similar to the following:<br><br>```
at-5000-4atm1#sh lane database
LANE Config Server database table 'cwsiLecsDb'
no default elan
elan 'vlanElanTest': un-restricted server
47.00918100000000603E899701.00E01431A421.01
(prio 0)
LANE Config Server database table
'lecsdb_57_87.3' bound to interface/s: ATM0
default elan: default
elan 'default': un-restricted server
47.00918100000000603E899701.00E01431A421.01
(prio 0) active
elan 'vlan9': un-restricted server
47.00918100000000603E899701.00E01431A421.09
(prio 0) active
``` |
| The ATM-VLAN may be associated with a VTP VLAN with a different name. | In the VlanDirector application, a VTP VLAN with an associated ATM-VLAN is represented under the VTP Domain folder as one entry with an ATM cloud icon beside it. For example, when a VTP VLAN with the name X is associated with an ATM-VLAN with the name Y, it is represented as one entry under the VTP Domain folder as X with an ATM cloud icon beside it. The name Y does not appear anywhere. |
| These solutions do not resolve the problem. | Enable **trace** and **debug** entering the following command:<br><br>```
ani -trace frontend -debug vlad -debug lane -debug ilmi -
trace pnni -debug vmpsadmin -trace devices
-debug devices.C5K -debug devices.C5K.C5500 -debug devices.LS1010
-debug devices.Router -debug devices.C3K -debug devices.C2800 -
logfile ani.log
``` |

Table 24-9   *Incorrect or Missing Association between VTP VLAN and ATM-VLAN*

Probable Cause	Possible Solution
This is the same as the probable cause in Table 24-7's contents in rows 1 through 4.	Check the corresponding solutions in the same rows in Table 24-7.
No LANE clients exist for the ATM-VLAN.	Configure LANE clients for appropriate ATM-VLANs. See the "Configuring and Monitoring LANE Services" scenario in the *Getting Started with CWSI Campus* publication. See the software configuration guide for your specific device.
LANE clients exist but are not discovered.	Make sure that devices are not timing out.
LANE servers exist on devices that do not have enough memory.	If the configuration server resides on a Catalyst 5000 series switch, verify that the device has at least 16 MB of memory.
No rediscovery is done after configuring VLANs with LANE services enabled.	**Step 1** From the CWSI Campus Map window, select View; Rediscover Map. **Step 2** Start the VlanDirector application by selecting Tools; VlanDirector from the CWSI Campus Map. **Step 3** From the VlanDirector Names window, select File; Refresh. See the *Using the Campus VlanDirector Application* publication for additional assistance.
These solutions do not resolve the problem.	Enable **trace** and **debug** entering the following command: ani -trace frontend -debug vlad -debug lane -debug ilmi -trace pnni -debug vmpsadmin -trace devices -debug devices.C5K -debug devices.C5K.C5500 -debug devices.LS1010 -debug devices.Router -debug devices.C3K -debug devices.C2800 -logfile ani.log

Table 24-10 *Cannot Create or Modify a VLAN with LANE Services Enabled*

Probable Cause	Possible Solution
This is the same as the probable cause in Table 24-7's contents in rows 1 through 4.	Check the corresponding solutions in the same rows in Table 24-7.
LE server was not created.	Increase the timeout for the device on which you have configured the LE server.
The configuration server could not be configured.	The LE server ATM address already exists in the configuration server database. Make sure that the ATM address of the newly created LE server is not already present in the configuration server database.
These solutions do not resolve the problem.	Enable **trace** and **debug** entering the following command: ```ani -trace frontend -debug vlad -debug lane -debug ilmi -trace pnni -debug vmpsadmin -trace devices -debug devices.C5K -debug devices.C5K.C5500 -debug devices.LS1010 -debug devices.Router -debug devices.C3K -debug devices.C2800 -logfile ani.log```

Table 24-11 *Cannot Configure the Configuration Server*

Probable Cause	Possible Solution
This is the same as the probable cause in Table 24-7's contents in rows 1 through 4.	Check the corresponding solutions in the same rows in Table 24-7.
The configuration server database was not configured.	Increase the timeout for the device on which you have configured the configuration server.

The configuration server already exists.	Using the CLI, remove the existing configuration server database. The following is a sample configuration:
	
	```interface ATM0```
	```mut 1500```
	```atm pvc 1 0 5 qsaal```
	```atm pvc 2 0 16 ilmi```
	```atm ilmi-keepalive 5```
	```lange config database xxxx```
	
	Remove this line:
	
	```Lange config database xxxx```

Table 24-11 *Cannot Configure the Configuration Server (Continued)*

Probable Cause	Possible Solution
ATM addresses could not be assigned to the configuration server.	Using the CLI, remove the ATM address association, if it already exists. The following is a sample configuration: ``` interface ATM0 mtu 1500 atm pvc 1 0 5 qsaal atm pvc 2 0 16 ilmi atm ilmi-keepalive 5 lane config fixed-config-atm-address lane config auto-config-atm-address lane config config-atm-address lane config database xxxx ``` Remove these lines: ``` lane config fixed-config-atm-address lane config auto-config-atm-address lane config config-atm-address lane config database xxxx ```
The configuration server's ATM address could not be configured on the ATM switches.	Verify the community strings and increase the SNMP timeout. To check the community strings and increase the SNMP timeout, select Edit; SNMP Communities from the CWSI Campus map. See "Preparing for Network Discovery" of the *Getting Started with CWSI Campus* publication if you need additional assistance entering the correct community strings and timeout value.
These solutions do not resolve the problem.	Enable **trace** and **debug** entering the following command: ``` ani -trace frontend -debug vlad -debug lane -debug ilmi - trace pnni -debug vmpsadmin -trace devices -debug devices.C5K -debug devices.C5K.C5500 -debug devices.LS1010 -debug devices.Router -debug devices.C3K -debug devices.C2800 - logfile ani.log ```

Troubleshooting AtmDirector

This subsection describes how you can use the tools within the AtmDirector application to troubleshoot and enhance your network.

Logging Messages

The AtmDirector application logs error and debug messages that are useful when you need to troubleshoot your network or to resolve any problems. The error and debug messages are automatically recorded (by default) in the $CWSIROOT/log/atmd.log file.

To set the logging option on or off, follow these steps:

Step 1   Select Preferences; Options from the AtmDirector main window. The Global Preferences window opens.

Step 2   Select the Miscellaneous index tab. The Miscellaneous options are displayed.

Step 3   Click the On button to log error and debug messages, or click the Off button to stop logging the error and debug messages. Topology and discovery messages are automatically logged if the On button is selected. This is the default.

Note	If the discovery process is polling, messages are logged after Discovery has completed polling.

Step 4   Click OK.

You can start or stop logging the error and debug messages while the AtmDirector application is running. The option that you select (On or Off) will not change when the application is terminated.

Note	It is recommended that you keep the debug option On.

Analyzing the Log

You can begin to troubleshoot your network and resolve any problems by analyzing the error and debug messages that have been recorded in the logfile of the AtmDirector application. The logfile with the error and debug messages is kept in the $CWSIROOT/log/atmd.log file.

NOTE	If there are no error or debug messages in the logfile, the logging option was not On.

The error and debug messages in the $CWSIROOT/log/atmd.log file are in the following format:

```
<timestamp> AtmDirector:<severity>:<component>:<message>
```

Example error and debug messages include the following:

```
1998/07/29 17:09:15.55 AtmDirector:Info:GUI:Started AtmDirector Initialization...
1998/07/29 17:09:15.56 AtmDirector:Debug:Topology:Running in Debug All mode.
1998/07/29 17:09:17.08 AtmDirector:Debug:ORB:EVENTCHANNEL CONNECTED...
1998/07/29 17:09:30.37 AtmDirector:Info:GUI:Finished AtmDirector Initialization.
```

Checking the Status of Devices and Links

The AtmDirector application monitors devices and links at defined intervals and shows their status on the topology map by changing the colors of the affected device icons and indicating the status of the links.

You can redefine the intervals by changing the SNMP polling. The polling parameters (Timeout, Retries, Data Collection Polling Interval, and Utilization Polling Interval) are displayed in the Global Preferences window.

The Timeout parameter default is 5 seconds. If the polling process does not receive a response from a device in the time specified, the device is considered unreachable.

The Retries parameter default is three attempts. If the discovery process cannot reach a device in the specified number of attempts, the device is considered unreachable.

The Data Collection Polling Interval parameter default is 30 minutes. This polling interval is used by RMON.

The Utilization Polling Interval parameter default is 10 seconds. This polling interval is used for the utilization calculations in the VC list.

Checking ATM Networks

You can troubleshoot your ATM network or monitor the traffic and usage of its virtual channels (VCs) by using specific reports and graphical displays provided by the AtmDirector application. Refer to the following sections of online AtmDirector manual, located at http://cio.cisco.com/univercd/cc/td/doc/product/rtrmgmt/cw2000/camp_mgr/cwsi_2x/c2si _2_2/atmd_c/vcs.htm#xtocid2851315 for the information that you need:

- List Virtual Channels
- Selecting Virtual Channels
- Checking Link Utilization
- Checking Virtual Channel Utilization
- Plotting Utilization
- Tracing Virtual Channels
- Display Trace Reports in Tabular Form
- Display Trace Reports Graphically
- Clearing Trace Reports
- Display Virtual Channels Between Devices
- Checking Virtual Channel Connectivity
- Triggering OAM Pings

- Display an OAM Ping Report
- Setting Up Soft Permanent Virtual Channels or Paths
- Setting the Interface Configuration

Checking ATM-VLAN Networks

You can troubleshoot your ATM-VLAN network by monitoring its LANE components and virtual channels, and by using specific reports and graphical displays provided by the AtmDirector application. Refer to the following sections of online AtmDirector manual, located at
http://cio.cisco.com/unviercd/cc/td/doc/product/rtrmgmt/cw2000/camp_mgr/cwsi_2x/cwsi_2_2/atmd_c/lanetopo.htm for the information that you need:

- Displaying ATM-VLAN Information for Fabric Devices
- Displaying Summary Information for an ATM-VLAN
- Viewing Client Summary Information
- Viewing LE Server/Broadcast Server Summary Information
- Viewing Configuration Server Summary Information
- Viewing the Configuration Server Database
- Viewing the Configuration Server ATM-VLAN Configuration Table
- Monitoring Control Connections for a LANE Component
- Monitoring Data Direct Connections for a Client
- Monitoring Client Status and Control Parameters
- Monitoring the LE_ARP Table
- Monitoring LE Server Status
- Monitoring Configuration Server Addresses
- Graphing Client Performance Information
- Graphing Broadcast Server Performance Information

Checking PNNI Networks

You can use the AtmDirector application to troubleshoot your PNNI network by checking the node configurations (including the PNNI timers), monitoring the link status of neighboring peers and PNNI addresses, and tuning the PNNI parameters. Refer to the following sections of online AtmDirector manual, located at the following web addresses, for the information you need:

http://cio.cisco.com/unviercd/cc/td/doc/product/rtrmgmt/cw2000/camp_mgr/cwsi_2x/cwsi_2_2/atmd_c/pnnicfg.htm
http://cio.cisco.com/unviercd/cc/td/doc/product/rtrmgmt/cw2000/camp_mgr/cwsi_2x/cwsi_2_2/atmd_c/pnniaddr.htm
http://cio.cisco.com/unviercd/cc/td/doc/product/rtrmgmt/cw2000/camp_mgr/cwsi_2x/cwsi_2_2/atmd_c/pnnimgmt.htm

- Displaying the Node Configuration and Information
- Modifying the Node Configuration
- Displaying Link Information
- Displaying the Values of the PNNI Timers
- Modifying the Values of the PNNI Timers
- Displaying Neighboring Peer Link and Status Information
- Display Address Summaries
- Modify an Address Summary
- Add an Address Summary
- Delete an Address Summary
- Displaying Reachable Addresses
- Modify a Reachable Address
- Add a Reachable Address
- Delete a Reachable Address
- Display Address Scope Mapping
- Modify Address Scope Mapping
- Display PNNI Interface Parameters
- Modify PNNI Interface Parameters

Collecting Data for Troubleshooting

The AtmDirector application has some features that require you to enable data collection for troubleshooting purposes. The collected data is used to help you perform the following tasks:

- Display top N active hosts in a fabric or clients in an ATM-VLAN
- Display traffic between hosts or between clients
- Display a graphical analysis of call failures to and from devices in a fabric or ATM-VLAN

Refer to the following sections of online AtmDirector manual, located at
http://cio/cisco/com/univercd/cc/td/doc/product/rtrmgmt/cw2000/camp_mgr/cwsi_2x/cws
i_2_2/atmd_c/enable2.htm#xtocid56365 for the information that you need to collect data:

- Enabling Data Collection
- Setting Up Port Select Groups
- Viewing Enabled Switches
- Graphing Top N Active Hosts
- Graphing Traffic Between Hosts
- Graphing Call Failures
- Graphing a Broadcast Server Frame Analysis
- Disabling Data Collection

Problem Solving

Table 24-12 displays problems that you might encounter while using the AtmDirector
application and provides probable causes and possible solutions.

Table 24-12 *Troubleshooting Problems*

Problem	Probable Cause	Possible Solution
An end host cannot be discovered.	ILMI is not enabled.	Enable ILMI on the affected end host.
	No SNMP connection to the end host exists.	Set up the SNMP connection to the end host. Make sure that all device requirements are met.
The LEC does not appear in ELAN map.	Device where LEC resides is not SNMP reachable, or it was incapable of joining the ELAN.	Check to see if the LEC exists in the ELAN, and check to see if the device is SNMP reachable.
The LEC cannot join an ELAN.	The LEC was not discovered as a valid LEC.	Check to see if the device where the LEC resides is SNMP-reachable.
	The LEC was discovered at one time, but it went down and could not rejoin the ELAN.	Check the status of the LEC; make sure its address is configured correctly on the LightStream 1010.
		Check the last failure state of the LEC.
No connectivity exists between clients.	Clients belong to different ELANs.	Verify that both clients belong to the same ELAN.

Table 24-12 *Troubleshooting Problems (Continued)*

Problem	Probable Cause	Possible Solution
	One client is unknown to the other.	Check the client ARP information to see if it is known to the LE client.
	Client(s) are not registered with the LES.	Check the LES status parameters window.
The BUS performance graph indicates high usage.	A client is using the maximum amount of bandwidth.	Determine which LEC is generating heavy broadcast usage. Check the TopN clients.
An unexpected volume of control frames is present.	Configuration is incorrect.	Check the menu item "Graphing Client Performance Information" to get information about the control frames and to change the configuration accordingly. For example, if the OUT ARP requests have a high volume, you probably need to change the ARP response time.
The device must be taken offline for maintenance purposes.	Possible effects will take place on ELANs.	Check the ATM-VLAN catalog from the fabric map to list all the ELAN components residing on a device.
The PNNI node does not appear on the topology map.	The PNNI node is not enabled.	Use CiscoView or the CLI to verify that the PNNI node (node index = 1) is enabled. Then select the LightStream 1010 switch that contains the node, and rediscover the device.
The PNNI node is isolated from the PNNI network.	The ANI server did not find a PNNI link for this node during the previous discovery cycle.	Select the PNNI node from the PNNI topology map. Then check to see if the level of the PNNI node is the same as the other nodes. Also check to see if any interfaces for this node are configured to PNNI.
		Note: If the node level and interface information is correct, you need to rediscover the device. The PNNI link takes approximately 2 to 3 minutes to synchronize with the neighboring nodes, and the ANI server might not have found a PNNI link from this node in the previous discovery cycle.

Troubleshooting TrafficDirector

In some cases, the TrafficDirector environment does not work as you would expect. This subsection includes tips for troubleshooting your TrafficDirector environment. It explains the following:

- The impact of security settings at both the TrafficDirector management console and the SwitchProbe device
- SwitchProbe and Network Analysis Module security, and the Properties file installation
- How to test the operational status of an agent on the network for agents, Frame Relay agents, and switches

Ensuring Access to SwitchProbe Devices

Because the operations personnel who set up and configured your SwitchProbe devices may be different than the TrafficDirector administrator, a quick review of the implications of configuration settings at the SwitchProbe device can help you isolate possible problems.

Before the TrafficDirector application can access SwitchProbe data, the parameters must be properly set using the SwitchProbe agent configuration utility, including those special parameters required for tracking Frame Relay, ATM, and WAN statistics.

For more information, see the following sections:

- VLAN Monitor, SMON MIB, and ART MIB Options
- NetFlow and Resource Monitor Options—SwitchProbe Devices
- SwitchProbe and Network Analysis Module Security
- VLAN Monitor, SMON MIB, and ART MIB Options

NOTE   The ARTMIB option is available only on SwitchProbe devices.

Before the TrafficDirector application can access the proper data required in the VLAN Monitor or ART Monitor applications, you must verify that the VLAN option is enabled at the SwitchProbe device or Network Analysis Module to support VLAN Monitor, and that the ARTMIB option is enabled at the device to support ART Monitor.

NetFlow and Resource Monitor Options—SwitchProbe Devices

Before the TrafficDirector application can reflect NetFlow and Resource Monitor activity, verify that the NetFlow option is enabled at the SwitchProbe device to support viewing of proxy SNMP and round-trip delay data (with Resource Manager only) and NetFlow statistics.

NetFlow Option—Network Analysis Module

Before the TrafficDirector application can support viewing of NetFlow statistics on the Network Analysis Module, you must verify that the NetFlow option is enabled on the device.

SwitchProbe and Network Analysis Module Security

To ensure that the TrafficDirector administrator has access privileges to the local console on the SwitchProbe device using the TrafficDirector Remote Login application, you must grant the optional administrative privileges (read and write access) to the TrafficDirector administrator.

User access privileges, if set at the SwitchProbe device, allow you to view the console settings but not to edit them. This user-level security setting is useful if you have multiple sites where operations personnel may be asked to track down but not necessarily fix a SwitchProbe agent problem.

If you do not know the administrative password at the SwitchProbe device and one is set, you cannot use the Remote Login application. These SwitchProbe security features are independent of the security options that you can enable for access to TrafficDirector administrator applications.

The following section contains more information.

Properties File Installation

To ensure that properties files can be reinstalled automatically when SwitchProbe devices are rebooted, follow these steps:

Step 1 Use the default scripts to run dvcfg (either startup for most agents, or fstartup for Frame Relay agents).

Step 2 Set the SwitchProbe server address to the IP address of the TrafficDirector management station.

Step 3 Verify that the TrafficDirector dvtrap daemon is running.

If these conditions are met, you do not need to manually reinstall the properties files through the Configuration Manager.

Network Access to SwitchProbe Devices

To test for network connectivity to the SwitchProbe device, use the Test Agents application. The test agent tool indicates whether an agent is operational and what options are supported, and it indicates the general health of the device's UDP/IP connection.

For more information about agent configuration issues, see the *Cisco SwitchProbe Installation and Configuration Guide.*

Testing Agents, Switches, and Frame Relay Agents

NOTE The Test Agent feature does not update the SPAN port information under Roving Information when the SPAN port is set on the switch through the command line. It will always reflect the information about the port that was roved from the TrafficDirector application and is not updated. To test an agent, Frame Relay agent, or switch, follow these steps:

Step 1 Select the agent you want to test from the agent list box, either from the TrafficDirector main window or from Configuration Manager.

Step 2 Do *one* of the following:

— In the TrafficDirector main window, click the Test Agent icon.

— In Configuration Manager, click Test.

If the agent is operational, the Agent Test window opens (see Figure 24-3).

Figure 24-3 *Agent Test Window*

Interpreting Test Agent Messages

When a test is successful, the information in Table 24-13 is displayed. When you have finished viewing the information, click OK to close the Agent Test window.

Table 24-13 *Information Displayed Upon Successful Agent Test*

Field	Description
IP Address	IP address of the agent management interface.
Ping	The ping (query) result: **Passed**—The connection is fully operational. **Not Supported**—The connection is fully operational but is not supported by the Resource Monitor option.
Read Community	The agent read community name (as entered in the Configuration Manager application), and whether this name is the same as the agent's established read community name (OK) or is not (Failed).
Write Community	The agent write community name (as entered in the Configuration Manager application), and whether this name is the same as the agent's established write community name (OK) or is not (Failed).
Protocol Monitoring	Whether the agent supports RMON2 network layer protocol monitoring.
Application Monitoring	Whether the agent supports RMON2 application layer protocol monitoring.
High Capacity Monitoring	Whether the agent supports HCRMON as a high-speed device.
VLAN Monitoring	Whether the VLAN Monitor option is enabled in the agent.
Application Response Time	Whether the ARTMIB option is enabled in the agent.
Resource Monitoring	Whether Resource Monitor is enabled in the agent. Resource Monitor is required to configure RT delays and proxy SNMP gets.
Interface Number	The number of the agent interface used to monitor activity on a network segment.
Description	The media type of the interface specified in the Interface Number field.
Interface Type	The type of interface distinguished according to the physical link protocol, as described in RFC 1213.
Physical Address	The MAC address of the agent.
Number of Interfaces	The number of network interfaces on the agent.

continues

Table 24-13 *Information Displayed Upon Successful Agent Test (Continued)*

Field	Description
Net Speed	The estimated bandwidth for the current interface in bits per second (bps).
DTE Speed	The estimated DTE circuit speed (in bps). Full-duplex links only.
DCE Speed	The estimated DCE circuit speed (in bps). Full-duplex links only.
Description	The device model, as defined by the network administrator.
Contact	The name of the person responsible for the agent, and how to contact that person.
SysName	The administratively assigned name of the agent.
Location	The physical location of the agent, as defined by the system administrator in the Configuration Manager.
UpSince	The date and time that the agent became operational on the network. Also, when the agent was last booted.

Interpreting Switch Agent Test Messages

The test information that is generated when communicating with a switch is slightly different from the information generated when you test an agent.

When you test a switch, the TrafficDirector software queries the switch and informs you if the query passed or failed. Figure 24-4 shows the Switch Test window.

Figure 24-4 *Switch Test Window*

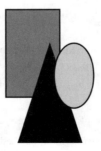

When a test is successful, the information in Table 24-14 is displayed.

Table 24-14 *Information Displayed Upon Successful Switch Test*

Field	Description
IP Address	IP address of the switch management interface.
Ping	The ping (query) result: **Passed**—The connection is fully operational. **Not Supported**—The connection is fully operational but is not supported by the Resource Monitor option.
Read Community	The switch read community name (as entered in the Configuration Manager application), and whether this name is the same as the agent's established read community name (OK) or is not (Failed).
Write Community	The switch write community name (as entered in the Configuration Manager application), and whether this name is the same as the agent's established write community name (OK) or is not (Failed).
IP Address	The IP address of the switch's management interface.
Description	The device model, as defined by the network administrator.
Contact	The name of the person responsible for the switch, and how to contact that person.
SysName	The system name for the switch.
Location	The physical location of the switch, as described by the system administrator in the Configuration Manager.
UpSince	The date and time that the switch became operational on the network. Also, when the switch was last booted.
Roving Agent	The name of the roving agent defined for the switch, if any.
Analyzer Port	The name of the switch port that the roving agent is physically connected to, if applicable.
Monitor Port	The currently roved port, if any. The monitor port contains the name of the switch port that the roving agent is currently monitoring.

You receive the same message as an agent or Frame Relay agent, if the test failed.

Troubleshooting CiscoView

This subsection provides the following information on how to troubleshoot any problems that you might encounter when using CiscoView application and how to identify device problems using CiscoView.

The Cvinstall.cshrc and the Cvinstall.sh Files and System Performance Issue

The CVinstall.cshrc and the CVinstall.sh files automatically set all environmental variables required for CiscoView. If there are errors starting CiscoView, source one of these files.

CiscoView opens each device in a separate window, by default. On large networks, this can consume too much RAM and slow performance. To decrease RAM use, you can open devices in the same window by changing operating characteristics. Select Options; Properties. Choose Same Window in the Launch CiscoView In option.

Also, multiple sessions of CiscoView might degrade system performance because of the use of X resources. Reduce the number of sessions running on an X server by selecting the option Same Window in Options; Properties. This causes successive invocations of CiscoView on an X server to reuse a single session.

Fixing Display Problems

If CiscoView fails to display a device, the following message appears:

```
"<hostname>: unmanageable"
```

This message suggests one of the following conditions:

- The SNMP agent is not running on the device, although the device is accessible from the management session.

  — You should be able to **ping** the device from the management session.

- You entered an incorrect community string.

  — To re-enter a community string, select Options; Properties.

- The management station cannot reach and successfully **ping** the device.

  — Check your device package and compare the date with the CCO device package version. Upgrade your device package to the latest version, if required.

- You encountered an unsupported card error.

  — CiscoView displays the "Unsupported Card" or "Unknown Card" error messages instead of displaying the contents of the card when a device package does not support the card. You might have to contact CCO and check the upgrade planner for the device package. If the device package is supposed to support the card, try upgrading the device package to the latest version from CCO.

- You received the error message: "Can't read DD(...) not set."

  — CiscoView generates this error message when any of the following conditions are true:

- The IOS version is not supported by the device package.

- The physical device might not contain a card component, or it might not have been configured properly.
- The IOS may not have the feature that supports the card. In this case, you might have to upgrade the IOS to the proper version.
- There is a problem with the device package.

For the previous conditions, check whether the device package supports the IOS version of the device under consideration. Upgrade the IOS/switch version.

- CiscoView rolls back after a device package installation or deinstallation.
    - When a device package is installed, CiscoView runs a static check utility (cvtest) on all existing device packages to determine if installation or deinstallation destabilized CiscoView.

    There are two possible reasons why the device package may roll back:

    - A package was installed without the requisite installation of a dependent device package. For example, the 3600 package needs to be installed before installation of the AS5800, and the CPW1420.pkg requires installation of the Cat2820.

Note   If you encounter this problem during incremental installations, check the list of installed packages and verify that all dependent packages are installed.

    - The device package's installation did not pass the static check utility. Contact the Cisco TAC with the following file: $NMSROOT/CVinstall.log.
    - List the packages installed on the system and their version numbers. Note the name of the device package that failed and its version number.

Identifying Device Problems (Dashboard Monitor)

Perform any of the following tasks in CiscoView to isolate the cause of a problem:

- Check the color-coded legend to determine the status of a port.
- Check the port configuration information and determine that the port is active. (See the menu item "Displaying Configuration").
- Check the performance information by examining the dashboard display.
- Check the utilization and error information for ports and the memory information for a device.
- Check the status bar for SNMP or other error messages.

Interpreting SNMP Error Messages

CiscoView displays the following SNMP error messages, shown in Table 24-15, resulting from failed command requests in the status bar message area:

Table 24-15 *SNMP Error Messages*

Message	Explanation
timeout	You can no longer reach the device in the time specified in the CiscoView Properties window.
tooBig	The request that you made cannot fit into a single packet. Generally, CiscoView splits requests for physical view status until the device can respond. In certain cases, CiscoView assumes that if an agent times out on 20 or more variables, the agent might not be capable of responding because the request is too big; it splits the request and resends it. Check that the MTU size on the SNMP interface is as large as possible so that CiscoView does not waste bandwidth by sending more than one request.
genErr	This is a collective message name for problems that do not have a unique error message.
noSuchName	A request for a variable was sent to an inaccessible variable. This occurs if you are not using the correct community string.
badValue	The agent did not respond within the time interval specified by the timeout/retries field in the CiscoView Properties window. This can also indicate the use of an incorrect community string.
	While performing a set operation on a MIB object, the value specified for writing does not follow the proper syntax for the MIB object. It could be because of type mismatches or out-of-range values.

Before Calling Cisco Systems' TAC Team

Before calling Cisco Systems's Technical Assistance Center (TAC), make sure that you have read through this chapter and completed the actions suggested for your system or application's problem.

Additionally, do the following and document the results so that we can better assist you. Please be prepared to provide the following information:

- What version of CiscoWorks 2000 it is (RME2.2/CWSI2.4, RME2.1/CWSI2.3, RME2.0/CWSI2.2, or so on)
- What type of operating system platform it is on (Windows NT4.0, Solaris 2.5.1/2.6, HPUX10.20/11.0, IBM AIX 4.2.1/4.3.2)
- System hardware information: CPU model and speed, available RAM, available hard drive space

- If your problem is with a web-based application (such as RME), the browser type and version information
- What type of operation is failing/giving the message

What the exact error message is, and a description of the problem behavior or the error message text

- What type of device you are applying the operation to
- The IOS version or switch software version
- An explanation about how to reproduce the problem

Additional Sources

The following books have information in both hard-copy and online copy on CCO:

- *Addendum: Using the Campus TrafficDirector Application*—
  http://cio.cisco.com/univercd/cc/td/doc/product/rtrmgmt/sw_ntman/td_main/td_5_7/td57add.htm
- *Getting Started with CiscoView 4.2(1)*—
  http://cio.cisco.com/univercd/cc/td/doc/product/rtrmgmt/cvparnt/cview/cvovr42/index.htm
- *Getting Started with CWSI Campus*—
  http://cio.cisco.com/univercd/cc/td/doc/product/rtrmgmt/cw2000/camp_mgr/cwsi_2x/cwsi_2_2/gsg_cwsi/index.htm
- *Getting Started with Resource Manager Essentials*—
  http://cio.cisco.com/univercd/cc/td/doc/product/rtrmgmt/cw2000/cw2000e/e_2_x/rm_2_0/rme_gs/index.htm
- *Installing Resource Manager Essentials/CWSI Campus on AIX*—
  http://cio.cisco.com/univercd/cc/td/doc/product/rtrmgmt/cw2000/camp_mgr/cwsi_2x/cwsi_2_3/mgr_aix/index.htm
- *Installing Resource Manager Essentials/CWSI Campus on HP-UX*—
  http://cio.cisco.com/univercd/cc/td/doc/product/rtrmgmt/cw2000/camp_mgr/cwsi_2x/cwsi_2_3/mgr_hpux/index.htm
- *Installing Resource Manager Essentials/CWSI Campus on Solaris*—
  http://cio.cisco.com/univercd/cc/td/doc/product/rtrmgmt/cw2000/camp_mgr/cwsi_2x/cwsi_2_3/mgr_sol/index.htm
- *Installing Resource Manager Essentials/CWSI Campus on Windows*—
  http://cio.cisco.com/univercd/cc/td/doc/product/rtrmgmt/cw2000/camp_mgr/cwsi_2x/cwsi_2_4/mgr_win/index.htm

- *Release Notes for Resource Manager Essentials 2.2/CWSI Campus 2.4*—
http://cio.cisco.com/univercd/cc/td/doc/product/rtrmgmt/cw2000/camp_mgr/cwsi_2
x/cwsi_2_4/relnt2_3/index.htm

- *Supported Devices for CWSI Campus 2.4*—
http://www.cisco.com/univercd/cc/td/doc/product/rtrmgmt/cw2000/c2_4.htm

- *Supported Devices in Essentials 2.1/2.2*—
http://cio.cisco.com/univercd/cc/td/doc/product/rtrmgmt/cw2000/cw2000e/dev_sup/
index.htm

- *Using the Campus AtmDirector Application*—
http://cio.cisco.com/univercd/cc/td/doc/product/rtrmgmt/cw2000/camp_mgr/cwsi_2
x/cwsi_2_2/atmd_c/index.htm

- *Using the Campus TrafficDirector Application*—
http://cio.cisco.com/univercd/cc/td/doc/product/rtrmgmt/sw_ntman/td_main/td_5_6/
traf5_6/index.htm

- *Using the Campus UserTracking Application*—
http://cio.cisco.com/univercd/cc/td/doc/product/rtrmgmt/cw2000/camp_mgr/cwsi_2
x/cwsi_2_2/us_c/index.htm

- *Using the Campus VlanDirector Application*—
http://cio.cisco.com/univercd/cc/td/doc/product/rtrmgmt/cw2000/camp_mgr/cwsi_2
x/cwsi_2_2/vd_c/index.htm

## CHAPTER 25

Troubleshooting Security Implementations

This chapter covers several of the security products used to protect the network. It includes scanning software (CiscoSecure Scanner, formerly known as NetSonar), intrusion-detection software (CiscoSecure Intrusion Detection System, formerly known as NetRanger), firewall software (Cisco PIX Firewall), and router and switch password recovery.

As the Internet grows, so does the possibility of illegal activities. These activities can range from denial-of-service attacks to the compromising of propriety data. Many products have been developed to protect networks.

Firewalls were the first security products introduced to prevent unauthorized entry into the protected network. They allow network access only to specifically configured protocols and network objects. Next came intrusion-detection software products. These products track authorized traffic permitted by the firewall, while searching for unauthorized activity such as hacking attempts or denial-of-service attacks. Finally there was scanning software, which allowed administrators to detect security vulnerabilities in their network design.

This chapter assists a network administrator in debugging the security products mentioned here that have been installed in the network. This chapter assumes that the reader is familiar with the installation and operation of the software products to be debugged.

Only debugging commands are discussed in this chapter. For more information about the command syntax or explanation for each software product, refer to the user manual. You can also find the commands under "Service and Support" in the "Technical Documentation" section of Cisco Connection Online (CCO).

In the creation of this chapter, care was taken to use only the latest versions of software. If you have earlier versions of software than those discussed here, refer to the user's manual for your product for proper commands and syntax.

Objectives

The objective of this chapter is to help those already familiar with installed security software products to do some basic troubleshooting or debugging.

Troubleshooting CiscoSecure Scanner

The majority (75 percent) of the CiscoSecure Scanner (NetSonar) problems deal with licensing. The license issues are being addressed and will change with the next release.

Table 25-1 describes the other 25 percent of common problems.

Table 25-1   *Common Problems with NetSonar*

Symptom	Possible Problem	Suggested Actions
The following NetSonar components are not showing up in the HTML browser: report, grid, chart, and NSDB.	NetSonar does not have the correct path to the browser.	Check the HTML Browser tab on the Preferences tab, and make sure that the path to your browser is correct.
You receive the following error message: "Not enough room for axis."	NetSonar license is invalid, or the user rules are not correct.	Make sure that you have a valid license file. Check the user.rules file, and make sure that the syntax is correct for any rules that you have added.
The server starts, but the client will not start.	NetRanger is running on the same machine as NetSonar.	Make sure that you stop NetRanger before executing any NetSonar scans or probes.
You are at your machine and cannot view the data that NetSonar obtained from a scheduled scan.	Your machine is not the machine on which NetSonar is installed and from which the scan was run.	You can view scan and probe only data from the machine on which NetSonar is installed and from which the scan or probe was run.
Suddenly you are allowed to scan only one host.	Your license is expired or invalid. NetSonar has reverted to the original demo license.	If you have an evaluation license, go to www.cisco.com/go/netsonar-eval to renew it, or contact your sales representative to purchase a license.
You have closed the NetSonar GUI. When you reopen it, NetSonar is not working correctly.	You have an open NetSonar browser.	Make sure that you close all NetSonar browsers when you exit NetSonar.

Before Calling Cisco Systems' TAC Team

Before calling Cisco Systems's Technical Assistance Center (TAC), make sure that you have read through this chapter and completed the actions suggested for your system's problem.

In addition, note and document the following information so that we may better assist you:

- Operating system (Solaris or Windows NT) version
- CiscoSecure Scanner version

Troubleshooting CiscoSecure Intrusion Detection System (NetRanger)

The main objective of this section is to help diagnose problems that may occur when running CiscoSecure Intrusion Detection System (IDS). There are three parts to the IDS: the Director, and the Sensor, and the Post Office. The Sensor discussed in this section is the appliance, not the feature that is now available in the IOS. The Post Office is the communication backbone that allows NetRanger services and hosts to communicate with each other. All communication is supported by a proprietary, connection-based protocol that can switch between alternate routes to maintain point-to-point connections.

Commands That Can Be Used to Troubleshoot the Application

CiscoSecure IDS comes with several commands and logs that are highly valuable when troubleshooting a problem with the software. This section gives a brief description of each command and each log file, followed by an example. Later sections discuss when to use each command.

The following commands are used when troubleshooting:

- **nrvers**—Used to extract the version number of each of the processes running. This is especially helpful after upgrading the software.

```
netrangr@director>nrvers
Application Versions for director.rtp
  postofficed v2.2.1      (release)       99/07/19-22:30
  loggerd v2.2.1          (release)       99/07/19-22:31
  packetd v2.2.1          (release)       99/07/19-22:44
  managed v2.2.1          (release)      99/07/19-22:29
  configd v2.2.1          (release)      99/07/19-22:29
  sapd v2.2.1              (release)       99/07/19-22:31
  fileXfer v2.2.1         (release)       99/07/19-22:36
```

- **nrstatus**—Used to find the current status of all daemons. The command displays all daemons that are currently running on the system.

```
netrangr@director>nrstatus
netrangr 28906     1 99    Feb 05 ?      8295:01 /usr/nr/bin/nr.managed
```

```
netrangr 28921    1  0   Feb 05 ?         0:04 /usr/nr/bin/nr.configd
netrangr 28948    1  0   Feb 05 ?         0:09 /usr/nr/bin/nr.fileXferd
netrangr 28936    1  0   Feb 05 ?         0:04 /usr/nr/bin/nr.sapd
netrangr 28877    1  0   Feb 05 ?         0:29 /usr/nr/bin/nr.loggerd
netrangr 28891    1  0   Feb 05 ?         6:17 /usr/nr/bin/nr.packetd
netrangr 28217    1  0   Feb 05 ?         6:47 /usr/nr/bin/nr.postofficed
```

- **nrconns**—Used to determine the currently configured connections and their status. Things to look for in the output include the IP address of the host and the information in brackets []. In the example that follows, [Established] means the communication is up and running. [SynSent] means that the Director sent a packet to sensor2 and never received a response.

```
netrangr@director>nrconns
Connection Status for director.rtp
        sensor.rtp Connection 1: 171.68.120.214   45000 1 [Established]
sto:0002 with Version 1
        sensor2.rtp Connection 1: 171.68.120.213   45000 1 [SynSent] sto:0002
with Version 1
```

- **nrest**—Is the same command as **nrconns**, but it shows only established connections. It will *not* display any other connections except for those already established.

```
netrangr@director>nrest
Established Connections for director.rtp
        sensor.rtp Connection 1: 171.68.120.214   45000 1 [Established]
sto:0002 with Version 1
```

- **nrstop**—Used to force all IDS daemons to gracefully shut down.

```
netrangr@director>nrstop
done
```

- **nrstart**—Used to start all IDS daemons. This command reads the file /usr/nr/etc/daemons and starts all the IDS daemons listed.

```
netrangr@director>nrstart
starting netranger services:
netrangr  1671    1  0 09:28:49 pts/0     0:00 /usr/nr/bin/nr.postofficed
netrangr  1781    1  0 09:28:51 ?         0:00 /usr/nr/bin/nr.configd
netrangr  1741    1  0 09:28:50 ?         0:00 /usr/nr/bin/nr.loggerd
netrangr  1823    1  0 09:28:51 pts/0     0:00 /usr/nr/bin/nr.fileXferd
netrangr  1751    1  0 09:28:50 ?         0:00 /usr/nr/bin/nr.packetd
netrangr  1766    1  0 09:28:50 ?         0:00 /usr/nr/bin/nr.managed
netrangr  1796    1  0 09:28:51 ?         0:00 /usr/nr/bin/nr.sapd
netranger startup done.
```

Error Files Used for Debugging Application Errors

The following files are located in the /usr/nr/etc directory. Each is created when you run the application the first time. If you delete these files and stop and start the application, these files will be re-created. However, if you do not delete these files, information will be appended on to it. Each file contains the error associated with that daemon. For example, communication errors would be found in the errors.postoffice file.

On the Sensor or appliance:

- **errors.fileXferd**—Errors with transferring files between the Sensor and the Director. This type of file transfers normally happen when configuring the Sensor.

- **errors.managed**—Errors occurring while creating the access list on the router or when trying to communicate with the router.

- **errors.packetd**—Errors occurring while capturing traffic of the network.

- **errors.postofficed**—Errors occurring with the communication infrastructure.

- **errors.sapd**—Errors occurring during file management.

On the Director:

- **errors.postofficed**—Errors occurring with the communication infrastructure.

- **errors.sapd**—Errors occurring during file management. This includes Oracle on the Director.

- **errors.configd**—Errors occurring during the configuration process of Sensors.

- **errors.smid**—Errors occurring with OpenView.

- **errors.eventd**—Errors occurring when trying to run an event. This is normally the paging process but can be any script that you would like to run.

- **errors.fileXferd**—Errors with transferring files between the Sensor and the Director. This type of file transfer normally happens when configuring the Sensor.

- **errors.loggerd**—Errors occurring while trying to log data to the log files.

- **errors.nrConfigure**—Errors occurring with the configuration graphical user interface (GUI).

Table 25-2 shows symptoms, possible problems, and suggested actions to be taken when troubleshooting CiscoSecure IDS.

Table 25-2 *Troubleshooting NetRanger*

Symptom	Possible Problem	Suggested Actions
Director not running		
You see the following error message: "Cannot write message to Director, errno =2."	This error occurs when smid tries to write to a socket that does not exist. This may occur because the Director's nrdirmap application has not created its communication socket in /usr/nr/tmp because the HP OpenView user interface (ovw) was not started.	First ensure that the underlying NetRanger services, such as postofficed and smid, are running by typing **nrstatus** at the command line. If the services are not running, type **nrstart** to manually start them. Then start HP OpenView by typing **ovw & at** the command line.

continues

Table 25-2   *Troubleshooting NetRanger (Continued)*

Symptom	Possible Problem	Suggested Actions
You see the following error message: "Cannot write message to Director, errno = 233."	This error message is generated when smid writes to a socket whose buffer is overflowing. This can occur when the Director's nrdirmap application is not running.	Ensure that the HP OpenView user interface (ovw) is running by executing ovw &. This will automatically start nrdirmap.
You see the following error message: "Cannot write message to Director, errno = 239."	This error message occurs when smid and nrdirmap do not have adequate permissions to communicate via sockets in /usr/nr/tmp.	Ensure that the smid process is owned by user netrangr and that nrdirmap runs as SUID netrangr.

You see the following error message: "nrdirmap: fatal: libovw.so.1: can't open file: errno=2."	The LD_LIBRARY_PATH environment variable is not set properly in your user environment. This may indicate that you are logged on to the Director platform as the wrong user.	Follow the instructions in "Installation and Configuration," for setting up an HP OpenView environment for user accounts other than netrangr. If the user account is based on either the Bourne or the Korn shell, the following lines should exist in the user's $HOME/.profile:
		
		`if [ -d /opt/OV ] ; then`
		`    . /opt/OV/bin/ov.envvars.sh`
		`      PATH=$OV_BIN:$PATH`
		`      export PATH`
		
		`LD_LIBRARY_PATH=$OV_LIB:$LD_LI`
		`BRARY_PATH`
		`      export LD_LIBRARY_PATH`
		
		`fi`
		
		If the user must use a shell other than ksh, then the preceding lines must be translated into the appropriate scripting language and placed in the appropriate startup file.

Table 25-2   *Troubleshooting NetRanger (Continued)*

Symptom	Possible Problem	Suggested Actions
Director running		
The Director's security map contains a Sensor icon but fails to show any events for that Sensor.	The Director's Severity Status attributes are set higher than the level of alarms being generated by the Sensor.	On the Director interface, highlight the icon for the Sensor system and then either press Ctrl-O or click Describe/Modify on the Edit menu. Then select NetRanger/Director and click View/Modify. Ensure that the Minimum Marginal and Minimum Critical status thresholds are low enough to register events from the Sensor in question.
The Director's security map contains a Sensor icon but fails to show any events for that Sensor.	The level of alarms generated by the Sensor system fall below the routing threshold set in the /usr/nr/etc/destinations file.	If the Director Severity Status thresholds are set properly, ensure that the routing threshold in the Sensor's /usr/nr/etc/destinations file is set low enough to route information to the Director.
You see the following error message: "Application AppId.HostId.OrgId has reached maximum number of alarms."	The application mentioned in the error message has 1000 alarm icons represented on its HP OpenView child submap. The Director will not create more than 1000 icons on a submap (window) because HP OpenView can behave unpredictably when this happens.	Delete the alarm icons on the crowded submap. The Director will resume creating alarm icons on the submap for any new events. To view iconic representations of the events that nrdirmap diverted to /usr/nr/var, delete the icons on the map, and then shut down and restart the user interface. **Note**: The Director saves any additional alarm data for that application to a file named nrdirmap.buffer.ovw_map_name in the /usr/nr/var directory, where ovw_map_name is the name of the ovw map.

continues

Table 25-2   *Troubleshooting NetRanger (Continued)*

Symptom	Possible Problem	Suggested Actions
A Sensor's alarms are properly displayed on the Director security map, but information on those alarms does not appear in the Show Current Events window, and the event log file in the Director's /usr/nr/var directory does not contain any records from that Sensor.	The Director loggerd service is not listed as a destination in either the Sensor or the Director's configuration files.	Use nrConfigure to create an entry in the Sensor's /usr/nr/etc/destinations file for the Director's loggerd service, or create a DupDestination entry in the Director's /usr/nr/etc/smid.conf file to redirect event data to loggerd from smid.
Information is properly displayed in the Director's Show Current Events window, but the cursor turns into an hourglass and never changes back.	The current events utility continues to pull information from the Director log files as long as the window is up.	Click Stop to terminate the filtering application. You can then use the scrollbars and menu options to look at the data. Click Close to exit this window.
Connectivity		
A Sensor or any of the NetRanger services running on the system cannot be accessed.	The Sensor services are not running properly.	Telnet to the Sensor and run nrstop. Examine the error files in /usr/nr/var. Restart the Sensor by typing **nrstart**.
Sensor		
The NetRanger daemon processes cannot be started or stopped when running nrstart or nrstop.	You are trying to run these utilities from an account that does not have access rights to the Sensor daemons.	Ensure that you are logged on to the Sensor or Director systems under the same user account that was used to start its daemon services. (The default is user netrangr.)

Table 25-2   *Troubleshooting NetRanger (Continued)*

Symptom	Possible Problem	Suggested Actions
Oracle		
Cannot determine if Oracle is installed.		Check local and mounted file systems using commands **df**, **mount**, and **find**. Look for oracle and product/.
Cannot determine if Oracle is running.		Run **ps -ef	grep ora** from the command line to check whether Oracle is running.
Oracle Installer (orainst) could not find any products to install.	start.sh was not run before starting orainst.	Run /cdrom/cdrom0/orainst/start.sh to prepare your environment for the orainst program.
One of the following messages is displayed: "sqlplus: not found" "sqlldr: not found"	The Oracle bin directory is not present or specified properly in your $PATH.	Set $PATH to include $ORACLE_HOME/bin.
The following error message is displayed when you try to run sqlplus: "~~~/oracle/product /7.3.2/bin/sqlplus: cannot open."	The shell finds sqlplus, but it cannot be executed. This can occur when your $PATH includes references to the wrong versions of the Oracle binaries. For example, you have mounted the wrong Oracle directories from a file server. Therefore, you are trying to execute HPUX binaries on a SPARC system.	Ensure that the $ORACLE_HOME directory contains the proper binaries for the platform you are running. Refer to "Installing an Oracle RDBMS" in *RDBMS Reference*.
sqlplus, sqlldr, or sapx fail with the following SID error message: "ERROR: ORA-01034: ORACLE not available" "ORA-07200: slsid: oracle_sid not set"	The ORACLE_SID environment variable, which identifies which database instance to use, was not set properly before starting sqlplus.	Set the ORACLE_SID environment variable to the name of your database instance. You can find out your database instance name by running **ps -ef	grep ora**. The string after the last underbar in the returned text is the database instance name.

continues

Table 25-2 *Troubleshooting NetRanger (Continued)*

Symptom	Possible Problem	Suggested Actions

sqlplus, sqlldr, or sapx fails with the following libc error message: "libc.so.xxx: can't do something"	$ORACLE_HOME/lib is not part of the LD_LIBRARY_PATH environment variable.	Add ORACLE_HOME/lib to the LD_LIBRARY_PATH environment variable. If you are running either the Bourne or the Korn shell, ensure that your $HOME/.profile contains the following entries:
		
		`LD_LIBRARY_PATH=$LD_LIBRARY_PA`
		`TH:$ORACLE_HOME/lib`
		`export LD_LIBRARAY_PATH`

sqlplus, sqlldr, or sapx fail with the following TNS error message: "ERROR: ORA-12154: TNS: could not resolve service name"	Oracle cannot understand the name specified in your connect string.	Ensure that the Oracle file tnsnames.ora resides in its proper location (usually $ORACLE_HOME/admin/network) and that it is properly formatted. Then use the tnsping utility to test sqlnet connectivity to your remote database.
sqlplus, sqlldr, or sapx return a TNS or USER/PASSWORD error message.	Improper connect string.	Correct the syntax on the connect string. If specifying the password on the command line, type **sqlplus user/password@host**. Otherwise, type **sqlplus user@host**, and sqlplus will prompt for a password.
Data management package		
Instrumentation shows proper configuration, but no actions are being performed.	If there are no FM_Action items in sapd.conf, then the install procedure did not properly copy files into sapd.conf because of an upgrade from NetRanger 1.2.x to 1.3.x or 2.x.	Manually copy the sapd.conf.nsx or sapd.conf.director from /usr/nr/etc/wgc/templates into /usr/nr/etc/, replacing the sapd.conf file. **Note**: The file /usr/nr/etc/wgc/templates/sapd.conf contains descriptions of the tokens used by sapd. This file does not contain any real token values. It is intended as a reference for setting triggers in the sapd.conf file in the /usr/nr/etc directory.

Table 25-2   *Troubleshooting NetRanger (Continued)*

Symptom	Possible Problem	Suggested Actions
There are extraneous files in the /usr/nr/var directory structure, and a /usr/nr/var/old directory exists.	You have upgraded from NetRanger 1.2.x to 1.3.x or 2.x, which does away with the /usr/nr/var/old directory. The upgrade has also left behind many files in /usr/nr/var.	Clean the extraneous files, delete the /usr/nr/var/old directory, and archive the /usr/nr/var/dump directory.
SQL queries do not display data.	You did not enter % as a wildcard.	Use % as a wildcard in your SQL queries.
From the SQLPLUS prompt, typing **@event1**, **@space1**, **@time1**, or **@system1** does not return proper data.	You are using the wrong command-line parameter.	SAP 1.3.x requires that you type either **@event**, **@space**, **@time**, or **@system**. You will be prompted for the desired drill-down level (for example, 1, 2, 3).
Queries do not display new signatures.	You have upgraded from NetRanger 1.2.x to 1.3.x or 2.x without updating the nr_sigs and nr_orgs tables.	Update the nr_sigs table with /usr/nr/etc/signatures, and update the nr_orgs table with /usr/nr/etc/organizations. Use the code at the end of nrdb_master_create for this purpose.
Instrumentation shows a successful notify, but no mail notification has been sent.	The mailx feature cannot be invoked through the command-line interface.	To ensure that mail can be sent from a command line, from the command line, use mailx to send mail to yourself. If mail is not sent, set the domain name by typing **domainname your_domain_name** from the command line (on Solaris, you can add the name of your domain to the /etc/defaultdomain file). Then add your mail server information to /etc/hosts, with the following format: IP_address server_name mailhost, where IP_address is the IP address of your mail server and server_name is its DNS server name.

continues

Table 25-2   *Troubleshooting NetRanger (Continued)*

Symptom	Possible Problem	Suggested Actions
The sapx database loader fails with a JDBC-related error message (ora-1461).	You are using the NT Oracle 8 database server.	You have three options for bypassing this error:
		1. Bypass the default sapx loader by using the alternate loading templates in /usr/nr/bin/sap/sql/skel.
		2. Use a UNIX Ora7 or Ora8 server. Cisco has successfully tested the server software on Solaris Sparc, x86, HP-UX, and AIX.
		3. Upgrade NT Ora 8.0.4.0.0 to 8.0.4.0.4. This upgrade should solve the JDBC problems, but it has not been tested.
nrConfigure		
During initial startup, nrConfigure will cause a core dump.		Restart nrConfigure. nrConfigure will then restart without error.
HP-UX performance problems		
HP-UX versions of nrConfigure run slowly on some HP machines.	There is not a reliable JIT Java Compiler on HP-UX. This performance problem can sometimes lead to confusion when the user interface is sluggish and users initiate actions several times because of poor performance. For example, rapid successive mouse clicks can lead to unexpected behavior by nrConfigure. Another case involves Java errors scrolling on console and the Java application screens crashing.	Retry your previous steps. In most cases, a second or third attempt is successful.

Table 25-2   *Troubleshooting NetRanger (Continued)*

Symptom	Possible Problem	Suggested Actions
File transfer problems		
You receive the following error message during file transfer between Sensors and Directors: Error transferring file from source_file to destination_file.	Occasionally, errors occur in file transfer between Sensors and Directors. However, if too many of these errors occur, there is a problem with fileXferd.	To ensure that communication is occurring, run the **nrstatus** and **nrvers** commands on both the Sensors and the Directors. Both the **nrvers** and **nrstatus** command outputs should indicate that fileXferd is running. If either command indicates that fileXferd is not running (for example, fileXferd does not appear in the process list), perform an **nrstop** and **nrstart** on the Sensors and Directors.

If fileXferd is running, then another possibility is that the nrConfigure databases have incorrect file permissions.

You can confirm the ownership of the nrConfigure databases by running the following command on the Director:

`ls -l /usr/nr/var/nrConfigure`

If any subdirectories are owned by user root, then perform the following steps:

Step 1   Use the **su** command to become user root.

Step 2   Type this command:

`rm -rf /usr/nr/var/nrConfigure`

Step 3   Use the **su** command to become user netrangr.

Step 4   Start the Director interface with the **ovw &** command.

Step 5   Click Advanced, nrConfigure DB, Create on the Security menu.

continues

Table 25-2 *Troubleshooting NetRanger (Continued)*

Symptom	Possible Problem	Suggested Actions
You receive the following error message during file transfer between Sensors and Directors: Error transferring file from source_file to destination_file *(continued)*		If none of the subdirectories are owned by user root, follow these steps: **Step 1** Start the Director interface with the **ovw &** command. **Caution**: Ensure that no Machine icons are selected before continuing with the next steps. If you select any Machine icons, then nrConfigure deletes and creates databases on the selected machines only. **Step 2** Click Advanced, nrConfigure DB, Delete on the Security menu. **Step 3** Click Advanced, nrConfigure DB, Create on the Security menu. Another problem may occur if you answer **no** when nrConfigure prompts you to download the latest configuration files. The solution for the problem is to delete and re-create new nrConfigure databases, as outlined previously.
Launching the NSDB or online help launches a new copy of the HTML browser, instead of refreshing the existing HTML browser window.		If you use Netscape, you can configure NetRanger to load all HTML pages into a single browser window. To do this, follow these steps: **Step 1** Open the /usr/nr/etc/nrConfigure.con f file in a text editor.

Table 25-2 *Troubleshooting NetRanger (Continued)*

Symptom	Possible Problem	Suggested Actions

Launching the NSDB or online help launches a new copy of the HTML browser, instead of refreshing the existing HTML browser window. *(continued)*		**Step 2** Change the value of the Browser token to the following value:
		
		`Browser=/usr/nr/bin/director/n`
		`rSingleBrowser`
		
		Step 3 Change the value of the NetscapeLocation token to the following value:
		
		`NetscapeLocation=/opt/netscape`
		`/netscape`
		
		Step 4 Save your changes and close the editing session.

Before Calling Cisco Systems' TAC Team

Before calling Cisco Systems's Technical Assistance Center (TAC), make sure that you have read through this chapter and completed the actions suggested for your system's problem.

In addition, note and document the following information so that we can better assist you:

- Versions of each daemon. Use the **nrvers** command.
- Operating systems installed on the hardware. This is especially important on the Director.
- Compress the /usr/nr/etc and the error files in the /usr/nr/var directory.

Troubleshooting PIX Firewall

To debug the PIX Firewall, you must first breakdown the task at hand. The following is a possible breakdown of a task, followed by solutions to possible problems, error codes, and **debug** commands. The symptoms and their likely solutions are included in Table 25-3. The error codes and their definitions should help in the interpretation of errors found in various logs. The **debug** commands are listed and accompanied by examples to assist in their use.

Finding the Real Problem

The PIX is the gateway to the Internet for the network and is normally blamed for problems that occur when a user cannot get out to the Internet. Although the PIX might be the problem, there are many other elements involved that might be causing the problem. Here you will find a list of other areas that could be causing the problem with a quick checklist.

- User's host machine
  - — Can the host machine **ping** to anything else on the inside network?
  - — Is the proper default gateway assigned?
  - — Can the host machine **ping** the inside interface of the PIX?
- Protected inside router
  - — Can the router **ping** the inside interface of the PIX?
  - — Can the router **ping** the user's host?
  - — Can the router get to anything on the external network?
- PIX
  - — Can the PIX **ping** the outside router?
  - — Can the PIX get to an external site past the outside router?
  - — IS the host's address defined in the **nat** command?
  - — Are there enough addresses defined in the global pool for all the internal hosts?
- Unprotected outside router
  - — Can the outside router get to the Internet?
  - — Does the outside router see packets coming from the PIX?

As you can see, many other factors are involved when troubleshooting the PIX Firewall.

debug Commands

The following commands are helpful when debugging the PIX Firewall.

- **show debug**—Used to display what debugging is turned on.
- **show debug**
- **debug icmp trace off**
- **debug packet off**
- **debug sqlnet off**

- **debug icmp trace**—When a host is **ping**ed through the PIX Firewall from any interface, **trace** output displays on the console. The following example shows a successful **ping** from an external host (192.150.50.42) to the PIX Firewall's outside interface (200.200.200.1).

```
router#debug icmp trace
Inbound ICMP echo reply (len 32 id 1 seq 256) 192.150.50.1 > 192.150.50.42
Outbound ICMP echo request (len 32 id 1 seq 512) 192.150.50.42 > 192.150.50.1
Inbound ICMP echo reply (len 32 id 1 seq 512) 192.150.50.1 > 192.150.50.42
Outbound ICMP echo request (len 32 id 1 seq 768) 192.150.50.42 > 192.150.50.1
Inbound ICMP echo reply (len 32 id 1 seq 768) 192.150.50.1 > 192.150.50.42
Outbound ICMP echo request (len 32 id 1 seq 1024) 192.150.50.42 > 192.150.50.1
Inbound ICMP echo reply (len 32 id 1 seq 1024) 192.150.50.1 > 192.150.50.42
```

- **debug packet** *if_name*—Used to debug a packet. The following example lists the information as it appears in a packet.

```
router#debug packet inside
--------PACKET ---------
-- IP --
4.3.2.1 ==>     255.3.2.1
        ver = 0x4       hlen = 0x5      tos = 0x0       tlen = 0x60
        id = 0x3902     flags = 0x0     frag off=0x0
        ttl = 0x20      proto=0x11      chksum = 0x5885
        -—UDP --
                source port = 0x89      dest port = 0x89
                len = 0x4c      checksum = 0xa6a0
        -—DATA --
                00000014:                                       00 01 00 00¦
        ....
                00000024: 00 00 00 01 20 45 49 45 50 45 47 45 47 45 46 46¦ ..
.. EIEPEGEGEFF
                00000034: 43 43 4e 46 41 45 44 43 41 43 41 43 41 43 41 43¦ CC
NFAEDCACACACAC
                00000044: 41 43 41 41 41 00 00 20 00 01 c0 0c 00 20 00 01¦ AC
AAA.. ...... ..
                00000054: 00 04 93 e0 00 06 60 00 01 02 03 04 00¦ ..
....\Q......
--------END OF PACKET ---------
```

- **debug packet** *if_name* **[src source_ip [netmask mask]] [dst dest_ip [netmask mask]] [[proto icmp] | [proto tcp [sport src_port] [dport dest_port]] | [proto udp [sport src_port] [dport dest_port]] [rx|tx|both]**—Used to see the contents of packets as it travels between two destinations.

Syntax description:

— *if_name*—Interface name from which the packets are arriving; for example, to monitor packets coming into the PIX Firewall from the outside, set *if_name* to outside.

— **src** *source*—Source IP address.

— **netmask** *mask*—Network mask.

— **dst** *dest_ip*—Destination IP address.

— **proto icmp**—Display ICMP packets only.

— **proto tcp**—Display TCP packets only.

— **sport** *src_port*—Source port. See the "Ports" section in "Introduction" for a list of valid port literal names.

— **dport** *dest_port*—Destination port.

— **proto udp**—Display UDP packets only.

— **rx**—Display only packets received at the PIX Firewall.

— **tx**—Display only packets that were transmitted from the PIX Firewall.

— **both**—Display both received and transmitted packets.

In the following example, the contents of the tcp packets on port 25 with the source address of 200.200.200.20 and the destination address of 100.100.100.10 are displayed.

```
debug packet outside src 200.200.200.20 dst 100.100.100.10 proto tcp dport 25 both
```

NOTE   Use of the **debug packet** command on a PIX Firewall experiencing a heavy load may result in the output displaying so fast that it may be impossible to stop the output by entering the **no debug packet** command from the console. You can enter the **no debug packet** command from a Telnet session.

Additional Debug Command Notes

The **debug icmp trace** command now sends output to the Trace Channel. The location of the Trace Channel depends on whether you have a simultaneous Telnet console session running at the same time as the console session, or if you are using only the PIX Firewall serial console.

If you are using only the PIX Firewall serial console, all **debug** commands display on the serial console.

If you have both a serial console session and a Telnet console session accessing the console, then no matter where you enter the **debug icmp trace** or the **debug sqlnet** commands, the output displays on the Telnet console session.

If you have two or more Telnet console sessions, the first session is the Trace Channel. If that session closes, the serial console session becomes the Trace Channel. The next Telnet console session that accesses the console will then become the Trace Channel.

The **debug packet** command displays only on the serial console. However, you can enable or disable this command from either the serial console or a Telnet console sessions.

The **debug** commands are shared between all Telnet and serial console sessions.

NOTE	The downside of the Trace Channel feature is that if one administrator is using the serial console and another administrator starts a Telnet console session, the serial console **debug icmp trace** and **debug sqlnet** output will suddenly stop without warning. In addition, the administrator on the Telnet console session will suddenly be viewing **debug** output, which may be unexpected. If you are using the serial console and **debug** output is not appearing, use the **who** command to see if a Telnet console session is running.

NOTE	To let users ping through the PIX Firewall, add the **conduit permit icmp any** command to the configuration. This lets **ping**s go outbound and inbound.

Troubleshooting Steps

The first example deals with an internal user who cannot access the Internet. These are recommended troubleshooting steps to follow, but note that these steps may not solve every instance of this problem.

Step 1 Go to the end user's machine and have the user **ping** the PIX's internal interface. If you get a response, go to the next step. If you do not get a response, check the following for possible solutions:

— User cannot ping any internal address. Check interface card on the user's system.

— User can **ping** other systems on the same network but cannot **ping** the PIX. This assumes that there is a router between the user's system and the PIX. Check the following:

(a) The default route on the user's system.

(b) The default route or static route on the inside router. Make sure that the inside router is configured to route the traffic both ways.

— PIX cannot **ping** user's system. If not on the same network, check the internal router. If the PIX can **ping** the internal router but not beyond, make sure that the PIX knows how to get to that subnet.

(a) Check the default inside route on the PIX. In the following example, the default route would be 100.100.100.2.

```
Route inside 0.0.0.0 0.0.0.0 100.100.100.2 1
Route inside 0.0.0.0 0.0.0.0 100.100.100.2 1
```

(b) Check the routing table on the inside router to make sure that the inside router knows how to properly route the packets.

Step 2   On the PIX, turn on **debug icmp trace**.

— Allow ICMP traffic through the PIX. To do this enter the following command:

```
conduit permit icmp any any
```

Note   Use of the **debug packet** command on a PIX Firewall experiencing a heavy load may result in the output displaying so fast that it may be impossible to stop the output by entering the **no debug packet** command from the console. You can enter the **no debug packet** command from a Telnet session.

— Next find out if the user's system has a translated address. To do this, use the following command:

```
show xlate local ip_address
```

— If there is a translated address, you will need to clear the address. Use the following command:

```
clear xlate local ip_address
```

Step 3   Try to access a web site from the user's system.

Step 4   Check the translation table to make sure that a translation was built for the user's system. Refer to the command in Step 2.

Step 5   If there was no translation built, have the user's system try to **ping** an outside system, and then watch the output from the **debug** command. If you do not see any output, then the packet is not making it to the PIX. If the packet is making it to the PIX, then check the syslog output and check to make sure that there are enough addresses in the global command. Verify that the user's address is included in the **nat** command addresses. Check other items between the PIX and the user's system. Confirm that there is a valid default route.

Step 6   If there was a translation built, turn on debugging of the packet, and see if the packet is traveling through the PIX.

Step 7 If the packet goes out but you do not get a return, then the outside router does not know how to return the traffic. Check the routing table on the outside router.

External Users Cannot Access an Internal System (Web Server, Mail Server)

The following six steps provide a practical approach to troubleshooting common problems associated with external users having difficulty accessing a company's internet/mail servers.

Step 1 The first step in this type of debugging is to allow **ping**s from the external source for testing purposes. Use this command:

```
conduit permit icmp any any
```

Step 2 Next turn on **debug icmp trace**.

NOTE   Use of the **debug packet** command on a PIX Firewall experiencing a heavy load may result in the output displaying so fast that it may be impossible to stop the output by entering the **no debug packet** command from the console. You can enter the **no debug packet** command from a Telnet session.

Step 3 Have an external site try to **ping** the internal system via the translated address. For example, if your web server has an internal address of 10.10.10.1 and a translated address of 200.200.200.1, have the external site **ping** the 200.200.200.1 address.

Step 4 If you do not see the packets on the PIX, check the external router to ensure that they are making it to there. If they are, then check the routing table on the external router to make sure that the router knows how to route the packet. If the routing tables are correct, then check the ARP table on the router to make sure that it has the proper MAC address for the packet. It should be the same as the PIX's external MAC address.

Step 5 Check the static and conduit statements in the configuration on the PIX for the server in question, and ensure that they are correct. You can also check by the following two commands:

— **show static**—This will show all the static addresses currently assigned.

— **show conduit**—This will show all the conduits that are currently applied.

Step 6   If the packet goes through, then have the external site try to get to the server again. This time, use port 80 (web browsing). If the external user cannot get to the server, check the log for their address. Check to see if the address is getting denied.

Troubleshooting Techniques

Table 25-3 suggests what actions to take when presented with the two most common Pix firewall connectivity problems.

Table 25-3   *Troubleshooting Techniques*

Symptom	Possible Problem	Suggested Actions
The internal host cannot access a host on the Internet.	The Network Translation Table does not include the network that the host is on.	Make sure that the NAT command includes the network the host is on. For example: `Host address 171.68.101.1 nat (inside,outside) 1 171.68.0.0 255.255.0.0`

	There are no more addresses in the global statement to handle the number of internal hosts.	Make sure that there are sufficient global addresses for all the internal hosts.
		
		`global (outside) 1 200.200.200.2-200.200.200.250`
		
		Or, use port address translation (PAT):
		
		`global (outside) 1 200.200.200.2-200.200.200.2`

	The host's default gateway is not set to the proper address.	If the host is on the same network as the PIX, it must have the PIX's inside interface for its default gateway.
	The router on the outside of the PIX does not know how to route the addresses that you have defined in the **global** pool back to the PIX. This is normally caused by using addresses in the **global** pool definition that are on a different network than the outside interface of the PIX.	Have a static route for those **global** addresses put on the outside router.

Table 25-3 *Troubleshooting Techniques (Continued)*

Symptom	Possible Problem	Suggested Actions
	The PIX was recently changed or replaced, and the ARP table on the outside router has not cleared yet.	Use the **clear arp** command on the outside router.
	The host's default gateway is not set to the proper address.	Check the default gateway on the user's host.
The external host cannot access a host on the local network (for example, a web server).	The outside address does not know how to route the packets.	Make sure that the router connected to the outside of the router knows how to route the static address of the server.
	There is no static or conduit statement for the server.	Whether it is a WEB server or an e-mail server, it must have a static statement and a conduit statement on the PIX. The static statement statically maps an internal addresses to an external address. The conduit command opens a hole for traffic to come through the PIX and get to the server. The following is an example for a WWW server with an internal address of 10.10.10.20 and an external (translated) address of 200.200.200.20: `static (inside,outside) 200.200.200.20 10.10.10.20 netmask 255.255.255.255 conduit permit tcp host 200.200.200.20 eq www any`
	The PIX does not know how to route the traffic to the server.	This will happen only if the server is on a different network than the PIX. Check the inside route statement, and make sure that the PIX knows how to route the traffic. Use the **show route** command.

Before Calling Cisco Systems' TAC Team

Before calling Cisco Systems' Technical Assistance Center (TAC), make sure that you have read through this chapter and completed the actions suggested for your system's problem.

Additionally, do the following and document the results so that we can better assist you:

- Obtain the version of the PIX IOS software
- Obtain as much hardware information as possible

Additional Sources

Books:

- Atkins, Derek. *Internet Security Professional Reference*, Second Edition. Indianapolis: New Riders Publishing, 1997.
- Kaeo, Merike. *Designing Network Security.* Indianapolis: Cisco Press, 1999.

URLs:

- Internet: www.securityfocus.com (SecurityFocus.com is a single place, or community, on the Internet where people and corporations can go to find security information and have security questions answered by leading authorities in the industry. This site provides access to security links and resources including news, books, mailing lists, tools and products, and security services.)
- Internet: www.finjan.com (Finjan makes filters and other countermeasures to block the Java Scripts used to execute session hijacking, session replay attacks, and other "mobile code" attacks.)
- Newsgroups: alt.2600 (This is a newsgroup of interest to hackers and security experts. It has a vast amount of information on network intrusion and protection techniques.)

PIX Maintenance

The PIX has two important maintenance features:

- Password recovery
- Software upgrades

These are discussed in the next sections.

Password Recovery

The password recovery for the PIX 515 requires a TFTP server to download the password data to it because that model does not have a floppy drive. For the other PIX models, use the following procedure.

A password recovery image will be available. This image will need to be copied using TFTP to the PIX just like any new upgrade image.

The TFTP capabilities directly take the place of the floppy loader, so, all previous functions that were handled with a floppy will be handled with TFTP.

Please note the following:

- TFTP on the PIX requires that you reboot the PIX.
- When you enter the ROM monitor, the PIX application *will not* be running, so no traffic will pass in your network while this operation is being performed.
- The TFTP server should be on the most secure part of the network (preferably on the inside).
- Using TFTP for a new image or password recovery will require your network to be offline until this activity is complete.
- Once the system is rebooted, the addresses used during the TFTP process do not remain in the configuration or memory.

PIX 520 Password Recovery Procedure

The following is the recommended process for recovering lost passwords in PIX 520 firewalls.

Step 1   Download Nppix.bin and rawrite.exe from: www.cisco.com/warp/customer/110/34.shtml into the same directory on a PC. (You will need a CCO login to download.)

Step 2   When you have retrieved the two files, execute RAWRITE: C:\TEMP>RAWRITE.

RaWrite 1.2—Write the disk file to a raw floppy disk.

Step 3   Enter source filename: NPPIX.BIN.

Step 4   Enter destination drive A.

Step 5   Insert a formatted disk into drive A, and press Enter.

The Rawrite program then writes the password recovery image to disk.

Step 6   Boot your PIX with that disk, which will clear the old password.

Downloading a PIX 515 Image over TFTP

Because the PIX 515 does not have a floppy drive, the only method of password recovery available is by downloading a recovery program from a TFTP server. The TFTP capabilities directly take the place of the floppy loader, so all previous functions that were handled with a floppy will be handled with TFTP.

Please note the following:

- TFTP on the PIX requires that you reboot the PIX.

- When you enter the ROM monitor, the PIX application *will not* be running, so no traffic will pass in your network while this operation is being performed.

- The TFTP server should be on the most secure part of the network (preferably on the inside).

- Using TFTP to copy a new image or password recovery will require your network to be offline until this activity is complete.

- Once the system is rebooted, the addresses used during the TFTP process do not remain in the configuration or memory.

The PIX 515 receives its boot image either from Flash memory or by downloading the image from a TFTP server.

This section describes the **monitor** command, which you will invoke while the PIX 515 is booting by sending a Break character or pressing the Escape key.

Because the PIX 515 does not have a disk drive, you need to send a binary image to the PIX 515 using TFTP.

The PIX 515 has a special mode called monitor mode that lets you retrieve the binary image over the network. When you power on or reboot the PIX 515, it waits 10 seconds, during which you can send a break character or press the Escape key to activate monitor mode.

If you do not want to enter the boot mode, press the Spacebar to start the normal boot immediately, or wait until the 10 seconds have finished, and the PIX 515 will boot normally.

While in monitor mode, you can enter commands that let you specify the location of the binary image, download it, and reboot the PIX 515 from the new image. If you do not activate monitor mode, the PIX 515 boots normally from Flash memory.

Monitor mode also lets you **ping** the TFTP server to see if it is online and to specify the IP address of the nearest router if the image is not on a subnet shared with a PIX 515 interface.

The monitor feature works only on the PIX 515 and not with earlier models of the PIX Firewall. TFTP does not perform authentication when transferring files, so a username and password on the TFTP server are not required.

If you are using Windows Hyperterminal, you can press the Esc (Escape) key or send a Break character by pressing the Ctrl and break keys.

From a Telnet session to a terminal server that has serial access to the PIX 515, use Ctrl-] to get the Telnet command prompt, and then enter the **send break** command.

If the TFTP service stops receiving data requests during a file transfer, it waits 4 seconds and then closes the connection.

To download an image over TFTP, use the following procedure:

Step 1   Immediately after you power on the PIX Firewall and the startup messages appears, send a Break character, or press the Esc (Escape) key.

The monitor prompt appears.

Step 2   If desired, enter a question mark (?) to list available commands.

Step 3   Use the **interface** command to specify which interface the **ping** traffic should use. If the PIX 515 has only two interfaces, the **monitor** command defaults to the inside interface.

Step 4   Use the **address** command to specify the IP address of the PIX Firewalls interface.

Step 5   Use the **server** command to specify the IP address of the remote server.

Step 6   Use the **file** command to specify the filename of the PIX Firewall image.

Step 7   If needed, enter the **gateway** command to specify the IP address of a router gateway through which the server is accessible.

Step 8   If needed, use the **ping** command to verify accessibility. If this command fails, configure access to the server before continuing.

Step 9 Use the **TFTP** command to start the download.

Step 10 After the download is complete, reboot the PIX and install a new password.

Software Upgrade Paths

The software upgrade procedure that you follow depends on whether you want to keep your configuration files intact. If you do, use the procedure outlined in Table 25-4.

Table 25-4 *Software Upgrade*

If Your PIX Firewall Version Is:	Install This Version:
2.7x	3.0, and then upgrade to the next version
3.0	4.0.7, and then upgrade to the next version
4.0.7	4.1(7), and then upgrade to the next version
4.1(5) or later	4.2(x), and then upgrade to the next version
4.2(x)	4.4

If you don't care about retaining the configuration information, you can upgrade directly from the current version to the latest version.

Recovering a Lost Password

This section describes the procedures required to recover a lost login or enable password. The procedures differ, depending on the platform and the software used, but in all cases, password recovery requires that the router be taken out of operation and powered down.

If you need to perform one of the following procedures, make certain that secondary systems can temporarily serve the functions of the router undergoing the procedure. If this is not possible, advise all potential users and, if possible, perform the procedure during low-use hours.

NOTE Make a note of your password and store it in a secure place.

All the procedures for recovering lost passwords depend on changing the configuration register of the router. Depending on the platform and software you are using, this will be done by reconfiguring the router software or by physically moving a jumper or DIP switch on the router.

Table 25-5 shows which platforms have configuration registers in software and which require that you change the jumper or DIP switch position to change the configuration register.

Table 25-5 *Configuration Registers for Specific Cisco Platforms and Software*

Platform (and Software, If Applicable)	Software Configuration Register	Hardware Configuration Register (Jumper)	Hardware Configuration Register (DIP Switch)
Cisco 2000 series	Yes	—	—
Cisco 2500 series	Yes	—	—
Cisco 3000 series	Yes	—	—
Cisco 4000 series	Yes	—	—
Cisco 7000 series running Software Release 9.17(4) or later (Flash) or Cisco IOS Release 10.0 or later (ROM)	Yes	—	—
Cisco 7000 running Software Release 9.21 or earlier from ROM	—	Yes	—
Cisco 7200	Yes	—	—
Cisco 7500	Yes	—	—
Cisco IGS running Software Release 9.1 or later	Yes	—	—
Cisco IGS running software prior to Software Release 9.1	—	—	Yes
Cisco CGS	—	Yes	—
Cisco MGS	—	Yes	—
Cisco AGS	—	Yes	—
Cisco AGS+	—	Yes	—

Password-Recovery Procedure:
Platforms Running Current Cisco IOS Releases

Recent Cisco platforms run from Flash memory or are booted from the network and can ignore the contents of nonvolatile RAM (NVRAM) upon booting. (Cisco 7000 series routers that boot from Flash memory or netboot have this capability as well; a Cisco 7000 that boots from ROM has this capability if it is running Cisco IOS Release 10.0 or later.) Ignoring the contents of NVRAM permits you to bypass the configuration file (which contains the passwords) and to gain complete access to the router. You can then recover the lost password or configure a new one.

NOTE   If your password is encrypted, you cannot recover it. You must configure a new password.

Figure 25-1 shows a flowchart describing the password-recovery procedure for the following platforms:

- Cisco 2000, Cisco 2500, Cisco 3000, and Cisco 4000 series access servers and routers

- Cisco 7000 series routers running Software Release 9.17(4) and later from Flash or Cisco IOS Release 10.0 or later from ROM

- Cisco IGS routers running Software Release 9.1 or later

- Cisco CGS, MGS, AGS, and AGS+ routers running Software Release 9.1(7) or later

- Cisco 7000 series routers running Software Release 9.17(4) through 9.21 from ROM

Some of these platforms are configurable in software. Others require that you physically change the position of the configuration register jumper on the processor card. Figure 25-1 shows diverging paths, when necessary, to take you through the steps required for the platform and software with which you are working.

Refer to Table 25-5 to determine whether the platform with which you are working is configurable in software, or if it requires you to physically move the jumper.

Figure 25-1 *Password Recovery: Platforms Running Current Cisco IOS Releases and Recent Software Releases*

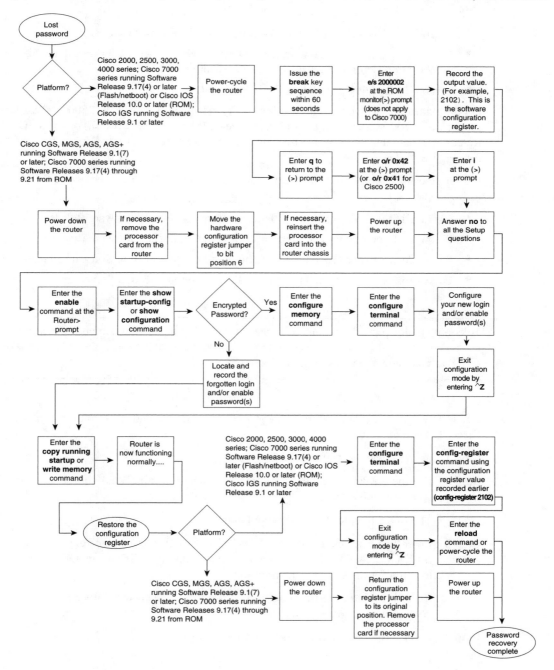

The next procedure describes the password-recovery process for the following platforms only:

- Cisco 2000, Cisco 2500, Cisco 3000, and Cisco 4000 series routers
- Cisco 7000 series routers running Software Release 9.17(4) or later (Flash memory or netboot) or Cisco IOS Release 10.0 or later from ROM
- Cisco IGS Running Software Release 9.1 or later

For the platforms listed, be certain to follow the path labeled "Cisco 2000, 2500, 3000, 4000 series; Cisco 7000 series running Software Release 9.17(4) or later (Flash) or Cisco IOS Release 10.0 or later (ROM); IGS running Software Release 9.1 or later" in the flowchart (see Figure 25-1).

For the step-by-step password recovery sequence for other platforms, see one of the following sections:

- Password-Recovery Procedure: Platforms Running Recent Software Releases
- Password-Recovery Procedure: Platforms Running Earlier Software Releases
- Password-Recovery Procedure: IGS Running Software Prior to Software Release 9.1
- Password-Recovery Procedure: Cisco 500-CS Communication Server

NOTE   To complete this procedure, you must have a terminal or a personal computer (running terminal-emulation software) connected to the console port of the router. In addition, make sure that you know the break command key sequence.

The following is the password-recovery procedure for Cisco platforms running current Cisco IOS software:

Step 1   Power-cycle the router.

Step 2   Use the break key sequence for your terminal or terminal emulation software within 60 seconds of turning on the power.

The ROM monitor (>) prompt will appear.

Step 3   Enter the command **e/s 2000002**. (For Cisco 7000 series routers, enter **e/s XXXXXXXX**.) This command examines the short (16-bit) memory location for the software configuration register.

Record the output resulting from this command. This is the software configuration register value.

Step 4   Enter **q** (quit) to return to the ROM monitor (>) prompt.

Step 5   Enter the **o/r 0x42** command. The value 42 sets the software configuration register bit to position 6, which allows the router to ignore the contents of NVRAM when booting. (Be sure to enter **0x** followed by the configuration register value.)

Step 6   Enter **i** (initialize) at the ROM monitor (>) prompt. The router will reboot.

Step 7   Answer **no** to all the setup questions.

Step 8   Enter the **enable** exec command at the Router prompt.

Step 9   Enter the **show startup-config** or **show configuration** privileged exec command to see whether your password is clear-text (is not encrypted) or encrypted.

Step 10 If your password is clear-text, proceed to Step 14.

If your password is encrypted, continue with Step 11.

Step 11 If your password is encrypted, enter the **configure memory** privileged exec command. This transfers the stored configuration into running memory.

Step 12 Enter the **configure terminal** privileged exec command to enter router configuration mode.

Step 13 If you lost the enable password, use the **enable password** global configuration command to configure a new password, and press ^Z to exit configuration mode. The following is the command syntax for the **enable password** command:

enable password [*level level*] {*password* | *encryption-type encrypted-password*}

Syntax description:

— *level level*—(Optional) Level for which the password applies. You can specify up to 16 privilege levels, using numbers 0 through 15. Level 1 is normal exec-mode user privileges. If this argument is not specified in the command, or if the **no** form of the command is used, the privilege level defaults to 15 (traditional enable privileges).

— *password*—The password that users type to enter enable mode.

— *encryption-type*—(Optional) Cisco-proprietary algorithm used to encrypt the password. Currently, the only encryption type available is 7. If you specify an encryption type, the next that argument you supply must be an encrypted password (a password already encrypted by a Cisco router).

— *encrypted-password*—The encrypted password that you enter, copied from another router configuration.

Example:

In the following example, the password pswd2 is enabled for privilege level 2:

```
enable password level 2 pswd2
```

If you lost the login password, configure the console line using the login and password line configuration commands. Enter **CTRL Z** to exit configuration mode, and proceed to Step 15.

Syntax:

To enable password checking at login, use the **login** line configuration command:

login [*local* | *tacacs*]

Syntax description:

— *local*—(Optional) Selects local password checking. Authentication is based on the username specified with the **username** global configuration command.

— *tacacs*—(Optional) Selects the TACACS-style user ID and password-checking mechanism.

Examples:

The following example sets the password letmein on virtual terminal line 4:

```
line vty 4
password letmein
login
```

Syntax:

To specify a password on a line, use the **password** line configuration command:

password *password*

Syntax description:

— *password*—Character string that specifies the line password. The first character cannot be a number. The string can contain any alphanumeric characters, including spaces, up to 80 characters. You cannot specify the password in the format number-space-anything. The space after the number causes problems. For example, **hello 21** is a legal password, but **21 hello** is not. The password checking is case-sensitive. For example, the password **Secret** is different from the password **secret**.

When an exec process is started on a line with password protection, the exec prompts for the password. If the user enters the correct password, the exec prints its normal privileged prompt. The user can try three times to enter a password before the exec exits and returns the terminal to the idle state.

Example:

The following example removes the password from virtual terminal lines 1 to 4:

```
line vty 1 4
  no password
```

Step 14 If you lost the enable password, locate the **enable-password** global configuration command entry in the configuration, and record the password.

If you lost the login password, find the configuration entries for the console line, and record the password indicated by the password line configuration command.

Step 15 Use the **copy running-config startup-config** or **write memory** privileged exec command to write the configuration into NVRAM.

NOTE   Issuing the **copy running-config startup-config** or **write memory** command at this point on a Cisco 2500, Cisco 3000, or Cisco 4000 will overwrite the configuration. Make certain that you have a backup of your configuration file.

The router is now fully functional, and you can use your recovered or reconfigured passwords as usual.

<table>
<tr><td>NOTE</td><td>Restore the software configuration register to its original value as soon as possible. If it is not returned to the value that you noted in Step 3, the router will always ignore the contents of NVRAM and will enter the Setup routine upon booting. Continue with Step 17 to return the software configuration register to its original value.</td></tr>
</table>

Step 16 In privileged exec mode, enter router configuration mode using the **configure terminal** privileged exec command.

Step 17 Change the software configuration register to its original value by using the **config-register** global configuration command. You must enter **0x** and then the software configuration register value that you recorded in Step 3. Using the sample value 2102, the command would be **config-register 0x2102**.

Syntax:

The following is the syntax for **config-register** command:

config-register *value*   ·

Syntax description:

— *value*—Hexadecimal or decimal value that represents the 16-bit configuration register value that you want to use the next time the router is restarted. The value range is from 0x0 to 0xFFFF (0 to 65535, in decimal).

Step 18 Exit router configuration mode by entering **^Z**.

The next time the router is power-cycled or restarted with the **reload** privileged exec command, the bootup process will proceed as normal. Use your new or recovered password to gain access to the router after it reboots.

Password-Recovery Procedure:
Platforms Running Recent Software Releases

The Cisco CGS, MGS, AGS, and AGS+ platforms, and the Cisco 7000 series routers running software prior to Cisco IOS Release 10.0 from ROM all have their configuration registers in hardware, so you must physically change the position of the configuration register jumper during the password-recovery process.

It might be necessary to remove the processor card from the router chassis to access the hardware configuration register jumper. Consult your hardware documentation for detailed instructions on removing and inserting the processor card from the router chassis, if necessary.

Moving the hardware configuration register jumper to bit position 6 allows the router to ignore the contents of NVRAM while booting. This permits you to bypass the configuration file (and, therefore, the passwords) and gain complete access to the router. You can then recover the lost password or configure a new one.

NOTE	If your password is encrypted, you cannot recover it. You must configure a new password.

Figure 25-1 shows a flowchart describing the password-recovery procedure for the following platforms:

- Cisco 2000, Cisco 2500, Cisco 3000, and Cisco 4000 series access servers and routers
- Cisco 7000 series routers running Software Release 9.17(4) and later from Flash memory/netboot, or Cisco 7000 series routers running Cisco IOS Release 10.0 or later from ROM
- Cisco IGS routers running Software Release 9.1 or later
- Cisco CGS, MGS, AGS, and AGS+ routers running Software Release 9.1(7) or later
- Cisco 7000 series routers running Software Release 9.17(4) through 9.21 from ROM

Some of these platforms are configurable in software and do not require a hardware change. Others require that you physically change the position of the configuration register jumper on the processor card.

Refer to Table 25-5 to determine whether the platform on which you are working is configurable in the software, or whether it requires you to physically move the jumper.

The following procedure describes the password-recovery process for the following platforms only:

- Cisco CGS, MGS, AGS, and AGS+ routers running Software Release 9.1(7) and later
- Cisco 7000 series routers running Software Release 9.17(4) through 9.21 from ROM

For these platforms, follow the path labeled "Cisco CGS, MGS, AGS, AGS+ running Software Release 9.1(7) or later; Cisco 7000 series running Software Release 9.17(4) through 9.21 from ROM" in the flowchart (see Figure 25-1).

For the step-by-step password recovery sequence for other platforms, see one of the following sections:

- Password-Recovery Procedure: Platforms Running Current Cisco IOS Releases
- Password-Recovery Procedure: Platforms Running Earlier Software Releases
- Password-Recovery Procedure: IGS Running Software Prior to Software Release 9.1
- Password-Recovery Procedure: Cisco 500-CS Communication Server

NOTE   To complete this procedure, you must have a terminal or a personal computer (running terminal emulation software) connected to the console port of the router.

The following is the password-recovery procedure for Cisco platforms running recent software releases:

Step 1   Power down the router.

Step 2   Change the hardware configuration register by moving the jumper from bit position 0 or 1 to bit position 6. This will force the router to ignore the contents of NVRAM and, therefore, the configuration file after it loads the operating system. Note the original position of the jumper.

NOTE   To move the hardware configuration register jumper, you might need to remove the processor card from the router chassis. This is the case with the Route Processor (RP) card in Cisco 7000 series routers. Refer to your hardware documentation for complete instructions on removing and inserting the processor card. If you had to remove the processor card, reinsert it before continuing.

Step 3   Power up the router.

The router will boot but will ignore the contents of NVRAM and enter the Setup routine.

Step 4   Answer **no** to all the setup questions.

The Router prompt appears.

Step 5   Enter the **enable** exec command.

Step 6   Enter the **show configuration** privileged exec command to see whether the password is in clear text (is not encrypted) or if it is encrypted.

If the password is in clear text, go to Step 10. If the password is encrypted, continue with Step 7.

Step 7   If the password is encrypted, enter the **configure memory** privileged exec command. This writes the stored configuration into running memory.

Step 8   Enter the **configure terminal privileged exec** command to enter router configuration mode.

Step 9   If you have lost the enable password, use the **enable-password global** configuration command to configure a new password.

If you have lost the login password, configure the console line with a new login password using the **login** and **password** line configuration commands. Press CTRL-Z to exit configuration mode. Proceed to Step 11.

Syntax:

To enable password checking at login, use the **login** line configuration command:

login [*local* | *tacacs*]

Syntax description:

— *local*—(Optional) Selects local password checking. Authentication is based on the username specified with the username global configuration command.

— *tacacs*—(Optional) Selects the TACACS-style user ID and password-checking mechanism.

Examples:

The following example sets the password letmein on virtual terminal line 4:

```
line vty 4
password letmein
login
```

Syntax:

To specify a password on a line, use the **password** line configuration command:

password *password*

Syntax description:

— *password*—Character string that specifies the line password. The first character cannot be a number. The string can contain any alphanumeric characters, including spaces, up to 80 characters. You cannot specify the password in the format number-space-anything. The space after the number causes problems. For example, **hello 21** is a legal password, but **21 hello** is not. The password checking is case-sensitive. For example, the password **Secret** is different from the password **secret**.

When an exec process is started on a line with password protection, the exec prompts for the password. If the user enters the correct password, the exec prints its normal privileged prompt. The user can try three times to enter a password before the exec exits and returns the terminal to the idle state.

Example:

The following example removes the password from virtual terminal lines 1 to 4:

```
line vty 1 4
 no password
```

Step 10 If you have lost the enable password, locate the **enable-password** global configuration command entry, and record the password.

If you have lost the login password, find the configuration entries for the console line, and record the password indicated by the **password** line configuration command.

Step 11 Use the **write memory** privileged exec command to write the configuration into running memory.

Step 12 The router is now fully functional, and you can use your recovered or reconfigured passwords as usual.

NOTE Return the hardware configuration register jumper to its original position as soon as possible. If the jumper is not returned to the bit position that you noted in Step 2, the router will always ignore the contents of NVRAM and will enter the Setup routine upon booting. Continue with Step 13 to return the jumper to its original position.

Step 13 Power down the router.

Step 14 Move the hardware configuration register jumper from bit position 6 to its original position (the position that you noted in Step 2).

It might be necessary to remove the processor card to gain access to the jumper. Consult your hardware documentation for complete instructions on removing and inserting the processor card, if necessary. If you had to remove the processor card, reinsert it before continuing.

Step 15 Power up the router. Use your new or recovered password to gain access to the router.

Password-Recovery Procedure:
Platforms Running Earlier Software Releases

Cisco CGS, MGS, AGS, and AGS+ platforms, and Cisco 7000 series routers running software prior to Cisco IOS Release 10.0 from ROM all have their configuration registers in the hardware, so you must physically change the position of the configuration register jumper during the password-recovery process.

It might be necessary to remove the processor card from the router chassis to access the hardware configuration register jumper. Consult your hardware documentation for detailed instructions on removing and inserting the processor card from the router chassis, if necessary.

NOTE   If your password is encrypted, you cannot recover it. You must configure a new password.

Figure 25-2 shows a flowchart that describes the password-recovery procedure for the following platforms:

- CGS, MGS, AGS, and AGS+ routers running Software Release 9.1(6) and earlier
- Cisco 7000 series routers running Software Release 9.17(3) and earlier from ROM

The step-by-step procedure that follows and the password recovery flowchart shown in Figure 25-2 apply only to the indicated platforms running the indicated software. There is another procedure for recovering a password on these platforms if they are running more recent software. See the previous section, "Password-Recovery Procedure: Platforms Running Recent Software Releases."

Figure 25-2 *Password Recovery: Platforms Running Earlier Software Releases*

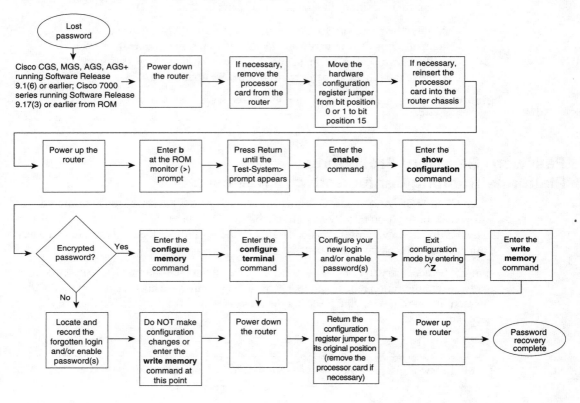

NOTE   To complete this procedure, you must have a terminal or a personal computer (running terminal emulation software) connected to the console port of the router.

The following is the password-recovery procedure for Cisco platforms running earlier software releases:

Step 1   Power down the router.

Step 2   Change the hardware configuration register by moving the jumper from bit position 0 or 1 to bit position 15.

Note the original position of the jumper.

Note	To move the hardware configuration register jumper, you might need to remove the processor card from the router chassis. This is the case with the RP card in Cisco 7000 series routers. Consult your hardware documentation for complete instructions on removing and inserting the processor card. If you had to remove the processor card, reinsert it before continuing.

Step 3 Power up the router. The ROM monitor (>) prompt appears.

Step 4 Enter **b** (bootstrap) at the (>) prompt.

Step 5 Press the Return key until the Test-System prompt appears.

Step 6 Enter privileged mode by issuing the **enable** exec command.

Step 7 Enter the **show configuration** privileged exec command to see whether the password is clear-text (is not encrypted) or is encrypted.

If the password is clear-text, go to Step 12.

If the password is encrypted, continue with Step 8.

Step 8 If the password is encrypted, enter the **configure memory** privileged exec command.

This writes the stored configuration into running memory.

Step 9 Enter the **configure terminal** privileged exec command to enter router configuration mode.

Step 10 If you have lost the enable password, use the **enable-password** global configuration command to configure a new password, and press CTRL-Z to exit configuration mode.

If you have lost the login password, configure the console line with a new password using the login and password line configuration commands. Press CTRL-Z to exit configuration mode.

Syntax:

To enable password checking at login, use the **login** line configuration command:

login [*local* | *tacacs*]

Syntax description:

— *local*—(Optional) Selects local password checking. Authentication is based on the username specified with the **username** global configuration command.

— *tacacs*—(Optional) Selects the TACACS-style user ID and password-checking mechanism.

Examples:

The following example sets the password letmein on virtual terminal line 4:

```
line vty 4
password letmein
login
```

Syntax:

To specify a password on a line, use the **password** line configuration command:

password *password*

Syntax description:

— *password*—Character string that specifies the line password. The first character cannot be a number. The string can contain any alphanumeric characters, including spaces, up to 80 characters. You cannot specify the password in the format number-space-anything. The space after the number causes problems. For example, **hello 21** is a legal password, but **21 hello** is not. The password checking is case-sensitive. For example, the password **Secret** is different from the password **secret**.

When an exec process is started on a line with password protection, the exec prompts for the password. If the user enters the correct password, the exec prints its normal privileged prompt. The user can try three times to enter a password before the exec exits and returns the terminal to the idle state.

Example:

The following example removes the password from virtual terminal lines 1 to 4:

```
line vty 1 4
 no password
```

Step 11 Use the **write memory** privileged exec command to write the configuration into running memory. Proceed to Step 13.

Step 12 If you have lost the enable password, locate the **enable-password** global configuration command entry in the configuration, and record the password.

If you have lost the login password, find the configuration entries for the console line, and record the password indicated by the **password** line configuration command. Do not make configuration changes or use the **write memory** command at this time.

Step 13 Power down the router.

Step 14 Remove the processor card, and move the hardware configuration register jumper from bit position 15 to its original position (the position that you noted in Step 2).

Step 15 Power up the router. Use your new or recovered password to gain access to the router.

Password-Recovery Procedure:
IGS Running Software Prior to Software Release 9.1

Cisco IGS routers have a bank of DIP switches located on the rear panel. These DIP switches are used to set the hardware configuration register and must be used in the password-recovery process if the router is running system software prior to Software Release 9.1.

NOTE   If your password is encrypted, you cannot recover it. You must configure a new password.

Figure 25-3 shows the password-recovery procedure for the Cisco IGS running software prior to Software Release 9.1. There is another procedure for the IGS platform if it is running Software Release 9.1 or later. See the section "Password-Recovery Procedure: Platforms Running Current Cisco IOS Releases."

NOTE   To complete this procedure, you must have a terminal or a personal computer (running terminal emulation software) connected to the console port of the router.

The following is the password-recovery procedure for IGS routers running software prior to Software Release 9.1:

Step 1 Power down the router.

Step 2 Record the settings of the DIP switches located on the rear panel of the router. You will need to return these switches to their original positions after you have recovered your password.

Figure 25-3 *Password Recovery: IGS Running Software Release Prior to 9.1*

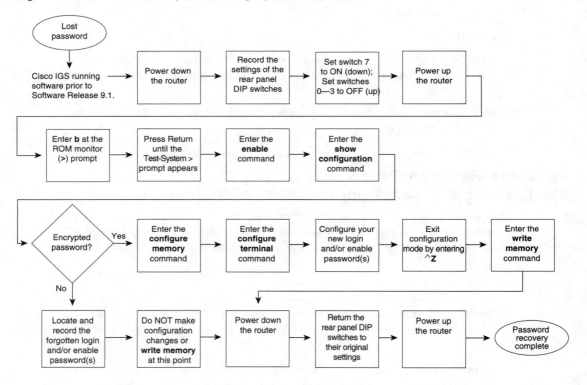

Step 3 Set switch number 7 to the ON position (down).

Step 4 Set switches 0–3 to the OFF position (up).

Step 5 Power up the router.

The router will boot up, and the terminal will display the ROM monitor (>) prompt.

Step 6   Enter **b** (bootstrap) at the (>) prompt.

Step 7   Press the Return key until the Test-System prompt appears.

Step 8   Enter the **enable** privileged exec command at the Test-System prompt.

Step 9   If the password is clear-text (is not encrypted), go to Step 14.

If the password is encrypted, continue with Step 10.

Step 10 If the password is encrypted, enter the **configure memory** privileged exec command. This writes the stored configuration into running memory.

Step 11 Enter the **configure terminal** privileged exec command to enter router configuration mode.

Step 12 If you have lost the enable password, use the **enable-passwo**rd global configuration command to configure a new password, and press ^Z to exit configuration mode.

If you have lost the login password, configure a new password on the console line using the **login** and **password** line configuration commands. Press ^Z to exit configuration mode.

Syntax:

To enable password checking at login, use the **login** line configuration command:

login [*local* | *tacacs*]

Syntax description:

— *local*—(Optional) Selects local password checking. Authentication is based on the username specified with the username global configuration command.

— *tacacs*—(Optional) Selects the TACACS-style user ID and password-checking mechanism.

Examples:

The following example sets the password letmein on virtual terminal line 4:

```
line vty 4
password letmein
login
```

Syntax:

To specify a password on a line, use the **password** line configuration command:

password *password*

Syntax description:

— *password*—Character string that specifies the line password. The first character cannot be a number. The string can contain any alphanumeric characters, including spaces, up to 80 characters. You cannot specify the password in the format number-space-anything. The space after the number causes problems. For example, **hello 21** is a legal password, but **21 hello** is not. The password checking is case-sensitive. For example, the password **Secret** is different from the password **secret**.

When an exec process is started on a line with password protection, the exec prompts for the password. If the user enters the correct password, the exec prints its normal privileged prompt. The user can try three times to enter a password before the exec exits and returns the terminal to the idle state.

Example:

The following example removes the password from virtual terminal lines 1 to 4:

```
line vty 1 4
  no password
```

Step 13 Enter the **write memory** privileged exec command to write the configuration changes into stored memory. Proceed to Step 16.

Step 14 If your password is clear-text (is not encrypted), enter the **show configuration** privileged exec command.

Step 15 If you have lost the enable password, locate the **enable-password** global configuration command entry in the configuration, and record the password.

If you have lost the login password, find the configuration entries for the console line and record the password indicated by the **password** line configuration command. Do not make configuration changes or use the **write memory** command at this time.

Step 16 Power down the router.

Step 17 Return the hardware configuration register DIP switches located on the back panel of the router to their original settings (the settings that you noted in Step 2).

Step 18 Power up the router. Use your new or recovered password to gain access to the router.

Password-Recovery Procedure:
Cisco 500-CS Communication Server

Lost passwords cannot be recovered from Cisco 500-CS communication servers. The only way to recover from a lost password is to return the communication server to its factory default configuration using the Reset button located on the top of the case.

The following procedure describes how to restore the Cisco 500-CS to its default configuration.

CAUTION   When you perform this procedure, your configuration will be lost.

Step 1 Power down the communication server.

Step 2 Press and hold down the Reset button on the top of the case while turning on the power to the communication server.

Step 3 The 500-CS is returned to its factory default configuration.

You must reconfigure the communication server.

Appendixes

Creating Core Dumps

When a router crashes, it is sometimes useful to obtain a full copy of the memory image (called a *core dump*) to identify the cause of the crash. Core dumps are generally very useful to your technical support representative. Not all crash types will produce a core dump. The different crash types are discussed in more details in Appendix B, "Memory Maps."

CAUTION   Use the commands discussed in this appendix only under the direction of a technical support representative. Creating a core dump while the router is functioning in a network can disrupt network operation.

Basic Setup

Four basic ways exist for setting up the router to generate a core dump:

- Using Trivial File Transfer Protocol (TFTP)
- Using File Transfer Protocol (FTP)
- Using remote copy protocol (rcp)
- Using a Flash disk

Using TFTP

If TFTP is used to dump the core file to the TFTP server, the router will dump only the first 16 MB of the core file. This is a limitation of most TFTP applications. Therefore, if your router's main memory is more than 16 MB, do not use TFTP.

The following is the router configuration needed for getting a core dump using TFTP:

```
exception dump a.b.c.d
```

Here, *a.b.c.d* is the IP address of the TFTP server.

The core dump is written to a file named *hostname*-core on the TFTP server, where *hostname* is the name of the router. You can change the name of the core file by adding the **exception core-file** *filename* configuration command.

Depending on the TFTP server application used, it may be necessary to create on the TFTP server the empty target file to which the router can write the core. Also make sure that you have enough memory on your TFTP server to hold the complete core dump.

Using FTP

To configure the router for core dump using FTP, use the following configuration commands:

```
ip ftp usename username
ip ftp password password
exception protocol ftp
exception dump a.b.c.d
```

Here, *a.b.c.d* is the IP address of the FTP server. If the username and password are not configured, the router will attempt anonymous FTP.

Using rcp

Remote copy protocol (rcp) can also be used to capture a core dump. Enabling rcp on a router will not be covered in this appendix. Refer to the Cisco IOS Software Configuration document for configuring rcp.

After rcp is enabled on the router, the following commands must be added to capture the core dump using rcp:

```
exception protocol rcp
exception dump a.b.c.d
```

Here, *a.b.c.d* is the IP address of the host enabled for rcp.

Using a Flash Disk

Some router platforms support the Flash disk as an alternative to the linear Flash memory or PCMCIA Flash card. The large storage capacity of these Flash disks makes them good candidates for another means of capturing core dump. For information on the router platforms and IOS versions that support the Flash disk, refer to the Cisco IOS Release Notes.

The following is the router configuration command needed to set up a core dump using a Flash disk:

```
exception flash <procmem¦iomem¦all> <device_name[:partition_number]> <erase ¦
no_erase>
```

The **show flash all** command will give you a list of devices that you can use for the **exception flash** command.

Advanced Setup

The configuration commands in this section may be used in addition to those described in the "Basic Setup" section.

Exception Memory

During the debugging process, you can cause the router to create a core dump and reboot when certain memory size parameters are violated. The following **exception memory** commands are used to trigger a core dump:

```
exception memory minimum size
```

The previous code is used to define the minimum free memory pool size.

```
exception memory fragment size
```

The previous code is used to define the minimum size of contiguous block of memory in the free pool.

The value of *size* is in bytes and is checked every 60 seconds. If you enter a size that is greater than the free memory, and if the **exception dump** command has been configured, a core dump and router reload is generated after 60 seconds. If the **exception dump** command is not configured, the router reloads without generating a core dump.

Debug Sanity

In some cases, the technical support representative will request that **debug sanity** be enabled when setting up the core dump. This is a hidden command in most IOS releases, but it sometimes is necessary to debug memory corruption. With **debug sanity**, every buffer that is used in the system is sanity-checked when it is allocated and when it is freed.

The **debug sanity** command must be issued in privileged exec mode (enable mode) and involves some CPU utilization. However, it will not significantly affect the router's functionality.

Not all types of crash require **debug sanity** to be enabled. Use this command only when your technical support representative requires it.

To disable **debug sanity**, use the privileged exec command **undebug sanity**.

Testing the Core Dump Setup

When the router is configured for core dump, it may be useful to test whether the setup works.

The IOS provides a special command to test or trigger a core dump:

```
write core
```

Use this command in privileged exec mode (enable mode). This command will cause a crash, and the content of the memory will be dumped accordingly. If it no core dump is generated, the whole setup and config must be reviewed.

CAUTION	The **write core** command will have an impact on a production network. It will cause the router to crash and will prevent it from coming up before dumping the content of its memory. This might take some time, depending on the amount of DRAM present on the router. Use the command with utmost caution.

Memory Maps

This appendix presents memory maps for selected product platforms, processors, and interface cards. Memory map information is useful for technically qualified users who understand concepts of low-level operating systems, bus structures, and address mapping in computer systems.

Troubleshooting Crashes

When a system crashes, the ROM monitor detects the error, prints a message to the console and stores the stack information at the time of the crash. We refer to this crash information as a stack trace, and it is seen from the **show stack** command. This data is overwritten when the system is reloaded, so you might want to check your configuration register settings and decide how you want to recover from system crashes. Stack traces can be used by qualified technical support representatives who have access to symbol tables, object files, and source code needed to decode the stack.

When using this appendix, be aware of the distinct difference between program counter values and operand addresses. Figure B-1 shows part of the **show stack** output to identify these.

Figure B-1   **show stack** *Output Identifying Difference Between Program Counter Values and Operand Addresses*

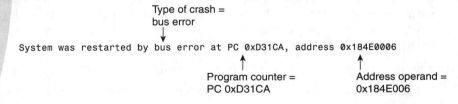

Type of crash =
bus error

System was restarted by bus error at PC 0xD31CA, address 0x184E0006

Program counter =
PC 0xD31CA

Address operand =
0x184E006

NOTE   The addresses that appear in this appendix are operand values and should not be confused
               with program counter values. All memory addresses are in hexadecimal, unless otherwise
               noted.

Memory map information can be useful when you are determining whether a problem
exists in the software or in the hardware. The system software can provide information
about the reasons for a system crash.

Always collect the **show stack**, **show version**, and **show run**, and the **logs**. A **show tech**
output may provide additional information, especially on the Cisco 7500 and 7200 series
platforms.

Types of Crashes and Their Causes

Examples of crash types are listed here:

- Bus error/SegV exception
- Software-forced crash
- Address error
- Watchdog timeout
- Parity error
- Other types

These crashes will be discussed in greater detail in the next sections.

Bus Error/SegV Exception

Bus errors and SegV exceptions are the most common types of crashes. They occur when
the processor tries to access a memory-mapped address that either does not exist (software
error) or does not respond in time (hardware problem). A SegV exception occurs only on
the RISC processors when the memory-mapped address does not exist.

The type of processor (RISC or 68000) is seen using the **show version** command.

Figure B-2 shows the important information that you see in the output of **show version**
taken from two different routers.

Figure B-2 *Important Information from Output of* **show version** *from Two Different Routers*

```
cisco 3640 (R4700) processor (revision 0x00) with 49152K/16384K bytes of memory.
```
            ↑
            The R indicates
            a RISC processor

```
cisco 2500 (68030) processor (revision D) with 8192K/2048K bytes of memory.
```
            ↑
            This indicates
            a non-RISC processor

The address that the processor was trying to access when the system crashed provides some indication as to whether the failure occurred in software or hardware.

For the 68000 processors, if the operand address is a valid physical memory address in the memory map, the problem is probably in the hardware. Bus errors on an address not in the map usually indicate a software bug. Get the **show stack** output decoded.

For the RISC processors, the rule about addressing errors due to hardware when the address is valid doesn't work anymore. This is because some memory regions do not support all types of CPU accesses, and the hardware will correctly return an error if the software incorrectly uses the wrong access mode. On RISC processors, the virtual addresses are used instead of directly accessing the physical addresses. Get confirmation from an experienced engineer before swapping hardware based on an addressing error.

Software-Forced Crash

The router IOS has certain health-checking routines that occur frequently to guard against corruption of various types and infinite loops. If the IOS finds a corruption of data or code in memory or detects that it is stuck in an infinite loop, it will crash itself by calling a crashdump routine to attempt to write a core file. Get the **show stack** output decoded. If the decode indicates a memory corruption, additional data such as a core dump may be needed to identify the cause of the corruption. Refer to Appendix A, "Creating Core Dumps," for more information on setting up a core dump.

Address Error

Address errors occur when the software tries to access data on incorrectly aligned boundaries. For example, 2- and 4-byte accesses are allowed only on even addresses. An address error usually indicates a software bug.

Watchdog Timeout

Cisco processors have timers that guard against certain types of system hangs. The CPU periodically resets a watchdog timer. If the timer is not reset, a trap will occur. Failure to service the watchdog timer indicates either a hardware bug or a software bug.

Parity Error

Parity errors indicate that internal hardware error checks have failed. A parity failure is almost always due to a hardware problem. Use the memory maps listed later in this chapter to identify the affected hardware.

Other Types

There are many other types of crashes, but they are more rare. Some are caused by hardware, and some are caused by code corruption that is stepped on before they are found by the IOS routines. A stack decode mentioned earlier is needed to find the routines that caused the crash.

Memory Maps

The following tables summarize memory map information for the various Cisco platforms:

Table B-1 describes the Cisco 12000-GRP memory map.

Table B-2 describes the Cisco 12000 linecard memory map.

Table B-3 describes the Cisco 8540CSR memory map.

Table B-4 describes the Cisco RSP memory map.

Table B-5 describes the Cisco RSP4 memory map.

Table B-6 describes the Cisco 7000 Series RP memory map.

Table B-7 describes the Cisco 7200 Series NPE memory map.

Table B-8 describes the Cisco 7100 memory map.

Table B-9 describes the Cisco 6400-NRP memory map.

Table B-10 describes the Cisco 6400-NSP memory map.

Table B-11 describes the Cisco 6200 memory map.

Table B-12 describes the Cisco 6260 memory map.

Table B-13 describes the Cisco 4000-M memory map.

Table B-14 describes the Cisco 4500–4700 memory map.

Table B-15 describes the Cisco 3620 memory map.

Table B-16 describes the Cisco 3640 memory map.

Table B-17 describes the Cisco 3660 memory map.

Table B-18 describes the Cisco 2600 memory map.

Table B-19 describes the Cisco 2500 memory map.

Table B-20 describes the Cisco 1720 memory map.

Table B-21 describes the Cisco 1600 memory map.

Table B-22 describes the Cisco 1400 memory map.

Table B-23 describes the Cisco AS5200 memory map.

Table B-24 describes the Cisco AS5300 memory map.

Table B-25 describes the Cisco AS5800 memory map.

Table B-26 describes the Cisco 1000, 1003/1004/1005 memory map.

Table B-27 describes the Cisco VIP2 memory map.

Table B-1: 12000-GRP Memory Map

General MIPS Addressing

Most displayed addresses are virtual addresses, to be interpreted according to a platform's virtual memory map. However, some messages contain physical address, such as write bus error reports. There is no foolproof way to know from an address itself whether it is virtual or physical; knowledge of the display context is required.

Table B-1   *GRP Virtual Memory Map*

Address	Description
bfc00000 to bfc7ffff	Boot PROM
b7000000 to b7ffffff	PCMCIA
a0000000 to a7ffffff	Alternate view of the first 128 MB of DRAM used by ROM monitor
60000000 to 7fffffff	Up to 512 MB of main memory DRAM
3e850000 to 3e857fff	Ethernet interface
3e84a000 to 3e84bfff	Fabric receive registers
3e848000 to 3e849fff	Fabric transmit registers

continues

Table B-1 *GRP Virtual Memory Map (Continued)*

Address	Description
3e840000 to 3e841fff	I/O registers
3e000000 to 3e07ffff	Config NVRAM
38000000 to 39ffffff	Onboard Flash SIMM
28090000 to 28097fff	Fabric interface FPGA
28000000 to 2807ffff	Fabric interface memory

Table B-1a *GRP Physical Memory Map*

Address	Description
60000000 to 7fffffff	Up to 512 MB of main memory DRAM
1fc00000 to 1fc7ffff	Boot PROM
1e850000 to 1e857fff	Ethernet interface
1e84a000 to 1e84bfff	Fabric receive registers
1e848000 to 1e849fff	Fabric transmit registers
1e840000 to 1e841fff	I/O registers
1e000000 to 1e07ffff	Config NVRAM
18000000 to 19ffffff	Onboard Flash SIMM
17000000 to 17ffffff	PCMCIA
08090000 to 08097fff	Fabric interface FPGA
08000000 to 0807ffff	Fabric interface memory
00000000 to 07ffffff	First 128 MB of main memory DRAM

Table B-2: 12000 Linecard Memory Map

Terminology:

FIA—Switch fabric interface ASIC
BMA—Buffer management ASIC
L3—Layer 3 ASIC
MBUS—Maintenance bus
PLIM—Physical Layer Interface Module

Table B-2   *Linecard Virtual Memory Map*

Address	Description
BFC00000 to BFCFFFFF	Boot ROM
A0000000 to B7FFFFFF	Alternate view of the first 128 MB of DRAM used by ROM monitor
80000000 to 87FFFFFF	Alternate view of the first 128 MB of DRAM used by ROM monitor and IOS scheduler
40000000 to 7FFFFFFF	Up to 512 MB of main memory
30000000 to 3FFFFFFF	RX SDRAM (packet memory)
20000000 to 2FFFFFFF	TX SDRAM (packet memory)
12000000 to 17FFFFFF	PLIM address space
11C00000 to 11FFFFFF	MBUS address space
11800000 to 11BFFFFF	RX FIA ASIC address space
11400000 to 117FFFFF	TX FIA ASIC address space
10C00000 to 113FFFFF	RX BMA ASIC address space
10400000 to 10BFFFFF	TX BMA ASIC address space
10000000 to 103FFFFF	L3 ASIC address space

Table B-2a   *Linecard Physical Memory Map*

Address	Description
E0000000 to EFFFFFFF	RX SDRAM (packet memory)
C0000000 to CFFFFFFF	TX SDRAM (packet memory)
40000000 to 7FFFFFFF	Up to 1 GB of main memory
1FC00000 to 1FFFFFFF	Boot ROM
12000000 to 17FFFFFF	PLIM address space
11C00000 to 11FFFFFF	MBUS address space
11800000 to 11BFFFFF	RX FIA ASIC address space
11400000 to 117FFFFF	TX FIA ASIC address space
10C00000 to 113FFFFF	RX BMA ASIC address space
10400000 to 10BFFFFF	TX BMA ASIC address space
10000000 to 103FFFFF	L3 ASIC address space
00000000 to 0FFFFFFF	First 256 MB of main memory (EDO DRAM)

Table B-3: Catalyst 8540CSR Memory Map

Table B-3   *Catalyst 8540CSR Memory Map*

Address Space Name	Byte Address Start End	Length in Bytes	Notes	Function
DRAM	0000 0000 07FF FFFF	128 MB	Alias of address 6000 0000	Serves as the main DRAM that holds data and code
MEMD	0800 0000 08FF FFFF	16 MB	Alias of addresses 4000 0000 and 5000 0000	Holds the message data to/from the CPU and the switch fabric
	0900 0000 0FFF FFFF	112 MB	Invalid address; access will cause bus error or interrupt.	
I/O	1000 0000 1FFF FFFF	256 MB	Alias of address 3000 0000	
Empty	2000 0000 2FFF FFFF	256 MB	Invalid address; access will cause bus error or interrupt.	
I/O	3000 0000 3FFF FFFF	256 MB	Alias of address 1000 0000	
MEMD	4000 0000 40FF FFFF	16 MB	Alias of addresses 0800 0000 and 5000 0000	Holds the message data to/from the CPU and the switch fabric
	4100 0000 4FFF FFFF	240 MB	Invalid address; access will cause bus error or interrupt.	
	5000 0000 50FF FFFF	16 MB	Alias of addresses 0800 0000 and 4000 0000	Holds the message data to/from the CPU and the switch fabric
	5100 0000 5FFF FFFF	240 MB	Invalid address; access will cause bus error or interrupt.	
DRAM	6000 0000 67FF FFFF	128 MB	Alias of address 0000 0000	Serves as the main DRAM that holds data and code
	6800 0000 7FFF FFFF	384 MB	This space not accessible at address 0000 0000	
Empty	8000 0000 FFFF FFFF	2048 MB	Invalid address; access will cause bus error or interrupt.	

Table B-3a *MEMD Space Physical Address Map*

Physical Device	Byte Address Start End	Length in Bytes	Width in Bits	Function
SAR SRAM	0800 0000 080F FFFF	1 MB	64	
None	0810 0000 08DF FFFF	14 MB	64	
CUBI FPGA	08E0 0000 08EF FFFF	1 MB	64	CUBI FPGA control and status registers
CUBI FPGA	08F0 0000 08FF FFFF	1 MB	64	CUBI FPGA control and status registers

Table B-3b *I/O Space Physical Address Map*

Physical Device	Byte Address Start End	Length in Bytes	Width in Bits	Function
None	1000 0000 16FF FFFF			
PCMCIA cards	1700 0000 17FF FFFF	16 MB	16	Access for the contents of the cards plugged into the PCMCIA slots. The exact address at which the cards appear must be programmed via the PCMCIA controller. Card address spaces larger than 16 MB can be used via the windowing scheme that the PCMCIA controller provides.
Flash SIMM	1800 0000 1BFF FFFF	64 MB	32	SIMM socket wired for a single 32-bit-wide Flash SIMM. The wiring supports 32 MB, but what is actually stuffed during production is a customer option. This SIMM holds the boot system image, config, and so on—whatever software wants to put here.
PAM bus	1C00 0000 1CFF FFFF	16 MB	32	See PAM space table.

continues

Table B-3b *I/O Space Physical Address Map (Continued)*

Physical Device	Byte Address Start End	Length in Bytes	Width in Bits	Function
SWC bus	1D00 0000 1DFF FFFF	16 MB	16	See SWC space table.
NVRAM	1E00 0000 1E07 FFFE	512 K-1	8	Nonvolatile static RAM used for whatever software wants.
Time of day	1E07 FFFF	1	1	The NVRAM provides a TOD function that is read through the same address space as the NVRAM.
None	1E08 0000 1E83 FFFF			
Tiger ASIC	1E84 0000 1E84 00FF	256	16	Tiger control and status registers.
CIDR FPGA	1E84 0100 1E84 02FF	512	16	Various control and status registers.
None	1E84 0300 1E84 03DF			
PCMCIA controller	1E84 03E0 (index) 1E84 03E1 (data)	2	8	Control and status registers for configuring the PCMCIA slots. This is one of those lovely chips where you write an index register and then access a data register that uses the index register as the address.
None	1E84 03E2 1E84 03FF			
DUART	1E84 0400 1E84 047F	128	8	Dual UART for console port and out-of-band RP to RP communications.
None	1E84 0480 1E84 FFFF			
Ethernet controller	1E85 0000 1E85 FFFF	64 KB	16	10-Mbps Ethernet interface.
Ethernet SRAM	1E86 0000 1E87 FFFF	128 KB	32	

Table B-3b   *I/O Space Physical Address Map (Continued)*

Physical Device	Byte Address Start End	Length in Bytes	Width in Bits	Function
Network clock module	1E88 0000 1E88 00FF	256	8	
None	1E88 0100 1FBF FFFF			
Boot Flash PROM	1FC0 0000 1FC7 FFFF	512 KB	8	Holder for R5000 initial start-up code. This part is a Flash part and can be rewritten in system.
None	1FC8 0000 1FFF FFFF			

Table B-4: RSP Memory Map

Table B-4   *RSP Memory Map*

Address	Bit Width	Description
80000000 to FFFFFFFF		Available for expansion
60000000 to 77FFFFFF		Main memory
		Common
40000000 to 5FFFFFFF		Packet memory canonical address bit ordering bits in byte-swapped packet memory
		Common
38000000 to 3FFFFFFF		Boot EPROM and I/O space
30000000 to 37FFFFFF		System Flash memory
20000000 to 2FFFFFFF		Reserved platform-specific address space
18000000 to 1FFFFFFF		Boot EPROM and I/O space
10000000 to 17FFFFFF		System Flash memory
08000000 to 0FFFFFFF		Packet memory
00000000 to 07FFFFFF		Main memory
Individual addresses:		
11110000	16	System control
11110100	32	System status
11120000	8	Counter timer
11120040	8	Counter control register

continues

Table B-4 *RSP Memory Map (Continued)*

Address	Bit Width	Description
11120100-1112013F	8	Serial I/O ports
11120200	16	Environmental monitor control
11120300	32	Environmental monitor status
1115FFFF	1	Calendar (1 bit "bit 0")
111104000	8	Flash card status
Virtual address:		
E00000		Slot 0
E20000		Slot 1
E40000		Slot 2
E60000		Slot 3
E80000		Slot 4
EA0000		Slot 5
EC0000		Slot 6
EE0000		Slot 7
F00000		Slot 8
F20000		Slot 9
F40000		Slot 10
F60000		Slot 11
F80000		Slot 12

Table B-5: RSP4 Memory Map

Table B-5 *RSP4 Memory Map*

Memory Base	Memory Limit	Size	Device
0x0000 0000	0x07FF FFFF	Up to 128 Mb	Main memory
0x0800 0000	0x0F00 0000	Up to 128 Mb	Packet memory
0x1000 0000	0x16FF FFFF		System Flash memory
0x1700 0000	0x17FF FFFF		PCMCIA slots
0x1800 0000	0x1BFF FFFF		RxBootFlash
0x1C00 0000	0x1DFF FFFF		SLOT I/O
0x1E00 0000	0x1E7F FFFF		NVRAM

Table B-5   *RSP4 Memory Map (Continued)*

Memory Base	Memory Limit	Size	Device
0x1E80 0000	0x1EFF FFFF		I/O registers
0x1F00 0000	0x1FFF FFFF		BootPROM
0x2000 0000	0x2FFF FFFF		Reserved——Platform-specific address space
0x3000 0000	0x37FF FFFF	128 Mb	System Flash memory
0x3800 0000	0x3FFF FFFF		BootEPROM and I/O space
0x4000 0000	0x5FFF FFFF		Packet memory
0x6000 0000	0x7FFF FFFF		Main memory
0x8000 0000	0xFFFF FFFF		Available for expansion

Table B-6: Cisco 7000 Series RP Memory Map

Table B-6   *Cisco 7000 Series RP Memory Map*

Address	Bit Width	Description	Comments
00000000 to 0FFFFFFF		DRAM	
10000000 to 100FFFFF		ROML	
10400000 to 104FFFFF		ROMU	
11000000 to 110FFFFF		Multibus memory	
11100000 to 1110FFFF		Multibus I/O	
11110000 to 1112FFFF		Local I/O	
11130000 to 11130FFF		Diagnostic bus	
11131000 to 111314FF		ID PROM	
11140000 to 1115FFFF		NVRAM	
12000000 to 13FFFFFF		Internal Flash memory	
14000000 to 15FFFFFF		External Flash memory card	
11110000	16	System control	
11110100	32	System status register	
11110400		Flash memory card status	
11110C00		I/O address base	SwitchBus address space. Each unit occupies 64 bytes (0x40)
11120000	8	Counter timer	

continues

Table B-6 *Cisco 7000 Series RP Memory Map (Continued)*

Address	Bit Width	Description	Comments
11120040	8	Counter control register	
11120100 to 1112013F	8	Serial I/O ports	
11120200		Environmental monitor control	16 bits
11120300		Environmental monitor status	32 bits
11130000		Diagnostic bus	
11131000		ID PROM	
11140000		NVRAM	
1115FC00		Environmental monitor NVRAM base address	
1115FFFF	1	Real-time calendar bit	1 bit (bit 0)
11200000 to 11FFFFFF		Reserved	14 MB reserved
12000000		Onboard Flash memory	
14000000		External Flash memory	

Table B-7: Cisco 7200 Series NPE Memory Map

Table B-7 *Cisco 7200 Series NPE Memory Map*

Base	Until	Size	Device	Bus
0x0 0000 0000	0x0 07FF FFFF	128 MB	System DRAM	
0x0 0800 0000	0x0 0FFF FFFF	128 MB	System DRAM (rsvd)	
0x0 1000 0000	0x0 13FF FFFF	62 MB	Reserved	
0x0 1400 0000	0x0 141F FFFF	2 MB	GT-64010 registers	
0x0 1420 0000	0x0 19FF FFFF	94 MB	Reserved	
0x0 1A00 0000	0x0 1A3F FFFF	4 MB	Internal Flash SIMM	I/O
0x0 1A40 0000	0x0 1BFF FFFF	28 MB	Reserved: more Flash	I/O
0x0 1C00 0000	0x0 1DFF FFFF	32 MB	Reserved	
0x0 1E00 0000	0x0 1E1F FFFF	2 MB	NVRAM	I/O
0x0 1E20 0000	0x0 1E7F FFFF	6 MB	Reserved	
0x0 1E80 0000	0x0 1E9F FFFF	2 MB	I/O registers	I/O
0x0 1EA0 0000	0x0 1EFF FFFF	6 MB	Reserved	

Table B-7   *Cisco 7200 Series NPE Memory Map (Continued)*

Base	Until	Size	Device	Bus
0x0 1F00 0000	0x0 1FBF FFFF	12 MB	Reserved	
0x0 1FC0 0000	0x0 1FDF FFFF	2 MB	Boot EPROM	
0x0 1FE0 0000	0x0 3FFF FFFF	x MB	Reserved	
0x0 4000 0000	0x0 43FF FFFF	64 MB	PCI-to-PCMCIA interface (top slot)	
0x0 4400 0000	0x0 47FF FFFF	64 MB	PCI-to-PCMCIA interface (bottom slot)	
0x0 4800 0000	0x0 487F FFFF	8 MB	Fast Ethernet—memory-mapped I/O	
0x0 4880 0000	0x0 48FF FFFF	8 MB	PA1 memory-mapped I/O	
0x0 4900 0000	0x0 497F FFFF	8 MB	PA3 memory-mapped I/O	
0x0 4800 0000	0x0 49FF FFFF	8 MB	PA5 memory-mapped I/O	
0x0 4A00 0000	0x0 4A7F FFFF	8 MB	PA7 memory-mapped I/O	
0x0 4A80 0000	0x0 4AFF FFFF	8 MB	PA9 memory-mapped I/O	
0x0 4B00 0000	0x0 4B0F FFFF	1 MB	PCI PM, first 1 M, no byte swap	
0x0 4B10 0000	0x0 4B7F FFFF	7 MB	PCI PM, larger PM, no swap (rsvd)	
0x0 4B80 0000	0x0 4B8F FFFF	1 MB	PCI PM, first 1 M, byte swap	
0x0 4B90 0000	0x0 4BFF FFFF	7 MB	PCI PM, larger PM, byte swap (rsvd)	
0x0 4C00 0000	0x0 4C0F FFFF	1 MB	PCI alias, first 1 M, no byte swap	
0x0 4C10 0000	0x0 4C7F FFFF	7 MB	PCI alias, larger PM, no swap (rsvd)	
0x0 4C80 0000	0x0 4C8F FFFF	1 MB	PCI alias, first 1M, byte swap	
0x0 4C90 0000	0x0 4CFF FFFF	7 MB	PCI alias, larger PM, byte swap (rsvd)	
0x0 4D00 0000	0x0 4D7F FFFF	8 MB	PA2 memory-mapped IO	
0x0 4D80 0000	0x0 4DFF FFFF	8 MB	PA4 memory-mapped IO	
0x0 4E00 0000	0x0 4E7F FFFF	8 MB	PA6 memory-mapped IO	
0x0 4E80 0000	0x0 4EFF FFFF	8 MB	PA8 memory-mapped IO (rsvd)	
0x0 4F00 0000	0x0 4F7F FFFF	8 MB	PA10 memory-mapped IO (rsvd)	
0x0 4F80 0000	0x0 4FFF FFFF	8 MB	IO assy memory-mapped IO (rsvd)	
0x0 5000 0000	0x0 FFFF FFFF	x MB	Reserved	
0x1 0000 0000	0x0 001F FFFF	2 MB	PCI I/O address space	
0x1 0020 0000	0x1 4B7F FFFF	About 1 GB	Reserved	
0x1 4B00 0000	0x1 4B0F FFFF	1 MB	CPU PM, first 1M, no byte swap	

continues

Table B-7 *Cisco 7200 Series NPE Memory Map (Continued)*

Base	Until	Size	Device	Bus
0x1 4B10 0000	0x1 4B7F FFFF	7 MB	CPU PM, larger PM, no swap (rsvd)	
0x1 4B80 0000	0x1 FFFF FFFF	About 0 GB	Reserved	
0x2 0000 0000	0x3 FFFF FFFF	8 GB	L2 cache disabled (alias) for low 8 GB	
0x4 0000 0000	0x7 FFFF FFFF	16 GB	Cache controller tag Op 0	
0x8 0000 0000	0xF FFFF FFFF	32 GB	Cache controller tag Op 1	

Table B-7a *Cisco 7200 NPE-200 Memory Map*

Base	Until	Size	Device	Bus
0x0 0000 0000	0x0 07FF FFFF	128 MB	System DRAM	
0x0 0000 0000	0x0 0FFF FFFF	128 MB	System DRAM (rsvd)	
0x0 1000 0000	0x0 13FF FFFF	62 MB	Reserved	
0x0 1400 0000	0x0 141F FFFF	2 MB	GT-64010 registers	
0x0 1420 0000	0x0 19FF FFFF	94 MB	Reserved	
0x0 1A00 0000	0x0 1A3F FFFF	4 MB	Internal Flash SIMM	
0x0 1A40 0000	0x0 1BFF FFFF	28 MB	Larger Flash SIMM (rsvd)	
0x0 1C00 0000	0x0 1D00 0000	32 MB	Reserved	
0x0 1E00 0000	0x0 1E1F FFFF	2 MB	NVRAM (TOD)	
0x0 1E20 0000	0x0 1E7F FFFF	6 MB	Reserved	
0x0 1E80 0000	0x0 1E9F FFFF	2 MB	I/O registers	
0x0 1EA0 0000	0x0 1EFF FFFF	6 MB	Reserved	
0x0 1F00 0000	0x0 1FBF FFFF	12 MB	Bit bucket (read/write null)	
0x0 1FC0 0000	0x0 1FDF FFFF	2 MB	Boot EPROM	
0x0 1FE0 0000	0x0 3FFF FFFF	x MB	Reserved	
0x0 4000 0000	0x0 43FF FFFF	64 MB	PCI-to-PCMCIA interface (top slot)	
0x0 4400 0000	0x0 47FF FFFF	64 MB	PCI-to-PCMCIA interface (bottom slot)	
0x0 4800 0000	0x0 487F FFFF	8 MB	Fast Ethernet——memory-mapped IO	
0x0 4880 0000	0x0 48FF FFFF	8 MB	PA1 memory-mapped IO	
0x0 4900 0000	0x0 497F FFFF	8 MB	PA3 memory-mapped IO	

Table B-7a   *Cisco 7200 NPE-200 Memory Map (Continued)*

Base	Until	Size	Device	Bus
0x0 4980 0000	0x0 49FF FFFF	8 MB	PA5 memory-mapped IO	
0x0 4A00 0000	0x0 4A7F FFFF	8 MB	PA7 memory-mapped IO (rsvd)	
0x0 4A80 0000	0x0 4AFF FFFF	8 MB	PA9 memory-mapped IO (rsvd)	
0x0 4B00 0000	0x0 4B3F FFFF	4 MB	PCI PM, first 4 M, no byte swap	
0x0 4B40 0000	0x0 4B7F FFFF	4 MB	PCI PM, larger PM, no swap (rsvd)	
0x0 4B80 0000	0x0 4BBF FFFF	4 MB	PCI PM, first 4 M, byte swap	
0x0 4BC0 0000	0x0 4BFF FFFF	4 MB	PCI PM, larger PM, byte swap (rsvd)	
0x0 4C00 0000	0x0 4C3F FFFF	4 MB	PCI alias PM, first 4 M, no byte swap	
0x0 4C40 0000	0x0 4C7F FFFF	4 MB	PCI alias PM, larger PM, no swap (rsvd)	
0x0 4C80 0000	0x0 4CBF FFFF	4 MB	PCI alias PM, first 4 M, byte swap	
0x0 4CC0 0000	0x0 4CFF FFFF	4 MB	PCI alias PM, larger PM, byte swap (rsvd)	
0x0 4D00 0000	0x0 4D7F FFFF	8 MB	PA2 memory-mapped IO	
0x0 4D80 0000	0x0 4DFF FFFF	8 MB	PA4 memory-mapped IO	
0x0 4E00 0000	0x0 4E7F FFFF	8 MB	PA6 memory-mapped IO	
0x0 4E80 0000	0x0 4EFF FFFF	8 MB	PA8 memory-mapped IO (rsvd)	
0x0 4F00 0000	0x0 4F7F FFFF	8 MB	PA10 memory-mapped IO (rsvd)	
0x0 4F80 0000	0x0 4FFF FFFF	8 MB	IO assy memory-mapped IO (rsvd)	
0x0 5000 0000	0x0 FFFF FFFF	x MB	Reserved	
0x1 0000 0000	0x0 001F FFFF	2 MB	PCI I/O address space	
0x1 0020 0000	0x1 4B7F FFFF	About 1 GB	Reserved	
0x1 4B00 0000	0x1 4B3F FFFF	4 MB	CPU PM, first 4 M, no byte swap	
0x1 4B40 0000	0x1 4B7F FFFF	4 MB	CPU PM, larger PM, no swap (rsvd)	
0x1 4B80 0000	0x1 FFFF FFFF	About 0 GB	Reserved	
0x2 0000 0000	0x3 FFFF FFFF	8 GB	L2 cache disabled (alias) for low 8 GB	
0x4 0000 0000	0x7 FFFF FFFF	16 GB	Cache controller tag Op 0	
0x8 0000 0000	0xF FFFF FFFF	32 GB	Cache controller tag Op 1	

Table B-7b *Cisco 7200 NPE-300 Memory Map*

Base	Until	Size	Device	Bus
0x0 0000 0000	0x0 0FFF FFFF	256 MB	System SDRAM; configurable	
0x0 1000 0000	0x0 13FF FFFF	64 MB	Reserved	
0x0 1400 0000	0x0 141F FFFF	2 MB	GT-64120 registers	
0x0 1420 0000	0x0 14FF FFFF	14 MB	Reserved	
0x0 1500 0000	0x0 151F FFFF	2 MB	GT-64120 registers	
0x0 1520 0000	0x0 19FF FFFF	78 MB	Reserved	
0x0 1A00 0000	0x0 1A3F FFFF	4 MB	Internal Flash SIMM	
0x0 1A40 0000	0x0 1BFF FFFF	28 MB	Larger Flash SIMM (rsvd)	
0x0 1C00 0000	0x0 1D00 0000	32 MB	Reserved	
0x0 1E00 0000	0x0 1E1F FFFF	2 MB	NVRAM (TOD)	
0x0 1E20 0000	0x0 1E7F FFFF	6 MB	Reserved	
0x0 1E80 0000	0x0 1E9F FFFF	2 MB	I/O registers	
0x0 1EA0 0000	0x0 1EFF FFFF	6 MB	Reserved	
0x0 1F00 0000	0x0 1FBF FFFF	12 MB	Bit bucket (read/write null)	
0x0 1FC0 0000	0x0 1FDF FFFF	2 MB	Boot EPROM	
0x0 1FE0 0000	0x0 1FFF FFFF	2 MB	Reserved	
0x0 2000 0000	0x0 21FF FFFF	32 MB	System SDRAM (I/O memory); fixed	
0x0 2200 0000	0x0 2FFF FFFF	224 MB	System SDRAM (rsvd)	
0x0 3000 0000	0x0 3FFF FFFF	256 MB	Reserved	
0x0 4000 0000	0x0 43FF FFFF	64 MB	PCI-to-PCMCIA interface (top slot)	
0x0 4400 0000	0x0 47FF FFFF	64 MB	PCI-to-PCMCIA interface (bottom slot)	
0x0 4800 0000	0x0 487F FFFF	8 MB	I/O card Fast Ethernet——memory-mapped IO	
0x0 4880 0000	0x0 48FF FFFF	8 MB	PA1 memory-mapped IO	
0x0 4900 0000	0x0 497F FFFF	8 MB	PA3 memory-mapped IO	
0x0 4980 0000	0x0 49FF FFFF	8 MB	PA5 memory-mapped IO	
0x0 4A00 0000	0x0 4A7F FFFF	8 MB	PA7 memory-mapped IO (rsvd)	
0x0 4A80 0000	0x0 4AFF FFFF	8 MB	PA9 memory-mapped IO (rsvd)	
0x0 4B00 0000	0x0 4CFF FFFF	32 MB	Reserved	

Table B-7b *Cisco 7200 NPE-300 Memory Map (Continued)*

Base	Until	Size	Device	Bus
0x0 4D00 0000	0x0 4D7F FFFF	8 MB	PA2 memory-mapped IO	
0x0 4D80 0000	0x0 4DFF FFFF	8 MB	PA4 memory-mapped IO	
0x0 4E00 0000	0x0 4E7F FFFF	8 MB	PA6 memory-mapped IO	
0x0 4E80 0000	0x0 4EFF FFFF	8 MB	PA8 memory-mapped IO (rsvd)	
0x0 4F00 0000	0x0 4F7F FFFF	8 MB	PA10 memory-mapped IO (rsvd)	
0x0 4F80 0000	0x0 4FFF FFFF	8 MB	IO assy memory-mapped IO (rsvd)	
0x0 5000 0000	0x0 BFFF FFFF	1792 MB	Reserved	
0x0 C000 0000	0x0 CFFF FFFF	256 MB	Lower system SDRAM, PCI byte swapped	
0x0 D000 0000	0x0 DFFF FFFF	256 MB	Reserved	
0x0 E000 0000	0x0 EFFF FFFF	256 MB	Upper system SDRAM, PCI byte swapped	
0x0 F000 0000	0x0 FFFF FFFF	256 MB	Reserved	
0x1 0000 0000	0x1 001F FFFF	2 MB	PCI I/O address space	
0x1 0020 0000	0xF FFFF FFFF		Reserved	

Table B-7c *Cisco 7200 NPE-175 Memory Map*

Base	Until	Size	Device	Bus
0x0 0000 0000	0x0 0FFF FFFF	256 MB	System SDRAM and packet memory	
0x0 1000 0000	0x0 13FF FFFF	64 MB	Reserved	
0x0 1400 0000	0x0 141F FFFF	2 MB	GT-64120 registers	
0x0 1420 0000	0x0 14FF FFFF	14 MB	Reserved	
0x0 1A00 0000	0x0 1A3F FFFF	4 MB	Internal Flash SIMM	
0x0 1A40 0000	0x0 1BFF FFFF	28 MB	Larger Flash SIMM (rsvd)	
0x0 1C00 0000	0x0 1DFF FFFF	32 MB	Reserved	
0x0 1E00 0000	0x0 1E1F FFFF	2 MB	NVRAM (TOD)	
0x0 1E20 0000	0x0 1E7F FFFF	6 MB	Reserved	
0x0 1E80 0000	0x0 1E9F FFFF	2 MB	I/O registers	
0x0 1EA0 0000	0x0 1EFF FFFF	6 MB	Reserved	

continues

Table B-7c *Cisco 7200 NPE-175 Memory Map (Continued)*

Base	Until	Size	Device	Bus
0x0 1F00 0000	0x0 1FBF FFFF	12 MB	Bit bucket (read/write null)	
0x0 1FC0 0000	0x0 1FDF FFFF	2 MB	Boot EPROM	
0x0 1FE0 0000	0x0 1FFF FFFF	2 MB	Reserved	
0x0 2000 0000	0x0 2FFF FFFF	256 MB	Reserved	
0x0 3000 0000	0x0 3FFF FFFF	256 MB	Reserved	
0x0 4000 0000	0x0 43FF FFFF	64 MB	PCI-to-PCMCIA interface (top slot)	
0x0 4400 0000	0x0 47FF FFFF	64 MB	PCI-to-PCMCIA interface (bottom slot)	
0x0 4800 0000	0x0 487F FFFF	8 MB	Fast Ethernet—memory-mapped IO	
0x0 4880 0000	0x0 48FF FFFF	8 MB	PA1 memory-mapped IO	
0x0 4900 0000	0x0 497F FFFF	8 MB	PA3 memory-mapped IO	
0x0 4980 0000	0x0 49FF FFFF	8 MB	PA5 memory-mapped IO	
0x0 4A00 0000	0x0 4A7F FFFF	8 MB	PA7 memory-mapped IO (rsvd)	
0x0 4A80 0000	0x0 4AFF FFFF	8 MB	PA9 memory-mapped IO (rsvd)	
0x0 4B00 0000	0x0 4CFF FFFF	32 MB	Reserved	
0x0 4D00 0000	0x0 4D7F FFFF	8 MB	PA2 memory-mapped IO	
0x0 4D80 0000	0x0 4DFF FFFF	8 MB	PA4 memory-mapped IO	
0x0 4E00 0000	0x0 4E7F FFFF	8 MB	PA6 memory-mapped IO	
0x0 4E80 0000	0x0 4EFF FFFF	8 MB	PA8 memory-mapped IO (rsvd)	
0x0 4F00 0000	0x0 4F7F FFFF	8 MB	PA10 memory-mapped IO (rsvd)	
0x0 4F80 0000	0x0 4FFF FFFF	8 MB	IO assy memory-mapped IO (rsvd)	
0x0 5000 0000	0x0 7FFF FFFF	768 MB	Reserved	
0x0 8000 0000	0x0 8FFF FFFF	256 MB	System SDRAM, PCI byte swapped	
0x0 9000 0000	0x0 9FFF FFFF	256 MB	Reserved	
0x0 A000 0000	0x0 AFFF FFFF	256 MB	Reserved	
0x0 B000 0000	0x0 FFFF FFFF	1280 MB	Reserved	
0x1 0000 0000	0x1 001F FFFF	2 MB	PCI I/O address space	
0x1 0020 0000	0x1 FFFF FFFF	2MB	Reserved	

Table B-7d   *Cisco 7200 NPE-225 Memory Map*

Base	Until	Size	Device	Bus
0x0 0000 0000	0x0 0FFF FFFF	256 MB	System SDRAM and packet memory	
0x0 1000 0000	0x0 13FF FFFF	64 MB	Reserved	
0x0 1400 0000	0x0 141F FFFF	2 MB	GT-64120 registers	
0x0 1420 0000	0x0 19FF FFFF	14 MB	Reserved	
0x0 1A00 0000	0x0 1A3F FFFF	4 MB	Internal Flash SIMM	
0x0 1A40 0000	0x0 1BFF FFFF	28 MB	Larger Flash SIMM (rsvd)	
0x0 1C00 0000	0x0 1D00 0000	32 MB	Reserved	
0x0 1E00 0000	0x0 1E1F FFFF	2 MB	NVRAM (TOD)	
0x0 1E20 0000	0x0 1E7F FFFF	6 MB	Reserved	
0x0 1E80 0000	0x0 1E9F FFFF	2 MB	I/O registers	
0x0 1EA0 0000	0x0 1EFF FFFF	6 MB	Reserved	
0x0 1F00 0000	0x0 1FBF FFFF	12 MB	Bit bucket (read/write null)	
0x0 1FC0 0000	0x0 1FDF FFFF	2 MB	Boot EPROM	
0x0 1FE0 0000	0x0 1FFF FFFF	2 MB	Reserved	
0x0 2000 0000	0x0 2FFF FFFF	256 MB	Reserved	
0x0 3000 0000	0x0 3FFF FFFF	256 MB	Reserved	
0x0 4000 0000	0x0 43FF FFFF	64 MB	PCI-to-PCMCIA interface (top slot)	
0x0 4400 0000	0x0 47FF FFFF	64 MB	PCI-to-PCMCIA interface (bottom slot)	
0x0 4800 0000	0x0 487F FFFF	8 MB	Fast Ethernet——memory-mapped IO	
0x0 4880 0000	0x0 48FF FFFF	8 MB	PA1 memory-mapped IO	
0x0 4900 0000	0x0 497F FFFF	8 MB	PA3 memory-mapped IO	
0x0 4980 0000	0x0 49FF FFFF	8 MB	PA5 memory-mapped IO	
0x0 4A00 0000	0x0 4A7F FFFF	8 MB	PA7 memory-mapped IO (rsvd)	
0x0 4A80 0000	0x0 4AFF FFFF	8 MB	PA9 memory-mapped IO (rsvd)	
0x0 4B00 0000	0x0 4CFF FFFF	32 MB	Reserved	
0x0 4D00 0000	0x0 4D7F FFFF	8 MB	PA2 memory-mapped IO	
0x0 4D80 0000	0x0 4DFF FFFF	8 MB	PA4 memory-mapped IO	
0x0 4E00 0000	0x0 4E7F FFFF	8 MB	PA6 memory-mapped IO	
0x0 4E80 0000	0x0 4EFF FFFF	8 MB	PA8 memory-mapped IO (rsvd)	
0x0 4F00 0000	0x0 4F7F FFFF	8 MB	PA10 memory-mapped IO (rsvd)	

continues

Table B-7d *Cisco 7200 NPE-225 Memory Map (Continued)*

Base	Until	Size	Device	Bus
0x0 4F80 0000	0x0 4FFF FFFF	8 MB	IO assy memory-mapped IO (rsvd)	
0x0 5000 0000	0x0 7FFF FFFF	768 MB	Reserved	
0x0 8000 0000	0x0 8FFF FFFF	256 MB	System SDRAM, PCI byte swapped	
0x0 9000 0000	0x0 9FFF FFFF	256 MB	Reserved	
0x0 A000 0000	0x0 AFFF FFFF	256 MB	Reserved	
0x0 B000 0000	0x0 FFFF FFFF	256 MB	Reserved	
0x1 0000 0000	0x1 001F FFFF	2 MB	PCI I/O address space	
0x1 0020 0000	0xF FFFF FFFF		Reserved	

Table B-8: Cisco 7100 Memory Map

Table B-8 *Cisco 7100 Memory Map*

Memory Base	Memory Limit	Size	Device
0x0 0000 0000	0x0 0FFF FFFF	256 MB	Reserved
0x0 1000 0000	0x0 13FF FFFF	62 MB	Reserved
0x0 1400 0000	>0x0 141F FFFF	2 MB	GT-64120 registers
0x0 1420 0000	0x0 19FF FFFF	94 MB	Reserved
0x0 1A00 0000	0x0 1A3F FFFF	4 MB	Internal Flash SIMM
0x0 1A40 0000	0x0 1BFF FFFF	28 MB	Larger Flash SIMM (rsvd)
0x0 1C00 0000	0x0 1DFF FFFF	32 MB	Reserved
0x0 1E00 0000	0x0 1E3F FFFF	4 MB	NVRAM (first socket)
0x0 1E40 0000	0x0 1E47 FFFF	512 KB	NVRAM/TOD (second socket)
0x0 1E48 0000	0x0 1E7F FFFF		Reserved
0x0 1E80 0000	0x0 1E9F FFFF	2 MB	I/O registers
0x0 1EA0 0000	0x0 1EFF FFFF	6 MB	Reserved
0x0 1F00 0000	0x0 1FBF FFFF	12 MB	Bit bucket (read/write null)
0x0 1FC0 0000	0x0 1FDF FFFF	2 MB	Boot EPROM
0x0 1FE0 0000	0x0 1FFF FFFF	x MB	Reserved

Table B-8 *Cisco 7100 Memory Map (Continued)*

Memory Base	Memory Limit	Size	Device
0x0 4D00 0000	0x0 4E7F FFFF	24M	L0 local PCI bus
0x0 4D00 0000	0x0 4D7F FFFF	8 MB	Slot 1, WAN adapter 1
0x0 4D80 0000	0x0 4DFF FFFF	8 MB	Slot 3, port adapter 1
0x0 4E00 0000	0x0 4E7F FFFF	8 MB	Slot 5, service adapter
0x0 4000 0000	0x0 497F FFFF	24M	L1 local PCI bus
0x0 4000 0000	0x0 47FF FFFF	128 MB	Slot 0, PCMCIA
0x0 4800 0000	0x0 487F FFFF	8 MB	Slot 0, FE0, FE1
0x0 4880 0000	0x0 48FF FFFF	8 MB	Slot 2, WAN adapter 2
0x0 4900 0000	0x0 497F FFFF	8 MB	Slot 4, port adapter 2
0x0 5000 0000	0x0 5FFF FFFF	512 MB	Reserved
			Packet SDRAM
0x0 6000 0000	0x067FF FFFF	128 MB	Packet SDRAM
0x0 6800 0000	0x0 7FFF FFFF	384 MB	Packet SDRAM reserved
			Code/data SDRAM
			Code/data SDRAM
			Code/data SDRAM reserved
0x0 5000 0000	0x0FFFF FFFF	2816 MB	Reserved
0x1 0000 0000	0x0 001F FFFF	2 MB	PCI I/O address space

Table B-9: Cisco 6400-NRP Memory Map

Four categories of devices exist: device reserved, memory reserved, undefined, and I/O reserved. A processor reference to a reserved location will generate either a bus error (on a read) or a system controller interrupt (on a write). Both of these are sourced from the system controller. A processor reference to an undefined location will silently return undefined data on a read or will silently accept data on a write. Writing to an undefined location may generate an undesired side effect. Accessing an I/O reserved location will generate an I/O address error interrupt for either a read or a write. Note that the Rev 1 board memory maps have been copied to the end of the document until the Rev 2 boards are functional and have replaced the Rev 1 boards. All registers are big-endian.

Table B-9 *Cisco 6400-NRP Memory Map*

Memory Base	Memory Limit	Size	Device
0x0 0000 0000	0x0 07FF FFFF	128 MB	System DRAM
0x0 0800 0000	0x0 13FF FFFF	128 MB	Reserved
0x0 1400 0000	0x0 141F FFFF	2 MB	Galileo GT-64010A registers
0x0 1420 0000	0x0 19FF FFFF	94 MB	Reserved
0x0 1A00 0000	0x0 1AFF FFFF	16 MB	Flash SIMM
0x0 1B00 0000	0x0 1BFF FFFF	16 MB	Undefined (decodes to Flash SIMM socket)
0x0 1C00 0000	0x0 1C1F FFFF	2 MB	I/O space
0x0 1C20 0000	0x0 1DFF FFFF	30 MB	Undefined
0x0 1E00 0000	0x0 1E1F FFFF	2 MB	NVRAM (TOD)
0x0 1E20 0000	0x0 1E7F FFFF	6 MB	Reserved
0x0 1E80 0000	0x0 1EBF FFFF	4 MB	Boot Flash
0x0 1EA0 0000	0x0 1FBF FFFF	18 MB	Reserved
0x0 1FC0 0000	0x0 1FDF FFFF	2 MB	Boot EPROM space
0x0 1FE0 0000	0x0 47FF FFFF	642 MB	Reserved
0x0 4800 0000	0x0 487F FFFF	8 MB	BPE Ethernet controller
0x0 4880 0000	0x0 48FF FFFF	8 MB	NME Ethernet controller
0x0 4900 0000	0x0 497F FFFF	8 MB	CSE Ethernet controller
0x0 4980 0000	0x0 49FF FFFF	8 MB	Undefined (PCI bus timeout)
0x0 4A00 0000	0x0 4A7F FFFF	8 MB	SAR
0x0 4A80 0000	0x0 4AFF FFFF	8 MB	Undefined (PCI bus timeout)
0x0 4B00 0000	0x0 4B3F FFFF	4 MB	PCI packet memory, no byte swap
0x0 4B40 0000	0x0 4B7F FFFF	4 MB	Undefined (PCI bus timeout)
0x0 4B80 0000	0x0 4BBF FFFF	4 MB	PCI packet memory, byte swap
0x0 4BC0 0000	0x0 4BFF FFFF	4 MB	Undefined (PCI bus timeout)
0x0 4C00 0000	0x0 5FFF FFFF	320 MB	Reserved
0x0 6000 0000	0x0 601F FFFF	2 MB	PCI I/O address space

Table B-9   *Cisco 6400-NRP Memory Map (Continued)*

Memory Base	Memory Limit	Size	Device
0x0 6020 0000	0x0 BFFF FFFF	About 1.5 GB	Reserved
0x0 C000 0000	0x0 C7FF FFFF	128 MB	PCI bus access to DRAM with byte swap
0x0 C800 0000	0x1 4AFF FFFF	About 2 GB	Reserved
0x1 4B00 0000	0x1 4B3F FFFF	4 MB	CPU packet memory, no byte swap
0x1 4B40 0000	0x1 8AFF FFFF	About 1 GB	Reserved
0x1 8B00 0000	0x1 8C3F FFFF	4 MB	L2 cache tag test range (Valid only when the L2 cache tag test bit of the control register is set. Otherwise, this space is reserved.)
0x1 8C40 0000	0x1 FFFF FFFF	About 2 GB	Reserved
0x2 0000 0000	0x3 FFFF FFFF	8 GB	L2 cache disabled alias for memory space
0x4 0000 0000	0x7 FFFF FFFF	16 GB	L2 cache controller tag Op 0 (invalidate entry, no writeback) TagOp[0]:1, TagOp[1]: 0
0x8 0000 0000	0xF FFFF FFFF	32 GB	L2 cache controller tag Op 1 (flush all entries, no writeback) TagOp[0]:0, TagOp[1]: 1

Table B-9a   *System Memory Map Detailed*

Memory Base	Memory Limit	Size	Device
0x0 0000 0000	0x0 07FF FFFF	128 MB	System DRAM
0x0 0800 0000	0x0 13FF FFFF	128 MB	Reserved
0x0 1400 0000	0x0 141F FFFF	2 MB	Galileo GT-64010A registers
0x0 1400 0000	0x0 1400 0007	8 bytes	CPU interface configuration
0x0 1400 0008	0x0 1400 000F	8 bytes	RAS[1:0] low decode address
0x0 1400 0010	0x0 1400 0017	8 bytes	RAS[1:0] high decode address
0x0 1400 0018	0x0 1400 001F	8 bytes	RAS[3:2] low decode address
0x0 1400 0020	0x0 1400 0027	8 bytes	RAS[3:2] high decode address
0x0 1400 0028	0x0 1400 002F	8 bytes	CS[2:0] low decode address
0x0 1400 0030	0x0 1400 0037	8 bytes	CS[2:0] high decode address
0x0 1400 0038	0x0 1400 003F	8 bytes	CS[3] and BootCS low decode address

continues

Table B-9a *System Memory Map Detailed (Continued)*

Memory Base	Memory Limit	Size	Device
0x0 1400 0040	0x0 1400 0047	8 bytes	CS[3] and BootCS high decode address
0x0 1400 0048	0x0 1400 004F	8 bytes	PCI I/O low decode address
0x0 1400 0050	0x0 1400 0057	8 bytes	PCI I/O high decode address
0x0 1400 0058	0x0 1400 005F	8 bytes	PCI memory low decode address
0x0 1400 0060	0x0 1400 0067	8 bytes	PCI memory high decode address
0x0 1400 0068	0x0 1400 006F	8 bytes	Internal space decode
0x0 1400 0070	0x0 1400 0077	8 bytes	BUS error address low
0x0 1400 0078	0x0 1400 007F	8 bytes	BUS error address high
0x0 1400 0080	0x0 1400 03FF	896 bytes	Undefined
0x0 1400 0400	0x0 1400 0403	4 bytes	RAS[0] low decode address
0x0 1400 0404	0x0 1400 0407	4 bytes	RAS[0] high decode address
0x0 1400 0408	0x0 1400 040B	4 bytes	RAS[1] low decode address
0x0 1400 040C	0x0 1400 040F	4 bytes	RAS[1] high decode address
0x0 1400 0410	0x0 1400 0413	4 bytes	RAS[2] low decode address
0x0 1400 0414	0x0 1400 0417	4 bytes	RAS[2] high decode address
0x0 1400 0418	0x0 1400 041B	4 bytes	RAS[3] low decode address
0x0 1400 041C	0x0 1400 041F	4 bytes	RAS[3] high decode address
0x0 1400 0420	0x0 1400 0423	4 bytes	CS[0] low decode address
0x0 1400 0424	0x0 1400 0427	4 bytes	CS[0] high decode address
0x0 1400 0428	0x0 1400 042B	4 bytes	CS[1] low decode address
0x0 1400 042C	0x0 1400 042F	4 bytes	CS[1] high decode address
0x0 1400 0430	0x0 1400 0433	4 bytes	CS[2] low decode address
0x0 1400 0434	0x0 1400 0437	4 bytes	CS[2] high decode address
0x0 1400 0438	0x0 1400 043B	4 bytes	CS[3] low decode address
0x0 1400 043C	0x0 1400 043F	4 bytes	CS[3] high decode address
0x0 1400 0440	0x0 1400 0443	4 bytes	BootCS low decode address
0x0 1400 0444	0x0 1400 0447	4 bytes	BootCS high decode address
0x0 1400 0448	044B	4 bytes	DRAM configuration
0x0 1400 044C	0x0 1400 044F	4 bytes	DRAM Bank0 parameters
0x0 1400 0450	0x0 1400 0453	4 bytes	DRAM Bank1 parameters

Table B-9a *System Memory Map Detailed (Continued)*

Memory Base	Memory Limit	Size	Device
0x0 1400 0454	0x0 1400 0457	4 bytes	DRAM Bank2 parameters
0x0 1400 0458	0x0 1400 045B	4 bytes	DRAM Bank3 parameters
0x0 1400 045C	0x0 1400 045F	4 bytes	Device Bank0 parameters
0x0 1400 0460	0x0 1400 0463	4 bytes	Device Bank1 parameters
0x0 1400 0464	0x0 1400 0467	4 bytes	Device Bank2 parameters
0x0 1400 0468	0x0 1400 046B	4 bytes	Device Bank3 parameters
0x0 1400 046C	0x0 1400 046F	4 bytes	Device boot bank parameters
0x0 1400 0470	0x0 1400 0473	4 bytes	Address decode error
0x0 1400 0474	0x0 1400 07FF	908 bytes	Undefined
0x0 1400 0800	0x0 1400 0803	4 bytes	Channel 0 DMA byte count
0x0 1400 0804	0x0 1400 0807	4 bytes	Channel 1 DMA byte count
0x0 1400 0808	0x0 1400 080B	4 bytes	Channel 2 DMA byte count
0x0 1400 080C	0x0 1400 080F	4 bytes	Channel 3 DMA byte count
0x0 1400 0810	0x0 1400 0813	4 bytes	Channel 0 DMA source address
0x0 1400 0814	0x0 1400 0817	4 bytes	Channel 1 DMA source address
0x0 1400 0818	0x0 1400 081B	4 bytes	Channel 2 DMA source address
0x0 1400 081C	0x0 1400 081F	4 bytes	Channel 3 DMA source address
0x0 1400 0820	0x0 1400 0823	4 bytes	Channel 0 DMA destination address
0x0 1400 0824	0x0 1400 0827	4 bytes	Channel 1 DMA destination address
0x0 1400 0828	0x0 1400 082B	4 bytes	Channel 2 DMA destination address
0x0 1400 082C	0x0 1400 082F	4 bytes	Channel 3 DMA destination address
0x0 1400 0830	0x0 1400 0833	4 bytes	Channel 0 DMA next record pointer
0x0 1400 0834	0x0 1400 0837	4 bytes	Channel 1 DMA next record pointer
0x0 1400 0838	0x0 1400 083B	4 bytes	Channel 2 DMA next record pointer
0x0 1400 083C	0x0 1400 083F	4 bytes	Channel 3 DMA next record pointer
0x0 1400 0840	0x0 1400 0843	4 bytes	Channel 0 DMA control
0x0 1400 0844	0x0 1400 0847	4 bytes	Channel 1 DMA control
0x0 1400 0848	0x0 1400 084B	4 bytes	Channel 2 DMA control
0x0 1400 084C	0x0 1400 084F	4 bytes	Channel 3 DMA control
0x0 1400 0850	0x0 1400 0853	4 bytes	Timer/counter 0

continues

Table B-9a *System Memory Map Detailed (Continued)*

Memory Base	Memory Limit	Size	Device
0x0 1400 0854	0x0 1400 0857	4 bytes	Timer/counter 1
0x0 1400 0858	0x0 1400 085B	4 bytes	Timer/counter 2
0x0 1400 085C	0x0 1400 085F	4 bytes	Timer/counter 3
0x0 1400 0860	0x0 1400 0863	4 bytes	DMA arbiter control
0x0 1400 0864	0x0 1400 0867	4 bytes	Timer/counter control
0x0 1400 0868	0x0 1400 0BFF	920 bytes	Undefined
0x0 1400 0C00	0x0 1400 0C03	4 bytes	PCI command
0x0 1400 0C04	0x0 1400 0C07	4 bytes	PCI time out and retry
0x0 1400 0C08	0x0 1400 0C0B	4 bytes	PCI RAS[1:0] bank size
0x0 1400 0C0C	0x0 1400 0C0F	4 bytes	PCI RAS[3:2] bank size
0x0 1400 0C10	0x0 1400 0C13	4 bytes	PCI CS[2:0] bank size
0x0 1400 0C14	0x0 1400 0C17	4 bytes	PCI CS[3] and boot CS bank size
0x0 1400 0C18	0x0 1400 0C1B	4 bytes	Interrupt cause
0x0 1400 0C1C	0x0 1400 0C1F	4 bytes	CPU mask
0x0 1400 0C20	0x0 1400 0C23	4 bytes	Undefined
0x0 1400 0C24	0x0 1400 0C27	4 bytes	PCI mask
0x0 1400 0C28	0x0 1400 0C2B	4 bytes	PCI SErr mask
0x0 1400 0C2C	0x0 1400 0C33	8 bytes	Undefined
0x0 1400 0C34	0x0 1400 0C37	4 bytes	PCI interrupt acknowledge
0x0 1400 0C38	0x0 1400 0CF7	192 bytes	Undefined
0x0 1400 0CF8	0x0 1400 0CFB	4 bytes	PCI configuration address
0x0 1400 0CFC	0x0 1400 0CFF	4 bytes	PCI configuration data
0x0 1400 0D00	0x0 141F FFFF	About 2044 KB	Undefined
0x0 1420 0000	0x0 19FF FFFF	94 MB	Reserved
0x0 1A00 0000	0x0 1BFF FFFF	32 MB	Flash SIMM
0x0 1C00 0000	0x0 1C1F FFFF	2 MB	I/O space
0x0 1C00 0000	0x0 1C00 0003	4 bytes	NRP-1 config register
0x0 1C00 0004	0x0 1C00 0007	4 bytes	NRP-1 control register
0x0 1C00 0008	0x0 1C00 000B	4 bytes	Reset reason register
0x0 1C00 000C	0x0 1C00 000F	4 bytes	Interrupt status register

Table B-9a *System Memory Map Detailed (Continued)*

Memory Base	Memory Limit	Size	Device
0x0 1C00 0010	0x0 1C00 0013	4 bytes	Interrupt mask register
0x0 1C00 0014	0x0 1C00 0017	4 bytes	EHSA register
0x0 1C00 0018	0x0 1C00 001B	4 bytes	Watchdog register
0x0 1C00 001C	0x0 1C00 001F	4 bytes	LED register
0x0 1C00 0020	0x0 1C00 0023	4 bytes	MICE register
0x0 1C00 0024	0x0 1C00 0027	4 bytes	PMPCI FPGA program register
0x0 1C00 0028	0x0 1C00 002F	4 bytes	Network interface control register
0x0 1C00 0030	0x0 1C00 FFFF	64 KB	I/O reserved
0x0 1C01 0000	0x0 1C01 1FFF	8 KB	IDPROM (2 KB size, byte access on word boundary)
0x0 1C01 2000	0x0 1C02 FFFF	119 KB	I/O reserved
0x0 1C03 0000	0x0 1C03 1FFF	8 KB	PAM bus mailbox memory (2 KB size, byte access on word boundary) Address range accessible only from the NRP-1 processor, not the NSP
0x0 1C03 2000	>0x0 1C03 FFFF	55 KB	I/O reserved
0x0 1C04 0000	0x0 1C04 0003	4 bytes	Undefined
0x0 1C04 0000	0x0 1C04 003F	64 bytes	Console UART (8-bit device on 64-bit boundary)
0x0 1C04 0004	0x0 1C04 0004	1 bytes	Console UART mode register (MR1A, MR2A)
0x0 1C04 0005	0x0 1C04 000B	7 bytes	Undefined
0x0 1C04 000C	0x0 1C04 000C	1 bytes	Console UARTRead: status register (SRA) Write: clock select register (CSRA)
0x0 1C04 000D	0x0 1C04 0013	7 bytes	Undefined
0x0 1C04 0014	0x0 1C04 0014	1 bytes	Console UARTRead: undefined Write: command register (CRA)
0x0 1C04 0015	0x0 1C04 001B	7 bytes	Undefined
0x0 1C04 001C	0x0 1C04 001C	1 bytes	Console UART Read: Rx holding register (RHRA) Write: Tx holding register (THRA)
0x0 1C04 001D	0x0 1C04 0023	7 bytes	Undefined

continues

Table B-9a   *System Memory Map Detailed (Continued)*

Memory Base	Memory Limit	Size	Device
0x0 1C04 0024	0x0 1C04 0024	1 bytes	Console UART Read: input port change register (IPCR)
			Write: aux control register (ACR)
0x0 1C04 0025	0x0 1C04 002B	7 bytes	Undefined
0x0 1C04 002C	0x0 1C04 002C	1 bytes	Console UART Read: interrupt status register (ISR)
			Write: interrupt mask register (IMR)
0x0 1C04 002D	0x0 1C04 0033	7 bytes	Undefined
0x0 1C04 0034	0x0 1C04 0034	1 bytes	Console UART Read: counter/timer upper (CTU)
			Write: C/T upper register (CRUR)
0x0 1C04 0035	0x0 1C04 003B	7 bytes	Undefined
0x0 1C04 003C	0x0 1C04 003C	1 bytes	Console UART Read: counter/timer lower (CTL)
			Write: C/T lower register (CTLR)
0x0 1C04 003D	0x0 1C04 0043	7 bytes	Undefined
0x0 1C04 0044	0x0 1C04 007F	64 bytes	Modem UART
0x0 1C04 0044	0x0 1C04 0044	1 bytes	Modem UART mode register (MR1B, MR2B)
0x0 1C04 0045	0x0 1C04 004B	7 bytes	Undefined
0x0 1C04 004C	0x0 1C04 004C	1 bytes	Modem UART Read: status register (SRB)
			Write: clock select register (CSRB)
0x0 1C04 004D	0x0 1C04 0053	7 bytes	Undefined
0x0 1C04 0054	0x0 1C04 0054	1 bytes	Modem UART Read: undefined
			Write: command register (CRB)
0x0 1C04 0055	0x0 1C04 005B	7 bytes	Undefined
0x0 1C04 005C	0x0 1C04 005C	1 bytes	Modem UART Read: Rx holding register (RHRB)
			Write: Tx holding register (THRB)
0x0 1C04 005D	0x0 1C04 0063	7 bytes	Undefined
0x0 1C04 0064	0x0 1C04 0064	1 bytes	Modem UART Read: undefined
			Write: undefined

Table B-9a   *System Memory Map Detailed (Continued)*

Memory Base	Memory Limit	Size	Device
0x0 1C04 0065	0x0 1C04 006B	7 bytes	Undefined
0x0 1C04 006C	0x0 1C04 006C	1 bytes	Modem UARTRead: input port Write: output port conf register (OPCR)
0x0 1C04 006D	0x0 1C04 0073	7 bytes	Undefined
0x0 1C04 0074	0x0 1C04 0074	1 bytes	Modem UARTRead: start counter command Write: set output port bits command
0x0 1C04 0075	0x0 1C04 007B	7 bytes	Undefined
0x0 1C04 007C	0x0 1C04 007C	1 bytes	Modem UARTRead: stop counter command Write: reset output port bits command
0x0 1C04 007D	0x0 1C04 007F	3 bytes	Undefined
0x0 1C04 0080	0x0 1C04 00FF	64 bytes	Undefined
0x0 1C04 0100	0x0 1C04 FFFF	64 KB	Undefined
0x0 1C05 0000	0x0 1C05 0003	4 bytes	NRP-to-NSP control register
0x0 1C05 0004	0x0 1C05 0007	4 bytes	NSP-to-NRP control register
0x0 1C05 0008	0x0 1C05 000B	4 bytes	NRP-to-NSP interrupting semaphore
0x0 1C05 000C	0x0 1C05 000F	4 bytes	NRP-to-NSP interrupting semaphore
0x0 1C05 0010	0x0 1C05 0013	4 bytes	GP semaphore 0
0x0 1C05 0014	0x0 1C05 0017	4 bytes	GP semaphore 1
0x0 1C05 0018	0x0 1C05 001B	4 bytes	GP semaphore 2
0x0 1C05 001C	0x0 1C05 001F	4 bytes	GP semaphore 3
0x0 1C05 0020	0x0 1C05 0023	4 bytes	IDPROM write enable/lock
0x0 1C05 0024	0x0 1C1F FFFF	1.8 MB	I/O reserved
0x0 1C02 0000	0x0 1DFF FFFF	32 MB	Reserved
0x0 1E00 0000	0x0 1E01 FFFF	128 KB	NVRAM
0x0 1E02 0000	0x0 1E7F FFFF	8 MB	Reserved
0x0 1E80 0000	0x0 1EB FFFF	4 MB	Boot Flash
0x0 1EC0 0000	0x0 1FBF FFFF	16 MB	Reserved
0x0 1FC0 0000	0x0 1FC7 FFFF	512 KB	Boot EPROM

continues

Table B-9a   *System Memory Map Detailed (Continued)*

Memory Base	Memory Limit	Size	Device
0x0 1FC8 0000	0x0 1FDF FFFF	1536 KB	Undefined (boot EPROM decode)
0x0 1FE0 0000	0x0 3FFF FFFF	514 MB	Reserved
0x0 4800 0000	0x0 487F FFFF	8 MB	BPE Ethernet controller
0x0 4880 0000	0x0 48FF FFFF	8 MB	NME Ethernet controller
0x0 4900 0000	0x0 497F FFFF	8 MB	CSE Ethernet controller
0x0 4980 0000	0x0 49FF FFFF	8 MB	Undefined (PCI bus timeout)
0x0 4A00 0000	0x0 4A7F FFFF	8 MB	SAR
0x0 4A80 0000	0x0 4AFF FFFF	8 MB	Undefined (PCI bus timeout)
0x0 4B00 0000	0x0 4B3F FFFF	4 MB	PCI packet memory, no byte swap
0x0 4B40 0000	0x0 4B7F FFFF	4 MB	Undefined (PCI bus timeout)
0x0 4B80 0000	0x0 4BBF FFFF	4 MB	PCI packet memory, byte swap
0x0 4C00 0000	0x0 4CFF FFFF	16 MB	Undefined (PCI bus timeout)
0x0 4D00 0000	0x0 5FFF FFFF	320 MB	Reserved
0x0 6000 0000	0x0 601F FFFF	2 MB	PCI I/O address space
0x0 6020 0000	0x0 BFFF FFFF	About 1.5 GB	Reserved
0x0 C000 0000	0x0 C7FF FFFF	128 MB	PCI bus access to DRAM with byte swap
0x0 C800 0000	0x1 4AFF FFFF	About 2 GB	Reserved
0x1 4B00 0000	0x1 4B3F FFFF	4 MB	CPU packet memory, no byte swap
0x1 4B40 0000	0x1 FFFF FFFF	About 3 GB	Reserved
0x2 0000 0000	0x3 FFFF FFFF	8 GB	L2 cache disabled alias for memory space
0x4 0000 0000	0x7 FFFF FFFF	16 GB	L2 cache controller tag Op 0 (invalidate entry)
0x8 0000 0000	0xF FFFF FFFF	32 GB	L2 cache controller tag Op 1 (flush entry)

Table B-10: Cisco 6400-NSP Memory Map

All registers and memories on the NSP switch card reside in the MEMD (CPU-Switch bus) space of the NSP processor card. Table B-10 lists all addresses that the NSP-SC decodes for itself or for other cards that it interfaces with. Note that all accesses are 32 bits.

Table B-10 *Cisco 6400-NSP Memory Map*

MEMD Address		Description	Bits Used
0800 0000	0800 007C	MMC switch controller registers	31:0
0800 0080	0800 00FC	Reserved	
0800 0100	0800 010C	Accordian registers	31:0
0800 0110	0800 01FC	Reserved	
0800 0200	0800 02D4	NSP-SC registers	
0800 0200		Redundancy control	31:16
0800 0204		Redundancy active	31:16
0800 0208		Linecard sense	31:16
0800 020C		Linecard ready	31:16
0800 0210		NSP/PEM/fan sense	19:16
0800 0214		NSP/PEM/fan ready	19:16
0800 0280		Slot ID	16
0800 0284		EHSA control	19:16
0800 0288		Mastership	16
0800 028C		NRP processor resets	31:16
0800 0290		Network timing	17:16
0800 0294		BITS clock receiver	18:16
0800 0298		Power adjust	17:16
0800 029C	0807 FFFC	Reserved	
0808 0000	0808 1FFC	NSP-SC ID PROM (2 K × 8)	31:24
0808 2000	0817 FFFC	Reserved	
0818 0000	0818 007C	BPE Ethernet controller	31:0
0818 0080	0827 FFFC	Reserved	
0828 0000	0829 FFFC	BPE Ethernet packet buffer SRAM	31:0
082A 0000	082F FFFC	Reserved	
0830 0000	087F FFFC	NSP feature card	31:0
0880 0000	08BF FFFC	PAM bus X (linecards/NRPs 0 to 7)	31:0
08C0 0000	08FF FFFC	PAM bus Y (linecards/NRPs 8 to 15)	31:0
0900 0000	0FFF FFFC	Reserved	

Table B-11: Cisco 6200 Memory Map

Table B-11 *Cisco 6200 Memory Map*

Type	Address Range	Description
System memory	0x00000000 to 0x007FFFFF	System DRAM (8 MB)
	0x00800000 to 0x01FFFFFF	Reserved (24 MB)
	0x02000000 to 0x0FFFFFFF	Reserved
PCI I/O space	0x10000000 to 0x10000003	PCMCIA controller
	0x10000004 to 0x11FFFFFF	Reserved
PCI memory space	0x12000000 to 0x1200001F	Ethernet 1 (10BaseT)
	0x12000020 to 0x1200003F	Ethernet 2 (10Base2)
	0x12000040 to 0x120FFFFF	Reserved
	0x12100000 to 0x121FFFFF	TNETA1570 (SAR)
	0x12200000 to 0x13FFFFFF	Reserved
GT64011	0x14000000 to 0x141FFFFF	System controller
PCMCIA slot 0	0x15000000 to 0x15FFFFFF	Tuple
	0x16000000 to 0x17400000	Memory space
	0x17400000 to 0x17FFFFFF	Reserved
PCMCIA slot 1	0x18000000 to 0x18FFFFFF	Tuple
	0x19000000 to 0x1A3FFFFF	Memory space
	0x1B000000 to 0x1BFFFFFF	Reserved
Local GT bus	0x1C000000 to 0x1C7FFFFF	(CS0) DUART
	0x1C800000 to 0x1CFFFFFF	(CS1) NVRAM/TOD
	0x1D000000 to 0x1DFFFFFF	(CS2) Internal Flash SIMM
	0x1F000000 to 0x1FBFFFFF	(CS3) IO FPGA
	0x1FC00000 to 0x1FFFFFFF	(BootCS) Boot EPROM
	0x20000000 to 0x3FFFFFFF	Reserved
PCMICA mapped space	0x40000000 to 0x43FFFFFF	PCMCIA slot 0
	0x44000000 to 0x47FFFFFF	PCMICA slot 1
	0x48000000 to 0xFFFFFF	Reserved

Table B-12: Cisco 6260 Memory Map

Table B-12 *Cisco 6260 Memory Map*

Type	Address Range	Description
System memory	0x00000000 to 0x03F00000	System DRAM (64 MB)
	0x04000000 to 0x07F00000	Reserved (64 MB)
PCI memory space two	0x08000000 to 0x0BFFFFFF	Switch cell buffer memory (64 MB)
	0x0C000000 to 0x0CFFFFFF	Switch header table memory (16 MB)
	0x0D000000 to 0x0D7FFFFF	Switch link memory (8 MB)
	0x0D800000 to 0x0D8000FF	Switch registers (64 MB)
	0x0D900000 to 0x0D9027FF	Queue memory
	0x0DA00000 to 0x0DA01FFF	Modem input queue count memory
	0x0DB00000 to 0x0DB003FF	Shaper memory
	0x0DB00400 to 0x0FFFFFFF	Reserved
PCI I/O space	0x10000000 to 0x11FFFFFF	Reserved
PCI memory space one	0x12000000 to 0x1200001F	AM79C970A (10BastT Ethernet)
	0x12000020 to 0x12000FFF	Reserved
	0x12001000 to 0x12001FFF	IDT77252 SAR internal registers
	0x12100000 to 0x124FFFFF	IDT77252 SAR external SRAM
	0x13000000 to 0x137FFFFF	Upstream FPGA
	0x13800000 to 0x13FFFFFF	Downstream FPGA
GT64121	0x14000000 to 0x141FFFFF	System controller
	0x14200000 to 0x1BFFFFFF	Reserved
Local GT bus	0x1C000000 to 0x1C7FFFFF	(CS0) DUART—console and aux
	0x1C800000 to 0x1CFFFFFF	(CS1) NVRAM/TOD
	0x1D000000 to 0x1DFFFFFF	(CS2) Flash SIMM
	0x1E000000 to 0x1EFFFFFF	Reserved
	0x1F000000 to 0x1F1FFFFF	(CS3) CP EPLD
	0x1F200000 to 0x1F200007	(CS3) PCF8584 I2C controller
	0x1F200008 to 0x1F3FFFFF	Reserved
	0x1F400000 to 0x1F7FFFFF	(CS3) Bootflash
	0x1F800000 to 0x1FBFFFFF	Reserved
	0x1FC00000 to 0x1FFFFFFF	(BootCS) Boot EPROM—ROM MON
	0x20000000 to 0xFFFFFFFF	Reserved

Table B-13: Cisco 4000 Memory Map

Table B-13 *Cisco 4000 Memory Map*

Address	Bit Width	Description	Comments
00000000 to 0003FFFF	32	System SRAM	256 KB, fixed; 0 wait read, 1 wait write
00040000 to 00FFFFFF	32	System DRAM memory (SIMMs)	8-, 16-, 32-bit unaligned access supported; 4, 8, 16, or 32 MB
00040000 to 003FFFFF		4 MB	
00040000 to 00FFFFFF		16 MB	
01000000 to 01FFFFFF	16	Boot EPROM	2 MB, fixed
01000000 to 010FFFFF		1 MB	
01000000 to 011FFFFF		2 MB	
01000000 to 013FFFFF		4 MB	
01000000 to 017FFFFF		8 MB	
02000000 to 02FFFFFF	8 or 32	Onboard resources	
02020000		System I/O	
03000000 to 03FFFFFF	32	Flash memory EPROM or EPROM	32-bit read/write access
03000000 to 031FFFFF		2 MB	
03000000 to 033FFFFF		4 MB	
03000000 to 037FFFFF		8 MB	
05000000		System DRAM	Upper 16 MB of 32-MB configuration
06000000 to 06FFFFFF	32	Shared (I/O) memory	8-, 16-, 32-bit unaligned access supported; 1 to 16 MB
06000000 to 060FFFFF		1 MB	
06000000 to 063FFFFF		4 MB	
06000000 to 067FFFFF		8 MB	
04000000 to 05FFFFFF		Undefined	
07000000 to 07FFFFFF		Undefined	
08000000 to 08FFFFFF	32	I/O expansion	NIM slots
08000000 to 080FFFFF	16	NIM at I/O expansion slot 1	16-bit aligned access only
08100000 to 081FFFFF	16	NIM at I/O expansion slot 2	16-bit aligned access only

Table B-13 *Cisco 4000 Memory Map (Continued)*

Address	Bit Width	Description	Comments
08200000 to 082FFFFF	16	NIM at I/O expansion slot 3	16-bit aligned access only

1 Only the Cisco 4000-M supports 32 MB DRAM. The 32-MB configuration is split into two discontiguous pieces, with the upper 16 MB mapped to begin at location 05000000.

2 Only the Cisco 4000-M supports 8 MB Flash memory.

Table B-13a *Cisco 4000 Memory Map of Onboard Resources*

Address	Bit Width	Description	Comments
02000000 to 0201FFFF	8	NVRAM battery backed-up CMOS SRAM	128 KB, fixed; also accommodates 32 KB × 8 and 8 KB × 8
02110000	32	System status and control registers	
02110002		Hardware revision	
02110040 to 0211005F	8	System ID PROM cookie	24 bytes
02110100	32	Shared memory control register	
02120000	8	Counter timer	
02120040	8	Counter interrupt control register	
02120100 to 0212013F	8	Control serial I/O	

Table B-14: Cisco 4500, 4500-M, 4700, 4700-M Memory Map

Table B-14 *Cisco 4500, 4500-M, 4700, 4700-M Memory Map*

Address	Bit Width	Description	Comments
60000000 to 61FFFFFF	64	System DRAM	Capable of 8- to 64-bit access, cached
60000000 to 607FFFFF		8 MB	
60000000 to 60FFFFFF		16 MB	
60000000 to 61FFFFFF		32 MB	
BFC00000 to BFC7FFFF	8	Boot EPROM	
BFC00000 to BFC1FFFF		128 KB	
BFC00000 to BFC7FFFF		512 KB	
3E000000 to 3EFFFFFF	8	Onboard resources	

continues

Table B-14 *Cisco 4500, 4500-M, 4700, 4700-M Memory Map (Continued)*

Address	Bit Width	Description	Comments
30000000 to 30FFFFFF	32	System Flash memory EPROM	
30000000 to 303FFFFF		4 MB	
30000000 to 307FFFFF		8 MB	
30000000 to 30FFFFFF		16 MB	
38000000 to 387FFFFF	32	Boot Flash memory EPROM	
38000000 to 383FFFFF		4 MB	
38000000 to 387FFFFF		8 MB	
40000000 to 40FFFFFF	32	Shared memory	8-, 16-, 32-bit access
40000000 to 403FFFFF		4 MB	
40000000 to 40FFFFFF		16 MB	

Table B-14a *Cisco 4500, 4500-M, 4700, 4700-M Memory Map of Onboard Resources*

Address	Bit Width	Description	Comments
3E000000 to 3E07FFFF	8	NVRAM	Battery backed-up SRAM
3E000000 to 3E01FFFF	8	128 KB	
3E000000 to 3E07FFFF	8	512 KB	
3E000000	8	Time of day clock	
3E800400	8	System ID PROM cookie	

Table B-15: Cisco 3620 Memory Map

Table B-15 *Cisco 3620 Memory Map*

Memory Base	Memory Limit	Size	Device
0x0 0000 0000	0x0 03FF FFFF	Up to 32 Mb	Main DRAM (four 72 -pin simms)
0x0 0400 0000	0x0 0FFF FFFF		Reserved
0x0 1400 0000	0x0 14FF FFFF		GT64010 registers
0x0 1E80 0000	0x0 1E9F FFFF	Up to 1 MB	Board registers, DUART
0x0 1EC0 0000	0x0 1EFF FFFF	Up to 1 MB	Bit bucket
0x0 1FC0 0000	0x0 1FDF FFFF	Up to 1 MB	ROM monitor
0x0 1FE0 0000	0x0 1FFF FFFF	Up to 64 KB	NVRAM

Table B-15   *Cisco 3620 Memory Map (Continued)*

Memory Base	Memory Limit	Size	Device
0x0 3000 0000	0x0 3FFF FFFF	Up to 48 MB	Main Flash (two 80-pin simms)
0x0 4000 0000	0x0 43FF FFFF	Up to 64 MB	PCMCIA slot 1
0x0 4400 0000	0x0 47FF FFFF	Up to 64 MB	PCMCIA slot 2
0x0 4D00 0000	0x0 4D7F FFFF	Up to 8 MB	PM 0, PCI memory
0x0 4D80 0000	0x0 4DFF FFFF	Up to 8 MB	PM 1, PCI memory
0x1 0000 0000	0x1 0000 7FFF	Up to 32 KB	General PCI I/O
0x1 0000 8000	0x1 0000 9FFF	Up to 8 KB	PM 0, PCI I/O
0x1 0000 A000	0x1 0000 BFFF	Up to 8 KB	PM 1, PCI I/O

Table B-16: Cisco 3640 Memory Map

Table B-16   *Cisco 3640 Memory Map*

Memory Base	Memory Limit	Size	Device
0x0 0000 0000	0x0 07FF FFFF	Up to 64 Mb	Main DRAM (four 72-pin simms)
0x0 0800 0000	0x0 0FFF FFFF		Reserved
0x0 1400 0000	0x0 14FF FFFF		GT64010 registers
0x0 1E80 0000	0x0 1E9F FFFF	Up to 1 MB	Board registers, DUART test CS
0x0 1EC0 0000	0x0 1EFF FFFF	Up to 1 MB	Bit bucket
0x0 1FC0 0000	0x0 1FDF FFFF	Up to 1 MB	ROM monitor
0x0 1FE0 0000	0x0 1FFF FFFF	Up to 1 MB	NVRAM
0x0 3000 0000	0x0 3FFF FFFF	Up to 48 MB	Main Flash (two 80-pin simms)
0x0 4000 0000	0x0 43FF FFFF	Up to 64 MB	PCMCIA slot 0
0x0 4400 0000	0x0 47FF FFFF	Up to 64 MB	PCMCIA slot 1
0x0 4D00 0000	0x0 4D7F FFFF	Up to 8 MB	PM 0, PCI memory
0x0 4D80 0000	0x0 4DFF FFFF	Up to 8 MB	PM 2, PCI memory
0x0 4E00 0000	0x0 4E7F FFFF	Up to 8 MB	PM 1, PCI memory
0x0 4E80 0000	0x0 4EFF FFFF	Up to 8 MB	PM 3, PCI memory
0x1 0000 0000	0x1 0000 7FFF	Up to 32 KB	General PCI I/O
0x1 0000 8000	0x1 0000 9FFF	Up to 8 KB	PM 0, PCI I/O
0x1 0000 A000	0x1 0000 BFFF	Up to 8 KB	PM 2, PCI I/O
0x1 0000 C000	0x1 0000 DFFF	Up to 8 KB	PM 1, PCI I/O
0x1 0000 E000	0x1 0000 FFFF	Up to 8 KB	PM 3, PCI I/O

Table B-17: Cisco 3660 Memory Map

Table B-17 *Cisco 3660 Memory Map*

Memory Base	Memory Limit	Size	Device
0x0 0000 0000	0x0 0FFF FFFF	Up to 128 Mb	Main SDRAM (two 168-pin dimms)
0x0 1400 0000	0x0 14FF FFFF		GT64120 registers
0x0 1E00 0000	0x0 1E7F FFFF	Up to 8 MB	Bit bucket
0x0 1E80 0000	0x0 1E83 FFFF	Up to 1 MB	Board registers
0x0 1E84 0000	0x0 1E84 FFFF	Up to 1 MB	DUART
0x0 1FC0 0000	0x0 1FDF FFFF	Up to 1 MB	ROM monitor
0x0 1FE0 0000	0x0 1FFF FFFF	Up to 64 KB	NVRAM
0x0 3000 0000	0x0 33FF FFFF	Up to 64 MB	Main Flash (two 80-pin simms)
0x0 3C00 0000	0x0 3C0F FFFF	Up to 1 MB	TDM switch
0x0 4000 0000	0x0 43FF FFFF	Up to 64 MB	PCMCIA slot 0
0x0 4400 0000	0x0 47FF FFFF	Up to 64 MB	PCMCIA slot 1
0x0 4800 0000	0x0 487F FFFF	Up to 8 MB	FE 0/0, PCI memory
0x0 4880 0000	0x0 48FF FFFF	Up to 8 MB	FE 0/1, PCI memory
0x0 4A00 0000	0x0 4A7F FFFF	Up to 8 MB	AIM 0, PCI memory
0x0 4A80 0000	0x0 4AFF FFFF	Up to 8 MB	AIM 1, PCI memory
0x0 4D00 0000	0x0 4D7F FFFF	Up to 8 MB	NM 1, PCI memory
0x0 4D80 0000	0x0 4DFF FFFF	Up to 8 MB	NM 3, PCI memory
0x0 4E00 0000	0x0 4E7F FFFF	Up to 8 MB	NM 2, PCI memory
0x0 4E80 0000	0x0 4EFF FFFF	Up to 8 MB	NM 4, PCI memory
0x0 4F00 0000	0x0 4F7F FFFF	Up to 8 MB	NM 5, PCI memory
0x0 4F80 0000	0x0 4FFF FFFF	Up to 8 MB	NM 6, PCI memory
0x1 0000 0000	0x1 0000 7FFF	Up to 32 KB	General PCI I/O
0x1 0000 8000	0x1 0000 9FFF	Up to 8 KB	AIM 0, PCI I/O
0x1 0000 A000	0x1 0000 BFFF	Up to 8 KB	AIM 1, PCI I/O
0x1 0020 0000	0x1 0020 1FFF	Up to 8 KB	NM 1, PCI I/O
0x1 0020 2000	0x1 0020 3FFF	Up to 8 KB	NM 3, PCI I/O
0x1 0020 4000	0x1 0020 5FFF	Up to 8 KB	NM 2, PCI I/O
0x1 0020 6000	0x1 0020 7FFF	Up to 8 KB	NM 4, PCI I/O
0x1 0020 8000	0x1 0020 9FFF	Up to 8 KB	NM 5, PCI I/O
0x1 0020 A000	0x1 0020 BFFF	Up to 8 KB	NM 6, PCI I/O

Table B-18: Cisco 2600 Memory Map

Table B-18   *Cisco 2600 Memory Map*

Memory Base	Memory Limit	Size	Device
0x0000 0000	0x03FF FFFF	Up to 64 Mb	Physical address space
0x4000 0000	0x4FFF FFFF	16 Mb	PCI memory space
0x6000 0000	0x60FF FFFF	Up to 16 Mb	Flash
0x6700 0000	0x67FF FFFF	64 Kb	NVRAM, WIC, internal regs
0x6800 0000	0x6800 FFFF		PCI config/IO spze
0x6801 0000	0x6801 FFFF	64 Kb	PowerQUICC regs
0x8000 0000	0x83FF FFFF	Up to 64 Mb	Virtual address space

Table B-19: Cisco 2500 Memory Map

Table B-19   *Cisco 2500 Memory Map*

Address	Bit Width	Description	Comments
00000000 to 00FFFFFF	32	DRAM	2, 4, 8, or 16 MB
00000000 to 001FFFFF	32	DRAM 2 MB	
00000000 to 003FFFFF	32	DRAM 4 MB	
00000000 to 007FFFFF	32	DRAM 8 MB	
00000000 to 00FFFFFF	32	DRAM 16 MB	
00000000 to 001FFFFF	8/16	Boot Flash memory	1 or 2 MB, when Flash memory PCMCIA card is not installed
00000000 to 001FFFFF	16	Flash memory PCMCIA card	Boot mode
01000000 to 011FFFFF	16	Boot EPROMs for ROM monitor and RXBOOT images	1 or 2 MB ROM; 2 MB Flash memory
01000000 to 011FFFFF	16	Flash memory PCMCIA card	When installed
02000000 to 0201FFFF	8	Configuration NVRAM	32 or 128 KB
02000000 to 02007FFF	8	Configuration NVRAM (32 KB)	
02000000 to 0201FFFF	8	Configuration NVRAM (128 KB)	

continues

Table B-19 *Cisco 2500 Memory Map (Continued)*

Address	Bit Width	Description	Comments
02100000 to 0213FFFF	8/16	Onboard I/O registers and chips	
03000000 to 03FFFFFF	32	Flash memory RAM (SIMMs)	4, 8, or 16 MB
03000000 to 033FFFFF	32	Flash memory RAM (4 MB)	
03000000 to 037FFFFF	32	Flash memory RAM (8 MB)	
03000000 to 03FFFFFF	32	Flash memory RAM (16 MB)	
08000000 to 081FFFFF	8/16	Onboard boot EPROMs (remapped)	1 or 2 MB, when PCMCIA Flash memory card is installed

Table B-20: Cisco 1720 Memory Map

Table B-20 *Cisco 1720 Memory Map*

Memory Base	Memory Limit	Size	Device
0x0000 0000	0x027F FFFF	40 Mb	DRAM
0x4000 0000	0x4FFF FFFF	64 Mb	PCI memory space
0x5000 0000	0x5000 0FFF		Compression
0x5008 0000	0x5008 0FFF		Encryption
0x6000 0000	0x63FF FFFF	64 Mb reserved; 16 Mb used	Flash
0x6800 0000	0x68FF FFFF	64 Kb	NVRAM, WIC, internal regs
0x7000 0000	0x7000 FFFF	4 Kb	Q-SPAN regs
0xFF00 0000	0xFF00 3FFF	16 Kb	PowerQUICC regs
0xFFF0 0000	0xFFFF FFFF	1 Mb	Boot ROM

Table B-21: Cisco 1600 Memory Map

Table B-21 *Cisco 1600 Memory Map*

Item	Beginning Address	Ending Address
ROM	0x00000000	0x003fffff
RAM	0x2000000	0x03ffffff

Table B-21   *Cisco 1600 Memory Map (Continued)*

Item	Beginning Address	Ending Address
ROM (–d flag)	0x04000000	0x043fffff
PC card (Flash)	0x08000000	0x08ffffff
PC card (attribute)	0x09000000	0x09ffffff
Misc registers	0x0d000000	0x0dffffff
NVRAM	0x0e000000	0x0e007fff
DPR	0x0ff00000	0x0ff00fff

Table B-22: Cisco 1400 Memory Map

Table B-22   *Cisco 1400 Memory Map*

Start Address	End Address	Width	CS	DSACK Source	Description
0x02000000	0x03FFFFFF	LongWord	CS1	Internal	SIMM DRAM
0x05000000	0x07FFFFFF		CS2		SIMM DRAM
			CS5		Onboard DRAM
			CS6		Onboard DRAM
0x04000000	0x043FFFFF	Word	CS0	Internal	ROM
0x08000000	0x08FFFFFF	Byte/word	CS4	External	PC card common memory
0x09000000	0x09FFFFFF	Byte/word	CS4	External	PC card attribute memory
0x0A000000	0x0AFFFFFF	Byte/word	CS4	External	PC card
0x0B000000	0x0BFFFFFF	Byte/word	CS4	External	PC card
0x0D000000	0x0DFFFFFF	Byte	CS3	External	Total CS3 address space allocation
0x0D010000	0x0D01FFFF	Byte	CS3	External	Dummy cycles location
0x0D020000	0x0D02FFFF	Byte	CS3	External	Reserved
0x0D030000	0x0D03FFFF	Byte	CS3	External	PC card control registers
0x0D040000	0x0D04FFFF	Byte	CS3	External	Reserved
0x0D050000	0x0D05FFFF	Byte	CS3	External	Reserved for WIC registers
0x0D060000	0x0D06FFFF	Byte	CS3	External	Reserved

continues

Table B-22   *Cisco 1400 Memory Map (Continued)*

Start Address	End Address	Width	CS	DSACK Source	Description
0x0D070000	0x0D07FFFF	Byte	CS3	External	Reserved
0x0D080000	0x0D080000	Byte	CS3	External	Status register
0x0D080001	0x0D080001	Byte	CS3	External	Control register (LEDs)
0x0D080004	0x0D080004	Byte	CS3	External	External interrupt mask
0x0D080005	0x0D080005	Byte	CS3	External	External interrupt read/clear (wr)
0x0D080006	0x0D080006	Byte	CS3	External	NVRAM protect (hex 05 enables writes)
0x0D08000F	0x0D08000F	Byte	CS3	External	Reserved for WIC reset
0x0D880000	0x0D88FFFF	Byte	CS3	External	NVRAM
0x0E000000	0x0E7FFFFF	LongWord	CS7	External	PCI register space
0x0E800000	0x0E8FFFFF	LongWord	CS7	External	PCI memory space

Table B-23: AS5200 Memory Map

Table B-23   *AS5200 Memory Map*

Start Address	End Address	Block Name	# Bits
00000000	001FFFFF	DRAM 2 MB	×32
00000000	003FFFFF	DRAM 4 MB	×32
00000000	007FFFFF	DRAM 8 MB	×32
00000000	00FFFFFF	DRAM 16 MB	×32
00000000	001FFFFF	Flash PCMCIA card Boot mode	×16
00000000	000FFFFF	Boot Flash 1 MB Boot mode, no Flash card	×8/16
00000000	001FFFFF	Boot Flash 2 MB Boot mode, no Flash card	×8/16
01000000	011FFFFF	FLASH PCMCIA card When installed	×16

Table B-23   *AS5200 Memory Map (Continued)*

Start Address	End Address	Block Name	# Bits
01000000	010FFFFF	Boot Flash 1 MB When Flash card is not in	×8/16
01000000	011FFFFF	Boot Flash 2 MB When Flash card is not in	×8/16
02000000	02007FFF	Config RAM 32 K	×8
02000000	0201FFFF	Config RAM 128 K	×8
02100000	0218FFFF	Memory-mapped I/O	×8/16
03000000	033FFFFF	Flash 4 MB	×32
03000000	037FFFFF	Flash 8 MB	×32
03000000	03FFFFFF	Flash 16 MB	×32
04000000	041FFFFF	Reserved when 16 MB DRAM SIMM is installed	×32
08000000	080FFFFF	Boot Flash 1 MB When Flash card is installed	×8/16

Table B-23a   *I/O Map*

Start Address	End Address	Block Name	# Bits
02100000	021001FF	Reserved	×16
02110000	02110001	SCR 1	×16
02110002	02110003	SCR 2	×16
02110004	02110005	SCR 3	×16
02110006	02110007	SCR 4	×16
0211000A	0211000B	ASIC REG	×16
02110010	02110013	BP ADDR REG H / L	×16
02110014	02110017	BP MASK REG H / L	×16
02110018	02110018	FC REG/MASK REG	×8
02110019	02110019	BP control reg	×8
02110060	02110060	Cookie reg	×8
02120040	02120040	Counter control reg	×8
02120050	02120051	Counter 0	×16
02120060	02120061	Counter 1	×16
02120070	02120071	Counter 2	×16

continues

Table B-23a *I/O Map (Continued)*

Start Address	End Address	Block Name	# Bits
02120100	0212013F	2681 DUART (console)	×8
E 021300	02130003	Ethernet ChA	×16
R 021310	0213100F	Token Ring ChA	×16
02131010	02131011	Token Ring ChA reg0	×16
02131012	02131013	Token Ring ChA reg1	×16
T 021320	021320FF	DUAL serial ChB	×16
02132100	02132101	Serial 0 modem reg	×16
02132102	02132103	Serial 1 modem reg	×16
02132104	02132105	S0 ack(RD)/LED(wr)	×16
02132106	02132107	S1 ack(RD)/LED(wr)	×16
02134000	02134001	COPAN status reg	×16
02135000	02135001	Motherboard ID	×16
02135002	02135003	Motherboard REV	×16
02135004	02135005	MB config	×16
02135006	02135007	MB Cntl #1 reg	×16
02135008	02135009	MB status reg	×16
0213500A	0213500B	MB ISR #1 reg	×16
0213500C	0213500D	MB ISR #2 reg	×16
0213500E	0213500F	MB Cntl #2 reg	×16
02135010	02135011	MB Cntl #3 reg	×16
02135012	02135013	MB Cntl #4 reg	×16
02135014	02135015	MB IRQ vector reg	×16
02135016	021350FF	Reserved	×16
02135100	0213517F	Motherboard TDM I/F	×16
02135180	02135181	TDM output disable	×16
02135182	02135183	TDM PLL reg	×16
02135184	02135FFF	Reserved	×16
02136000	02136001	Compress ID	×16
02136002	02136003	Compress REV	×16
02136004	02137fff	Reserved for C.M.	×16

Table B-23a *I/O Map (Continued)*

Start Address	End Address	Block Name	# Bits
02138000	02138001	Slot 0 ID	×16
02138002	02138003	Slot 0 REV	×16
02138004	021380FF	Slot 0-specific	×16
02138100	0213817F	Slot 0 TDM I/F	×16
02138180	02139FFF	Slot 0-specific	×16
0213A000	0213A001	Slot 1 ID	×16
0213A002	0213A003	Slot 1 REV	×16
0213A004	0213A0FF	Slot 1-specific	×16
0213A100	0213A17F	Slot 1 TDM I/F	×16
0213A180	0213BFFF	Slot 1-specific	×16
0213C000	0213C001	Slot 2 ID	×16
0213C002	0213C003	Slot 2 REV	×16
0213C004	0213C0FF	Slot 2-specific	×16
0213C100	0213C17F	Slot 2 TDM I/F	×16
0213C180	021DFFFF	Slot 2-specific	×16

Table B-24: AS5300 Memory Map

Table B-24 *AS5300 Memory Map*

KUSEG			
Virtual Address	**Physical Address**	**Description**	**# Bits**
6000.0000 to 7FFF.FFFF	6000.0000 to 7FFF.FFFF	Main DRAM	64
4000.0000 to 4FFF.FFFF	4000.0000 to 4FFF.FFFF	Shared DRAM	32
3000.0000 to 37FF.FFFF	3000.0000 to 37FF.FFFF	System Flash	32
3800.0000 to 3BFF.FFFF	3800.0000 to 3BFF.FFFF	RxBoot Flash	32
3C00.0000 to 3DFF.FFFF	3C00.0000 to 3DFF.FFFF	Fixed NIM/	
		slot I/O	16
3E00.0000 to 3E7F.FFFF	3E00.0000 to 3E7F.FFFF	NVRAM	8
3E80.0000 to 3EFF.FFFF	3E80.0000 to 3EFF.FFFF	CPU I/O	16
3F00.0000 to 3FFF.FFFF	3F00.0000 to 3FFF.FFFF	Boot EPROM	8

continues

Table B-24   *AS5300 Memory Map (Continued)*

KSEG 0

Virtual Address	Physical Address	Description	# Bits
8000.0000 to 87FF.FFFF	0000.0000 to 07FF.FFFF	Main DRAM	64
5000.0000 to 5FFF.FFFF	0800.0000 to 0FFF.FFFF	Shared DRAM	32
9000.0000 to 97FF.FFFF	1000.0000 to 17FF.FFFF	System Flash	32
9800.0000 to 9BFF.FFFF	1800.0000 to 1BFF.FFFF	RxBoot Flash	32
9C00.0000 to 9DFF.FFFF	1C00.0000 to 1DFF.FFFF	Fixed NIM/	
		slot I/O	16
9E00.0000 to 9E7F.FFFF	1E00.0000 to 1E7F.FFFF	NVRAM	8
9E80.0000 to 9EFF.FFFF	1E80.0000 to 1EFF.FFFF	CPU I/O	16
9F00.0000 to 9FFF.FFFF	1F00.0000 to 1FFF.FFFF	Boot EPROM	8

KSEG 1

Virtual Address	Physical Address	Description	# Bits
A000.0000 to A7FF.FFFF	0000.0000 to 07FF.FFFF	Main DRAM	64
A800.0000 to AFFF.FFFF	0800.0000 to 0FFF.FFFF	Shared DRAM	32
B000.0000 to B7FF.FFFF	1000.0000 to 17FF.FFFF	System Flash	32
B800.0000 to BBFF.FFFF	1800.0000 to 1BFF.FFFF	RxBoot Flash	32
BC00.0000 to BDFF.FFFF	1C00.0000 to 1DFF.FFFF	Fixed NIM/	
		slot I/O	16
BE00.0000 to BE7F.FFFF	1E00.0000 to 1E7F.FFFF	NVRAM	8
BE80.0000 to BEFF.FFFF	1E80.0000 to 1EFF.FFFF	CPU I/O	16
BF00.0000 to BFFF.FFFF	1F00.0000 to 1FFF.FFFF	Boot EPROM	8

Table B-25: AS5800 Memory Map

Table B-25   *AS5800 Memory Map—NPE-200 Memory Map*

Base	Until	Size	Device	Bus
0x0 0000 0000	0x0 07FF FFFF	128 MB	System DRAM	
0x0 0800 0000	0x0 0FFF FFFF	128 MB	System DRAM (rsvd)	
0x0 1000 0000	0x0 13FF FFFF	62 MB	Reserved	
0x0 1400 0000	0x0 141F FFFF	2 MB	GT-64010 registers	
0x0 1420 0000	0x0 19FF FFFF	94 MB	Reserved	

Table B-25   *AS5800 Memory Map—NPE-200 Memory Map (Continued)*

Base	Until	Size	Device	Bus
0x0 1A00 0000	0x0 1A3F FFFF	4 MB	Internal Flash SIMM	
0x0 1A40 0000	0x0 1BFF FFFF	28 MB	Larger Flash SIMM (rsvd)	
0x0 1C00 0000	0x0 1D00 0000	32 MB	Reserved	
0x0 1E00 0000	0x0 1E1F FFFF	2 MB	NVRAM (TOD)	
0x0 1E20 0000	0x0 1E7F FFFF	6 MB	Reserved	
0x0 1E80 0000	0x0 1E9F FFFF	2 MB	I/O registers	
0x0 1EA0 0000	0x0 1EFF FFFF	6 MB	Reserved	
0x0 1F00 0000	0x0 1FBF FFFF	12 MB	Bit bucket (read/write null)	
0x0 1FC0 0000	0x0 1FDF FFFF	2 MB	Boot EPROM	
0x0 1FE0 0000	0x0 3FFF FFFF	x MB	Reserved	
0x0 4000 0000	0x0 43FF FFFF	64 MB	PCI-to-PCMCIA interface (top slot)	
0x0 4400 0000	0x0 47FF FFFF	64 MB	PCI-to-PCMCIA interface (bottom slot)	
0x0 4800 0000	0x0 487F FFFF	8 MB	Fast Ethernet——memory-mapped IO	
0x0 4880 0000	0x0 48FF FFFF	8 MB	PA1 memory-mapped IO	
0x0 4900 0000	0x0 497F FFFF	8 MB	PA3 memory-mapped IO	
0x0 4980 0000	0x0 49FF FFFF	8 MB	PA5 memory-mapped IO	
0x0 4A00 0000	0x0 4A7F FFFF	8 MB	PA7 memory-mapped IO (rsvd)	
0x0 4A80 0000	0x0 4AFF FFFF	8 MB	PA9 memory-mapped IO (rsvd)	
0x0 4B00 0000	0x0 4B3F FFFF	4 MB	PCI PM, first 4 M, no byte swap	
0x0 4B40 0000	0x0 4B7F FFFF	4 MB	PCI PM, larger PM, no swap (rsvd)	
0x0 4B80 0000	0x0 4BBF FFFF	4 MB	PCI PM, first 4 M, byte swap	
0x0 4BC0 0000	0x0 4BFF FFFF	4 MB	PCI PM, larger PM, byte swap (rsvd)	
0x0 4C00 0000	0x0 4C3F FFFF	4 MB	PCI alias PM, first 4 M, no byte swap	
0x0 4C40 0000	0x0 4C7F FFFF	4 MB	PCI alias PM, larger PM, no swap (rsvd)	
0x0 4C80 0000	0x0 4CBF FFFF	4 MB	PCI alias PM, first 4 M, byte swap	
0x0 4CC0 0000	0x0 4CFF FFFF	4 MB	PCI alias PM, larger PM, byte swap (rsvd)	
0x0 4D00 0000	0x0 4D7F FFFF	8 MB	PA2 memory-mapped IO	
0x0 4D80 0000	0x0 4DFF FFFF	8 MB	PA4 memory-mapped IO	

continues

Table B-25   *AS5800 Memory Map—NPE-200 Memory Map (Continued)*

Base	Until	Size	Device	Bus
0x0 4E00 0000	0x0 4E7F FFFF	8 MB	PA6 memory-mapped IO	
0x0 4E80 0000	0x0 4EFF FFFF	8 MB	PA8 memory-mapped IO (rsvd)	
0x0 4F00 0000	0x0 4F7F FFFF	8 MB	PA10 memory-mapped IO (rsvd)	
0x0 4F80 0000	0x0 4FFF FFFF	8 MB	IO assy memory-mapped IO (rsvd)	
0x0 5000 0000	0x0 FFFF FFFF	x MB	Reserved	
0x1 0000 0000	0x0 001F FFFF	2 MB	PCI I/O address space	
0x1 0020 0000	0x1 4B7F FFFF	About 1 GB	Reserved	
0x1 4B00 0000	0x1 4B3F FFFF	4 MB	CPU PM, first 4 M, no byte swap	
0x1 4B40 0000	0x1 4B7F FFFF	4 MB	CPU PM, larger PM, no swap (rsvd)	
0x1 4B80 0000	0x1 FFFF FFFF	About 0 GB	Reserved	
0x2 0000 0000	0x3 FFFF FFFF	8 GB	L2 cache is disabled (alias) for low 8 GB	
0x4 0000 0000	0x7 FFFF FFFF	16 GB	Cache controller tag Op 0	
0x8 0000 0000	0xF FFFF FFFF	32 GB	Cache controller tag Op 1	

Table B-25a   *AS5800 Memory Map—DSC Memory Map*

Base	Until	Size	Device	Bus
0x0 0000 0000	0x0 03FF0 FFFF	64 MB	System DRAM	
0x0 0400 0000	0x0 0FFF FFFF	192 MB	Reserved for larger DRAM	
0x0 1000 0000	0x0 13FF FFFF	62 MB	Reserved	
0x0 1400 0000	0x0 141F FFFF	2 MB	GT-64010 registers	
0x0 1420 0000	0x0 19FF FFFF	94 MB	Reserved	
0x0 1A00 0000	0x0 1A3F FFFF	8 MB	Internal Flash SIMM	I/O
0x0 1A40 0000	0x0 1BFF FFFF	24 MB	Reserved: more Flash	I/O
0x0 1C00 0000	0x0 1DFF FFFF	32 MB	Reserved	
0x0 1E00 0000	0x0 1E01 FFFF	128 KB	NVRAM default config	I/O
0x0 1E02 0000	0x0 1E1F FFFF	About 2 MB	Reserved for larger NVRAM	I/O
0x0 1E20 0000	0x0 1E7F FFFF	6 MB	Reserved	
0x0 1E80 0000	0x0 1E9F FFFF	2 MB	I/O registers	I/O

Table B-25a *AS5800 Memory Map—DSC Memory Map (Continued)*

Base	Until	Size	Device	Bus
0x0 1EA0 0000	0x0 1EFF FFFF	6 MB	Reserved	
0x0 1F00 0000	0x0 1FBF FFFF	12 MB	Reserved	
0x0 1FC0 0000	0x0 1FC7 FFFF	512 KB	Boot EPROM	
0x0 1FC8 0000	0x0 1FDF FFFF	1536 KB	Reserved: more EPROM	
0x0 1FE0 0000	0x0 3FFF FFFF	x MB	Reserved	
0x0 4000 0000	0x0 43FF FFFF	64 MB	PCI-to-PCMCIA interface (top slot)	MB0
0x0 4400 0000	0x0 47FF FFFF	64 MB	PCI-to-PCMCIA interface (bottom slot)	MB0
0x0 4800 0000	0x0 4800 07FF	2 KB	Backplane interconnect: Fast Ethernet-0	MB0
0x0 4800 0800	0x0 4800 0FFF	2 KB	Backplane interconnect: Fast Ethernet-1	MB0
0x0 4800 1000	0x0 4800 17FF	2 KB	Backplane interconnect: Fast Ethernet-2 (inter-DSC)	MB0
0x0 4800 1800	0x0 4800 1FFF	2 KB	Front panel 10BaseT MAC	MB0
0x0 4800 2000	0x0 487F FFFF	About 8 KB	Reserved: PCI memory-mapped device	MB0
0x0 4880 0000	0x0 4BFF FFFF	56 MB	PCI memory-mapped device (MB1 in trunk cards)	MB0
0x0 4C00 0000	0x0 4F7F FFFF	56 MB	PCI memory-mapped device (MB2 in CE1 card)	MB0
0x0 4F80 0000	0x0 4FFF FFFF	8 MB	Reserved: PCI memory-mapped device	MB0
0x0 5000 0000	0x0 FFFF FFFF	x MB	Reserved	
0x1 0000 0000	0x0 001F FFFF	2 MB	PCI I/O address space	MB0
0x1 0020 0000	0x1 FFFF FFFF	About 4 GB	Reserved	
0x2 0000 0000	0x3 FFFF FFFF	8 GB	Alias—low 8 GB, L2 cache disabled	
0x4 0000 0000	0x7 FFFF FFFF	16 GB	Cache controller tag Op 0[1]	
0x8 0000 0000	0xF FFFF FFFF	32 GB	Cache controller tag Op 1[2]	

[1]When this space is accessed, the L2 cache for its alias in low 8 GB is flushed, and the corresponding tag is invalidated.

[2]When this space is accessed, the entire L2 cache is flushed and invalidated.

Table B-25b *AS5800 Memory Map—Modem Card Memory Map*

Base	Until	Size	Device	Bus
0x0 0000 0000	0x0 03FF0FFFF	64 MB	System DRAM	
0x0 0400 0000	0x0 0FFF FFFF	192 MB	Reserved for larger DRAM	
0x0 1000 0000	0x0 13FF FFFF	62 MB	Reserved	
0x0 1400 0000	0x0 141F FFFF	2 MB	GT-64010 registers	
0x0 1420 0000	0x0 19FF FFFF	94 MB	Reserved	
0x0 1A00 0000	0x0 1BFF FFFF	32 MB	Reserved (Flash on DSC)	I/O
0x0 1C00 0000	0x0 1DFF FFFF	32 MB	Reserved	
0x0 1E00 0000	0x0 1E01 FFFF	128 KB	Reserved (NVRAM on DSC)	I/O
0x0 1E02 0000	0x0 1E1F FFFF	About 2 MB	Reserved	I/O
0x0 1E20 0000	0x0 1E7F FFFF	6 MB	Reserved	
0x0 1E80 0000	0x0 1E9F FFFF	2 MB	I/O registers	I/O
0x0 1EA0 0000	0x0 1EFF FFFF	6 MB	Reserved	
0x0 1F00 0000	0x0 1FBF FFFF	12 MB	Reserved	
0x0 1FC0 0000	0x0 1FC7 FFFF	512 KB	Boot EPROM	I/O
0x0 1FC8 0000	0x0 1FDF FFFF	1536 KB	Reserved: more EPROM	I/O
0x0 1FE0 0000	0x0 3FFF FFFF	x MB	Reserved	
0x0 4000 0000	0x0 47FF FFFF	128 MB	Reserved (PCMCIA on DSC)	MB0
0x0 4800 0000	0x0 4800 07FF	2 KB	Backplane interconnect: Fast Ethernet Tx MAC	MB0
0x0 4800 0800	0x0 4800 0FFF	2 KB	Backplane interconnect: Fast Ethernet Rx MAC	MB0
0x0 4800 1000	0x0 4800 18FF	About 2 KB	Reserved	MB0
0x0 4800 1900	0x0 4800 19FF	256 KB	Memory access to PLX9060SD runtime registers	MB0
0x0 4800 1A00	0x0 49FF FFFF	About 32 KB	Reserved: PCI memory-mapped device	MB0
0x0 4A00 0000	0x0 4BFF FFFF	32 MB	Modem card-specific PCI memory-mapped device	MB0
0x0 4C00 0000	0x0 4FFF FFFF	64 MB	Reserved PCI memory-mapped device	MB0
0x0 5000 0000	0x0 FFFF FFFF	x MB	Reserved	
0x1 0000 0000	0x0 001F FFFF	2 MB	PCI I/O address space	MB0

Table B-25b *AS5800 Memory Map—Modem Card Memory Map (Continued)*

Base	Until	Size	Device	Bus
0x1 0020 0000	0x1 FFFF FFFF	About 4 GB	Reserved	
0x2 0000 0000	0x3 FFFF FFFF	8 GB	Alias—low 8 GB, L2 cache disabled	
0x4 0000 0000	0x7 FFFF FFFF	16 GB	Cache controller tag Op 0[1]	
0x8 0000 0000	0xF FFFF FFFF	32 GB	Cache controller tag Op 1[2]	

[1]When this space is accessed, the L2 cache for its alias in the low 8 GB is flushed, and the corresponding tag is invalidated.

[2]When this space is accessed, the entire L2 cache is flushed and invalidated.

Table B-25c *AS5800 Memory Map—Trunk Card Memory Map*

Base	Until	Size	Device	Bus
0x0 0000 0000	0x0 03FF FFFF	64 MB	System DRAM	
0x0 0400 0000	0x0 0FFF FFFF	192 MB	Reserved for larger DRAM	
0x0 1000 0000	0x0 13FF FFFF	62 MB	Generate bus error illegal address	
0x0 1400 0000	0x0 141F FFFF	2 MB	Gt64010A registers	
0x0 1420 0000	0x0 14FF FFFF	X MB	Legal address decode WatchDog timeout	Internal
0x0 1500 0000	0x0 1E7F FFFF	X MB	Generate bus error illegal address	
0x0 1E80 0000	0x0 1E8F FFFF	2 MB	I/O registers	I/O
0x0 1E90 0000	0x0 1FBF FFFF		Generate bus error illegal address	
0x0 1FC0 0000	0x0 1FC7 FFFF	512 KB	Boot EPROM	I/O
0x0 1FC8 0000	0x0 1FDF FFFF	1536 KB	Reserved for larger EPROM	I/O
0x0 1FE0 0000	0x0 47FF FFFF	128 MB	Generate bus error illegal address	
0x0 4800 0000	0x0 4800 07FF	2 KB	BIC Fast Ethernet-0	MB0
0x0 4800 0800	0x0 4800 0FFF	2 KB	BIC Fast Ethernet-1	MB0
0x0 4800 1000	0x0 4800 18FF	2 KB	Reserved	MB0
0x0 4800 2000	0x0 4800 2FFF	4 KB	Gt64011 Reg's PCI memory mapped	MB0
0x0 4820 0000	0x0 482F FFFF	1 MB	FDL DRAM PCI memory mapped	MB0
0x0 4830 0000	0x0 487F FFFF	5 MB	Future DRAM PCI memory mapped	MB0
0x0 487F FFFF	0x0 48BF FFFF	4 MB	M32x 0 PCI memory mapped	MB1
0x0 48C0 0000	0x0 48FF FFFF	4 MB	M32x 1 PCI memory mapped	MB1
0x0 4900 0000	0x0 493F FFFF	4 MB	M32x 2 PCI memory mapped	MB1

Table B-26: Cisco 1000, 1003/1004/1005 Memory Map

Table B-26   *Cisco 1000, 1003/1004/1005 Memory Map*

Address	Size	Chip Select	Description
0000000 to 00FFFFF	1 MB	CS0	ROM
2000000 to 2FFFFFF	16 MB	CS1, 2	DRAM up to 16 MB
6000000 to 600FFFF	64 Kb	CS6	PCMCIA I/O space
8000000 to 800FFFF	16 MB	CS5	PCMCIA/PC card attribute memory
8010000 to 8FFFFFF	16 MB	CS5	PCMCIA/PC card common memory
C0003E0 to C0003E1	64 Kb	CS4	PCMCIA controller index and data register
E000000 to E007FFF	32 Kb	CS7	NVRAM
FF00000 to FF00FFF	1 MB	360DPR	68360 dual port memory (top 1 MB)
CPU Space:			
003ff00 to 003ff03	4 bytes		MBAR for 68360

Table B-27: VIP2 Memory Map

Table B-27   *VIP2 Memory Map*

Physical Address	Segment	Size	Reno Mode	CPU Parity Checked	Description
0000 0000 to 07FF FFFF	kseg 0/1	128 MB	0	Yes	64-bit main DRAM (64 bit)
0800 0000 to 0FFF FFFF		128 MB	1+3	Yes	Unused (32-bit target)
1000 0000 to 1003 FFFF	kseg 0/1	256 KB	2+3		PMA ASIC config space (32 bit)
1004 0000 to 1003 FFFF	kseg 0/1	256 KB	2+3		CYA ASIC config space (32 bit)
1008 0000 to 10FF FFFF		15.5 MB	2+3		Unused (32-bit target)
1100 0000 to 11FF FFFF	kseg 0/1	16 MB	2+3		Cbus/MEMD memory (32 bit)
1200 0000 to 12FF FFFF	kseg 0/1	16 MB	2+3		PCI/SRAM memory (32 bit)

Table B-27   *VIP2 Memory Map (Continued)*

Physical Address	Segment	Size	Reno Mode	CPU Parity Checked	Description
1300 0000 to 13FF FFFF	kseg 0/1	16 MB	2+3		PCI bus: I/O space (32 bit)
1400 0000 to 17FF FFFF	kseg 0/1	64 MB	2+3		PCI bus: memory space (32 bit)
1800 0000 to 1BFF FFFF		64 MB	2+3		Unused (32-bit target)
1C00 0000 to 1C03 FFFF	kseg 0/1	256 KB	1+3		Interrupt controller (16 bit)
1C04 0000 to 1DFF FFFF		About 32 MB	1+3		Unused (16-bit target)
1E00 0000 to 1E7F FFFF		8 MB	2+3		Unused (8-bit target)
1E80 0000 to 1EBF FFFF		4 MB	2+3		Unused (32-bit target)
1EC0 0000 to 1ECF FFFF	kseg 0/1	1 MB	0		32-bit address exception register: DRAM Reno
1ED0 0000 to 1EFF FFFF	kseg 0/1	1 MB	1+3		32-bit address exception register: I/O Reno
1F00 0000 to 1FBF FFFF	kseg 0	12 MB	2+3		Unused (8-bit target)
1FC00 0000 to 1FFF FFFF	kseg 0	4 MB	2+3		8-bit boot PROM
2000 0000 to 27FF FFFF		128 MB	1+3		Unused (32-bit target)
2800 0000 to 2FFF FFFF		128 MB	2+3		Unused (32-bit target)
3000 0000 to 3003 FFFF	kuseg	256 KB	2+3		PMA ASIC config space (32 bit)
3004 0000 to 3007 FFFF	kuseg	256 KB	2+3		CYA ASIC config space (32 bit)
3008 0000 to 30FF FFFF	kuseg	15.5 MB	2+3		Unused (32-bit target)
3100 0000 to 31FF FFFF	kuseg	16 MB	2+3		Cbus/MEMD memory (32 bit)

continues

Table B-27 *VIP2 Memory Map (Continued)*

Physical Address	Segment	Size	Reno Mode	CPU Parity Checked	Description
3200 0000 to 32FF FFFF	kuseg	16 MB	2+3		PCI/SRAM memory (32 bit)
3300 0000 to 33FF FFFF	kuseg	16 MB	2+3		PCI bus: I/O space (32 bit)
3400 0000 to 37FF FFFF	kuseg	64 MB	2+3		PCI bus: memory space (32 bit)
3800 0000 to 3BFF FFFF	kuseg	64 MB	2+3		Unused (32-bit target)

Technical Support Information

When you have a problem that you cannot resolve, the resource of last resort is your Cisco Systems technical support representative. To analyze a problem, your technical support representative will need certain information about the situation and the symptoms that you are experiencing. To speed up the problem isolation and resolution process, collect the necessary data before you contact your representative.

This appendix describes how to collect relevant information about your internetwork and how to present that information to your technical support representative. Refer to the appropriate chapter within this book for specific information that you need to collect for each technology. In addition, some sections describe Cisco Connection Online, Cisco's primary, real-time support channel on the World Wide Web (WWW), and Cisco Connection Documentation, Cisco's library of product information on CD-ROM. Both are valuable resources in troubleshooting network problems. Make sure that you search CCO for documentation regarding your problem before you contact your technical representative.

Gathering Information About Your Internetwork

Before gathering any specific data, compile a list of all relevant symptoms that users have reported on the network (such as connections dropping or slow host response).

The next step is to gather specific information. Typical information needed to troubleshoot internetworking problems falls into two general categories: information required for any situation, and information specific to the topology, technology, protocol, or problem.

Information that is always required by technical support engineers includes the following:

- Configuration listing of all routers involved
- Complete specifications of all routers involved
- Description of changes, if any, made to the network prior to the problem/symptom
- Description of the nature of the problem (whether the problem occurs intermittently, what errors are being observed, and so on)
- Version numbers of software (obtained with the **show version** command) and firmware (obtained with the **show controllers** command) on all relevant routers

- Network topology map
- List of hosts and servers (host and server type, number and function of each host/server on the network, description of host operating systems implemented)
- List of network layer protocols, versions, and vendors

To assist you in gathering this required data, the **show tech-support** exec command has been added in Cisco IOS Release 11.1(4) and later. This command provides general information about the router that you can provide to your technical support representative when you are reporting a problem.

The **show tech-support** command outputs the equivalent of the **show version, show running-config, show controllers, show stacks, show interfaces, show buffers, show process memory**, and **show process cpu** exec commands. In many cases, the **show tech-support** command outputs can be long and can affect router performance.

Specific requirements that vary depending on the situation include the following:

- Output from general **show** commands:

    show interfaces

    show controllers

    show processes {**cpu** | **mem**}

    show buffer

    show mem summary

- Output from protocol-specific show commands:

    show *protocol* **route**

    show *protocol* **traffic**

    show *protocol* **interfaces**

    show *protocol* **arp**

    show appletalk globals (AppleTalk only)

    show ipx servers (Novell IPX only)

- Output from relevant **debug** privileged exec commands
- Output from protocol-specific **ping** and **trace** diagnostic tests, as appropriate
- Network analyzer traces, as appropriate
- Core dumps obtained using the **exception dump** router configuration command, or using the **write core** router configuration command, if the system is operational, as appropriate

Getting the Data from Your Router

You must tailor the way that you obtain information from the router to the platform that you are using to collect the information. Following are some hints for different platforms:

- **PC and Macintosh**—Connect a PC or a Macintosh to the console port of the router, and log all outputs to a disk file (using a terminal emulation program). The exact procedure varies, depending on the communication package used with the system.

- **Terminal connected to console port or remote terminal**—The only way to get information with a terminal connected to the console port or with a remote terminal is to attach a printer to the auxiliary port on the terminal (if one exists) and force all screen output to go to the printer. This method is undesirable because there is no way to capture the output data to a file.

- **UNIX workstation**—At the UNIX prompt, enter the command **script** *filename*, where *filename* is the destination file for the log, and then Telnet to the router. The UNIX **script** command captures screen outputs to the specified filename. To stop capturing output and close the file, enter the end-of-file character (typically **^D**) for your UNIX system.

NOTE   To get your system to automatically log specific error messages or operational information to a UNIX syslog server, use the **logging** *internet-address* router configuration command. For more information about using the **logging** command and setting up a syslog server, refer to the Cisco IOS configuration guides and command references.

Remote Console Port and Auxiliary Port Access

You can access a router from a remote location without a router being connected to a network by dialing directly to the console or auxiliary port on a router. In general, the console port is recommended because it displays router startup messages, whereas the auxiliary port does not provide this information. In addition, if a router hangs in the read-only memory monitor, you can reboot the system if you are connected using the console port. However, if you have a local terminal connected to your console, you might have no other choice than to connect to the auxiliary port. The following discussions provide the general requirements for connecting to a Cisco router remotely via the console or auxiliary ports.

Console Port Connected Modem

To connect remotely to the console port on a Cisco router, you need the following:

- Null modem cable

- PC or equivalent with suitable communications software
- 14.4 kbps–capable modem

When you have your communications software installed, set your PC's comm port (or equivalent) to 9600 baud (a software setting).

The modem attached to your router's console port must be configured as follows:

- Lock the DTE speed to 9600
- Set no flow control
- Set autoanswer
- Set no echo
- Set no result

NOTE   Refer to your modem documentation to determine the commands required to set these options on your modem. Refer to your modem and router hardware documentation for specific cabling requirements.

Auxiliary Port Connected Modem

To connect remotely to the console port on a Cisco router, you need the following:

- Straight-through serial cable
- PC or equivalent with suitable communications software
- 14.4 kbps–capable modem

NOTE   Refer to your modem documentation to determine the commands required to set these options on your modem. Refer to your modem and router hardware documentation for specific cabling requirements.

To use the router's auxiliary port for remote access, you must include several configuration commands. The required commands are as follows:

```
line aux 0
modem inout
```

If you are using software prior to Cisco IOS 11.1, set the modem options as specified for the console port.

If you are using Cisco IOS 11.1 or later, you do not need to set the modem configuration manually, but you must include the **modem autoconfigure discovery** line configuration subcommand.

NOTE   You can also refer to Chapter 16, "Troubleshooting Dialup Connections," for additional related information.

CCO

CCO, formerly Cisco Information Online (CIO), is Cisco Systems' primary, real-time support channel. Maintenance customers and partners can self-register on CCO to obtain additional content and services.

Available 24 hours a day, seven days a week, CCO provides a wealth of standard and value-added services to Cisco's customers and business partners. CCO services include product information, software updates, release notes, technical tips, the Bug Navigator, the Troubleshooting Engine, configuration notes, brochures, descriptions of service offerings, and download access to public and authorized files.

CCO serves a wide variety of users through two interfaces that are updated and enhanced simultaneously: a multimedia version that resides on the WWW, and a character-based version. The WWW version of CCO provides richly formatted documents with photographs, figures, graphics, and video, as well as hyperlinks to related information, official documentation, and technical tips. The character-based CCO supports Zmodem, Kermit, Xmodem, FTP, Internet e-mail, and fax download options, and it is excellent for quick access to information over lower bandwidths.

You can access CCO in the following ways:

- WWW: www.cisco.com.
- Telnet: cco.cisco.com.
- Modem: From North America, 408-526-8070; from Europe, 33 1 64 46 40 82. Use the following terminal settings: VT100 emulation; databits: 8; stop bits: 1; parity: none; baud rate: up to 14.4 kbps.

For a copy of CCO's frequently asked questions (FAQ), send e-mail to cco—help@cisco.com. For additional information, send e-mail to cco—team@cisco.com.

CCO Troubleshooting Services

Registered CCO users can take advantage of a number of WWW-based support services offered by Cisco's Customer Support Engineering organization. These services are offered to help you diagnose and resolve problems in your network. These tools are accessible to registered CCO users through the Technical Assistance Center (TAC) page within CCO. WWW-based troubleshooting services/tools include the following:

- **Open Q&A Forum**—This interactive tool that provides database searches for quick answers to technical questions. For more difficult questions, you receive access to CCIE qualified experts to help solve your problem.

- **Automated TAC Case Management**—Problem cases can be opened, updated, and monitored through CCO's Case tools.

- **Troubleshooting Assistant**—This tool resolves a variety of common internetworking problems using an intuitive web interface. It supports a variety of technologies and protocols.

- **Stack Decoder**—This tool analyzes and diagnoses stack traces from Cisco IOS routers. You can paste the output from the **show stack** exec command into the tool and receive the results on the screen or by e-mail.

- **Hardware/Software Compatibility Matrix**—This tool can be used to determine the compatibility between hardware product numbers and software versions.

- **Software Bug Toolkit**—This tool is used to search for software bugs based on version and feature sets.

All CCO users—registered users and guests alike—can obtain answers to frequently asked questions, implementation case studies, technical tips, implementation procedures, sample configurations, and more at CCO's public site (www.cisco.com/public/Support_root.shtml).

You can sign up as a registered CCO user at www.cisco.com/public/registration.shtml.

Providing Data to Your Technical Support Representative

If you need technical assistance with a Cisco product that is under warranty or covered by a maintenance contract, contact Cisco's Technical Assistance Center (TAC) to open a case. Contact the TAC with a phone call or an e-mail message:

- **North America**—800-553-2447; e-mail: tac@cisco.com
- **Europe**—32 2 704 5555; e-mail: euro-tac@cisco.com
- **Asia-Pacific**—61 2 8448 7107; e-mail: asiapac-tac@cisco.com

Refer to the TAC web page on CCO for more information about contacting the TAC center nearest you.

When submitting information to your technical support representative, electronic data is preferred. Electronic data significantly eases the transfer of information between technical support personnel and development staff. Common electronic formats include data sent via electronic mail and files sent using FTP.

If you are submitting data to your technical support representative, use the following list to determine the preferred method for submission:

- The preferred method of information submission is via File Transfer Protocol (FTP) service over the Internet. If your environment supports FTP, you can place your file in the incoming directory on the host cco.cisco.com.

- The next best method is to send data by e-mail. Before using this method, be sure to contact your technical support representative, especially when transferring binary core dumps or other large files.

- If you use e-mail, do not use encoding methods such as binhex or zip. Only MIME-compliant mail should be used.

- Transfer via a PC-based communications protocol, such as Kermit, to upload files to (CCO). Again, be sure to contact your technical support representative before attempting any transfer.

- Transfer by disk or tape.

- The least favorable method is hard-copy transfer by fax or postal service.

Symbols

A

E

G

H

I

J–K

L

M

N

P

Q

R

S

W

Cisco Interactive Mentor

The Cisco Interactive Mentor product line is a series of e-learning solutions designed to provide entry-level networking professionals with the opportunity to gain practical, hands-on experience through self-paced instruction and network lab simulation exercises. This combination of computer-based training with lab exercises offers users a unique learning environment that eliminates the cost overhead necessary with the actual network devices, while offering the same degree of real-world experience. Current releases include:

Router Basics
1-58720-011-2

$149.95

AVAILABLE NOW

LAN Switching
1-58720-021-X

$199.95

AVAILABLE NOW

IP Routing: Distance Vector Protocols
1-58720-012-0

$149.95

AVAILABLE NOW

Access ISDN
1-58720-025-2

$199.95

AVAILABLE NOW

Expert Labs: IP Routing
1-58720-010-4

$149.95

AVAILABLE NOW

Voice Internetworking: Basic Voice over IP
1-58720-023-6

$149.95

AVAILABLE NOW

Cisco Career Certifications

Building Cisco Remote Access Networks
Cisco Systems, Inc., edited by Catherine Paquet
1-57870-091-4 • AVAILABLE NOW

Based on the Cisco Systems instructor-led course available worldwide, *Building Cisco Remote Access Networks* teaches you how to design, set up, configure, maintain, and scale a remote access network using Cisco products. In addition, *Building Cisco Remote Access Networks* provides chapter-ending questions to help you assess your understanding of key concepts and start you down the path for attaining your CCNP certification.

Building Cisco Multilayer Switched Networks
Cisco Systems, Inc./Karen Webb, CCIE
1-57870-093-0 • AVAILABLE NOW

Based on the Cisco Systems course taught worldwide, *Building Cisco Multilayer Switched Networks* teaches you how to build and manage campus networks using multilayer switching technologies. BCMSN provides in-depth coverage of Layer 2 switching technologies, Layer 3 routing services, switched campus network security, and applying Layer 3 traffic management to the campus network. Prepare for CCNP and CCDP certification while learning the fundamentals of multilayer switched networks.

Building Scalable Cisco Networks
Cisco Systems, Inc./Diane Teare and Catherine Paquet
1-57870-228-3 • AVAILABLE NOW

Based on the Cisco Systems course taught worldwide, *Building Scalable Cisco Networks* addresses tasks that network managers and engineers need to perform when managing access and controlling overhead traffic in growing, routed networks. The book discusses router capabilities used to control multiprotocol traffic over LANs and WANs, as well as connecting corporate network to an ISP. Prepare for CCNP and CCDP certification while learning advanced routing concepts.

Cisco Internetwork Troubleshooting
Cisco Systems, Inc., edited by Laura Chappell and Dan Farkas, CCIE
1-57870-092-2 • AVAILABLE NOW

Based on the Cisco Systems instructor-led course available worldwide, *Cisco Internetwork Troubleshooting* teaches you how to perform fundamental hardware maintenance and troubleshooting on Cisco routers and switches. If you are pursuing CCNP certification and anticipate taking the CCNP Support exam, this book is a logical starting point.

www.ciscopress.com

Cisco Career Certifications

CCNP Remote Access Exam Certification Guide

Brian Morgan, CCIE #4865 and Craig Dennis

1-58720-003-1 • AVAILABLE NOW

CCNP Remote Access Exam Certification Guide is a comprehensive study tool for the Cisco Certified Network Professional Remote Access Exam #640-505. The new exam evaluates your ability to build a remote access network to interconnect central sites to branch offices and home office/telecommuters, control access to the central site, as well as maximize bandwidth utilization over the remote links. This book provides you with concise reviews of all the major topics covered on the Remote Access Exam. You'll gain full mastery of all the concepts and technologies upon which you will be tested, including selecting the proper equipment, assembling and cabling WAN components, configuring asynchronous connections with modems, configuring PPP and controlling network access, using ISDN and DDR, establishing X.25 and Frame Relay connections, managing network performance, scaling IP addresses with NAT, and monitoring the access and use of the network with AAA. Includes comprehensive testing engine on CD-ROM.

CCNP Switching Exam Certification Guide

David Hucaby, CCIE #4594 and Tim Boyles

1-58720-000-7 • AVAILABLE NOW

CCNP Switching Exam Certification Guide is a comprehensive study tool for the Cisco Certified Network Professional Switching Exam #640-504. The new exam evaluates your ability to build campus networks using multilayer switching technologies and to manage campus network traffic. This book provides you with concise reviews of all the major topics covered on the Switching Exam. You'll gain full mastery of all the concepts and technologies upon which you will be tested, including switched Ethernet, trunking, multicasting, multilayer switching, VLANs, ATM, LANE, interVLAN routing, HSRP, network traffic control, and monitoring and troubleshooting techniques. Includes comprehensive testing engine on CD-ROM.

Cisco Career Certifications

CCNP Support Exam Certification Guide

Amir Ranjbar

0-7357-0995-5 • AVAILABLE NOW

Cisco Support Exam Certification Guide is a comprehensive study tool for the Cisco Certified Network Professional Support Exam #640-506. The exam evaluates your ability to diagnose, isolate, and correct network problems in a variety of environments. This book provides you with concise reviews of all the major topics covered on the Support Exam. You'll gain full mastery of all the concepts and technologies upon which you will be tested, including troubleshooting resources, tools, and methodology, understanding data-link layer troubleshooting, fast switching methods, and buffering technologies, network layer protocol troubleshooting, troubleshooting Catalyst 5000 switches, and troubleshooting WAN connections. Includes comprehensive testing engine on CD-ROM.

CCNP Routing Exam Certification Guide

Clare Gough

1-58720-001-5 • AVAILABLE NOW

Cisco CCNP Routing Exam Certification Guide is a comprehensive study tool for the Cisco Certified Network Professional Routing Exam #640-503. The exam evaluates you ability to support and implement scalable routed internetworks for any size environment. This book provides you with concise reviews of all the major topic areas and objectives for the Routing exam. You'll gain full mastery of all the concepts and technologies upon which you will be tested, including principles of scalable internetworks, scalable routing protocols, managing traffic and access, and optimizing scalable internetworks. Includes comprehensive testing engine on CD-ROM.

Cisco Internetwork Design

Cisco Systems, Inc., edited by Matthew H. Birkner, CCIE

1-57870-171-6 • AVAILABLE NOW

Based on the Cisco Systems instructor-led course available worldwide, *Cisco Internetwork Design* teaches you how to plan and design a network using various internetworking technologies. Created for those seeking to attain CCDP certification, this book presents the fundamental, technical, and design issue associated with campus LANs; TCP/IP networks; IPX, AppleTalk, and Windows-based networks; WANs, and SNA networks.

CISCO SYSTEMS

CISCO PRESS

www.ciscopress.com

Cisco Press

Committed to being your long-term resource as you grow as a Cisco Networking professional

Help Cisco Press **stay connected** to the issues and challenges you face on a daily basis by registering your product and filling out our brief survey. Complete and mail this form, or better yet ...

Register online and enter to win a FREE book!

Jump to **www.ciscopress.com/register** and register your product online. Each complete entry will be eligible for our monthly drawing to win a FREE book of the winner's choice from the Cisco Press library.

May we contact you via e-mail with information about **new releases, special promotions** and customer benefits?

❐ Yes   ❐ No

E-mail address _____

Name _____

Address _____

City _____ State/Province _____

Country _____ Zip/Post code _____

Where did you buy this product?

❐ Bookstore   ❐ Computer store/electronics store
❐ Online retailer   ❐ Direct from Cisco Press
❐ Mail order   ❐ Class/Seminar
❐ Other_____

When did you buy this product? _____ Month _____ Year

What price did you pay for this product?

❐ Full retail price   ❐ Discounted price   ❐ Gift

How did you learn about this product?

❐ Friend   ❐ Store personnel   ❐ In-store ad
❐ Cisco Press Catalog   ❐ Postcard in the mail   ❐ Saw it on the shelf
❐ Other Catalog   ❐ Magazine ad   ❐ Article or review
❐ School   ❐ Professional Organization   ❐ Used other products
❐ Other_____

What will this product be used for?

❐ Business use   ❐ School/Education
❐ Other_____

Cisco Press
201 West 103rd Street
Indianapolis, IN 46290
ciscopress.com

Cisco Press
Customer Registration—CP0500227
P.O. Box #781046
Indianapolis, IN 46278-8046

Internetworking Troubleshooting Handbook, Second Edition (1-58705-005-6)

Thank you for completing this survey and registration. Please fold here, seal, and mail to Cisco Press.

Do you have any additional comments or suggestions?

On what topics would you like to see more coverage?

Have you purchased a Cisco Press product before?
☐ Yes   ☐ No

What is your formal education background?
☐ High school   ☐ Vocational/Technical degree   ☐ College degree
☐ Some college   ☐ Masters degree   ☐ Professional or Doctoral degree

Which best describes your job function?
☐ Corporate Management   ☐ Systems Engineering   ☐ IS Management
☐ Network Design   ☐ Network Support   ☐ Webmaster
☐ Marketing/Sales   ☐ Consultant   ☐ Student
☐ Professor/Teacher   ☐ Other

How many years have you been employed in a computer-related industry?
☐ 2 years or less   ☐ 3-5 years   ☐ 5+ years

Cisco Press
c i s c o p r e s s . c o m

PACKET

Packet magazine serves as the premier publication linking customers to Cisco Systems, Inc. Delivering complete coverage of cutting-edge networking trends and innovations, *Packet* is a magazine for technical, hands-on users. It delivers industry-specific information for enterprise, service provider, and small and midsized business market segments. A toolchest for planners and decision makers, *Packet* contains a vast array of practical information, boasting sample configurations, real-life customer examples, and tips on getting the most from your Cisco Systems' investments. Simply put, *Packet* magazine is straight talk straight from the worldwide leader in networking for the Internet, Cisco Systems, Inc.

We hope you'll take advantage of this useful resource. I look forward to hearing from you!

Jennifer Biondi
Packet Circulation Manager
packet@cisco.com
www.cisco.com/go/packet

☐ **YES!** I'm requesting a **free** subscription to *Packet*™ magazine.

☐ No. I'm not interested at this time.

☐ Mr.
☐ Ms.

First Name (Please Print)   Last Name

Title/Position (Required)

Company (Required)

Address

City   State/Province

Zip/Postal Code   Country

Telephone (Include country and area codes)   Fax

E-mail

Signature (Required)   Date

☐ I would like to receive additional information on Cisco's services and products by e-mail.

1.0 Do you or your company:
A ☐ Use Cisco products   C ☐ Both
B ☐ Resell Cisco products   D ☐ Neither

1. Your organization's relationship to Cisco Systems:
A ☐ Customer/End User   DI ☐ Non-Authorized Reseller   J ☐ Consultant
B ☐ Prospective Customer   E ☐ Integrator   K ☐ Other (specify):
C ☐ Cisco Reseller   G ☐ Cisco Training Partner
D ☐ Cisco Distributor   I ☐ Cisco OEM

2. How would you classify your business?
A ☐ Small/Medium-Sized   B ☐ Enterprise   C ☐ Service Provider

3. Your involvement in network equipment purchases:
A ☐ Recommend   B ☐ Approve   C ☐ Neither

4. Your personal involvement in networking:
A ☐ Entire enterprise at all sites   F ☐ Public network
B ☐ Departments or network segments at more than one site   D ☐ No involvement
C ☐ Single department or network segment   E ☐ Other (specify):

5. Your Industry:
A ☐ Aerospace   G ☐ a. Education (K–12)   K ☐ Health Care
B ☐ Agriculture/Mining/Construction   ☐ b. Education (College/Univ.)   L ☐ Telecommunications
C ☐ Banking/Finance   H ☐ Government—Federal   M ☐ Utilities/Transportation
D ☐ Chemical/Pharmaceutical   I ☐ Government—State   N ☐ Other (specify):
E ☐ Consultant   J ☐ Government—Local
F ☐ Computer/Systems/Electronics

PACKET